Ways of Knowing Muslim Cultures and Societies

Social, Economic and Political Studies of the Middle East and Asia

FOUNDING EDITOR: C.A.O. VAN NIEUWENHUIJZE

Editor

Dale F. Eickelman

Advisory Board

Fariba Adelkhah (*SciencesPo/CERI, Paris*)
Ruth Mandel (*University College London*)
Roger Owen (*Harvard University*)
Armando Salvatore (*McGill University*)

VOLUME 122

The titles published in this series are listed at *brill.com/seps*

Prof. Dr. Dr. h.c. Gudrun Krämer. Photo courtesy of Marcus Bleyl.

Ways of Knowing Muslim Cultures and Societies

Studies in Honour of Gudrun Krämer

Edited by

Bettina Gräf
Birgit Krawietz
Schirin Amir-Moazami
Ulrike Freitag
Konrad Hirschler

TUTA SUB AEGIDE PALLAS · 1683 ·

BRILL

LEIDEN | BOSTON

Cover illustration: Cairo International Book Fair 2013 Photographer: Marcel Behrens

The Library of Congress Cataloging-in-Publication Data is available online at http://catalog.loc.gov

Typeface for the Latin, Greek, and Cyrillic scripts: "Brill". See and download: brill.com/brill-typeface.

ISSN 1385-3376
ISBN 978-90-04-37754-7 (hardback)
ISBN 978-90-04-38689-1 (e-book)

This book is printed on acid-free paper and produced in a sustainable manner.

Contents

Editors' Preface: Ways of Knowing Muslim Cultures and Societies XI
The Underneath of Academic Life: Gudrun Krämer and Islamic Studies Today XXVI
Dale F. Eickelman
List of Illustrations XXXV
List of Contributors XXXVII
Tabula Gratulatoria XL
Bibliography Gudrun Krämer XLIII
Primary Supervision of Doctoral Theses by Gudrun Krämer at Freie Universität Berlin LII

PART 1
Islamic Studies Inside Out

1 Between Europe and Asia: Arabic and Islamic Studies in Imperial Russia 3
Alexander Knysh

2 Kairo 1869 – Eine historische Collage 27
Reinhard Schulze

PART 2
Empires, Corporations, and Nations

3 Muḥammad Rashīd Riḍā's Reformist Project to Establish a True Caliphate: Prospects and Challenges 55
Ahmed Ibrahim Abushouk

4 Ottoman Corporatism, Eighteenth to Twentieth Centuries: Beyond the State-Society Paradigm in Middle Eastern History 81
Johann Büssow and Astrid Meier

5 Family Portraits: Visual Sources for a Social History of the Late Ottoman Empire 111
Elke Hartmann

6 The Position of Philosophy in the Late Ottoman Educational Reforms 132
M. Sait Özervarlı

PART 3
Islam, Ethics, and Languages

7 Pratique religieuse et comportement moral 147
Abdou Filali-Ansary

8 The Emerging Field of Ethics in the Context of Modern Egypt 157
Mutaz al-Khatib

9 Religion as Discourse: Conversion and Commitment to *Jihād* in South Africa 181
Abdulkader Tayob

PART 4
Media Perspectives and Material Approaches

10 From the Pocketbook to Facebook: Maktabat Wahba, Publishing, and Political Ideas in Cairo since the 1940s 223
Bettina Gräf

11 Reading between the Lines: Arabic Script, Islamic Calligraphy, and the Question of Legibility 246
Alina Kokoschka

12 Dimensions of "Giving Voice:" Discursive Agency and Intellectual Practice on Swahili Islamic Radio, in Mombasa 2005–2006 265
Kai Kresse

13 Shāh Walī Allāh of Delhi, His Successors, and the Qur'ān 280
Muhammad Qasim Zaman

PART 5
The Politics of Body and Gender

14 #ItsMensTurn: Of Hashtags and Shīʿī Discourses in Iran 301
Katajun Amirpur

15 Contested Genderscapes: Islamic Languages of Women's Rights in the Arab Region 310
Bettina Dennerlein

16 On Coming to Grips with Turkish Oil Wrestling: Conceptualising Muscular Islam and Islamic Martial Arts 327
Birgit Krawietz

PART 6
Dominant Minorities and Dominant Majorities

17 Domination, Resilience, and Power: Religious Minorities in the Imperial and Post-Imperial Middle East 357
Hamit Bozarslan

18 Carving Out a Space for Equal Political Citizenship? Muslim Politics of Remembrance in Uganda 376
Dorothea E. Schulz

PART 7
Arab Revolutions and Their Impact on Research about the Middle East

19 Understanding Transformation, Elite Change, and New Social Mobilisation in the Arab World: An Actor-Centred and Policy-Oriented Research Project 397
Muriel Asseburg

20 Understanding Politics in Egypt "From Below" 411
Cilja Harders

PART 8
Muslims Inside Out

21 Recognition and its Traps in Liberal Secular Conditions: The Case of Muslims in Europe 427
Schirin Amir-Moazami

22 The Refugee and the Dog 441
Ruth Mas

Index 469

Editors' Preface: Ways of Knowing Muslim Cultures and Societies

Ways

At the centre of this collection of articles honouring Gudrun Krämer is a variety of approaches to the academic exploration of Muslim social and cultural settings. The volume brings together international colleagues and colleagues closer to home and presents multiple ways of studying the Islamic tradition and Muslim beliefs and practices in the year 2018.

As an internationally renowned scholar, Gudrun Krämer has crossed paths with a wide range of people in many contexts. Simply assembling those who work closely with her in the academic landscape of Berlin—not to mention scholars from around the world with whom she has cultivated long-term and ongoing academic relationships—would have been impossible for this edited volume. With the limitation of a single volume, what we aimed for in organising this collection was to highlight the breadth of disciplines reflected in Gudrun Krämer's own work: Islamic studies, history, anthropology, political science, political theory, and religious studies. In addition, the articles of this volume address the notion of Islam in different geographies—including the contemporary and historical dimensions of various cultures and languages—at the same time capturing the epistemological and political underpinnings of this enterprise.

These introductory words are written from a German, and even what one might call a Berlinese perspective. Besides introducing the book in your hands, we will touch on some of the stages of Gudrun Krämer's academic career, considered against the larger framework of political and academic developments in Germany and beyond.

Knowing

Islam has been a subject of intense study since its earliest days, with the resulting knowledge assembled and conveyed first and foremost by Muslims themselves, but also by non-Muslims, especially by Christians, and later by secularised Christians, self-proclaimed liberals, positivists, atheists, Marxists, and many others, most of them elites from the northern shores of the Mediterranean. The purposes were various, among them the fight against heresy (Rodinson 1980), the self-assured assertion of one's own beliefs and practices

(MacIntyre 1990), and the romantic construction of the culture of the "other" that would mirror one's own desires (for German Orientalism, cf. Polaschegg 2005; for the French, Stemmler 2004, and Schulze in this volume). However, at the turn of the twentieth century, inquiry into Islam became more specifically related to questions of culture and history, especially the history of civilisation and its presumed hierarchies within so-called world history (*Weltgeschichte*). The search for knowledge was at that point tightly bound to colonial policies and ambitions, and consciously so. Each empire and, after World War I, each evolving nation-state in Europe had its own strategies, interests, and politics, and therefore Middle Eastern studies and/or Islamic studies has developed within the framework of national interests (cf. Knysh in this volume).

In Germany the academic discipline of Islamic studies (*Islamwissenschaft*) was born in the early twentieth century and is closely connected to the name Carl Heinrich Becker (Jung 2011, Schäbler 2008), carrying the heritage of nineteenth-century historicism and defining the Orient and Islam (or the Islamic Orient) as cultural or civilisational entities. Islamic studies probably strengthened the Eurocentrism of German humanities, rather than helping "to develop a potential of resistance against it" (Johansen 1990, 87). Under National Socialism and during World War II, many scholars of Islam had to leave the country because of their Jewish background or their stance against the regime and its totalitarianism and racism—or for both reasons. Others collaborated with the Nazis and adopted their ideology of cultural and ethnic supremacy (Ellinger 2006; Höpp et al. 2004). After World War II, research and publications about Islam and Islam-related topics increased in Germany in different ways on either side of the Cold War—as a form of area studies in the East (Hafez 1995) and as an expression of a preference for remote historical times, with little focus on contemporary themes, in the West.

However, research on modernity and on contemporary questions of social and political change slowly found their way into West German Islamic studies. Gudrun Krämer's research has been pioneering in this respect and it has reached an international audience: her work on the political thinking of the Egyptian Muslim Brothers and related independent thinkers and activists was among the first of its kind in Germany. From 1982 to 1994, in parallel with her research and in contrast to most of her colleagues at that time, she worked at the Stiftung Wissenschaft und Politik in Ebenhausen, an institution that was founded in 1962 in order "to make up for the deficiencies in German Oriental studies practiced at universities" (Johansen 1990, 95; see also Asseburg in this volume).

In the framework of this dedicated turn towards the present, concepts, methods, and perspectives borrowed from other disciplines entered into the disciplinary investigation of Islam. This gained pace in the 1990s, and with the support of scholars such as Gudrun Krämer, approaches from anthropology, sociology, cultural and media studies, film studies, gender studies, and political theory were brought into the fold of Islamwissenschaft to analyse and interpret political developments in Germany and internationally (see Eickelman in this volume).

However, this has only rarely translated into politics or informed the ways in which politicians would deal with the increasing Muslim population in Germany. On the contrary, there is a widespread tendency among the German public to listen to alarmist voices. We have witnessed a process of inquiring into Muslim thought and practice, examining the subject matter with every tool available, from the microscope to statistical analysis, since at least 9/11, if not since the fall of the Wall in 1989, thereby oscillating between acknowledging the other as other and turning those others into one's own voice (cf. Amir-Moazami in this volume). In public memory, much of the earlier academic cultural essentialism-cum-Eurocentrism seems to prevail (cf. Mas in this volume). German politicians have had different opinions about whether Islam is part of German history and the present (carefully not addressing Muslims directly). On 3 October 2010 Christian Wulff (Christian-Democratic Union, CDU) was the first President of Germany to publicly acknowledge that Islam is now part of Germany ("Der Islam gehört inzwischen auch zu Deutschland"; Hildebrandt 2015). This welcoming gesture, far from being universally shared, has triggered a wide-ranging debate. While the German Chancellor Angela Merkel agrees, fellow politician Horst Seehofer (Christian Social Union, CSU), former Minister President of Bavaria, expressed precisely the opposite view ("Der Islam gehört nicht zu Deutschland") in an official statement on 16 March 2018, shortly after he was appointed Minister of the Interior in the newly formed German government (cf. Tasemir 2018).

Being trained in Islamic Studies at the Freie Universität Berlin from the mid-1990s on, with Gudrun Krämer as one of the young professors at that time (she became professor there in 1996), meant to become sensitive to these issues. Students became aware of and careful about their impact as researchers of Islam in a newly unified Germany that was still looking to determine its political course, both internally (how to deal with the inhabitants of the former GDR, on the one hand, and its Muslims on the other) and externally (the question of whether Germany's size and economic power obliged it to play a bigger role in global politics again: the bombardment of Yugoslavia by the German air force during the Kosovo war in 1999 to support the Albanian Muslim population was a case in point). For students and graduates, amidst an evolving awareness of these configurations, the moral fulcrum was embodied in the conscious—or at least as-conscious-as-possible—decision on research topics to be pursued. At the same time, in terms of time and place, it was a unique opportunity, since students were being trained by scholars of Islam from both West Germany and East Germany (cf. Hennig 2018).

Gudrun Krämer was a role model when it came to the question of choosing research topics. All of her own topics seemed to be challenging, politically speaking—certainly her work on the history of the Jews in modern Egypt (her PhD dissertation, published in 1989) fit into this category, as did her book on contemporary Muslim thinking on democracy, human rights, and Islam (her habilitation, published in 1999); her history of Palestine until 1948 (2002; English translation, 2008, now in its third edition; also translated into Spanish, 2006); and her book on Ḥasan al-Bannā, the founder of the Egyptian Muslim Brothers (2010). (The full list of her publications is included in this volume). She has described herself as a specialist in Islamic studies *and* a historian. A recent example of her devotion to historical detail, combined with the ability to provide a masterful overview of time and space, is the massive *Der Vordere Orient und Nordafrika ab 1500* (2016). Providing the reading public with ready access to material evidence has been, in her experience, the only way to win over others, by challenging their convictions and possibly erroneous assumptions. This straightforwardness was key to her being awarded the prestigious Gerda Henkel Prize in 2010. When she received the award, her work was praised as enlightening, nuanced, very clear in her language, and a pleasure to read.

In 2018, she was accorded the honour of being appointed to the Wissenschaftsrat, the German Council of Science and Humanities, which advises the German government on matters of higher education and research, further recognition of the significance of her contributions to this vitally important field of study.

Muslim

For many students it was the Gulf War of 1990 to 1991 that led them to Islamic studies and prompted them to learn Arabic, Persian, Turkish, and other Eastern languages. They were not perhaps concerned with Islam at first but wanted to understand their own geopolitical circumstances and the world around them. However, there were other students, too, in the cohort at Freie Universität in Berlin, German students with Turkish, Palestinian, Tunisian, and Armenian backgrounds. They had a variegated notion of the tradition of Islam and Muslim practices and beliefs, and linked that notion to many other categories, such as music, poetry, architecture, colonial struggle, class struggle, commitment, oppression, home, invasion, and exile. Soon most of the students discovered that learning about Islam and Muslims meant learning about everything else as well. They studied colonial histories and the role of different knowledge regimes in various practices of belief in the regions of concern (topics they had not encountered in school, regardless of whether they had been educated in East or West Germany). They would learn about orthodox and heterodox practices in various times and places, related or unrelated to Christian practices, and about Muslim majorities that have been suppressed and minorities that have been in power, and the other way around (cf. Bozarslan, Hartmann, Schulz, and Tayob in this volume).

In the end, they would comprehend the need to look for the relationships between their own histories and the histories of Islam, whether in terms of political, economic, cultural, ethical, or legal dimensions. They would come to understand that Islam might be a notion, a religion, a tradition, and a lived practice all at once, reported and mediated to them in many different ways (cf. Krawietz in this volume). They would learn, especially from Gudrun Krämer, that a discursive tradition (cf. Asad 1986), one that focusses on and interprets a set of fixed texts in different ways at different times—and thus opening, rather than closing, various possible histories and futures—is not unique to Islam. Indeed, Islam is no exception here to any other discursive tradition one might study, such as Catholicism, for example (MacIntyre 1990). One can maintain, though, that the tradition of Islam is exceptional in the way it has been situated in the geopolitical field (cf. Asad 1993, 2003; Salvatore 2007, as well as Filali-Ansary, al-Khatib, Kresse, and Tayob in this volume).

Accordingly, it has become all the more important to dive into the details of this tradition. Gudrun Krämer has mastered the contemporary complexity of Islam-related questions with encyclopaedic knowledge. In recognition of her expertise, in 2001 she was invited to join the editorial board of the *Encyclopaedia of Islam, THREE* (*EI3*), a crucial and vast knowledge venture that had been planned even before the Second Edition of the encyclopaedia, which had begun publication in 1960, was finished, in 2004. As of this writing, she continues in her position as an editor of *EI3*, an exacting and demanding responsibility for all those involved that represents a significant and ongoing contribution to the field.

Cultures and Societies

The Berlin Graduate School Muslim Cultures and Societies (BGSMCS) at Freie Universität Berlin, of which Gudrun Krämer was one of the founding members and its long-standing director, was founded in 2007. The success of the first—and hitherto only—"Graduate School Muslim Cultures and Societies" during the German Excellence Initiative reshaped Islamic studies in Germany, not only transforming the academic landscape on the regional and national scale but also drawing the attention of scholars and students from all over the world. The villa in Berlin-Dahlem, the location of the BGSMCS, became a truly multifaceted space. The first cohort started its cooperative research in 2008 (cf. Kokoschka in this volume, who is one of the first alumni; see also the list of PhD students Gudrun Krämer has supervised).

The two notions of culture and society (set in the plural) are programmatic for this volume too: They are broad enough to encourage thinking about and discussion of the Islamic tradition and Muslim practices, while avoiding the trap of essentialism and Eurocentrism. Moreover, these terms are not necessarily confined to given geopolitical entities such as empires or nations and their borders. The advantage is that subjects such as the internal and foreign policies of individual states, the global political economy connected to the region, terrorism, and war might be discussed, but not necessarily or exclusively. In this volume, we propose an inquiry into Muslim cultures and societies utilising variegated methodological and self-reflexive tools that extend well beyond the necessity of merely cultivating the languages—an approach very different from that of Heinrich Leberecht Fleischer, who taught Oriental studies in Leipzig from 1835 to 1888, and who, in Baber Johansen's words, "transformed the Orient into grammar and lexicography" (Johansen 1990, 77).

The Volume

The volume is introduced with an essay, directly following this preface, by Dale Eickelman, who describes the state of international Islamic studies today and highlights Gudrun Krämer's role in it. He shows how Krämer has "contributed to building new academic spaces and made such spaces an integral part of her scholarly presence," thus shaping and reshaping Islamic studies in the last thirty years in many different contexts.

Following from the design of the Berlin Graduate School Muslim Cultures and Societies, the ways of studying Islam, the Islamic tradition, and Muslim beliefs and practices presented here are characterised by a wide geographical scope, a broad timeline, an historically informed focus on contemporary phenomena, and transdisciplinary perspectives. We have divided the twenty-two contributions into the following eight categories:

1) In the first category, *Islamic Studies Inside Out*, Alexander Knysh and Reinhard Schulze teach us anew and in gratifying detail the degree to which the description and analysis of Muslim societies and cultures in the nineteenth

century were intertwined with the internal and external agendas of different empires and states, in this case the Russian Empire, on the one hand, and the French on the other. Thus, the knowledge that was gained within the newly created discipline of Islamic Studies cannot be seen as essentially true to the actual object of inquiry but should always be considered in its relationship to contemporary politics.

2) The articles that comprise the second category, *Empires, Corporations, and Nations*, contributions by Ahmed Abushouk, Johann Büssow and Astrid Meier, Elke Hartmann, and M. Sait Özervarlı, are closely related to the first category in historical terms. These articles deal with the late Ottoman Empire and present reflections on and analysis of a time of change and transitional orders in the final phase of the empire. Abushouk discusses Muḥammad Rashīd Riḍā's active support of the old order in the form of the Ottoman caliphate, through the lens of his journal *al-Manār*. Büssow and Meier reflect on an alternative understanding of the social and political order within the Ottoman Empire, which they call "Ottoman corporatism," with the intention of complicating the stiff and sometimes misleading state-society distinction. Hartmann, in her paper, demonstrates the usefulness of incorporating visual sources, in the form of photographic family portraits, into a social history of the Ottoman Empire. In his article, Özervarlı portrays the evolving differentiation of the discipline of philosophy (*hikmet, felsefe-i cedide*) in the late Ottoman reforms within the two educational systems that developed in parallel and sometimes overlapped: the classical learning institution, or *madrasa*, and the newly built European institutions.

3) In his contribution, which is placed in the third section, *Islam, Ethics, and Languages*, Mutaz al-Khatib is similarly concerned with the history of philosophy, especially with moral philosophy and ethical thinking (*al-tafkīr al-akhlāqī*), as he calls it. He narrates the evolution of this sub-field of philosophy, which reflected the influence of European—and especially French—thought, covering the same period of time as Özervalı's contribution, but in this case for Egypt. In the last part of his article he draws attention to the new field of Islamic ethics that evolved in the last decades of the twentieth century. In this same category, Abdou Filali-Ansary discusses the relationship between morals and religious practice in different Muslim settings. He is especially interested in the dimension of the secular in connection with public morals and public religiosity. Abdulkader Tayob, in turn, analyses a highly publicised conversion to the notion of *jihād* in the South African context, which occurred after the invasion of Iraq by the United States and its allies in 2003 and the subsequent formation of the Islamic state in Iraq and Syria (ISIS). The three articles of this section reflect the increasing interconnectedness of various regions and

normative orders since the nineteenth century, with respect to ethics and moral action. Languages and translation politics play an important part in this regard and display at least three important points: the complexity of the issue, the frequent confusion within transregional communication, and the role of hegemonic language regimes within the conceptions of moral inquiry.

4) The closely related question of media representation is discussed in section four, *Media Perspectives and Material Approaches* to the study of Muslim cultures and societies. Following a constructivist line of thinking, one can argue that there is no knowledge without mediation. Thus, in this category the different media practices involved in any form of inquiry and their relation to material conditions are highlighted. Alina Kokoschka investigates the Arabic script, Islamic calligraphy, and the question of legibility. She asks about the deeper sense of a writing that is difficult to read. This question leads her to the importance of materiality and, further, to the "art of the line," a calligraphy that reaches beyond words and invites reading between the lines.

Muhammad Qasim Zaman deals with practices around the translation of the Qurʾān and *ḥadīth* in eighteenth- and nineteenth-century South Asia. He points out that, although the Ṣūfī scholar Shāh Walī Allāh (d. 1176/1762) was not the first to render the Qurʾān into Persian on the Indian subcontinent, his translation had considerable influence on generations of translators and exegetes. Zaman argues that this impact was backed by claims to religious authority that in themselves owed much to the technology of print.

Bettina Gräf, in her article, is also concerned with the interrelation of media technology, social relations, and the promulgation of knowledge, albeit in a different setting. She investigates visions of social change in connection with materiality in forms as different as pocketbooks and Facebook, and explores questions of ownership and censorship in Egypt. She argues that individual and/or group expression in public—and therefore individual and/or group agency—is bound to economic constraints, on the one hand, and to constant interventions by the modern state on the other. Unlike in the South Asian case Zaman examines and the time and space he is concerned with, promises of social change connected to new media technologies thus glimmer for only brief moments in time and are very much bound to the experiences of one generation and their media biographies.

Kai Kresse pushes the discussion in yet another direction while looking at internal debates among coastal Muslims in postcolonial Kenya. He investigates discursive agency and intellectual practices on Swahili Islamic Radio in Mombasa in the years 2005 and 2006, emphasising the ways in which the radio programme's listeners and makers address and negotiate internal conflict. Kresse's analysis highlights, on the one hand, the specific ethical dimensions of intellectual practice on the Swahili coast and, on the other, questions the dominance of Eurocentric categories in academic analytic language in general.

5) The fifth category of inquiry, titled *The Politics of Body and Gender*, is closely related to the fourth. Just like reflections on the material conditions of communication, the topic of body and gender permeates time and space. These relatively new perspectives form an important part of critical studies about Muslim cultures and societies.

Birgit Krawietz investigates the cultural multiplicity of Turkish oil wrestling, drawing on the late Shahab Ahmed's postulation of a "Balkans-to-Bengal" complex. In contrast to the homogenising and for many decades utterly nation-bound narrative of republican Turkey imposed on the sport, her contribution points to a much broader scope of influences. Discussing concepts such as Muscular Islam and Islamic martial arts, she draws attention to neo-traditional, modified wrestling practices related to the oil wrestling hub of Edirne and the newly introduced Ethnosports Cultural Festival in Istanbul.

Katajun Amirpur and Bettina Dennerlein provide new insights into the politics of gender in Muslim contexts: Amirpur's article deals with the solidarity many Iranian men demonstrated with Iranian women in a Facebook campaign initiated in December 2009 called *Men in Hijabs*. These interventions—which were originally meant as support for an Iranian man, Majīd Tavakkolī, who had given a speech against oppression on National Student Day—became an impetus for rethinking notions of gender, masculinity, femininity, public and private, and their epistemological underpinnings. Similarly, Dennerlein sheds light on the intellectual dynamics of current debates on gender in the Arab World. Her starting point is a text by the Egyptian political scientist and Islamic thinker Hiba Raʾūf ʿIzzat, published in 2005, in which she critiques transnational women's rights activism. In the tradition of modern Islamic thought, ʿIzzat inserts herself into differently aligned debates and addresses diverse national and international publics, while questioning the "ideological dominance of the secular-religious binary."

6) Our sixth category, titled *Dominant Minorities and Dominant Majorities*, with contributions by Hamit Bozarslan and Dorothea Schulz, is not intended to highlight the often-problematic terminology of minorities and majorities in nation-state settings, but rather to draw attention to the different possible hierarchies involved in sectarian tensions and to reconsider the assumptions that underlie much of the research on the Middle East in the social sciences since the 1990s and 2000s. Bozarslan deals with the different handling of ethnic and confessionally bound groups in empires and nations and compares the "civility of the empires with the citizenship of the states," using the late Ottoman Empire as an example. His article simultaneously speaks very much to the

second category of this volume, *Empires, Corporations, and Nations*. Dorothea Schulz's article focusses on Muslim minorities in a Christian-dominated African context, addressing how Muslims in southwestern Uganda enact rituals of remembrance and commemoration of traumatic experiences of marginality, forceful expulsion, and existential threat, as hopeful gestures evoking the possibility of peaceful coexistence, equal treatment, and pluralism. She also offers an insightful contribution to the scholarship on trauma, mourning, and public commemoration by showing how these historical experiences of violence and bereavement are embedded in regimes of memory and state-orchestrated silencing.

7) Issues of sectarianism and nationalism played an important role in the latest Arab revolutions in 2011 and 2012 too. These issues were not the reason for the revolutions—which in the first place called for economic, social, and political change, wrapped in the slogans for bread (*ʿaish*), dignity (*karāma*), and social justice (*ʿadāla ijtimāʿiyya*)—but rather were used in countering the revolutions. The major crackdown on the Egyptian Muslim Brothers after the coup d'état in Egypt in August 2013 and the ensuing discrimination and prosecution directed against them is one case in point. In their articles categorised under the heading *Arab Revolutions and Their Impact on Research about the Middle East*, Muriel Asseburg and Cilja Harders show the impact of the revolutions in terms of political science approaches to authoritarianism and political mobilisation. While Asseburg focusses on elite perspectives and elite change in four countries—Egypt, Libya, Tunisia, and Yemen—Harders is interested in what Asef Bayat has called "the politics from below" and its long-term influences among those who represented the generation of Egyptian youth in 2011.

8) The last section of this volume, *Muslims Inside Out*, addresses the grounds on which Muslims are accepted into or excluded from European nation-states. Schirin Amir-Moazami's chapter investigates the ways in which Europe's politics of recognising Muslims are recurrently promoted as a means of opposing ongoing measures of securitisation that target Muslims. However, as she demonstrates, the paradigms of recognition, which are inscribed in a liberal-secular matrix of Western European democracies, are also riddled with contradictions and exclusionary mechanisms. This becomes especially obvious in the way in which Muslims are simultanously inserted into a secular nation-state framework and at the same time marked as "religious" through ever-changing conditions of acceptance. The critique of the paradigm of recognition offered by Amir-Moazami is extended by Ruth Mas's consideration of the structural and legal mechanisms at play in deciding the inside and outside status of Muslims in Germany and Europe. Set in the context of the ongoing refugee crisis, Mas traces the genealogy of equivalencies established between the animal and the

human in order to argue that the disciplining feature of law functions as a means to secularly domesticate Muslims, especially Muslim refugees.

These eight categories clearly relate to certain academic disciplines, but they also show the cross-disciplinary approaches applied in mastering the complexities of the issues. However, the volume does not seek simply to address "complexity." The most interesting observation we can draw from the various contributions is the relatedness of academic knowledge production within space and time. Obviously, it is not unimportant to reflect about who is speaking and from where and from what point of view. What we can see today with regard to Islamic studies is a change in consciousness and in balance. At least since the 1980s, with discussions of the postmodern condition (Lyotard 1979, Jameson 1984) and postcoloniality (Shohat 1992, Mbembe 2001), heterogenous voices from many places around the world are present within the academy. This volume in honour of Gudrun Krämer and her work thus displays a certain stage of critical inquiry, politics, and self-reflection on the matter of hierarchies and power relations within academic writing related to the Islamic tradition. We very much hope, in line with ideas expressed in Achille Mbembe's *Critique de la raison nègre* (2013), that the academic (and any other) clocks will not in the future be turned back.

Acknowledgements

First and foremost, we would like to express our deepest gratitude to Gudrun Krämer for generously sharing with us her enormous range of ways of knowing Muslim cultures and societies. We further wish to express our gratitude to Dale Eickelman for hosting this volume in his fine series "Social, Economic and Political Studies of the Middle East and Asia," published in Leiden by Brill, and to Maurits van den Boogert and the entire production team at Brill. When we approached Brill with the project of this Festschrift they wholeheartedly picked it up and offered generous help and support. Our special thanks go to Abdurraouf Oueslati, project manager of *EI3*, who administered communications with the authors and oversaw the production process, and to Linda George for expert English copy editing. It was a real pleasure to work with your professional, collaborative, and encouraging minds throughout the production of this volume. We will certainly miss your presence in our inboxes. We are also grateful to Marie-Pascale Pieretti for the French copy editing, and to Amir Dastmalchian for assistance with the Persian. We would further like to thank Ulrike Freitag and Konrad Hirschler, who provided valuable feedback and who supported us throughout the entire process with advice and assistance in various matters.

Furthermore, we are grateful to Verena Klemm and Dorothée Sack, who were of great help at the beginning of the project.

Several others had to bear with an additional workload and diligently devoted themselves to the book project, including the student assistants Juli Singer (Ludwig-Maximilians-Universität München), David Battefeld (Freie Universität Berlin), and Farid al-Ghawaby (Freie Universität Berlin). Christina Stark (BGSMCS) was so kind to help in preparing the index. We are also grateful to the secretaries of the Institute of Islamic Studies at Freie Universität Berlin, Angela Ballaschk and Sonja Eising, as well as the secretary of the BGSMCS, Jutta Schmidbauer, for their extensive support. In addition we relied on the services of the PhD Office at the Department for History and Cultural Studies (Freie Universität Berlin), and we thank Michaela Köppen and Irina Golubko for their assistance in checking data for us there.

We extend our thanks to those listed in the Tabula Gratulatoria, and offer special gratitude to the contributors to this volume. We very much appreciate your positive response to the enterprise.

Bettina Gräf, Birgit Krawietz, and Schirin Amir-Moazami,
Berlin, June 2018

Bibliography

Asad, Talal. 1986. *The Idea of an Anthropology of Islam.* Washington D.C.: Center for Contemporary Arab Studies, Georgetown University.

Asad, Talal. 1993. *Genealogies of Religion: Discipline and Reasons of Power in Christianity and Islam.* Baltimore and London: The Johns Hopkins University Press.

Asad, Talal. 2003. *Formations of the Secular: Christianity, Islam, Modernity.* Stanford: Stanford University Press.

Ellinger, Ekkehard. 2006. *Deutsche Orientalistik zur Zeit des Nationalsozialismus 1933–1945.* Edingen-Neckarhausen: Deux mondes.

Hafez, Kai. 1995. *Orientwissenschaft in der DDR: Zwischen Dogma und Anpassung, 1969–1989.* Hamburg: Deutsches Orient-Institut.

Hennig, Jochen. 2018. "Frank Hörnigks Erinnerungen an die Neuformierung der Berliner Wissenschaftslandschaft nach 1989." In Deirdre Byrnes, Jean E. Conacher, and Gisela Holfter (eds.), *German Reunification and the Legacy of GDR Literature and Culture.* Leiden and Boston: Brill, 181–84.

Hildebrandt, Tina. 2015. "Der Islam gehört zu Deutschland." ZEIT ONLINE, 12 March. https://www.zeit.de/2015/09/christian-wulff-angela-merkel-islam-deutschland; accessed 29 May 2018.

Höpp, Gerhard, Peter Wien, and René Wildangel (eds.). 2004. *Blind für die Geschichte? Arabische Begegnungen mit dem Nationalsozialismus*. ZMO-Studien 19. Berlin: Klaus Schwarz.

Jameson, Frederic. 1984. "Postmodernism, or the Cultural Logic of Late Capitalism." *New Left Review* 146, Jul-Aug: 53–92.

Johansen, Baber. 1990. "Politics and Scholarship: The Development of Islamic Studies in the Federal Republic of Germany." In Tareq Y. Ismael (ed.), *Middle East Studies: International Perspectives on the State of the Art*. New York: Praeger, 71–130.

Jung, Dietrich. 2011. *Orientalists, Islamists and the Global Public Sphere: A Genealogy of the Modern Essentialist Image of Islam*. Sheffield, UK: Equinox Publishing.

Krämer, Gudrun. 1989. *The Jews in Modern Egypt, 1914–1952*. London: I.B. Tauris.

Krämer, Gudrun. 1999. *Gottes Staat als Republik: Reflexionen zeitgenössischer Muslime zu Islam, Menschenrechten und Demokratie*. Baden-Baden: Nomos.

Krämer, Gudrun. 2002. *Geschichte Palästinas: Von der osmanischen Eroberung bis zur Gründung des Staates Israel*. Munich: Beck.

Krämer, Gudrun. 2010. *Hasan al-Banna*. Oxford: Oneworld Publications.

Krämer, Gudrun. 2016. *Der Vordere Orient und Nordafrika ab 1500*. Frankfurt am Main: S. Fischer.

Lyotard, Jean-François. 1979. *La Condition postmodern: Rapport sur le savoir*. Paris: Édition de Minuit.

MacIntyre, Alasdair. 1990. *Three Rival Versions of Moral Enquiry: Encyclopaedia, Genealogy, and Tradition*. Notre Dame, Indiana: University of Notre Dame Press.

Mbembe, Achille. 2001. *On the Postcolony*. Berkeley and Los Angeles: University of California Press.

Mbembe, Achille. 2013. *Critique de la raison nègre*. Paris: La Découverte.

Polaschegg, Andrea. 2005. *Der andere Orientalismus: Regeln deutsch-morgenländischer Imagination im 19. Jahrhundert*. Berlin and New York: de Gruyter.

Rodinson, Maxime. 1980. *La Fascination de l'Islam*, Paris: Maspero.

Salvatore, Armando. 2007. *The Public Sphere: Liberal Modernity, Catholicism, Islam*. New York: Palgrave Macmillan.

Schäbler, Birgit. 2008. "Historismus versus Orientalismus? Oder: Zur Geschichte einer Wahlverwandtschaft." In Abbas Poya and Maurus Reinkowski (eds.), *Das Unbehagen in der Islamwissenschaft: Ein klassisches Fach im Scheinwerferlicht der Politik und der Medien*. Bielefeld: transcript Verlag, 51–70.

Shohat, Ella. 1992. "Notes on the Post-Colonial." *Social Text* 31/32, Third World and Post-Colonial Issues: 99–113.

Stemmler, Susanne. 2004. *Topografien des Blicks: Eine Phänomenologie literarischer Orientalismen des 19. Jahrhunderts in Frankreich*. Bielefeld: transcript Verlag.

Tasemir, Ebru. 2018 "Der Islam gehört nicht zu Deutschland" *TAZ*, 22 March 2018. http://www.taz.de/!5493389/; accessed 29 May 2018.

The Underneath of Academic Life: Gudrun Krämer and Islamic Studies Today

Dale F. Eickelman

The *métier* of academic life usually foregrounds writings over the backstage of proposals, committee meetings, and lobbying governments and foundations for support. Academics downplay these ancillary activities. It is easy to let them detract from academic projects and not all scholars get the balance right. "Underneath" here describes how Gudrun Krämer has contributed to building new academic spaces and made such spaces an integral part of her scholarly presence. A keen observer of how universities work, she has used her knowledge of how things work and her negotiating skills to reshape Islamic studies.

How Institutions Work

In most appraisals of academic careers, administrative skills and the learned craft of making committees function successfully form only a background to academic achievement, or are assumed to be "natural" skills effortlessly acquired. In Krämer's[1] case, programme- and institution-building are an essential part of her academic persona, linked to her skill in organising both peers and junior colleagues and students, bringing them together to add scholarly value to her own work and to theirs, but without converting the best and the brightest into disciples obliged to follow a party line. From distant North America, I inevitably miss the finer nuances of the academic life of Germany and Berlin, but the distance also allows me to see the wider context in which Krämer's skills have developed over the twenty years that we have worked together, never as co-authors but sometimes as co-consultants or co-organisers, joining efforts to make Islamic studies realise its full potential in the face of evolving challenges.

As an anthropologist, I am fascinated by how institutions work, including academic institutions. In the 1970s and 1980s, this interest took the form of exploring the habits of thought, or cognitive style, inculcated by Islamic mosque-universities (Eickelman 1978, Eickelman 1985).[2] It is not much of a stretch to

1 Americans easily lapse into the familiar use of the first name alone with professional colleagues. Gudrun and I are on a first-name basis when we meet. In more formal settings, I am uncomfortable using "Professor Dr." My compromise here is to use "Krämer" most of the time, allowing the friendship and professional respect to follow in between the lines.

2 For an assessment of contemporary university education, see Eickelman 2017.

use the same ethnographic (and historical) approach to understand how we operate in contemporary academic space, learning to create transnational and transdisciplinary spaces that shape intellectual inquiry—and to learn the strengths and limits of our own respective national academic *habitus*, or ways of thinking and acting, to use a term that Pierre Bourdieu brought into the sociological mainstream (Eickelman 1979).

ISIM as a Noble Experiment

Marburg-born Krämer and Evergreen Park-born Eickelman shared at least one crucial place of learning to shape transnational and transdisciplinary Islamic Studies together. We were both founding members of the Academic Committee of the International Institute for the Study of Islam in the Modern World (ISIM) (1998-2009), now sadly defunct. I was present at the Committee's first meeting, which coincided with its formal inauguration—including a major disruption by Iranian émigrés protesting the inclusion of a pro-regime speaker. For a brief initial period, I was the only advisory committee member who was neither a Dutch citizen nor of Dutch origin. Professor Krämer—a rank she already had attained in 1996—joined for the second meeting. Until the Committee's dissolution in 2002, she remained one of its most articulate and persuasive members.

ISIM was an unusual academic experiment. At the outset, it took on the shape of its successful predecessor for Asia, the International Institute for Asian Studies (IIAS), founded in 1993 by Wim Stokhof, a talented polymath whose vision ranged far beyond his initial specialty of Austronesian and Papuan linguistics. He also launched ISIM, in 1998, and became its first director-in-charge. Governance was in the hands of the presidents of three Dutch universities—Leiden, Amsterdam, and Utrecht—later expanded to include the president of Nijmegen. In my private notes, I referred to the governing board as the Four Horsemen of the Apocalypse. This was not because of their fearsome personalities—and I got to know several of them reasonably well—but because of the inherent challenge of sustaining cooperation among four distinct and competing universities. Some saw Islamic Studies in Leiden as detracting from other priorities. In retrospect, others might argue that resistance to such an ambitious programme was inevitable, and that its survival for eleven years was not a bad outcome.

In the late 1990s, ISIM was an influential game-changer. It hit the ground running, with an impressive series of conferences and working groups, and reports on an array of topics—including Muslims in Europe, visions of Islamic modernity, health care and the family in Turkey, Shīʿī Ṣūfism, Algerian cultural history, Islam in Brunei, and the appearance of influential new periodicals in the Muslim-majority world. The scope of ISIM's activities was vast, and its print flagship was the *ISIM Newsletter*, a widely circulated tabloid-style document containing short, pithy articles accessible across disciplinary lines and for a wide audience. ISIM intended to change how Islamic studies were done, and for a time it succeeded.

The task of the Advisory Committee was to identify themes and talent. We also contributed articles to the *ISIM Newsletter*, distributed worldwide for free in postal and online delivery to anyone capable of requesting a subscription. Thus, Krämer's first written contribution to the *Newsletter* was "On Difference and Understanding: The Use and Abuse of the Study of Islam," based on the third annual ISIM lecture, which she delivered 15 March 2000 (Krämer 2000).[3]

The Context of Krämer's "Use and Abuse"

Krämer's essay was appropriately magisterial. It elaborated on ways of knowing earlier introduced in Islamic studies by Gustav von Grunebaum in his edited volume *Unity and Variety in Muslim Civilization* (von Grunebaum 1955). Astonishingly for the 1950s, the American Anthropological Association, not known for publishing works by scholars seen as "Orientalists," sponsored the book. The term "Orientalist" had not yet taken on a negative meaning in the 1950s. Like von Grunebaum, Krämer blended the close reading of texts with an evocation of their social and historical contexts. Of course, there was a generational difference between the two: von Grunebaum was born in 1909 and Krämer in 1953. Another difference was that von Grunebaum was a *bricoleur* in combining disciplinary approaches. He led by example, without explaining what was new and mildly different in his approach. Krämer came to scholarly maturity in a different era. She was, and remains, skeptical of arguments that lump all predecessors together into crude categories such as "Orientalist," "colonialist," "post-modern," or (more recently) "intersectional." There is a place for such labels, but not as conversation-stoppers—to use philosopher Richard Rorty's apt phrase—that block attention to how one thinks about religion, society, or history outside circles of like-minded believers (Keane 1998).

To give a sense of the mid-twentieth-century context for Islamic studies, let me describe the distinguished historian who led my first-ever seminar in Islamic history at McGill University in 1964, informing our class that the key texts

3 Issues remain accessible online at https://openaccess.leidenuniv.nl/bitstream/handle/1887/10073/newsl_13.pdf;sequence=1.

had all been established by the "greats" of an earlier generation—including Theodor Nöldeke (1836-1930), Ignaz Goldziher (1850-1921), and others. The role of our generation, it was explained, was to ferret out typographical errors and other minor imperfections. As for Islam as a religion, we were also informed that we non-Muslims should respect the boundaries of "faith." We should report on but not criticise theological debates, or pursue too far such issues as how *ḥadīth*, the sayings of the prophet Muḥammad, were authenticated.

My Pakistani classmates—some of us remain in contact to this day—reveled in the discovery that when they did not want, or were unprepared, to discuss certain topics, it sufficed to assert that the non-Muslim instructor was treading on a tenet of faith. It was not that they objected to "critical" studies of religious texts, but rather they saw how they could use others' perceptions of interfaith dialogue pragmatically to deflect unwelcome questions.

Further background is needed to how we studied. McGill's Institute for Islamic Studies was founded by Wilfred Cantwell Smith (1916-2000), with support from the Rockefeller Foundation. Smith left McGill University for Harvard in the spring of 1964, and I joined McGill in the Fall of that year. The composition of the student body was almost unique to the Institute. When the Institute had sufficient funds, and it still did in the mid-1960s, the goal was to recruit 30 graduate students per year. Of these, 14 were Christian, 14 Muslim, plus—said some advanced students—one Jew and one social scientist. I think that I fell into the latter category. Of course, there was no explicit policy of which we students were aware, but the "balance" of admitted students held for the years I was at McGill.

The idea of such numerical diversity was to stimulate dialogue. Yet if one instructor relegated us to scanning the works of leading predecessors for typographical errors, informing us that all major scholarship had been completed, this was not Smith's founding vision. His influential book *The Meaning and End of Religion*, published in 1963, made a powerful argument for how the analytical category of "religion" evolved over time both in the English language and in Arabic, and had a powerful influence on the comparative study of religion (Smith 1963). Thus, thinking about religion in earlier eras was far from immobile, and from the nineteenth century onward necessitated making explicit the categories by which we think about faith and society.[4]

For rigidity and fixed ideas, nothing beat the arrogant assumptions of "modernisation" theory in the mid-twentieth century. The received wisdom was

4 For a discussion of how the categories by which we think about religion and society are implicitly and consciously transformed, see Eickelman 2015.

to attribute a positive role to religion in earlier historical periods, but to assert that religion in the modern world played an increasingly marginal role in public life. At least the social scientists who advocated this view produced memorable quotes. One claimed that the Muslim world faced an unpalatable choice: either a "neo-Islamic totalitarianism" intent on "resurrecting the past," or a "reformist Islam" that would open "the sluice gates and [be] swamped by the deluge" (Halpern 1963, 129). Another wrote: Middle Eastern societies faced the stark choice of "Mecca or mechanization" (Lerner 1964, 405).

Evoking these academic and public understandings toward religion and the Muslim world offers insight into the challenge of institution-building faced by Krämer in Europe and those of us in North America. For example, after several years' discussions that began in the late 1970s, the Social Science Research Council (SSRC) established in 1983 (with the American Council of Learned Societies, ACLS) a Joint Committee for the Comparative Study of Muslim Societies, and I was a founding member. This Committee, dissolved in 1991, came into being over the strenuous objections of the SSRC's Middle East Studies Committee, which strongly felt that the study of any religion was "epiphenomenal," unlike the study of the hard surfaces of economics and politics, which was presumably "real."

The voices of political scientists such as Benedict Anderson and James Scott, who took peoples' ideas and ideologies as seriously as the so-called "hard surfaces," were just beginning to reach a wider public (Anderson 1993; Scott 1985). In one of our early workshops, intended to bring together advanced doctoral students and recent doctorates from different disciplines, one participant, then a philologically-oriented pre-doctoral historian and now a tenured full professor, said at the concluding session that it was "diverting" to hear the views of sociologists, political scientists, and anthropologists, but that he would now return to the "real" work of history, presumably in his view, text-based, with unexamined implicit contextual understandings.

ISIM and Its Sequel

The pervasive ideological divide among disciplines and ideologies continued long after Krämer's 2000 ISIM annual lecture, when slogans such as the "West versus the rest" continued to prevail. Unfortunately, she was correct that the idea of "culture" still invoked by some in the 1990s was an outmoded notion of the concept of "culture" as inflexible and static, rather than as contested, contingent, and emerging, and therefore easier to integrate into both social history and the study of contemporary societies. As Krämer wrote, "Scholars now insist on the openness of historical processes that are neither linear nor homogeneous" (Krämer 2000, 6).

The ten members of the ISIM academic committee were equally divided between Dutch and non-Dutch members. Discussions were robust but never acrimonious, although Dutch members of the board would sometimes explain to me, and perhaps to others, the points of contention among the Dutch themselves, usually related to the allocation of resources. Before September 2001, there was a disinclination to focus on the policy issues of Muslims and Muslim institutions in Europe, although this reluctance was gradually overcome—although not resistance to doing the bidding of policy-makers.

Our work consisted of the fine art of academic investment, reviewing projects and activities that should be funded and advanced, with particular emphasis given to projects and personnel with the capacity to influence disciplinary and academic trends across disciplines and topics, including women and religious politics, the mainstreaming of Islamic banking, the representations in architecture and speech of religious authority, inter-communal violence in South Asia and Indonesia, Islam in European schools, religious brotherhoods in the contemporary world, parallels in Jewish and Islamic studies, and homosexuals and *imāms*. The tools to explore these and other topics included conferences and workshops held in Leiden and elsewhere, degree programmes, the *ISIM Newsletter*, lectures, and occasional papers. Krämer's ability to connect historical with contemporary studies—a passion that I share—and to range across disciplines, stood out. In 2002, budget cuts and reorganisation led to the dissolution of ISIM's academic committee, but our paths continued to converge.

Concurrently with our responsibilities on the ISIM Academic Committee, I saw firsthand Krämer's ability to work with students and recent post-doctoral scholars during the year that I spent at the Wissenschaftskolleg zu Berlin, from August 2000 through July 2001. From January through May 2001 we co-directed a Berlin-wide non-credit graduate seminar/working group on Islam and Modernity (Islam und Moderne). Gudrun socialised me into managing a German seminar, one with a diversity of nationalities and academic levels—graduate students and recent post-doctoral fellows. We both were challenged to keep discussions on track and to convey that direct questioning and comment were acceptable in a successful seminar.

Since 1996, Krämer's scholarly career has been based in Berlin. She maintained her focus on scholarship in what must have been a challenging and sometimes tense administrative and political environment. I recall attending an African Studies conference at the Freie Universität Berlin just after Draconian reductions in the size of its political science department had been announced in the early Fall of 2000. Throughout academic Berlin, there was considerable anxiety about overlapping universities and academic centres, not to mention the multiplicity of state-sponsored music and theatre groups left over from the unique status of Berlin. Funds were short. Added to the sense of uncertainty was the fate of the Zentrum Moderner Orient (ZMO, now the Leibniz-Zentrum Moderner Orient), an institution about which Gudrun cared deeply. After several shaky starts after German reunification, it appeared to come into its own in 1998 with the appointment of Ulrich Haarmann (1942–1999), who died not long after his appointment. For several years it was in the hands of interim or caretaker heads. The anxious discussions about what to do next finally resulted in the appointment of Ulrike Freitag, who has been the director of the ZMO and professor at the Institute for Islamic Studies at the Freie Universität Berlin since 2002. Thus the Institute for Islamic Studies has served to tie together several of Berlin's interrelated academic centres focussed on Islam and the Middle East.

Trouble in Tahiti (and Berlin)

Gudrun Krämer considered—at least briefly—leaving Berlin for Los Angeles in 2003. This unrealised flight allows me to invoke Leonard Bernstein's 1951 "Trouble in Tahiti," a Broadway musical about a troubled couple in seemingly perfect American suburbia. Berlin, of course, is as remote from an American suburb (or Tahiti) as one can imagine, but the turbulence of academic institutions in Berlin at the dawn of the twenty-first century can only be imagined. Perhaps her interest in becoming a candidate to direct the Middle East Center at the University of California, Los Angeles, was in part inspired by her 2001 participation on the selection committee for the Levi della Vida award, which at the time was still administered by UCLA.

Having chaired an external review committee for UCLA's Center for Near Eastern Studies in October 2001, I shared with her what I knew of the position.[5] It had enormous potential and Gudrun would have been ideal for the position. However complex the academic politics of Berlin and the challenges to secure funding, the skills in one setting did not readily transpose to the other equally complex setting. In my view, as an academic, Krämer would have excelled at UCLA, but UCLA had institutional and political challenges of its own. As head of a major programme inevitably caught up in American public politics,

5 At the time I was the Bin Laden Fellow at the Centre for Islamic Studies at the University of Oxford.

especially at a state university where controversies in the Middle East readily merged with domestic U.S. and California ones, she would have been as much at sea as would an American navigating the subtle and not-so-subtle contest of institutions and wills in Berlin. As a learning experience that helped Krämer sharpen her skills in making Islamic studies in Berlin realise their full potential, her brief UCLA candidacy, and perhaps others of which I am unaware, and of course the ISIM experience, no doubt brought into focus what she could accomplish in Berlin and how to go about it.

My sense of Gudrun's comprehensive grasp of issues and how to make institutions work was further reinforced when we once again collaborated, this time in Jerusalem in January 2005, co-conducting an external review of the M.A. in Islamic Studies programme at the Hebrew University of Jerusalem. Such external reviews intensively cram into two or three days the evaluation of how other people's students and faculty work together. Both of us were familiar with Islamic and Middle Eastern studies in Israel, and Krämer in particular was at ease in noting the strong parallels between Jewish and Islamic approaches to the study of text and context.

Ideas and Institutions

In scope, authority, timeliness, substance, and ability to communicate across a wide range of disciplines, Krämer offers the conceptual framework and organisational skills necessary to reshape how we think about Islam, religion, and modernity. To have attained a professorship at the Freie Universität Berlin in 1996 indicates an early recognition of her talent. The collection *Speaking for Islam* (2006), which she co-edited with Sabine Schmidtke, shows her ability to infuse solid scholarship with commentary on changing academic fashion. Both her co-introduction to the volume and her essay on Yūsuf al-Qaraḍāwī's views on apostasy use with skill the academic tropes of the day, including in her title, "Drawing Boundaries." But the essay also points out the irony of "(post-) modern" scholars drawing fixed boundaries of what is "right" and "wrong" that offer strong parallels to the habits they condemn among their predecessors (Krämer 2006, 181). Her preface to *Global Mufti* (2009) exemplifies her style in succinctly presenting the work of colleagues and students without claiming explicit credit for making things work for others (Krämer 2009, ix–xi).

I lack firsthand knowledge of the behind-the-scenes efforts involved in creating the Berlin Graduate School Muslim Cultures and Societies (BGSMCS) in 2007, for which Krämer has served as director from its inception until today. It is clear that in scope and substance, any graduate programme based in two universities—the Freie Universität Berlin and the Humboldt-Universität zu Berlin—and an independent research centre, the Leibniz-Zentrum Moderner Orient, conjoined with federal and state German funding as a centre of excellence, suggests a strong ability to work with and persuade others, not only immediate colleagues in Islamic studies but also educational policy-makers and high-level deciders on the allocation of scarce resources. From distant North America, it appears that BGSMCS is now assuming the mantle of intellectual leadership and training to which ISIM in the Netherlands aspired but was unable to sustain.

What makes the Berlin Graduate School stand out from other programmes is its emphasis on graduate training—a long-term investment in higher education open to Germans and non-Germans alike—facilitating the work of advanced students, recent post-doctorates, and advanced scholars who can make use of the multiple resources available in Berlin. BGSMCS is further abetted by Krämer's *modus operandi*. From the first time that I met Dr. Krämer in her "natural habitat" of Berlin in 2000–2001, she introduced me promptly to her students and junior colleagues—a habit of opening networks to others that cannot be taken for granted. After BGSMCS was launched in 2007, her concern with creating opportunities for the next generation became all the more apparent. In April 2010, I took part in a BGSMCS conference on "Integrating Media and Transcultural Communication Research within Islamic and Area Studies." The conference was vintage Krämer in at least two ways. It was actually organised by then-junior colleagues with a special interest in Islamic and media studies, Bettina Gräf and Nadja-Christina Schneider. It brought together a number of younger scholars, not all of whom were working on Islamic themes. Some were involved in other aspects of media studies, and the conference was an effort to find common ground among scholars and practitioners with different skills and understanding of the implications of the new communications media. Krämer's style was to let others learn to lead and organise, with her preparing the way. My contribution as an "elder" was to link these new directions in media studies with earlier approaches.[6] Krämer's contribution was quietly to level the playing field in academic life between women and men, and advanced scholars and those whose careers were just beginning. Sometimes the most dramatic changes come not through proclamations, but by example. Between words and practice, Krämer has been a powerful voice in shaping Islamic studies today.

Many of us can write books and share good ideas in conferences and seminars. What distinguishes a few scholars such as Gudrun Krämer is the ability

6 For my contribution, see Eickelman 2011.

to lead, persuade, and organise, by words and deeds, creating the space and structure for promising contemporaries and successors.

A distinctive Krämer characteristic is the ability to seize the particular, as with her earlier work on Jews in Egypt in the first half of the twentieth century and her important later work on Egypt's Ḥasan al-Bannā (d. 1949), founder of the Muslim Brotherhood, and to relate such "specifics" to wider issues central to contemporary social thought. She communicates her ideas to wide audiences and works with others to enhance their own skills at research, interpretation, and communication. BGSMCS was not the heroic creation of one person, but one can impute to Krämer the ability to create "ties that bind," enabling the creation of institutions and habits of thinking likely to endure for years to come.

Krämer's work is good to think with, as Lévi-Strauss might say. She translates key concepts across global and national lines, bringing clarity to ongoing debates. Her knowledge of historical and present-day contexts contributes significantly to our understanding of major issues of religious and secular authority, and how the struggle over people's imaginations in public and political space has played out earlier in history and today. Her writings and activities advance scholarship, and she addresses issues that have immediate implications for European and global policy issues. In a word, she has had a global impact. An important part of her enduring legacy will be BGSMCS, recently awarded the Einstein Award for Doctoral Programmes.

Bibliography

Anderson, Benedict. 1993^2 [1983]. *Imagined Communities: Reflections on the Origin and Spread of Nationalism*. New York: Verso.

Eickelman, Dale F. 1978. "The Art of Memory: Islamic Education and Its Social Reproduction." *Comparative Studies in Society and History* 20/4: 485–516.

Eickelman, Dale F. 1979. "The Political Economy of Meaning." *American Ethnologist* 6/2: 386–93.

Eickelman, Dale F. 1985. *Knowledge and Power in Morocco: The Education of a Twentieth-Century Notable*. Princeton: Princeton University Press.

Eickelman, Dale F. 2011. "Media in Islamic and Area Studies: Personal Encounters." *Oriente Moderno* 91/1: 13–22.

Eickelman, Dale F. 2015^2. "Anthropology of Knowledge." *International Encyclopedia of the Social and Behavioral Sciences*, vol. 13. Oxford: Elsevier, 70–73.

Eickelman, Dale F. 2017. "Building Universities that Lead: The Arabian Peninsula." In Dale F. Eickelman and Rogaia Mustafa Abusharaf (eds.), *Higher Education Investment in the Arab States of the Gulf: Strategies for Excellence and Diversity*. Berlin: Gerlach Press, 8–22.

von Grunebaum, Gustav E. (ed.). 1955. *Unity and Variety in Muslim Civilization*. Chicago: University of Chicago Press.

Halpern, Manfred. 1963. *The Politics of Social Change in the Middle East and North Africa*. Princeton: Princeton University Press.

Keane, John. 1998. "The Limits of Secularism." *Times Literary Supplement*, January 9.

Krämer, Gudrun. 2000. "On Difference and Understanding: The Use and Abuse of the Study of Islam." *ISIM Newsletter* 5 (June 2000), 6–7. Accessible online at https://openaccess.leidenuniv.nl/bitstream/handle/1887/17393/ISIM_5_On_Difference_and_Understanding-The_Use_and_Abuse_of_the_Study_of_Islam.pdf?sequence=1.

Krämer, Gudrun. 2006. "Drawing Boundaries: Yūsuf al-Qaraḍāwī on Apostasy." In Gudrun Krämer and Sabine Schmidtke (eds.), *Speaking for Islam: Religious Authorities in Muslim Societies*. Leiden: Brill, 181–217.

Krämer, Gudrun. 2009. "Preface." In Bettina Gräf and Jakob Skovgaard-Peterson (eds.), *Global Mufti: The Phenomenon of Yūsuf al-Qaraḍāwī*. London: Hurst, ix–xi.

Lerner, Daniel. 1964 [1958]. *The Passing of Traditional Society: Modernizing the Middle East*. New York: Free Press.

Scott, James C. 1985. *Weapons of the Weak: Everyday Forms of Peasant Resistance*. New Haven: Yale University Press.

Smith, Wilfred Cantwell. 1963. *The Meaning and End of Religion: A New Approach to the Religious Traditions of Mankind*. New York: Macmillan.

Illustrations

4.1 *Surname-i Vehbi*, Procession of the guilds; in the foreground, the representatives of the jewellers and goldsmiths. 82

5.1 Wedding photograph of Boghos Kaboulian and Rebecca Najarian, Agn/Eğin, ca. 1898 (Kaboulian coll., USA / Houshamadyan). 116

5.2 Wedding photograph of Arshalous Kasabashian (born Shahabian) and Yervant Kasabashian, Shabin-Karahisar, 1908 (Kasabach and Getoor coll., Southfield, MI, USA / Houshamadyan). 117

5.3 The post-mortem photograph of Mahdesi Avedis Toumajan, Gürün (Toumajan coll., Southfield, MI, USA / Houshamadyan). 118

5.4 Armenian family from Agn/Eğin (Jamgochian coll., USA / Houshamadyan). 120

5.5 The Kurkjian family, ca. 1901, Eğin/Agn or Erzincan/Yerznga (Gloria Korkoian coll., Dearborn, MI, USA / Houshamadyan). 122

5.6 The Der Matossian family, Keghi, before 1912 (ODA/Americas/Gloria Korkoian coll., Dearborn, MI, USA / Houshamadyan). 124

11.1 The letter *nūn* may take many different shapes depending on the letter that follows. Figure taken from "Text Layout Requirements for the Arabic Script." W3C Editor's Draft 03 August 2017, https://w3c.github.io/alreq/. 249

11.2 Nazar talisman, to ward off the Evil Eye, Turkey 2012. Blue glass, golden glitter, and plastic pearls, with printed motive showing the Kaʿba. 250

11.3 Shop window in Istanbul 2012 with oversized "Muḥammad" lettering in an especially twisted ligature. 251

11.4 Silver dirham dated 208/823-24. Photograph by Pernille Klemp for The David Collection, Copenhagen,
Inv.No C 32. 253

11.5 Beirut 2017 255

11.6 On the fence surrounding the building site for the new Bauhaus Museum, to open in 2018, the slogan "Bauhaus Museum in the city of Dessau" is rendered in various languages. The Arabic version shows the three most common mistakes that word processing programmes cause: Writing is from left to right instead of right to left, letters are reversed, and all are unconnected. 256

11.7 Programming Language *qalb* ("heart," a recursive acronym for *lugha barmaja*) with the implementation of the Fibonacci sequence algorithm, which is frequently used in demonstrations of new programming languages. 257

11.8 Dervish's staff, Iran, 18th-19th century. Photograph by Pernille Klemp for the David Collection, Copenhagen, Inv.No 15/1994. 258

11.9 In the shop of the Great Mosque of Xi'an, China, this calligraphy was displayed for sale in 2015. It shows a vase full of flowers that is formed out of words. The centre section of the vase reads *raḥmat Allāh* (God's Mercy). 259
11.10 A Turkish restaurant in Berlin uses the basmalah in the shape of a tulip as a neon-lit shop sign. 260
11.11 In this Bektashi Ṣūfī paper silhouette (1280/1863–64), cut with a sharp knife rather than scissors, ʿAlī is personified as a lion. 261
22.1 Arrival. Illustration by Anton Jones, 2018. 442
22.2 Crossing. Illustration by Anton Jones, 2018. 457
22.3 Detention. Illustration by Anton Jones, 2018. 463

Contributors

Ahmed Ibrahim Abushouk
is Professor of Modern and Contemporary History and Associate Dean for Academic Affairs at the College of Arts and Sciences, Qatar University, Qatar.

Schirin Amir-Moazami
is Professor of Islamic Studies at the Institute for Islamic Studies, Freie Universität Berlin, Germany.

Katajun Amirpur
is Professor of Islamic Studies at the University of Cologne, Germany.

Muriel Asseburg
PhD, is Senior Fellow at the Stiftung Wissenschaft und Politik (SWP), Berlin, Germany.

Hamit Bozarslan
PhD, is Director of Studies at the École des Hautes Études en Sciences Sociales (EHESS), CETObaC, Paris, France.

Johann Büssow
is Professor of Islamic History and Culture at the Ruhr-Universität Bochum, Germany.

Bettina Dennerlein
is Professor of Gender Studies and Islamic Studies at the University of Zurich, Switzerland.

Dale F. Eickelman
is Ralph and Richard Lazarus Professor of Anthropology and Human Relations Emeritus and Research Professor of Anthropology at Dartmouth College, Hanover, New Hampshire, USA.

Abdou Filali-Ansary
is Professor Emeritus, Aga Khan University, Institute for the Study of Muslim Civilisations, London, United Kingdom.

Bettina Gräf
PhD, is Lecturer at the Institute for the Near and Middle East at Ludwig-Maximilians-Universität München, Germany.

Cilja Harders
is Professor of Political Science and Head of the Center for Middle Eastern and North African Politics, Otto-Suhr-Institut, Freie Universität Berlin, Germany.

Elke Hartmann
PhD, is Visiting Professor of Cultural Studies of the Middle East at the Universität Bamberg, Germany.

Mutaz al-Khatib
is Assistant Professor at the Research Center for Islamic Legislation and Ethics (CILE), Hamad Bin Khalifa University, Qatar.

Alexander Knysh
is Professor of Islamic Studies at the University of Michigan, Ann Arbor, Michigan, USA, and St. Petersburg State University, St. Petersburg, Russia.

Alina Kokoschka
PhD, is a Postdoctoral Researcher at the Institute for Islamic Studies and the Berlin Graduate School Muslim Cultures and Societies, Freie Universität Berlin, Germany.

Birgit Krawietz
is Professor of Islamic Studies at the Institute for Islamic Studies, Freie Universität Berlin, Germany.

Kai Kresse
is Associate Professor of Middle Eastern, South Asian, and African Studies at Columbia University, New York, New York, USA.

Ruth Mas
PhD, New York, New York, USA.

Astrid Meier
is Professor of Islamic Studies at the Martin-Luther-Universität Halle-Wittenberg, Germany.

M. Sait Özervarlı
is Professor of Intellectual History and Head of the Department of Humanities and Social Sciences at Yildiz Technical University, Istanbul, Turkey.

Dorothea Schulz
is Professor of Anthropology at the Department of Social Anthropology, University of Münster, Germany.

Reinhard Schulze
is Professor Emeritus of Islamic Studies and Oriental Philology and head of the Forum Islam and Middle East at the Universität Bern, Switzerland.

Abdulkader Tayob
is Professor of Islam, African Publics, and Religious Values at the University of Cape Town, South Africa.

Muhammad Qasim Zaman
is the Robert H. Niehaus '77 Professor of Near Eastern Studies and Religion at Princeton University, Princeton, New Jersey, USA.

Tabula Gratulatoria

The essays in this volume testify to both the breadth and depth of Gudrun Krämer's scholarship in Middle Eastern and Islamic studies, but they cannot capture the full range of her influence in these fields and the personal side of her interactions with scholarly colleagues. Having missed meeting her by a few months in Cairo in 1980, I finally caught up with her in 2001, when we were recruited as two of the executive editors of the third edition of the Encyclopaedia of Islam, and I quickly came to appreciate her impact on the field in its widest sense. From Berkeley to Beijing, Gudrun has edified and charmed colleagues in a wide variety of disciplines, as testified to by this Tabula Gratulatoria.

Everett Rowson

—

Dauda Abubakar
Ahmed Ibrahim Abushouk
Manan Ahmed
Olly Akkerman
Sarah Albrecht
Peter-André Alt
Schirin Amir-Moazami
Katajun Amirpur
Abdullahi A. An-Na'im
Muriel Asseburg
Nadia Al-Bagdadi
Ingeborg Baldauf
Thomas Bauer
Lale Behzadi
Ildikó Bellér-Hann
Teresa Bernheimer
Sheila Blair
Verena Blechinger-Talcott
Jonathan Bloom
Philip Bockholt
Ralph Bodenstein
Anabelle Böttcher
Michael Bongardt
Maurits van den Boogert
Michael Borgolte
Antonia Bosanquet
Hamit Bozarslan
Gabriele vom Bruck
Rainer Brunner
Johann Büssow
Léon Buskens
Alexandre Caeiro
Sebastian Conrad
Nadja Danilenko
Amir Dastmalchian
Bettina Dennerlein
Nora Derbal
Hansjörg Dilger
Hans-Georg Ebert
Saeid Edalatnejad
Dale F. Eickelman
Joed Elich
Khaled El-Rouayheb
Sebastian Elsässer
Sarah Eltantawi
Werner Ende
Farid Esack
Markus Fiebig
Abdou Filali-Ansary
Kate Fleet
Regula Forster
Britta Frede

Gabriele Freitag
Ulrike Freitag
Josephine Gelhar
Linda George
Farid al-Ghawaby
Nicholas Gjorvad
Karin Gludovatz
Bettina Gräf
Hannes Grandits
Nile Green
Martin Grötschel
Beatrice Gründler
Annette Grüters-Kieslich
Nora Haakh
Claus-Peter Haase
Kai Hafez
Veronika Hager
Dyala Hamzah
Cilja Harders
Alan H. Hartley
Elke Hartmann
Axel Havemann
Peter Heine
Arnim Heinemann
Konrad Hirschler
Nicolette van der Hoek
Albert Hoffstadt
Livnat Holtzman
Vincent Houben
Ahmed Fekry Ibrahim
Oliver Janz
Hans Joas
Baber Johansen
Brian Johnson
Hilary Kalmbach
Andreas Kaplony
Nico Kaptein
Omar Kasmani
Elizabeth Suzanne Kassab
Frank Kelleter
Barbara Kellner-Heinkele
Georges Khalil
Mutaz al-Khatib
Hans Kippenberg
Verena Klemm
Alexander Knysh
Florian Kohstall
Alina Kokoschka
Jakob Krais
Birgit Krawietz
Klaus Kreiser
Kai Kresse
Hermann Kreutzmann
Anke von Kügelgen
Winrich Kühne
Mirjam Künkler
Nora Lafi
Christian Lange
Peter Lange
Aleksandra Lewicki
Amélie Le Renard
Zachary Lockman
Roman Loimeier
Christoph Markschies
Ruth Mas
Denis Matringe
Astrid Meier
Rahina Muazu
Christian Müller
Jutta Müller-Tamm
Nefissa Naguib
John Nawas
Christoph Neumann
Jørgen Nielsen
Katja Niethammer
Giorgio Nogara
Ulrich Nolte
M. Sait Özervarlı
M'hamed Oualdi
Abdurraouf Oueslati
Lars Ostermeier
Friedericke Pannewick

Margrit Pernau
Volker Perthes
Frank Peter
Johanna Pink
Andrea Polaschegg
Dietrich Reetz
A. Kevin Reinhart
Nils Riecken
Olivier Roy
D. Fairchild Ruggles
Umar Ryad
Dorothée Sack
Samuli Schielke
Werner Schiffauer
Sabine Schmidtke
Nadja-Christina Schneider
Cornelia Schöck
Anja Schoene
Dorothea Schulz
Reinhard Schulze
Roman Seidel
Wendy Shaw
Ayman Shihadeh
Katrin Simon
Udo Steinbach
Manja Stephan-Emmrich
Shabo Talay
George Tamer
Abdulkader Tayob
Hanan Toukan
Leslie Tramontini
Torsten Tschacher
Markus Wachowski
Stefan Weber
Isabelle Werenfels
Christoph Werner
Stefan Wild
Torsten Wollina
Anna Würth
Ronny Vollandt
Muhammad Qasim Zaman
Hartmut Zinser

Bibliography Gudrun Krämer

Books

2016. *Der Vordere Orient und Nordafrika ab 1500*. Frankfurt am Main: Fischer.

2011. *Demokratie im Islam*. Munich: C.H. Beck Verlag.

2010. *Hasan al-Banna*. Oxford: Oneworld Publications.

2008. *A History of Palestine: From the Ottoman Conquest to the Founding of the State of Israel*. Princeton: Princeton University Press.

2005. *Geschichte des Islam*. Munich: C.H. Beck Verlag.

2002. *Geschichte Palästinas: Von der osmanischen Eroberung bis zur Gründung des Staates Israel*. Munich: C.H. Beck Verlag.

2000. *Responsabilité, égalité, pluralisme: Réflexions sur quelques notions-clés d'un ordre islamique moderne*. Casablanca: éd. Le Fennec.

1999. *Gottes Staat als Republik: Reflexionen zeitgenössischer Muslime zu Islam, Menschenrechten und Demokratie*. Baden-Baden: Nomos.

1989. *The Jews in Modern Egypt, 1914–1952*. London: I.B. Tauris.

1986. *Ägypten unter Mubarak: Identität und nationales Interesse*. Baden-Baden: Nomos.

1982. *Minderheit, Millet, Nation?: Die Juden in Ägypten, 1914–1952*. Wiesbaden: Harrassowitz.

Book Chapters

2018. "Piety, Politics, and Identity: Configurations of Secularity in Egypt." In Mirjam Künkler, John Madeley, and Shylashri Shankar (eds.), *A Secular Age beyond the West: Religion, Law and the State in Asia, the Middle East and North Africa*. Cambridge: Cambridge University Press, 295–316.

2015. "Arabische Welt." In Friedrich Jaeger, Wolfgang Knöbl, and Ute Schneider (eds.), *Handbuch Moderneforschung*. Stuttgart and Weimar: J.B. Metzler, 27–37.

2015. "Die Erziehung des aktiven Muslims: Hasan al-Banna, die ägyptischen Muslimbrüder und das Projekt der islamischen Reform." In Tobias Georges, Jens J. Scheiner, and Ilinca Tanaseanu-Döbler (eds.), *Bedeutende Lehrerfiguren: Von Platon bis Hasan al-Banna*. Tübingen: Mohr Siebeck, 333–58.

2015. "Making Modern Muslims: Islamic Reform, Hasan al-Banna, and the Egyptian Muslim Brotherhood." In Sven Trakulhun, Ralph Weber, and Pheng Cheah (eds.), *Delimiting Modernities: Conceptual Challenges and Regional Responses*. Lanham, MD: Lexington Books, 197–213.

2015. "Pluralism and Tolerance." In Gerhard Böwering (ed.), *Islamic Political Thought: An Introduction*. Princeton: Princeton University Press, 169–84.

2015. "Secularity Contested: Religion, Identity and the Public Order in the Arab Middle East." In Marian Burchardt, Monika Wohlrab-Sahr, and Matthias Middell (eds.), *Multiple Secularities beyond the West: Religion and Modernity in the Global Age*. Vol. 1, *Religion and Its Others*. Berlin and Boston: de Gruyter, 121–37.

2015. "Von Normen und Werten: Religion, Recht und Politik im modernen Islam." In Helmut König and Manfred Sicking (eds.), *Der Irak-Krieg und die Zukunft Europas*. Bielefeld: transcript, 171–90.

2014. "Der Reiz des Gesellschaftsvergleichs: Kategorien sozialer Ordnung im islamisch geprägten Vorderen Orient." In Tillmann Lohse and Benjamin Scheller (eds.), *Europa in der Welt des Mittelalters: Ein Colloquium für und mit Michael Borgolte*. Berlin and Boston: de Gruyter, 101–18.

2013. "Gottes-Recht bricht Menschen-Recht: Theokratische Entwürfe im zeitgenössischen Islam." In Kai Trampedach and Andreas Pečar (eds.), *Theokratie und theokratischer Diskurs: Die Rede von der Gottesherrschaft und ihre politisch-sozialen Auswirkungen im interkulturellen Vergleich*. Tübingen: Mohr Siebeck, 493–515.

2012. "Islamische Reform und gesellschaftliche Erneuerung oder: Was ist 'kritische Islamwissenschaft'?" In Mouhanad Khorchide and Marco Schöller (eds.), *Das Verhältnis zwischen Islamwissenschaft und islamischer Theologie: Beiträge der Konferenz Münster, 1.-2. Juli 2011*. Vol. 1, *Masa'il*. Münster: Agenda Verlag, 109–114.

2012. "Kommentar." In Michael Borgolte and Matthias M. Tischler (eds.), *Transkulturelle Verflechtungen im mittelalterlichen Jahrtausend: Europa, Ostasien, Afrika*. Darmstadt: Wissenschaftliche Buchgesellschaft, 187–94.

2011. "Islam, Kapitalismus und die protestantische Ethik." In Gunilla-Friederike Budde (ed.), *Kapitalismus: Historische Annäherungen*. Göttingen and Oakville CT: Vandenhoeck & Ruprecht, 116–46.

2011. "Zum Verhältnis von Religion, Recht und Politik: Säkularisierung im Islam." In Elke Ariëns, Helmut König, and Manfred Sicking (eds.), *Glaubensfragen in Europa: Religion und Politik im Konflikt*. Bielefeld: transcript, 127–48.

2010. "Toleranz im Islam: Ein Blick in Geschichte und Gegenwart." In Angelika Neuwirth and Günter Stock (eds.), *Europa im Nahen Osten, der Nahe Osten in Europa*. Berlin: Akademie Verlag, 39–52.

2009. "Einheit, Vielfalt und die Spannung zwischen diesen beiden: Eine Einführung in den Islam." In Karl Lehmann (ed.), *Weltreligionen: Verstehen, Verständigung, Verantwortung*. Frankfurt am Main: Verlag der Weltreligionen, 137–56.

2009. "Islam and Secularization." In Hans Joas and Klaus Wiegandt (eds.), *Secularization and the World Religions*. Liverpool: Liverpool University Press.

2009. "Foreword." In Bettina Gräf and Jakob Skovgaard-Petersen (eds.), *Global Mufti: The Phenomenon of Yūsuf al-Qaraḍāwī*. London: Hurst, 9–11.

2008. “The Contest of Values: Notes on Contemporary Islamic Discourse.” In Hans Joas and Klaus Wiegandt (eds.), *The Cultural Values of Europe*. Liverpool: Liverpool University Press, 338–56.

2008. “Hohe Religiosität und Vielfalt: Muslimische Aspekte des Religionsmonitors.” In Bertelsmann Stiftung (ed.), *Religionsmonitor* [...]. Gütersloh: Verlag Bertelsmann Stiftung, 219–29.

2008. “Ist der Islam eine politische Religion?” In Konrad Paul Liessmann (ed.), *Die Gretchenfrage: “Nun sag', wie hast du's mit der Religion?”* Vienna: Zsolnay, 82–103.

2008. “Ja, er kann: Islam als Empowerment.” In D. Ganten (ed.), *Was ist der Mensch?* Humanprojekt: Interdisziplinäre Anthropologie 3. Berlin: de Gruyter, 159–61.

2008. “Moving out of Place: Minorities in Middle Eastern Urban Societies, 1800–1914.” In Peter Sluglett (ed.), *The Urban Social History of the Middle East, 1750–1950*. Syracuse NY: Syracuse University Press, 182–223.

2008. “Unterscheiden und Verstehen: Über Nutzen und Missbrauch der Islamwissenschaft.“ In Abbas Poya & Maurus Reinkowski (eds.), *Das Unbehagen in der Islamwissenschaft.* Bielefeld: transcript, 263–70.

2008. “Vision und Kritik des Staates im Islamismus.” In Peter Pawelka (ed.), *Der Staat im Vorderen Orient: Konstruktion und Legitimation politischer Herrschaft*. Baden-Baden: Nomos, 82–103.

2007. “Islam, Menschenrechte und Demokratie: Anmerkungen zu einem schwierigen Verhältnis.” In Nicole Janz & Thomas Risse-Kappen (eds.), *Menschenrechte—globale Dimensionen eines universellen Anspruchs*. Baden-Baden: Nomos, 39–54.

2007. “Justice in Modern Islamic Thought.” In Abbas Amanat and Frank Griffel (eds.), *Shari'a: Islamic Law in the Contemporary Context*. Stanford: Stanford University Press, 20–37; 187–96.

2007. “Zum Verhältnis von Religion, Recht und Politik: Säkularisierung im Islam.” In Hans Joas and Klaus Wiegandt (eds.), *Säkularisierung und die Weltreligionen*. Frankfurt am Main: Fischer, 172–93.

2006. “Drawing Boundaries: Yūsuf al-Qaraḍāwī on Apostasy.” In Gudrun Krämer and Sabine Schmidtke (eds.), *Speaking for Islam: Religious Authorities in Muslim Societies.* Leiden and Boston: Brill, 181–217.

2006. (with Sabine Schmidtke) “Religious Authority and Religious Authorities in Muslim Societies: A Critical Overview.” In Gudrun Krämer and Sabine Schmidtke (eds.), *Speaking for Islam: Religious Authorities in Muslim Societies.* Leiden and Boston: Brill, 1–14.

2006. “Gewaltpotentiale im Islam.” In Reinhard Hempelmann and Johannes Kandel (eds.), *Religionen und Gewalt: Konflikt- und Friedenspotentiale in den Weltreligionen*. Göttingen: V&R unipress, 239–47.

2006. “Introduction.” In Zahiduddin I. Munavvarov and Reinhard J. Krumm (eds.), *The Role of Women in Modern Muslim Societies*. Tashkent: Center of al-Imam Bukhari and Friedrich Ebert Stiftung, 117–24.

2006. "'Kein Zwang in der Religion'?: Religiöse Toleranz im Islam." In Matthias Mahlmann and Hubert Rottleuthner (eds.), *Ein neuer Kampf der Religionen? Staat, Recht und religiöse Toleranz*. Berlin: Duncker & Humblot, 141–60.

2005. "State and Religion in the Modern Islamic World: Introductory Remarks." In: Zahiduddin I. Munavvarov and Reinhard J. Krumm (eds.), *Secularity and Religion in Muslim Countries: Searching for a Rational Balance*. Tashkent: Friedrich Ebert Stiftung, *150–54*.

2005. "Wettstreit der Werte: Anmerkungen zum zeitgenössischen islamischen Diskurs." In Helmut Heit (ed.), *Die Werte Europas: Verfassungspatriotismus und Wertegemeinschaft in der EU?*. Münster: LIT Verlag, 469–93.

2004. "Juden, Christen und Muslime in der 'Heiligen Stadt'." In Helmut Hubel and Tilman Seidensticker (eds.), *Jerusalem im Widerstreit politischer und religiöser Interessen: Die "Heilige Stadt aus interdisziplinärer Sicht*. Frankfurt am Main: Peter Lang, 41–58.

2004. "Aus Erfahrung lernen? Die islamische Bewegung in Ägypten." In Clemens Six, Martin Riesebrodt & Siegfried Haas (eds.), *Religiöser Fundamentalismus: Vom Kolonialismus zur Globalisierung*. Innsbruck: StudienVerlag, 185–200.

2004. "Introduction." In Zahiduddin I. Munavvarov & Reinhard J. Krumm (eds.), *State and Religion in Countries with a Muslim Population*. Tashkent: Center of al-Imam Bukhari and Friedrich Ebert Stiftung, 154–58.

2003. "'Der Islam ist Religion und Staat': Zum Verhältnis von Religion, Recht und Politik im Islam." In Wolfgang Schluchter (ed.), *Fundamentalismus, Terrorismus, Krieg*. Weilerswist: Velbrück Wissenschaft, 45–59.

2003. "Islam, Menschenrechte und Demokratie: Anmerkungen zu einem schwierigen Verhältnis." *Bertha Benz-Vorlesung* 20. Ladenburg: Gottlieb Daimler- und Karl Benz-Stiftung.

2003. "Islam, Menschenrechte und Demokratie: Anmerkungen zu einem schwierigen Verhältnis." In Deutscher Hochschulverband (ed.), *Glanzlichter der Wissenschaft: Ein Almanach*. Saarwellingen: Licius & Licius Verlag, 93–103.

2003. "Zum Verhältnis von Religion, Recht und Politik im Islam." In Zahiduddin I. Munavvarov (ed.), *Islam und säkularer Staat: Dokumentation des Internationalen Symposiums "Islam und Säkularer Staat," 5./6.6.2002*. Tashkent: Internat. Stiftung al-Imam al-Buhari, Friedrich-Ebert-Stiftung, 199–208.

2001. "Toleranz und Bürgerrecht: Nichtmuslime in muslimischen Gesellschaften." In Hilmar Hoffmann and Wilfried F. Schoeller (eds.), *Wendepunkt 11. September 2001: Terror, Islam und Demokratie*. Cologne: DuMont, 157–73.

2000. "Die Entdeckung der Zivilgesellschaft: Ein kritischer Überblick." In Franz Peter Lang and M. Reza Asghari (eds.), *Islam und sozio-ökonomische Entwicklung*. Essen: MA, Akademie Verlags- und Druck-Gesellschaft, 55–67.

2000. "Good Counsel to the King: The Islamist Opposition in Saudi Arabia, Jordan and Morocco." In Joseph Kostiner (ed.), *Middle East Monarchies: The Challenge of Modernity*. Boulder, CO: Lynne Rienner Publishers, 257–87.

2000. "Les juifs d'Égypte: Communauté une et divisible." In Christian Décobert (ed.), *Valeur et distance: Identités et sociétés en Égypte.* Paris: Maisonneuve et Larose, Maison Méditerranéenne des Sciences de l'Homme, 199–208.

2000. "Visions of an Islamic Republic: Good Governance according to the Islamists." In Kai Hafez (ed.), *The Islamic World and the West.* Leiden: Brill, 33–45.

1999. "Moderner Staat, kolonialer Staat? Ägypten und der Fruchtbare Halbmond." In Wolfgang Reinhard (ed.), *Verstaatlichung der Welt? Europäische Staatsmodelle und außereuropäische Machtprozesse.* Munich: Oldenbourg, 165–88.

1999. "Techniques and Values: Contemporary Muslim Debates on Islam and Democracy." In Gema Martin Munoz (ed.), *Islam, Modernism and the West: Cultural and Political Relations at the End of the Millenium.* London and New York: I.B. Tauris, 174–90.

1998. "Die arabische Welt im 20. Jahrhundert." In Albrecht Noth and Jürgen Paul (eds.), *Der islamische Orient: Grundzüge seiner Geschichte.* Würzburg: Ergon, 439–504.

1997. "Der „Gottesstaat" als Republik? Islam und Demokratie." In Kai Hafez (ed.), *Der Islam und der Westen: Anstiftung zum Dialog.* Frankfurt am Main: Fischer Taschenbuch, 44–55.

1997. "Liberalisierung in der arabischen Welt." In Wilfried von Bredow (ed.), *Demokratie und Entwicklung: Theorie und Praxis der Demokratisierung in der Dritten Welt.* Opladen: Leske + Budrich, 51–60.

1996. "Order and Interest: The Gulf War and the Arab State System." In Wolfgang F. Danspeckgruber and Charles Tripp (eds.), *The Iraqi Aggression against Kuwait: Strategic Lessons and Implications for Europe*. Boulder CO: Westview Press, 51–64.

1995. "Cross-Links and Double Talk? Islamist Movements in the Political Process." In Laura Guazzone (ed.), *The Islamist Dilemma: The Political Role of Islamist Movements in the Contemporary Arab World.* Reading: Ithaca Press, 39–67.

1995. "Dhimmi ou citoyen: Réflexions réformistes sur le statut des non-musulmans en société islamique." In Alain Roussillon (ed.), *Entre Réforme sociale et mouvement national: Identité et modernisation en Égypte (1882–1962)*. Cairo: CEDEJ, 577–90.

1995. "Islam and Pluralism." In Rex Brynen, Bahgat Korany, and Paul Noble (eds.), *Political Liberalization and Democratization in the Arab World.* Vol. 1, Theoretical Perspectives. Boulder and London: Lynne Rienner Publishers, 113–28.

1994. "The Integration of the Integrists: A Comparative Study of Egypt, Jordan and Tunisia." In Ghassan Salamé (ed.), *Democracy without Democrats? The Renewal of Politics in the Muslim World.* London and New York: I.B. Tauris, 200–26.

1992. "Konfliktmuster und Konfliktmöglichkeiten im Nahen Osten und am Golf." In Wolfgang Heydrich, J. Krause, Uwe Nerlich, J. Nötzold, and Reinhardt Rummel (eds.), *Sicherheitspolitik Deutschlands: Neue Konstellationen, Risiken, Instrumente*. Baden-Baden: Nomos, 439–57.

1992. "Kritik und Selbstkritik: Reformistisches Denken im Islam." In Michael Lüders (ed.), *Der Islam im Aufbruch? Perspektiven der arabischen Welt*. Munich and Zurich: Piper Verlag, 207–29.

1991 "Die Golfkrise und das arabische Staatensystem." In Peter Pawelka et al. (eds.), *Die Golfregion in der Weltpolitik*. Stuttgart, Cologne, and Berlin: Verlag W. Kohlhammer, 9–20.

1989. "Macht und Allmacht: Die Konfliktlage im Nahen Osten." In Dieter Senghaas (ed.), *Regionalkonflikte in der Dritten Welt: Autonomie und Fremdbestimmung*. Baden-Baden: Nomos, 149–66.

1988. "Ägypten: Probleme der inneren Ordnung." In Helmut Hubel (ed.): *Nordafrika in der internationalen Politik*. Munich: R. Oldenbourg Verlag, 73–84.

1987. "Political Participation of the Jews in Egypt, World War I to the Revolution of 1952." In Shimon Shamir (ed.), *The Jews of Egypt: A Mediterranean Society in Modern Times*. Boulder and London: Westview Press, 68–82.

1984. "*Zionism in Egypt, 1917–1948*." In Amnon Cohen and Gabriel Baer (eds.), *Egypt and Palestine*. New York: St. Martin's, and Jerusalem: Ben Zvi Institute.

1983. "'Radical' Nationalists, Fundamentalists, and the Jews in Egypt or, Who is a Real Egyptian?" In Gabriel Warburg and Uri M. Kupferschmidt (eds.), *Islam, Nationalism, and Radicalism in Egypt and the Sudan*. New York: Praeger, 354–71.

1981. "Face à la modernité: Les Juifs d'Égypte aus XIXe et XXe siècles." In Jacques Hassoun (ed.), *Juifs du Nil*. Paris: Sycomore, 81–106.

Editorship

2007-. *The Encyclopaedia of Islam THREE*. Edited by Kate Fleet, Gudrun Krämer, Denis Matringe, John Nawas, and Everett Rowson. Leiden and Boston: Brill.

2006. (with Sabine Schmidtke) *Speaking for Islam: Religious Authorities in Muslim Societies*. Leiden and Boston: Brill.

2006. Anti-Semitism in the Muslim World. In *Die Welt des Islams* 46/3.

Journal Articles and Reviews

2014. "M. Emon, Anver: *Religious Pluralism and Islamic Law: Dhimmīs and Others in the Empire of Law* (Review)." *Bulletin of the School of Oriental and African Studies* 77: 205–6.

2013. "Modern but Not Secular: Religion, Identity and the *ordre public* in the Arab Middle East." *International Sociology* 28/6: 629–44.

2009. "'New Fiqh' Applied: Yūsuf al-Qaraḍāwī on Non-Muslims in Islamic Society." *Jerusalem Studies in Arabic and Islam* 36: 489–515.

2006. "Anti-Semitism in the Arab World: A Critical Review." *Die Welt des Islams* 46/3: 243–76.

2005. "Gute Regierungsführung: Neue Stimmen aus der islamischen Welt." *Verfassung und Recht in Übersee* 38/3: 258–75.

2005. "Islam und Toleranz." *Blätter für deutsche und internationale Politik* 50/9: 1119–29.

2004. "Moral Policy or Good Islamic Governance." *Vingtième siècle* 82: 131–43.

2004. "La politique morale ou bien gouverner à l'islamique." *Vingtième siècle* 82: 131–43.

2003. "Islam, Menschenrechte und Demokratie: Anmerkungen zu einem schwierigen Verhältnis." *Wirtschaft und Wissenschaft* 11: 36–47.

2001. "Nachdenken über Islam, Menschenrechte und Demokratie." *Gewerkschaftliche Monatshefte* 52/11–12: 679–85.

2000. "On Difference and Understanding: The Use and Abuse of the Study of Islam. Annual Lecture, International Institute for the Study of Islam in the Modern World (ISIM)." *ISIM Newsletter* 5: 6–7.

1999. "Law and Order: The Application of the Shari'a in the Middle East." *Middle Eastern Lectures* 3: 57–68.

1997. "Ein 'Orchideenfach'? Islamwissenschaft im Porträt." *Forschung & Lehre* 4/8: 422–24.

1996. "Kein Zwang in der Religion?" *Zeitschrift für Kulturaustausch* 46/4: 51–56.

1996. "Keine Demokratisierung ohne die Opposition: Soll man die Islamisten über Wahlen einbinden?" *Der Überblick: Hamburg* 32/4: 15–18.

1994. "Die Attraktion des politischen Islam: Fallbeispiel Ägypten." *Comparativ: Leipziger Beiträge zur Universalgeschichte und vergleichenden Gesellschaftsforschung* 4/6: 58–77.

1994. "Islam ist nicht gleich Islam: Einheit der Lehre, Vielfalt der Lebenswelten." *du: die Zeitschrift der Kultur* 54/7: 27–29.

1993. "Islamist Notions of Democracy." *Middle East Report* 183: 2–8.

1994. "Die Korrektur der Irrtümer: Innerislamische Debatten um Theorie und Praxis der islamischen Bewegungen." In *Zeitschrift der Deutschen Morgenländischen Gesellschaft, Suppl. 10: XXV. Deutscher Orientalistentag in München, Vorträge*, 8.-13.4.1991, ed. Cornelia Wunsch. Stuttgart: Franz Steiner Verlag, 183–91.

1992. "*Nationalism and National Identity*, by Abraham Ashkenasi (Review)." *Middle East Studies Association Bulletin* 26/1: 79–80.

1992. "Liberalization and Democracy in the Arab World." *Middle East Report* 174: 22–25, 35.

1989. "Milton J. Esman, Itamar Rabinovich (eds.), *Ethnicity, Pluralism, and the State in the Middle East*, Ithaca/London: Cornell University Press 1988 (Review)." *Der Islam* 66/1: 151.

1989. "Ronald L. Nettler: *Post Trials Present Tribulations: A Muslim Fundamentalist's View of the Jews*, Oxford: Pergamon Press 1988 (Review)." *Der Islam* 66/1: 164–65.

1987/88. "The Change of Paradigm: Political Pluralism in Contemporary Egypt." In *Peuples Méditerranéens* 41–42: 283–302.

1986. "Das 'Ende' von Camp David." *Internationale Politik 1983–84*: 256–68.

1985. "*Tibi, Bassam: Die Krise des modernen Islams; eine vorindustrielle Kultur im wissenschaftlich-technischen Zeitalter* (Review)." *MERIP Reports* 130: 28–29.

1984. "The May 1984 Parliamentary Elections in Egypt - Parties, Programs and Prospects." *Orient* 25/3: 361–75.

1984. "Die Wahl zum ägyptischen Abgeordnetenhaus vom Mai 1984 - Parteien, Wahlprogramme und Ergebnisse." *Orient* 25/3: 361–75.

1984. "Piscatori, James P., *Islam in the Political Process* (Review)." *Middle East Studies Association Bulletin* 18/1: 88–89.

1983. (with Jean-Pierre Péroncel-Hugoz) "Correspondance." *Politique étrangère* 48/4: 1066.

1983. "L'Égypte du président Moubarak." *Politique Étrangère* 48/3: 633–646.

1983. "Die Juden als Minderheit in Ägypten, 1914–1956: *Islamische Toleranz im Zeichen des Antikolonialismus und des Antizionismus*." *Saeculum* 34/1: 36–69.

1980. "Deutsche Orientalistik—am Beispiel Tübingens. Arabistische und islamkundliche Studien." *Middle East Studies Association Bulletin* 14/2: 76–78.

Encyclopedia Entries

2016. "Political Islam." In Richard C. Martin (ed.), *Encyclopedia of Islam and the Muslim World*, 2nd ed., Farmington Hills: Macmillan Reference.

2015. "Arabische Welt." In Friedrich Jaeger, Wolfgang Knöbl, and Ute Schneider (eds.), *Handbuch Moderneforschung*. Stuttgart: Verlag J.B. Metzler, 27–37.

2015. "Nationalism, Historical Aspects of the Arab World." In James D. Wright (ed.), *International Encyclopedia of the Social & Behavioral Sciences*. Amsterdam: Elsevier, 271–74.

2013. "Hasan al-Banna." In Gerhard Böwering, Patricia Crone, and Mahan Mirza (eds.), *The Princeton Encyclopedia of Islamic Political Thought*. Princeton: Princeton University Press, 12–15.

2013. "Pluralism and Tolerance." In Gerhard Böwering, Patricia Crone, and Mahan Mirza (eds.), *The Princeton Encyclopedia of Islamic Political Thought*. Princeton: Princeton University Press, 419–27.

2007. "Justice and Righteousness: VIII. Islam." In Hans Dieter Betz (ed.), *Religion Past & Present: Encyclopedia of Theology and Religion*. Leiden and Boston: Brill.

1995. "Minorities in Muslim Societies." In John L. Esposito (ed.), *Oxford Encyclopedia of the Modern Islamic World*. New York and Oxford: Oxford University Press, 108–11.
1987. "Ägypten." In Udo Steinbach and Rüdiger Robert (eds.), *Handbuch: Der Nahe und Mittlere Osten.* Leverkusen: Leske Verlag+ Budrich GmbH, vol. 2, 9–39.

Primary Supervision of Doctoral Theses by Gudrun Krämer at Freie Universität Berlin

2018. Danilenko, Nadja. *Picturing the Islamicate World in the Tenth Century: The Story of al-Iṣṭakhrī's Book of Routes and Realms.*

2018. Bockholt, Philip. *Weltgeschichtsschreibung zwischen Schia und Sunna: Ḫvāndamīrs (gest. 1535/6) Ḥabīb as-siyar und seine Rezeption im Handschriftenzeitalter.*

2018. Gjorvad, Nicholas. *The "Black Hole" of the Brotherhood: The Evolution of a Youth Group to a Political Party.*

2016. Al-Zaid, Saud. *Modernity's Other: An Intellectual Anthropology of Radical Islamic Thought.*

2016. Hünefeld, Kerstin. *Islamic Governance in Yemen: Imām Yaḥyā's Protection of the Jews and the Negotiation of Power.*

2015. Kokoschka, Alina. *Warenwelt Islam Konsumkultur und Ästhetik der Waren im zeitgenössischen Syrien.*

2014. Krais, Jakob. *Geschichte als Widerstand: Das Libyan Studies Centre und die antikoloniale Neuschreibung der libyschen Nationalgeschichte (1978–2010).*

2014. Albrecht, Sarah. *Dār al-Islām Revisited: Territoriality in Contemporary Islamic Legal Discourse on Muslims in the West.*

2014. Hartmann, Elke. *Die Reichweite des Staates: Wehrpflicht und moderne Staatlichkeit in der Spätzeit des Osmanischen Reiches (1878–1910).*

2013. Wollina, Torsten. *Zwanzig Jahre Alltag: Das Journal des Ahmad ibn Tauq als Selbstzeugnis.*

2013. Saßmannshausen, Christian. *Reform in Translation: Family, Distinction, and Social Mediation in Late Ottoman Tripoli.*

2012. Simon, Katrin. *"Race matters:" Afroamerikanische Muslime zwischen Widerstand und Anpassung.*

2012. Elsässer, Sebastian. *The Coptic Question in Contemporary Egypt: Debating National Identity, Religion, and Citizenship.*

2009. Edalatnejad, Saeid. *Shiite Tradition, Rationalism and Modernity: The Codification of the Rights of Religious Minorities in Iranian Law (1906–2004).*

2009. Gräf, Bettina. *Islamische Rechtsgutachten und elektronische Medien: Veränderungen im religiös-rechtlichen Diskurs am Beispiel des Rechtsgelehrten Yūsuf 'Abdallāh al-Qaraḍāwī.*

2008. Büssow, Johann. *Politik und Gesellschaft im spätosmanischen Palästina (ca. 1876–1917).*

2008. Hamzah, Dyala. *L'intérêt général (maslaha 'âmma) ou le triomphe de l'opinion: Fondation délibératoire (et esquisses délibératives) dans les écrits du publiciste syro-égyptien Muhammad Rashîd Ridâ (1865–1935)* (Freie Universität Berlin and EHESS Paris).
2008. Niethammer, Katja. *Arabische Wege zu Rechtsstaatlichkeit, Partizipation und Demokratie? Der Reformprozess im Königreich Bahrain.*
2006. Hermann, Katja. *"Palästina in Israel:" Formen und Funktionen palästinensischer Zivilgesellschaft am Beispiel von NGOs in Israel.*
2006. Rohde, Achim. *Facing Dictatorship: State-Society Relations in Baʿthist Iraq.*
2005. Mohr, Irka-Christin. *Lehrtexte für den islamischen Religionsunterricht aus Nordrhein-Westfalen, Wien und Rotterdam: Beispiele muslimischer Selbstverortung im Vergleich.*
2003. Safi, Khaled Mohammed. *The Egyptian Rule in Palestine 1831–1840: A Critical Reassessment.*
2003. Niam, Khoirun. *Muslim Intellectuals in Contemporary Indonesia: Survey of Muslim Intellectual Affiliation and Thought (1966–2001).*
2001. Weber, Stefan. *Zeugnisse kulturellen Wandels: Stadt, Architektur und Gesellschaft im 19. und frühen 20. Jahrhundert.*
2000. Steinberg, Guido. *Religion und Staat in Saudi-Arabien: Eine Sozialgeschichte der wahhabitischen Gelehrten 1912–1953.*

PART 1

Islamic Studies Inside Out

CHAPTER 1

Between Europe and Asia: Arabic and Islamic Studies in Imperial Russia

Alexander Knysh

> The humanities could almost be defined as those disciplines in which the reconstruction of a disciplinary past inextricably belongs to the core of the discipline.
>
> WOLF LEPENIES and PETER WEINGART (quoted in Ursula Wokoeck, *German Orientalism*, 19)

1 Introduction

This chapter takes as its primary geographic focus the major Russian cities of St. Petersburg, Moscow, and Kazan, with occasional references to the Arabic and Islamic scholarship produced in Central Asia, the Caucasus, and Ukraine. Chronologically, it concentrates on the first one hundred and fifty years of the development of Arabic and Islamic studies as a distinctive academic discipline within the broader field of the study of the Orient known in Russian as *orientalistika* (Oriental studies) or *vostokovedenie* (Orientology).

The term "Orientalism" is avoided here, because of the negative connotations associated with the term since the publication in 1978 of Edward Said's (1935–2003) *Orientalism,* in which he accused Western specialists in Oriental studies ("Orientalists") of: (a) distorting the image of Islam, the Arabs, and Muslims generally, and (b) complicity in facilitating and justifying Western (primarily European) colonisation of the Muslim world.[1] The accuracy of Edward Said's analysis will be tested throughout this chapter.

Although teaching in the United States now for many years, the author still regards himself as heir to the tradition of Russian Arabic and Islamic studies examined below. In line with the general theme of the present volume,

1 For a thorough critical assessment of the validity of Said's arguments see, among others, Varisco 2007; Irwin 2008; Burke III and Prochaska 2008; Bobrovnikov and Miri 2016.

 | DOI:10.1163/9789004386891_002

special attention is accorded to Russian parallels with the German school of *Orientalistik*, whose representatives, as will be shown, played a critical role in the establishment and encouragement of that school's Russian counterpart.[2]

2 Managing Islam under Catherine the Great

Whereas St. Petersburg and Moscow had developed significant Orientology centres before 1855, a pivotal year for the history of Islamic and Arabic Studies in the Russian Empire, the flagship locale for the field was undeniably Kazan. Situated in the Volga region, which had a substantial Muslim population of Turkic-speaking Tatars, Bashkirs, and other, less populous ethnicities, it housed the famous Kazan University. Founded in 1804, it boasted the largest body of faculty and students specialising in various Oriental languages and cultures.

Instruction in Turkic languages at the Kazan Gymnasium dates back to the second half of the eighteenth century, when Catherine the Great (1729–96) abandoned the theretofore largely ineffective policy of suppressing the Islamic religion and its learned representatives and instead embarked on a programme aimed at cultivating the Muslim religious elite (Shofman and Shamov, 1956; cf. Schimmelpenninck van der Oye 2010, 96). This change was supposed to establish the latter as a vital intermediary between the Russian state and its Muslim population. In adopting this measure, Catherine followed in the footsteps of Peter the Great (1672–1725), who had effectively co-opted the Russian Orthodox clergy into the state bureaucracy and thus rendered it completely pliant and dependent on the monarch's will. In practice, the aim of Catherine's policy was to integrate Muslim leaders of the Volga region into the Russian state machinery. New mosques were constructed and departments of local languages (primarily Tatar Turkic) were established. The spirit of the Tsarina's reforms did not die with her. When Kazan University was founded at the turn of the nineteenth century, it already offered instruction in the major Islamic languages: Arabic, Persian, and Turkic/Tatar. Under the close supervision of the imperial state, a cautious revival of religious education was given the green

2 The author's major source for German *Orientalistik* is Ursula Wokoeck's 2009 monograph, *German Orientalism: The Study of the Middle East and Islam from 1800 to 1945*. This paper also draws on the excellent historical surveys of Islamic and Arabic studies produced in Russian Orientology by scholars such as V.V. Bartol'd (1869–1930) and I.Iu. Krachkovskii (1883–1951).

light. This meant, among other things, that local religious communities were allowed to set up religious colleges to train Muslim clergy.[3]

3 The Kazan University

In December 1805, the Russian Ministry of Education issued a decree that established the legal and institutional framework for restructuring the first Russian universities. It contained provisions pertaining to the teaching of "Eastern" or "Oriental" languages (*vostochnye iazyki*). The decree led to the establishment of chairs of Oriental languages at the country's first universities, in Moscow, Kazan, and Khar'kov.[4]

In Kazan, the academic study and teaching of Arabic language and literature was centred at Kazan University. Its Arabic-Persian chair was part of the "Class (*razriad*) of Oriental Philology." The chair was occupied in succession by the German scholars Christian-Martin Frähn (1782–1851) and Franz (Fedor) Erdmann (1793–1863), neither of whom knew Russian and who conducted their classes in Latin, which severely limited their audience—students who read or spoke Latin were in short supply in Kazan.[5]

In 1826, the Department of Oriental languages hired Aleksandr Kazem-Bek (1802–70) as a lecturer in Turkic languages. A Persian (or Azeri-Persian) convert to Protestantism who was fluent in Arabic, Persian, and Turkish, as well as the major European languages, Kazem-Bek cut a unique figure. He combined traditional Islamic learning with proficiency in European scholarship acquired through self-directed study (Krachkovskii 1950, 173; cf. Morrison 2009, 623–24). His later career as professor of Arabic and Persian in Kazan (1846–49) and of Persian in St. Petersburg (1849–55), and finally also as dean of the newly founded Faculty of Oriental Languages at St. Petersburg University is especially remarkable because he had no formal academic diploma (Bartol'd 1977, 9:46–47; Kononov 1957, 10). Kazem-Bek's teaching philosophy in Kazan was strictly and consciously utilitarian. He saw his principal task as supplying

3 The long-ranging and variegated ramifications of Catherine's experiments in "managing Islam" have been discussed by different authors: Khabutdinov 2010; Crews 2006; Frank 1998; Kemper 1998.

4 Khar'kov later fell victim to the centralisation act of 1855, when Oriental studies faculties were transferred to St. Petersburg. Kononov 1957, 7; cf. Schimmelpenninck van der Oye 2010, 95–96.

5 Kim and Shastitko 1990, 157, and Valeev 1998, 101; for an illuminating assessment of their contribution to Russian scholarship on the Orient see Schimmelpenninck van der Oye 2010, 98–99.

the Russian state with career diplomats, military officers, statesmen, and interpreters, all of whom he considered indispensable for Russia's proper functioning on the world stage (Schimmelpenninck van der Oye 2010, 120–21). He was much less enthusiastic about training academics steeped in ancient texts and cultural artefacts (Bartol'd 1977,48). Kazem-Bek's teaching philosophy remained unchanged after he left Kazan for St. Petersburg in 1849.

His chair of Arabic and Persian languages at Kazan University was taken over by the German scholar Joseph (Iosif) Gottwald (1813–97). Gottwald was a fine and dedicated academic. His chief contribution to Arabic studies was the publication in 1861–63 of an Arabic-Russian dictionary based on the vocabulary of the Qur'ān, seven *mu'allaqāt*, and the poems of the pre-Islamic poet Imru' al-Qays (d. ca. 550 CE), the first such reference book in Russian.[6] He also published a catalogue of the Kazan collection of Oriental manuscripts that was transferred to St. Petersburg following the establishment of the Faculty of Oriental Languages there in 1855.

4 The Missionary Division at the Spiritual Academy in Kazan

For the purpose of comparing developments in the Russian Empire with other regions, it is important to point out that despite the ostensibly "Islam-friendly" policies implemented by the Russian imperial administration in the Volga region, the country's Christian rulers did not give up hope of wooing their Muslim subjects away from Islam and converting them to Christianity. To this end, in 1854 the Missionary Division at the Kazan Spiritual (or Theological) Academy was established by an imperial edict, with the mandate to train anti-Muslim polemicists and missionaries (Schimmelpenninck van der Oye 2010, 127; and especially Geraci 2001). The Division's goal was to convert Russia's Muslims to Orthodox Christianity, or at least to prevent the Tatars who had already been baptised (called *kryasheny*) from "falling back" into Islam.

In accordance with this goal, the cadres of the Missionary Division willy-nilly had to acquire a good command of Arabic, the language of Islamic revelation, and to be well versed in the fundamentals of Islamic history and religion. Their task was to engage local Muslim scholars in a polemical dialogue, intellectually defeat them, and, in so doing, demonstrate the superiority of (Orthodox)

6 Krachkovskii 1950, 175–76. The full title of Gottwald's work is "Opyt arabsko-russkogo slovaria na Koran, sem' moallakat i stikhotvoreniia Imruelkaisa," Kazan 1863, an offprint from the "Transactions of Kazan University" II–IV, 1861. When the Kazan Faculty of Oriental Languages was closed in 1855, Gottwald was demoted to the position of librarian.

Christianity, in the hope of convincing them to embrace the Christian faith. Although the missionaries of the Kazan Spiritual Academy were able to win over a handful of converts from among Tatar and Bashkir Muslims, in the end their activities proved ineffective. Unwittingly, members of the Missionary Division, including several Christian Arabs affiliated with it, became Russia's first experts on Islam as an intellectual and theological tradition (Schimmelpenninck van der Oye 2010, 152). In the first half of the nineteenth century the Kazan anti-Muslim missionaries vigorously pursued the study of Islam in its historical development (Kim and Shastitko 1990, 164–67). Some of them, including Nikolai Il'minskii (1822–91), even traveled to Egypt and stayed there to learn Islamic sciences from the leading scholars of the world affiliated with the renowned al-Azhar University (Kim and Shastitko 1990, 158; cf. Schimmelpenninck van der Oye 2010, 132).

5 First Translation of the Qur'ān from Arabic into Russian by Gordii Sablukov

It is hardly accidental that the first relatively accurate and readable translation of the Qur'ān from Arabic into Russian, published in 1878, was accomplished by Il'minskii's successor as chair of Arabic and Turkic languages at the Kazan Spiritual Academy, Gordii Sablukov (1804–80).[7] Sablukov's painstaking monographic studies of the Qur'ān's themes and diction render him the first Russian expert on the Muslim scripture (Krachkovskii 1955, 212–24). In accordance with his Christian convictions, Sablukov considered the Qur'ān to be the creation of Muḥammad's poetic genius and a faithful reflection of the social and cultural realities of "Bedouin Arabia." Basing his work on this assumption, Sablukov consistently collated the text of the Qur'ān with the masterpieces of pre-Islamic poetry by the tribal poets of the Arabian Peninsula. Despite the fact that in his study of the Qur'ān Sablukov relied almost exclusively on Muslim sources and consciously avoided any references to Western scholarship

7 Krachkovskii 1950, 181–83. The second and third editions of Sablukov's *Koran* appeared in 1894 and 1907. Previous translations were made from European languages; the first Russian translation of the Qur'ān was completed by Piotr Postnikov in 1716, based on the French translation of André du Ryer; see Rezvan 1991, 14; and Rezvan 1998. The Qur'ān translation by the Russian general Dmitrii Boguslvaskii (1826–93), which was completed at about the same time as Sablukov's (in the late 1870s), was not published until recently. On Boguslavskii, see Krachkovskii 1955, 119–23; Rezvan 1995. Boguslavskii's authorship of this translation has, however, been questioned by the Moscow Arabist Dmitrii Frolov (Frolov's lecture on the Qur'ān and Qur'ānic studies delivered at the Kazan Federal University on 6 July 2012).

(Krachkovskii 1955, 224), he arrived at basically the same conclusions as his European colleagues, especially Theodor Nöldeke (1836–1930). For instance, Sablukov consistently stressed the difference between the diction and themes found in the Meccan period of the Qur'ān's history and the Medinan period, which he tried to correlate with the changing circumstances of Muḥammad's life and the socio-political environment in which he lived.[8]

6 The Kazan Spiritual Academy at the Turn of the 20th Century

In a similar vein, Il'minskii's students and Sablukov's successors Efim Malov (1835–1918) and Nikolai Ostroumov (1846–1930), who were also affiliated with "the chair of anti-Muslim subjects" (Kim and Shastitko 1990, 38–39), produced a considerable amount of instructional materials for survey courses on Islam. Whereas Malov's works contained some "small pearls" of genuine scholarship,[9] they were inherently vitiated by their underlying missionary and anti-Islamic agendas. The same is generally true of the work of Ostroumov, who left Kazan in 1877. Having established himself as "the foremost expert on Islam" in Russia, he was dispatched to the newly conquered Turkestan region in Central Asia, where he served as a senior administrator in charge of "public schools."[10] Between 1910 and 1914 Ostroumov, who in spite of his close association with the Kazan Spiritual Academy was not an ordained priest, produced a series of manuals that covered the principal subfields of Islamic studies.[11]

One of the hallmarks of missionary-directed Islamic studies in Kazan was its abiding interest in Islam's origins in the pre-Islamic society of Arabia. The last major representative of this trend, Mikhail Mashanov (1852–1924), was rightly regarded as the foremost expert on the subject in his age.[12] Like any serious scholar of Islam, Mashanov dabbled in various themes of classical Islamic sciences, especially theology (*kalām*), jurisprudence (*fiqh*), Ṣūfism, and

---

8 Kim and Shastitko 1990, 36–37; Krachkovskii 1950, 182. One should point out that the bulk of Sablukov's studies were accomplished following his resignation from the "chair of anti-Muslim subjects" (*kafedra protivomusul'manskikh predmetov*) at the Kazan Spiritual Academy.

9 Krachkovskii 1950, 184, quoting their contemporary and the doyen of the St. Petersburg school of Arabic and Islamic studies, Viktor Rozen (1849–1908).

10 Krachkovskii 1950, 188. On the paradoxical aspects of Ostroumov's relation to Islam, see a perceptive article by Morrison 2009.

11 For example "Arabia, the Cradle of Islam" (1910), "The Qur'an" (1912), "The Dogmas of the Qur'an" (1912), "Shari'at" (1912), and, finally, "Introduction to Islamic Studies" (1914).

12 Kim and Shastitko 1990, 43; his study was published in Kazan in 1885.

Islamic "sects" (Kim and Shastitko 1990, 368–71). Nevertheless, despite his first-hand knowledge of Arabic culture and Islamic religion (he had spent two years studying in Cairo and Jidda), Mashanov's research was decisively shaped by the demands of anti-Muslim polemics. In addition to his studies of classical Islam, he also wrote treatises in defence of the Tatar converts to Orthodox Christianity and on other issues related to the exigencies of Christian missionary activities among the Turkic-speaking Muslim minorities of the Russian Empire (Kim and Shastitko 1990, 233–65).

Unusual among the alumni of the Missionary Division of the Kazan Spiritual Academy is Panteleimon Zhuze (Jawzi) (1871–1942),[13] a Palestinian Arab who obtained his master's degree from Kazan University in 1899.[14] Important is the fact that, like his predecessors, Zhuze took an interest in Arabic sources pertaining to the history and geography of the Russian Empire. In 1905 he edited and published an Arabic account of Georgia by the Archdeacon Paul of Aleppo (1627–69). Following his move to Baku (Azerbaijan), Zhuze continued to collect and translate Arabic historical and geographical texts related to the Caucasus, such as the third/ninth-century chronicles of al-Yaʿqūbī and al-Balādhurī (Krachkovskii 1950, 233).

Although the study of Islam for missionary purposes by the members of the Kazan Spiritual Academy was inherently biased and perhaps irrevocably flawed, the primacy of these studies in the major subfields of Islamic studies is impossible to deny.[15] At a time when the Arabists of Russia's two capitals were preoccupied with the intricacies of pre-Islamic and classical poetry or Arabic geographical and historical texts pertaining to Russian or East European history, the missionary scholars of Kazan were engaged in a serious investigation of the formative period of Islam, the Qur'ān, and *ḥadīth,* as well as traditional Islamic sciences such as *tafsīr*, *fiqh,* and *kalām*. This phenomenon can be seen as one of the many paradoxes of Russian scholarship on Arabs and Islam.[16]

13 His Arabic name was Bandali Saliba Jawzi.

14 Krachkovskii 1950, 185; Zhuze was a runner-up in the competition for "the chair of Arabic language and denunciation (*oblichenie*) of Mohammedanism," vacated by Mashanov in 1911; the chair was eventually given to Mashanov's student, Mikhail Ivanov. Zhuze's life and work, especially his controversial study of Islamic thought *Min taʾrīkh al-ḥaraka al-fikriyya fī l-Islām* (1928), are analyzed in Sonn 1996.

15 For the ongoing debates over the validity and usefulness of its legacy for today's Islamology, see, e.g., Valeev 1998, 198–218; and Khabibullin 2006, 375–81.

16 The publications of the Kazan missionaries drew scathing criticism from the contemporary academic scholar Viktor Rozen, who, in line with his secularist and positivistic convictions, considered their works incompatible with the standards of what he regarded as "objective" academic scholarship. Khabibullin 2006, 364–65; and Batunskii 2003, 3:47–50.

7 The Faculty of Oriental Languages in St. Petersburg

When the St. Petersburg Pedagogical Institute was granted university status in 1819, it already had chairs in the Arabic and Persian languages. These chairs were occupied, respectively, by two students of the great French Orientalist scholar Silvestre de Sacy (1758–1838): Jean-François Demange (1789–1839) and François-Bernard Charmoy (1793–1868) (Kononov 1957, 7; Schimmelpenninck van der Oye 2010, 159). Three years after the French academics had started to teach courses in Arabic and Persian, they left their posts for the newly created Department of Oriental Languages at the Russian Ministry of Foreign Affairs, to provide linguistic training to aspiring members of Russia's diplomatic corps (Kononov 1957, 8). The French scholars were succeeded by the talented Polish autodidact Osip Senkovskii (1800–58), who had learned Arabic during his travels in Syria and Egypt. Senkovskii, both a scholar and a novelist, whose literary work was praised by Aleksandr Pushkin himself (Krachkovskii 1955, 225), held the chair of Oriental languages at St. Petersburg University until 1847.[17]

The inauguration of the Faculty of Oriental Languages in St. Petersburg in August 1855 marked the end of Kazan University's role as the principal centre of Oriental studies in Russia. In accordance with the centralising logic of the Russian imperial state, all provincial academic institutions specialising in this field were shut down and their resources (libraries, textbooks, and faculty) were relocated to St. Petersburg.[18] The faculty was the chief beneficiary of this centralisation, which now housed fourteen language programmes. No European university of that age could boast such breadth and diversity of linguistic and cultural expertise on Oriental subjects.[19] Kazan University, on the other hand, bore the brunt of this imperial drive for centralisation, because it lost almost all of its Oriental faculty and library resources, including the collection of precious Oriental manuscripts.[20] The Kazan Spiritual Academy, however,

17 For a perceptive account of Senkovskii's academic and literary career, see Schimmelpenninck van der Oye 2010, 160–68.

18 The opening of the faculty in St. Petersburg was the last stage in the academic drama that was started in 1851 by edict of the tsar Nicholas I, which ordained "the termination of the study of Oriental languages at the Kazan University"; see Valeev 1998, 106–7.

19 Farzaliev, 2005; an unpublished article that was kindly shared with me by the author; Schimmelpenninck van der Oye 2010, 197.

20 Valeev 1998, 107–8; the Richelieu College in Odessa was also shut down and its faculty lost their positions; see Kim and Shastitko 1990, 159. Only six years later, in 1861, did the teaching of Arabic language and literature resume at Kazan University, with the appointment of Ivan Kholmogorov (d. ca. 1870), and then continued only until 1868 (Kim and Shastitko 1990, 161). The teaching of "Islamic" languages resumed on a rather modest scale only at the end of the 1880s, Krachkovskii 1950, 177.

had survived, because, as a clerical institution, it did not fall under the jurisdiction of the Ministry of Education.

8 Curricula at St. Petersburg's Faculty of Oriental Languages

The study of Arabic literature and culture at St. Petersburg's Faculty of Oriental Languages existed side by side with programmes in Persian, Turkish, and Semitic studies (Hebrew, Syriac, and Chaldean). Many students were studying several languages simultaneously (Schimmelpenninck van der Oye 2010, 174). Although the history and geopolitical realities of imperial Russia determined the special attraction for Russian students of Persian and Turkic languages and literatures, their teachers advised them that their expertise would be incomplete without at least a basic proficiency in Arabic and Islamic studies. Such students became the principal constituency for courses in these subjects, alongside the less numerous Arabists.[21]

This curriculum remained largely unchanged throughout the second half of the nineteenth and the first two decades of the twentieth century. Even a cursory glance at the subjects taught by instructors associated with the Arabic faculty is enough to confirm the predominantly philological orientation of this academic programme. Expertise in Islam and Islamic culture and history was clearly and unapologetically subordinate to the acquisition of linguistic proficiency (cf. Wokoeck 2009, 211).

Historical and cultural information was presented to students in the form of short passages culled by their instructors from medieval Arabic chronicles and presented under the elastic rubric of "literature" (Kim and Shastitko 1990, 160). These textual fragments were read primarily as grammatical exercises, with minimal historical commentary provided by the instructor. There was, as far as one can tell, no effort on the part of the instructors to place these excerpts into a meaningful historical context or analyse them as pieces of historical, religious, or cultural evidence that could be used to reconstruct a certain Islamic society during a given epoch. Survey courses on Islam and Middle Eastern history and culture were rather rare and poorly structured. In this respect, Russian academic Orientalism seems to have lagged behind its European counterparts in Germany, Austria, France, Holland, and Britain.

21 The difficulties involved in mastering all three languages were cited in an unfavorable report on the state of Oriental studies at St. Petersburg University in 1892; its author, a Turkologist from Kiev, suggested that students would do better concentrating on just one language. See Schimmelpenninck van der Oye 2010, 175–76.

The high regard that Russian scholars had for European academic study of the Orient is attested by the fact that some of them traveled to Europe to undertake apprenticeships under major luminaries.[22] At the same time, Russian scholars of the Orient never tired of emphasising the distinctive nature of their scholarship vis-à-vis that of their Western European colleagues.[23] This distinctiveness was attributed to Russia's geographical position on the border (both cultural and geographic) between Asia and Europe,[24] its contiguity with its "Asiatic" neighbours, and, as a consequence, the indebtedness of Russian culture and statehood to its primeval Oriental "roots" (Tolz 2011, 80–83). The ambivalent attitude of Russian academics toward "Russia's own Orient" persisted throughout the remainder of the nineteenth century, reached its peak in the twentieth century under the Soviet regime, and is still in evidence today. It reflects the much broader ambivalence of Russian society (today as in the past) toward its identity and intellectual and cultural orientation.[25]

9 Coming of Age: St. Petersburg and Vladimir Girgas (1835–1887)

During the first decade of its existence, the St. Petersburg Faculty of Oriental Languages produced a cohort of scholars who were destined to invigorate the field of Arabic and Islamic studies in Russian academia and to elevate it to the standards set by their European colleagues. Among these pioneering academics was Vladimir Girgas (or Girgass, 1835–87). After acquiring a basic knowledge of Arabic language and culture at the Faculty, the young scholar of (Baltic) German extraction chose not to continue his studies at his home institution. Instead, he traveled to Paris at his own expense and attached himself to the two distinguished French Arabists of the age, Armand Caussin de Perceval (1795–1871) and Joseph Reinaud (1795–1867). To support himself during his educational sojourn in Paris he offered private lessons to children (Kim and Shastitko 1990, 166). Upon his return to St. Petersburg in 1860, Girgas

22 For example, Girgas, Rozen, and Shmidt; see Tolz 2008.

23 For details, see Chapter 4 of Tolz 2011.

24 See, e.g., Schimmelpenninck van der Oye 2010, 1-11.

25 The question of the implications of this "dual identity" for the study of the Orient by Russian academics and practitioners of "applied Orientalism" has been the subject of a recent study by Alexander Morrison, who argues that Russia's uniqueness in this respect vis-à-vis the other European colonial powers has been greatly exaggerated. He concedes, however, that "Russia's distinctness may lie in the fact that we find a much greater interpenetration of the worlds of scholarship and colonial rule than in the British Empire" (Morrison 2009, 644).

defended a bachelor's thesis on the conquest of Egypt by the Ottoman sultan Selim I (Bartol'd 1977, 129–30). His choice of topic (which seems to be at odds with his life-long interest in Arabic philology) was in all probability dictated by the recent events of the Crimean War (1853–56) and the interest in Ottoman history that it had ignited among educated Russians. If this was indeed the case, then Girgas's bachelor's thesis may serve as testimony to the fact that some Russian scholars were more responsive to the "public interest in the region" (that is, the Middle East and North Africa) than were their German colleagues who, on the whole, were prone to ignore it in favour of "the pursuit of Oriental languages, manuscripts, books, as well as artifacts" (Wokoeck 2009, 219).

In the winter of 1881, the administration of St. Petersburg University sent Girgas to the Middle East (Bartol'd 1977, 130). In the Levant, Girgas witnessed the beginnings of the Arabic literary and cultural "renaissance" (*al-nahḍa*) and the debates it had generated among Arab intellectuals. About two decades before his arrival in Syria, the first Arabic newspaper, *Ḥadīqat al-akhbār* ("The garden of news"), was published in Beirut. It became an important forum for lively discussions of the future of Arabic language and culture. During his stay in the Middle East Girgas was engaged in philological investigations, collecting Arabic words not attested in Western and Russian dictionaries, recording folk sayings and proverbs, and working in local archives and manuscript collections. His interest in the living language and folklore of the Arabs was unusual in an age when Western scholars were still preoccupied almost exclusively with the cultural legacy of the "Golden Age" of Arabic-Islamic civilisation, viewing its present condition as one of "paralysis" and "decline."[26] In this respect, he anticipated the "discovery" of modern Arabic literature that is usually associated with the name of Ignatii Krachkovskii, who himself readily acknowledged the primacy of his senior colleague in this academic pursuit (Krachkovskii 1955, 127–32).

Upon his return to St. Petersburg Girgas defended his master's thesis. Once again, he chose a topic that was only tangentially related to his philological interests: "The Rights of the Christians in the East, According to Islamic Laws" (Bartol'd 1977, 147). His choice was in all likelihood dictated by the interest in the subject evidenced among the Russian public at large following the massacre of Christians in Lebanon in 1860 (Kim and Shastitko 1990, 168). Only while writing his doctoral dissertation did Girgas finally allow himself to tackle a purely philological topic, a comprehensive and thorough description of Arabic grammar, which he completed in 1873.

26 For a critical discussion of this issue, see Knysh 2006, 235–36.

10 The *Arabic Chrestomathy*

Among the subsequent generations of Russian Arabists and Islamologists, Girgas is remembered (together with his student Viktor Rozen) primarily as the author of the *Arabic Chrestomathy* (*Arabskaia khrestomatia*; 1876). This selection of Arabic texts from the "Golden Age" of Islamic civilisation has served as the main introductory textbook for students of Arabic in St. Petersburg/Leningrad/St. Petersburg ever since. Arranged in the order of difficulty and length of the texts, the *Arabic Chrestomathy* was used at the initial stages of language acquisition by students of the Faculty of Oriental Studies for almost a century (Kim and Shastitko 1990, 169). From a selection of simple Arabic proverbs (*amthāl*) and anecdotes (*nawādir*) the *Chrestomathy* progresses to the more challenging *ḥadīth* (Prophetic traditions), followed by excerpts from historical, geographical, and grammatical texts, and culminates with the more challenging historical narratives and poetry (Beliaev and Vinnikov 1960, 101).

However, this fine collection of primary texts (many of which were based on Arabic manuscripts from the academic libraries of the Russian capital) was of limited value without a comprehensive Arabic-Russian dictionary. Earlier Russian dictionaries were insufficient for readers of the *Chrestomathy*, whereas European ones (such as Albert [de] Biberstein-Kazimirski's *Dictionnaire Arabe-Français*, 1860) were expensive and difficult to procure (Kim and Shastitko 1990, 169). The solution came in the form of the *Arabic-Russian Dictionary for the Arabic Chrestomathy and the Qur'an*, which was compiled by Girgas himself and published in Kazan in 1881.[27] A second edition of the *Dictionary* appeared in 2006, attesting to its abiding usefulness for students of classical Arabic and Islamic culture in Russia.

Comparatively speaking, oral and communicative skills were downplayed. This approach prevailed until the end of twentieth century, when more emphasis came to be placed on communication skills and active use of vocabulary in real-life situations. One can thus argue that following their publication in the last decades of the nineteenth century, the *Chrestomathy* and the *Dictionary* have served as the textual foundation for training specialists in Arabic and Islamic studies at St. Petersburg and later also at Leningrad University (Batsieva 1972, 276).

27 Kazan had an Arabic printing press that had been built by order of Catherine the Great in the late 18th century.

11 Baron Viktor Rozen (1848–1908) and the Academic Journal *Transactions of the Oriental Division of the Imperial Russian Archeological Society*

One of the most distinguished products of this text-based educational philosophy was Baron Viktor Rozen (von Rosen). Son of a Baltic German and a half-Russian-half-Georgian mother (Krachkovskii 1955, 68), Rozen began his studies at the Faculty of Oriental Languages shortly after Girgas had joined its faculty. After graduation, he spent one year in Leipzig, where he studied under the supervision of the renowned German Arabist Heinrich Fleischer (1801–88). Fortuitously, his co-student was the famous Hungarian Islamologist Ignaz Goldziher (1850–1921), and the two young men became friends. Upon his return to St. Petersburg in 1872, Rozen successfully defended a master's thesis titled "Ancient Arabic Poetry and Its Analysis."

Like Goldziher, Rozen felt that the disciplinary confines of Arabic philology were too narrow for his talent. Both students of Fleischer viewed it as a means to something broader and more intellectually stimulating rather than an end in itself (Bartol'd 1977, 721). At a time when Islamic studies had only begun to emerge as a freestanding academic discipline in both Germany and Russia, the two men concentrated their intellectual energies on the study of Islam's multifaceted intellectual and institutional manifestations (Wokoeck 2009, 218–19).

Rozen was lucky to have Girgas as his mentor. Their partnership lasted for fourteen years. Upon the latter's resignation from his professorial post in 1886 due to a grave illness, Rozen became the sole representative of Arabic studies at the Faculty of Oriental Languages. The situation changed a few years later when the Faculty hired his students Nikolai Mednikov (1855–1918) and Aleksandr Shmidt (1871–1939) (Kim and Shastitko 1990, 170). Endowed with "the unique intellectual and psychological qualities of a leader" (Batunskii 2003, 3:32), Rozen became the *spiritus movens* not only of Arabic and Islamic studies but also of the entire Oriental studies community of the Russian Empire (Krachkovskii 1950, 142). The fact that he was able to realise his ambitious academic agenda was due in part to the high administrative positions he occupied at both St. Petersburg University and the Russian Academy of Sciences. From 1893 to 1902 Rozen served as dean of the Faculty of Oriental Languages, and in 1885 he was appointed head of the Oriental Division of the Russian Archeological Society (Beliaev and Vinnikov 1960, 103–4).

His wide-ranging influence on his colleagues was also a result in part of his position as the editor in chief of the newly created (1886) academic journal

Transactions of the Oriental Division of the Imperial Russian Archeological Society (*Zapiski Vostochnogo otdeleniia Imperatorskogo Russkogo arkheologicheskogo obshchestva*). This academic post enabled Rozen to disseminate his ideas and rigourous standards of scholarship among Russian academics and the educated public at large (Bartol'd 1977, 591–92). Under Rozen's leadership, *Transactions* became the main mouthpiece of Oriental studies in imperial Russia and "an important vehicle for promoting the achievements of Russian Orientology in the West" (Schimmelpenninck van der Oye 2010, 187). Both the Society and its journal can be considered the Russian equivalents of the *Deutsche Morgenländische Gesellschaft* and the *Zeitschrift für die Kunde des Morgenlandes*, founded in Germany in 1845 and 1838, respectively (Wokoeck 2009, 110). As in Germany, where the institution and the journal served as a "rallying point ... for Oriental studies and 'its promoters and friends'" (Wokoeck 2009, 136), the role of their Russian counterparts in the advancement of academic Orientology in Russia is impossible to overestimate. Note, however, the time lag of about fifty years, which has proved extremely difficult for Russian Orientology to overcome.[28] Thus, as in many other academic disciplines, here too, Russian academics were doomed to play the game of catch-up vis-à-vis their European colleagues.

In his study of Russian Islamology, Mark Batunskii described Rozen's academic creed as consciously and unapologetically positivistic (Batunskii 2003, 3:9, 48–49). There is some truth to it. Rozen flatly rejected anything that smacked of "engaged" scholarship, be it a missionary "analysis" of Islam or applying racial/racist theories to Islamic societies, both of which were quite common among Russian and European academics of that age (Tolz 2011, 73–74 and 78–79; cf. Khabibullin 2006, 9, 16, 301, 364–66).

In agreement with the views of some of his German colleagues,[29] Rozen was a firm believer in the critical role of religion in shaping the history of mankind. This theoretical assumption is evident in the close attention to Islam that we find in the work of one of Rozen's foremost students, Vasilii Bartol'd (1869–1930).[30] This is not to say that Rozen's students were uniformly committed to

---

28 "Russia was latecomer in this respect. Already toward the end of the eighteenth century William Jones's Asiatic Society in Bengal had begun publishing its *Asiatic Researches*, while the French *Journal asiatique* first appeared in 1823, followed some twenty-five years later by the German Oriental Society's *Zeitschrift* (Journal)" (Schimmelpenninck van der Oye 2010, 187). On Jones, see Arberry 1946.

29 As articulated by leading European scholars of the Orient committed to the concept of *Kulturgeschichte*, such as Alfred von Kremer (1828–89), Ignaz Goldziher (1850–1921), Martin Hartmann (1851–1918), and Carl Becker (1876–1933); according to Ursula Wokoeck (2009, 170–72), this view of Islam remained marginal among German university academics until the first decades of the twentieth century.

30 For an illuminating summary of his life and work, see Bregel 1980.

Islamic studies: another renowned student of Rozen's, Ignatii Krachkovskii (1871–1951), chose to pursue the more traditional path of philological inquiry, which had been the hallmark of the St. Petersburg school of Oriental studies from its inception.

12 Arabic and Islamic Studies in Moscow and Aleksei Boldyrev (1780–1842)

Although the St. Petersburg school had the critical advantage of being located in Russia's capital (and thus close to sources of state funding and patronage), Moscow's contribution to the formation and development of Oriental studies was quite substantial, albeit different from that of St. Petersburg. It is at Moscow University that we find the first ethnically Russian professor of Arabic and Persian, Aleksei Boldyrev (1780–1842). A graduate of Moscow University in 1806, Boldyrev seems to have learned Semitic languages on his own. Be this as it may, the promising young man was recommended for the study of Oriental languages abroad and spent several years in Göttingen and Paris, studying with, among others, Silvestre de Sacy.[31] Upon his return to Moscow in 1811 Boldyrev began teaching the Arabic and Hebrew languages as well as the "history of Jews and Arabs, [their] religion, laws, sciences, arts, customs and traditions" (Bartol'd 1977, 50). He prepared and published several useful lithographic editions of Arabic and Persian texts (chrestomathies), which "remained popular among the subsequent generations of scholars of the Moscow University" (Krachkovskii 1950, 80). Boldyrev's Arabic chrestomathy served Russian students of Arabic for more than forty years, until it was replaced by the already mentioned "canonical" chrestomathy of Girgas and Rozen. A collection of short stories, anecdotes, and other narrative "curiosities," Boldyrev's sourcebook played a notable role in the "Orientalisation" of Russian literature in the 1820s through the 1830s. Together with Senkovskii's "Oriental" novels and short stories,[32] translations of Boldyrev's selections exposed the general Russian reader to Oriental(ist) themes and motifs, laying the groundwork for their extensive use by Russian writers and poets in the decades that followed (Krachkovskii 1950, 82).

Boldyrev published two Arabic grammars (in 1827 and 1836). They were used by Russian students until the publication of the more detailed and sophisticated Arabic grammar by Mikhail Navrotskii (1823–71) of St. Petersburg Univer-

31 Bartol'd 1977, 49; Krachkovskii 1950, 79–80; on the role of de Sacy in shaping German *Orientalistik*, see Wokoeck 2009, 14–15 and passim.

32 Senkovskii's penname was "Baron Brambeus;" for details of his literary career see Hope 2003; see also Schimmelpenninck van der Oye 2010, 160–68.

sity (Krachkovskii 1955, 302–3). In the final account, the majority of Boldyrev's students pursued careers outside academia; some distinguished themselves as creative writers and literary critics. Boldyrev's own academic career came to an abrupt end in 1837, when he had to resign from his post as rector of Moscow University, after he had, in his capacity as censor, allowed the publication of the "scandalous" "Philosophical Epistles" by the liberal thinker and Europhile Pyotr Chaadaev (1794–1856) (Krachkovskii 1950, 85; Bartol'd 1977, 50; cf. Schimmelpenninck van der Oye 2010, 265, note 13).

Following Boldyrev's departure, Arabic and Islamic studies at Moscow University suffered a protracted decline. Boldyrev's personal catastrophe led to the suspension of the entire discipline of Oriental studies at Moscow University (Krachkovskii 1950, 156). The teaching of Arabic there resumed only in 1852, when taken up again by a student of Boldyrev's named Pavel Petrov (1814–75). However, Petrov's interests lay elsewhere (primarily in the Indian languages), and in the 1870s the teaching of Arabic was discontinued once again, to reappear only after the Communist revolution of 1917.

13 The Lazarev Institute of Oriental Languages in Moscow and Agafangel Krymskii (1871–1942)

In Moscow, training in Oriental languages for career purposes was offered also by the privately funded Lazarev Institute (Lazarevskii Institut), which was established by a wealthy Armenian family in 1814 (Baziiants 1963, 6:270–301). Following the adoption of new bylaws, so-called "special classes" for language instruction were created at the Institute. They comprised chairs of Arabic, Armenian, Persian, Russian, Turkic-Tatar languages, and history of the Orient. Unlike the Oriental departments of the St. Petersburg and Moscow universities, the Lazarev programmes did not include instruction in the languages of the Far East and India. In accordance with its original raison d'être, the Lazarev Institute emphasised oral and reading proficiency in the "living" Oriental vernaculars over and against a more academic and historically grounded study of Middle Eastern cultures and literatures that prevailed in St. Petersburg after Kazem-Bek's resignation as dean of the Faculty of Oriental Languages. The Institute's director Georgii Kananov (1881–97) is even quoted as explicitly advising his younger faculty against engaging in subjects (especially history and religion) that were not directly relevant to the task of training professional diplomats, consular workers, and military and civil officials, as well as interpreters (Kuznetsova 1984, 130–31). One consequence of this utilitarian, applied teaching philosophy was that the Institute's hiring policy consistently gave preference to native speakers of the languages of instruction. Typical in this respect are the Arabic language lecturer Mikhail Attaya (1851–1921), a Syrian Arab who compiled several Arabic textbooks, an Arabic-Russian dictionary, and other teaching aids, and Georgii Murkos, Russia's second Arab professor (after Muḥammad ʿAyād al-Ṭanṭāwī).[33]

The flowering and expansion of Arabic and Islamic studies at the Lazarev Institute at the turn of the twentieth century is associated with Agafangel Krymskii (1871–1942). A litterateur, polyglot, and man of truly encyclopedic intellectual interests, his role in Moscow's academic life of the first decade of the twentieth century is comparable to that of Viktor Rozen in St. Petersburg. Krymskii's life-long agenda was to translate the masterpieces of Islamic high culture into his native Ukrainian and to reveal Oriental influences on Ukrainian literature and folklore (Smilianskaia 1971, 209). Krymskii himself acknowledged that, at times, his poetic vision of reality and human history came into conflict with his "analytic intellect" (Smilianskaia 1971, 211). At the same time, his training as an historian and his breadth of intellectual interests prevented Krymskii from limiting himself to purely philological and literary pursuits. He took an acute interest in broad historical processes, viewing both religion and economic factors as their principal driving forces. This is evident from his abiding concern with the socio-economic roots of Islam and the religious life of the Arabs before and after Islam's appearance on the historical scene (Batunskii 2003, 3:67–68). In this respect Krymskii is similar to his older contemporary Vasilii Bartol'd in St. Petersburg. One may venture a guess that the interest that both men took in the global processes that had shaped the social, political, and economic conditions in the region of their specialisation was indicative of a new trend in Russian Orientology in the first decades of the twentieth century (for Bartol'd, see Tolz 2011, 90). The same trend seems to have been taking shape in the German *Orientalistik* of that age (Wokoeck 2009, 175–80).

The fact that Krymskii was the section editor for the Middle East for the Russian version of the widely read *Encyclopedia of Brockhaus and Efron* and that the celebrated Russian novelist Leo Tolstoy "learned the Koran from Krymskii" (Krachkovskii 1950, 169) speak for themselves. It is impossible to deny that before his departure for Kiev in 1918, Krymskii was able to create a distinctive school of Arabic and Islamic studies in Moscow (Kim and Shastitko 1990, 176).

33 Krachkovskii 1950, 161–64. The Egyptian scholar Muḥammad ʿAyād al-Ṭanṭāwī (1810–61), a graduate of al-Azhar, was the third holder of the Arabic chair at St. Petersburg University's Faculty of Oriental Languages (after Jean-François Demange and Osip Senkovskii); see Krachkovskii 1955, 94–98.

The aim of Krymskii's school to reach out to broader audiences complemented (and occasionally competed with) the more pedantic, academic approach characteristic of the Arabic and Islamic studies centres based in St. Petersburg. This "division of academic labor" persisted, at least in the mental imagery of the Russian educated public, under Soviet rule and is still being often invoked today in private and public discourses.

There was hardly any aspect of Arabic and Islamic studies that escaped Krymskii's attention. His choice of topics was dictated by either his teaching responsibilities (especially his survey courses on Islamic literatures and history) or his own spiritual and artistic inclinations. The latter prompted him to undertake a study of Ṣūfism, which he treated as an ideology of passive protest on the part of the Muslim masses against the injustices, oppression, and cruelty of the ruling elite. In the Ṣūfī quest for spiritual perfection and serenity, Krymskii saw the ultimate expression of the Oriental ideal of freedom—an ideal that, in his romantic imagination, prefigured the moral and ethical values depicted in the novels of Dostoevsky and Tolstoy (Batunskii 2003, 3:66). Thus, Krymskii believed that Ṣūfism's pacifism and tolerance of other religious attitudes anticipated Tolstoy's doctrine of non-resistance to evil and violence (Smilianskaia 1971, 211–12).

During his sojourn in Syria at the beginning of his academic career, Krymskii assembled a considerable body of printed materials pertaining to the beginnings of the "new" (that is, modern) Arabic literature and Levantine folklore. For a long time, Krymskii's numerous responsibilities prevented him from converting them into a scholarly monograph. He returned to these materials only much later, on the eve of the Second World War, when he was in Kiev.[34] In his massive (almost 800 printed pages) study of the vicissitudes of Arabic belles-lettres in the modern epoch, Krymskii sought to identify the reasons for the decline of traditional/post-classical Arabic literature. He was also eager to show the influence of Levantine folklore on the formation of the new Arabic style and literary canon. To this end, he examined the role of "progressive" Arabic journals, newspapers, and other periodicals in the elaboration and canonisation of this new diction. Additionally, Krymskii took an interest in the literature of Arab emigrants to the West, the Arab-Christian literature of the Levant, the formation of "new" literary circles and clubs in Beirut, Aleppo, Damascus, Homs, and other Levantine cities, and other related topics (Gurnitskii 1980, 155–56). Krymskii sent a manuscript of the first volume of his study of the "new" (modern) Arabic literary scene to Leningrad to be published by the publishing

34 He moved to Kiev to preside over the reconstruction of Ukrainian scientific institutions in 1918; see Smilianskaia 1971, 214–15.

arm of the Soviet Academy of Sciences. Unfortunately, the publication process was interrupted by the Nazi invasion of the Soviet Union in June 1941.[35]

Despite his demanding positions as secretary of the Ukrainian Academy of Sciences (1918–28), head of the historical-philosophical section of the same academy, and chair of Arabic and Iranian Philology at Kiev University (in addition to his numerous other academic and teaching commitments), Krymskii continued to maintain an active research agenda, until the Nazi army occupied the outskirts of Kiev in 1941. Together with other top-ranking Ukrainian academics he was evacuated to Kazakhstan, where he died in 1942 (Gurnitskii 1980, 162–63).

14 Ignatii Krachkovskii (1883–1951) and the Emergence of an Interdisciplinary View of Arab-Islamic History and Culture

Ignatii Krachkovskii is rightfully regarded as the doyen of Arabic studies in Russia of the first half of the twentieth century. Like Bartol'd and Krymskii, he survived the ravages of the Russian revolution and civil war (1917–21)[36] and managed to pursue a successful and productive career under the heavy hand and suspicious eyes of the Communist regime.[37]

Krachkovskii's article "The Historical Novel in Contemporary Arabic Literature," first published in 1911, was truly groundbreaking, and it determined the development of Western perceptions of this emerging literary phenomenon for years to come (Kim and Shastiko 1990, 187). Again, it is worth pointing out that Krachkovskii's experiences in the Orient are unique in that they combined his acquaintance with "native" Arab scholarship with exposure to European Orientology—a fact that may explain why he subsequently became such an influential and prolific contributor to both. Krachkovskii's interest in modern literary developments in the Arab world did not distract him from his original interest in classical Arabic literature. Here, too, he sought to go beyond the rather limited horizons of European Arabic studies (Krachkovskii 1955, 14). In contradistinction to their narrowly focused philological approach to the Arabic poetic corpus, Krachkovskii called on his colleagues to appreciate

35 For many years, his manuscript lingered in an academic archive. It was published thirty years later under the editorship of Anas Khalidov (1929–2001); Gurnitskii 1980, 154. See Krymskii 1971.

36 For detailed overviews of the period in question, see Kemper and Conermann 2011; Kemper 2009a; and Kemper 2009b.

37 For a vivid description of the harassment and ostracism to which he was subjected in the late 1940s, see Dolinina 1994, 370–98, and Kemper 2009b, 111–14.

Arabic poetry's artistic merits and imagery and to apply to them the latest tools of literary criticism already tested on the masterpieces of European literature. The philological, grammar-and-lexicology-based approach characteristic of the school established by the French scholar Silvestre de Sacy, which had dominated the field since the beginning of the nineteenth century (Wokoeck 2009, 4, 14–15, 113–16), was gradually abandoned in favour of a more interdisciplinary and contextualised vision of Arab-Islamic history and culture. This tendency was not unique to Russian Orientology, but is attested for the German *Orientalistik* as well, whose major representatives had grown tired of pure philology and its "neglect of the study of *Realien,*" understood as politics, religion, and culture (Wokoeck 2009, 174, 175, and 177–84).

15 Conclusion

Based on the materials examined in this chapter, the following conclusions and general observations can be proposed. European interest in Muslim societies and cultures was laden with the heavy historical baggage of military confrontation, cerebral animosity, and religious polemic.[38] However, with the political and technological power of Western nation-states on the rise and the military threat from the Muslim world no longer imminent, this negative intellectual and emotional baggage took a back seat to new visions. In the triumphal and self-confident European societies of the nineteenth century, the Muslim "Orient" was drastically "re-imagined" and integrated into the collective European imagery of the "modern self" that we usually associate with the rise of the European nation-state and nationalism. This re-imagining of the self and the non-European "other" was not as homogenous as Edward Said's works might have us believe (Burke III and Prochaska 2008, 18, 22, and 46). Recent studies have shown that the way in which various European countries represented themselves and others varied considerably, often drastically, from one country to another (Burke III and Prochaska 2008, 48–49; Wokoeck 2009, 7–11, 16, 95–97, 219, and 221).

Russia, as has been pointed out, had its "own Orient" within its borders.[39] Some parallels with German *Orientalistik* are illuminating. Russia's education and scholarship, including Oriental studies, at first lagged behind their German

38 For a helpful survey of attitudes toward Islam in various European contexts see Kalmar 2012.

39 Russia's specificity in this respect has been demonstrated convincingly in the recent studies by Michael Kemper (and his collaborators), Vera Tolz, and David Schimmelpenninck

predecessors and tried to imitate them in many, albeit not all respects. Throughout the first half of the nineteenth century there is little evidence that German states had any colonial aspirations, or even any political interest in the Orient (Wokoeck 2009, 90; cf. 91). While this observation obviously does not apply to the Russian Empire, the latter's academic and teaching institutions specialising in Oriental studies were, somewhat paradoxically, patterned on those of German universities. Even though the Russian state wanted its Orientalists to participate actively in its colonial projects and management of "Muslim affairs" within the country, in the end, this was a choice made by individual scholars. Thus, as we have seen, Kazem-Bek had no compunctions about placing his expertise at the service of the empire, whereas his colleagues at the Faculty of Oriental Languages in St. Petersburg were almost uniformly opposed to being distracted from their pursuit of the "unbiased truth" (Tolz 2011, 79). As David Schimmelpenninck van der Oye has observed, they were in favour of a more theoretical, academic approach grounded in the traditions of German philology (Schimmelpenninck van der Oye 2010, 120). What is even more remarkable is that this "ivory tower" approach eventually won the day. The fact that Russian scholars of the late nineteenth and early twentieth centuries consistently debunked both missionary studies of Islam and the amateurish Orientalist dabbling of imperial administrators in the Russian colonies as inferior to the "pure scholarship" of university- and academy-based faculty speaks for itself. It is noteworthy that they presented the *Orientalistik* of Germany, a country with no major Oriental colonies, as a model to be emulated in Russia (Tolz 2011, 78.)

What does this tell us about Russian Orientalogists? Even when some of them presented their "unbiased" scholarship as a more adequate foundation for imperial decision-making than the "tainted" wisdom of their missionary and practically oriented counterparts working with actual Muslims, not Muslim texts,[40] they could not expect the government to follow their advice. Indeed, the experience of many generations of academic Orientologists in Russia and elsewhere has demonstrated that good professional advice is routinely ignored by the powers-that-be in favour of their own practical reasoning, prejudices, and ideological agendas.[41] And yet, as any scholars dedicated to their profession, the Russian Arabists and Islamologists now as before still entertain

van der Oye. Note, however, should be taken of the counter-argument advanced by Alexander Morrison 2009.

40 To use the definition of Alexander Morrison 2009; see also Knysh 1991, 121–30.

41 As argued by Alexander Morrison 2009, 643–46.

an inflated perception of the power of their discipline to change the world for the better. This noble-minded if somewhat self-serving conviction comes to the fore, for example, in Vasilii Bartol'd's suggestion that one of the major reasons for Russia's defeat in its war with Japan in 1904–1905 was the government's failure to invest in "the study of Japan and the Japanese language" (Tolz 2011, 79). Similar sentiments were expressed seventy-five years later by several Soviet academic experts on Afghanistan, who first warned against, then bemoaned the decision of the Soviet leadership to invade that country in December 1979 (Paterson 2011). Had the advice of Bartol'd and his Soviet successors been heeded, we may have lived in a better world today, although this hypothesis, alas, is impossible to prove.

Bibliography

Arberry, Arthur J. 1946. *Asiatic Jones: The Life and Influence of Sir William Jones (1746–1794), Pioneer of Indian Studies.* London and New York: Longmans, Green.

Bartol'd, Vasilii. 1977. *Sochineniia.* Vol. 9. *Raboty po istorii vostokovedeniia.* Moscow: Nauka.

Batsieva, Svetlana. 1972. "Arabistika," *Aziatskii musei–Leningradskoe otdelenie instituta vostokovedeniia AN SSSR.* Ed. A.P. Baziiants et al. Moscow: Nauka.

Batunskii, Mark. 2003. *Rossiia i Islam.* Moscow: Progress-Traditsiia, 3 volumes.

Baziiants, Ashot. 1963. "Sozdanie instituta vostochnykh iazykov v Moskve." *Ocherki po istorii russkogo vostokovedeniia* 6: 270–301.

Beliaev, Viktor, and Isaak Vinnikov. 1960. "Arabistika i semitologia na vostochom fakul'tete." *Uchenye zapiski Leningradskogo universiteta: Seriia vostokovednykh nauk* 13: 98–110.

Bobrovnikov, Vladimir, and Seyed Javad Miri (eds.). 2016. *Orientalizm vs. Orientalistika: Sbornik statei.* Moscow: Institut vostokovedeniia RAN and OOO Sadra.

Bregel, Yuri. 1980. "Bartol'd and Modern Oriental Studies." *International Journal of Middle East Studies* 12: 385–403.

Burke III, Edmund, and David Prochaska. 2008. "Introduction: Orientalism from Postcolonial Theory to World History." In Edmund Burke III and David Prochaska (eds.), *Genealogies of Orientalism: History, Theory, Politics.* Lincoln NE and London: University of Nebraska Press, 1–73.

Crews, Robert. 2006. *For Prophet and Tsar: Islam and Empire in Russia and Central Asia.* Cambridge MA and London: Harvard University Press.

Dolinina, Anna. 1994. *Nevol'nik dolga.* St. Petersburg: Peterburgskoe vostokovedenie.

Farzaliev, Akif. 2005. *Mirza Kazem-Bek (1802–1870).* Unpublished article.

Frank, Allen J. 1998. *Islamic Historiography and "Bulghar" Identity among the Tatars and Bashkirs of Russia.* Leiden: Brill.

Geraci, Robert P. 2001. *Window on the East: National and Imperial Identities in Late Tsarist Russia*. Ithaca NY and London: Cornell University Press.

Gottwald, Josef. 1863. *Opyt arabsko-russkogo slovaria na Koran, sem' moallakat i stikhotvoreniia Imruelkaisa*, Kazan, 1863; an offprint from the "Transactions of Kazan University" II–IV, 1961. Kazan: Kazan University.

Gurnitskii, Kazimir. 1980. *Agafangel Efimovich Krymskii*. Moscow: Nauka.

Hope, John. 2003. "Manifestations of Russian Literary Orientalism." PhD dissertation. Ann Arbor: University of Michigan.

Irwin, Robert. 2008. *Dangerous Knowledge: Orientalism and Its Discontents*. Woodstock NY: Overlook Press.

Kalmar, Ivan. 2012. *Early Orientalism: Imagined Islam and the Notion of Sublime Power*. London and New York: Routledge.

Kemper, Michael. 1998. *Sufis und Gelehrte in Tatarien und Baschkirien, 1789–1889: Der islamische Diskurs unter russischer Herrschaft*. Berlin: K. Schwarz.

Kemper, Michael. 2009a. "The Soviet Discourse on the Origin and Class Character of Islam, 1923–1933." *Die Welt des Islams* 49: 1–48.

Kemper, Michael. 2009b. "Ljucian Klimovič: Der ideologische Bluthund der sowjetischen Islamkunde und Zentralasienliteratur." *Asiatische Studien* 63/1: 93–133.

Kemper, Michael, and Stephan Conermann (eds.). 2011. *The Heritage of Soviet Oriental Studies*. London and New York: Routledge.

Khabibullin, Mars. 2006. *Mikhail Aleksandrovich Mashanov – professor Kazanskoi dukhovnoi akademii, missioner i islamoved*. Kazan: Alma-Lit.

Khabutdinov, Aidar Iu. 2010. *Istoriia Orenburgskogo magometanskogo dukhovnogo sobraniia (1788–1917): Instituty, idei, liudi*. Moscow: Nizhnii Novgorod.

Kim, G.F., and P.M. Shastitko (eds.). 1990. *Istoriia otechestvennogo vostokovedeniia do serediny XIX veka*. Moscow: Nauka.

Knysh, Alexander. 1991. "Sufizm." In S.M. Prozorov (ed.). *Islam: Istoriograficheskie ocherki*. Moscow: Nauka, 109–207.

Knysh, Alexander. 2006. "Historiography of Sufi Studies in the West and in Russia." *Pis'mennye pamiatniki Vostoka/Written Monuments of the Orient* 1/4: 206–38.

Kononov, Andrei. 1957. "Vostochnyi fakul'tet Leningradskogo universiteta (1855–1955)." *Vestnik Leningradskogo universiteta* 8: 5–22.

Krachkovskii, Ignatii. 1950. *Ocherki po istorii russkoi arabistiki*. Moscow and Leningrad: Izdatel'stvo Akademii nauk.

Krachkovskii, Ignatii. 1955. *Izbrannye sochineniia*. Vol. 1. Ed. V.I. Beliaev and G.V. Tsereteli. Moscow: Izdatel'stvo Akademii nauk.

Krymskii, Agafangel E. 1971. *Istoriia novoi arabskoi literatury*. Ed. A.B. Khalidov. Moscow: Nauka.

Kuznetsova, N. 1984. "Vostokovedy-lazarevtsy na rubezhe dvukh vekov po ikh pis'mam." In *Formirovanie gumanisticheskikh traditsii otechestvennogo vostokovedenia (do 1917 goda)*. Moscow: Nauka, 122–44.

Morrison, Alexander. 2009. "'Applied Orientalism' in British India and Tsarist Turkestan." *Comparative Studies in Society and History* 51/3: 619–47.

Paterson, Anna. 2011. "Scholars, Advisers and State-Builders: Soviet Afghan Studies in the Light of Present-day Afghan Development." In Michael Kemper and Stephan Conermann (eds.), *The Heritage of Soviet Oriental Studies.* London and New York: Routledge, 124–44.

Rezvan, Efim (ed.). 1995. *Koran: Perevod i kommentarii D.N. Boguslavskogo*. St. Petersburg: Peterburgskoe vostokovedenie.

Rezvan, Efim. 1991. "Koran i koranistika." In S.M. Prozorov (ed.), *Islam: Istoriograficheskie ocherki.* Moscow: Nauka, 7–84.

Rezvan, Efim. 1998. "Koran v Rossii." In S.M. Prozorov (ed.), *Islam na territorii byvshei Rossiiskoi imperii.* Moscow: Nauka, 1: 47–58.

Said, Edward. 1978. *Orientalism.* New York: Pantheon.

Schimmelpenninck van der Oye, David. 2010. *Russian Orientalism.* New Haven and London: Yale University Press.

Shofman, Arkadii, and Georgii Shamov. 1956. "Vostochnyi raziad Kazanskogo universiteta." *Ocherki po istorii russkogo vostokovedeniia* 2: 418–48.

Smilianskaia, Irina. 1971. "Agafangel Efimovich Krymskii." *Narody Azii i Afriki* 4: 209–15.

Sonn, Tamara. 1996. *Interpreting Islam: Bandali Jawzi's Islamic Intellectual History.* Oxford: Oxford University Press.

Tolz, Vera. 2008. "European, National, and (Anti-) Imperial." *Kritika: Explorations in Russian and Eurasian History* 9/1: 53–81.

Tolz, Vera. 2011. *Russia's Own Orient: The Politics of Identity and Oriental Studies in the Late Imperial and Early Soviet Periods.* Oxford: Oxford University Press.

Valeev, Ravil. 1998. *Kazanskoe vostokovedenie: Istoki i razvitie.* Kazan: Izdatel'stvo Kazanskogo universiteta.

Varisco, Daniel. 2007. *Reading Orientalism: Said and the Unsaid.* Seattle and London: University of Washington Press.

Wokoeck, Ursula. 2009. *German Orientalism: The Study of the Middle East and Islam from 1800 to 1945*. London: Routledge.

CHAPTER 2

Kairo 1869 – Eine historische Collage

Reinhard Schulze

Schon in der frühen ägyptischen Nationalgeschichtsschreibung galt das Jahr 1869 als ein Höhepunkt der Durchsetzung einer "neuen Ordnung" (*al-niẓām al-jadīd*). Natürlich spielte dabei die Tatsache eine Rolle, dass im November jenes Jahres der Suez-Kanal nach zehnjähriger Bauzeit in Betrieb genommen werden konnte. Zumindest hinsichtlich der Schifffahrt war Ägypten nun untrennbar mit Europa verbunden. Die einheimischen Eliten rückten diese Verbundenheit in das Zentrum ihrer Vorstellungswelten, die nun mehr und mehr um den Leitbegriff der Zivilisation kreisten. Zwar galt die Verbundenheit der Sache nach der Gesamtheit Europas, doch tatsächlich privilegierten sie Frankreich oder besser noch Paris. Die französische Metropole, dominantes urbanes Modell einer Zivilisationsordnung, war auch für die Kairoer Eliten das Abbild einer erhofften Zukunft. Doch auch wenn das Jahr 1869 den Höhepunkt einer *mondialisation* Kairos und damit Ägyptens bedeuten sollte, auch wenn sich damit die Konvergenz zwischen europäischen und ägyptischen Ordnungsvorstellungen hin zu einer angeblichen gemeinsamen, global erscheinenden Zukunft abbildete, deuteten sich zugleich schon Prozesse der Divergenz an, die die Verbundenheit rissig und asymmetrisch werden ließ. Es ist kaum zu verleugnen, dass bis in die siebziger Jahre des 19. Jahrhunderts die Kairoer Eliten davon ausgingen, selbst Teil einer universellen Moderne zu sein, die nicht im Widerspruch zu ihrer eigenen islamischen, christlichen oder jüdischen Tradition stand. Zivilisation war für sie noch die universelle Bezeichnung für das Telos "sittlicher", sozialer und wirtschaftlicher Entwicklung, an deren Ende eine – heute würde man sagen – "transnationale" Gemeinschaft der Moderne stehen sollte. Diese schon von den Saint-Simonisten propagierte Vision hatte nach 1834 zunächst unter manchen Angehörigen der ägyptischen Staatseliten Freunde gefunden und bis in die Zeit der 1860er Jahre die sozialen Vorstellungswelten der Eliten dominiert. Allerdings zeigte sich schon 1869, dass die Hegemonie über diesen Zivilisationsdiskurs keineswegs unumstritten war. 1869 war auch das Jahr, in dem Vertreter der europäischen Öffentlichkeit mehr und mehr darauf pochten, dass die Hegemonie über die Zivilisation und die Moderne ihnen gebühre und dass die Ägypter in prinzipieller Differenz zu dieser Moderne zu sehen seien. Dies lohnt die Frage, wie sich für die Stadt Kairo das

 | DOI:10.1163/9789004386891_003

Jahr 1869 darstellen lässt. Mir schien es sinnvoll, dass Porträt als eine Collage in vier Bildern, die sich an den vier Jahreszeiten orientieren, auszuführen. Hilfreich war, dass das Jahr 1869 eben wegen der Eröffnung des Suez-Kanals unter sehr genauer Beobachtung gestanden hatte und dass es daher auch eine breite historische Literatur gibt, die für ein solches Porträt genutzt werden kann.[1]

1 Der Frühling 1869

Das Jahr 1869 beginnt für Kairo wie als Aufbruch in eine *belle époche* (Mostyn 2006). Der ägyptische Pädagoge Rifāʿa Rāfiʿ al-Ṭahṭāwī, nun 67 oder 68-jährig, hatte gerade seine Schrift *manāhij al-albāb* beendet, in der er unter anderem grundsätzliche Betrachtungen über die Konvergenz und Divergenz der europäischen und ägyptischen Staatsordnungen angestellt hatte.[2] Seine Vision galt nun einem durch Grenzen und Zugehörigkeit klar definierten Ägypten, dessen Entwicklungsmodell er in den europäischen Mächten sah. So hegte er die Hoffnung, dass eines Tages Ägypten mitsamt seiner islamischen Identität zu einem festen Bestandteil Europas werden würde (Powell 2003, 52). Die Konvergenz zwischen Ägypten und den europäischen Mächten ergäbe sich in der Machtgestaltung als ruhmreiches Empire, das die Integration der Bevölkerung als "Nation" gewährleisten würde. Al-Ṭahṭāwī widmete sich nun ganz seinem Amt im Kultusministerium und schrieb an einer neuen arabischen Grammatik, die er noch in jenem Jahr veröffentlichen konnte. Das Arabische sollte neben dem Französischen die moderne Sprache der Kairoer Bürger werden; al-Ṭahṭāwīs sprachpolitische Bemühungen hatten Erfolg: wie später im Sprachenerlass vom 9.1.1870 festgelegt wurde, galten diese beiden Sprachen fortan als gleichberechtigte Nationalsprachen, die nun endgültig die osmanische Sprache und damit auch die osmanische Kultur, die zwischen 1820 und 1860 eine bemerkenswerte Aufwertung in Kairo erfahren hatte, zu verdrängen halfen.

In dem Kairoer Stadtteil Ezbekīya (Azbakiyya) war die Sprachkonvergenz für eine kleine bürgerliche Gesellschaft[3] schon Wirklichkeit geworden (Kīlānī

1 Sāmī Bāshā 1915; Douin 1933–1938; Rifaat 1947; Sabry 1934; Sabry 1924; Sammarco 1937; al-Rāfiʿī 1932; Jerrold 1879; Farman 1908; Guindi and Tagher 1946; Mestyan 2017.

2 Gedruckt durch Būlāq: al-Maṭbaʿa al-Miṣrīya, 1869. In jenem Jahr wurden etwa 25 arabische Bücher in den Druckereien von Kairo publiziert, vornehmlich aus der Traditionsliteratur, so Werke von al-Jazarī, al-Mināwī, al-ʿAqbāwī, al-Samhūdī, al-Bayjūrī, al-Bukhārī, Ibn ʿĀbidīn, Ibn Ḥijāzī, Ibn Iyās, Ḫafājī, al-Maʿarrī, al-Manīnī, al-Sharqāwī, al-Suyūṭī, al-Tibrīzī, und al-Zamaḫsharī.

3 Hierzu demnächst mehr in Schulze, "Zur Genealogie bürgerlicher Selbstkonzepte in nahöstlichen Gesellschaften" (im Druck).

1959, 681–704; Mostyn 2006, 69). Wie in Berlin oder Wien war auch hier das Französische zum Etikett einer gebildeten Schicht geworden, die durch die Aufnahme der Sprache des 19. Jahrhunderts Anteil an der Zivilisation der Moderne haben wollte. Am 4. Januar 1869 war in der Ezbekīya, dem reichsten Stadtteil Kairos, gerade das neue französische Théatre de la Comédie eröffnet worden, in dem als erstes Jacques Offenbachs "Die Schöne Helena" aufgeführt wurde, nicht ohne dem Publikum eine arabische Übersetzung des Librettos in die Hand zu geben (Douin 1933–1938, 104; Mestyan 2017, 124). Wie bei allen Theaterbauten, die der Hof bestellt hatte, wirkte auch hier der deutsch-österreichische Architekt Julius Franz (1831–1915) als Baumeister. Wie selbstverständlich wurde nun das Theater als Teil der modernen ägyptischen Zivilisation angesehen. Schon Ḥabīb Ablā Mālṭī hatte um 1855 in dem Vorwort zu seinem arabischen Theaterstück *al-Aḥmaq al-basīṭ* (der einfältige Narr oder einfach der Simplicius) behauptet, dass Ägypten als Heimstatt aller menschlichen Zivilisation auch ein Anrecht auf das habe, was damals in Europa als Errungenschaft des Fortschrittes gefeiert wurde. Und dazu gehöre selbstverständlich auch das Theater. Selbst wenn es in der jüngeren ägyptischen Geschichte das "bürgerliche Theater" nicht gegeben habe, müsse es auch als Teil der ägyptischen Tradition angesehen werden.[4]

Das gerade einmal 0,24 km² große Ezbekīya-Viertel war zum Symbol einer kulturellen Konvergenz geworden. In diesem Stadtteil, der nun endgültig den Platz des älteren Europäerviertels Muskī eingenommen hatte, lebten 1869 etwa 40.000 besser gestellte Kairoer, also vielleicht 15% der Gesamtbevölkerung. Sie konnten sich in den 25 Cafés erfreuen, die rings um den in jenem Jahr neu gestalteten Ezbekīya-Garten angesiedelt waren. Hotels wie das 1841 eröffnete Shepheard-Hotel oder die verschiedenen Logen, darunter besonders die 1865 vom Prinzen Muḥammad ʿAbd al-Ḥalīm (1831–1894) gegründete ägyptische Großloge[5], boten den europäischen wie den Kairoer Bürgern reichlich Möglichkeiten, Geschäftsbeziehungen zu knüpfen oder sich von den berühmten Terrassen aus das Treiben auf den Straßen anzuschauen. Der Hauch eines

4 Neue Ausgabe von *al-Aḥmaq al-basīṭ* durch Shmuel More und Mūsā Shawāriba. Haifa: Gustav Heinemann-Institut, Univ. Haifa, 1997.

5 Der erste Versuch, eine ägyptische Loge zu gründen, geht auf Prinz Muḥammad ʿAbd al-Ḥalīm Pāshā (1831–1894) zurück, der 1864/6 in Kairo eine erste ägyptische Großloge gegründet hat, die unter der Leitung der Loge des Großen Orients Italiens stand und die als Großer Orient Ägyptens und zugleich als nationale Großloge Ägyptens wirkte. Nach seiner kurzen Exilzeit in England brachte er 1867 ein Patent für eine Distriktgroßloge der englischen Großloge mit, die er bis 1872 leitete; die ägyptische Loge wurde von Salvatore Zola geführt. Daneben gab es allein in Kairo acht weitere englische Logen. Lennhof and Posner 1930, 30f., 658. Siehe Sommer 2015, 79f.; zu ʿAbd al-Ḥalīm siehe Fairman 1884; Gendzier 1966, 28, 45–48; Landau 1965; Douin 1933–1938, 96–98; Sabry 1924, 139–43.

Empire libéral umgab die Ezbekīya und die südwestlich angrenzenden Stadtteile. Zwar vermieden es Kairoer wie europäische Bürger, von dem Ezbekīya-Garten aus in die nordöstlich gelegenen Teile der Altstadt zu wandern, galten diese Viertel doch schon 1869 als die verrufensten Orte Kairos. Doch warum sollten die Bürger denn auch in ein Kairoer East End gehen?

Im Januar 1869 nahmen auch die Arbeiten an dem neuen Kairoer West End Konturen an. Bis 1874 sollte sich die Gesamtfläche urbaner Bebauung in Kairo um fast 2 km² vergrößern (Arnaud 1993). 1870 wurden das erste Mal Gasleitungen verlegt; mehr und mehr für Kutschen geeignete Straßen durchzogen nun die Stadt, und auch die Planungen für Wasserleitungen machten große Fortschritte. Nach dem überragenden Erfolg der ägyptischen Ausstellungspavillons auf der Pariser Weltausstellung von 1867 fühlten sich diejenigen Kairoer bestätigt, die als Ausdruck einer symmetrischen Stadtentwicklung zwischen Kairo und Paris im Südwesten der Ezbekīya einen neuen Stadtteil aufbauen wollten. Noch vor Chicago sollte Kairo nach dem Modell von Paris zur zweiten Weltstadt, zur zweiten Hauptstadt des 19. Jahrhunderts umgestaltet werden. Doch während sich in Paris die Umgestaltung nach den Erfahrungen der großen Stadtrevolten von 1830 und 1848 vorrangig auf die alten Stadtteile bezog, wurden die Altstadtviertel Kairos nur sehr oberflächlich in die Stadtplanung mit einbezogen und die Baumaßnahmen im Altstadtbereich waren fast nur auf die Ezbekīya begrenzt. Stattdessen schien es so, als ob in Kairo nach Londoner Vorbild ein pompöses West End gebaut wurde.[6] Hier waren die bestehenden Herrschaftsbauten wie der vizekönigliche Palast in Zamālek, der am 18. Januar 1869 mit einem Ball als Gezira Palace Hotel neu eröffnet wurde,[7] integriert worden. Innerhalb von zwei Jahren sollte der neue Stadtteil Ismāʿīlīya fertiggestellt sein. In der Stadtplanung von 1869 kündigte sich damit schon die spätere Konvergenzbrechung an: denn das "alte Kairo" sollte nicht in die neue Hauptstadt eingebunden werden. Im Gegenteil: das "alte Kairo" war gehalten – dem Zeitgeschmack entsprechend – seinen mittelalterlichen Charakter zu bewahren. Und mittelalterlich ist hier wörtlich zu nehmen: denn das ägyptisch-arabische Kulturideal war noch 1869 deutlich auf die fatimidische, ayyubische und frühmamlukische Zeit ausgerichtet.

In Kairo, wo damals auf etwa 10 km² mehr als 300.000 Menschen lebten, stritt 1869 die kosmopolitische Moderne des Bürgertums mit einer ägyptischen romantischen Nostalgie, die sich sowohl einem "islamischen Mittelalter"

6 Allerdings lässt sich durchaus auch eine Parallele zur Stadtplanung in Berlin ziehen, so Prestel 2017.

7 Der Ball fand anlässlich von Ismāʿīls Thronjubiläum statt, siehe z.B. *Illustrated London News* 13.2.1869, 168.

wie auch einer vorislamischen, ägyptischen Zeit verpflichtet fühlte. 1863 war bereits das ägyptische Museum gegründet worden, und 1869 wurde die École d'Égyptologie eröffnet, an der ab 1870 Heinrich Ferdinand Karl Brugsch (1827–94) unterrichten sollte. Brugschs Aufgabe war die eines Gründungsrektors einer neuen ägyptischen "Universität." Er selbst sollte zugleich der Abteilung für Sprache und Literatur vorstehen. Der Institution wurden nun ein vorbereitendes Gymnasium und ein Polytechnikum angeschlossen; hinzu kamen 1869 eine Rechtsabteilung, Abteilungen für technisches Zeichnen und für Wirtschaft und die erwähnte Schule für Ägyptologie. Amtlicher Leiter des ganzen Vorhabens, für das nur kurzzeitig der Begriff "Universität" gewählt worden war, war der Minister für fromme Stiftungen und stellvertretende Kultusminister ʿAlī Mubārak (1823–93), der Teile der Schule in einem alten Palast am *Darb al-gamāmīz* untergebracht hatte.[8] Diese oft fotografierte Straße, in der Mubārak 1870 auch die neue vizekönigliche Bibliothek in dem ehemaligen Palast von Muṣṭafā Fāḍil (1830–75), dem Bruder des Khediven, errichten ließ, sollte auf der Weltausstellung in Paris 1889 als Rue du Caire nachgebaut werden. Zum Nachbau gehörte dann natürlich auch der "Bauchtanz", zu dem der Lithograph Georges Coutan alias Pasquin eine Darstellung ebenfalls unter dem Titel "La rue du Caire" anfertigte und mit der spöttischen Bemerkung versah: "Concert égyptien, c'est ici la vraie, l'unique danse du ventre!"[9]

Der Philologe und Schüler al-Ṭahṭāwīs ʿAbdallāh Abū l-Suʿūd (1821–1878) publizierte im Frühjahr 1869 die arabische Übersetzung des Museumkatalogs, der auch den arabischen Bürgern einen Zugang zur zeitgenössischen Präsentation der altägyptischen Kultur erlaubte und damit erstmals ein modernes Museumskonzept begründete (Mariette 1869). Das Indigénat égyptien (*al-raʿāwīya al-jinsīya al-maḥallīya*), das 1867 der Khedive[10] Ismāʿīl proklamiert hatte, sollte folglich national wie kosmopolitisch sein, Teil eines universellen zivilisatorischen Prozesses der Moderne.[11] Für Ismāʿīl selbst, der zusammen mit seinem älteren Bruder in Paris aufgewachsen war und der bis zur Übernahme des Amts als Vizekönig 1863 mehrfach Europa besuchte hatte, war diese

8 Mubārak war 1869 zum Vorsteher des *waqf*-Ministeriums ernannt worden; im August 1869 folgte seine Ernennung als Minister für öffentliche Arbeiten; dieses Amt verlor er schon im September desselben Jahres. Im Januar 1870 übernahm er die Schul- und Kultusbehörde. Zu den Bauten an dieser Gasse siehe Mubārak 1886–1888, 92 f.

9 L'Exposition pour rire. *Revue comique*, [1889], abgedruckt in Demeulenaere-Douyère 2014.

10 Diesen Titel erhielt er im osmanischen Firman vom 8.6.1867; vgl. zu seiner Person immer noch Crabitès 1933.

11 Das *indigénat* wird aber auch als Beispiel einer "Provinznationalität" gesehen, Parolin 2009, 74f., Fn. 5. Der Begriff ist also hier nicht bedeutungsgleich mit dem *indigénat*-Konzept des französischen Kolonialismus.

"transmigratorische" Situation selbstverständlich. Das osmanische Staatsbürgerschaftsgesetz vom 19.1.1869 demzufolge "jeder, der einen osmanischen Vater und eine osmanische Mutter oder nur einen osmanischen Vater hat, osmanischer Staatsbürger" sei, hatte auf Ägypten zunächst keine nachhaltigen Auswirkungen. In einem Zirkular vom 18. April 1869 wurde klargestellt, dass osmanische Untertanen in Ägypten dem ägyptischen Gesetz und ägyptischen Gerichten unterstellt seien, sofern die Kapitulationen dem nicht widersprächen (Abécassis und Le Gall-Kazazian 1992).

Die kulturellen Trennlinien in Kairo verliefen allerdings nicht nach dem Muster hier europäische Zivilisation, dort islamisch-arabische Tradition; vielmehr erlaubte die ägyptische Ausdeutung der Konvergenzbeziehung, beide Traditionen so zu verflechten, dass keiner ein eindeutiges Privileg zukam. Am 4. Februar 1869 brach am Spätnachmittag die alljährliche *maḥmal*-Karawane nach Mekka auf und wurde von den Kairoer Bürgern und den Europäern der Ezbekīya prunkvoll verabschiedet. Am selben Abend dann gingen die Zuschauer in die Comédie, um dort Offenbachs Opéra bouffo "La Grande Duchesse de Gérolstein" und vor allem die Diva Catherine Schneider, genannt Hortense, zu sehen (Douin 1933–1938, 108; *Neue Berliner Musikzeitung* 06.01.1869, 4).

Die Saison in Kairo hatte, dem Klima angepasst, im Winter begonnen und erreichte im Februar ihren Höhepunkt. Inzwischen war auch die Zahl prominenter Orientreisender gewachsen. Mitte Januar 1869 waren schon die österreichischen Erzherzöge Rainer und Ernst sowie die Erzherzogin Marie eingereist. Zu ihnen gehörten des weiteren die Prinzessin von Wales, Alexandra Caroline von Dänemark (1844–1925), George Sutherland-Leveson-Gower, 3. Duke of Sutherland (1828–92), der zusammen mit dem Naturforscher Richard Owen (1804–92), dem irisch-britischen Kriegsberichterstatter und Journalisten William Howard Russell (1821–1907) und dem Ingenieur John Fowler (1817–98) im Februar 1869 in Kairo Station machte. Ihnen schloss sich bald auch der Afrikaforscher Samuel White Baker (1821–93) an, der später im Jahr von Ismāʿīl für vier Jahre zum Gouverneur der Provinz Äquatoria ernannt werden sollte. Im April kam dann auch der britische Kronprinz Albert Edward nach Kairo. Die großen und prunkvollen Feste in den Stadtpalais, die Bälle, die der Khedive in seinen Palästen organisieren ließ (*The Illustrated London News* 13.2.1869), und die zahllosen offiziellen Empfänge boten zwar Möglichkeiten, Geschäftsbeziehungen zu knüpfen; zum Beispiel erhielt anlässlich eines solchen Festes eine französische Firma den Auftrag zum Bau einer Nilbrücke. Für musikalische Unterhaltung war gesorgt. Ende Februar reiste sogar aus Wien "Josefine Weinlich's Damen-Kapelle" an. Politische Beziehungen aber ließen sich kaum knüpfen, denn Kairo war eine machtlose Hauptstadt. Für die öffentlichen Arbeiten in Kairo wurden nur etwa 200.000 £E ausgegeben, obwohl 1869 allein die reichsten Kairoer Stadtteile Ashrāqīya, Ezbekīya und Jamālīya etwa 1 Million £ Steuern zu zahlen hatten. Der Baumwollboom der Jahre 1863–1865 hatte die Agrarmentalität des ausländischen wie des einheimischen ägyptischen Kapitals so gestärkt, dass nach der Rezession von 1866 an einer Aufgabe der agrarorientierten Kapitalisierung Ägyptens nicht zu denken war. Schließlich wurde der Staatsetat 1869 zu 92% aus der Grundsteuer und zu 8% aus den Einnahmen der Staatsbahnen finanziert. Für Kairo bedeutete dies den Verzicht auf die Ansiedlung einer weiterverarbeitenden Industrie, welche die Stadt politisch auf eigene Füße hätte stellen können. Der Dampf, Zeichen des Fortschritts, qualmte eben in Oberägypten und am Suez-Kanal, nicht aber in Kairo.

Dafür aber hatte Kairo auch noch nicht den Tribut an den Fortschritt zahlen müssen. Kairo war 1865 von der letzten, aber auch schlimmsten Cholera-Epidemie, die in Oberägypten gewütet und eine der letzten großen Hungersnöte in Ägypten begleitet hatte, kaum betroffen gewesen. Noch im Sommer 1865 hatten in Oberägypten Cholera und Hunger 350.000 Menschenleben gefordert.[12] In Kairo starben damals über 6.000 Menschen an der Seuche. Doch vier Jahre genügten, um die Opfer vergessen zu machen. In der Ezbekīya und der Muskī waren die Kairoer Bürger vor Not und Hunger sicher. Die Viertel wurden im Frühjahr 1869 durch die Einführung der Gasbeleuchtung illuminiert, die das "alte Kairo" östlich des Khalīj, in dem es noch kein Gaslicht gab, im Dunkeln verschwinden ließ.

Am 2. April 1869 entdeckte ein Maschinist des Theaters an der Tür zur Loge des Khediven eine Zündschnur, die zu einer Bombe unter dem Sitz des Khediven führte, die offenbar am Abend desselben Tages, an dem der Khedive eine Theateraufführung verfolgen wollte, zur Explosion gebracht werden sollte. Der Khedive wurde rechtzeitig gewarnt; die Attentäter konnten allerdings nicht ausfindig gemacht werden. Der Khedive, der schon am 22. September 1868 in Alexandria bei seiner Rückkehr von seiner Reise nach Konstantinopel einem Attentatsversuch entronnen war, verdächtigte erneut seinen Onkel, Prinz Ḥalīm oder seinen eigenen Bruder Muṣṭafā Fāḍil, die Attentäter gedungen zu haben.[13] Ḥalīm, der vor allem als Industrieller gewirkt hatte und dessen Villa in Shubrā in Nordkairo zugleich Mittelpunkt eines beachtlichen agrarwirtschaftlichen Unternehmens gewesen war, hatte offenbar große Schwierigkeiten, sich mit der Zurücksetzung in der Thronfolge zu arrangieren, die durch den osmanischen Erlass vom 8. Juni 1867 zusammen mit der Verleihung des Titels "Khedive" an den Vizekönig zugunsten einer Primogenitur geändert

12 Zur Cholera-Pandemie 1863–1875 siehe Hays 2005, 267–71.

13 So schon beim Alexandria-Attentatsversuch, siehe Douin 1933–38, 88, 115.

worden war. Prinz Ḥalīm war 1868 nach Konstantinopel emigriert und lebte zeitweise auch in Paris. Am 3. April wurden der armenisch-osmanische Theaterdirektor Séraphin Manasse (1837–1888) und einige Schauspieler verhaftet. Die Untersuchungsbehörden aber fanden keine Anhaltspunkte, die den Verdacht bestätigten. Manasse entschied sich, sicherheitshalber das Land zu verlassen und wirkte ab Juli 1870 als Direktor des Théâtre Déjazet in Paris.

Frohlocken hingegen konnte der Khedive gleich doppelt: zum einen war er im Frühjahr 1869 zum fünften Mal Vater geworden. Jamīla Fāḍila (gest. 1896), Tochter seiner Ehefrau Jīhān-hanum, sollte später als mystische Dichterin berühmt werden. Zum anderen heiratete im März 1869 seine älteste Tochter Tawḥīda-hanum den damaligen stellvertretenden Kriegsminister Manṣūr Pāshā Yegen; bei den Feierlichkeiten im Theater des al-Bāb al-Ālī-Palast[14] traten nicht nur einheimische Musikanten auf, sondern auch der Star unter den osmanischen Zauberern, der Magier Meḥmed Shukrī, und die damals weltberühmte französische Zirkustruppe von Théodore Rancy (1818–1892) (Mestyan 2011, 76).[15]

Zudem hatte die französische Kaiserin öffentlich bekundet, dass sie zur Eröffnung des Suez-Kanals, die damals noch für den 15. Oktober 1869 geplant war, nach Ägypten kommen wollte. Am 17. Mai 1869 reiste Ismāʿīl auf seiner Jacht Maḥrūsa über Korfu nach Venedig, welches das Schiff am 21. Mai erreichte. Auf seiner anschließenden zweimonatigen Europareise standen Besuche in Florenz, Triest, Wien, Berlin, Paris, London Brüssel, nochmals Paris und Toulon auf dem Programm.

2 Der Sommer

Am 17. Mai 1869 endete daher die Saison in Kairo. Der Hof war aus der Stadt abgereist und begab sich nun nach Europa. Der Khedive beabsichtigte, dort selbst Gäste für die im November geplante prunkvolle Eröffnung des Suez-Kanals einzuladen. Neben verschiedenen europäischen Potentaten sollten auch eine Anzahl von französischen Literaten und Künstlern geladen werden. Ismāʿīl hatte Großes vor: Der Suez-Kanal war zwar ein wichtiges Prestigeobjekt, er stand jedoch nicht im Mittelpunkt seines Interesses.

Der Konvergenz folgend sah sich Ismāʿīl als europäischen Herrscher; die Tribute an das Osmanische Reich, die 1866 verdoppelt worden waren,

14 Der Palast war Anfang der 1820er Jahre am heutigen Mīdān al-Taḥrīr für den Prinzen Ibrāhīm erbaut worden.

15 Siehe hierzu *Le Monde illustré* 24.4.1869, 257, 262, 264; siehe ausführlich Konrad 2008, 363f.

hinderten ihn nicht daran, eine eigene Militärstreitmacht aufbauen zu wollen, die mit der seines Großvaters Muḥammad ʿAlī konkurrieren sollte. Die ägyptische Armee wurde im Sommer 1869 auf 160.000 Mann erhöht;[16] in Europa sollten nicht nur Gäste geladen, sondern vor allem Waffen, insbesondere vier Panzerfregatten und Gewehre gekauft werden, die Ismāʿīl für seine imperialen Absichten einzusetzen gedachte. Das politische Ziel war die Gründung eines ägyptischen Empires, das sich politisch eng an Frankreich, militärisch an den USA anlehnen und geographisch vor allem nach Afrika expandieren sollte (Green 2007, 11–32). Erste engere Militärbeziehungen zu den USA waren schon 1866 zustande gekommen, als ägyptische Truppen auf Kreta zur Bekämpfung der Arkadi-Revolte eingesetzt worden waren (Elz 1988).[17] Weiterhin hatte der Khedive im Frühjahr 1869 den amerikanischen "Glücksritter" Thaddeus Phelps Mott (1831–1894) kontaktiert, der ihm empfohlen hatte, ehemalige Offiziere aus dem amerikanischen Bürgerkrieg für die ägyptische Armee anzuwerben. Mott kam Ende April 1869 nach Kairo und wurde im September desselben Jahres zum Kammerherrn des Khediven ernannt. Eine direkte Kontaktaufnahme mit der amerikanischen Regierung war nicht angesagt, da der Khedive nominell noch immer Untertan des osmanischen Sultans war. Tatsächlich konnten so Offiziere wie Charles Pomeroy Stone (1824–1887) oder Henry Hopkins Sibley (1816–1886) rekrutiert und im Herbst 1869 in die ägyptische Armee aufgenommen werden (Crabitès 1931, Dunn 2006). Am 30. Juni 1869 hatte General Claude-Etienne Minié Bey (1804–1879), der Leiter der ägyptischen Gefechtsschule, in London einen Vertrag mit dem Waffenbauer E. Remington über die Herstellung und Lieferung von 60.000 speziell für die ägyptische Armee produzierten Gewehren unterzeichnet, worüber sich die britischen Stellen sehr beunruhigt zeigten (Dunn 2005, 66). Auch Schweizer spielten hier eine wichtige Rolle: Schweizer bildeten schon einen wichtigen Rückhalt in den Polizeitruppen in Kairo und Alexandria. Nun wurde sogar daran gedacht, eine Elitetruppe von 1.000 Schweizer Soldaten aufzustellen. Doch die Pläne scheiterten schon im Spätsommer 1869 (Dunn 2005, 54).

Das Osmanische Reich, selbst gerade mit einer weitreichenden Armeereform befasst (Hartmann 2016, 99–128), reagierte verstimmt auf die ägyptische Aufrüstung: im Juli 1869 verlangte Istanbul, die ägyptische Armee wieder auf

16 Noch Ende Januar 1869 soll es ein "Übereinkommen" gegeben haben, wonach sich der Khedive zu einer Reduktion der Truppen auf 15.000 Mann bereit erklärt habe, *Times* (London), 1.2.1869.

17 Die ägyptischen Truppen waren noch im Sommer 1869 auf Kreta aktiv und unterstanden einem osmanischen Kommando (Muṣṭafā Naʿīlī Pāshā, ʿUmar Pāshā und dem Großwesir ʿAlī Pāshā).

die alte Sollstärke von 30.000 Mann zu reduzieren[18] und die Waffenkäufe in Europa einzustellen. Ismāʿīl aber, gerade von den europäischen Höfen zurückgekehrt und nun mehr Europäer als Osmane, sah darin einen unberechtigten Eingriff in die 1867 gewährten Autonomierechte[19] und versuchte, durch eine bewusst prunkvolle Eröffnung des Suez-Kanals die europäischen Mächte indirekt zu einer Anerkennung des ägyptischen Empires zu bewegen. Die ägyptisch-osmanische Krise, die im Grunde schon 1867 begonnen hatte, drohte sich zu einem Hegemonialkonflikt auszuweiten. Beide Seiten spannten die europäische Öffentlichkeit ein, um durch die Publikation ihrer Depeschen und Gutachten die Mächte auf ihre Seite zu ziehen. Die Vision des Khediven, ein ägyptisches Reich, das sich vom östlichen Mittelmeer einschließlich Kreta bis nach Abessinien und die somalischen Länder erstrecken sollte, zu errichten, war mehr als nur ein bloßer Traum: Bakers Ernennung als Gouverneur von Äquatoria und der Beginn des ägyptisch-abessinischen Krieges im November 1869 deuteten darauf hin, dass Ismāʿīl ernsthaft gewillt war, dieser Vision Taten folgen zu lassen. Für das Osmanische Reich, das nach dem Abschluss der *tanẓīmāt*-Reformen nun bemüht war, durch eine Modernisierung der politischen Strukturen die Hoheit über die Reichsgebiete zurückzuerlangen, wirkten die Ambitionen des Khediven fast wie eine Bedrohung.

In Kairo brachte der August 1869 eine Überraschung: in den Cafés und Salons der Ezbekīya trat erstmals Jamāl al-Dīn al-Afghānī (1838–1897) auf, der sich für 40 Tage in Kairo aufhielt und dann nach Istanbul weiterreisen sollte.[20] Später wird man ihm nachsagen, er habe sich vorzugsweise in einer Bierhalle in der Ezbekīya aufgehalten, wo er auch den Kontakt zu einem "europäischen Schankmädchen" gesucht habe (al-Wardī 1969, 311). Der später als Journalist tätige Syrer Salīm ʿAnhūrī (1856–1933) berichtete, dass al-Afghānī darüber hinaus eine Vorliebe für Zigarren und Cognac gehegt habe.[21] Er schien damals noch den Lebensstil eines Dandys gepflegt zu haben. Zugleich aber hat er wohl auch Gelehrte an der Azhar getroffen und Vorlesungen gehalten, so zum Buch *al-Ishārāt wa-l-tanbīhāt* von Ibn Sīnā. Seine bei der Eröffnung der Istanbuler *dār al-ʿulūm* gehaltene Rede über den "Fortschritt der Wissenschaften und Künste" (al-Sanūsī 1976, 275–77)[22] mag einen Eindruck von dem vermitteln,

18 Dies war die Zahl, die in der *irāde* vom 27.5.1866 durch den osmanischen Sultan festgeschrieben worden war.

19 Ismāʿīl hatte schon 1867 die Hoffnung gehegt, einen Allianzvertrag mit Griechenland abschließen zu können.

20 Al-Afġānī wohnte im Ḫān al-Ḫalīlī, so Riḍā 1906–26, 23–25; Hourani 1962, 131f.

21 Dies berichtete zumindest Riḍā 1906–1926, 41, 52.

22 Widerlegung von al-Fīlībāwī (Halil Fevzi Filibeli, 1805–1884) 1872, cit. Berkes 1964, 185, Fn. 48, dort findet sich auch eine Diskussion des Textes.

was der Perser in den Kairoer Cafés vielleicht schon angesprochen hatte: Seine wichtigste These war, dass jedes Prophetentum nichts anderes als ein normales menschliches Handwerk sei, das sich jeder aneignen könne, der danach strebe. Die metaphorische Verwendung der Prophetie für selbständiges politisches Handeln, wie al-Afghānīs Rudimente einer Sozialphilosophie überhaupt, wirkten im apolitischen Kairo auf die Zuhörer wie den damals 20jährigen Studenten Muḥammad ʿAbduh, der sich gerade um Zugang zu islamisch-philosophischen Texten etwa von Miskawayh bemühte, sicherlich überraschend: Wenn jeder Bürger sich das Recht auf Prophetie aneignen könne, dann stünde auch jedem Bürger das Recht auf politische Machtbeteiligung zu. Durch solche Diskussionen, die in Kairo sicherlich erst nach al-Afghānīs Rückkehr 1871 zu wirken begannen, konnte die Stadt allmählich ihre unpolitische Stellung im Staat zugunsten einer wirkungsvollen Machtbeteiligung verändern. Für die Kairoer Bürger brachte das *Empire libéral* des Khediven so einen Hauch politischer Freiheit, die al-Afghānī auszukosten verstand. Aber auch der Khedive wusste das Klima zu nutzen: Im Frühjahr war sein Bruder Muṣṭafā Fāḍil aus dem Pariser Exil nach Kairo zurückgekehrt. Fāḍil hatte sich in Istanbul für eine liberale Verfassung des Osmanischen Reichs eingesetzt und war dafür 1866 des Landes verwiesen worden.[23] Die politische Realität aber sah anders aus: In einer Rede auf der dritten Sitzung der ägyptischen Ratsversammlung vom 28.1. bis zum 22.3.1869 machte Ismāʿīl den Kairoer Bürgern nochmals klar, dass sie politisch kein wirkliches Mitspracherecht hätten und es auch nicht reklamieren könnten (al-Rāfiʿī 1937, 123–27; Sammarco 1937, 416–24; Douin 1933–1938, 128–36). Tatsächlich kamen nur drei der 75 Abgeordneten aus Kairo!

In Kairo schloss sich Fāḍil einem kleinen Kreis von Intellektuellen an, die der *Jamʿīyat al-Maʿārif*, der Gesellschaft der Schönen Künste, nahestanden (al-Rāfiʿī 1932, 271). Diese war von dem Kaufmannssohn Ibrāhīm al-Muwayliḥī (1844–1906) zusammen mit ʿUthmān Jalāl (1829–1898) 1868 gegründet worden. Al-Muwayliḥī hatte außerdem im Frühsommer 1869 eine Druckerei der Gesellschaft eröffnet und zwei Nummern seiner politischen Zeitschrift *Nuzhat al-Afkār* publiziert, die aber bald von der Regierung verboten wurden. Das Verbot politischer Opposition war immer ein Teil des *Empire libéral*.

Spott und Satire waren auch in Kairo ein Mittel, um die tatsächliche politische Ohnmacht der Stadt zu mildern. ʿAbdallāh Abū l-Suʿūd nahm sich in seiner 1866 gegründeten Zeitschrift *Wādī l-Nīl* süffisant dieser Ohnmacht an und der damals 30jährige Yaʿqūb Ṣanūʿ, der sich vielleicht schon 1869 mit al-Afghānī getroffen hatte, beschäftigte sich mit seinen Plänen, in Kairo ein eigenes, arabisches satirisches Theater zu gründen. Ṣanūʿ bezog, wie Rotraud

23 Vgl. Brief von Fāḍil an Sultan ʿAbd al-ʿAzīz, publ. in Paris am 24.3.1867.

Wielandt zeigte, die apolitische *à la franca*-Attitude der ägyptischen Bürger in seinen Spott mit ein und kündete damit seinerseits schon die baldige kulturelle Konvergenzbrechung an.[24]

Die Kairoer Bürger der reichen Stadtteile hatten die Stadt im Sommer wieder für sich; sie bejubelten noch ihre Sängerin Sakne (1801–1890), die sie gerne mit der schwedischen Nachtigall Jenny Lind verglichen.[25] Sakne gehörte zu den Sängerinnen (*ʿālma*) der höheren Gesellschaft; bis in die Zeit der Regentschaft Ismāʿīls war sie vornehmlich in Privathäusern aufgetreten und hatte pro Auftritt die beachtliche Summe von 500 Piastern vom Auftraggeber und nochmals dieselbe Summe von den Gästen erhalten (*Das Ausland* 119, 19.5.1851, 476). Sakne galt als außerordentlich reich, ihr Haus in Sayyida Zaynab glich einem kleinen Palast, und Lucy Duff-Gordon, die am 13. Juli 1869 in Kairo verstarb, hatte süffisant in einem Brief vom 11. November 1862 bemerkt:

> Sákneh, the Arab Grisi, is fifty-five. Her face is ugly, I am told. She was veiled, and we only saw her eyes and glimpses of her mouth when she drank water; but she has the figure of a leopard, all grace and beauty, and a splendid voice of its kind – harsh but thrilling, like Malibran's. I guessed her thirty, or perhaps thirty-five.
>
> DUFF-GORDON 1865, 13f.[26]

Nach 1867/8 aber boten die neuen Salons, Cafés und Theater den Sängerinnen eine neue Öffentlichkeit. Der Khedive, dessen Vorgänger Muḥammad ʿAlī in einem Edikt im Juni 1834 Sängerinnen und Prostituierte noch aus Kairo verbannt wissen wollte,[27] zahlte ihr nun selbst fürstliche Gagen, und bald schon kostete ein Auftritt von ihr über 1.000 Piaster (Von Kremer 1863, 299). Doch ihre gefeierten Sänger ʿAbduh al-Ḥāmūlī (1836 o. 1841–1901), der später mit der "kleinen Sakne" (Sukayna, 1860–1896), die sich Almāẓ nannte,[28] verheiratet war, und Muḥammad ʿUthmān (1855–1900) waren mit nach Europa gereist. Die fast 900 offiziell zur Eröffnung des Suez-Kanals eingeladenen Gäste, die nun nach und nach in Kairo ankamen, waren gewiss etwas enttäuscht, da die Stars noch abwesend waren (Belleface 1987/1988).[29]

---

24 Ein ähnlicher Tenor findet sich schon in der Erzählung *Way iḏan lastu bi-Ifranjī* von Khalīl al-Khūrī (al-Khūrī 1860); Wielandt 1980, 131ff.

25 Allerdings war Sakne zuvor vor allem in ihrer Geburtsstadt Alexandria in der Villa Antoniadis aufgetreten.

26 Gemeint sind die französische Opernsängerin María de la Felicidad Malibran (1808–1836) und die italienische Opernsängerin Giulia Grisi (1811–1869).

27 Das Edikt war Anfang der 1850er Jahre aufgehoben worden, allerdings durften Sängerinnen immer noch nicht in öffentlichen Räumen auftreten.

28 Almāẓ, aus armen Verhältnissen stammend, hatte in der Truppe von Sakne ihre Karriere begonnen. Vgl. Fraser 2015; Van Nieuwkerk 1995, 35ff.

29 Oft musizierte man in der Tradition des Damaszeners Shākir, der 1820 nach Kairo gekommen war und dort große Triumphe gefeiert hatte.

Um sie herum aber war das Leben voller Aktivität. Die Bautätigkeiten im Südwesten der Ezbekīya deuteten daraufhin, dass Kairo inzwischen das Schicksal der meisten Metropolen der Zeit teilte: die alte Bausubstanz, vor allem des 18. Jahrhunderts, wurde zugunsten schnell hochgezogener Sandsteinbauten zerstört. Schon zeitgenössische Beobachter sprachen von einer "Haussmannisierung" Kairos. Am Südrand des Ezbekīya-Platzes waren im Mai 1869 die Arbeiten an der Errichtung der neuen Oper aufgenommen worden; alte mamlukische Stadtpaläste und Medresen wurden in Bürogebäude der staatlichen Verwaltung umgebaut; ganze Straßenzüge wurden für die Gasleitungen aufgerissen. Mit dem von Louis Maurice Linant Pasha (1799–1883), der auch als Chefingenieur beim Bau des Suez-Kanals wirkte, geleiteten Bau der Stahlbrücke über den Nil, die Qaṣr al-Nīl mit dem Südende der Jazīra verband und die im Winter 1871 fertiggestellt wurde, zeichnete sich eine ganz neue Orientierung der Stadtentwicklung ab. Die Kairoer nahmen aber diese Unbill wohl gelassen hin. Schließlich hatten auch die wohlhabenden Kairoer Kaufleute gefordert, die wichtigsten Einfallsstrassen in "ihre" Altstadt zu verbreitern, damit die größeren Kutschen auf zwei Fahrbahnen ihren Weg finden konnten. Hieß es doch, dass das schwierigste, was Napoleon je gemacht habe, gewesen sei, mit einem Vierspänner durch Kairo zu fahren. In Istanbul hingegen wurde nie ein kaiserliches Opernhaus gebaut. Hier setzte man eher auf das Musiktheater.

Im Osten der Stadt, in den Altstadtvierteln nördlich und südlich der Azhar, waren die traditionellen Eliten mit anderen Problemen beschäftigt. Die Schul- und Hochschulreform, die der damals noch stellvertretende Kultus- und Bauminister ʿAlī Mubārak nach dem Schulgesetz von 1868 in Angriff genommen hatte, provozierte Zustimmung und Widerspruch unter den etwa 230 Azhar-Gelehrten. Der Anspruch des Staates auf die Kontrolle der Ausbildung wurde allein schon damit legitimiert, dass etwa 2/3 der Schul- und Hochschulabgänger in der Armee und der Verwaltung beschäftigt wurden. Innerhalb der Azhar war der damalige Rektor Muṣṭafā al-ʿArūsī, der von 1864 bis 1870 amtierte, keineswegs unumstritten – im Gegenteil, für die einen, wie für den späteren Rektor Muḥammad al-ʿAbbāsī al-Mahdī (amtierte 1870–1882), war er zu reformfeindlich, für die anderen, angeführt von dem Maghrebiner Muḥammad ʿIllaysh, war er zu reformfreundlich. Al-ʿArūsī hatte schon 1865 einen weitgehenden Reformvorschlag für die Organisation und die Curricula der Azhar gemacht, die ganz dem Willen des Vizekönigs entsprechend zu einer stärkeren Hierarchisierung des Lehrpersonals und der Professorenschaft sowie zu einer Aufnahme nichtreligiöser Wissenschaften in die Curricula führen sollten. Im Sommer 1869 erreichte der Streit an der Azhar einen neuen Höhepunkt: die shāfiʿitischen Gelehrten, die seit fast 150 Jahren an der Azhar die Oberhand hatten, mussten anerkennen, dass im Zuge der Integration der Azhar in die staatlichen Ausbildungsstrategien die ḥanafitische Rechtsschule deutlich aufgewertet wurde. Immer mehr Studenten ließen sich 1869 in den ḥanafitischen Kollegs (*riwāq*) einschreiben, in der Hoffnung, dann eher eine Beschäftigung im Staatsdienst zu finden. Dem Khediven erschien al-ʿArūsī aber wohl als zu halbherzig, sodass er ihn 1870 durch al-Mahdī ersetzte, dem es sehr bald gelang, das Reformprojekt umzusetzen.

Im August erhielt der Khedive einen ausführlichen Brief des osmanischen Großwesirs Meḥmed Emīn ʿAlī Bāshā, selbst ein eifriger Verfechter der osmanischen Staats- und Verwaltungsreformen. Der Großwesir mahnte den Khediven unverblümt, zu den Bestimmungen früherer Firman zurückzukehren und sich ganz als Untertan des osmanischen Sultans zu verhalten, andernfalls drohte er damit, dass die dem Khediven gewährten Privilegien durchaus auch rückgängig gemacht werden könnten. Hierzu gehörte vor allem der Verzicht auf eine eigenständige Außenpolitik und Diplomatie wie auf eine vom Osmanischen Reich unkontrollierte Rüstungspolitik. Ismāʿīls Ambitionen zur Errichtung eines ägyptischen Empire weckten natürlich die Befürchtungen auf osmanischer Seite, der Khedive könnte in die Fußstapfen seines Großvaters Muḥammad ʿAlī treten wollen, der 1831 dem Reich gar den Krieg erklärt hatte. Der Khedive antwortete noch im September an den Sultan über den Großwesir und führte aus, dass sich seine Politik nicht gegen das Osmanische Reich richten würde, sondern allein den Interessen Ägyptens diene.[30] Noch bestand zwischen dem Khediven und dem Osmanischen Reich eine Pattsituation, die sich aber zum Ende des Jahres ändern sollte.

3 Der Herbst

ʿAlī Mubārak war beauftragt worden, sich persönlich um die Feierlichkeiten zur Eröffnung des Suez-Kanals zu kümmern. Auf einer Aktionärsversammlung in Paris war der 16.11.1869 als Eröffnungstermin festgesetzt worden. Der Khedive selbst hatte eigentlich den 15. Oktober vorgesehen. Das Osmanische Reich wurde vom Eröffnungstermin offiziell nicht informiert. Mubārak reiste im August kurz nach Paris, um die Gästeliste durchzugehen. Immerhin mussten etwa 900 geladene Gäste in Kairo untergebracht und versorgt werden, je nach Rang und Stellung in den ersten Hotels der Stadt, die zum Teil eigens für diesen Anlass errichtet worden waren; zudem mussten zahlreiche Droschken beschafft werden, die den Gästen jeder Zeit zur Verfügung zu stehen hätten. Eine Durchsicht der Gästeliste erweckt den Verdacht, dass die ägyptische

30 *New York Times* 2.9.1869 und 4.9.1869. Zum Kontext: Davison 1963, 234–69.

Regierung bewusst das Jahr 1798 nachzustellen versuchte: damals waren die französischen Wissenschaftler und Künstler noch als Entdecker nach Ägypten gekommen; diesmal sollte ihnen ein grandioses Schauspiel geboten werden, welches ihnen zu zeigen hatte, dass Ägypten jetzt kulturell in jeder Hinsicht Frankreich ebenbürtig sei.

Doch die französischen Gäste, die am 16. Oktober in Kairo eintrafen, spielten nicht mit. Wie Gérard de Nerval schon früher ausgeführt hatte, lag ihr Orient nicht mehr in Kairo, sondern allenfalls in der Pariser Oper. Schon am 6. September 1843 hatte Nerval, voller Trauer über den an Europa verlorenen Orient, seinem Freund Gautier geschrieben: "Oh! reste à Paris, et puisse le succès de ton ballet se prolonger jusqu'à mon retour! Je retrouverai à l'Opéra le Caire véritable, l'Egypte immaculée, l'Orient qui m'échappe, et qui t'a souri d'un rayon de ses yeux divins."[31] Sie erwarteten die Bestätigung ihrer nostalgischen Sehnsucht nach einem Orient, den sie nur noch selbst zu vertreten meinten. Gautier, der das französische Publikum im *Journal Officiel* vom 17.1. bis 8.5.1870 über seine Reise unterrichtete, pointierte: "Notre Caire, bâti avec les matériaux des Mille et une nuits se groupait autour de La Place de l'Esbekieh de Marilhat, un tableau singulier et violent" (Gautier 1902, 187). Ihr Kairo war eben nur das Ölbild, das Prosper Marilhat 1834 als Trost für die gescheiterte Juli-Revolution gemalt hatte. Der Maler, der seine Briefe aus Ägypten gerne mit "l'égyptien Prosper Marilhat" unterschrieben hatte und der von dem österreichischen Baron Carl Alexander von Hügel als Zeichner im Rahmen von dessen Ägypten-Expedition 1831–1833 angestellt worden war, wurde von Gautier geradezu hymnisch als veristisches Ideal eines Orientalen gepriesen. Immer wieder betonte Gautier, dass der Orient seinen eigentlichen Platz mitten in Paris habe, dass er, ohne je in Ägypten gewesen zu sein, ein echter "Türke aus Ägypten" sei und dass dieser Orient vor der Banalität der orientalischen Wirklichkeit zu schützen sei.[32]

Gautier haderte mit der Wirklichkeit, als er erstmals in Istanbul mit der Europäizität des Orients konfrontiert wurde (Gautier 1902, 68–100). Als er 1869 endlich in Kairo ankam, verzichtete er auf große Erkundungstouren und zog es vor, den Luxus, den ihnen die ägyptische Regierung bot, zu genießen. An Kairo zeigte er kein Interesse mehr. Die Reisenden waren, so schrieb er später, schon vorab von Touristen informiert worden, dass der wirkliche Ezbekīya-Platz nichts (mehr) mit dem gemein hatte, den Marilhat gemalt hatte. So gab

31 *Le journal de Constantinople* 7.9.1843 in de Nerval, 1986, 878–79, 882–83; hier zitiert nach Moussa 2017, 151–66, hier 153; außerdem Moussa 2016, 103–16. Siehe auch Moussa 2015, 590–96.

32 Vgl. Gautier 1973, 4–8; Moussa 1994, 106, 168–87, hier 183; Neumann 2006, 133–50, hier 134.

Gautier vor, sich den Fuß verstaucht zu haben, so dass er die meiste Zeit auf der Terrasse des Shepheard-Hotels verbrachte, "wo man uns in unseren Träumen unterbrachte."[33] Dort meinten die Touristen, ihren Traum zu finden. Das reale Kairo symbolisierte für sie der Esel, den orientalischen Traum hingegen das Kamel. Kamele aber waren in Kairo 1869 nur noch selten zu finden; man musste sich schon aus der Stadt heraus bemühen, in die Unzivilisiertheit, wie Gautier sagte. Gautiers Reisegenosse, der Künstler und Schriftsteller Eugène Fromentin (1820–1876), erschlagen und ermüdet von der Stadt Kairo, verzichtete ganz darauf, seinen Aufenthalt in der Stadt vom 16. bis 21. Oktober 1869 zu beschreiben (Fromentin 1935, 46).[34] Spottend, im Grunde verärgert, vermerkte Gautier wie fast jeder Orientreisende jener Zeit, dass alles, was ihm begegnete, wenn er das Hotel verließ, Esel und die Rufe der Treiber "Donkey Donkey" waren.

Am 22. Oktober reisten die meisten geladenen Gäste nach Oberägypten. Sie verpassten daher die Eröffnung der Kairoer Oper, die am 1.11.1869 mit einer Aufführung von Verdis Rigoletto feierlich begangen wurde. Die 950 Gäste der Premiere waren durchweg Mitglieder der europäischen und der ägyptischen oberen Gesellschaft, die nach dem heißen und selbst für ägyptische Verhältnisse ungewöhnlich trockenen Sommer "ihre Saison" eröffneten. Ursprünglich hatte der Khedive Verdi dafür gewinnen wollen, wenigsten eine Eröffnungshymne zu komponieren, doch der Maestro lehnte ab. Erst im Frühsommer 1870 ließ er sich überreden eine Oper zu schreiben. Es sollte noch bis zum 24.12.1871 dauern, bis endlich die Oper Aida, deren Libretto Abū l-Suʿūd ins Arabische übersetzt hatte, in Kairo uraufgeführt wurde.

Immerhin: Für die Rigoletto-Aufführung konnte der Khedive den Bariton Cesare Boccolini (Rigoletto) und die Sopransängerin Giuseppina Vitali (Gilda) engagieren lassen. Den Kritiken nach scheint der Dirigent und Freund Verdis, Emanuele Muzio (1821–1890), den der Intendant der Oper, der griechische Chemiker Paul Draneht (eigentlich Paul Pavlides[35]) aus Mailand nach Kairo kommen gelassen hatte, das Orchester zur Zufriedenheit des Publikums geleitet zu haben (*Fremden-Blatt* 314, 13.11.1869). Das neue Opernhaus war allerdings nach der zweiten Aufführung des Rigoletto (3.11.1869) fast abgebrannt, und

33 "On nous logeait dans notre rêves." Gautier 1902, 2: 190; Kabbani 1986, 74.

34 Nach der Rückkehr von der Oberägyptenreise blieb ihm nur der 14. November für einen kurzen Besuch der Bazare. Ausführlicher berichtete der Diplomat Charles Taglioni 1870, 34–66.

35 Pavlidis war von Muḥammad ʿAlī nach Paris zum Studium geschickt worden und sollte dort als "Orientale" auftreten; hierzu sollte er sich einen "orientalischen Namen" zulegen. Sein Lehrer, Baron Thénard, schlug vor, dass sich Pavlidis Thénard in rückwärts buchstabierter Form (also Draneht) nennen sollte, siehe Mostyn 2006, 28.

später verhinderte der Krieg in Frankreich eine rechtzeitige Anlieferung der monumentalen Bühnenbilder.

Die öffentliche Verschuldung betrug im Oktober 1869 schon £ 29.000.000. Doch bis 1869 hielten sich die Schulden noch die Waage mit dem ökonomischen Potential der agrarischen Exportwirtschaft, zu deren Gunsten massiv in Bewässerung, Gütertransport per Eisenbahn, Baumwollplantagen (*ʿizab*) und Ausbildung mit meist französischem und britischem Kapital investiert worden war. Nach 1869 bot das Land aber keinen Gegenwert zu den Schulden mehr an. Schon 1876 waren nur noch knapp 10% der inzwischen auf 100 Millionen £ angewachsenen Verschuldung des Landes durch Werte (z.B. Kronland und Suezkanal-Aktien) gedeckt.

Die Eröffnung des Suez-Kanals am 17.11.1869, die allein etwa 1 Million £ gekostet haben sollen, war der festliche Höhepunkt des Jahres. Brugsch fungierte als Reiseleiter für hochgestellte Persönlichkeiten, von denen es viele aber vorzogen, an Bord ihrer Jachten zu bleiben, da es keine "angemessenen Unterkünfte" gäbe. Die französischen Gäste, die ihrem orientalischen Traum nachhingen, hatten den Anspruch der ägyptischen Eliten, europäisch zu sein, mit Wehmut aufgenommen, mussten sie doch erleben, dass damit "ihr" Ägypten an Europa verloren gegangen war. Der französische Maler Jean-Léon Gérôme, der seit 1850 schon dreimal in Kairo gewesen war, besuchte nun im November erneut die Stadt und porträtierte mit einer fast fotografischen Präzision seine Visionen (Lane-Poole 1898, 288). Nur war das für die Mehrheit der nostalgischen Europäer alles andere als erstrebenswert.[36] Sie beklagten den Verlust "ihres Ägyptens" und wollten gleichzeitig nicht anerkennen, dass zumindest Kairo tatsächlich schon in Europa lag. Die Konvergenz musste gebrochen werden, um den orientalischen Traum zu bewahren. So verwundert es nicht, dass in Kairo schliesslich auch so manche orientalischen Phantasien der Europäer bewahrheitet wurden: auf dem Ezbekīya-Platz, der nun nach und nach vom französischen Landschaftsarchitekten Jean-Pierre Barillet-Deschamps (1824–1873) zu einem Garten umgestaltet wurde[37], wurde im November 1869 ein "echtes" orientalisches Cafés eröffnet, mit "echten" Mohren als Garçons und "echtem" orientalischen Mocca. Gleich nebenan aber gab es auch das "europäische" Café, in dem man gepflegt von einer sicheren Warte aus "in den Orient" schauen und dabei die französisch-ägyptischen Zeitungen *L'Égypte*, *Le Nil* oder *Le Progrès égyptien* lesen konnte. Später kamen Schießbuden, Tabakläden und noch mehr Cafés hinzu. Eine türkisch-europäische Musikkappelle

---

36 Es gab natürlich auch Ausnahmen, siehe z.B. Plauchut 1889, 22.

37 Hier hatte sich Kairo verspätet: in Konstantinopel war schon 1869 der Taksim-Garten eröffnet worden, vgl. Çelik 1986, 40.

unterhielt die Flaneure mit Militärmusik (Abouseif 1985). Und später dann, als erstmals der Bauchtanz in Kairo vorgeführt werden sollte, war ein erster Höhepunkt der Orientalisierung des Orients erreicht.[38] Die Eliten wehrten sich noch, auch wenn einige vielleicht schon erkannten, dass sich hinter dieser Orientalisierung eine Geschäftsidee verbergen sollte, die manchen Kairoer Kaufleuten von Vorteil sein sollte. Bōghōṣ Nūbār Pāshā (1825–1899), damals Premierminister, sollte 1878 für den Khedive Ismāʿīl einen Redetext formulieren, in dem es hieß: "Mon pays n'est plus en Afrique, nous faisons partie de l'Europe actuellement" (zitiert nach Sabry 1924, 132).

Der Orientalismus wandelte sich nun zu einer hegemonialen Ordnung: die neue Modernität des ägyptischen Empire wurde den ägyptischen Eliten wieder entrissen, nachdem sich schon Orientalisten und Ägyptologen der islamischen beziehungsweise pharaonischen Geschichte des Landes bemächtigt hatten. Das Moderne könne eben nur, wie Lane-Poole ausführt, als Importprodukt verstanden werden, nicht als kreative Leistung der ägyptischen Gesellschaft. Den Kairoern blieb nichts: der Orient war zum europäischen Traum geronnen, die Moderne in Ägypten zum Privileg Europas geworden. So hatte schon 1861 der damalige bourbonische Thronprätendent Heinrich V de Chambord im Verlaufe seiner Ägyptenreise notiert: "Tous ce peuples orientaux ne prennent qu'une apparence de civilisation; à la premiére occasion le barbare se retrouve" (Comte de Chambord 1984, 245).

Bis etwa 1870 war unter den arabischen Eliten dagegen die Überzeugung von der Gültigkeit der zivilisatorischen Konvergenz zwischen der islamischen und der europäisch-christlichen Welt sehr populär; sie erlaubte den Kulturvergleich (*muqābala*), den 1869 Autoren wie ʿAbdallāh Abū l-Suʿūd, Ṣāliḥ Majdī, ʿAbdallāh Fikrī al-Ṭahṭāwī[39] und ʿAlī Mubārak in Kairo, Buṭrus al-Bustānī in

38 Von *danse du ventre* sprachen wohl erstmals französische Zeitungen im Kontext von Gérômes Bild *l'Almée*, siehe Léo Lagrange, "Le salon de 1864", in: *Gazette des beaux-arts* (1864), S. 502–36, hier S. 529 und Ch. Asselineau, "Le salon de 1864" in: *Revue nationale et étrangère, politique, scientifique et littéraire* 17 (1864), S. 171–77, hier S. 175f., ausserdem *Le Figaro* 27.3.1864, S. 5; das Bild von Gérôme, das im Salon von 1864 ausgestellt wurde, wurde in *Le Figaro* (1.5.1864) als "Attenat auf die Sitten" bezeichnet. Am 17. Oktober 1869 war auch die französische Literatin Louise Colet nach Ägypten gekommen und hatte in der oberägyptischen Stadt nach jener syrisch-ägyptischen Tänzerin gefahndet, die nacheinander George William Curtis und Gustave Flaubert 1848/1851 besucht hatten und die gemeinhin als *küçek hanum* («Fräulein») bekannt war. Sie wurde von ihnen und anderen für ihren «Bienentanz» gefeiert. Colet, die wohl sehr eifersüchtig auf Flauberts Beziehung zu Küçek Hanum reagiert hatte, traf die Tänzerin aber nicht an (Barnes 1984, 109–10, 122–24, 137–52).

39 1869 wirkte der spätere klassizistische Autor und Staatsangestellte Fikrī in Kairo noch als Erzieher des Prinzen Tawfīq.

Beirut oder besonders Aḥmad Fāris al-Shidyāq in Istanbul selbstbewusst anstellten (al-Bustānī 1869; al-Shidyāq 1855); sie gestattete die bruchlose und historisch berechtigt erscheinende Rezeption europäischer Denktraditionen, die nur als Teil einer gemeinsamen Zivilisation angesehen wurden; und sie ermöglichte das Leben in der Moderne, ohne Zweifel an der Berechtigung eines solchen Lebens aufkommen zu lassen.

4 Der Winter

Die Moderne hat die ägyptische Gesellschaft 31.379.000 £ Sterling gekostet, die der Staat als Anleihen aufgenommen hatte. Diese Summe aber war für damalige Verhältnisse nicht spektakulär. Es war aber eine Verschuldung, welche die Divergenz der ägyptischen Gesellschaft kennzeichnete. Um die Schulden bedienen zu können, war die ägyptische Regierung gezwungen, immer mehr Teile der Infrastruktur des Landes zu verkaufen, Konzessionen zu erteilen und Einkünfte zu verpachten. Kairo, politisch entmachtet und wirtschaftlich wenig produktiv, war nicht in der Lage, die Agrarmentalität des ägyptischen Hofes zu brechen und selbst für eine Schuldenregelung zu sorgen. Dadurch war die Finanzpolitik weiterhin in der Hand des Landes, das durch die Stabilisierung der Baumwoll- und Zuckerexportwerte 1869 seine ökonomische Autonomie noch wahren konnte. Doch schon 1869 überstiegen die Steuerschulden in Kairo erstmals die Produktivität der Stadt. Der privatwirtschaftliche Kolonialismus, der 1820 in Ägypten wirksam geworden war, hatte diese strukturelle Divergenz hervorgerufen, die politisch den Hof stützte, die Stadt aber vollkommen entmündigte. Die Moderne in Kairo, die 1869 einen Höhepunkt erreichte, erlag schließlich den durch den Kolonialismus vorgegebenen Machtstrukturen. Die politische Macht lag nun in den europäischen Städten, die sich mit dem ägyptischen Land verbündet hatten.

Wem die Hegemonie in dieser Machtordnung gebührte, stand fest: Vom 6. bis zum 24. November 1869 war zudem ein internationaler Handelskongress erneut in Kairo zusammengetreten, zu dem die europäischen Mächte, aber auch kleinere Staaten wie Hamburg, hochrangige Delegierte entsandt hatten. Der eigentlich von den am Kanalbau beteiligten Gesellschaften getragene Kongress hatte die Aufgabe, die Rahmenbedingungen für eine freie Schifffahrt auf dem Suez-Kanal zu diskutieren (*Der österreichische Ökonomist* 8.1.1870, 12).

Schon am 29.11.1869 machte sich die ägyptische Finanzpolitik negativ bemerkbar: der osmanische Sultan erließ einen Firman, in dem er die Kontrolle des ägyptischen Staatshaushalts, die Abrüstung der ägyptischen Armee auf 30.000 Mann und die Einstellung der Waffenkäufe forderte. Zudem versuchte das Osmanische Reich, die Steuerhoheit über Ägypten zurückzuerlangen. Ismāʿīl musste nachgeben, wenn auch halbherzig: Obwohl er sich der Sache des Friedens unterwerfe, betrachte er doch seine Rechte und Privilegien weiterhin als gerade so umfassend, wie sie bisher waren. Doch die Pforte verlangte ultimativ die Übergabe von 200.000 Gewehren und die noch in Toulon auf der Reede liegenden, eigentlich für Ägypten bestimmten Panzerfregatten. Vergeblich versuchte der Khedive dagegen zu halten und orderte die Schiffe zunächst zurück nach Alexandria. Doch verliefen seine Bemühungen im Sand. Im März 1870 musste er die Schiffe schließlich doch an das osmanische Kriegsministerium abliefern. Trotzdem verfolgte der Khedive weiterhin seine Verschuldungspolitik und nahm schon 1870 eine neue Anleihe in Höhe von £7.142.860 auf, für die er aber nur 5 Millionen £ ausgezahlt bekam. Das Osmanische Reich, das nach dem Krim-Krieg zumindest bis zur Orientalischen Krise von 1875/6 seine Zugehörigkeit zum europäischen Westen erreicht hatte, zerstörte erstaunlich selbstbewusst den Traum von einem ägyptischen Empire. Die Brechung der Konvergenz war erreicht. Mit dem Beginn des politischen Kolonialismus zu Beginn der siebziger Jahre wurde der Anspruch der ägyptischen Eliten, gleichberechtigt an der Zivilisation der Moderne teilzuhaben, zunichte gemacht. An die Stelle des kulturellen Vergleichs und des zivilisatorischen Wettbewerbs trat nun die Distanz, welche die Kolonisierten von den Kolonisierenden trennen sollte. Als al-Afghānī 1871 nach Kairo zurückkehrte, war die kulturelle Brechung nicht mehr zu übersehen. Die Moderne begann sich in die Neustadt al-Ismāʿīlīya zurückzuziehen. Zwar gab es noch die Ezbekīya, den Ort der ägyptischen Moderne, doch die Auslagerung der europäischen Kultur und die Zuordnung der ägyptischen Kultur zur Altstadt war nicht mehr aufzuhalten. Das neue Jahrzehnt leitete die koloniale Situation ein, die Ägypten über Jahrzehnte prägen sollte.

Bibliographie

Zeitungen

Das Ausland
Der österreichische Ökonomist
Fremden-Blatt (Wien)
Gazette des beaux-arts
Illustrated London News
Journal Officiel
Le Figaro

Le Journal de Constantinople
Le Monde illustré
Neue Berliner Musikzeitung
New York Times
Revue nationale et étrangère, politique, scientifique et littéraire
The Illustrated London News
Times (London)

Literatur

Abécassis, Frédéric und Anne Le Gall-Kazazian. 1992. "L'identité au miroir du droit: Le statut des personnes en Égypte (fin XIXe - milieu XXe siècle)." *À propos de la nationalité. Égypte/Monde arabe* 11: 11–38.

Arnaud, Jean-Luc. 1993. "Maps of Cairo and the Development of the City at the End of the 19th Century." In Attilo Petruccioli (ed.), *Environmental Design: Journal of the Islamic Environmental Design Research Centre* 1/2. Rome: Dell'oca Editore, 82–91.

Asselineau, Ch. 1864. "Le salon de 1864." *Revue nationale et étrangère, politique, scientifique et littéraire* 17 (1864), 171–77, S. 175f.

Barnes, Julian. 1984. *Flaubert's Parrot.* New York: Vintage.

Behrens-Abouseif, Doris. 1985. *Azbakiyya and its Environment from Azbak to Ismāʿīl, 1476–1879.* Kairo: IFAO.

Berkes, Niyazi. 1964. *The Development of Secularism in Turkey.* Montreal: McGill University Press.

Belleface, Jean-François. 1987/1988. "Turath, classisisme et variétés: L'orchestre oriental au Caire au XXe siècle." *Bulletin des études orientales* 39/40: 39–65.

al-Bustānī, Buṭrus. 1869. *Khiṭāb fi l-hay'a al-ijtimāʿiyya wa-l-muqābala bayna l-ʿawā'id al-ʿarabiyya wa-l-ifranjiyya.* Beirut: Maṭbaʿat al-maʿārif.

Çelik, Zeynep.1986. *The Remaking of Istanbul: Portrait of an Ottoman City in the Nineteenth Century.* Berkeley: University of California Press.

Comte de Chambord. 1984. *Journal de Voyage en Orient 1861.* Paris: Tallandier.

Crabitès, Pierre. 1931. *Americans in the Egyptian Army.* London: Routledge.

Crabitès, Pierre. 1933. *Ismail, the Maligned Khedive.* London: Routledge.

Davison, Roderic H. 1963. *Reform of the Ottoman Empire, 1856–1876.* Princeton: Princeton University Press.

Demeulenaere-Douyère, Christiane. 2014. "L'Égypte, la modernité et les expositions universelles." *Bulletin de la Sabix – Société des amis de la Bibliothèque et de l'Histoire de l'École polytechnique* 54: 37–41.

Douin, Georges. 1933–38. *Histoire du règne du khédive Ismaïl,* Rome: Stampata [...] nell Ìstituto poligrafico dello stato per la Reale società di geografia d'Egitto. I–III/1–2.

Duff-Gordon, Lucy. 1865. *Letters from Egypt 1863–65*. London: Macmillan.

Dunn, John P. 2005. *Khedive Ismail's Army*. London and New York: Routledge.

Dunn, John P. 2006. "Americans in the Nineteenth Century Egyptian Army: A Selected Bibliography." *The Journal of Military History* 70/1 (2006): 123–36.

Elz, Wolfgang. 1988. *Die europäischen Grossmächte und der kretische Aufstand, 1866–1867*. Stuttgart: Steiner.

Fairman, Edward St. John.1884. *Prince Halim Pacha, of Egypt, a Freemason: Egyptian Affairs, or, How Ismail Pacha Found, and Left, Egypt, the Cause and Origin of the Egyptian Question, and the Only, Because the Just, Solution*. London: Published by the author, Edward Saint John Fairman.

Farman, Elbert Eli. 1908. *Egypt and Its Betrayal: An Account of the Country during the Periods of Ismaîl and Tewfik Pashas, and of How England Acquired a New Empire*. New York: Grafton.

al-Fīlībāwī, Khalīl Fawzī (Halil Fevzi Filibeli). 1872. *al-Suyūf al-qawāṭiʿ*. Istanbul, o.V.; osmanisch: *Süyūfü l-qavâṭiʿ li-men qāla inne n-nübüvvete sanʿatün mine ṣ-ṣanāʾiʿ*. Istanbul: o.V., 1881.

Fraser, Kathleen W. 2015. *Before They Were Belly Dancers: European Accounts of Female Entertainers in Egypt, 1760–1870*. Jefferson NC: McFarland.

Fromentin, Eugène. 1935. *Voyage en Égypte (1869): Journal publié d'après le carnet manuscrit avec introduction et notes par Jean-Marie Carré*. Paris: Aubier.

Gautier, Théophile. 1902. *L'Orient*. I–II. Paris: G. Charpentier et E. Fasquelle, II.

Gautier, Théophile. 1973. "Prosper Marilhat." In *Prosper Marilhat, Vertaison 1811–Paris 1847: Peintures, dessins, gravures: Exposition ville de Clermont-Ferrand: Musée Bargoin, Juin-septembre 1973*. Clermont-Ferrand: Musée Bargoin, 4–8.

Gendzier, Irene L. 1966. *The Practical Visions of Yaʿqub Sanuʿ*. Cambridge MA: Harvard University Press.

Green, Dominic. 2007. *Three Empires on the Nile: The Victorian Jihad, 1869–1899*. New York: Free Press.

Guindi, Georges und Jacques Tagher. 1946. *Ismail d'après les documents officiels avec avant-propos et Introduction historique: Ouvrage publié à l'occasion du cinquantenaire de la mort du Khedive Ismail 1895–1945*. Kairo: Institut français d'archéologie orientale.

Hartmann, Elke. 2016. *Die Reichweite des Staates: Wehrpflicht und moderne Staatlichkeit im Osmanischen Reich, 1869–1910*. Paderborn: Schöningh.

Hays, J. N. 2005. *Epidemics and Pandemics: Their Impacts on Human History*. Santa Barbara CA: ABC-Clio, 267–71.

Hourani, Albert. 1962. *Arabic Thought in the Liberal Age, 1798–1939*. London: Oxford University Press.

Jerrold, Blanchard. 1879. *Egypt Under Ismail Pacha: Being Some Chapters of Contemporary History*. London: Tinsley.

Kabbani, Rana. 1986. *Europe's Myths of Orient: Devise and Rule*. London: Macmillan.

al-Khūrī, Khalīl. 1860. *Way idhan lastu bi-Ifranjī*. Beirut: al-Maṭbaʿa al-Sūriyya.

Kīlānī, Muḥammad Sayyid. 1959. *Fī rubūʿ al-Azbakīya: Dirāsa adabīya, tārīkhīya, ijtimāʿiyya*. Kairo: Dār al-ʿArab.

Konrad, Felix 2008. *Der Hof der Khediven von Ägypten: Herrscherhaushalt, Hofgesellschaft und Hofhaltung, 1840–1880*. Würzburg: Ergon-Verlag.

Landau, Jacob. 1965. "Prolegomena to a Study of Secret Societies in Modern Egypt." *Middle Easterm Studies* 1/2: 135–86.

Lane-Poole, Stanley. 1898. *Cairo: Sketches of Its History, Monuments, and Social Life*. London: J.S. Virtue.

Lennhof, Eugen und Oskar Posner. 1930. *Internationales Freimaurer-Lexikon*. Wien: Amalthea-Verlag.

Mariette, Auguste. 1869. *Furjat al-mutafarrij ʿalā al-Antīqa Khāna al-Khidiwiyya al-kāʾina bi-Būlāq Miṣr al-maḥmīya: Wa-hiya ʿibāra ʿan waṣf nukhbat al-āthār al-qadīma al-Miṣriiyya al-mawjūda fī Khazīnat al-Tuḥaf al-ʿIlmiyya al-Miṣriyya*. Kairo: Maṭbaʿat Wādī l-Nīl.

Mestyan, Adam. 2011. *"A Garden with Mellow Fruits of Refinement:" Music Theaters and Cultural Politics in Cairo and Istanbul, 1867–1892*. PhD dissertation, Central European University, Budapest.

Mestyan, Adam. 2013. "Power and Music in Cairo: Azbakiyya." *Urban History* 40/4: 681–704

Mestyan, Adam. 2017. *Arab Patriotism: The Ideology and Culture of Power in Late Ottoman Egypt*. Princeton: Princeton University Press.

Mostyn, Trevor. 2006. *Egypt's Belle Epoque*. London: I.B. Tauris.

Moussa, Sarga. 1994. "Les premiers 'touristes' en Orient." *Romanische Forschungen* 106: 168–87.

Moussa, Sarga. 2015. "L'Égypte nervalienne." In Florence Quentin (Hg.), *Le Livre des Égyptes*. Paris: Robert Laffont, 590–96.

Moussa, Sarga. 2016. "Le Caire rêvé, Le Caire parodié: Gautier et Nerval, correspondance croisée (1843)." In Anne Geisler-Szmulewicz und Sarga Moussa (Hg.), *Gautier et Nerval: Collaborations, solidarités, différences*. Nîmes: Lucie éditeur, 103–16.

Moussa, Sarga. 2017. "Le voyage en orient de Nerval ou la possibilité d'un orientalisme hybride." In Véronique Porra und Gregor Wedekind (Hg.), *Orient - Zur (De-)Konstruktion eines Phantasmas*. Bielefeld: transcript, 151–66.

Mubārak, ʿAlī. 1887. *al-Khiṭaṭ al-Tawfīqiyya al-jadīda li-Miṣr al-Qāhira wa-mudunihā wa-bilādihā al-qadīma wa-l-shahīra*. I–XX. Būlāq: al-Maṭbaʿa al-kubrā al-amīriyya, 1886–88.

Neumann, Martin. 2006. "Le roman de la momie: Ägyptische Kunst und Kultur als Konkretisation eines ästhetischen Ideals." In Michael Bernsen und Martin Neumann (eds.), *Die französische Literatur des 19. Jahrhunderts und der Orientalismus.* Tübingen: Niemeyer, 133–50.

Parolin, Gianluca P. 2009. *Citizenship in the Arab World: Kin, Religion and Nation-State.* Amsterdam: Amsterdam University Press.

Plauchut, Edmond. 1889. *L'Egypte et l'occupation anglaise.* Paris: Plon.

Powell, Eve Troutt. 2003. *A Different Shade of Colonialism: Egypt, Great Britain, and the Mastery of the Sudan.* Berkeley: University of California Press.

Prestel, Joseph Ben. 2017. *Emotional Cities: Debates on Urban Change in Berlin and Cairo, 1860–1910.* Oxford: Oxford University Press.

al-Rāfiʿī, ʿAbd al-Raḥmān. 1932. *ʿAṣr Ismāʿīl.* I–II. Kairo: Maṭbaʿat al-Nahḍa.

Riḍā, Muḥammad Rashīd. 1324–44 [1906–1926]. *Tārīkh al-ustāḏ al-imām al-shaykh Muḥammad ʿAbduh.* I–III. Kairo: al-Manār, I.

Rifaat, Mohammed. 1947. *The Awakening of Modern Egypt.* London: Longmans, Green.

Sabry, Mohammed. 1924. *La genèse de l'esprit national Egyptien, 1863–1882.* Paris: Librairie Picart.

Sabry, Mohammed. 1934. *L'Empire Égyptien sous Ismail et l'ingérence Anglo-Française (1863–1869).* Paris: Geuthner.

Sāmī Bāshā, Amīn. 1915. *Taqwīm al-Nīl wa-asmāʾ man tawallā amr Miṣr wa-muddat ḥukmihim ʿalayhā wa-mulāḥaẓāt taʾrīkhiyya ʿan aḥwāl al-khilāfa al-ʿāmma wa-shuʾūn Miṣr al-khāṣṣa ʿan al-mudda al-munḥaṣira bayna l-sana al-ūlā wa-sanat 1333 al-hijriyya, (622–1915 milādiyya).* Kairo: Maṭbaʿat al-Amīriyya, 1–3: 1916–1936, Bd. 3/2 (ʿan al-mudda min ghuḍūn sanat 1279–1289 hijriyya (1863–1872 milādiyya).

Sammarco, Angelo. 1937. *Histoire de l'Egypte moderne, III: Le règne du Khédive Ismail de 1863 à 1879.* Kairo: Impr. de l'Institut francais d'archeologie orientale.

al-Sanūsī, Muhammad. 1976. *al-Riḥla al-ḥijāziyya.* ʿAlī al-Shanūfī (Hg.), I–III. Tunis: al-Shirka al-Tūnisīya li-l-Tawzīʿ, III.

Schulze, Reinhard. "Zur Genealogie bürgerlicher Selbstkonzepte in nahöstlichen Gesellschaften." In Manfred Hettling (Hg.), *Bürgertum: Bilanzen, Perspektiven, Begriffe.* Göttingen: Vandenhoeck und Ruprecht (2019, im Druck).

al-Shidyāq, Aḥmad Fāris. 1855. *Kitāb al-sāq ʿalā l-sāq fī-mā huwa al-Fāriyāq aw Ayyām wa-shuhūr wa-aʿwām fī ʿajm al-ʿArab wa-l-Aʿjām* = La vie et les aventures de Fariac: Relation de ses voyages avec ses observations critiques sur les arabes et sur les autres peuples. Paris: Duprat.

Sommer, Dorothe. 2015. *Freemasonry in the Ottoman Empire: A History of the Fraternity and Its Influence in Syria and the Levant.* London: I.B. Tauris.

Taglioni, Charles. 1870. *Deux mois en Egypte: Journal d'un invité du Khédive.* Paris: Amyot.

van Nieuwkerk, Karin. 1995. *A Trade Like Any Other: Female Singers and Dancers in Egypt.* Austin: University of Texas Press.

von Kremer, Alfred. 1863. *Aegypten: Forschungen über Land und Volk während eines zehnjährigen Aufenthalts.* I–II. Leipzig: Brockhaus, II.

al-Wardī, ʿAlī. 1969. *Lamaḥāt ijtimāʿiyya min taʾrīkh al-ʿIrāq al-ḥadīth*. I–VI. Bagdad: Maṭbaʿat al-irshād, III.

Wielandt, Rotraud. 1980. *Das Bild der Europäer in der modernen arabischen Erzähl- und Theaterliteratur*. Beirut: Orient-Institut der Deutschen Morgenländischen Gesellschaft.

PART 2

Empires, Corporations, and Nations

CHAPTER 3

Muḥammad Rashīd Riḍā's Reformist Project to Establish a True Caliphate: Prospects and Challenges

Ahmed Ibrahim Abushouk

1 Introduction

Muḥammad Rashīd Riḍā (1865–1935) was the most prominent and active supporter of the Ottoman caliphate in its last three decades of existence. The primary objective of his reformist project was to support the caliphate in its struggle against European colonialism and the nationalist movements that had emerged in several Muslim countries. The present contribution endeavours to examine Riḍā's reformist project with reference to his role as a conservative Sunnī jurist (*al-faqīh al-sunnī al-muḥāfiẓ*), who was much concerned with the unity of the Muslim *umma* (community) and its independence vis-à-vis the growing threat of European imperialism and Arab nationalism, and how these concerns affected his theological priorities.

The contribution starts with a survey of the available literature on Riḍā's reformist project dealing with the caliphate. The second part focusses on the socio-political and intellectual world into which Riḍā was born, received his education, and began his career as a journalist—in Beirut, before leaving for Cairo in 1897. The third part highlights the features of Riḍā's reformist project and the phases of its development and modification in light of the political crisis that occurred before and continued after the separation of the Ottoman sultanate and the caliphate in 1922. Finally, the analysis examines the political challenges that faced Riḍā's reformist project and his political stance towards the ruling authority in Istanbul and his political rivals in the Arab region.

2 State of Research

Riḍā's reformist project has received special attention from several scholars tackling it from different perspectives, covering Riḍā's role as a journalist (Hamzah 2003 and 2013), political activist (Haddad 1997), and Muslim reformer (Skovgaard-Petersen 2001), and as a figure whose ideas influenced twentieth-

 | DOI:10.1163/9789004386891_004

century Muslim thinkers and politicians in developing a political philosophy of an Islamic state. The caliphate as an institution of governance remained at the core of his reformist project, which attempted to develop the caliphate of conquest (that is, the Ottoman caliphate) into a true caliphate. A few studies have addressed his reformist project with special emphasis on the concept of the caliphate, such as Mahmoud Haddad's article "Arab Religious Nationalism in the Colonial Era: Reading Rashīd Riḍā's Ideas on the Caliphate" (1997). Haddad strikes a balance between Riḍā's reformist text and the socio-political and intellectual setting in which the text was shaped. The merit of Haddad's work is that he moves beyond the classical textual analysis by Malcom Kerr, which dealt with Riḍā's reformist project from a legal and political standpoint in order to examine its success in reconciling medieval Islamic political thought with the requirements of modernity (Kerr 1966). Haddad scrutinises Riḍā's thinking on the issue of the caliphate in the context of the four interrelated phases of his life, ranging from the period of Abdülhamid II's rule (1876–1909) to the period after the abolition of the Ottoman caliphate in 1924 (Haddad 1997, 254). This approach enables Haddad to analyse Riḍā's reformist project on the caliphate and the result of the separation of the two authorities (temporal and spiritual). Apart from his thorough discussion, Haddad criticises Riḍā, arguing that he sacrificed his theological considerations, bowing to the political pressures of his time. However, this critique seems to pay little attention to the role of Riḍā as a conservative Sunnī jurist worried about the unity of the Muslim *umma* and the protection of the caliphate as a symbol of maintaining this unity.

Another work relevant to the theme of this chapter is that of Hamid Enayat, titled *Modern Islamic Political Thought* (2001). One of its chapters is devoted to "The Concept of an Islamic State: Muḥammad Rashīd Riḍā," and in it the author builds his argument on the political crisis that emerged in the Muslim world after the separation of the sultanate and the caliphate in 1922. Enayat examines Riḍā's treatise on the caliphate and emphasises that its author was torn between his support for the Ottoman caliphate "in the name of the Islamic universalism" and the demands of Arab nationalism, which dominated the Arab political landscape during the post-First World War period (Enayat 2001, 106). This hypothesis seems to have misled the author into seeing Riḍā's preference for Arab nationalism, at a certain political juncture, as a departure from his commitment to an Islamic universalism that would establish an Arab-Islamic state under the leadership of an Arab caliph, to be headquartered in the Ḥijāz. A close reading of Riḍā's reformist project does not support Enayat's conclusion, in that Riḍā had remained "a pan-Islamist all his life, and even though he placed special emphasis on the Arabs' role in Islam, he never was a regionalist or nationalist" (Busool 1984, 84).[1] Enayat's misinterpretation appears to have followed from his textual analysis, which discounts the role political scenarios played in shifting Riḍā's theological views without, however, compromising the core of his reformist mission.

In this chapter, the discussion of Riḍā's reformist project for a true caliphate is not based on a textual analysis, but rather on a mixture of textual and contextual analysis, examining the political and intellectual setting in which Riḍā's project was shaped.[2] This approach partially agrees with that of Haddad, who labels Riḍā a "pragmatic reformer" rather than classifying him as a consistent Muslim thinker who produced a new model of governance that would overcome the challenges of the Muslim *umma* (Haddad 1997, 277). Haddad attributes this inconsistency in Riḍā's political stance to his main concern, which was the political independence of Muslim lands against the aggression of European colonial forces (ibid., 265). The critique of inconsistency also appears in the work of Dyala Hamzah, in her assessment of Riḍā's contributions as a Muslim reformer, on the one hand, and as a journalist, on the other. She classifies his journalistic work as "the chronicle of a world in tremendous turmoil, dictated by events and written by an author in the process of shaping his craft and in the process of being shaped by it" (Hamzah 2003, 3). Wajīh Kawtharānī justifies Riḍā's inconsistency in terms of his role as *al-faqīh al-sunnī al-muḥāfiẓ* whose aim was to produce solutions to the challenges facing the Muslim *umma* without being restricted by the theological concept of the caliphate and its various aspects (Kawtharānī 1980, 58–9).

In light of the available literature and primary sources, the present chapter attempts to examine Riḍā's reformist project on the caliphate in terms of the political situation that shaped its mission and formed its theological considerations. This approach leads us to raise the following questions:

1. What are the main political factors that encouraged Riḍā to produce a reformist project on the caliphate?
2. How did he use his top-down approach to promote and implement his reformist project in the Muslim world?
3. Why did this reformist project fail to achieve its primary objectives?

3 Rashīd Riḍā in a Changing Muslim World

Muḥammad Rashīd Riḍā was born in al-Qalamūn village in Ottoman Syria (now Lebanon), at a time when the Muslim world was passing through a series

1 Busool based his argument on the account of Nuseibeh 1956, 124.

2 See, for a similar approach and further literature, Brunner 2017.

of profound changes that affected its socio-political and economic structures. The changes were mainly associated with the territorial expansion of European colonial forces in the Muslim world, aimed at utilising the region's natural resources, finding cheap labour for European industry, and opening new and highly profitable markets for European manufactured products (Reichmuth 2017). Against these imperialist agendas, the Ottoman caliphate failed to protect its territories in the Balkan region and the Middle East.

About a decade after the birth of Riḍā, a traditional ceremony of *bayʿa* (oath of allegiance) was held in Istanbul, where Abdülhamid II (r. 1293–1327/1876–1909) was given the titles of Sultan and Caliph of the Ottoman Caliphate. The two titles were confirmed in the third and fourth articles of the 1876 Ottoman Constitution, which stated: "The Exalted Ottoman Sultanate possesses the Great Islamic Caliphate, which is held by the eldest member of the Ottoman Dynasty in accordance with ancient practice.... His Imperial Majesty, The Padişah, by virtue of the Caliphate, is the protector of the religion of Islam and the Ruler and Emperor of all Ottoman subjects" (quoted in Katz 2016, 214). The combination of the two authorities in the hands of one person had generated a heated debate in London, where scholars and politicians praised the separation of temporal and religious powers, and suggested the transfer of the seat of the caliphate from Istanbul to Jidda, in Saudi Arabia, or to Cairo, in Egypt. They assumed that the separation of powers would undermine the position of Sultan Abdülhamid and give the British government full control over the Muslim world (Buzpinar 1996, 64). The idea of transferring the caliphate to Mecca was encouraged by British officers who had worked in India, such as George Birdwood (1832–1917). He argued that "it is a great pity that we do not get the Muhammedans of India to look up to the Shareef of Mecca as the Caliph of Islam for he lives by the side of our road to India and would be as completely in our power as the Suez Canal."[3] Other British officers attempted to put the separation of the two powers in a theological context by claiming that Sultan Abdülhamid and his predecessors were disqualified from being recognised as caliph for two reasons. First, the last of the ʿAbbāsid caliphs (r. 132–923/750–1517) in Cairo had not stepped down in favour of Sultan Selim I (r. 918–26/1512–20), nor had he acknowledged the sultan's leadership of the Muslim *umma.* Secondly, the Ottoman sultans who had claimed leadership of the caliphate were not descendants of the Quraysh, the tribe of the prophet Muḥammad.

This anti-Ottoman campaign was later championed by W.S. Blunt,[4] who had set up contacts with "liberal" Muslims in certain Arab capitals and encouraged

3 *The Times Newspaper,* London, 12 June 1877, 8. Cited in Buzpinar 1996, 65.

4 Wilfrid Scawen Blunt (1840–1922) was an English poet best known for his elegant erotic verse and his anti-imperialism. He entered the diplomatic service in 1858 and traveled frequently

them to create an Arab caliphate that would enjoy full autonomy from Istanbul. Buzpinar characterises Blunt's anti-Ottoman activities as follows:

> This was the beginning of a chapter in Blunt's life and thought which was devoted to the love of Arabs and the hatred of Turks. Especially during the honeymoon period of this romanticism, from 1878 to 1882, he came up with several schemes for separating the Arabs from the Ottoman Empire and for setting up an Arab government with the moral and material backing of the British government.
>
> BUZPINAR 1996, 81

His schemes did not receive great support from the British government until Sir William E. Gladstone became prime minister (for a second time) in 1880, and advised Blunt to communicate with his private secretary Edward Hamilton and the Foreign Office. In his memorandum of July 1880, Blunt warned the Foreign Office that a revival of the Ottoman Caliphate would not serve Great Britain's interests, which, he claimed, would be supported by the establishment of an Arab caliphate in Mecca under England's protection, in that this proposed caliphate would secure permanent control over India for Great Britain.[5]

As a consequence of this negative propaganda, Muslim political activists in different parts of the Muslim world were divided into two major groups. The first group supported Sultan ʿAbdülhamid as the legitimate caliph of the Ottoman caliphate and a symbol of Muslim unity against European colonialism. The other group denounced his legitimacy and called for a political change that would force him to step down (Buzpinar 1996, 75). This state of discontent and resistance manifested itself in different forms. In Egypt in 1881, a social-political revolution broke out in Cairo against the intervention of Great Britain and France in the administration of the country. The short-lived success of this revolution resulted in the formation of a nationalist government chaired by Maḥmūd Sāmī al-Bārūdī (d. 1904), with Aḥmad ʿUrābī (d. 1911) as minister of war, under the slogan "Miṣr lil-Miṣriyyīn" (Egypt for the Egyptians). The growing popularity of the nationalist government created a great threat to the newly appointed Khedive Muḥammad Tawfīq (r. 1879–92), who invited the support of Great Britain and France. The interference of British and French troops in Egypt led to a series of riots and a popular resistance that proclaimed the

in Egypt, Asia Minor, and Arabia. He became known as an ardent sympathiser with Muslim aspirations, and in *The Future of Islam* (1882) he directed attention to the forces that had produced Pan-Islamism and Mahdism. He was a violent opponent of British policy in the Sudan and supported the national party in Egypt.

5 Cited from "Memoir" by W. S. Blunt, on the position of the Ottoman sultans towards Islam. In David S. Katz 2016, 218.

khedive a traitor. British troops seized the opportunity and occupied Egypt in 1882, claiming this action was necessary to protect the rights of European creditors and maintain security and order in the country (Galbraith and al-Sayyid Marsot 1978, 471–88).

The outbreak of the ʿUrābī revolution in Egypt in 1881 coincided with the eruption of the Mahdist revolution in the Sudan, where a Ṣūfī *shaykh* named Muḥammad Aḥmad b. ʿAbdallāh, declared himself the expected *mahdī* (messiah), who would fill the earth with justice and equity just as it had been filled with oppression and tyranny. With this his cause, he declared *jihād* against the Ottoman caliphate, whose leaders were branded as infidels who did not follow the teachings of the Qurʾān and the Sunna. The revolution succeeded in overthrowing the Ottoman administration in the Sudan in 1885 and establishing a nationalist government that ruled there until British and Egyptian troops invaded the country in 1898 (Abushouk 2009, 43–60). In response to the success of the Mahdist revolution, Blunt recorded an entry in his diary about the views of the reformist Jamāl al-Dīn al-Afghānī (1838–97) on the future of the Ottoman caliphate:

> A long talk with Jemal-ed-Din [al-Afghānī] about prospects at Constantinople and about the Caliphate. He is for the [Sudanese] Mahdi for the Mahdi's successor taking the Sultan's place, or the Sharif Own [of Mecca], or the Imam of Sunna—any of these he thought might now take the lead, but Constantinople must remain the seat of the Caliphate, as Arabia or Africa would be mere places of exile. Amongst other things, he told me that it was he himself who had suggested to the Sherif el-Huseyn [of Mecca] to claim the Caliphate, but El Huseyn had said it was impossible without armed support, and the Arabs could never unite except in the name of religion.
>
> BLUNT 2016, 218

Before the outbreak of the two revolutions mentioned above—the Mahdist in Sudan and the ʿUrābī in Egypt—the Berlin Congress of 1878 had authorised France to assume control of Tunisia, having already accepted the occupation of Ottoman Cyprus by the British in 1878. In 1881 the French troops occupied Tunisia on the grounds that some Tunisian tribesmen had crossed the border with Algeria and created a state of instability in the region. The defeated Bey, Muḥammad III al-Ṣiddīq, signed a treaty that authorised French military forces to occupy the country. In return, he agreed to tackle domestic affairs and accept a French minister resident in Tunis to facilitate his contact with the French authorities (Lewis 2008).

This political situation as a whole seems to have provoked the Ottoman leadership and led the Sultan and his closest associates to search for an ideology that would help them to unite Muslims behind the banner of the caliphate and against the growing influence of European powers in their countries. This call for political unity expressed itself in various forms. The most significant one of them was that of Sultan ʿAbdülhamid, who sent delegates throughout the Muslim world to urge Muslims to unite under his leadership and the Ottoman caliphate. His version of pan-Islamism was adopted and promoted by members of his ruling bureaucracy and intellectuals, such as Jamāl al-Dīn al-Afghānī and Muḥammad ʿAbduh (1849–1905), who was the principal representative of modern Muslim reformism in Egypt. Muslim scholars and nationalists in the Arab countries, the Indian sub-continent, and the Malay world supported the caliphs from the point of view of their being a symbol of Muslim unity and a counterweighing power against European colonial forces. Nevertheless, these expectations did not come true, and the call for pan-Islamism gradually lost sway and disappeared from the political scene, leaving the Muslim world under the hegemony of the European colonial powers (Abushouk 2003, 9–12).

4 Riḍā's Life and His Reformist Project and Its Prospects

Rashīd Riḍā began his education at al-Rashīdiyya Primary School in Tripoli, Lebanon, where he studied Arabic language, Islamic jurisprudence, and Ṣūfism. He then continued his education at the Islamic National School in Beirut and established a close relationship with its director, Shaykh Ḥusayn al-Jisr (1845–1909). After receiving his diploma in Islamic studies in 1892, he began his career as a journalist and a freelance preacher in several mosques. During this period, he continued his education in Islamic studies with the help of various Syrian scholars and joined the Naqshbandiyya Ṣūfī order. After familiarising himself with the works of al-Afghānī and ʿAbduh, he quit his Ṣūfī order, describing this qualitative shift in the following words:

> I found several copies of *al-ʿUrwa al-Wuthqā* among my father's papers, and every issue of it was like an electric current striking me, giving my soul a shock, and setting it in a blaze, carrying me from one state to another, and giving me a new understanding of Islam. My concern was limited to the rectification of Muslim doctrine, preventing Muslims from doing evil deeds and instead urging them to the good. I became concerned with guiding Muslims to civilisation, protecting their sovereignty,

> and competing with other nations in the sciences, art, industry, and all the fundamentals of life.
>
> RIḌĀ, 2006, 1: 303[6]

The magazine *al-'Urwa al-Wuthqā* had clearly changed Riḍā's thinking profoundly, increasing his awareness of the challenges facing the leadership of the Ottoman caliphate in Istanbul that threatened the unity of the Muslim *umma*. This intellectual shift early in his life put him in conflict with the traditional leadership of political and Islamic institutions in Syria. It also motivated Riḍā to establish contact with al-Afghānī in Istanbul and 'Abduh, who was in exile in Beirut (1886–1989), before returning to Cairo in 1889. The outcome of these contacts culminated in his move to Cairo in 1897, where he joined 'Abduh's intellectual circle and became his closest associate, leading disciple, biographer, and spokesman for his ideas, which can be summarised by the following goals:

- The purification of Islam from all innovations (*bid'a*) that affected its pristine purity based on the Qur'ān and the Sunna;
- The liberation of Islamic jurisprudence from blind imitation of the traditional schools of law;
- The exercise of *ijtihād* (independent reasoning) as the best means for bridging the gap between historical Islam and modernity;
- The introduction of a modern educational system that would reconcile religious and secular disciplines;
- The revival of Arabic linguistics as a means of facilitating interpretation of the authentic sources of Islam (the Qur'ān and the Sunna).[7]

The attraction of 'Abduh's reformist ideas seems to have encouraged Riḍā in founding his journal *al-Manār* in 1898. In the inaugural issue, the objectives of the journal were stated as follows:

> To promote social, religious and economic reforms; to prove the suitability of Islam as a religious system under present conditions and the practicability of divine law as an instrument of government; to remove superstitions and beliefs that do not belong to Islam; to counteract false teachings and interpretations of Muslim beliefs, such as the prevalent ideas of pre-destination, the bigotry of different schools or rites of canon law, and the abuses connected with the cult of saints and practices of Ṣūfī orders; to encourage tolerance and unity among the different sects; to promote general education; to encourage progress in the sciences and

6 Translations are the author's, unless otherwise noted.

7 For further details, see Muḥammad 'Imāra 1972, 1985; Bluhm-Warn 1997.

> arts; to arouse the Muslim nations to competition with other nations in all matters that are essential to national progress.
>
> RIḌĀ 1898, 11–12

The first issue of the journal appeared on 22 Shawwāl 1315/17 March 1898, as a weekly journal of eight pages, dealing with current affairs and including special articles on topics related to Islam. A year later, it was transformed into a monthly journal divided into two main parts. The first part included ʿAbduh's commentary on the Qur'ān and Riḍā's *fatwā*s, which "revealed his outstanding knowledge and independence of thought particularly with questions regarding modern issues" (Shahin 1993, 9). The second part focussed on a variety of subjects that addressed social, political, economic, religious, and literary matters. A special section was devoted to Riḍā's speeches and talks delivered on various occasions as well as his comments on letters received from readers. It also included the intellectual contributions of key Muslim figures such as Jamāl al-Dīn al-Afghānī, Muḥammad ʿAbduh, ʿAbd al-Raḥmān al-Kawākibī (d. 1902), Muḥammad Tawfīq Ṣidqī (d. 1920), and Shakīb Arslān (d. 1946). The regular contributions of these distinguished writers made *al-Manār* an intellectual platform for Muslim correspondents, readers, and activists to exchange ideas and views with Riḍā in Cairo, request his legal opinion on certain issues, and voice their grievances against European hegemony in the Muslim world (Jomier 1991, 360–1).[8]

5 The Reformist Project, First Phase

The key question here is how did Riḍā address and promote his reformist project of the true caliphate to his fellow Muslims and to non-Muslim readers? To answer this question we need to examine first the development of the theological political concept of the caliphate throughout the four phases of Riḍā's life, which stemmed from his relationship with Sultan Abdülhamid in 1898 up to the abolition of the Ottoman caliphate in 1924. During the Hamidian phase (1898–1909), Riḍā showed a higher degree of support for the Ottoman caliphate, introducing his journal, *al-Manār*, as "an Ottoman oriented" journal, voicing "Hamidian views." Its primary objective was stated as defending the Ottoman caliphate (*al-dawla al-ʿāliya*) and serving the interest of "our lord the great sultan" (Riḍā 1898, 13). This support manifested itself in the journal's campaign for the two major projects launched by Sultan Abdülhamid: the construction of

8 For further detail on *al-Manār*, see Abushouk 2007; Hamzah 2013; and Ryad 2009.

the Ḥijāz railway and the call for pan-Islamism. The call for pan-Islamism was initiated by Abdülhamid as a means of facing the growing threat of European imperialism in his territories and the challenge of the Turkish and Arab nationalists who had lost faith in his leadership. In 1899, Riḍā published a series of articles on pan-Islamism in *al-Manār*, discussing the origin of the concept, its primary objectives, and its supporters. Riḍā traced its origin back to al-Afghānī "who first wrote and preached on the explanation of the social ills of Muslims, and illuminated their diseases and treatment" (Riḍā 12 August 1899, 2/22: 337–48). He built his pan-Islamism call on two associations: the worldly and the spiritual. The worldly association, from his perspective, should include all subjects of the Ottoman caliphate, who would be treated equally as Ottoman citizens regardless of their religious and social affiliation. The spiritual association would be composed of all Muslims who believe in "Allah, His angels, His books, His messengers, and the judgement day," and their unity would be cemented by the spread of the Arabic language and the standardisation of the educational system (Riḍā 5 August 1899, 2/21: 321–27). Thus, Riḍā advocated for

> the creation of an Islamic association, under the auspices of the caliph, its headquarters to be in Mecca, with branches in all Muslim countries.… Its mission is the standardisation of Muslim doctrine, ethical and moral teachings, judicial and civil rulings, and the [Arabic] language. Its activities are the rectification of innovations and evil teachings, and the improvement of discourse and the proselytisation of Islam. The expected results are the unification of Islamic governments.
>
> RIḌĀ 12 August 1899, 2/22: 345

He assumed that the achievement of this pan-Islamism project would lead to a solidification of a Muslim identity that would draw its essence from the Arabic language and Islamic religion. On the contrary, if a nation were not to sustain its language and religion, its identity and cultural value would be lost (Riḍā 1988, 98–101.)

This topic of pan-Islamism circulated by *al-Manār* received special attention from newspapers and magazines issued in the Muslim world, where Muslim and Christian journalists criticised Riḍā's reformist project for pan-Islamism, claiming that the project did not acknowledge the separation of religion and state, and the caliphate and sultanate. As they argued, the caliph should be responsible for spiritual affairs of Muslims and the sultan in charge of political affairs of Muslims and non-Muslims, assuming that this separation would strengthen the unity of the Ottoman caliphate and reduce political and religious tensions among different sectors of society. Riḍā appears to have been dissatisfied with these assertions, and in response he wrote a long plea, defining the concept of religion in Islam and that of state in Muslim history, and finally describing the caliphate as a form of deputation by the prophet Muḥammad, aimed at protecting the *dīn* (religion) and managing the affairs of the world (Riḍā 12 August 1899 22/2: 343–60). Hence, the holder of the position of caliph must be responsible for both temporal and spiritual powers in the Muslim world. Riḍā's argument was built on the following ten responsibilities of the caliph, which he copied verbatim from the fifth/eleventh-century jurist al-Māwardī[9]:

1. The caliph must guard the *dīn* as it was established in its original form and about which the first generations of the *umma* are agreed; if an innovator appears, or someone of dubious character deviates from this *dīn*, he should make clear to him the legal proof of his error, explain the right way to him, and take the appropriate measures regarding his liability and his punishment, such that the *dīn* is protected from blemish and the *umma* is prevented from going astray;
2. He must execute legal judgments between contestants and bring to an end any dispute between two litigants so that equity prevails and the weak are not oppressed;
3. He must protect the territory of Islam and defend the sanctuaries, so that people may earn their sustenance and travel, safe from any threat to their persons or belongings;
4. He must establish the *ḥadd*-punishments in order to protect what Allah, may He be exalted, has made inviolable from being violated and prevent the rights of His servants from being abused;
5. He must fortify the border outposts against attack and defend them with force against an enemy who might appear unexpectedly and violate what is sacred or shed the blood of Muslims or *dhimmī*s [members of protected religions, who are] protected by a pact;
6. He must make *jihād* against those who resist Islam after having been called to it, until they submit or accept to live as a protected *dhimmī*-community, so that Allah's rights, may He be exalted, "be made uppermost above all [other] religions" (Q 9:33);
7. He must collect the *fay'* and *zakāh* taxes from those on whom the *sharīʿa* and legal judgment have made it an obligation to pay, and this without fear or oppression;

9 Abū l-Ḥasan ʿAlī b. Muḥammad b. Ḥabīb al-Māwardī (d. 450/1058) was a Sunnī Muslim jurist and author of *al-Aḥkām al-sulṭāniyya* ("The laws of Islamic governance"). His book is one of the most significant sources on the history of political theory in Islam.

8. He must apportion the stipends and whatever is due from the *bayt al-māl* [the treasury] without wastefulness or meanness, and make payments punctually, neither before their time nor after it;
9. He must ensure the employment of trustworthy persons and the appointment of worthy counsellors capable of undertaking those tasks delegated to them and of safeguarding monies made over to them;
10. He must personally supervise the Muslims' affairs and execute the policy of the *umma* and defend the nation, without over-reliance on the delegation of authority, lest he devote himself to pleasure-seeking or worship, for this may lead even the trustworthy to deceive and counsellors to behave dishonestly: Allah, may He be exalted, has said: "O Dāwūd, surely I have made a *khalīfa* on the earth, so decide equitably between people and do not follow passions lest you be led astray from the way of Allah" (Q 38:26). So Allah does confine the matter of delegating duties to someone who does not participate directly in the affairs himself; nor does He grant him an excuse to follow his passions as He has described this as going astray. Although it is a duty incumbent on Dāwūd from the point of view of the *dīn* and the office of *khalīfa*, it is nevertheless a duty of every subject to manage his affairs properly. The Prophet said (may the peace and blessings of Allah be upon him): "Each of you is a shepherd and each of you is responsible for his flock." (Riḍā 19 August 1899, 2/23: 355–6)[10]

At this juncture, Riḍā consulted al-Māwardī's "manual" in order to attract the support of conservative Muslims who perceived the Ottoman caliphate as the only legitimate power in the Muslim world that would defend Muslim lands against European aggression (Fahmī 1910, 934). Riḍā's reformist project was not in harmony with the publications of some distinguished scholars, such as ʿAbd al-Raḥmān al-Kawākibī, who opposed the reform of the Ottoman caliphate. His publications challenged Riḍā's reformist project on three points. The first point was associated with al-Kawākibī's view of the leadership of Sultan Abdülhamid, whom he described as an authoritarian ruler who should be held responsible for the decline of Muslim communities and the encroachment of European colonial forces in the Muslim world. He attributed the political deterioration of the Ottoman caliphate to "the absence of representative institutions, such as the mechanism of *shūrā* (consultation), which once allowed the Arabs a measure of democratic participation as well as a mode of decision-making that reflected the will of the citizenry" (Funatsu 2006, 7f.). Al-Kawākibī also criticised "the delegation of authority over the provinces of the empire

10 The English translation is based on al-Māwardī, n.d., trans. Yate, 27–9.

to authorize governors who lacked any affinity with the local inhabitants." He added to these major problems, "the absence of a consistent and harmonious body of laws; and the imposition [of] a single administrative and criminal legal code throughout the empire, irrespective of differences among national and local customs" (Funatsu 2006, 7f.). Al-Kawākibī's publications created an unhealthy atmosphere for the promotion of Riḍā's reformist project under the patronage of the sultan. The second point of al-Kawākibī's challenge to Riḍā's reformist project was his call for the installment of an Arab caliph of Qurayshī descent in Mecca, who would have spiritual authority over the Muslim world. The holder of this position, he suggested, would exercise his authority via an advisory council, supported by appointed or elected members from all Muslim countries. The third point was al-Kawākibī's conviction that the religion "is what the individual believes in, not what the crowds believe in." In other words, he called for the separation of temporal and religious authority and, at the same time, encouraged Arab activists to take over leadership of the Ottoman caliphate. This nationalist attitude led some scholars to see him as a pioneer of Arab nationalism, criticising the hegemony of the Turks over the leadership of the Ottoman caliphate.

Riḍā did not see the proposal for the appointment of an Arab caliph as a political threat to Ottoman temporal leadership of the Muslim world. Rather, he considered it a process that would shift the spiritual power of the Ottoman caliphate from the Turks to the Arabs. Thus, he attributed al-Kawākibī's stand to his distrust in the leadership of the sultan (Fahmī 1910, 936). In spite of this justification, Riḍā disagreed with al-Kawākibī's argument for the separation of temporal and religious authority (Riḍā 1902, 279).

6 Second and Third Phase

During the second phase of his life (1908–14) Riḍā joined the Ottoman Consultative Society (Jamʿiyyat al-Shūrā al-ʿUthmāniyya), founded in 1907 in Cairo. In *al-Manār*, Riḍā reported its formation and objectives as follows:

> This society was established in Cairo by individuals from the Turks, Arabs, Armenians, Romanians, and Kurds. Its objective is to unite the Ottoman peoples of different races and religions to work together to make the Ottoman government a consultative and just one. This is the ideal way of protecting the state from disintegration. The causes of this disintegration are internal disagreement, tyranny, and enslavement.
>
> RIḌĀ 1907, 950–51

The primary objectives of this society indicate that Riḍā had lost his confidence in the autocratic regime of Sultan Abdülhamid and instead advocated for the democratisation of the political system of the Ottoman caliphate to a more consultative model. When the Young Turks took over and reinstated the constitution of 1876, he wrote in *al-Manār*:

> On this holiday the Ottomans reinstated their constitution and the *umma* Council.... They reinstated them through the efforts of the liberals and with the reinforcement of the great army. This is a festive day for the Ottoman *umma,* with its different nationalities and religious affiliations. Today the Ottomans breathed the air of political and social life, and tasted the sweetness of liberty.... The difference between the past and the present is like the difference between day and night, or dark and light, snow and hot wind, truth and falsehood, knowledge and ignorance, and power and weakness.
>
> RIḌĀ 1908, 417, 423

After the nomination of the first government of the Young Turks, Riḍā paid a year-long visit to Istanbul in 1908 with the intention of getting moral and financial support for his two sub-projects, which were the basic components of his reformist goals: the first of these sub-projects was the establishment of a "School of Propagation and Guidance" in Istanbul, with the objective of training Muslim students, who would graduate as professional preachers and Muslim scholars who would be leaders for reform in Muslim communities. The second sub-project grew from his interest in reuniting the Turks and the Arabs, based on his belief that their genuine collaboration would contribute to the reform of the Ottoman caliphate and the unification of the Muslim *umma*. The two sub-projects did not attract the attention of the new rulers of Istanbul. The matter led Riḍā to lose faith in the Young Turks and create the secret Society of the Arab League (Munaẓẓamat al-Jamʿiyya al-ʿArabiyya) in Cairo in 1909. He urged the Arabs to secede from the Ottoman caliphate and establish their own state, which would include the Arabian Peninsula, Syria, and Iraq. He excluded the rest of the Arab countries because they were under the control of European colonial powers. Scholars have interpreted this shift in his political discourse as a departure from Islamic universalism to Arab nationalism, in that he perceived the Arab awakening as "an essential prerequisite for the renaissance of Islam that he was working for" (Tauber 1994, 196).

His move in this direction became clearer in the third phase of his life, which coincided with the First World War (1914–18). During this era, Riḍā supported Sharīf Ḥusayn of Mecca as a legitimate leader of the proposed Arab state, which would take primary responsiblity for the protection of the holy places in the Ḥijāz from the aggression of the European imperial forces hoping to divide the Ottoman caliphate. After the declaration of the Sykes-Picot Agreement of 1916, Riḍā terminated his political relationship with the Sharīf family and instead intensified his contact with ʿAbd al-ʿAzīz b. Suʿūd (known as Ibn Saʿūd, 1880–1953), Imām Ḥamīd al-Dīn (1869–1948) of Yemen, and Muḥammad ʿAlī al-Idrīsī (1876–1923) of ʿAsīr, urging them to set up joint leadership for the administration of the Ḥijāz. Nevertheless, the call for this joint leadership ended in complete failure, leading him to limit his support to Ibn Saʿūd, whom he saw as a competent leader for the proposed state of the Ḥijāz and the betterment of the Muslim nation (Abushouk 2014, 37–44).

7 Riḍā's True Caliphate

The constant shift in Riḍā's choices detailed above suggests that Riḍā was in a real political dilemma in his quest to find a legitimate and powerful state that would protect the unity and legacy of the Muslim *umma* vis-à-vis the threat of European colonialism. As Kawtharānī rightly argues, this shifting of options can be understood only in the context of a conservative Muslim jurist concerned with protecting the Ottoman caliphate one way or another—whether under the wide umbrella of the Turks or the narrow one of the Arabs. Riḍā began to feel that his reformist project was at risk, particularly when the Kemalists abolished the sultanate in 1922, entrusted its temporal authority to the Grand National Assembly, and limited the powers of the caliph in Istanbul to spiritual and ceremonial matters. In his speech of the first of November 1922 to the Grand National Assembly in Ankara, Mustafa Kemal commended the separation of the sultanate from the caliphate. He proclaimed that this separation was not a new phenomenon in Muslim history. It had been in existence since the time of the ʿAbbāsids in Baghdad and Cairo, when the caliphs functioned as figureheads, leaving the temporal powers to chief ministers and later to Mamlūk sultans.

In contrast, Riḍā criticised the abolition of the sultanate and the separation of the two authorities, claiming that these actions did not have roots in the history of Muslim practices and were not in harmony with the fundamental principles of Islam. In one of his articles published in *al-Manār* he wrote:

> Al-Ghāzī Mustafa Kemal Pasha was mistaken in what he mentioned in his speech [hoping] to prove that the caliphate is not legitimate and does not serve the interest of the nation. Our lord ʿUmar [b. al-Khaṭṭāb, the

> second caliph, r. 13–23/634–44] knew [that the caliphate was legitimate], and paved the way for another regime, based on the *shūrā* in the election of his successor. He [Kemal] was wrong in his claim that the Umayyads [r. 41–132/661–750], the ʿAbbāsids, and the Ottomans had failed to establish such a caliphate, just as he was wrong in his assertion that the Companions of the Prophet had established the caliphate based on the power of racial solidarity. The result was that he was misguided in his own judgment that the true or right thing had been done by those who confiscated the power of the first caliphs and made their title as a tool of blessing.... All these are invalid actions carried out by force and in violation of the Sharīʿa.... We have explained that in articles published in this volume. We have written a letter to al-Ghāzī Mustafa Kemal, outlining the right plan for the revival of the caliphate and for its benefit. This happened before the occurrence of this last event [i.e., the separation of the caliphate]. We hope that [the Kemalists] will correct their mistake after reconciliation, and consult distinguished Muslim scholars from all countries.
>
> RIḌĀ 1922, 784–5

The passage reveals that Riḍā anticipated that the Kemalists were capable of leading the revival of the Islamic caliphate. In the introduction to his treatise on the caliphate, published in 1923, he appealed to the Turks, as the most competent nation in the Muslim world, to translate his reformist project into action. His project was based on his conviction that "Islam is the greatest moral power on earth, which could revive Eastern civilisation and rescue Western civilisation.... This cannot be achieved without the revival of the government of the Islamic Caliphate," which would combine "the guidance of the religion and civilisation to serve humanity" (Riḍā 1988, 10–11). He then dedicated his treatise to the leadership of the Turkish nation, as a manual that could help them implement his reformist project. He appealed to the Turks saying:

> O Turkish people, I dedicated to you these chapters written to explain the reality of the caliphate and its rules, some of its history and high status, how all mankind needs it, and how Muslims perpetrate a crime against themselves by misusing it and straying from its objective, and to explain what now faces its revival and what will be the solution.
>
> RIḌĀ 1988, 11

Riḍā's treatise on the caliphate is divided into two parts. The first part deals with the theological foundations of the caliphate, based on the works of classical Muslim jurists, such as al-Māwardī (d. 648/1058), al-Taftazānī (d. 792/1390), and Ibn Khaldūn (d. 809/1406). In his discussion, he focusses on the concept of the caliphate, the obligation to appoint a caliph and the requirements of the office, the oath of allegiance and its form, the issue of succession, the forms of the caliphate, and the *ahl al-ḥall wa-l-ʿaqd* and their role.[11] Three issues that received his special attention are: the obligation of appointing a caliph who would function as head of the Islamic state, vested with temporal and religious powers; the headquarters of the true caliphate; and the qualifications of the candidate.

7.1 *The Obligation of Appointing a Caliph*

Riḍā considered this appointment as necessity and denied the separation of temporal and religious authorities. He perceived the election of a caliph as a collective obligation for all Muslims, and that every Muslim should give his oath of allegiance to the elected caliph. The individuality of this obligation drew its validity from the Prophetic tradition that says: "Whosoever dies without a *bayʿa* on his neck dies the death of *Jāhiliyya* [the age of ignorance, before the coming of Islam]" (Aḥmad b. Hanbal n.d., 4:96). The necessity of having a caliph led Riḍā to distinguish between three forms of the caliphate. The first one is the true/ideal caliphate, where the caliph should fulfil the seven conditions mentioned by al-Māwardī.[12] The second form of caliphate was the caliphate of necessity, which would take its shape when the *ahl al-ḥall wa-l-ʿaqd* appointed a caliph who did not fulfil all the requirements of his office but received the *bayʿa* (the oath of allegiance) of the masses. Under this format, several Umayyad and ʿAbbāsid caliphs were appointed, even though they lacked justice and were not competent to exercise *ijtihād*. The third form was

11 The phrase *ahl al-ḥall wa-l-ʿaqd* literally means "the people who loosen and bind." It refers to "the qualified representatives of the Muslim community who act on their behalf in appointing and deposing a ruler (*khalīfa*). These influential people must enjoy certain qualities: they must be Muslims, male, of age, free, and capable of judging who is best qualified to fill the office. The current orthodox view would identify these electors with the whole of the nation, with Parliament, or with the body of religious scholars and jurists" (Moten and El-Fatih 2005, 4).

12 1. Justice together with all its conditions; 2. Knowledge, which equips them [the caliphs] for *ijtihād* in unforeseen matters and for arriving at relevant judgments; 3. Good health in their faculties of hearing, sight, and speech, such that they may arrive at a sound assessment of whatever they perceive; 4. Sound in limb, free of any deficiency that might prevent them from normal movement; 5. Judgement capable of organising the people and managing the offices of administration; 6. Courage and bravery enabling them to defend the territory of Islam and to mount *jihād* against the enemy; 7. Descent from the family of Quraysh, because of the *ḥadīth* on the matter and by virtue of consensus (al-Māwardī n.d., 4:12).

the caliphate of conquest by force (*khilāfat al-taghallub bi-l-quwwa*), where the caliph came to office by force, without the support of *ahl al-ḥall wa-l-ʿaqd*. This classification permitted Riḍā to argue that the Ottoman caliphate was a caliphate of conquest and its caliphs based their political legitimacy on their hereditary right and force. Therefore, Muslims were obligated to support them in order to maintain the unity of the Muslim countries that were either under the hegemony of European colonial powers or local leaderships, or were not competent to defend their territories against European aggression (Riḍā 1988, 56–9).

In this first part of his treatise, Riḍā did not make a breakthrough in the legacy of his predecessors, but rather agreed with them on the necessity of the caliphate as an institution of governance. Muslims are collectively responsible for electing their own caliph, who will be equipped with temporal and religious powers (Riḍā 1988, 13–65). In the second part of his treatise, Riḍā examined three semi-religious and semi-secular themes associated with his reformist project that focused on the revival of the true caliphate. The first theme appeared in the way that he restructured the membership of *ahl al-ḥall wa-l-ʿaqd,* whose role it was to elect or depose a caliph on behalf of the Muslim community. He opened the membership of this group to certain individuals from different sectors of the Muslim community, whom he labeled "the leaders of the nation" who won "its trust in sciences, businesses, and interests that are required for the maintenance of the nation's life" (Riḍā 1988, 66). He did not determine the total number of members of this group, the quorum for taking serious decisions on behalf of the Muslim community, or how members would be chosen or elected to this group. To avoid the issue of group election, Riḍā categorised the activists in the Muslim world into three groups, in terms of their qualifications to be members of *ahl al-ḥall wa-l-ʿaqd*. The first group was Europeanised Muslims, who received their education in European schools or were influenced by the material development that had taken place in European countries. Both factions of this group considered Islam as a major cause of the backwardness of their communities and opted for the secularisation of their states and societies. Some of them supported the idea of confining the powers of the caliph to spiritual and ceremonial matters, similar to the Catholic papacy (Riḍā 1988, 13–65). The second group was that of the dogmatic Muslim jurists, who were in favour of Islamisation of states and societies more in line with the teachings of the Ḥanafī school of law. Riḍā questioned the legislative capability of this group to enact military, financial, and political laws that would solve the contemporary problems of Muslim communities (Riḍā 1988, 72–4). The third group, which could maintain a middle way between the two extremes, was the reformist party, which, as Riḍā argues, had an independent understanding of Islamic jurisprudence and the ability to reconcile the *sharīʿa* with the values of European civilisation. He named this group "the party of al-Imām Muḥammad ʿAbduh," whom he praised as the pioneer of the modern Muslim reformist movement. He claimed that this party had widespread support among Muslim scholars in India, Turkey, and some Arab countries, support that would qualify this group to lead his reformist project, with the aim of reviving the true caliphate, whose head (the caliph) would be elected by the representatives of this reformist party (Riḍā 1988, 60–70).

7.2 *The Headquarters of the True Caliphate*

The second theme that attracted Riḍā's attention was the headquarters of the true caliphate, whether it should be in Istanbul, the traditional capital of the Ottoman caliphate, in the Hijāz (Mecca and Medina), where the Muslims laid down the foundations of the first Islamic State, or in Mosul, in northern Iraq, where the Arabs, Turks, and Kurds lived together. The pros and cons of these three proposals were outlined by Riḍā, who finally suggested the transfer of the headquarters of the proposed caliphate to the Hijāz, if the three proposals were rejected by Muslim representatives. The dilemma of Riḍā was that the Hijāz was not the ideal place for the headquarters of the true caliphate, and the Kemalists were not eager to maintain the Islamic legacy of their Ottoman forerunners. Their strategy was to abolish the caliphate and consolidate the powers of their republican and secular state in Turkey (Riḍā 1988, 80–6).

7.3 *The Qualifications of the Candidate*

The third theme was the necessary qualifications of a candidate who could be elected caliph. As was mentioned earlier, al-Māwardī had fixed seven requirements for a candidate for the position of caliph. Riḍā suggested the establishment of "a high school to graduate candidates for the Great Imamate and *ijtihād*. From the graduates of this school, the staff of the private caliphate office, judges and jurists, and public law makers will be selected" (Riḍā 1988, 88). The caliph, who would be elected from among graduates of this school, would function as "the true Imam and the deputy of the prophet Muḥammad in the establishment of the religion and world politics" (Riḍā 1988, 88). Muslims should then obey his decisions and commands in all matters that might serve their public affairs and which were not contrary to the fundamentals of Islam. As al-Marrākushī argues, this proposal can be justified from a theoretical viewpoint, but its implementation on the ground would be impractical, since the majority of Muslim countries were neither united nor politically free to make their own decision (al-Marrākushī 1985, 140). Because of this situation, according to al-Marrākushī, Riḍā's text fell short of understanding the reality of the political situation in the Muslim world and did not satisfy the individual expectations of Muslim countries.

For the implementation of his reformist project, Riḍā suggested three programmes and nine councils that would facilitate the process of electing a caliph and the management of his duties and responsibilities. His proposal included a programme for a high school that would graduate future caliphs and Muslim scholars; a programme for the caliphal election; and a programme for the administrative and financial administration of the Caliphate Office. The councils include the following areas of responsibility: general consultation (*shūrā*); *fatāwā* and religious publications; delegation of powers to governors; judges and legal jurists; general supervision of government; propaganda and missionary work, prayer, sermons, proselytisation, guidance, and *ḥisba* (the function of regulating the marketplace); *zakāt* (almsgiving) and its recipients; *ḥajj* amīrate (leadership) and service of the two Holy Places (Mecca and Medina); and general correspondence (Riḍā 1988, 88). Riḍā considered the proposed programmes and councils as a step towards the establishment of a necessary transitional government that would first demonstrate the competency of the elected caliph in administrating the religious and temporal affairs of Muslims, and secondly pave the way for the revival of a true caliphate that would resemble the ideological end of his reformist project.

8 Riḍā's Reformist Project at the Crossroads in 1924

A year after the separation of the sultanate from the caliphate, the Kemalists signed the Second Peace Treaty with the Allies in the city of Lausanne, Switzerland, on 24 July 1923. This treaty permitted them to restore their control over Anatolia and eastern Thrace, and demarcated the political borders of their newly born state (modern Turkey). In October 1923, the Grand National Assembly declared Ankara the capital of the Turkish Republic, adopted the new Constitution of the Republic of Turkey, and elected Mustafa Kemal Ataturk as its first president and Asmat Anoun as its first prime minister. These political developments gave the Kemalists solid recognition in Turkey and motivated them to abolish the Ottoman caliphate on 3 March 1924. With this decision, they put the final nail in the coffin of the Ottoman caliphate and by doing so created a serious challenge to Riḍā's reformist project. (Shaw and Shaw 1992, 365–9)

The supporters of the caliphate considered the abolition decision politically apostate, requiring revision and repentance, while critics of the caliphate commended it as a step towards political reform and renewal. ʿAlī ʿAbd al-Rāziq

(1888–1966), for instance, published a controversial treatise titled *Islam and the Foundations of Government* in April 1925, in which he labelled the caliphate as a mere political illusion that has no basis in the Qurʾān, prophetic traditions, or Muslim consensus.[13] In his view, Muslims should feel free to establish their own governments, based on their own reason and experience. His thesis provoked outrage from a wide range of Muslim scholars, particularly the conservative ones, who condemned his work and called for it to be barred from circulation and for its author to be punished. As a result, a high council of senior scholars was held at al-Azhar, in Cairo, where the treatise of ʿAbd al-Rāziq was assessed and its author investigated. After a series of investigations, the collective decision of the council was as follows:

> We, the shaykhs of al-Azhar Mosque, with the consensus of the twenty-four scholars among us from the High Council of Scholars, have ruled to dismiss ʿAlī ʿAbd al-Rāziq—one of the scholars of al-Azhar Mosque, judge of the Manṣūra Sharīʿa Court of First Instance, and author of the book *Islam and the Foundations of Government*—from the corps of scholars.
>
> RIḌĀ, in Anonymous 1925, 383

Riḍā supported this decision by publishing a series of articles in *al-Manār*, accusing ʿAbd al-Rāziq of apostasy because he denied the Islamic roots of the caliphate as the institution of governance. He described al-Rāziq's treatise as "a new call to blow up the building of the caliphate ... and a kind of political and scientific war against Islam and Muslims. It is worse than the crusader war in the name of religion" (*al-Manār*, 1925, 100).

The whole scenario reveals that after the publication of *Islam and Fundamentals of Government* the reformist project of Riḍā had lost its theoretical appeal and after the abolition of the Ottoman caliphate 1924 its implementation in the near future had become very difficult. The only avenue left for Riḍā to promote his project was to extend invitations to Muslim scholars to an international conference on the future of the caliphate and the possibility of restoring it. Three conferences on the topic were held, in Mecca (1924), Cairo (1926), and Jerusalem (1931), but their outcomes did not meet with Riḍā's expectations. Eventually his reformist project became a distant dream and was never translated into political action (Kramer 1986, 80–141).

---

13 For further details on ʿAlī ʿAbd al-Rāziq and his book, see Wegner 2001, Tagelsir 2004, Broucek 2012.

9 Conclusion

As the foregoing discussion demonstrates, the Ottoman caliphate had different connotations to its supporters and detractors. The supporters promoted it as a tool of Islamic unity that would permit them to protect their lands from the aggression of European imperialism and enhance their communal identity against the internal threats of newly emerged nationalist movements and their secular agendas. The detractors perceived it as a symbol of a civilisation whose time had passed and saw its institutions as irrelevant to the contemporary needs of modern societies (Pankhurst 2013, 5). Riḍā was the most famous and the most active promoter of the caliphate in its different forms and in the various phases of its development. He maintained that its existence as the institution of governance was necessary and the reform of its conquest form (that is, the Ottoman caliphate) would lead to the revival of its ideal form (the true caliphate). To achieve this objective, he adopted a top-down approach for reform and revival. This approach and its surrounding political environment led him to see the caliphate as "an instrumental symbol for the unity and sovereignty of the Muslims rather than a theoretical or theological concept that has to be strictly adhered to" (Pankhurst 2013, 22). Therefore, his support of the Ottoman political elites and their counterparts in the region has to be examined in the context of his role as a Muslim jurist who was much concerned about the unity of the Muslim *umma* and saw the continuity of the caliphate as a tool for maintaining that unity. He therefore supported Sultan Abdülhamid II and his successors (1909–24), even though he was aware that their political agendas differed from what he considered ideal, and that, according to the set of requirements instituted by al-Māwardī and other classical Muslim jurists they were not qualified for those posts.

The most distinguished Muslim ideologue who was inspired by Riḍā's reformist project on the caliphate and tried to implement it with a bottom-up approach was Ḥasan al-Bannā (1906–49), who founded the Society of the Muslim Brothers in the city of al-Ismāʿīliyya, near the Suez Canal, in 1928 (Ushama 1995, Krämer 2010, Rubin 2010). His bottom-up approach included seven levels of reform that would eventually lead to the restoration of the caliphate. These seven levels of reform include "reforming oneself, one's family, and one's society, liberating society politically, establishing Islamic governance, re-establishing the Muslim *umma* leading to *khilāfa* (united leadership of Muslims), and providing leadership to the world to carry the *amāna* (trust) of guiding people to the true path" (Ushama 2005, 204–5). Al-Bannā supported the Egyptian nation state, even though he did not consider it to be politically legitimate because of its secular attitude; nevertheless he considered it a temporary step towards his ultimate ideological goal, the restoration of the caliphate.

Neither the top-down nor the bottom-up approach succeeded in translating into action the reformist projects of their authors (Riḍā and al-Bannā, respectively). As a result, the revival of the Islamic caliphate remained a distant dream for several Islamic political groups, which have different plans and agendas for its implementation on the ground. Here, one may single out Ḥizb al-Taḥrīr al-Islāmī (Islamic Party of Liberation), *al-Qāʿida,* and the Islamic State of Iraq and Syria (ISIS). Other political parties, such as the al-Nahḍa Movement in Tunisia and Jamaat-e-Islami in Pakistan, have accepted Western democracy and its political institutions as a channel that may qualify them to participate in governing their own countries via various forms of general elections. Their political agendas have been confined to the Islamic reforms put forth in their countries and societies from within, instead of being preoccupied with the revival of a caliphate resembling the ideological goal of their reformist predecessors.

Bibliography

Sources

Anonymous. 1925. "Ḥukm hayʾat kibār al-ʿulamā fi *l-Islām wa-usūl al-ḥukm* (The Verdict of the Organization of Senior Scholars on *Islam and Foundations of Government*)." *al-Manār* 26/5: 383–93.

Fahmī, ʿAlī Affandī. 1910. "Al-Khilāfa al-Islāmiyya wa-l-Jāmiʿa al-ʿUthmāniyya." *al-Manār* 13/12: 933–37.

Ibn Hanbal, Aḥmad. n.d. *Musnad,* 4: 96.

al-Māwardī, Abū l-Ḥasan. n.d. *Al-Aḥkām as-Sulṭāniyyah* = The Laws of Islamic Governance. Trans. Asadullah Yate. London: Ta-Ha Publishers.

Riḍā, Rashīd. 1898. "Fātiḥat al-Sana al-Ūlā." *al-Manār* 1/1: 9–14.

Riḍā, Rashīd. 1899a (5 August). "Al-Jinsiyya wa-l-dīn." *al-Manār* 2/21: 321–27.

Riḍā, Rashīd. 1899b (12 August). "Al-Jāmiʿa al-Islāmiyya." *al-Manār* 2/22: 338–48.

Riḍā, Rashīd. 1899c (19 August). "Al-Dīn wa-l-dawla aw al-khilāfa wa-l-sulṭa." *al-Manār* 2/23: 353–60.

Riḍā, Rashīd. 1902. "ʿAbd al-Raḥmān al-Kawākibī." *al-Manār* 5/6–7: 237–40, 276–80.

Riḍā, Rashīd. 1907. "Jamʿiyyat al-Shūrā al-ʿUthmāniyya." *al-Manār* 9/12: 950–51.

Riḍā, Rashīd. 1908. "ʿĪd al-umma al-ʿUthmāniyya." *al-Manār* 11/6: 417–24.

Riḍā, Rashīd. 1910. "Al-Khilāfa Islāmiyya wa-l-jāmiʿa al-ʿUthmāniyya." *al-Manār* 13: 713–20, 857–63, 933–37.

Riḍā, Rashīd. 1922. "Khuṭbat al-Ghāzī Muṣtafā Kamāl Pāshā." *al-Manār* 23/10: 784–85.

Riḍā, Rashīd. 1925. "Al-Islām wa-uṣūl al-ḥukm: Baḥth fi l-khilāfa wa-l-ḥukūma fi l-Islām." *al-Manār* 26/2: 100–4.

Riḍā, Rashīd. 1988. *Al-Khilāfa*. Cairo: Dār al-Zaharā lil-Iʿlām al-ʿArabī.

Riḍā, Rashīd. 2006². *Tārīkh al-Ustādh al-Imām al-Shaykh Muḥammad ʿAbduh*. vol. 1. Cairo: Dār al-Faḍīla.

Secondary Literature

Abushouk, Ahmed Ibrahim. 2003. "Muslim Unity: Lessons from History." *International Journal of Muslim Unity* 1/1: 9–20.

Abushouk, Ahmed Ibrahim. 2007. "Al-Manār and the Ḥadhramī Elite in the Malay-Indonesian World: Challenge and Response." *Journal of the Royal Asiatic Society* 17/3: 301–22.

Abushouk, Ahmed Ibrahim. 2009. "The Ideology of the Expected Mahdi in Muslim History: The Case of the Sudanese Mahdiyyah, 1881–1898." *The Pakistan Journal of History and Culture* 30/1: 43–60.

Abushouk, Ahmed Ibrahim. 2014. *Al-Malik ʿAbd al-ʿAzīz Āl Suʿūd fī majallat al-Manār*. Beirut: Arabic Scientific Publishers.

Ali, Souad Tagelsir. 2004. *ʿAli ʿAbd al-Raziq's al-Islam wa Usul al-Hukm: A Modern Liberal Development of Muslim Thought*. PhD dissertation, University of Utah, Salt Lake City, Utah.

Bluhm-Warn, Jutta. 1997. "*Al-Manār* and Ahmad Soorkatti: Links in the Chain of Transmission of Muḥammad Abduh's Ideas to the Malay-Speaking World." In Peter G. Riddell and Tony Street (eds.), *Islam: Essays on Scripture, Thought and Society: A Festschrift in Honour of Anthony H. Johns*. Leiden: Brill, 295–308.

Blunt, W.S. 2016. "Memoirs." In S. David. Katz, *The Shaping of Turkey in the British Imagination, 1776–1923*. London: Palgrave Macmillan, 218–20.

Broucek, James. 2012. *The Controversy of Shaykh ʿAli ʿAbd al-Raziq*. PhD dissertation, Florida State University, College of Arts and Sciences, Tallahassee, Florida.

Brunner, Rainer 2017. "The Pilgrim's Tale as a Means of Self-Promotion: Muḥammad Rashīd Riḍā's Journey to the Ḥijāz (1916)." In Michael Kemper and Ralf Elger (eds.), *The Piety of Learning: Islamic Studies in Honor of Stefan Reichmuth*. Leiden: Brill, 270–91.

Busool, Assad N. 1984 "Rashid Rida's Struggle to Establish A Modern Islamic State." *American Journal of Islamic Studies* 1: 83–99.

Buzpinar, Ş. Tufan. 1996. "Opposition to the Ottoman Caliphate in the Early Years of Abdülhamid II: 1877–1882." *Die Welt des Islams* 36/1: 59–89.

Enayat, Hamid. 2001. *Modern Islamic Political Thought*. Kuala Lumpur: Islamic Book Trust.

Funatsu, Ryuichi. 2006. "Al-Kawākibī's Thesis and Its Echoes in the Arab World Today." *Harvard Middle East and Islamic Review* 7: 1–40.

Galbraith, John S., and Afaf Lutfi al-Sayyid-Marsot. 1978. "The British Occupation of Egypt: Another View." *International Journal of Middle East Studies* 9/4: 471–88.

Haddad, Mahmoud. 1997. "Arab Religious Nationalism in the Colonial Era: Rereading Rashīd Riḍā's Ideas on the Caliphate." *Journal of the American Oriental Society* 117/2: 253–77.

Hamzah, Dyala. 2003. "Rashīd Riḍā: 'Alim, Islamic reformer or Journalist? Genre, Class and the Intellectual Craft during the Nahda." Presented to the Fourth Mediterranean Social and Political Research Meeting, Florence, Italy, 19–23 March 2003 (unpublished).

Hamzah, Dyala. 2013. "From 'Ilm to Sihafa or the Politics of the Public Interest (Maslaha): Muhammad Rashīd Ridā and his Journal *al-Manar* (1898–1935)." In Dyala Hamzah, *The Making of the Arab Intellectual: Empire, Public Sphere and the Colonial Coordinates of Selfhood*. London: Routledge, 90–127.

'Imāra, Muḥammad (ed.). 1972. *Al-A'māl al-Kāmila lil-Imām Muḥammad 'Abduh*. Beirut: al-Mu'assasa al-'Arabiyya lil-Dirasāt wa-l-Nashr, part II.

Jomier, J. 1991. "al-Manār." In *The Encyclopedia of Islam*, Second Edition.

Katz, David S. 2016. *The Shaping of Turkey in the British Imagination, 1776–1923*. London: Palgrave Macmillan.

Kausar, Zeenath (ed.). 2005. *Contemporary Islamic Political Thought: A Study of Eleven Islamic Thinkers*. Kuala Lumpur: International Islamic University Malaysia.

Kawtharānī, Wajīh. 1980. *Mukhtārāt Siyāsiyya min Majallat al-Manār*. Beirut: Dār al-Ṭalī'a.

Kerr, Malcolm H. 1966. *Islamic Reform: The Political and Legal Theories of Muḥammad 'Abduh and Rashīd Riḍā*. Berkeley and Los Angeles: University of California Press.

Krämer, Gudrun. 2010. *Hasan al-Banna*. London: Oneworld.

Kramer, Martin S. 1986. *Islam Assembled: The Advent of the Muslim Congresses*. New York: Columbia University Press.

Lewis, Mary Dewhurst. 2008. "Geographies of Power: The Tunisian Civic Order, Jurisdictional Politics, and Imperial Rivalry in the Mediterranean, 1881–1935." *The Journal of Modern History* 80/4: 791–830.

Moten, Abdul Rashīd, and A. Abdel Salam El-Fatih. 2005. *Glossary of Political Science Terms: Islamic and Western*. Kuala Lumpur: Thomson.

al-Marrākushī, Muḥammad Ṣāliḥ. 1985. *Tafkīr Muḥammad Rashīd Riḍā khilāl Majallat al-Manār, 1989–1935*. Tunis: Al-Dār al-Tūnisiyya lil-Nashr.

Nuseibeh, Hazim Zaki. 1956. *The Ideas of Arab Nationalism*. Ithaca: Cornell University Press.

Pankhurst, Reza. 2013. *The Inevitable Caliphate? A History of the Struggle for Global Islamic Union, 1924 to the Present*. London: C. Hurst & Co.

Reichmuth, Stefan. 2017. "Rashīd Riḍā: Introduction to the First Annual Volume of *al-Manār* (Egypt, 1909)." In Björn Bentlage, Marion Eggert, Hans-Martin Krämer, and

Stefan Reichmuth (eds.), *Religious Dynamics under the Impact of Imperialism and Colonialism: A Sourcebook.* Leiden: Brill, 293–304.

Rubin, B. 2010. *The Muslim Brotherhood: The Organization and Policies of a Global Islamist Movement.* New York: Palgrave Macmillan.

Ryad, Umar. 2009. "A Printed Muslim 'Lighthouse' in Cairo *al-Manār*'s Early Years, Religious Aspiration and Reception (1898–1903)." *Arabica* 56/1: 27–60.

Shahin, Emad Eldin. 1993. *Through Muslim Eyes: M. Rashīd Riḍā and the West.* Herndon VA: International Institute of Islamic Thought.

Shaw, Stanford J., and Ezel Kural Shaw. 1992[4]. *History of the Ottoman Empire and Modern Turkey.* 2 vols. Cambridge: Cambridge University Press.

Skovgaard-Petersen, Jakob. 2001. "Portrait of the Intellectual as a Young Man: Rashīd Ridā's Muhāwarāt al-muslih wa-al-muqallid (1906)." *Islam and Christian–Muslim Relations* 12/1: 93–104.

Tauber, Eliezer. 1994. "Three Approaches, One Idea: Religion and State in the Thought of ʿAbd al-Raḥmān al-Kawākibī, Najīb ʿAzūrī and Rashīd Riḍā." *British Journal of Middle Eastern Studies* 21/1: 190–8.

Ushama, Thameem. 1995. *Hasan al-Banna: Vision and Mission.* Kuala Lumpur: A.S. Noordeen.

Ushama, Thameem. 2005. "Hasan al-Banna's Life, Mission, Political Thought, and Reforms." In Zeenath Kausar (ed.), *Contemporary Islamic Political Thought: A Study of Eleven Islamic Thinkers.* Kuala Lumpur: International Islamic University Malaysia, 187–228.

Wegner, Mark Jonathan. 2001. *Islamic Government: The Medieval Sunnī Islamic Theory of the Caliphate and the Debate over the Revival of the Caliphate in Egypt, 1924–1926.* PhD dissertation, University of Chicago, Chicago, Illinois.

CHAPTER 4

Ottoman Corporatism, Eighteenth to Twentieth Centuries: Beyond the State-Society Paradigm in Middle Eastern History

Johann Büssow and Astrid Meier

1 Introduction

Written sources as well as pictorial representations from the Ottoman Empire regularly portray the subjects of the Ottoman sultan as organised in "groups" along religious, ethnic, professional, and other lines of social differentiation. Whether or not such groups carried administrative functions is not always clear—at least not for the modern reader or observer of such representations.

Consider, for example, the depiction of the guild of jewellers and goldsmiths, painted by Vehbi, parading past Sultan Ahmet III on the occasion of his son's circumcision in 1720 (Illustration 4.1). The painting sets the guild apart from other guilds, such as the beeswax sellers and tinsmiths, who follow next in line. The presence of the turbaned figure, riding on a horse and followed by what appears to be his personal guard, hints at an interior hierarchy among the guildsmen. The text accompanying the painting identifies him as the chief goldsmith (*kuyumcu başı*) of the Palace (Serban 2009, 3), the person representing his group vis-à-vis the sultan, and ensuring the proper fulfilment of collective responsibilities (Faroqhi 2010, 208). Vehbi's album (*Surname*) presents dozens of other such group representatives parading past the ruler and thereby suggests a well-entrenched social and political order with "groups" and "group heads" (Ott. Turk. *baş* or *re'is*) as its basic elements.

This Ottoman self-image seemingly depicting an overarching pattern of social-cum-political order has become the object of distorted and misleading interpretations. When European scholars and artists described the social order of the Ottoman Empire, they usually emphasised the importance of some such groups, in particular those defined in religious and tribal terms. This tendency became even more pronounced when European powers institutionalised their rule over parts of the Ottoman Middle East in the age of colonialism. Many analyses of contemporary Middle Eastern culture and politics, as they are produced across the globe by academics and non-academic intellectuals

 | DOI:10.1163/9789004386891_005

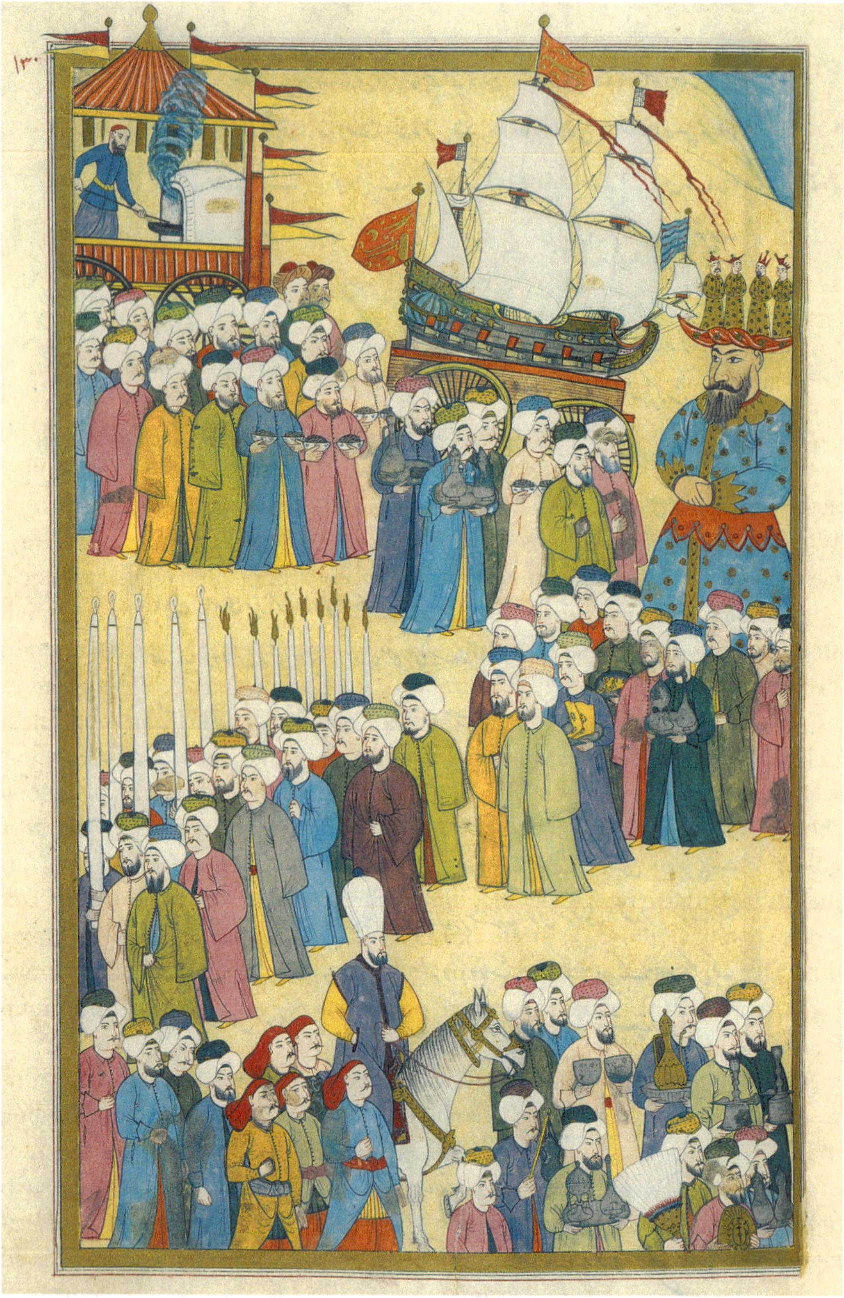

ILLUSTRATION 4.1 *Surname-i Vehbi*, Procession of the guilds; in the foreground, the representatives of the jewellers and goldsmiths.
SOURCE: ATIL 1999, 148.

today, still rely on easy but inaccurate representations of the importance of family, tribe, and religious "sect" as significant categories of social belonging in Middle Eastern countries, instead of confronting the difficulties of such categorisations.

In this article we posit that we can much better understand a number of classical topics in the historiography of the modern Middle East—among them the so-called "millet system," tribe-state relations, and the politics of notables—if we take a broader perspective, which encompasses the entire range of group formation and group dynamics, and which we propose to call "Ottoman corporatism." This, then, leads to a second and more fundamental point.

Drawing from observations from the Syrian lands between the eighteenth and twentieth centuries, we argue that in the early-modern and modern Ottoman domains, social organisation and state formation are continuous and intricately linked processes that cannot be grasped if looked at only through the lens of "state-society" relations. This concept, which presupposes a duality of two neatly separable entities interacting with one another has become a popular but again somewhat misleading perspective among Ottomanists in recent years (for an overview, see Mikhail and Philliou 2012). In particular, this perspective is not well suited to account for the Ottoman vision in which both political and social order were permeated by overarching patterns and ideals, and it also stands in the way of overcoming essentialising notions of family, tribe, and "sect."

Unfortunately, Ottoman "state-society" relations are rarely explored to the extent that they are with respect to other world regions. Even though it might be true, as it might be for any other empire, that "the Ottoman Empire *was not* like any other empire" (Mikhail and Philliou 2012, 743), the field can profit from the intellectual stimuli provided by the renewed attention paid lately to "empire" under the umbrella of global history (see, for example, Lester 2005). In our view, intellectual stimulus, or "Reiz," as Gudrun Krämer proposes (Krämer 2014), is one of the attractions of looking beyond one's own specialisation. As we will see, questioning specific historical and scholarly conceptions in the search for a common terminology can prove both stimulating and irritating, for example regarding the notions of state, society, and religion.

In our approach, we are stimulated by various avenues of questioning historical enquiry. Most important among them is the problem of how to conceptualise state and society. Here the general discussion has moved away from structuralist approaches as they still dominate Ottoman historiography towards a more processual concept. Patrick Joyce and Chandra Mukerji (Joyce 2013; Joyce and Mukerji 2017), for instance, understand states not as entities or unitary actors but as assemblages of various agencies and sites, which combine control of persons and things and which in modern times are increasingly integrated by infrastructural technology or "logistical power" (Joyce and Mukerji 2017, 1).[1] Michael Mann, highlighting the exponential increase of importance that such technology accorded the modern state, allowing it to "to penetrate civil society, and to implement logistically political decisions throughout the realm," has termed this phenomenon "infrastructural power" (Mann 1989 [1984], 113).[2]

For Joyce and Mukerji, the exercise of logistical power is an ongoing experiment and manifests itself in material formations of state power that act as "distributed tools of governance … independently of each other and even of officials" (Joyce and Mukerjee 2017, 2). Yet it is "the physical practices of bureaucracies, keen to delineate the boundaries of the state and produce state effects" that draw what Timothy Mitchell called the "state effect," that is, the line between state and non-state (Mitchell 1999 and 2002). As we have seen in Vehbi's representation of the guild parading before the sultan, the political here cannot be separated from notions of social order and the ways in which it is imagined and performed, through clothing, turbans, horses, processions, and the like. As Joyce and Mukerji write:

> As much as states need modes of social coordination, they also depend on cultural modes of imagination—not only the imagined communities of Benedict Anderson, but also imagined histories and destinies that seem real because they are visible in the design of things and lived out in and through … them in everyday life.
>
> JOYCE and MUKERJI 2017, 12

Combining an interest in the social, the political, the cultural, and the material, a second starting point for our "approach" or "way of knowing" Middle Eastern societies is what Max Weber has defined as a double interest in the structure of domination and society (cf. Weber 1985 [1921–22], 212, 541). Here we are indebted to Gudrun Krämer, who inspiringly adapted the discussion of many of

1 See also, for another perspective, the influential study "Headless State" by Sneath 2007, 1–2: "Viewing the state as a form of social relation rather than a central structure avoids the evolutionist dichotomy between state and nonstate society, and it makes it possible for us to conceive of a 'headless state', a configuration of statelike power formed by the horizontal relations between power holders, rather than a result of their mutual subordination to a political center."

2 The concept has been applied inter alia to the cases of the administration of late Ottoman Transjordan and Palestine and of the Ottoman police (see Rogan 1999, Büssow 2011a, and Ergut 2002).

Weber's categories to the modern Middle East. She, as an executive editor of the *Encyclopaedia of Islam THREE*, also put the authors of this study in contact in 2010, and thereby instigated what has become a long-standing scholarly cooperation. In her survey of Middle Eastern history since 1500 (Krämer 2016), she offers some broad observations on state and society in this world region. Two ideas that we found particularly thought provoking were her statement regarding the "primacy of politics" and her verdict that in the early-modern and modern Middle East "vertical" connections generally outweighed "horizontal" ones (Krämer 2016, 556; see also Krämer 2014). We try to develop this approach, based on our reading of some recent contributions to German social history, in particular Rudolf Schlögl's work on face-to-face communication in society and state formation (Schlögl 2014; 2008).

Responding to these diverse stimuli, we will argue that one can see important features of the changing modes of Ottoman governance (not only but also "governmentality") at play in the corporate nature of at least some social groups. We will discuss what we mean by "corporate nature" in detail in the following section. Suffice it to say that this approach challenges some well-known tenets concerning "Ottoman" or "Islamic" ways of social organisation. One might think immediately of Max Weber's claim, echoed by other social theorists, that the Ottoman Middle East as an "Islamic" society is characterised by the absence of "corporations," in contrast to the "Occident" (Weber 1985 [1921–22], 394, 429–40; Kuran 2011, 97–142; Salvatore 2016, 278–87).

One might also consider the idea of Middle Eastern society as segmented along the lines of religious, ethnic, and tribal communities—each of them being held together by strong "vertical" ties of authority and patronage but maintaining only very weak ties to other segments. This notion of segmentation is vividly captured in the metaphors of a "mosaic" (e.g., generalising Gibb and Bowen 1951, 1:159; critical review in Turner 2014 [1978], 39–52) or that of "a house of many mansions," a metaphor Kamal Salibi (1988) has used with regard to Lebanon. By reinforcing the voices that have refuted these arguments before us, our attempt at reconstructing the dual systemic logic of social organisation and governance is meant to transcend the exceptionalism that characterises much of the historiography of the Middle East—in tune with another long-standing aim of Gudrun Krämer's work.

We proceed in two steps. In the first section of our paper, we spell out what we mean by "Ottoman corporatism." Here we will also provide a short (and preliminary) inventory of terms and phenomena linked to social groups in the Ottoman context, and we suggest criteria for distinguishing among social groups with and those without corporate character. In the second section, we present two case studies of corporatism in the early-modern and modern

Ottoman countryside: villages and Bedouin tribal groups in the Syrian lands from the eighteenth to the twentieth centuries.

2 Corporate Groups and Ottoman Governance

It is an often repeated tenet that the absence of corporatist structures is characteristic of Muslim societies. Joseph Schacht, in his influential book *An Introduction to Islamic Law,* states bluntly:

> The concept of corporation does not exist in Islamic law (neither does that of a juristic person ....); only the *ʿāqila* [the group legally required to pay compensation] can be regarded as a rudimentary form of corporation.
> SCHACHT 1964, 155[3]

The focus of these discussions is Islamic law's apparent lack of a juridical concept of legal entity or "legal personality" (*juristische Person*), a term which, in Western legal traditions, is applied to diverse entities such as cities, universities, or business corporations (Behrens-Abouseif 2009).

In the perspective of most specialists of Islamic law, a society or community is made up of individuals, not groups.[4] In the meantime, the existence of corporate structures and institutions has been reaffirmed from multiple perspectives. David Santillana in his *Istituzioni di diritto musulmano* (1925–28), another influential introduction to Islamic law, devoted a whole chapter to the discussion of legal personalities,[5] for which there exists no term in Islamic law, even though these entities nevertheless exist, with effects, rights, and obligations (1925, vol.1:170–89; for the *waqf* as legal personality see Behrens-Abouseif 2009). According to Santillana, the jurists never developed a notion of "legal personality," even not for the above-mentioned guilds and professional corporations who are well-documented for the mediaeval Islamicate world (Santillana 1925, 171). Baber Johansen (1999, 411) revised this judgement by demonstrating that jurists in fact had developed the concept of the "professional group"

3 Cf. ibid., 186. The *ʿāqila* is the group of persons liable for the payment of compensation or "blood money" (*diya*) in cases of homicide by mistake, see Johansen 1999, 385 fn. 143. Customary law in the Arab Middle East applies compensation to a wider range of cases, including murder, bodily harm, and property damage.

4 For an overview of the relationship of individual and community rights, see Johansen 1999, 189–218; for the relationship between individual person and government in particular, see 213.

5 Santillana speaks of *persone giuridiche*, i.e., *juridical persons*, following the German "*juristische Person.*" This is in English "legal personality."

(*ahl al-ḥirfa*) as early as the eleventh century CE. Moreover, at least with respect to Ḥanafī penal law, Johansen sees not only rudimentary forms of corporations at play, as Schacht did, but talks about such corporate groups as an important institution in the relations between subject and authority.[6]

This is the starting point of our own contribution. If we now can concede the existence of corporate groups as well as a general idea of incorporation, what do we mean when we speak of Ottoman corporatism? As in other contexts, we need to acknowledge that corporatism (or "corporativism") is not a fixed concept, but "still elusive, owing to insufficient definition and ideological controversy," as Czada writes in his seminal article on the concept (Czada 2011, 458). "In its most basic meaning," he notes, "corporativism refers to a political power structure and practice of consensus formation based on the functional representation of professional groups" (Czada 2011, 458).

The importance of professional organisations has been evoked already several times in this article and the study of Ottoman "guilds" and professional associations has developed into a lively field since Gabriel Baer's (1970) provocative article about the functions of corporations (for an overview see Faroqhi 2010).[7] However, this is not the only kind of grouping we are interested in. Hence, we propose to use corporatism as a theoretical concept and regime type (cf. Czada 2011, 459), a conceptualisation that helps us understand widespread forms of collective solidarity and subsidiarity at work in the Ottoman polity.

In the context of this essay, we define corporations (or corporate groups) as social groups that bear collective responsibility and have some capacity for collective action (cf. Johansen 1998, 385 fn. 143 and 411–12 fn. 264). Usually, they become political actors only through representatives. The question remains what range of action is open to these collective actors. Autonomy, as Krämer asserts,

> counts among the most interesting aspects of societal action and organization, and not just of the Ottoman Empire and Palestine: Most village and urban communities appeared to their members and to outsiders as autonomous, and the defense of this autonomy greatly mattered to them. Yet autonomy should not be confused with isolation, splendid or otherwise, let alone with autarchy.
>
> KRÄMER 2008, 43

6 "Von der behaupteten Feindschaft des islamischen Rechts gegen Korporationen lässt sich im hanafitischen Strafrecht nichts finden" (Johansen 1998, 411; cf. 384).

7 For a discussion in a more comparative perspective emphasising the economic, see the work on European guilds by Sheilagh Ogilvie (2011, 2014).

In drawing new attention to corporate aspects of Ottoman social organisation and politics, we do not claim that all groups in Ottoman history are the same and have the same functions. The "doing and undoing" of difference is a common trait in the making of human communities, from the very small to the most aggregate (Hirschauer 2014). We are interested here only in those groups that appear as relevant elements of social ordering in the actual process of state formation. Thus we do not look at status groups (*Stände*), which in Weber's model of social stratification are differentiated according to non-economic qualities such as honour, prestige, religion, and so forth. The reason we disregard them is that they are analytical or descriptive categories, but not actual groups with the potential for collective action.

So what groups actually were corporations in our understanding, and which were not? In the following section we will take a cursory look at various groups that appear in our sources, trying to flesh out the concept.

2.1 *Terminology and Phenomenology of Social Groups in the Ottoman Context*

Any student of Ottoman history knows the sometimes rather disturbing fact that in the vast documentation available, terms are not used in a consistent manner. For example, *ṣinf/sınıf* (pl. *aṣnāf/esnaf*) seems to apply more specifically and consistently to occupational groups. However, as Baer observed, in Arabic as well as in Turkish texts from the Ottoman period, professional guilds are also frequently called *ṭāʾifa* (pl. *ṭawāʾif/tevaʾif*), a word that has the general sense of "group" and may also be used for inhabitants of a neighbourhood (*ḥāra/zukak* or *sokak, maḥalla/mahalle*), ethnic groups (e.g. Türkmen, Romani/*Kıbt*), or any religious or tribal community (Baer 1996, 29–30; Masters 1988, 43–45; cf. Reinkowski 2005, 253–58). When speaking of tribal communities, Ottoman administrators used terms such as *ʿashīra/ʿaşiret* and *qabīla/kabile* to cover a wide range of actual groups, ranging from small local communities to far-ranging tribal confederations.[8]

Our contention is that such usage of terminology, frustrating as it may be for historians, actually reflects the necessities of administrative practice. First of all, administrators, who mostly did not stay longer than one or two years in one province, did not have the time and motivation to deal with the intricacies of local communal life. Moreover, from an administrative point of view, all these groups were homologous entities: They were fiscal, political, and sometimes also military units and had one or more representatives vis-à-vis the state,

8 In one of the sixteenth-century tax lists, *qabīla* is rather exceptionally also used for subgroups of the Jewish community in the town of Ṣafad; see Hütteroth and Abdulfattah 1977, 39.

with whom the administrator had to deal. This deliberate abstraction from the facts "on the ground" is what James C. Scott in his book *Seeing Like a State* has described as the administrative technique of simplification. Scott writes:

> First, the knowledge that an official needs must give him or her a synoptic view of the ensemble; it must be cast in terms that are replicable across many cases. In this respect, such facts must lose their particularity and reappear in schematic or simplified form as a member of a class of facts. Second, in a meaning closely related to the first, the grouping of synoptic facts necessarily entails collapsing or ignoring distinctions that might otherwise be relevant.
>
> SCOTT 1998, 81

The potential list of social groups that acted as corporations is long and it goes far beyond the most common cases of professional, ethnic, or religious groups. Krämer has described some of them elsewhere as

> locally and/or personally defined communities of solidarity and liability which acted in the social, juridical and political spheres and which, in case of conflict, were held responsible by the authorities: urban quarters and neighbourhoods, village communities, nomadic clans, associations of young men and many more.
>
> KRÄMER 2014, 109

In specific places and during specific periods the blind or former slaves (*ʿabīd*) also appear as organised groups with their own headmen.[9] Ṣūfī brotherhoods and extended families should also be added to this list. Some of these groupings show characteristics of corporations, but their interaction with state agencies usually proceeded in much less formalised ways than with the other groups mentioned above. The question of where exactly to draw the line between corporate and non-corporate groups in such cases is beyond the limits of this article.

One of the most general terms for groups of all kinds and sizes is *jamāʿa/cemaʿat* (cf. Hütteroth and Abdulfattah 1977, 27–29). Its frequent use in administrative and legal writings drew our attention early on in our cooperation, and since then we have become convinced that a better understanding of this usage is crucial in order to grasp the day-to-day aspects of governing an empire.

---

9 For the organisation of the blind in eighteenth-century Cairo, see Meier 2015, 107; on the *ʿabīd* community of late Ottoman Jaffa, see Tarawneh 2000, 476–77.

As we are going to demonstrate in our examples below, the term can point to the importance of face-to-face interventions between what we usually call state and society.

In many cases, the persons present in such a *jamāʿa/cemaʿat* act as representatives for those groups that we identify as corporate groups. These groups are characterised by common objectives, solidarity, and joint liability, at least insofar as what concerns specific aspects of the group's activities. The question of self-government or self-rule, which is predominant in discussions of "the corporatist model of the European pre-modern society" (Hespanha 2014, 310) is not at the forefront of our concern, as in general we do not have the sources that would allow us to look inside such incorporated groups and discern how they worked internally. Nonetheless, it is important not to subscribe to "any idyllic vision of corporatism ... as a realm of self-government before the heteronomous rule of the state" (Hespanha 2014, 310).

2.2 *Mechanisms of Corporatist Governance*

If we want to understand what role such groups played in Ottoman governance, we have to rethink some central concepts. The most important is the relationship between state and society. In political science, where many authors in Ottoman historiography draw their inspiration, discussions of the role of the "modern" state centre on the development from collective to individual autonomy. Here we do not want to discuss the truth of claims of this branch of political theory, but rather explore more pragmatically the dynamic role of groups in Ottoman politics, in particular with respect to groups other than the professional.

Hence, we focus here on the interfaces—physical, personal, and virtual—through which Ottoman governance became possible. In Ottoman historiography, the function of such interfaces certainly has been addressed before in various ways, for instance under the rubric of intermediate powers (*intermediäre Gewalten*; Röhrborn 1978), the "politics of notables" (Hourani 1968; Khoury 1990, and many others), and the "age of the *aʿyān*" (McGowan 1994). The *aʿyān*, that is, the category designating the top level of Ottoman local elites (a term which, in the case of the Syrian lands, we find almost exclusively used in urban contexts)[10] have received most attention. Gudrun Krämer has made helpful observations on notables as mediators between the population and the government, based on her study of the *aʿyān* in late Ottoman and Mandate Palestine. In particular, she suggests as an area of particular interest the specific "instruments and mechanisms of leverage" that notables had at their

10 Cf. Ursinus 1995 on other usage of the term in Ottoman Europe.

disposal in order to press for the interests of their interlocutors "above" and "below" (Krämer 2008, 94). Büssow has further developed this model and has added observations on the *aʿyān*'s resources and on particular fields of their political activity, that is, patronage, dispute settlement, and public protest.[11] He also included material on the much-overlooked rural political elites (Büssow 2011a, 356–74).

As we have mentioned earlier, Ottomanist scholarship has not stopped here. Detailed studies have been devoted to professional, religious, and tribal groups. Taxation and petitioning—two central practices for corporatist group formation—have also been documented.[12] Petitions—some of which were signed by dozens, in some cases more than one hundred persons—document the ability of a group to articulate common interests, and the effect of such efforts may be seen as a measure of the group's political weight. The burden of taxation is a test for many things, among them the strength of social ties within the group, the representative's ability to balance different interests, and the authorities' ability to exert control over the group. In this way, disputes over taxation reveal what we would like to call the relative "carrying capacity" of corporate groups, as well as their degree of autonomy. Autonomy—and this concept also belongs to the many stimulating observations by Gudrun Krämer that continue to merit attention (see Krämer 2008, 43, quoted above)—as a social ideal may have been an important factor that made membership in corporate groups attractive for Ottoman subjects and that sustained acceptance of corporatist structures "from below."

An interesting example is the attempt of the Egyptian government during the period of Egyptian rule in Damascus in 1833 to organise taxation by a new system, in which individuals were to pay taxes via professional organisations and after payment received individualised tax receipts. This led to unsatisfying results. Afterwards the Egyptian government reverted to assessing the same tax on a neighbourhood level, and, according to a well-informed local chronicler, was able to more than double the amount of taxes collected per capita. Apparently, neighbourhood organisations were a more efficient means to carry out this unpopular task. We can only speculate what happened within the neighbourhoods, but probably the measure attained a higher degree of legitimacy

11 Regarding patronage, Schlögl (2008, 175 fn. 75) importantly remarks that what research has been established on patron-client relations needs to be transferred to kinship groups and 'corporations'. Only this will allow an understanding of the contribution of clientelist networks to early modern state-building.

12 On petitions from the late Ottoman period see Ben-Bassat 2013; Sievert 2014. On taxation, see Wilkins 2010; Barkey 2008; Demirci 2003 and 2001; Salzmann 2004, Chap. 2.

because it allowed for burden-sharing according to local rules (Büssow 2011b, 118–19).

Many more examples could be added here, and we will provide some more below. What we want to highlight here is that, to date, Ottoman historiography has described many important elements of corporatist governance but is lacking in a vision of the dynamic whole. Recent work by the historian of early-modern Germany Rudolf Schlögl contains some suggestions that may contribute to a more complete picture (Schlögl 2008, 2014). Schlögl proposes that we think about early-modern society in the German-speaking lands as a societal formation in its own right, with distinct institutions and ways of organising, not merely as an early or transit stage of what later becomes a modern society and state. At the centre of his model stands an elaborate notion of communication, derived from system theory, in the footsteps of sociologist Niklas Luhmann and others.

In early-modern social formations, writes Schlögl (2008, 178), state and societies cannot develop an all-encompassing structure that works from the face-to-face level to the boundaries of the state in question, and accordingly territorial rule remains an unfulfilled ideal. The result is that "society is imagined as an agglomeration of groups" (Schlögl 2008, 178) that interact in various ways and degrees, using various media.[13] The family as the social grouping that provides the most immediate level of interaction is of highest importance, but no less important are other groups defined by the face-to-face interaction among their members. The primary media that shape such groupings are spoken language, the use of the body and of material objects, and the reference to space and time. The mode of interaction within the group (Schlögl has "*Vergesellschaftung*")[14] is "presentist and performative." Only writing allows human actors to distance themselves from these conditions, to observe them from an abstract point of view and to create another mode of communication (Schlögl 2008, 171).

We have already pointed to some examples of face-to-face communication in the Ottoman context, which included public displays in parades, processions, inspection rounds, and demonstrations,[15] but also in the semi-public arrangements of receptions at court, of sessions of the administrative councils

13 Schlögl (2008, 168) defines media as "everything that serves to provide difference in a concrete situation" (our translation). Money, law, or power can be considered media in this way.

14 For the difficulties of rendering German terms such as "Vergesellschaftung" or "Vergemeinschaftung" into English, cf. Swedberg and Agevall 2016.

15 In nineteenth-century Syria, the Arabic term *ʿarāḍa* seems to have been used as a generic term for demonstrations. The anonymous chronicle edited and translated by Büssow and

and the sharīʿa courts. The groups concerned include guilds, confessional groups, and village, city, and neighbourhood communities, that is, the units that played an important role in the administration of taxes and services.[16]

Delegations represented the groups in question through the bodies of those individuals present. The arrangement of these bodies in space is highly significant for understanding internal hierarchies, as evident in the rather pompous performance of guild headmen, through the spoken word, through moving through or standing in a certain space and often in routinely repeated sequences of performances, for example, on the occasion of accession of new sultan or governor, religious holidays, annual pilgrimages, birthdays, and circumcision (*sünnet*) festivities in the sultan's household. These arrangements of people representing corporate groups are what Schlögl calls the "presentist and performative mode of group construction" (Schlögl 2008, 173). For him, their bodies are not a symbol, an abstract reference to something absent, but "iconic." The body becomes a "writing surface," on which clothes are arranged that make the larger order of things readable (ibid., 175). The absent members of the group are made accessible in the "experience of presence" of their representatives. "Iconisation" (ibid., 176) is the process through which "presentist/ face-to-face communication" or "communication within a culture of presence" (*Anwesenheitskommunikation*, ibid., 155) allows for socialisation across large territories.

These displays are the most visible signs or icons of social order and state formation. Yet the groups in question function in more complex constructions of the social and the political. Here speech and writing are of utmost importance, and Ottoman sources teaches us about the formalised processes of petitioning, adjudication, and administration, which together form the core of governing an empire. Violence is another important means of communicating via present bodies, for example, through rituals of initiation, acts of shaming, corporal punishment, and execution (Schlögl 2008, 176). Such incidents are frequently reported in the historical literature of the day for many Ottoman cities.

Even if we do not aim here to copy Schlögl's approach and apply it to the Ottoman Empire, we think it is worth our while to consider the consequences of his research for our enquiry. We are well informed about the importance

Safi describes a whole repertoire of "street politics," including parades, demonstrations, riots, military displays, inspection rounds, official visits, formal receptions, and protests at the provincial governor's offices (see Büssow and Safi 2013, and Büssow 2011b).

16 See, for instance, the welcome ceremonies in late Ottoman Jaffa and Jerusalem for newly arrived governors (Büssow 2011a, 42, 410).

of written communication in Ottoman state-making for the elaborate bureaucratic system that existed at least from the late fifteenth century onwards and adapted itself time and again to changing circumstances. In many cases we can safely state that the structures of corporatist governance that we observe in the sources were the result of cooperation between a bureaucratic government and local actors. What we do not fully understand is how this bureaucratic system interlinked with the local organisation of face-to-face groups in order to produce what we call the empire.

We will elaborate now on our idea of Ottoman corporatism, the presentist mode of dealing with groups that we see at work in two specific examples from our own research. Both come from an area of study that is relatively uncommon in Ottomanist research, namely rural society. We pay special attention to the terms with "presentist" implications, such as first and foremost *jamāʿa,* in contrast to other terms referring to groups.

3 Two Cases of Corporatism in the Ottoman Countryside: Villages and Bedouin Groups in the Syrian Lands

With the following two case studies we attempt to demonstrate the diversity of corporate groups as well as of corporate politics in different contexts and times. The materials for the two cases were collected for other projects, based primarily on Ottoman administrative and juridical sources. This choice has a decisive influence on the various degrees of visibility of the respective groups. Local authors or ethnographies may attenuate the resulting image, but this is beyond the scope of this article.

3.1 *Corporatist Village Politics Before the Age of Individuation: Face-to-Face Communication Meets Bureaucratic Government*

In an article on Ottoman water administration, Meier (2016; see also Marino and Meier 2012) pointed to two incidents in the history of the village of al-Kanākir, to the southeast of Damascus, near the Aʿwaj River, which are highly relevant to our enquiry. In April 1708, a group of about fifty village men came fully armed to a division point on the main water channel and hindered experts sent by the judge of Damascus to repair the channel and adjust the division of water. Some five years later the whole system of water distribution for a number of villages, including al-Kanākir, came to be revised during a long day of checking, repairing, and adjusting all equipment in and around Saʿsaʿ. Dozens of people followed in procession from one place to the other. On this occasion the people of al-Kanākir, who had solicited the judge for this inspection (*bi-ltimās ahālī qaryat al-Kanākir*), were represented by a group of five men (*jamāʿa min ahālī qaryat al-Kanākir*), one introduced as the local police officer (*subashi*) of the village.

Both moments are crucial for understanding the power relations in the countryside of Damascus. We see the village community, or at least its male component, as active participants in Ottoman policymaking.[17] Threatening violence, the armed group of village men was able to halt proceedings that had been initiated by the second highest instance of the provincial administration. In the seemingly peaceful solution of the water conflicts in the region some years later, the representatives of al-Kanākir attended the material manifestation of their victory over some of their rivals, when the mechanism of water division was adapted in their favour. Unfortunately, the negotiation processes between the parties implicated in these conflicts remain hidden. What is important to note is the ability of the parties to come to new solutions, not recurring to ancient custom or precedent. This new solution was sanctioned by the legal procedure of "inspection" (*kashf wa-wuqūf*) and registration of the act describing the proceedings in the Chief Judge's registers (for more details, see Marino and Meier 2012, 386–92). Face-to-face communication meets here the archival mind of the Ottoman bureaucracy.

Both incidents seem to confirm that in the Ottoman system village communities had both agency and ample room for manoeuvering. Yet historians need to be cautious not to overgeneralise by understanding the specific site of this instance of "logistical power." Village water channels are considered in Ḥanafī legal thought and in Ottoman legal practice as a sort of co-owned property (*milk mushtarak*) of the users, usually addressed also in legal texts as village communities. In contrast to many assumptions based on anthropological studies of the early twentieth century that stressed the importance of a fixed tradition and local custom, the administration of such secondary water channels was open for the renegotiation of rights, under the one condition that all shareholders must agree (Meier 2016, 23–24). Many cases illustrate this principle of "autonomy" in water-related issues.

This type of autonomy is not found in other fields of village politics. It is important to note that autonomy came in differing degrees, depending on the norms and rules that shaped the relevant issue. Rural communities seem to have been well informed about proper administrative and legal proceedings and historians do not deal with illiterate or ignorant people, notwithstanding the difficulties in discovering the "authentic" voice of village communities (Meier 2005; cf. Ben-Bassat 2013, 89–91).

17 For other aspects of village integration, i.e., economic, religious-cultural, and demographic, see Baer 1982, 50.

Village communities, usually called *qarya*, were not only controlling their water channels, water distribution, and land use within the boundaries of the village, they also were one of the basic units of Ottoman tax administration, (e.g., Hütteroth and Abdulfattah 1977, 26–27). Villages, like other administrative units, are often seen as relevant largely with respect to tax collection (e.g., Krämer 2008, 41). The paying of taxes and other regular and irregular impositions in kind and in cash were in fact the joint liability of the tax-paying population of a village. The many conflicts over taxes on record, about who had to pay how much to what collector, are themselves an illustration of the village community acting as a corporate group.[18] Such conflicts also raise the question of whether people could be forced to be a member of such a corporate group or forced out of it. One *fatwā* by the famous ʿAbd al-Ghanī al-Nābulusī (d. 1731) "supported the right of the people of a village to expel a man who failed to contribute his portion of the tax burden" (Mundy and Saumarez 2007, 26). A considerable number of lawsuits brought to court refer to attempts by tax collectors or other villagers to hinder people from moving freely from one place to another. In some cases on record, the community aspect prevailed over the individual right of freedom of movement, in others it did not (cf. Rafeq 1999, 83–86; Mundy and Saumarez 2007, 26–27).

The village communities were one power group in a triangle of forces that shaped access to resources, the other two being *waqf* institutions with landed revenue and intermediary agents of the state, such as fief-holders (timariots) and tax farmers. The conflicts between these groups can be perceived in the echoes they left in the written record of the many lawsuits presented to the courts or government councils in Damascus and elsewhere. They often involved more directly the one or two highest representatives of central authority in the province. Such dealings often brought face-to-face confrontations from the rural sites into the urban theatres of state representation, the judges' courts, and the governor's seat. A case in point is the convocation of the village of Ḥazrama to court in 1132/1720. Seven villagers faced three *waqf* administrators and three state agents. In the course of the long-drawn-out proceedings the villagers had also solicited a *fatwā* by the *şeyhülislam* in Istanbul (Meier 2005). This is exceptional, but not uncommon in cases involving villagers.[19]

In such cases, the room for negotiated solutions (*tawāfuq, tarāḍin, ṣulḥ*) is limited by Ottoman *qānūn* and *sharīʿa*, as far as the documentation allows us to follow the process. Autonomy was mostly restricted, but not non-existent,

18 See, for a number of examples, Meier 2005; Mundy and Saumarez 2007, 26–28; and for this point in particular, Taylor 2011, xiii and 57.

19 For another case, see Marino and Meier 2012, 412–14.

in the dealings of village communities with the appointed agents of the state, even if we do not take into consideration the growing indebtedness of whole village communities towards these men (cf. Rafeq 1992, 325–29). Contractual arrangements about the payment of taxes were often not upheld in court (Meier 2005), as only the sultan had the power to alter tax rates and to have them entered formally into the tax registers of the province.

The position of village communities seems most disadvantageous in their relations with the endowments (*waqf*) that controlled the income of village lands. Meier (2005) has shown in several cases how changes in *waqf* legal theory and the way Ottoman judges applied it in their courts helped endowments (legal personalities in their own right) gain the upper hand over village communities. According to the documentation available, such conflicts could last for decades, and the parties faced each other in court time and again to present the same claims and counterclaims without seemingly reaching a solution. We would need more detail about the practical effects of such proceedings to be able to judge the inherent logic of such repetitions and whether they could affect the power relations between the conflicting parties.

Another area of joint liability is penal law, with respect to which available source material only very seldom allows for insights into what happened in a village. An interesting case concerns an inspection that took place in July 1728,[20] when the Chief Judge of Damascus sent a delegation to investigate the accidental death of a child in the bath of Zibdīn, a village belonging to the Ghūṭa, the oasis of Damascus. The girl, who suffered from epilepsy, had suffered an attack inside the bath and drowned in the pool when left alone by her mother, who had gone outside for a drink of water. After confirming the death to be accidental, the inspector-judge heard the declaration (*iqrār*) of the mother that nobody was responsible for the death and liable for the payment of blood money. She lists among other parties the "people of the village" (*ahālī al-qarya*).[21]

The small number of cases from a limited geographical range referred to here, does not allow for generalising about the social patterns of rural communities (see Baer 1982, 86). Yet they point to the importance of community-based politics in the eighteenth century. During the nineteenth century, however,

20 MSD 33/227/365, end of Dhū al-Qaʿda 1140. This is a document from the registers of the Series *al-Maḥākim al-sharʿiyya* of Damascus, which are stored in the Syrian National Archives, *Dār al-Wathāʾiq al-Taʾrīkhiyya*, in Damascus. The document is referred to by three numbers and the registration date: register/page/document (Hijrī date).

21 For the responsibility of corporate groups in cases of homicides etc., see Johansen 1998, 384–85.

village communities seem to become more and more invisible to the historian, with the exception of those groups that mounted resistance against taxation and conscription and those connected to important water channels. The reforms regarding taxation and new property laws related to agricultural land led to profound transformations in the countryside, weakening the role of the village community:

> Although the village and urban quarter remained the administrative unit for summation, the 1840s profits (*temettuat*) registers took the individual agricultural family estate as a unit, including its fields, animal capital and other resources. The Arab provinces were excluded from the outset, but registration was carried through for Anatolia and Rumelia between 1842 and 1844.
>
> MUNDY and SAUMAREZ 2007, 42–43

Even in the Arab provinces, from the 1860s on at least, individuation took effect: "the impetus to link the registration of taxable property to that of persons was also to mark the long nineteenth century. ... individuation of tax responsibility was in good measure to be achieved by the last decades of the empire" (Mundy and Saumarez 2007, 43).

The control of tax evaluation went to the newly established regional councils, which came to have "the final say in the government of virtually all aspects of the province" (Mundy and Saumarez 2007, 43). Hence the administrative setup on the local and provincial level changed profoundly as did the ways in which to access those who represented the state. Tax farming and the last remaining military fiefs were not actively abolished, but no new holders were appointed. The famous Land Code of 1858 rendered the exercise of collective right even more difficult:

> Thus, treating the question of village self-government as one of types of land use, the Code protects certain collective rights but provides no mechanism for legal definition of such rights, save reference to established custom, acknowledged in previous government dealings with the village.
>
> MUNDY AND SAUMAREZ 2007, 46

Under the impact of the infrastructural power of the reforming empire, village communities lost much of the limited autonomy they had held under the Ottoman *ancien régime*. New mechanisms, such as official elections, also changed established patterns of representation. From 1864, the elected *muhtars*—the one or two headmen of a village—became the most important link serving as the representative of the Ottoman bureaucracy in the province, but also as the mouthpiece of the collective village population, as is evident in many petitions concerning taxation from Ottoman Palestine in the second half of the nineteenth century (Ben-Bassat 2013, 91; cf. Baer 1982, 109–45).

For Egypt, Timothy Mitchell sees a similar process at work, for a number of corporate groups in the rural sphere:

> another process, also usually omitted from histories of private property: the incorporation or erasure of political communities that occupied the margin, neither outside nor completely within the jurisdiction of Cairo. Before the middle of the nineteenth century, most people inhabiting parts of the Nile valley beyond the immediate reach of Cairo lived in autonomous political communities referred to as tribes or emirates, and were relatively independent of the Cairene authorities. Historical sources refer to these populations as *ʿarab*, a term usually translated as "Bedouin" and used in contrast to the fellahs, the settled villagers.
>
> MITCHELL 2002, 61

3.2 *The ʿAnaza Bedouins: Incorporating Tribally Organised Mobile People During the Bureaucracy's Advance into Hitherto Uncontrolled Territories*

In contrast to villages, where the sources suggest that liabilities became increasingly individualised during the late eighteenth and early nineteenth centuries, the role of tribal collectives and tribal representatives definitely grew during the same period, as the imperial government strove to gain control over peripheral lands. This subsection will discuss the ʿAnaza tribal confederation as an example of the incorporation of new tribal groups into the Ottoman Empire during the nineteenth century. We will try to show that tribal groups merit more attention in research and that, as in the better-studied urban contexts, governance in the thinly populated arid lands of Syria was a co-production of bureaucratic government and local actors.

In order to understand the salience of the tribal category, we would like to suggest, much can be gained from a comparison between tribally and religiously defined groups. While villages become less visible, tribal and religious groups both acquire increased visibility in our sources during the Ottoman reform period. Groups of both these categories wielded considerable autonomy and both could mount credible "threat scenarios" that forced the imperial government to act. Therefore, for Ottoman administrators, they were social forces to be reckoned with, for better or worse. By extension, both categories of social groups were objects of political strategising by imperial as well as local and foreign actors.

Religious groups, and first and foremost the Christian denominations, received support from European powers. Intercommunal violence could invite foreign intervention, as for example during the Greek War of Independence and during the civil war in Mount Lebanon of 1860. Arguably the most dramatic threat scenario by the end of the nineteenth century certainly was that of Russian intervention on behalf of the Armenians in Eastern Anatolia.

The special role of *tribal* groups in the Syrian lands derived from their military potential. Some but not all of them were military forces, capable of creating social unrest and forming alliances with potent rival military powers. Perhaps the most glaring case in point was the tribal migration from the Najd region during the eighteenth century, which around 1800 partly coalesced with the Saʿūdī-Wahhābī alliance (Meier and Büssow 2012). Beginning around the same period, European powers (in particular France, Britain, and Russia) toyed with the idea of tribal groups as instruments they could put to use for increasing their influence in Ottoman territories. From around 1900 the rising number of Arab nationalists also proposed similar ideas (Schäbler 2004; Büssow 2011a, 367–68).

Among the governing elites in Istanbul, too, there was considerable hope of mobilising the potential of tribal groups in favour of the empire, as loyal subjects, taxpayers, and auxiliary forces. Perhaps the most ambitious manifestations of this vision were a number of newly founded frontier districts in the Arab provinces, for example the District of Dayr al-Zawr (Deir ez-Zor), which was established in ʿAnaza territories in the Syrian steppe in 1869, the District of Nāṣiriyya, established in co-operation with the Muntafiq tribal confederation in southern Iraq in 1870, and the Subdistrict of Biʾr al-Sabʿ (Beersheba), which was established in the Negev desert (al-Naqab) in 1900.

In more routine circumstances, tribal groups in late Ottoman Syria fulfilled another important task, namely the control of the vast steppe and desert lands east of Aleppo and Damascus, which were commonly referred to as the "open country" (*bādiya*). As administering these vast expanses of very sparsely populated land in the usual way would have been very costly, "indirect rule" (as the British later termed it) through tribal proxies was an attractive option for an empire short on manpower.[22]

Large groups of camel herders, referred to as "ʿAnaza," came to the Syrian lands as part of a general tribal migration movement from the seventeenth

22 See Herzog 2012, 287–303, for a recent reassessment of Ottoman manpower in the nineteenth century.

to the nineteenth century (Meier and Büssow 2012). Even more alarming for Istanbul, some of the ʿAnaza groups collaborated with the forces of the Wahhābīs, who threatened to conquer Damascus in 1810. The Syrian Ḥajj caravan was attacked several times in the course of these larger upheavals. The Ottoman governors and military commanders needed to cooperate with the ʿAnaza if they wanted to restore order in the region. The following process can be described as one of "incorporation," during which groups of highly mobile people were progressively "encapsulated," as it were, within increasingly formalised tribal structures. Thereby mid-level tribal units emerged as the main actors, be it as antagonists or allies of the Ottomans. The main topics in the dealings between the government and these groups were road security, including the Ḥajj routes, and taxation on the immense animal wealth.[23]

Tribal groups of mobile herders, in contrast to the villages discussed before, had the tendency to group and re-group quickly at various levels and they were difficult to incorporate into any bureaucratic state structure. Therefore, a theme to be followed through the remainder of this section is where we find tribal groups as actual corporations, according to our definition, and where they are used as mere labels in order to come to terms with the complex and often opaque reality of highly mobile people in a vast land. More specifically we need to ask who exactly was capable of joint action, who was held liable collectively in case of conflict or crime, and who had an interest in autonomy.

In a first attempt to create stability, the Ottomans established privileged relations with two pioneering groups of the ʿAnaza migration, the Ḥasana and the Wuld ʿAlī, whose shaikhly families were widely considered as being particularly "noble" by descent. Most importantly, representatives of these two groups were entrusted with safeguarding the Ḥajj caravan from Damascus. Around 1812, Shaykh Muhanna of the Ḥasana is portrayed in local sources as a sort of de facto governor of Western Syria between Aleppo and Hama (e.g., Shihābī 1969, 3:583). Shortly after this new order seemed to crystallise, the above-mentioned Wahhābī incursions brought new, much larger groups with unclear contours to the Syrian lands. The terminology in contemporary reports mirrors the confusion on the ground. One of the largest and most powerful groups among the new arrivals were known as Fadʿān (Fedʿān) to local observers and Ottoman officials, who reported clashes "between Fadʿān and ʿAnaza."[24] Shihābī, a local Arabic chronicler, writes on events in the spring of 1230/1815:

---

23 Nineteenth-century Syria might have had the largest concentration of mobile pastoralists worldwide. See Weulersse 1946, 61.

24 See BOA, HAT 444/22259, 8 Şaban 1227 / 17 August 1812; Shihābī 1969, 3:592. This is a document from the Prime Ministry Ottoman Archives, Başbakanlık Osmanlı Arşivi, in Istanbul. It belongs to the series of Hattı Hümayun.

> In this year, the Bedouins (*ʿurbān*) from the domains of Najd came to the lands of Hama.... These Bedouins are known as 'Fadʿān' and consist of scattered groups (*ṭawāʾif mutafarriqa*)—their names (*alqāb*) are 'Sbāʿa', 'Āl Haddāl', 'al-Jaryā' and 'al-Nabī'—and some of the 'Ṭawārī'. All of them stem from the Fadʿān .... They filled these domains [i.e., the Hama region] and counted around 20,000 men on horse and on foot.
>
> SHIHĀBĪ 1969, 3:607

The names of the groups enumerated by Shihābī could not be found in the classical genealogical manuals and apparently group identities were in flux. It took some more decades—until around 1850—before a clear order of names had settled in by which actors in the field—Ottoman as well as local or foreign—were able to distinguish specific groups and authorities among the ʿAnaza. The Fadʿān were now counted as one of the main ʿAnaza tribes, and the Sbāʿa, whom Shihābī mentions as a subgroup of them, appear as another. Finally, the name "Āl Haddāl" came to be identified with the leading shaikhly family of the ʿAmārāt tribe.

At the time when these structures were in place, our sources suggest that the whole set of the "mechanisms" of corporatism that we sketched out above were at work. The leading Ottoman statesman of the time, Ahmed Cevdet (1822–95), describes in his memoirs how in the 1860s a *shaykh* of the Fadʿān was appointed as a supreme Bedouin representative in the province of Aleppo:

> The shaykh received a letter of agreement (*reʾy buyuruldusu*) from the governor. He then met with the governor and was dressed in a robe of honour. Immediately afterwards, the shaykh went to the market and sat down in some place where merchants and artisans passing by would see him. From then on it was the shaykh's duty to supervise those tribes that approached the agricultural lands. As both parties were now guaranteed security, a lively commerce developed between the Bedouins who came to the city and those merchants who before had bought camels in Anatolia but now bought them in the ʿAnaza camps. The ʿAnaza shaykh levied a tax of 20 kuruş on each camel sold, in addition to the 20 kuruş which he collected on behalf of the government. This tax was then officially registered as the 'camel tax' (*deve resmi*).
>
> AHMET CEVDET 1980, 192[25]

---

25 For an original appointment letter that fits this description see BOA, İ.MVL 97/2067, 26 Cemaziyelahir 1263 / 11 June 1847, agreement between Shaykh Ghubayn and the governor of Aleppo, Mustafa Mazhar Paşa. This is a document from the Prime Ministry Ottoman Archives, Başbakanlık Osmanlı Arşivi, in Istanbul. It belongs to the correspondence of the Supreme Council for Judicial Regulations (Meclis-i Vala-yı Ahkam-ı ʿAdliye).

The performative act of installing a new Bedouin representative described here seems to illustrate well what Schlögl has called the "iconic" mode of representation. There were various Bedouin groups in the province of Aleppo. However, ʿAnaza appear here in Ahmed Cevdet's account as the "natural" representatives of all Bedouins and as guarantors of law and order. Even though the image of peace and prosperity conveyed by Ahmed Cevdet might be quite stylised in order to bolster the author's image as the efficient reformer, by the mid-nineteenth century, archival sources confirm that the political order in the Syrian steppe had stabilised. So did the tribal structure of the ʿAnaza, who from then onwards are defined as a confederation of six major tribes known as ʿAmarāt, Fedʿān, Ḥasana, Ruwalā, Sbāʿa, and Wuld ʿAlī.

By the end of the nineteenth century, the sources point to a stable system, in which political order was co-produced by government and tribal actors, leading to hybrid structures. "Aristocratic" shaikhly households received special care as "bridgeheads" of imperial rule in the "open country." Some leading *shaykhs* received government stipends and modern weapons, and some were even able to acquire title deeds for large tracts of land, according to the rules of the Ottoman Land Code of 1858. The tribal guesthouse or *maḍāfa* became a routine meeting ground for face-to-face communication between tribespeople and government officials, where representatives of local groups could bring their grievances.[26] An increasing number of Bedouins also used the telegraph network for sending petitions to Istanbul in order to seek justice directly from the central government (Ben-Bassat 2015). In parallel, an all-encompassing spatial order was devised for Syria, which rested on a conceptual separation between a zone of cultivation and settled life (*maʿmūra*), where the government was to exercise sole control over the legitimate use of violence, and the "open country" (*bādiya*), where various Bedouin tribes enjoyed special privileges. In late Ottoman administrative discourse, the *maʿmūra* was the realm of the individual landholder, the *bādiya* that of the tribal collective.

Most importantly, members of incorporated tribal collectives had the right to carry weapons and to apply customary law, and they benefitted from a simplified system of taxation. On the other hand, breaches of the order on the part of the Bedouins were to be answered by punitive military measures from the Ottoman authorities. For these purposes, tribal groups as privileged and co-liable entities had to be defined more precisely than ever before.

On the eve of the First World War, the interaction between the Ottoman bureaucracy and the ʿAnaza, which had started as a chaotic and highly conflicted situation at the end of the eighteenth century, had given rise to an assemblage or "dispositive" of heterogeneous elements, such as forts, various armed forces,

26 For observations from the turn of the twenty-first century, see Schoel 2011.

various courts of law, *maḍāfas*, telegraph lines, genealogical books, and tribal maps. Most of the above-mentioned structures of hybrid governance proved durable and were even further formalised under French colonial rule (1920–1946). Many of them lasted into the period of the Syrian revolt and civil war that began in 2011, and at least some are likely to contribute to the shaping of an eventual post-war order in Syria.

However, it is also the case that the limits of corporatism became visible during the last decades of Ottoman rule. A perennial topic in this system of governance has been what we have discussed above as the "carrying capacity" of social groups. The more Bedouin tribal groups were integrated into governance structures and transformed into vehicles of government control, the more communal autonomy came under threat. Tribal structures headed by aristocratic households lost their attractiveness and internal cohesion, and *shaykh*s of lower ranks attempted to bypass the aristocratic household and to gain direct access to the government. In other words, acceptance of corporatism "from below" was shrinking.[27] Thus, from the perspective of the Syrian arid lands, Ottoman corporatism appears to have rested on a precarious balance. The more the bureaucratic government gained "infrastructural power" in the "open country," the more it eroded the corporatist foundations on which it had established itself.

4 Conclusion

The aim of this contribution was to show that the focus on the corporate aspects of Ottoman politics yields interesting results for understanding the dynamics of the co-constitutive processes that give shape to state and society. Following the infrastructural logic manifest in the role of corporate groups in various sites allows for insights into the everyday functioning of the empire and the ever-changing relationships between various corporate and non-corporate groups.

Our findings do not confirm what is often conferred by the image of the "mosaic society," that is, the peaceful coexistence of autonomous and self-governing entities. It also questions familiar notions about the predominance

27 Our sources show traces of this process during the late Ottoman period, but it became more pronounced under European colonial rule. An inflation of *shaykh*s and shaikhly authority in the Negev after the establishment of Beersheba in 1900 is reported in Arif 1933, 42–47. For the political dynamics of an ʿAnaza group in French Syria during the 1930s, see Büssow 2011c.

of vertical ties in Middle Eastern societies. Apparently, the capability of variously constituted social groups to organise burden sharing and to balance competing interests was so attractive that the Ottoman bureaucratic government preferred to rely on these groups instead of pursuing direct control. Thus horizontal ties might have been more important than commonly assumed, and the "primacy of politics" in Middle Eastern history might be at least partly an illusion. This deserves further investigation, in particular for understanding the crucial transition from the Ottoman "old regime" to a more reform-oriented modernising state.

We would like to suggest that, on the whole, horizontal ties might have been more important in the eighteenth century than they were afterwards (and perhaps they never were more important before). Yet corporate logic did not disappear altogether in the nineteenth century and could play an important role in new contexts, such as the integration of regions hitherto nearly inaccessible to bureaucrats and their logic. A stronger emphasis on corporate groups in future research projects might complement the results of investigations into the constitution of status groups such as military, administrators, or *ʿulamāʾ*.

However, there are also limits for what corporatism can bring to Ottoman historiography. We are conscious of the fact that the government perspective implicit in our approach relegates other lines of investigation to the background and obscures the agency and autonomy of what one could call civil society. To a large extent because of the available source material, the approach we chose to discuss in this article does not make clear how historians are to grasp processes such as the shaping of public opinion and decision-making *within* social groups, be it a village, a group of mobile pastoralists, or the jeweller-goldsmiths in Istanbul.

Such questions might become particularly important with regard to religious groups, which we have excluded for the moment, only for practical reasons, not because they are not relevant (cf. Salzmann 2010). On the contrary, coming to terms with the role of corporate religious groups in local, regional, and imperial politics might help overcome the impasse encountered in many discussions of the so-called "millet system:" the idea of an organised hierarchical group that could operate through the whole empire necessitates, as we can learn from Schlögl's analysis, certain media of communication that surpass the presentist logic of face-to-face groups.

Yet, also for those seeking to understand collective action of non-state actors in the Ottoman Empire, it will be important to ask to what extent they may have been shaped by Ottoman corporatism. This is also true for the post-Ottoman Middle East, where the legacy of Ottoman-era modes of social interaction and state-building was often forgotten, negated, vilified, or romanticised.

Bibliography

Al- ʿĀrif, ʿ Ārif. 1933. *al-Qaḍāʾ bayn al-Badw*. Jerusalem: Maṭbaʿat Bayt al-Maqdis.

Atıl, Esin. 1999. *Levni and the Surname: The Story of an Eighteenth-Century Ottoman Festival*. Istanbul: Koçbank.

Baer, Gabriel. 1970. "The Administrative, Economic and Social Functions of Turkish Guilds." *International Journal of Middle East Studies* 1/1: 28–50.

Baer, Gabriel. 1982. *Fellah and Townsman in the Middle East: Studies in Social History*. London: Frank Cass.

Barkey, Karen. 2008. *Empire of Difference: The Ottomans in Comparative Perspective*. Cambridge: Cambridge University Press.

Behrens-Abouseif, Doris. 2009. "The Waqf: A Legal Personality?" In Astrid Meier, Johannes Pahlitzsch, and Lucian Reinfandt (eds.), *Islamische Stiftungen zwischen juristischer Norm und sozialer Praxis*. Berlin: Akademie Verlag, 55–60.

Ben-Bassat, Yuval. 2013. *Petitioning the Sultan: Protests and Justice in Late Ottoman Palestine, 1865–1908*. London: I.B. Tauris.

Ben-Bassat, Yuval. 2015. "Bedouin Petitions from Late Ottoman Palestine: Evaluating the Effects of Sedentarization." *Journal of the Economic and Social History of the Orient* 58: 135–62.

Büssow, Johann. 2011a. *Hamidian Palestine: Politics and Society in the District of Jerusalem, 1872–1908*. Leiden and Boston: Brill.

Büssow, Johann. 2011b. "Street Politics in Damascus: Kinship and Other Social Categories as Bases of Political Action, 1830–1841." *History of the Family* 16/2: 108–25.

Büssow, Johann. 2011c. "Negotiating the Future of a Bedouin Polity in Mandatory Syria: Internal and External Political Dynamics of the Sbaʿa-ʿAbada during the 1930s." *Nomadic Peoples* 15/1: 68–92.

Büssow, Johann, and Khaled Safi. 2013. *Damascus Affairs: Egyptian Rule in Syria through the Eyes of an Anonymous Damascene Chronicler, 1831–1840*. Würzburg: Ergon.

Cevdet Paşa, Ahmet. 1980. *Marûzât*, ed. Yusuf Halaçoğlu. Istanbul: Çağrı Yayınları.

Czada, Roland. 2011. "Corporativism (Corporatism)." In Badie, Bertrand, Dirk Berg-Schlosser, and Leonardo Morlino (eds.), *International Encyclopedia of Political Science*. London: Sage, 2: 458–63.

Demirci, Suleyman. 2001. *The Functioning of Ottoman Avariz Taxation: An Aspect of the Relationship between Centre and Periphery; a Case Study of the Province of Karaman, 1621–1700*. Durham: Durham University Press.

Demirci, Suleyman. 2003. "Complaints about Avâriz Assessment and Payment in the Avâriz-Tax System: An Aspect of the Relationship between Centre and Periphery; a Case Study of Kayseri, 1618–1700." *Journal of the Economic and Social History of the Orient* 46/4: 437–74.

Ergut, Ferdan. 2002. "Policing the Poor in the Late Ottoman Empire." *Middle East Studies* 38/2: 149–64.

Faroqhi, Suraiya. 2010. *Artisans of Empire: Crafts and Craftspeople under the Ottomans*. London and New York: I.B. Tauris.

Gibb, Hamilton A. R., and Harold Bowen. 1951. *Islamic Society and the West: A Study of the Impact of Western Civilization on Moslem Culture in the Near East*. Vol. 1: Islamic Society in the Eighteenth Century, part 1. London: Oxford University Press.

Herzog, Christoph. 2012. *Osmanische Herrschaft und Modernisierung im Irak: Die Provinz Bagdad,* 1817–1917. Bamberg: University of Bamberg Press.

Hespanha, Antonio Manuel. 2014. "The Legal Patchwork of Empires: Review of Benton, Lauren, and Richard J. Ross (eds.), *Legal Pluralism and Empires, 1500–1850*. New York: New York University Press." *Rechtsgeschichte/Legal History* 22: 303–14.

Hirschauer, Stefan. 2014. "Un/doing Difference: Die Kontingenz sozialer Zugehörigkeiten." *Zeitschrift für Soziologie* 43/3: 170–91.

Hourani, Albert. 1968. "Ottoman Reform and the Politics of Notables." In William R. Polk and Richard L. Chambers (eds.), *Beginnings of Modernization in the Middle East: The Nineteenth Century*. Chicago: University of Chicago Press, 41–68.

Hütteroth, Wolf-Dieter, and Kamal Abdulfattah. 1977. *Historical Geography of Palestine, Transjordan and Southern Syria in the Late 16th Century*. Erlangen: Selbstverlag der Fränkischen Geographischen Gesellschaft.

İslamoğlu-İnan, Huri. 1994. *State and Peasant in the Ottoman Empire: Agrarian Power Relations and Regional Economic Development in Ottoman Anatolia during the Sixteenth Century*. Leiden: Brill.

Johansen, Baber. 1996. "Échange commercial et hiérarchies sociales en droit musulman." In Hervé Bleuchot (ed.), *Les institutions traditionnelles dans le monde arabe*. Marseille: IREMAM, 19–28.

Johansen, Baber. 1999. *Contingency in a Sacred Law: Legal and Ethical Norms in the Muslim* fiqh. Leiden: Brill.

Joyce, Patrick. 2010. "What is the Social in Social History?" *Past & Present* 206/1: 213–48.

Joyce, Patrick, and Chandra Mukerji. 2017. "The State of Things: State History and Theory Reconfigured." *Theory and Society* 46/1: 1–19.

Khoury, Philipp. 1990. "The Urban Notables Paradigm Revisited." *Revue des Mondes Musulmans et de la Méditerranée* 55–56: 215–28.

Krämer, Gudrun. 2008. *A History of Palestine: From the Ottoman Conquest to the Founding of the State of Israel*. Princeton: Princeton University Press.

Krämer, Gudrun. 2014. "Der Reiz des Gesellschaftsvergleichs: Kategorien sozialer Ordnung im islamisch geprägten Vorderen Orient." In Tillmann Lohse and Benjamin Scheller (eds.), *Europa in der Welt des Mittelalters: Ein Colloquium für und mit Michael Borgolte*. Berlin: De Gruyter, 101–18.

Krämer, Gudrun. 2016. *Der Vordere Orient und Nordafrika ab 1500*. Frankfurt am Main: S. Fischer.

Kuran, Timur. 2011. *The Long Divergence: How Islamic Law Held Back the Middle East*. Princeton: Princeton University Press.

Lester, Alan. 2005. "Imperial Circuits and Networks: Geographies of the British Empire." *History Compass* 4/1: 124–41.

Mann, Michael. 1989 [1984]. "The Autonomous Power of the State: Its Origins, Mechanisms, and Results." In John A. Hall (ed.), *States in History*. Oxford and Cambridge MA: Basil Blackwell.

Marino, Brigitte, and Astrid Meier. 2012. "L'eau à Damas et dans son environnement rural au xviiie siècle." *Bulletin d'Études Orientales* 61: 363–428.

Masters, Bruce A. 1988. *Origins of Western Economic Dominance in the Middle East: Mercantilism and the Islamic Economy in Aleppo, 1600–1750*. New York: New York University Press.

Masters, Bruce A. 2004. *Christians and Jews in the Ottoman Arab World: The Roots of Sectarianism*. Cambridge: Cambridge University Press.

McGowan, Bruce. 1994. "The Age of the Ayans, 1699–1812." In Halil İnalcik and Donald Quataert (eds.), *An Economic and Social History of the Ottoman Empire, 1300–1914*. Cambridge and New York: Cambridge University Press, 637–58.

Meier, Astrid. 2011. "Bedouins in the Ottoman Juridical Field: Select Cases from Syrian Court Records, Seventeenth to Nineteenth Centuries." *Eurasian Studies* 9/1–2: 187–211.

Meier, Astrid. 2015. "Stiftungen für die Blinden im osmanischen Damaskus: Eigeninteresse und Altruismus im islamischen Stiftungswesen." In Sita von Reden (ed.), *Stiftungen zwischen Politik und Wirtschaft: Geschichte und Gegenwart im Dialog*. Berlin: De Gruyter, 95–122.

Meier, Astrid. 2016. "The Materiality of Ottoman Water Administration in Eighteenth-Century Rural Damascus: A Historian's Perspective." In Stephen McPhillips and Paul D. Wordsworth (eds.), *Landscapes of the Islamic World: Archaeology, History, and Ethnography*. Philadelphia: University of Pennsylvania Press, 19–33.

Meier, Astrid, and Johann Büssow. 2012. "ʿAnaza." *Encyclopaedia of Islam, THREE.*

Mikhail, Alan, and Christine M. Philliou. 2012. "The Ottoman Empire and the Imperial Turn." *Comparative Studies in Society and History* 54/4: 721–45.

Mitchell, Timothy. 1999. "Society, Economy, and the State Effect." In George Steinmetz (ed.), *State/Culture: State-Formation after the Cultural Turn*. Ithaca: Cornell University Press, 76–97.

Mitchell, Timothy. 2002. *Rule of Experts: Egypt, Techno-Politics, Modernity*. Berkeley: University of California Press.

Mundy, Martha, and Richard Saumarez Smith. 2007. *Governing Property, Making the Modern State: Law, Administration, and Production in Ottoman Syria*. New York: I.B. Tauris.

Ogilvie, Sheilagh. 2011. *Institutions and European Trade: Merchant Guilds, 1000–1800*. Cambridge: Cambridge University Press.

Ogilvie, Sheilagh. 2014. "The Economics of Guilds." *Journal of Economic Perspectives* 28/4: 169–92.

Rafeq, Abdul-Karim. 1992. "City and Countryside in a Traditional Setting: The Case of Damascus in the First Quarter of the Eighteenth Century." In Thomas Philipp (ed.), *The Syrian Land in the 18th and 19th Century: The Common and the Specific in the Historical Experience*. Stuttgart: Steiner, 295–332.

Rafeq, Abdul-Karim. 1999a. "Injustice and Complaint (Ẓulm wa-Shikāyet) in Mid-Nineteenth-Century Syria (The Case of the *iʿāna* Tax)." In Markus Köhbach, Gisela Procházka-Eisl, and Claudia Römer (eds.), *Acta Viennensia Ottomanica: Akten des 13. CIEPO-Symposiums vom 21. bis 25. September 1998 in Wien*. Wien: Institut für Orientalistik, 293–301.

Rafeq, Abdul-Karim. 1999b. "Relations between the Syrian "ulamāʾ" and the Ottoman State in the Eighteenth Century." *Oriente Moderno* 79, 67–95.

Reinkowski, Maurus. 2005. *Die Dinge der Ordnung: Eine vergleichende Untersuchung über die osmanische Reformpolitik im 19. Jahrhundert*. Munich: R. Oldenbourg.

Rogan, Eugene L. 1999. *Frontiers of the State in the Late Ottoman Empire: Transjordan 1850–1921*. Cambridge: Cambridge University Press.

Röhrborn, Klaus. 1978. "Konfiskation und intermediäre Gewalten im Osmanischen Reich." *Der Islam* 55/2: 345–51.

Salibi, Kamal. 1988. *A House of Many Mansions: The History of Lebanon Reconsidered*. London: I.B. Tauris.

Salvatore, Armando. 2016. *The Sociology of Islam: Knowledge, Power and Civility*. Chichester: Wiley Blackwell.

Salzmann, Ariel. 2004. *Tocqueville in the Ottoman Empire: Rival Paths to the Modern State*. Leiden: Brill.

Salzmann, Ariel. 2010. "Is There a Moral Economy of State Formation? Religious Minorities and Repertoires of Regime Integration in the Middle East and Western Europe, 600–1614." *Theory and Society* 39/3–4: 299–313.

Santillana, David. 1925–38. *Istituzioni di diritto musulmano malichita con riguardo anche al sistema sciafiita*. 2 vols. Rome: lstituto per I'Oriente.

Schäbler, Birgit. 2004. "From Urban Notables to 'Noble Arab': Shifting Discourses in the Emergence of Nationalism in the Arab East, 1910–1916." In Thomas Philipp and Christoph Schumann (eds.), *From the Syrian Land to the States of Syria and Lebanon*. Würzburg: Ergon, 175–98.

Schacht, Joseph. 1964. *An Introduction to Islamic Law*. Oxford: Oxford University Press.

Schlögl, Rudolf. 2008. "Kommunikation und Vergesellschaftung unter Anwesenden: Formen des Sozialen und ihre Transformation in der frühen Neuzeit." *Geschichte und Gesellschaft* 34: 155–224.

Schlögl, Rudolf. 2014. *Anwesende und Abwesende: Grundriss für eine Gesellschaftsgeschichte der frühen Neuzeit*. Konstanz: Konstanz University Press.

Schoel, Thorsten. 2011. "The Ḥsana's Revenge: Syrian Tribes and Politics in Their Shaykh's Story." *Nomadic Peoples* 15/1: 96–113.

Scott, James C. 1998 *Seeing Like a State: How Certain Schemes to Improve the Human Condition Have Failed.* New Haven: Yale University Press.

Serban, Carrie. 2009. *A Study of the Ottoman Guilds as They are Depicted in Turkish Miniature Paintings.* Master's thesis. Montreal: McGill University.

Shihābī, Aḥmad Ḥaydar 1969. *Ghurar al-Ḥisān fī akhbār abnā' al-zamān* = Chéhab, Émir Haidar Ahmad. *Le Liban à l'époque des Émirs Chéhab*, ed. Asad Rustum and Fouad E. Boustany, vol. 3. Beirut: Publications de l'Université Libanaise.

Sievert, Henning. 2014. "Intermediaries and Local Knowledge in a Changing Political Environment: Complaints from Libya at the Turn of the 20th Century." *Die Welt des Islams* 54/3–4: 322–62.

Singer, Amy. 1994. *Palestinian Peasants and Ottoman Officials: Rural Administration around Sixteenth-Century Jerusalem.* Cambridge: Cambridge University Press.

Sneath, David. 2007. *The Headless State: Aristocratic Orders, Kinship Society, and Misrepresentations of Nomadic Inner Asia.* New York: Columbia University Press.

Swedberg, Richard and Ola Agevall. 2016 [2005]. *The Max Weber Dictionary: Key Words and Central Concepts.* Stanford: Stanford University Press.

Tarawneh, Muhammad Salim al- [Muḥammad Salīm al-Tarāwina], *Qaḍā' Yāfā: Dirāsa idāriyya iqtiṣādiyya ijtimā'iyya, 1281–1333/1864–1914* [The Subdistrict of Jaffa: An Administrative, Economic, and Social Study, 1281–1333/1864–1914]. Amman: Wizārat al-Thaqāfa.

Taylor, Malissa A. 2011. *Fragrant Gardens and Converging Waters: Ottoman Governance in Seventeenth-Century Damascus.* PhD dissertation. University of California Berkeley: UC Berkeley Electronic Theses and Dissertations, permalink http://escholarship.org/uc/item/4f14r9vf.

Turner, Bryan S. 2014 [1978]. *Marx and the End of Orientalism.* London: Routledge.

Ursinus, Michael. 1995. "*Hane* in Kalkandelen, *Rü'us* in Selanik: Regionalspezifische Verwaltungspraktiken und -begriffe im Osmanischen Reich bis zum Beginn der *Tanzimat.*" In Hans Georg Majer and Raoul Motika (eds.), *Türkische Wirtschafts- und Sozialgeschichte von 1071 bis 1920.* Wiesbaden: Harrassowitz, 343–61.

Weber, Max. 1985^5 [1921–22]. *Wirtschaft und Gesellschaft.* Tübingen: Mohr Siebeck.

Weulersse, Jacques. 1946. *Les Paysans de Syrie et du Proche-Orient.* Paris: Gallimard.

Wilkins, Charles L. 2010. *Forging Urban Solidarities: Ottoman Aleppo 1640–1700.* Leiden: Brill.

Winter, Stefan. 2013. "Aufstieg und Niedergang des osmanischen Wüstenemirats (1536–1741): Die Mawali-Beduinen zwischen Tribalisierung und Nomadenaristokratie." *Saeculum* 63/2: 249–63.

CHAPTER 5

Family Portraits: Visual Sources for a Social History of the Late Ottoman Empire

Elke Hartmann

1 Introduction: Ottoman Photography and the "Istanbul Bias"

In recent years, there has been a growing interest in the study of photography as a topic and more generally visual materials as sources for cultural and social history.

Ottoman photography is by no means an entirely new subject. In recent years, a growing number of studies and editions of Ottoman photography that consider various aspects of the corpus have been published. Several works give overviews of the history and development of photography in the Ottoman Empire from various perspectives (Çizgen 1987; El-Hage 2007; Micklewright 2003; Özendes 2013). Others focus on the photography of architecture and the quest for modernity (Çelik and Eldem 2015; Shaw 2009). A number of the most important and influential photo studios in Istanbul have been studied in fascinating monographs (Özendes 1998; Öztuncay 1992; Öztuncay 2003). Orientalism is also a topic well studied and almost always referred to in discussions of Ottoman photography (Behdad and Gartlan 2013; Jacobson 2007; Özendes 2007; Woodward 2003).

Most of these studies focus mainly on Istanbul. Exceptions to this "Istanbul bias" (as Edhem Eldem puts it) are those albums, published in increasing numbers in recent years, which assemble historic photographs of a city, region, or population group, thus creating colourful portraits of that place or community. However, these volumes (especially those on Anatolia; see, for example, Köker 2009) are less analytical studies than photographic memorials to cities and regions, to a landscape, a life, a population structure, and a *Lebenswelt* that no longer exist. Another regional exception is Jerusalem and the Holy Land (Nassar 2006; Sheehi 2016).

2 Portrayal and Self-Portrayal in the Quest for Identity and Memory

Looking at *what* was depicted in the photographs, we can see a variety of topics and motives, which can be categorised under the notion of "portrait" in

 | DOI:10.1163/9789004386891_006

the broadest sense. One important field is, figuratively, the portraiture of landscapes and cities, and general views of various cities of the Ottoman provinces were frequent motives on postcards. For Istanbul, besides the historical monuments, the new architecture and modernisation of the city were also often documented in photography.

Portrait photography, in the narrower sense of the word, depicted families and individuals. As the art of photography itself was a novelty of the era perceived as "modern," the topics dealt with in the work of Ottoman photographers were accordingly the basic questions that were posed by the upheavals of modernity and the process of modernisation. Representation and self-representation—as either modern or in search of the place and significance of tradition in the new order—can be seen as the overarching subject of photography. The quest for identity and authenticity were expressions of this theme (Baleva 2014; Graham-Brown 1988). The photographic vehicles for this quest were portraits of the individual and family pictures.

When photography became more affordable, the processes of self-portraying and self-assertion became an issue not only for the ruling elite but for different classes and various segments of the subject populations, too. If a central aspect of modernity and modernisation was the disturbance of the traditional order and the search for a new framework—that is, a period of mobility and of accelerated change of values and norms—the same uprooting of larger parts of the population also had a spatial dimension. Photography thus became a medium for keeping the connection to the lost, be this merely the distant (with at least a theoretical hope of being reunited one day) or the past (with no hope of coming back again). Alongside the various issues of self-assertion, search for identity, and self-representation, different aspects of memory became a core dimension of photography.[1]

3 Family Portraits as Historical Sources

Considering photographs and more specifically family portraits as a source for social and cultural history does not mean that they replace other categories of sources, most of which are written sources. However, photographs can offer a

1 Of course, these observations are not restricted to photography in the Middle East, but are equally true for many other regions as different from one another as Germany and India, and thus can be generalised. For the Ottoman Empire, and more specifically the Ottoman Armenians, see Marsoobian 2015.

glimpse into various phenomena and may lead us to new aspects, questions, and problematics that can be examined in addition to textual sources.

Family portraits exist in great variety and touch on many aspects of family life. In categorising Ottoman photography, one possible dimension of analysis could be along the lines of regional and/or ethno-religious difference. Many of the recently published albums (printed or digitally published online) choose this approach and concentrate on one region, focusing on one specific community within this region.[2] This kind of photographic collection and the selection of photographs in it show one population group, often highlighting their traditional costumes, thus portraying the ethno-religious group in its specificity as a proto-national community.

4 The Houshamadyan Collection

The photo collection that serves as examplar and, accordingly, as the basis for this article concentrates on only one Ottoman population group, in this case, the Armenians in the Ottoman Empire. The collection belongs to Houshamadyan, a research project and Internet platform founded in 2010 and based in Berlin, which aims to reconstruct Ottoman Armenian everyday life and culture (Hartmann 2012; Hartmann 2014).[3] The core of this collection is photographs kept by Armenian families throughout the world, whose parents or grandparents came from the Ottoman lands. The Houshamadyan Association collects these family archives, digitises them, and makes these heretofore unpublished and until now hidden resources accessible on its online platform, www.houshamadyan.org, as well as in book publications (Hartmann, forthcoming; Tachjian 2014). By assembling the scattered family archives and bringing together fragmented pieces of collective memory, it allows for the reconstruction of a broader picture of Armenian everyday life and culture in the Ottoman Empire before the genocide. The collection of private archives is enriched by a number of photos taken from books, travelogues, magazines, journals, and newspapers of various sorts.

As the Houshamadyan collection focusses mostly on the Ottoman Armenians, the family portraits analysed and discussed in this article highlight only

2 Examples include http://www.albanianphotography.net; http://circasvoices.blogspot.de/2014/09/pascal-sebahs-ottoman-circassian.html.

3 Relevant weblinks are http://www.houshamadyan.org/en/introduction/what-is-houshamadyan.html; http://www.houshamadyan.org/en/introduction/why-houshamadyan.html).

one segment of the population of the Ottoman Empire, namely the Armenians. But in this analysis the Armenians are not viewed in their specificity as Armenians, in contrast to other Ottoman communities, highlighting possible differences produced by ethno-religious identity. Instead, the Armenians are looked at as *pars pro toto* of Ottoman society as a whole. A future study comparing Ottoman Armenian family portraits with those of Ottoman Jewish, Ottoman Greek, or different Ottoman Muslim groups may reveal differences and confessional specificities. Some of these possible connections are already touched on in this article. But by and large, the Ottoman Armenian family portraits—with the Houshamadyan collection having already grown to several thousand items—seem to give a representative overview of the different regions of the empire as well as of its different social strata. The photographs show families from the capital, Istanbul, as well as from almost all the Ottoman provinces. Among the families portrayed are wealthy families, along with those of modest means, and even the very poor. The photographs also illustrate different ways of life, different social, cultural, and political self-perceptions, and different choices of self-representation between tradition and modernity.

5 Families and Households

At first glance, differences appear in the sizes of the families portrayed. In some cases, we find photographs of nuclear families, consisting of father, mother, and two to five or six children.[4] There are photographs of only one of the parents with some but not all of the children, or only the grandfather with one child,[5] or pictures of only the male or only the female members of the family.[6] The majority of the pictures show extended families comprising three, four, or even five generations.[7]

4 Examples include ODA/Americas/Jamgochian coll., Melkon Jamgochian with family; Constantian family; ODA/Americas/Nersesian coll., family from Tadem; ODA/Turkey/Mgrdichian coll., Kltian family; ODA/Armenia/Vorperian coll., Malatya 1890s. Most of the photographs given here as examples are displayed in the ODA section (Open Digital Archive) of the Houshamadyan website. In the following references, instead of the full weblink, the region and name of collection are indicated, in accordance with the structure of the Houshamadyan website.

5 Examples include ODA/Europe/Gayda coll.

6 As in ODA/Americas/Jorge Kurkdjian coll., Dischekenian family.

7 Examples include ODA/Americas/Gloria Korkoian coll., Kurkjian family, Der Matossian family; ODA/Americas/Jamgochian coll., family in Agn; ODA/Americas/Jorge Kurkdjian coll., Kurkdjian family; cf. Lynch 1901, 2: 221; *Keghouni* 1905, 59; Kévorkian and Paboudjian 1992, 235, 368, 369, 646.

An extended family being photographed together does not necessarily mean that they lived together in one household. There certainly were occasions where the extended family would meet and have their photograph taken as a memento of that particular event. Photographs might be taken to commemorate happy gatherings, as for instance family picnics.[8] Weddings seem not to have formed such occasions, as in the Houshamadyan digital archives there is not a single wedding photograph dated before 1915 that depicts wedding parties gathering extended families or village or *mahalle* communities. Wedding photographs usually portray only the couple, as in Illustrations 5.1 and 5.2.[9]

Obviously, there are many differences, according to region, social class, and rural vs. urban populations, as well as among the various religious communities. The photographs point to this topic, for which only further research will provide more details.

Probably the most important genre of family photographs showing extended families and the one with the most examples is the post-mortem photograph. Bahattin Öztuncay claims that post-mortem photographs, although a common feature in America and Europe, were "very rare" in the Ottoman Empire. "If portraits of living people were frowned upon by conservative Muslims, photographs of the deceased were nearly impossible," he explains, continuing, "the Ottoman post-mortem photographs that have survived are of non-Muslims. The rarity even of these indicates that Western-style post-mortem photographs were also in little demand in the Greek, Armenian, and Jewish communities" (Öztuncay 2015, 99).

While I cannot offer any generalisations about the Ottoman Greeks or Jews on the basis of the collection at my disposal, it seems to be true, at least for the Armenian community in the Ottoman Empire, that post-mortem and funeral photographs were taken by many Ottoman Armenian families throughout the empire. The Houshamadyan collection contains many examples, such as that shown in Illustration 5.3 (ODA/Americas/Toumadjan coll., post-mortem Mahdesi Avedis Toumadjan ca. 1895).[10] These photographs were enactments.

8 Examples include ODA/Europe/Shukurian coll., the Atamian and Erkeletian families at a picnic in Nevşehir, probably right after World War I.

9 Other wedding photographs include ODA/Americas/Miscellaneous USA, Kaboulian/Najarian, Masoumian/Kaboulian; ODA/Americas/Arslanian (Kazanjian) coll., Berberian/Arakelian; ODA/Americas/Kasabach/Getoor coll., Arshalous and Yervant Kasabashian.

10 Other examples of post-mortem photographs include ODA/Europe/Andreassian coll., funeral in Sivas 1910; funeral of Vartouhi Andreassian, née Achbayan, in Sivas (before 1913); funeral of Meridjan Ansourian in Sivas, 1923; funeral around 1890; funeral of Anna Zallakian, Sivas, probably 1920/21; ODA/Americas/Miscellaneous USA, child burial in Agn ca. 1910; ODA/Europe/Miscellaneous France, Kavedjian coll., Djknavorian funeral, Ordu, 1905 or 1906; Khatchig Vartian's funeral in Ordu 1913; and others.

ILLUSTRATION 5.1 Wedding photograph of Boghos Kaboulian and Rebecca Najarian, Agn/Eğin, ca. 1898.
KABOULIAN COLL., USA / HOUSHAMADYAN.

ILLUSTRATION 5.2 Wedding photograph of Arshalous Kasabashian (born Shahabian) and Yervant Kasabashian, Shabin-Karahisar, 1908.
KASABACH AND GETOOR COLL., SOUTHFIELD, MI, USA / HOUSHAMADYAN.

ILLUSTRATION 5.3 The post-mortem photograph of Mahdesi Avedis Toumajan, Gürün.
TOUMAJAN COLL., SOUTHFIELD, MI, USA / HOUSHAMADYAN.

The deceased is placed either in his/her coffin or seated on a chair. In the latter case, he or she would be dressed in clothing that displayed, where applicable, insignia of rank and honour (cf. Boghosian 1998, 2:250–51: The post-mortem photograph of Hagop Shahinian, deputy of Sivas in the first Ottoman parliament, taken in Sivas in 1898). The members of the family and household are placed around the deceased, bowing their heads to the dead father or mother in visible grief, sometimes in a lamenting pose.

The number of persons and generations assembled for these family portraits commemorating special occasions leads one to think about the size of the household. The photographs of a nuclear family or of only one parent with child are almost exclusively from Istanbul or one of the more important urban centres and show wealthy families in Western style (cf. the examples given above). In contrast, most of the family portraits from the provinces depict three (or even more) generations, possibly uniting several nuclear families in one household. Demographic studies usually assume an average household size of five persons (Quataert 1994, 785). Yet there are hints that suggest we might consider the Ottoman and more specifically the Ottoman Armenian household as a social unit comprising several nuclear families, presumably made up of the *pater familias* and his wife with their children, including their married sons with their wives and children, all sharing one table and a family business. So far, we lack a substantial study on households, which would include information on the size of households and the household's relation to living patterns and economic situations, as well as probable differences between the various communities in the Eastern Anatolian provinces (for mainly Western Anatolia, see Duben 1985; for Ottoman Palestine, Schmelz 1990; and the Arab provinces, Doumani 2003). For this question, family photographs certainly cannot provide any solid answers, but at least they hint at an area of inquiry that merits further study, if we are to understand the family and household in late Ottoman society as the nucleus of social structure, possibly varying among the religious communities of the empire.

Another clue to the number of members in a family comes from one of the most common items carried by Armenian genocide survivors to their places of refuge: a set of wooden spoons with a ladle. This set would usually hang at the entrance to the family home, with the number of spoons corresponding to the members of the household and the ladle representing the *pater familias,* which he would use for distributing food to the family.[11] Many of the spoon sets from the Ottoman eastern provinces now kept and displayed in the Armenian State Museum of Ethnography (Sardarabad) and the History Museum of Armenia (Yerevan) in today's Republic of Armenia represent family units of eight to ten persons, rather than the assumed average of five.

Much more informative than this rather assumptive observation are remarks that allude to the possibly different sizes of Armenian and Muslim households in the (eastern) provinces, comments that were put forth as part of an argument in the debate on extending the military draft to non-Muslims in 1909. The recruitment laws allowed exemptions for draftees who were the sole breadwinners of their families. Armenian commentators complained that this regulation applied mostly to Muslim households consisting of only the nuclear family, whereas the Armenians (and more generally the Christians) tended to live in larger households of extended families, where there would always be another male breadwinner to step in for the drafted soldier (Kalpakdjian 1909, 1).

---

11 Personal communication, Svetlana Poghosyan, Scientific Vice-Director of the Armenian State Museum of Ethnography, Sardarabad, 11 July 2013; also Marutyan 2001, 107–9.

6 Clothing, Habitus, and Pose

Probably the most fruitful field for the analysis of family portraits is the aspect of social, cultural, and to a certain extent also political placement alluded to through habitus and pose, clothing and accessories. As these photographs are certainly not naturalistic depictions of any reality, but rather carefully arranged stagings, they tell us how the portrayed family and each of its members depicted themselves and wanted to be seen. They tell us about self-perceptions, but also about expectations. Thus, they indirectly reveal a mentality and a way of life.

Photographic portraits of families show particularly clearly the range of possibilities for social, cultural, and political self-locating that was available through dress and the types of differences that could emerge, even among the generations and genders within a single family. In one exposure of an Armenian family from Agn (Eğin), on the plains of Kharpert (Harput), we encounter several generations and a variety of styles of dress (Illustration 5.4, ODA/Americas/Jamgotchian coll.).

ILLUSTRATION 5.4 Armenian family from Agn/Eğin.
JAMGOCHIAN COLL., USA / HOUSHAMADYAN.

The representatives of the oldest and youngest generations—the elderly couple sitting in the middle of the picture (first generation), the small child in the grandfather's lap and the two boys sitting in the front row—are dressed the most traditionally. The child held in the lap wears a dress of the light and dark striped material (called *manusa*), which was widespread throughout the entire region. The old patriarch and his two grandsons in the front of the picture wear *entaris* (tunics) with sashes, slippers, and half-length coats. The headgear of the old man is a fez, which was the head-covering that became obligatory for Ottoman officials in 1829 through the Tanzimat reforms and first spread through the realm following these measures (Quataert 1997, 403). Together with the fez, a European-style frock coat became the standard attire of the modernist state officials and citizens. In the photograph, we see the three sons, who stand behind their parents, wearing these so-called "Stambuli" jackets, together with fezzes. The mother's fur-trimmed coat and the fabric and rich embroideries of the dresses worn by the younger women attest to a certain level of affluence.

Just as the husband's and sons' fezzes betray association with the world of the state bureaucracy, the wife's fur-trimmed coat, besides indicating wealth, signals contact with the world of the merchants who moved between Anatolia and its eastern neighbours.[12] Coats of the same type can be seen in other photographs, either worn by long-distance traders and rich merchants or by urban dignitaries, among whom, in turn, the most affluent merchants of the city often numbered; they appeared as philanthropic patrons and were elected to the newly created political committees during the reform period.[13]

In contrast to his father, the eldest son, who sits with his wife next to his parents, wears narrow-fitting pants instead of pantaloons, or *entari,* and a European-style waistcoat and jacket, covering his head with a fez. Unlike his mother, who is dressed in fully traditional garb, including a colourfully striped and patterned sash, his wife's dress (as the dresses of all the younger female members of the family) reveals European influence. What appears here to be "European"—in contrast to the classic Western Armenian costume—are the materials and cuts; these became integrated into the traditional dress in

12 On the regional distribution and the social connotations of this type of coat, see Badrig 1967, 43, 33–34, 39, plates 67, 39 and 53; for examples of patterns, see Avakian 1983, 46, also cf. the photographs in the appendix, figs. 33, 31a and b; on the large trading routes through Armenia and their significance for traditional dress, see Avakian 1983, 18.

13 Cf., for example, the images in Kévorkian and Paboudjian 1992, 212 (long-distance traders from Sivri-Hisar), and 525 (the Patriarch of Constantinople and later the Catholicos of the Armenian Apostolic Church) Khrimian Hayrig, with notables from Van. A prosopographical study of the Armenian deputies in the first Ottoman parliament of 1877–78 as a case study for the Armenian provincial notables is provided in Hartmann 2010.

Eastern Armenian areas (and later also clearly in a few regions of Western Armenia) over the course of the nineteenth century (Avakian 1983, 25, and figs. 11a and b). The family is photographed in front of a wall of the house that was decked with carpets and curtains. Other pictures exhibit background arrangements, which instead of carpets—or perhaps combined with them—present European furnishings, very frequently end tables and floor clocks (e.g. Kévorkian and Paboudjian 1992, 212, 261; Boghosian 1998, 2:250, 251; Yarman 2001, 63).

Illustration 5.5 provides an example, where the choice of traditional garb or European-style costume not only differs among the generations but also according to gender within the same generation, contrasting the modern suit of the head of the family to the attire of his wife. In another Armenian family portrait, taken in 1913 by the French traveller Thérèse Roussel, the head of the family can be seen in a European three-piece suit, leather shoes, and fez; the women of the family wear headscarves and chin-veils with their plain, everyday wear, and one of the small children also wears a traditional head-covering (*Le Tour du Monde* 1913, 550). In yet another portrait of an urban

ILLUSTRATION 5.5 The Kurkjian family, ca. 1901, Eğin/Agn or Erzincan/Yerznga.
GLORIA KORKOIAN COLL., DEARBORN, MI, USA / HOUSHAMADYAN.

family from Southern Armenia we see the reverse setting. The father is presented in a traditional striped tunic with a sash, half-length coat, and fez, his sons can be recognised as pupils, while his wife and daughter wear European clothing, although the daughter has put on an elaborately crafted silver belt (Kévorkian and Paboudjian 1992, 62).

Another family, this one from the region of Sebastia (Sivas), demonstrates its status and position in exactly the opposite way (Kévorkian and Paboudjian 1992, 235). European furnishings can be discerned in the background of the picture. The family's small son, who stands at the edge of the photo slightly offset from the rest of the family, holds his school book under his arm and wears a typical school uniform. The book indicates his status as a pupil in a modern school, an element that can be found in many family photos, as in the portrait of the Der Matossian family shown in Illustration 5.6.[14] To return to the photo of the family from Sebastia, with the exception of the child in the school uniform, the entire family wears the traditional dress of the region, clearly made from expensive fabric. Everyone, including the small children, wears shoes. The men's pants are made of goat hair, fashioned through a special weaving technique (Shwartz-Be'eri 2000, 67–139). The sophisticated process of production appears to have elevated this article of clothing to an identifying status symbol for the rural elite of the Armenian highlands and Kurdistan. One illustrative example is a picture of Musa Bey, one of the most powerful Kurdish tribal chiefs in the region of Muş. In 1889, he was sued for robbery and abduction. The first process against him was held at the provincial court. But because the kidnapped girl, an Armenian named Gülizar, had established contact with British missionaries, who spread news of her fate as a story of martyrdom and resistance, her case soon became an international sensation and was dealt with in another court case in Istanbul (Şaşmaz 2003; Der Garabedian (Kevonian) 1946; Kévonian 2005). During this process both sides, Gülizar and Musa Bey, published postcards with their portraits for propaganda and to cover some of the expenses. Musa Bey let himself be photographed in a newly fabricated finely woven goat hair suit, indicating his wealth and status.

Musa Bey's dress can be traced back to the traditional clothing of the region. The quality of the workmanship evident in the garments in these photographs from the late nineteenth and early twentieth centuries suggests these clothes were worn on special festive occasions—especially so since at this time cheap,

14 Other examples showing children holding school books include ODA/Americas/Piranian coll., Piranian family in 1914; Kévorkian and Paboudjian 1992, 235, 496.

ILLUSTRATION 5.6 The Der Matossian family, Keghi, before 1912.
PHOTOGRAPHER: SAMUEL H. SRABIAN (ODA/AMERICAS/GLORIA KORKOIAN COLL., DEARBORN, MI, USA / HOUSHAMADYAN).

factory-made fabrics were also widely available in the provinces.[15] Accordingly, people can be seen in such finely fashioned traditional clothing especially

15 The Ottoman-English trade agreement of 1838 created a caesura, which opened the Ottoman market to English industrial goods (Shaw and Kural Shaw 1977, 2:122; Quataert 1993, 92–104).

in photos from weddings and other large celebrations (e.g. Kévorkian and Paboudjian 1992, 481). Another occasion for this sort of clothing might be to display the splendid regional dress for the cameras of European travellers. How much this costume could become part of a museum-like exhibition is demonstrated by the portrayal of a group of woodworkers from Shadakh, who carry out their work in entirely pristine—and thus recognisable as new—splendid costume (Kévorkian and Paboudjian 1992, 553).

7 Communicating with the Outside World

As is clear from these few examples, an abundance of social historical information can be read from the details of clothing. Nevertheless, there is still much research to be done. The entire range of social and cultural historical information that is transmitted through dress is revealed only if one can know an entire series of elements. One must be able to recognise the details of the production techniques and the fabrics and other materials utilised in articles of clothing, and thus be able to infer their value. One must have detailed knowledge of the regional distribution of certain fabrics and patterns as well as their use by certain groups (ethnic-religious, social, professional, etc.). One needs to be able to decipher the messages about status, prestige, function, and also confession that certain colours, patterns, or articles of clothing can convey. In short, one must be able to read the entire set of meanings that were inherent in the multifaceted clothing of the Ottoman Empire, which were familiar to contemporaries, and through which they could orient themselves.[16]

16 The ethnographic works on Armenian dress, above all Badrig 1967, provide a good orientation. Badrig's richly illustrated album gives a historical overview of Armenian dress from antiquity to modernity, with a subsequent overview of the different regions, based on ethnographic studies since the nineteenth century as well as the material found in the "memory books" (*houshamadyan*), which were compiled in exile by survivors of the genocide for many of the lost regions, cities, towns, and even villages. An addition to Badrig's album is the study by Avakian 1983. Even if restricted to the nineteenth and early twentieth centuries, it is the most important recent publication on the topic. It distinguishes five larger regions within the Armenian world, describes in detail the different fabrics and their production, with many drawings and photographs of the different articles of clothing (as individual components of the costume), their cuts, colours and patterns, head-coverings, stockings and shoes, as well as ornamentation and jewellery, and finally it ends with an extensive glossary that also comprises the different regional meanings of the terms. See also *Badgerakirk Haygagan Daraznerou* n.d. [1988], and Poghosyan 2001. There are also works on the clothing of the Ottoman Empire in general. To start, the dictionary by Koçu 1967 is useful, providing an overview of the technical terms and also the fabrics, manners of processing, patterns, etc. Some information on the different textiles and their quality can be gleaned from the already cited work by Quataert 1993; cf. additionally the

From an analytical perspective, one has to consider two additional factors. First, it is important to keep in mind that in addition to its capacity for conveying meaning within Ottoman society, clothing was also one of the most important media for communication with the world beyond Ottoman borders. This is especially true with respect to photography. At the Vienna World's Fair of 1873, the Ottoman Empire presented itself by exhibiting its regional, ethnic, and religious diversity, conceived of as diversity in unity, which was held together—and above all made possible—by the umbrella of the Ottoman state. The catalogue of this Ottoman contribution to the exhibition was published as a large-format, illustrated book (Hamdi Bey and de Launay 1873). This self-portrayal was visually translated as a photographic exhibition of costumes, in which all the different types of inhabitants of the empire were placed side by side. In many cases, the different groups encountered one another in real life either extremely rarely or mostly through conflict, as would have been the case, for instance, with the Armenian monk from the island of Akhtamar, in Lake Van, who is shown framed left and right by two Kurdish warriors (Hamdi Bey and de Launay 1873, 320). The example of the Ottoman costume album of 1873 reveals the strong suitability of clothing—and even more so of the photographic portraits of selected costumes—for transmitting very complex connections between political, social, and cultural living conditions and identities in ways that both simplify and seem directly evident.

The European travellers who visited the Ottoman provinces in growing numbers were greatly interested in "originality," and thus in the celebrations, customs, and clothing of the indigenous peoples. Part of this curiosity may be rooted in the nineteenth-century European Christian and missionary interest in life in the lands of the Bible and Paradise. It may have arisen from the European fascination, dating from the age of Enlightenment, with the ancient Eastern civilisations. It may also have been imbued by colonialist inclinations and

likewise already mentioned compilation by Faroqhi and Neumann 2004, and Gürtuna 1999. In general, it can be asserted that the clothing of the elites is better researched than that of the "simple people," and that the east—as is true for many other areas of Ottoman research—remains hazy in comparison with the west of the country, meaning that much less is known about the clothing and its social connotations for the provinces than for the capital, Istanbul. What is still lacking, according to my knowledge, is a study that compares the clothing of the different groups of people within a given region (cf. however, the perspective that Badrig provides by contrasting Armenian dress with a panorama of types worn by the neighbouring peoples in Central Asia; Badrig 1967, table 82).

prejudices in search of presumed Ottoman, Oriental, or Muslim backwardness. However that may be, the European travellers' presence and interest made them a simultaneously unexpected and important mouthpiece for the inhabitants of the provinces in communicating their often-difficult situations—which was especially the case for the Armenians in the Eastern Anatolian highlands. The countless pictures in European travel literature showing the misery of the villagers are also to be understood in this context as what Martin Schulze Wessel and Jörg Requate have described as an "appeal to Europe" (Schulze Wessel and Requate 2002), be that for political or charitable assistance.

As much as the postures of the photographed villagers appear at times posed to solicit pity, their rags and bare feet nonetheless also greatly attest to a reality excluded from the portraits of the photo studios (e.g. Kévorkian and Paboudjian 1992, 486, 490, 491, 492, etc.). Even though photography became affordable for increasing numbers of social classes, the family portrait still remained a status symbol of the better situated city-dwellers. Furthermore, the clothing with which those being photographed enacted a vision of themselves and gave expression to their self-positioning remained for most village inhabitants an unaffordable luxury. Western Armenia had experienced a period of increasing uncertainty and daily violence since the 1840s. The ravages of the Russian-Ottoman war left entire tracts of land barren and uprooted hundreds of thousands of Armenian farmers. The fields lay fallow, and the lost harvests meant a series of local famines in the 1880s. The increasing social tension finally erupted in the 1890s in the empire-wide massacres of Armenians, in which adult men were disproportionally targeted, leaving many families without their breadwinners (Hartmann 2013). Poverty and oppression were also experienced by many Muslims. Many of the Muslims who had fled the Caucasus and the Balkan countries were settled in the Ottoman provinces without any basis whatsoever for earning a livelihood. Many of the settled Kurds were just as exposed to the attacks of the armed tribes as the Armenians were. The rags worn by these farmers suggest the original form of the traditional clothing. They do not, however, reveal clues to any kind of lifestyle, belonging, or attitude, but attest solely to the misery and daily fight for survival of their wearers. The possibility of expressing oneself through clothing is reserved for those who can afford to choose their dress and costume.

In sum, family portraits and photographic depictions of town and village life in the Ottoman provinces have much more potential than being mere illustrations of what we learn from textual sources. They can replenish our knowledge, especially when used in microhistorical studies, and can inspire our research.

Bibliography

(all cited websites accessed 20 December 2017)

Avakian, Nazig. 1983. *Haygagan Joghovrtagan Daraze (XIX t.–XX t. sgizp)* ["Armenian Popular Costume, 19th Century—Beginning of 20th Century"]. Yerevan: Haygagan SSH KA hrad.

Badgerakirk Haygagan Daraznerou ["Album of Armenian Costumes"]. n.d. [1988]. Beirut: Hamazkayin Vahe Sethian Dbaran.

Badrig, Arakel. 1967. *Haygagan Daraz. Hnakuyn Jamanagnerits Mintchev Mer Orere* ["Armenian Costume. From Ancient Times to Our Days"]. Yerevan: Haygagan SSH KA hrad.

Baleva, Martina. 2014. "Revolution in the Darkroom: Nineteenth-Century Portrait Photography as a Visual Discourse of Authenticity in Historiography." *Hungarian Historical Review* 3/2: 363–90.

Behdad, Ali, and Luke Gartlan (eds.). 2013. *Photography's Orientalism: New Essays on Colonial Representation*. Los Angeles: Getty Research Institute.

Boghosian, Sarkis. 1998. *Iconographie Arménienne*. 2 vols. Paris: Boghosian.

Çelik, Zeynep, and Edhem Eldem (eds.). 2015. *Camera Ottomana: Photography and Modernity in the Ottoman Empire 1840–1914*. Istanbul: Koç University Press.

Çizgen, Engin. 1987. *Photography in the Ottoman Empire 1839–1919*. Istanbul: Haşet Kitabevi.

Der Garabedian (Kevonian), Armenouhi. 1946. *Giulizar*. Paris: Imp. A. Der Hagopian.

Doumani, Beshara (ed.). 2003. *Family History in the Middle East: Household, Property, and Gender*. Albany: State University of New York Press.

Duben, Alan. 1985. "Turkish Families and Households in Historical Perspective." *Journal of Family and History* 10/1: 75–97.

El-Hage, Badr. 2007. "Les Armeniéns et la photographie au Proche-Orient." In Mona Khazindar, Djamila Chakour, and Philippe Monsel (eds.), *L'Orient des photographes Arméniens*. Paris: Institut du Monde Arabe, 11–19.

Faroqhi, Suraiya, and Christoph K. Neumann (eds.). 2004. *Ottoman Costumes: From Textile to Identity*. Istanbul: Eren.

Graham-Brown, Sarah. 1988. *Images of Women: The Portrayal of Women in Photography of the Middle East 1860–1950*. London: Quartet Books.

Gürtuna, Sevgi. 1999. *Osmanlı Kadın Giysisi*. Ankara: Kültür Bakanlığı.

Hamdi Bey, Osman, and [Victor] Marie de Launay. 1873. *Les costumes populaires de la Turquie en 1873 (Elbise-i Osmaniyye)*. Constantinople: Imprimerie du "Levant Times & Shipping Gazette." Reprint 1999, Istanbul: Sabanci Univ. Press.

Hartmann, Elke. 2010. "The 'Loyal Nation' and Its Deputies: The Armenians in the First Ottoman Parliament." In Christoph Herzog and Malek Sharif (eds.), *The First Ottoman Experiment in Democracy*. Würzburg: Ergon, 187–222.

Hartmann, Elke. 2012. "Houshamadyan Projesi: Osmanlı Ermenilerinin Tarihine Yeni Bir Yaklaşım." *Toplumsal Tarih* 222: 8–10.

Hartmann, Elke. 2013. "The Central State in the Borderlands: Ottoman Eastern Anatolia in the Late Nineteenth Century." In Omer Bartov and Eric D. Weitz (eds.), *Shatterzone of Empires: Coexistence and Violence in the German, Habsburg, Russian, and Ottoman Borderlands*. Bloomington: Indiana University Press, 172–90.

Hartmann, Elke. 2014. "Das Projekt Houshamadyan—ein virtuelles Erinnerungsbuch." In Corry Guttstadt (ed.), *Wege ohne Heimkehr: Die Armenier, der Erste Weltkrieg und die Folgen*. Berlin and Hamburg: Assoziation A, 197–99.

Hartmann, Elke (ed.). Forthcoming. *Ottoman Armenians: Life, Culture, Society*. Vol. 2. Berlin: Houshamadyan.

http://www.albanianphotography.net.

http://circasvoices.blogspot.de/2014/09/pascal-sebahs-ottoman-circassian.html.

http://www.houshamadyan.org/en/introduction/what-is-houshamadyan.html.

http://www.houshamadyan.org/en/introduction/why-houshamadyan.html.

http://www.houshamadyan.org/en/oda/.

Jacobson, Ken. 2007. *Odalisques and Arabesques: Orientalist Photography 1839–1925*. London: Bernard Quaritch Ltd.

Kalpakdjian, A. 1909. "Votch-Islamnerou Zinvorakroutian Shourtch." *Jamanag* 09 October, 24. N. 1327: 1.

Keghouni. 1905. (An Armenian-language review edited by the Mekhitarists of San Lazzaro/Venice.).

Kévonian, Arménouhie. 2005. *Les noces noires de Gulizar*. Trans. Jacques Mouradian. Marseille: Éditions Parenthèses.

Kévorkian, Raymond H., and Paul B. Paboudjian. 1992. *Les Arméniens dans l'Empire Ottoman à la veille du genocide*. Paris: ARHIS.

Koçu, Reşad Ekrem. 1967. *Türk Giyim, Kuşam ve Süslenme Sözlüğü*. Ankara: Sümerbank Kültür Yay.

Köker, Osman (ed.). 2009. *Orlando Carlo Calumeno Koleksiyonu'ndan Kartpostallar ve Vital Cuinet'nin İstatistikleri ve Anlatımlarıyla Bir Zamanlar Izmir*. Istanbul: Birzamanlar Yay.

Le Tour du Monde. 1913. (French travel magazine.).

Lynch, Harry F.B. 1901. *Armenia: Travels and Studies*. 2 vols. London: Longmans, Green and Co.

Marsoobian, Armen T. 2015. *Fragments of a Lost Homeland: Remembering Armenia*. London: I.B. Tauris.

Marutyan, Harutyun. 2001. "Wood." In Levon Abrahamian and Nancy Sweezy (eds.), *Armenian Folk Arts, Culture, and Identity*. Bloomington and Indianapolis: Indiana University Press, 101–12.

Micklewright, Nancy. 2003. "Late Ottoman Photography: Family, Home, and New Identities." In Relli Shechter (ed.), *Transitions in Domestic Consumption and Family*

Life in the Modern Middle East: Houses in Motion. New York: Palgrave Macmillan, 65–83.

Nassar, Issam. 2006. "Familial Snapshots: Representing Palestine in the Work of the First Local Photographers." *History & Memory* 18/2: 139–55.

Özendes, Engin. 1998. *Abdullah Frères: Ottoman Court Photographers*. Istanbul: Yapı Kredi Publications.

Özendes, Engin. 2007. *From Sébah & Joaillier to Foto Sabah: Orientalism in Photography*. Istanbul: Yapı Kredi Publications.

Özendes, Engin. 2013. *Photography in the Ottoman Empire 1839–1923*. Istanbul: YEM Yay.

Öztuncay, Bahattin. 1992. *James Robertson: Pioneer of Photography in the Ottoman Empire*. Istanbul: Eren.

Öztuncay, Bahattin. 2003. *The Photographers of Constantinople: Pioneers, Studios and Artists from 19th Century Istanbul*. Istanbul: Aygaz.

Öztuncay, Bahattin. 2015. "The Origins and Development of Photography in Istanbul." In Zeynep Çelik and Edhem Eldem (eds.), *Camera Ottomana: Photography and Modernity in the Ottoman Empire 1840–1914*. Istanbul: Koç University Press, 66–105.

Poghosyan, Svetlana. 2001. "Costume." In Levon Abrahamian and Nancy Sweezy (eds.), *Armenian Folk Arts, Culture, and Identity*. Bloomington and Indianapolis: Indiana University Press, 177–93.

Quataert, Donald. 1993. *Ottoman Manufacturing in the Age of the Industrial Revolution*. Cambridge: Cambridge University Press, 92–104.

Quataert, Donald. 1994. "The Age of Reforms, 1812–1914." In Halil İnalcık and Donald Quataert (eds.), *An Economic and Social History of the Ottoman Empire*. Cambridge: Cambridge University Press, 2: 759–943.

Quataert, Donald. 1997. "Clothing Laws, State, and Society in the Ottoman Empire, 1720–1829." *International Journal of Middle East Studies* 29/3: 403–25.

Şaşmaz, Musa. 2003. *Kürt Musa Bey Olayı (1883–1890)*. Istanbul: Kitabevi.

Schmelz, U.O. 1990. "Population Characteristics of Jerusalem and Hebron Regions according to Ottoman Census of 1905." In Gad G. Gilbar (ed.), *Ottoman Palestine, 1800–1914*. Leiden: E.J. Brill, 15–67.

Schulze Wessel, Martin, and Jörg Requate (eds.). 2002. *Europäische Öffentlichkeit: Transnationale Kommunikation seit dem 18. Jahrhundert*. Frankfurt am Main: Campus.

Shaw, Stanford J., and Ezel Kural Shaw. 1977. Reprint 2002. *History of the Ottoman Empire and Modern Turkey*, vol. 2, *Reform, Revolution, and Republic: The Rise of Modern Turkey 1808–1975*. Cambridge: Cambridge University Press.

Shaw, Wendy M.K. 2009. "Ottoman Photography of the Late Nineteenth Century: An 'Innocent' Modernism?" *History of Photography* 33/1: 80–93.

Sheehi, Stephen. 2016. *The Arab Imago: A Social History of Portrait Photography, 1860–1910*. Princeton: Princeton University Press.

Shwartz-Be'eri, Ora. 2000 (first published in Hebrew, 1981). *The Jews of Kurdistan: Daily Life, Customs, Arts and Crafts*. Jerusalem: The Israel Museum, 2000.

Sweezy, Nancy, and Levon Abrahamian (eds.). 2001. *Armenian Folk Arts, Culture, and Identity*. Bloomington and Indianapolis: Indiana University Press.

Tachjian, Vahé (ed.). 2014. *Ottoman Armenians: Life, Culture, Society*. Vol. 1. Berlin: Houshamadyan.

Woodward, Michelle L. 2003. "Between Orientalist Clichés and Images of Modernization: Photographic Practice in the Late Ottoman Era." *History of Photography* 27/4: 363–74.

Yarman, Arsen. 2001. *Osmanlı Sağlık Hizmetlerinde Ermeniler ve Surp Pırgiç Ermeni Hastanesi Tarihi*. Istanbul: Surp Pırgiç Ermeni Hastansi Vakfı.

CHAPTER 6

The Position of Philosophy in the Late Ottoman Educational Reforms

M. Sait Özervarlı

The close relationship between novelty and continuity is usually difficult to identify, as it is often easier to categorise historical developments in a dichotomous way. The Ottoman Empire, with its long history in the pre-modern past, experienced one of the most complex and intertwined modernisation processes of the nineteenth century. The transition was long and meandering, accompanied by multi-faceted differences of opinion and disputes arising from the tension between the centuries-old institutions and practices on the one side, and, on the other, the need for change under the pressure of modernisation and reforms.

Educational institutions, along with other administrative structures, were at the centre of this wide-ranging transition process. Although initially established to teach Islamic jurisprudence along with Qur'ānic exegesis, Prophetic traditions, and Arabic language, the classical learning institution, or *madrasa*, in its historical stages also offered various sorts of instruction at varying levels in philosophy, logic, and the sciences, such as mathematics and astronomy. Over the course of history at various times, Ottoman *madrasa*s also showed interest in what was called the rational philosophical sciences (*akli ilimler*). However, with the rapid establishment of modern institutions and the need to train students for employment within the modernising state structure (Findley 1980, 62), in the second half of the nineteenth century *madrasa*s had to share their unique central position as institutions of learning with modern institutions that increasingly attracted young students and their families. These new circumstances created significant changes in the Ottoman educational system and resulted in two educational systems functioning in parallel throughout the century.

By the end of the eighteenth century, Ottoman administrators had already begun to demonstrate an interest in modern European institutions of higher learning and this interest gradually grew, mainly through the official commitment to adapting new science and technology. Following major modernisation attempts in the military, the first modern educational institution, the Imperial

 | DOI:10.1163/9789004386891_007

School of Naval Engineering (Muhendishane-i Bahr-i Hümayun), was founded in 1773, with the aid of the French military expert of Hungarian origin, François Baron de Tott (1733–93). Gelenbevi İsmail Efendi (1730–91), who combined traditional and modern sciences, taught mathematics there (Hitzel 1995, 813–26). In the last decade of the eighteenth century, Selim III (r. 1789–1807) initiated a reform programme called the New Order (Nizam-i Cedid) and established new administrative and military units. In 1795, the second engineering school, the Imperial School of Terrestrial Engineering (Mühendishane-i Berr-i Humayun), was founded. Sultan Mahmud II (r. 1808–39) continued the reform project and led the empire to the Tanzimat period (1839–76), which is perceived as the turning point in a decisive move towards modernisation. The difficult task of understanding, translating, and interpreting modern thought in a period of political and cultural transformation led the Tanzimat leaders to initiate some significant reform attempts in higher education, a process that was both caused and accelerated by the state reorganisation programme. The demand for modernisation was triggered by the increasing number of travelers from the empire to Western European countries, the establishment of new institutions and schools, and the growing interest in modern science and thought, among other cultural factors. State officials increasingly felt the need to bring about urgent changes in the Ottoman educational system and other administrative institutions.[1]

The abolition of the resisting forces of the Janissary Corps in 1826 and the publication of the first Ottoman weekly and official gazette, *Takvim-i Vekayi* ("The Calendar of Events"), in 1831 provided a major contribution to the gradual implementation of such state reforms. In addition to the previously established engineering schools, the sultan established higher-level schools of military science (1834), music (1836), judiciary studies (1838), medicine (1839), and literary studies (1839). At the same time, students were sent to Europe, and in particular to France, to learn foreign languages and carry out further studies there.[2] To provide further educational assistance l'École imperiale ottomane (Mekteb-i Osmani) was established in Paris in 1857.[3] With the foundation of another school (Mekteb-i Sultani) in Galatasaray, in Istanbul, in 1868, under the directorship of Ernest de Salve-Villedieu (1815–93), Ottoman students began to learn French and other languages with more professional

1 Alkan 2000; Somel 2001; Fortna 2002; Akiba 2003.

2 Şişman 2004. For educational relations with Germany and joint institutional activities in the later years, see Turan 2000; and Gencer 2003.

3 Bilim 1989; Şişman 1986; Chambers 1968. A similar school (l'École égyptienne) was established for Egyptian students in Paris.

instruction than had been available elsewhere (Şişman 1989). In addition to previously established institutions of higher education, a new school of political science (Mekteb-i Mülkiye, 1859) was founded.[4] It was believed that progress and development in Ottoman scholarship would be possible only through the strengthening of new-style schools (*mektebs*) (Tahir 1914–15, 241–42). The new scholars, educated in the new type of *mekteb,* were increasingly gaining the upper hand in communicative discourses and were seen as different from the *ulema* (scholars) of *madrasa* origin and referred to as *münevver,* or "enlightened," a concept translated from the French *éclairé.* A *münevver* was seen as a person who had taken knowledge from both modern European and Ottoman sources, and the expression gained considerable currency in journals, newspapers, and public discourses (Özervarlı 2013). Morever, the *mektebli* and *medreseli* dispute occupied most discussions in the late Ottoman and early Republican periods (İnançalp 1978). Disputes emerged from the circulation through journals and translations of materialistic and positivistic ideas among Ottomans educated in modern thought.[5] The translation movement in the late nineteenth and early twentieth century was the main channel for the diffusion of Western literary texts and modern philosophical ideas.[6]

The Ottoman educational movement culminated in a modern university (*darülfünun*) in Istanbul, Çemberlitaş, which was the last major step in higher education. The term *darülfünun* means "the house of sciences" and derives from the Arabic *dār al-funūn*, and these institutions were founded to systematically meet the needs of modern science and thought. (The term *fann/funūn* in Arabic generally means "art/arts," but taken into Turkish it has the meaning of "science.") Following early arrangements for building a campus and offering exemplary public seminars (1846–61) and instruction based on modern teaching practices (1863–65), efforts had to cease for a while because the elegant new building, which was constructed for the university by a Swiss-Italian architect named Gaspare Fossati (1809–83), was appropriated by the Ministry of Finance.

A second attempt came a few years later with the Darülfünun-i Osmani, in the building that is now the Press Museum (Basın Müzesi). This institution also offered courses on the philosophy of science, but it functioned for

4 For Western views on these early professional schools, see, for instance, MacFarlane 1850.

5 For the history of materialism and positivism in the late Ottoman era and the early Turkish republic, see Akgün 1988, and Korlaelçi 1986.

6 See Meral 2010. For some examples of the translated philosophical books, see Descartes 1894; Büchner 1911; and Heackel 1911; Bourdel 1913; Fonsegrive 1913; Barbe 1914; Bertrand 1915; Seailles 1923; Poincare 1927.

only three years (1870–73). Another attempt took place with another institution, the Darülfünun-i Sultani, founded in 1874, which included schools of law (Hukuk), civil engineering (Turuk ve Maʿabir), and literature (Edebiyat), located within the building of the Galatasaray until 1881. The School of Literature had, according to its programme, courses on philosophy (*hikmet*) taught by the French scholar M. Perrard, and logic (*mantık*) taught by a certain Kerim Efendi.

Following shortly after this series of interruptions, the university was renamed and reorganised in 1900 as the Darülfünun-i Şahane, with branches in religious sciences (*ulum-i diniye*), mathematics and natural sciences (*ulum-i riyaziyye ve tabiʿiyye*), and literature (*edebiyat*). Philosophy, logic, and ethics were the subjects of joint courses within the Faculty of Literature. Coupled with an increase in the number of courses offered and a modernised curriculum with the establishment of new divisions, such as law and medicine, the university was renamed again, in 1912, this time as the Dersaadet (Istanbul) Darülfünunu. In this latest iteration, philosophy was divided between two faculties: theology and literature. Both faculties taught philosophy courses according to their distinct needs and programme design.

During the First World War (1914–18), several visiting professors were invited from Germany with the help of Franz Schmidt, the German advisor to the Minister of Education, among whom a professor of philosophy named Günther Jacoby (1881–1969)[7] deserves mention, due to his significant contributions. Moreover, a separate university (İnas Darülfününu) was established for female students, which was united with the main institution in 1919 (Arslan, Selçuk, and Nam 2012). On 21 April 1924, the Republic of Turkey recognised the Darülfünun as a state university, and in 1925 its administrative autonomy was accepted. By early 1932, a Swiss pedagogue and professor at the University of Geneva, Albert Malche (1876–1956), was invited to examine the educational system and prepare an expert report for reforms.[8] Finally, on 1 August 1933, Darülfünun was replaced by Istanbul University, with a major restructuring that witnessed the elimination of several members of the academic staff, including professors of the faculty of theology.[9]

In the history of modern Ottoman educational institutions and especially that of the Darülfünun, there are signs of both change and continuity. When the opening of the Darülfünun-i Osmani was announced to the public, two

7 Von Freytag-Loringhoff 1961. For German professors invited to the Darülfünun, see Dölen 2013; and Widmann 1973.

8 Malche 1939; Kocatürk 1984.

9 Ayni 2007; Dölen 2009; İhsanoğlu 1995; İhsanoglu 2010; Dölen 2010.

aims were underlined: to educate a workforce for the modernising state institutions and for producing scholarly writings on history and traditional culture, while at the same time allowing for the spread of new and useful knowledge from Europe on the natural and technological sciences.[10] With the outspoken aspiration to combine local and modern cultures, it is easy to understand that the demand for three classical Ottoman languages—Turkish, Arabic, and Persian—could be expected only from those who somehow had been educated in the *madrasas*. European learning and languages were accessible mostly through modern schools and travels to the West. Therefore, the Darülfünun looked to both academic directions and it retained a connection between traditional and modern learning.

Even *mektebs*, which functioned separately, represented continuity in historical tradition, as they also included Islamic morality in their curricula, starting from middle school (Fortna 2000). As Fortna points out:

> The hybridity of the new-style schools suggests that instead of looking for contrasts between the "old" and the "new," we should be prepared for a continuum of possible permutations combining elements of both traditions, changing each one in the process.
>
> FORTNA 2000, 375

The hybrid nature of the modern Ottoman schools, which included both Western and Islamic aspects, blurs the dichotomised understanding of late Ottoman society.[11] It also corresponds to what Gudrun Krämer suggests in her analysis of Islamic reform:

> Contemporary Islamic discourse rests on a long tradition of religious renewal and reform that predates modernity as an era and a programme and by the same token, it is not merely the result of modern encounters with "the West." Yet it cannot be denied that since the late nineteenth century, when large parts of the Islamic world were successively brought under European control, the debate over change, renewal and reform has taken on a new character. Renewal and reform have always involved a certain amount of borrowing from outside the tradition defined as Islamic, and hence "authentic." But the establishment of pious endowments, the elaboration of Sufi ritual and the introduction of coffeehouses, guns and the printing press (all of them unknown to the Prophet), disputed

10 For the complete text of this announcement see Bilsel 1943.

11 Fortna 2000, 388. Also cf. Fortna 2002.

> though they were, did not shake the general sense of what it meant to be a Muslim and to live in a Muslim society, at least not for the majority of Muslims.
>
> KRÄMER 2013, 636

This interconnection of past and present, old and new is vital to understanding the overall character of the Ottoman modernisation process in general, and its reforms in educational and scholarly circles in particular. A good case in point is the emergence of "moderate religious thinkers as an alternative voice to the defenders of mere positivism in the process of the modernization of Ottoman thought, rejecting the notion of conflict both between Islamic tradition and modernization and between true religion and pure science" (Özervarlı 2007). Another example is the reinterpretation of Ottoman Islamic customary law in the light of Durkheimian social collectivism by sociologist Ziya Gökalp (1876–1924) and his followers (Özervarlı 2017).

Despite its explicit goal of being a new and modern institution, the Darülfünun was not perceived as totally disconnected from the long tradition of *madrasa* teaching. Early proposals indicate that it was even presented to the public as a "new scientific *madrasa*" (*medrese-i cedide-i ilmiye*) (İhsanoglu 2010, 1: 352–53). The author of the first history of the Darülfünun, Mehmed Ali Ayni (1869–1945), for instance, made a comparison between the new institution and the first *madrasa* of Istanbul (Ayni 2007 [1927]). Another significant sign of continuation at the Darülfünun was the appointment of professors of the enlightened *madrasa* style as its leading teachers.

Among the prominent professors of philosophy at Darülfünun-i Şahane were, for instance, Babanzade Ahmed Naim (1872–1934) and İzmirli Ismail Hakkı (1869–1946), who were educated both in *madrasa*s and in modern schools, and were admirers of the classical legacy of Arab and early Ottoman thinkers. Apart from their teaching responsibilities, they translated and commented on books in French on modern philosophy and adjusted them to what they saw as the current needs of Ottoman philosophical tradition.[12] A vibrant third example of this trend is Mehmed Fatin Gökmen (1877–1955), who was a *madrasa* graduate, studied mathematical and natural sciences at the Darülfünun, became a professor of astronomy there, and was later appointed as the founding director of the modern observatory in Kandilli, Istanbul (Dizdar 1996). Moreover, the existence of courses in Arabic, Persian, and European languages, along with literature and philosophy courses, and the teaching in the law departments of Roman, Islamic, and modern European law also implied

12 Naim 1912; Fonsegrive 1913; Hakkı 1908; Boirac, no. 3762.

a desire to learn from both Eastern and Western academic cultures. However, these intertwined facts of continuity and change do not diminish the transforming novel character of the institution.

The name of the Darülfünun was chosen for the university with the purpose of emphasising novelty. Moreover, at the Darülfünun the old concept of *ʿilim* (knowledge) was incorporated into the new concept of *fen* (science), expressions which were usually used in plural forms *ulum* and *fünun,* in order to emphasise the integrity between the old and new. Whereas the term *ʿilim* referred to classical disciplines, which were taught in *madrasas*, the term *fen* mostly signified modern natural and mathematical sciences. However, the words *ulum* and *fünun* were not treated as representing completely separate realms in Ottoman terminology, but were often cited together. The Darülfünun and the unavoidable influence of modern European philosophy on Ottoman intellectuals in general led scholars to rethink the legacy of their tradition of thought, as well as to accommodate it to what they called the "new philosophy" (*felsefe-i cedide*), thereby proclaiming that they did not equate philosophy only with Western thinking.[13]

The first prominent professor of philosophy at the Darülfünun-i Şahane was Emrullah Efendi (1858–1914), who taught psychology, philosophy, and history of philosophy, from 1900 until his death. He also had a huge impact on the transformation of Ottoman education as the Minister of Education (1910–12). After Emrullah Efendi's death, the next prominent scholar at the institution was Babanzade Ahmed Naim (1872–1934), who taught for a long period (1914–33), tutoring in philosophy, metaphysics, logic, psychology, and ethics. Other professors, also representatives of this new trend of an intertwined approach, included Mustafa Şekib (1886–1958, psychology and philosophy of religion), Filibeli Ahmed Hilmi (1865–1914, philosophical movements), Halil Nimetullah (1880–1957, ethics), Mehmed Izzet (1891–1930, social philosophy and ethics), the famous Ziya Gökalp (1876–1924, philosophy and sociology), Necmeddin Sadak (1890–1953, sociology, political philosophy, and history of philosophy), Mehmed Emin (1891–1965, ethics, political thought, and history of philosophy), İzmirli İsmail Hakkı (1878–1946, Islamic philosophy, history of philosophy), Rıza Tevfik (1869–1949 philosophy, metaphysics), and Orhan Sadeddin (dates unspecified, history of philosophy).

The first philosophy course was given by Ahmed Vefik Pasha (1823–1891), on the philosophy of history. Later under the rubric of theoretical philosophy (*hikmet-i nazariye*), four courses were taught—namely, psychology

13 Researchers have drawn attention to the common mistake of associating modernisation only with the West. See Voll, 1996.

(*ilm-i ahval-i nefs*), logic (*mantık*), ethics (*ahlak*), and aesthetics (*hikmet-i bedayi*). Instructors also contributed to the teaching of philosophy with textbooks on philosophy, some of which were taken from the course notes taken by class participants, but some instructors, such as Ahmed Midhat (1844–1912), Mehmed Ali Ayni (1868–1945), Rıza Tevfik (1869–1949), and Halil Nimetullah (1880–1957), wrote their own textbooks for the Darülfünun students.[14]

Professors and other scholars expressed their opinions on the programmes and methods of instruction at the university. For instance Mehmed İzzet (1891–1930), one of the professors of the Darülfünun, in his articles on philosophy courses at the university, suggests that in its new academic environment, philosophy should not remain a totally theoretical discipline, but should influence society through science, literature, and art. It is up to philosophy, he argues, to take the lead and provide a vision for other disciplines and save them from becoming narrow research areas. He points out that the task of the Darülfünun was to train both philosophy teachers and scholars of philosophy. However, he regrets that philosophy was taught only at the undergraduate level at the Darülfünun and emphasises the need to establish graduate programmes in philosophy. According to Izzet, advanced studies and new ideas in philosophy would require serious PhD programmes (İzzet 1925, 121–22).

In conclusion, Ottoman modernisation efforts and new educational institutions did not aim to disconnect from traditional cultural elements. Despite their enhanced endeavours to translate French, English, and German philosophical texts, modern schools and the Darülfünun deliberately absorbed aspects of local culture in their long path to modernisation influenced by European programmes and ideas. The institutional structures of these new educational centres were based on traditional and modern principles that represented both continuity and reform. The synthesising rapprochement of two cultures was the result of a continuous process of reforming institutions in order to fulfill the expectations of the new generations of a modernised people, who had either graduated from modern schools while growing up in Ottoman culture, or had a binary education in both modern and traditional institutions. Although the group that was educated in modern schools criticised some practices of the previous generations, especially with regard to the methodology of scholarship, its representatives did not totally distance themselves from the historically developed scholarly culture. With respect to the philosophy curriculum, such scholars taught both modern and Islamic philosophy within faculties of literature and theology and published modern textbooks, monographs, and journal articles. The late Ottoman Empire not only devised

14 Midhat 2016; Ayni 2016; Tevfik 2009; Nimetullah 2011.

a new and much more differentiated role with respect to philosophy, but this development also goes hand in hand with variegated experiences of institutional reform.

Bibliography

Akgün, Mehmet. 1988. *Materyalizmin Turkiye'ye Girişi ve İlk Etkileri*. Ankara: Kultur ve Turizm Bakanligi Yayinlari.

Akiba, Jun. 2003. "A New School for Qadis: Education of the Sharia Judges in the Late Ottoman Empire." *Turcica* 35: 125–63.

Alkan, Mehmet O. 2000. "Modernization from Empire to Republic and Education in the Process of Nationalism." In Kemal H. Karpat (ed.), *Ottoman Past and Today's Turkey*. Leiden: Brill, 47–132.

Arslan, Ali, Mustafa Selçuk, and Mehmet Nam. 2012. *Türkiye'nin İlk ve Tek Kız Üniversitesi: İnas Darülfünunu (1914–1919)*. Istanbul: İdil Yayıncılık.

Ayni, Mehmed Ali. 2007 [1927]. *Darülfünun Tarihi*. Rendered into modern Turkish by Aykut Kazancıgil. Istanbul: Kitabevi.

Ayni, Mehmed Ali. 2016 [1927]. *Darülfünun Tarih-i Felsefe Dersleri*. Transliterated and rendered into modern Turkish by Yakup Yıldız. Konya: Çizgi Kitabevi.

Barbe, Abbe E. 1914. *Tarih-i Felsefe* (*Histoire de la philosophie*). Trans. Bohor Israil. Istanbul: Matbaa-i Amire.

Bertrand, Alexis. 1915. *Mebadi-i Felsefe-i İlmiyye ve Felsefe-i Ahlakiyye* (*Principes de philosophie scientifique et de philosophie morale*). Trans. Salih Zeki. 2 vols. Istanbul: Matbaa-i Amire.

Bilim, Cahit. 1989. "Paris'teki Osmanlı Okulu: Mekteb-i Osmani." *Anadolu Üniversitesi Fen-Edebiyat Fakültesi Dergisi* 1/2: 215–31.

Bilsel, Cemil. 1943. *İstanbul Üniversitesi Tarihi*. Istanbul: İstanbul Üniversitesi Yayınları, 14–5.

Boirac, Emile. n.d. *Cours elementaire de la philosophie, Chapter on Ethics*: *Mülahhas İlm-i Ahlak*, MS Süleymaniye Library. İzmirli, no. 3762.

Bourdel, Charles. 1913. *İlim ve Felsefe* (*Le science et la philosopie*). Trans. Mehmed Ali Ayni. Istanbul: Matbaa-i Amire.

Büchner, Ludwig. 1911. *Madde ve Kuvvet* (*Kraft und Stoff*). Ed. and trans. from French Baha Tevfik and Ahmed Nebil. Istanbul: Dersaadet Kutuphanesi.

Chambers, Richard L. 1968. "Notes on the Mekteb-i Osmani in Paris 1857–1874." In William R. Polk and Richard L. Chambers (eds.), *Beginnings of Modernization in the Middle East: The Nineteenth Century*. Chicago: University of Chicago Press, 313–29.

Descartes, René. 1894. *Usul Hakkinda Nutuk* (*Discours de la méthode*). Trans. İbrahim Edhem. Istanbul: Mahmud Bey Matbaasi.

Dizdar, Muammer. 1996. "Gokmen, Mehmet Fatin." *Türkiye Diyanet Vakfi İslam Ansiklopedisi* 14: 142.

Dölen, Emre. 2009. *Türkiye Üniversite Tarihi: Osmanlı Döneminde Darülfünun (1863–1922)*. Istanbul: İstanbul Bilgi Üniversitesi.

Dölen, Emre. 2010. *Türkiye Üniversite Tarihi: Cumhuriyet Döneminde Osmanlı Darülfünunu 1922–1933*. Istanbul: İstanbul Bilgi Üniversitesi.

Dölen, Emre. 2013. *Istanbul Darülfünunu'nda Alman Müderrisler 1915–1918*. Istanbul: İstanbul Bilgi Üniversitesi.

Findley, Carter V. 1980. *Bureaucratic Reform in the Ottoman Empire: The Sublime Porte 1789–1922*. Princeton: Princeton University Press, 62.

Fonsegrive, George-Lespinasse. 1913. *Elements de philosophie: Psychologie I. Mebadi-i Felsefe 'den Birinci Kitap; İlmü'n-nefs*. Istanbul: Maarif-i Umumiye Nezareti.

Fonsegrive, Georges. 1989. "Mebadi-yi Felsefeden Ilmu'n-nefs (Eléments de philosophie: Psychologie)." Trans. Babanzade Ahmed Naim. Istanbul: Maarif-i Umumiye Nezareti, 1913. *Dergisi*, 1/2: 215–31.

Fortna, Benjamin C. 2000. "Islamic Morality in Late Ottoman 'Secular' Schools." *International Journal of Middle East Studies*, 32/3: 369–93.

Fortna, Benjamin C. 2002. *Imperial Classroom: Islam, the State, and Education in the Late Ottoman Empire*. Oxford: Oxford University Press.

Gencer, Mustafa. 2003. *Jöntürk Modernizmi ve "Alman Ruhu": 1908–1918 Dönemi Türk-Alman İlişkileri ve Eğitim*. Istanbul: İletişim.

Hakkı, İzmirli İsmail. 1908. *Felsefe-i İslamiyye Tarihi*. Istanbul: Darülfünun Matbaası.

Heackel, Ernst. 1911. *Vahdet-i Mevcud: Bir Tabiat Aliminin Dini (Monisme)*. Trans. Baha Tevfik. Istanbul: Dersaadet Kutubhanesi.

Hitzel, Frédéric. 1995. "Les écoles de mathematics turques et l'aide française (1775–1798)." In Daniel Panzac (ed.), *Histoire économique et sociale de l'Empire ottoman et de la Turquie (1326–1960)*. Paris: Peteers, 813–26.

İhsanoğlu, Ekmeleddin. 1995. "The Genesis of 'Darülfünun': An Overview of Attempts to Establish the First Ottoman University." In Daniel Panzac (ed.), *Histoire économique et sociale de l'Empire ottoman et de la Turquie (1326–1960)*. Paris: Peeters, 827–42.

İhsanoglu, Ekmeleddin. 2010. *Darülfünun: Osmanlı'da Kültürel Modernleşmenin Odağı*. 2 vols. Istanbul: IRCICA.

İnançalp, Muallim Naci. 1978. *Mekteb ve Medrese*. Edited in transliteration by Erdoğan Eriiz. Istanbul: Çınar Yayınevi.

İzzet, Mehmet. 1925. "Darülfünun'da Felsefe Dersleri." *Darülfünun Edebiyat Fakültesi Dergisi* 4/2: 121–22, 130.

Kocatürk, Utkan. 1984. "Atatürk'ün Üniversite Reformu ile İlgili Notları." *Atatürk Araştırma Merkezi Dergisi* 1/1: 3–96.

Korlaelçi, Murtaza. 1986. *Pozitivizmin Turkiye'ye Girişi ve İlk Etkileri*. Istanbul: İnsan Yayınları.

Krämer, Gudrun. 2013. "Modern but not Secular: Religion, Identity and the *Ordre Public* in the Arab Middle East." *International Sociology* 28/6: 629–44, specifically, 636.

MacFarlane, Charles. 1850. *Turkey and its Destiny: The Result of Journeys Made in 1847 and 1848 to Examine into the State of That Country*. London: J. Murray.

Malche, Albert. 1939. *İstanbul Üniversitesi Hakkında Rapor*. Istanbul: Maarif Vekaleti.

Meral, Arzu. 2010. *Western Ideas Percolating into Ottoman Minds: A Survey of Translation Activity and the Famous Case of Telemaque*. PhD Dissertation, Universiteit Leiden.

Midhat, Ahmed. 2016 [1911]. *Darülfünun Dersleri: Tarih-i Hikmet*. Transliterated and rendered into modern Turkish by Ali Utku, Sebahattin Çevikbaş. Konya: Çizgi Kitabevi.

Naim, Ahmed. 1912. *Felsefe Dersleri*. Istanbul: Matbaa-i Hukukiyye.

Nimetullah, Halil. 2011 [1912]. *Dârülfünûn'da Felsefe Dersleri*. Transliterated and rendered into modern Turkish by Ali Utku, Uğur Köroğlu. Konya: Çizgi Kitabevi.

Özervarlı, M. Sait. 2007. "Alternative Approaches to Modernization in the Late Ottoman Period: İzmirli İsmail Hakki's Religious Thought against Materialist Scientism." *International Journal of Middle East Studies* 39/1: 77–102, specifically 77.

Özervarlı, M. Sait. 2013. "Intellectual Foundations and Transformations in an Imperial City: Istanbul from the Late Ottoman to the Early Republican Periods." *The Muslim World* 103/4: 521–52.

Özervarlı, M. Sait. 2017. "Reading Durkheim through Ottoman Lenses: Interpretations of Customary Law, Religion, and Society by the School of Gökalp." *Modern Intellectual History* 14/2: 393–419.

Poincare, Henri. 1927. *İlim ve Faraziye: Felsefe-i İlmiye* (*La science et l'hypothèse*). Trans. Salih Zeki. Istanbul: Milli Matbaa.

Seailles, Paul Janet-Gabriel. 1923. *Tahlili Tarih-i Felsefe: Metalib ve Mezahib* (*Histoire de la philosophie: les problèmes et les écoles*). Trans. Elmalili Hamdi. Istanbul: Matbaa-i Amire.

Somel, Selçuk Akşin. 2001. *The Modernization of Public Education in the Ottoman Empire, 1839–1908: Islamization, Autocracy, and Discipline*. Leiden: Brill.

Şişman, Adnan. 1986. "Mekteb-i Osmani 1857–1864." *Osmanlı Araştırmaları Dergisi* 5: 83–160.

Şişman, Adnan. 2004. *Galatasaray Mekteb-i Sultanisi 'nin Kuruluşu ve İlk Öğretim Yıllan 1868–1871*. Istanbul: Edebiyat Fakültesi Matbaası.

Şişman, Adnan, *Tanzimat Döneminde Fransa'ya Gönderilen Osmanlı Öğrencileri* (*1839–1876*), Ankara: Atatürk Kültür Dil ve Tarih Yüksek Kurumu Türk Tarih Kurumu.

Tahir, Bursalı Mehmet. 1914–15. *Osmanlı Müellifleri*. Matbaa-i Amire, 241–42.

Tevfik, Rıza. 2009 [1917]. *Darülfünun Felsefe Ders Notları*. Transliterated and rendered into modern Turkish by Ali Utku, Erdoğan Erbay. Konya: Çizgi Kitabevi.

Turan, Kemal. 2000. *Türk-Alman Eğitim İlişkilerinin Tarihi Gelişimi*. Istanbul: Ayışığı Kitapları.

Voll, John O. 1996. "The Mistaken Identification of 'The West' with 'Modernity'." *American Journal of the Islamic Social Sciences* 13/1: 1–12.

Von Freytag-Loringhoff, Bruno. 1961. "Günther Jacoby 80 Jahre alt." *Zeitschrift fur philosophische Forschung* 15: 237–50.

Widmann, Horst. 1973. *Exil und Bildungshilfe: Die deutschsprachige akademische Emigration in die Türkei nach 1933 mit einer Bio-Bibliographie der emigrierten Hochschullehrer im Anhang*. Bern: Herbert Lang.

PART 3

Islam, Ethics, and Languages

CHAPTER 7

Pratique religieuse et comportement moral

Abdou Filali-Ansary

De nos jours, la question du rapport entre pratique religieuse et comportement moral relève de conversations engageant le grand public plutôt que d'interrogations savantes. Dans les sociétés du sud de la Méditerranée, elle revient avec insistance dans les conversations de tous les jours depuis l'intensification de ce qu'on a appelé le « retour du religieux », c'est-à-dire l'affichage étendu de signes extérieurs associés avec la religion (barbe, hijab, prière dans l'espace public etc.). Dans les contextes du nord de la Méditerranée, la question était d'actualité il y a environ un siècle, lorsqu'on se posait des questions sur le rapport de la morale avec la foi religieuse, et qu'on se demandait si la moralité avait besoin de la foi religieuse et si la perte de la foi équivalait ou conduisait à une perte de repères moraux, du temps où des figures comme celles de Tolstoï ou Nietzsche marquaient leur présence. De nos jours, comme le remarque Charles Taylor, la foi religieuse est devenue une option parmi d'autres, et on ne demande plus si on a besoin d'être croyant pour avoir une moralité (Taylor 2007, 352–76). La question que nous soulevons aujourd'hui est plutôt celle du sens que pourrait avoir le fait qu'on se pose ce genre de questions dans des sociétés où le « retour du religieux » se manifeste de façon visible et souvent envahissante, voire violente, mais où en même temps les plaintes relatives au désordre moral, à l'immoralité des agents sont régulières, insistantes et pesantes.

En effet, dans les contextes musulmans, il ne se passe peut-être pas de jour où l'on n'entend pas quelqu'un se plaindre du manque de discipline ou de sens civique chez ses concitoyens, de la faiblesse du civisme et parfois même d'une espèce de « guerre de tous contre tous » qui serait menée, en contraste avec la discipline et l'esprit de solidarité qui régneraient dans les sociétés du nord.

Une des formulations les plus éloquentes de la question a été proposée par l'écrivain égyptien Youssef al-Sebaï (1917–78) dont le roman *Arḍ al-nifāq* connutun grand succès lors de sa publication en 1949. Dans ce roman, le « héros » aurait absorbé des « doses » de courage et de générosité ayant pour effet d' atténuer ou de neutraliser l'effet d'autres « doses » de « qualités » telles que l'hypocrisie, qui auraient été administrées en masse à la société égyptienne. Le comportement de cet individu crée de telles perturbations que tout l'ordre social s'en trouve remis en question.

 | DOI:10.1163/9789004386891_008

1 Normes et comportements dans les contextes musulmans

Malcom Kerr, un universitaire qui a eu l'occasion d'observer de près des sociétés de musulmans, a commencé son premier ouvrage par la remarque suivante

> La pensée sociale chez les musulmans est habitée par une idée pessimiste selon laquelle il existerait une tension entre l'idéal et le réel, le spirituel et le temporel, la vertu et le pouvoir, les commandements divins et les comportements humains. Au cours des derniers siècles, les lettrés musulmans n'ont pas considéré comme faisant partie de leur mission de résoudre la tension entre ces deux groupes d'éléments contrastés. Ils se sont engagés plutôt dans l'élaboration de conceptions de l'idéal et ont laissé la société élaborer ses propres solutions pratiques, non reconnues au demeurant, aux plans psychologiques et sociaux. Toutefois, la pénétration de la culture séculière dans le monde musulman moderne a changé cette donne. Au lieu de rendre un tel sentiment de tension obsolète, elle l'a rendu encore plus aiguë, et a fait de sa résolution une nécessité vitale.
>
> KERR 1966, 7

Conversations privées et débats publics révèlent effectivement la question du rapport entre la norme et la réalité qui est une préoccupation importante. Le sentiment de tension entre les deux domine, même dans des domaines qui n'ont rien à voir avec la moralité. Ainsi par exemple, à travers le monde arabe, on perçoit une tension similaire dans le domaine linguistique, puisque des élites cultivées continuent à s'exprimer dans une langue formelle que personne ne parle dans la vie de tous les jours, considérant les idiomes parlés comme des formes altérées de la « vraie » langue, l'arabe classique hérité des générations de l'« âge d'or ». La conception défendue par ces intellectuels est que la langue classique aurait été donnée en premier lieu, parfaite ou quasi parfaite, alors que les vernaculaires ne seraient que des pratiques irrespectueuses des normes du parler correct. Le respect de l'identité authentique et de la nécessité de parler avec précision exigeraient d'appliquer strictement la norme classique. Ils s'inscrivent donc en continuité avec leurs prédécesseurs des siècles passés qui se sont régulièrement dressés contre ce qu'ils ont appelé *laḥn al-ʿawāmm* (déformations des usages populaires). En cela, ils ne se rendent pas compte de ce que les approches historiques et linguistiques modernes ont apporté, à savoir que les langues commencent par être des vernaculaires et que certains de ces vernaculaires font l'objet d'une mise à l'écrit, qui résulte souvent d'une décision prise par un pouvoir politique ou une autorité religieuse. Ils refusent de reconnaître que la forme écrite et toute la sophistication qu'elle apporte sont le résultat d'usages savants qui se produisent lorsqu'une langue est adoptée et consacrée par des structures de pouvoir. L'attachement à des conceptions et attitudes obsolètes va jusqu'à ne pas voir que certains vernaculaires se sont tellement écartés de la langue classique qu'ils sont devenus eux-mêmes des langues à part, produisant des mondes de sens donnant lieu et d'une façon significative, à une littérature de qualité. Ces intellectuels rejettent tout autant le constat fait par des éducateurs que le temps consacré par les jeunes apprenants à maîtriser la langue classique entrave l'apprentissage des matières essentielles dans l'éducation de base. La question linguistique va de pair avec la nécessité de défendre l'intégrité de l'héritage culturel et la continuité de cet héritage, ainsi que de tout ce qui constitue l'identité « authentique ».

Le domaine religieux vit de la même tension entre la norme et la réalité. Les clercs religieux traditionnels diffusent des conceptions héritées des siècles passés pour être offertes au grand public, à travers les prêches religieux, comme moyen de donner sens à sa religiosité. L'enseignement religieux dans les contextes musulmans entretient une espèce de « bulle », où sont enfermés les esprits des jeunes et du grand public. Aucune référence aux approches d'historiens, anciennes ou modernes, qui situent les traditions religieuses des musulmans dans des contextes de lieu et de temps, ainsi que dans des univers culturels bien particuliers. Le tout est présenté comme le produit d'un savoir (*ʿilm*) formé de « propositions vraies », comme la quintessence d'une science accomplie et non susceptible d'être mise en question. En même temps se développent des pratiques religieuses éloignées des discours normatifs, de telle façon que l'opposition entre un islam normatif, ou islam savant, et un islam populaire se trouve reproduite, avec des différences importantes, notamment le fait que, d'une part, le discours savant est réduit à un prêche simplifié et à une reformulation des prescriptions élémentaires alors que, d'autre part, les pratiques de l'islam populaire sont appropriées par de nouvelles élites, souvent éduquées dans les domaines scientifiques et techniques.

Que ce soit dans le domaine religieux ou dans celui de la langue, le rapport entre la norme et les formes d'expression spontanées reste basé sur ce contraste. La norme est supposée être fixe mais ne prend pas ou très peu en compte, les pratiques vivantes. Le constat fait par Malcolm Kerr au début du paragraphe cité plus haut reste donc, pour le moment, valide (Kerr 1966, 7).

2 Moralité ou conformisme ?

Quel rapport peut-il y avoir entre ce contraste et la plainte constamment exprimée de décalage entre pratiques religieuses et comportement moral ?

Un premier constat serait que les pratiques religieuses, telles que la fréquentation des mosquées, l'habillement et d'autres signes visibles constituent une façon de se conformer à une norme sociale mais n'indiquent pas nécessairement une plus grande imprégnation de sentiments religieux. Les individus qui optent pour cette forme de conformisme choisissent de s'aligner avec ce qu'ils perçoivent comme des codes de ralliement à une identité collective, sans que cela conduise nécessairement à un changement au niveau de leur spiritualité ou des principes qui guident leur action. Un tel constat va dans le sens de remarques formulées par plusieurs observateurs. On peut en choisir quelques-uns, dont le témoignage peut être jugé intéressant : parmi les réformistes musulmans qui ont visité l'Europe au XIXe siècle, certains ont relevé que les Européens semblaient avoir mieux intériorisé des sentiments « musulmans » que ne l'auraient fait les musulmans eux-mêmes. De leur côté, des penseurs européens ont remarqué que, dans les contextes où le christianisme a prévalu, on peut constater que la sécularisation prend la forme d'une atténuation de l'adhésion aux dogmes en même temps qu'une meilleure imprégnation par des principes d'éthique religieuse.

On pourrait ajouter que le fait de ressentir aussi vivement le contraste entre l'apparent engagement religieux et le comportement moral, comme le note M. Kerr, pourrait exprimer une aspiration apparue dans les contextes modernes de voir les comportements s'aligner aux normes, aspiration qui aurait remplacé la résignation pessimiste au décalage entre les deux qui avait prévalu dans les sociétés prémodernes.

Toutefois ces explications restent au niveau d'impressions générales et leur formulation ne saurait en faire des réponses réfléchies à la question posée. Si nous nous tournons vers des explications proposées par des historiens qui se sont intéressés à l'évolution des mentalités et aux attitudes sociales en général, il est possible de passer à ce qu'on pourrait considérer comme un autre niveau d'explication.

Charles Taylor par exemple, dans l'ouvrage déjà mentionné *A Secular Age*, relève que la sécularisation qui s'est accomplie dans les sociétés du nord-ouest de l'Europe et de ses extensions dans le monde a conduit à éliminer la référence à la transcendance dans la sphère publique, à affaiblir des pratiques religieuses telles que la fréquentation des lieux de culte et à faire de la foi religieuse une option individuelle. Il est aisé de voir qu'aucune de ces évolutions ne s'est produite dans les contextes musulmans. Dans ces derniers en effet, la référence à la transcendance continue d'être invoquée dans l'espace public, les pratiques religieuses paraissent loin de s'affaiblir et il demeure quasi impossible d'exprimer en public le renoncement à la foi religieuse. Nous sommes donc dans une situation où des expressions liées à la religion balisent l'espace social et font partie d'une normativité sociale, comme une sorte de constitution implicite de la société. La religiosité exprimée par des signes extérieurs persiste donc dans ces contextes particuliers sans y entraver une sécularisation qui, selon de nombreux observateurs, se produit et s'observe à d'autres niveaux, comme celui de la mise en place d'institutions modernes.

Rappelons qu'il est de tradition de distinguer la modernité en tant que vision et ensemble d'attitudes, de la modernité qui implique un ensemble complexe de changements historiques. Dans l'abondante littérature consacrée à ce sujet il est facile d'égrener la liste relativement longue de termes disponibles pour décrire ces changements. Industrialisation, urbanisation, sécularisation, bureaucratisation, fragmentation, démocratisation, etc. Pour notre propos, les traits forts identifiés par Hodgson comme caractéristiques majeures des changements historiques, sont particulièrement significatifs.

En effet dans sa narration des phénomènes historiques liés ou regroupés sous le titre de modernité, Hodgson, le plus [khaldounien] des historiens du XXe siècle, dans le sens où il évite la simple narration des événements à la manière des chroniqueurs, parle de *Grande transmutation Occidentale*. Nous savons ce que *mutation* veut dire dans le monde du vivant: changement radical, conversion, évolution profonde. Hodgson introduit ensuite deux substantifs qui ajoutent des dimensions supplémentaires aux descriptions de la modernité. Il mentionne en effet ce qu'il appelle la technicalisation et, d'autre part, ce qu'il décrit comme un *gentling of manners*. Pour lui en effet, le temps de la "Grande Transmutation Occidentale" (XVIIIe siècle, Europe du Nord-Ouest) a vu l'émergence de normes morales nettement inclinées vers la compassion et sans rapport direct avec l'esprit techniciste dominant. Le plus remarquable était l'apparition de ce qu'on pourrait appeler un adoucissement des mœurs (*gentling of manners*), fondé sur l'attente confiante de voir se produire dans la réalité ce qui était considéré comme relevant de l'idéal. Les mœurs des classes supérieures s'adoucissaient et se « civilisaient » peu à peu. Conformément à ces nouvelles tendances, même les hérétiques ont commencé à être tolérés et la torture, comme punition ou comme moyen d'obtenir des informations, a été abandonnée. L'idée qui émergeait était qu'avec une éducation plus philosophique ou plus naturelle, dotée de lois accordant des espaces de liberté plus grands, les esprits humains et les humeurs pourraient, d'une manière générale, devenir éclairés et pouvoir s'élever à la perfection.

Si la fabrication de dispositifs mécaniques existait bien avant les temps modernes (il suffit de penser par exemple aux "gadgets" déjà présents au Moyen-âge), l'idée de soumettre la plupart sinon toutes les activités humaines à des procédés relevant de la rationalité technique ne s'est imposée ou n'a commencé à s'imposer qu'au XVIIIe siècle. Ce mouvement aurait pris une telle importance qu'un état d'esprit nouveau est apparu et s'est imposé bien au-delà des changements dans les manières de faire et dans les procédés adoptés par les spécialistes des divers domaines où la technique pouvait être utilisée. Il paraît aussi remarquable que Hodgson puisse soutenir que le changement qu'on peut percevoir dans les attitudes prédominantes de certaines sociétés qui font que les individus deviennent plus respectueux des normes collectives et plus enclins à aider leurs prochains, se seraient produits dans l'histoire en même temps que certaines conditions particulières qui peuvent être identifiées et décrites.

Au-delà donc des substantifs par lesquels on décrit habituellement les processus de modernisation, telles qu'urbanisation, industrialisation, sécularisation etc. Hodgson en ajoute un sur ces changements extrêmes—la technicalisation—qui se réfère à une mentalité particulière qui impose une rationalité technicienne dans des domaines où il n'a jamais été question de l'envisager, ainsi que le *gentling of manners*, à savoir des changements d'attitudes sociales qui produisent des rapports nouveaux au sein de certains contextes en particulier. Les deux constituent des transformations qui se produisent à des moments historiques déterminés, et qui sont intimement liées. Dans les deux il y a des attentes particulières, pour reprendre l'expression souvent soulignée par Hodgson (1974, 3, 191ff.).

Prendre du recul par rapport aux traits particuliers des cultures islamiques, placer les parcours des sociétés musulmanes dans des contextes larges et prendre en considération des tournants qui se sont produits dans des contextes différents permet, comme Marshall Hodgson l'a montré, de proposer des clefs d'interprétation originales et utiles. Des changements historiques ayant affecté certaines sociétés humaines en particulier auraient conduit à une situation où la norme est devenue plus accessible ou plutôt, où s'est généralisé le sentiment que la norme est devenue plus accessible. Ce qui, par effet de contraste, pousserait à ressentir plus intensément le contraste qui semble se maintenir entre les deux.

3 Une « modernisation sans modernité » ?

La question qui se pose est donc la suivante : le décalage dont on se plaint régulièrement dans les contextes musulmans serait-il la norme dans toutes les sociétés humaines où la « transmutation occidentale » ne se serait pas produite ? Si l'attente d'alignement du comportement aux normes devient générale en conséquence de la « transmutation », n'y-a-t-il pas lieu de reconnaître que ce serait là l'exception, et que la règle serait plutôt celle où prévaut le dédoublement entre pratiques religieuses et comportement moral ? Si tel est le cas, le fait que la conscience du décalage devienne si aiguë dans les contextes musulmans serait peut-être simplement le résultat de la conscience qu'il existe des contextes où le décalage est surmonté ou même éliminé. Les plaintes qu'on entend à ce sujet seraient simplement des manières d'exprimer le regret de n'avoir pas eu l'équivalent de la transmutation occidentale, de ne pas se trouver dans une situation où les comportements effectifs sont alignés avec les normes. Le fait que certaines impressions puissent être exprimées de manière indirecte est reconnu depuis bien longtemps, bien avant l'apparition, par exemple, de la psychanalyse, qui se proposait de retrouver des sens cachés derrière des actes ou des expressions particulières. Rien n'interdit donc d'accepter que ces plaintes qui reviennent constamment dans les conversations partout dans les pays du sud de la Méditerranée soient une manière de formuler l'idée que, désormais, on devrait atteindre un meilleur alignement des comportements effectifs avec les normes morales et que, vu que cela ne se produit pas ou n'a pas l'air de se produire de manière satisfaisante, une frustration se forme et devient de plus en plus audible et pesante.

Mais alors, il parait important de s'interroger sur les caractéristiques de ce mode de fonctionnement social où se combinent des manifestations ostentatoires d'adhésion à la foi collective avec des comportements dictés strictement par des critères d'utilité individuelle, n'ayant rien à voir avec les principes enseignés par la religion ? Quel aurait été donc le mode de fonctionnement « normal » de ces sociétés, avant qu'elles ne prennent conscience de l'existence d'autres modes de fonctionnement qui se seraient généralisés chez les voisins du Nord ?

Le sujet que nous décrivons comme « mode de fonctionnement des sociétés » recouvre un grand nombre de questions et en fait a intéressé penseurs, historiens, poètes et écrivains… On peut dire qu'à ce propos, nous avons affaire à des thèmes de prédilection pour toutes sortes d'observateurs. Parmi ces derniers, un qui nous vient rapidement à l'esprit est ʿAbd al-Raḥmān Ibn Khaldūn (732–808/1332–1406).

Dans sa *Muqaddima*, l'un des thèmes qui l'ont intéressé a été le contraste entre les modes de vie dans les milieux tribaux et dans les milieux urbains. Ceux qui vivaient en milieu tribal devaient survivre dans une grande précarité, ainsi que face à des dangers provenant de la compétition entre différents groupes humains pour l'accès aux ressources rares qu'offrait leur environnement. Il en résultait qu'il fallait être non seulement constamment mobilisé, mais être aussi solidaire des membres du groupe social auquel on appartenait, pour pouvoir survivre face à des conditions de vie difficile et à la concurrence d'autres groupes humains. Ces conditions inculquaient donc à ceux, qui vivaient dans ces milieux, des vertus particulières, telles que le courage, la solidarité avec les siens, et l'absence d'artifice dans les relations humaines. En revanche, dans les milieux urbains, où des revenus substantiels pouvaient être obtenus par le commerce et l'artisanat, ou par l'accès au pouvoir politique, le poids de la précarité était moindre ou n'était pas ressenti par toutes les classes sociales. La disponibilité de ressources au-delà du nécessaire pour la survie encourageait donc la recherche du luxe, du raffinement et, en conséquence, un relâchement des vertus de solidarité avec le groupe et de courage. Ici, en suivant des indications que nous trouvons dans Ibn Khaldoun sans nous embarrasser de nuances, il parait aisément possible de conclure que, les plaintes entendues régulièrement de nos jours concernent le mode de fonctionnement des milieux urbains. Dans les contextes urbains prémodernes, il fallait bien se conformer à la norme d'appartenance collective, et donc adopter comme les autres les signes ostentatoires d'appartenance religieuse alors qu'en même temps on poursuivait ses fins égoïstes de toutes les manières possibles sans s'embarrasser de quelque principe moral que ce soit.

Est-il possible de vivre une modernisation sans qu'il y ait de véritable modernité dans les esprits, selon l'expression de Jean Copans (1998, 87f.)? Ou bien serions-nous en train de faire l'expérience d'une urbanisation générale, sans que les conditions d'une véritable vie urbaine soient à la portée de la majorité de la population ?

Il paraît remarquable que, dans les conditions d'aujourd'hui, de nombreux intellectuels paraissent être victimes d'une double illusion. La première serait que toutes les sociétés humaines devraient passer par les mêmes étapes pour aboutir à une « fin de l'histoire », où démocratie libérale et économie mondialisée se combinent pour donner aux individus, devenus autonomes, des opportunités de se réaliser selon les valeurs qu'ils auraient librement choisi d'adopter, ce qui permettrait une meilleure adéquation entre normes et formes d'action. N'est-il pas possible que, selon un scénario pessimiste envisagé par Hodgson, quelques sociétés humaines atteignent ce stade et laissent les autres derrière elles, toujours en état de déséquilibre, un déséquilibre qui se traduirait par des conflits interminables entre différentes sensibilités, conceptions du monde et choix d'avenir ?

La deuxième illusion est de type « intellectualiste ». Elle présuppose que tout individu bien éduqué et exposé au savoir moderne et aux procédés rationnels, devrait prendre ses distances vis-à-vis des interprétations littérales de l'héritage religieux. Ce fut peut-être l'illusion qui a berné Mohammed Arkoun pendant toute sa vie, où il a constamment plaidé pour le remplacement de prêches traditionnels par une « islamologie appliquée » fondée sur des approches de sciences humaines et sociales contemporaines. Peut-être que la variable de l'éducation n'a, en fin de compte, qu'un effet limité ou ne peut être opérationnelle que dans des cercles limités.

Nous savons aujourd'hui que des peuples peuvent se soulever comme un seul homme lors de mobilisations générales, comme lorsque, par exemple, ils doivent faire face à des agressions externes ou des catastrophes naturelles. Nous savons que les peuples peuvent également vivre des moments de grâce, lorsqu'ils sentent qu'ils ont accompli quelque chose de remarquable, comme la libération d'une domination étrangère ou parfois même de victoires sportives face à des concurrents redoutés. A ces moments-là, il se produit quelque chose qui ressemble au *gentling of manners* décrit par Marshall Hodgson, c'est-à-dire une attente confiante que les membres de la communauté se comportent de manière loyale et respectueuse vis-à-vis des autres, ce qui pousse chaque individu à agir dans ce sens.

Généralement il s'agit de moments brefs, du fait que le soulèvement contre l'agression extérieure ou contre des tyrans intérieurs se dissipe très vite, et laisse remonter à la surface les réflexes qui prévalent dans des conditions « normales ». Le changement décrit par Marshall Hodgson ressemble à une forme atténuée des sentiments de mobilisation générale ou d'état de grâce, qui le rend plus durable dans le temps et finalement devient l'état normal dans des contextes où il se produit.

Des constats de ce genre ont poussé de nombreux idéologues du réformisme musulman au XIXe siècle puis de la *nahḍa* (renaissance) arabe du XXe siècle, à appeler à une mobilisation collective du genre de celle qui s'est produite lors de moments fondateurs de la communauté musulmane. Celle-ci a vu des éléments tribaux dispersés dans des régions désertiques et constamment en guerre les uns contre les autres devenir une force majeure, en mesure de vaincre et absorber des puissances régionales, telles que l'empire persan ou l'empire byzantin. Il s'est produit en fait au cours du siècle dernier de brèves mobilisations à l'échelle d'Etats territoriaux qui étaient en cours de formation. Ce fut le cas en Irak, en Syrie, en Égypte et dans les pays du Maghreb, où des nationalismes naissants émergeaient sur le socle de sentiments d'appartenance religieuse. Il faut dire que les victoires des nouvelles “nations” ont été plutôt brèves et qu'elles ont été suivies de défaites cuisantes. Les mobilisations collectives déclenchées par des sentiments liés à l'idée de nation ont abouti à une impasse et les attentes, immenses et insensées, ont été déçues. Les masses populaires, formées essentiellement de populations déracinées de leur environnement rural et exposées à des formes de misère et de frustrations inconnues jusqu'alors, ont subi l'attrait d'autres formes de mobilisation collective au nom de l'identité religieuse. Là encore, Il semblait possible de créer l'état d'esprit collectif qui devait permettre la réalisation du développement économique et de l'émancipation politique.

La grande question pour les sociétés du Sud de notre temps est de savoir comment créer des conditions qui permettent l'émergence de cette « attente confiante » de respect des normes qui pousse tous les membres de la société au respect de soi et au respect des autres.

Est-ce un raisonnement circulaire, où l'objectif à atteindre se confond avec la condition de sa réalisation ? Probablement, mais cela reflète des attitudes dominantes dans le contexte des sociétés du Sud.

Bibliographie

ʿĀmir, Muḥammad Fahmī. 2015. "Mā warā' *Arḍ al-nifāq* li-Yūsuf al-Sibāʿī?" *Diwān al-ʿArab: Minbar ḥurr li-l-thaqāfa wa-l-fikr wa-l-adab.* 4 Mars 2015. Available at www.diwanalarab.com/spip.php?article41170. Accessed 22 June 2018.

"Youssef Al-Sebaï (10 juin 1917–18 février 1978)." 2014. *Al-Ahram Hebdo*, Numéro 1028. Available at http://hebdo.ahram.org.eg/NewsContent/1028/39/136/6091/Youssef-Al Seba%C3%AF--juin----f%C3%A9vrier-.aspx.

Copans, Jean. 1998. *La longue marche de la modernité africaine: Savoirs, intellectuels, démocratie.* Paris: Editions Karthala.

Hodgson, Marshall G.S. 1974. *The Venture of Islam: Conscience and History in a World Civilization.* Vol. 3. *The Gunpowder Empires and Modern Times.* Chicago: University of Chicago Press.

Kerr, Malcolm. 1966. *Islamic Reform: The Political and Legal Thought of Muḥammad ʿAbduh and Rashīd Riḍā.* Berkeley: University of California Press.

al-Sibāʿī, Yūsuf. 1949. *Arḍ al-nifāq.* Cairo: Mu'assasat al-Khānjī.

Taylor, Charles. 2007. *A Secular Age.* Cambridge MA: Harvard University Press.

CHAPTER 8

The Emerging Field of Ethics in the Context of Modern Egypt

Mutaz al-Khatib

1 Introduction

This article traces the emergence of ethical thinking (*al-tafkīr al-akhlāqī*) in Egypt since the late nineteenth century and the beginning of the twentieth century and seeks to identify the motives and contexts of the resurgence of the field of ethics. This era is informed by its connection in Arab thought to the *nahḍa,* the so-called Arab Awakening, and, equally, its coincidence with the movement for the revival of Arab tradition and its dissemination.

A great number of studies have examined the reform movement in the Muslim world (*iṣlāḥ*)[1] and highlighted its main theorists and their various and multifaceted contributions to modern Islamic thought.[2] Despite the richness of available literature, one easily notices the near complete absence of references to anything related to ethics within the legacy of this movement.[3] In this study, the purpose is to discover dimensions of reform other than the juristic on the one hand, and reform related to the objectives of the *sharīʿa* on the other, both of which have received a great deal of attention in academic research.

In the classical era ethics (*akhlāq*) was perceived as part of "practical wisdom" (*al-ḥikma al-ʿamaliyya*) and seen as comprised of three parts: politics (*tadbīr al-madīna*), economics or management of the household (*tadbīr al-manzil*), and ethics (*tadbīr al-nafs*), a perception that was based on the Greek philosophical tradition (Khalīfa 1941, 13–14). Although the Islamic tradition

---

* This article was translated from Arabic into English. For their help in editing the English version I would like to thank Linda George, Bettina Gräf, Lena Salaymeh, and Mohammad Ghaly.

1 Please note the terms reform (*iṣlāḥ*), renaissance (*nahḍa*), and civilisation (*tamaddun*) are used interchangeably. It is not the aim of this study to explore the possible nuances between these terms but rather to examine their relevance to the field of ethics.

2 Adams 1933; Hourani 1970; Commins 1990; Alatas 2009; Gesink 2010; Wood 2016.

3 To the best of my knowledge, only few studies briefly and broadly or partially have touched upon issues close to what we examine in this study, including Delanoue 1982; al-Ḥaddād 2003; Jadʿān 2010. Finally we also refer to Aḥmad ʿAbd al-Ḥalīm ʿAṭiyya (1990), who compiled an annotated bibliography of the contemporary works on ethics in the Arab world.

 | DOI:10.1163/9789004386891_009

has witnessed varied and intensive discussions related to the field of ethics that spread across several domains, such as speculative theology (*ʿilm al-kalām*), mysticism (*taṣawwuf*), and jurisprudence (*fiqh*) and its fundamentals (*uṣūl al-fiqh*), as well as courtesy (*adab*), one does not find any theoretical foundation for an independent science called ethics. Even in the centuries between the librarian and bibliographer Abū Isḥāq al-Nadīm (d. ca. 380/990) and the historian and geographer Ḥājjī Khalīfa (1067/1657), the Greek philosophical concept persisted, that is, the classification of ethics within the nomenclatural hierarchy of science, which takes ethics as a branch of philosophy and divides it into theoretical wisdom and practical wisdom.

As far as the classical Islamic debates on ethics are concerned, these can be divided into three categories. The first relates to the various discussions permeating the Islamic sciences, as mentioned above. The second refers to the independent philosophical writings in Arabic that follow in the path of Aristotle, Plato, and Galen, as found, for example, in works by Abū Bakr al-Rāzī (d. 320/932), Abū Naṣr al-Fārābī (d. 339/950), Abū l-Ḥasan al-ʿĀmirī (d. 381/991), Abū ʿAlī Miskawayh (d. 421/1030), and Abū ʿAlī Ibn Sīnā (Avicenna, d. 429/1036), among others. The third category concerns writings that deal with practical advice or assess human behaviours and characteristics, as found, for example, in the book *Risāla fī mudāwāt al-nufūs wa-tahdhīb al-akhlāq wa-l-zuhd fī l-radhāʾil*, by Ibn Ḥazm (d. 456/1064; "Treatise for the Cure of the Soul and the Refinement of Character and Asceticism with respect to Vices"; Drāz 1998, 4).

After the sixth/twelfth century, we find hardly any significant contributions to ethics.[4] Even the debates in the nineteenth century among the Arab proponents of *al-nahḍa*, which revolved around the call for ethical reform, the tackling of corrupt social values, the assessment of educational curricula, and the critique of prevailing customs, did not result in an Arabic philosophical category of values (Naṣṣār 2009, 247). This situation changed, however, in the early twentieth century, as interest in the discourse of ethics became palpable, manifesting itself in publications, critical reviews, translations, and independent studies. My understanding is that ethical thinking moved from the practical aspect, which characterised the writings of earlier centuries, to the theoretical and philosophical level.

4 There are some late works on ethics in Arabic, such as *al-Risāla al-shāhiyya fī al-akhlāq* by ʿAḍud al-Dīn al-Ījī (d. 756/1355); in Persian, such as *Akhlāq-i Nāṣirī* by Naṣīr al-Dīn Ṭūsī (d. 672/1274); and in Turkish, such as *Akhlāq al-ʿalāʾī* by Ibn al-Ḥannālī (d. 979/1571) (published by Maṭbaʿat Būlāq in 1833). But such works did not produce paradigm-shifting contributions, as did works by Miskawayh, which heavily influenced them.

While the first emergence of Islamic ethics as an independent research topic was followed by a decline in interest in the second half of the twentieth century, interest has strongly resurged in the last two decades.[5]

2 Ethical Thought in Shifting Contexts before the Twentieth Century

The mission sent to France in 1826 by the ruler of Egypt in the Ottoman period, Muḥammad ʿAlī Pasha (r. 1805–48), provided Egyptian intellectuals with an up-close view of European civilisation. The aim of the endeavour was, in the words of Rifāʿa al-Ṭahṭāwī (1801–73), the *imām* of the mission, to recover the "lost sciences" (*al-ʿulūm al-mafqūda*; al-Ṭahṭāwī 1848, 22). Overwhelmed by the sophistication of European civilisation, al-Ṭahṭāwī set out to record his own testimonials, reflections, and comparisons. His writings reflect the major challenge he felt as he witnessed the gap between modern civilisation (*al-tamaddun al-ḥadīth*) and Islamic civilisation. He experienced this as a dilemma, which is depicted in several of his works. While European countries were known for ubiquitous "indecencies, heresies, and perversities," they were at the same time "the wisest of the countries in the world and the lands of natural sciences (*al-ʿulūm al-barrāniyya*)." They were also the most just, and had, in his opinion, reached "the apogee of skillfulness in the science of wisdom" (al-Ṭahṭāwī 1848, 22, 65). Al-Ṭahṭāwī sought to create harmony between the two civilisations by fusing "*sharīʿa* standards" with the knowledge and civilisation of Europe, which was the purpose for which he went to Europe in the first place. The legacy of the tension between Islam and modern civilisation was also subsequently felt by the generation of the Egyptian reformer Muḥammad ʿAbduh (1849–1905) and his school of thought. Al-Ṭahṭāwī, ʿAbduh, and other *nahḍa* advocates were preoccupied with European civilisation and "modern" knowledge (*al-maʿārif al-ḥadītha*). They were not interested in ethics and viewed Islamic law as sufficient for their reform project.

The desire to modernise explains why al-Ṭahṭāwī and the nineteenth-century proponents of the *nahḍa* embarked on the translation of French scholarship, specifically in relation to modern civilisation and the rise of nations. It is worth noting that al-Ṭahṭāwī read about "natural rights" (*al-ḥuqūq al-ṭabīʿiyya*) and "the spirit of laws" (*rūḥ al-sharāʾiʿ*) and, when he wanted to describe French thought and the books he had read in French, he could do so

5 The causes and contexts of this (re)emergence cannot be tackled in this article; see, however, the introduction by Mohammed Ghaly to the Brill journal *Islamic Ethics* (Ghaly 2017). The journal is published in Arabic, English, and French.

in Arabic only by referring to the idea of "determining what is good and what is detestable" (al-Ṭahṭāwī 1848, 22; al-Ṭahṭāwī 1912, 187–88), which is an Islamic concept ascribed to the Muʿtazilī school in the second century of Islam. While al-Ṭahṭāwī rejected this doctrine (al-Ṭahṭāwī 1872, 131), Muḥammad ʿAbduh would later valourise it and express leanings toward it in his work *Risālat al-tawḥīd* ("Treatise on the Oneness of God"; ʿAbduh 1897). Accordingly, the concept of European civilisation (*al-tamaddun al-Ūrūbbī*) was first tackled from the perspective and with the language of *kalām* and *fiqh*, and the discussion was later to witness a debate on the claim that Islam is anti-civilisational, an issue that "intensified the Islamic intellectual atmosphere in the late nineteenth and early twentieth centuries" (Jadʿān 2010, 394). The most illustrative example here is Muḥammad ʿAbduh's book *al-Islām wa-l-Naṣrāniyya* ("Islam and Christianity"; ʿAbduh 1905).

Because they were interested in theological matters, the centrality of civilisation and its compatibility with Islam, the Christian-Islamic polemical debates, and the relationship between Islam and science, these Arab intellectuals did not pursue philosophical discussions related to the field of ethics. Indeed, the study of philosophy as an academic discipline was prohibited at al-Azhar in the nineteenth century during the Ottoman period (Riḍā 1907, 312; al-Bahy 1964, 224–25). It emerged from the writings of the proponents of the *nahḍa*, including al-Ṭahṭāwī, Muḥammad ʿAbduh, Aḥmad Fāris al-Shidyāq (d. 1887), and others, as we will see in the following, as a belief that ethical matters do not fall outside the purview of legal commands and prohibitions.

However, since the early twentieth century there has been palpable interest in moral philosophy in its own right, a shift that can be attributed to several factors evolving around two essential common features: exposure to European thought through various means such as missions, translation, and education, and interactions within the Egyptian context.

2.1 *Modern Civilisation* (al-tamaddun al-ḥadīth) *and Its Relationship to Ethics: al-Ṭahṭāwī, ʿAbduh, and Rashīd Riḍā*

The mission that was sent by Muḥammad ʿAlī Pasha to France had significant results. One of these was the establishment of the Madrasat al-Alsun ("School of Languages") in 1835 under the chairmanship of Rifāʿa al-Ṭahṭāwī. In 1863, during the era of Ismāʿīl Pasha (r. 1863–79), he also founded an office for translating the French laws, called Qalam al-Tarjama ("The Pen of Translation"; al-Ṭahṭāwī 1912, 7; Hourani 1970, 71). In fact, many of the books that Egyptians read about modern civilisation, ethics, and French laws and legislation emanated from these institutions. The translations acquainted Egyptians with new ideas and concepts that, in addition to stirring general interest in the country, might have boosted the enthusiasm of some young people to study in France.

Rifāʿa al-Ṭahṭāwī read many books in French dealing with a range of subjects, such as philosophy, law, history, and literature. He was also well versed in the history of European nations, their ethical systems, natural rights, the spirit of laws (*l'esprit des lois*), the social contract, and such (al-Ṭahṭāwī 1848, 185–91), and he accorded importance to the refinement of morals (*tahdhīb al-akhlāq*). He considered progress to be contingent upon two foundations: the refinement of morality through religious and human virtues (*tahdhīb al-khuluq ʿalā l-faḍāʾil al-dīniyya wa-l-insāniyya*), and economic activity that leads to wealth and the improvement of the human condition. According to him, the wealth of a nation is the product of moral excellence (*faḍīla*); thus it followed that Egypt would be prosperous when its social virtues were strong, and the key to those virtues was education (al-Ṭahṭāwī 1912, 7; Hourani 1968, 100–101; Hourani 1970, 68ff.). Among the translations that al-Ṭahṭāwī proposed after his return from Paris was Montesquieu's book *Considérations sur les causes de la grandeur des Romains et de leur décadence* (Montesquieu 2011), which includes a chapter on the corruption of the morals of the Romans, arguing that in all situations religion protects ethics (*al-ʿaqīda al-dīniyya taḥmī al-akhlāq*) and that Roman civilisation had the distinctive feature that religious passion was not separate from national zeal. This was compatible with al-Ṭahṭāwī's Islamic background and his belief that Islamic legislation (*al-tashrīʿ al-Islāmī*) is capable of adapting to the requirements of modern European civilisation, and he argued that "love of the homeland leads to the refinement of morals" (*maḥabbat al-waṭan tuʾaddī ilā damāthat al-akhlāq*).

Recognition of European progress led the vanguards of the *nahḍa* to search for its causes and the reasons for the "backwardness" of Muslims. This initiated various debates about the meaning of progress and modern civilisation in relation to ethics and the acquisition of knowledge. The focus of the proponents of the *nahḍa*, from the nineteenth century, had been on education and the reform of what they called "human society" (*al-hayʾa al-ijtimāʿiyya*), which included civilisation (*al-ʿumrān wa-l-madaniyya*). They perceived that education was the only effective way to achieve internal immunity and real independence. This idea owes much to the book of the French pedagogue Edmond Demolins (1852–1907), *À quoi tient la supériorité des Anglo-Saxons*, published in 1897 and translated into Arabic by Aḥmad Fatḥī Pasha Zaghlūl (d. 1914), a disciple of Muḥammad ʿAbduh. The book was cited on several occasions in the journal *al-Manār*, published by the Syrian reformer Muḥammad Rashīd Riḍā (1865–1935; *al-Manār* 16/1913, 550; and 17/1914, 472). Demolins believed that the refinement of morals alone is not enough to achieve progress but social and economic reform are needed as well (Demolins 1899, 303–33).

The scholars of *al-nahḍa* were exposed to two modes of European thinking. The first viewed human society as moving in accordance with the natural path of progress (*taqaddum*) toward an ideal universal stage dominated by reason and the expansion of individual freedom, and the prevalence of relations based on free contracts and individual interest. This first mode was represented by Ernest Renan (d. 1892), Herbert Spencer (d. 1903), and Émile Durkheim (d. 1917). The second group, however, saw that modern civilisation assumed a national character and that each nation therefore has a mental structure, which, like the physical structure, is formed as a result of a slow historical accumulation (Hourani 1968, 181). The second group is represented by Gustave Le Bon (1841–1931), who saw that the psychology of a nation formulates that nation's spirit, and from that, its history and civilisation are extrapolated, and that the ethics of a nation constitutes the *raison d'être* of its development and determines its future (Le Bon 1913).

Muḥammad ʿAbduh and his disciples Qāsim Amīn (1863–1908), ʿAbd al-Qādir al-Maghribī (d. 1956), and Rafīq al-ʿAẓm (d. 1925), among others, proceeded in the same direction by focussing on the primacy of human society in relation to ethics. In their view, ethics was a fundamental pillar, of no less importance than laws and legislation, and which, with them, must regulate the education of the individual and the society (Jadʿān 2010, 394; Sedgwick 2009; ʿAbduh 1905). Muḥammad ʿAbduh read the French politician and author François Guizot (1787–1874) and taught his book *Histoire générale de la civilisation en Europe*, published in 1828 (Guizot 1877). Guizot, who was a conservative liberal, accorded importance to the Protestant Reformation in the making of the European renaissance (*al-nahḍa al-Ūrūbbiyya*). He considered modern civilisation to be based on two elements: the growth of human society (political and social growth) and the growth of the human being (in terms of individual and moral growth), and these are inextricably related. Every change in human society is beneficial to individuals and vice versa, and he perceived external change to be linked to self-change (Guizot 1877). Guizot limited his focus in this book to the first element only, which is the growth of human society in the European nations, but he promised to take up at some later point the second element of modern civilisation, which lies in the self-transformation of individuals, focussing on France only, which represented the vanguard of European civilisation in his lifetime. This second part of Guizot's book would perhaps have helped us to understand the reasons for the growth of the ethical debates in France, especially the fact that ethical education became a component of the French school curricula.

One has to emphasise however, that although Muḥammad ʿAbduh's library included European works in the field of ethics, such as *Émile ou de l'éducation* by Jean Jacques Rousseau, Leo Tolstoy's *War and Peace* and *The Fruits of Enlightenment,* and Herbert Spencer's *The Principles of Ethics*,[6] the ethical vision that shaped his orientation derived from classical Islamic philosophy. He taught Abū ʿAlī Ibn Miskawayh's *Tahdhīb al-akhlāq* ("The Refinement of Morals"), and he tried to get this work included in the official educational curricula.[7] ʿAbduh also revised some of his speculative positions and gave preponderance to some Muʿtazilī views, reaching the conclusion that the concept of morals is absolutely not relative.

Therefore, Muḥammad ʿAbduh's ethical conception is based on spiritual elevation in the quest for individual happiness (*al-saʿāda al-fardiyya*). Human beings are called upon to achieve perfection, which is the *raison d'être* of their existence and the secret to happiness, and they are also called upon to reconcile the two forms of happiness: spiritual and physical, as well as the happiness of the individual and of the society. ʿAbduh views ethics as the overlapping of social involvement, universal integration, an upward movement toward primordial existence, and a civilisational movement toward the promotion of growth and prosperity on earth. Success in attaining perfection is linked to the individual endeavour to make the soul aspire to a higher level and to the collective endeavour to achieve the social advancement of society (al-Ḥaddād 2003, 126–59). One can say that the ethical in Muḥammad ʿAbduh's view was confined to speculative theology and Ṣūfī frameworks. The modern tendency in it, however, lies in its link to civilisation only as a general framework, for education, in his thinking, is bound by ethical objectives, whereby each and every individual is supposed to achieve his humanity by virtue of being in harmony with the collective spirit of the community. ʿAbduh's conception of education is classical, as it is not seen as a temporary stage whose purpose is to prepare the individual to adapt to the values of the community. Rather, it is an ongoing effort to achieve an objective for the next life, and the relationship between the teacher and the student is a paternal one and cannot be compared to the type of relationship that exists between a civil servant and a modern citizen (al-Ḥaddād 2003, 135f.).

Muḥammad Rashīd Riḍā carried out the work started by Muḥammad ʿAbduh. He saw "education and learning as the two pillars on which happiness

---

6 In his French dissertation on Muḥammad ʿAbduh, ʿUthmān Amīn lists the sources in his library. See also al-Ḥaddād 2003, 127 and Hourani 1970, 135.

7 See *al-Manār* 1906, vol. 8, 401; and ʿAbd al-Rāziq 1922, 520. See also Sedgwick 2009, 16, who translates the title of the book as "Training in Ethics."

is founded, and they are the factors that lead to prosperity. The aim of education is to help every member of the nation to preserve the harmony of its national and religious community" (Riḍā 1899a, 567). Riḍā also came under the spell of Ibn Miskawayh's book *The Refinement of Morals*, holding that among the virtues of the modern scientific renaissance (*al-nahḍa al-ʿilmiyya al-ḥadītha*) was that "it awakened in us an awareness of all the kinds of reform that we need, including the printing of books on ethics and education." He made this comment in the context of his praise for Ibn Miskawayh's *Tahdhīb al-akhlāq*, which had been reissued, hailing it as "the best that I have seen in our language on the philosophy of ethics.... I have more than once cherished reading this book and taught it to some students" (Riḍā 1900, 492). Analysing Riḍā's pronouncements on various occasions, we find that, although he celebrates ethics as a discipline, it does not, in his perception, fall outside the classical purview. It "exists only in the books of Ṣūfis and philosophers, and Ṣūfī books mention it in a religious manner," he states in *al-Manār* in 1899 (Riḍā 1899b, 722). Elsewhere, he calls the science of ethical refinement "spiritual medicine" (*al-ṭibb al-rūḥānī*), criticising the lack of attention to it. He defines its subject matter as the "forces of the human soul and the characteristics of the conscious spirit that controls the body and conducts its work, and its aim is real happiness, because happiness is the fruit of good and useful works" (Riḍā 1899c, 881).

2.2 *The Impact of Exposure to French Thought: ʿAbd al-Rāziq and Luṭfī al-Sayyid*

The subsequent scientific missions left an impact and led to the revival of interest in philosophy in Egypt. This period witnessed the emergence of a new generation of intellectuals who were educated in France and who studied nineteenth-century European thought under some eminent thinkers. For example, Muṣṭafā ʿAbd al-Rāziq (1885–1947), who later became the head of al-Azhar (1945–47), travelled to France in the company of Aḥmad Luṭfī al-Sayyid (1872–1963) in 1909, where he attended some of the lectures of Émile Durkheim (Khūrshīd 1984). These two figures would significantly influence Egyptian culture in two different ways: firstly, ʿAbd al-Rāziq emphasised elements of the Islamic tradition (*al-aṣāla al-Islāmiyya*) and secondly Aḥmad Luṭfī al-Sayyid, who translated Aristotle's book on ethics from French into Arabic, established a liberal trend. Both scholars and their visions would have an important impact on an entire generation of Egyptian intellectuals.

The discussions on moral philosophy taking place in France beginning in the late nineteenth and early twentieth centuries influenced the students who were sent there to study philosophy. Part of the philosophical discussions organised by the French Philosophy Society in 1906 revolved around the normativity of ethics and its relation to religion, which created a conducive environment for the emergence of the sociological trend within ethics. This trend arose at a time when discussions of morality were entangled with different approaches, as will be explained in section 2 of this paper, which describes the different developments in ethics within the Egyptian context (al-Ṭawīl 1949, 11).

Another important influence in this era came through university education in Egypt, then in its early phases, which contributed to the teaching of philosophy, including moral philosophy. The Egyptian University (now Cairo University) was founded in 1908, and Aḥmad Luṭfī al-Sayyid became its president. (For ease of reference, the institution will henceforth be referred to in this essay as Cairo University.) Sulṭān Bīk Muḥammad, who was a professor of Arabic philosophy and ethics at Cairo Universty,[8] gave lectures in 1911 on "Arabic Philosophy and Ethics," and those lectures were later published in two parts: the first dealing with Arabic philosophy and the second with ethics. The university attracted some Orientalists who joined as instructors, including Louis Massignon (1883–1963), who taught philosophical terminology there in 1912 and 1913. Massignon's students in Cairo included, among others, Manṣūr Fahmī (d. 1957) and Ṭāhā Ḥusayn (d. 1973), who subsequently became leaders of the Egyptian *nahḍa*.[9] The Comte de Galarza (1878–1938), the Spanish Orientalist who lectured in Cairo from 1913 until 1920, provided preliminary introductions to the definition of ethics and lectured on the most important eighteenth-century philosophers, including Immanuel Kant, whose philosophy he introduced through the critique and analysis of practical reason (Comte de Galarza 1920). The French philosopher André Lalande (1867–1963) taught the first cohort of graduates of the Department of Philosophy at Cairo University, and his lectures, delivered in the 1920s, were translated into Arabic by Aḥmad Ḥasan al-Zayyāt (d. 1968) and Yūsuf Karam (d. 1959), and revised by Ṭāhā Ḥusayn. In his lectures Lalande discussed normative judgements and issues related to moral philosophy (Lalande 1929).

In the 1920s several texts on moral philosophy appeared and became part of the school curriculum, to the extent that the Egyptian Ministry of Education introduced the subject into primary and secondary school curricula. Aḥmad Amīn (d. 1954) and Amīn Wāṣif Bīk (d. 1928) were among the pioneers who wrote books exclusively devoted to ethics for student readers. Interest in the

8 Unfortunately I could not find any biographical information about him.

9 See, in this regard, Ibrāhīm Madkūr's introduction to Massignon's lectures, delivered at Cairo University (Madkūr n.d.).

subject increased and resulted in the 1940s in an Islamic trend that became intrinsically linked to moral philosophy, while prior to that, the dominant influential paradigm in written texts had been the European philosophical model, especially the French. This Islamic trend appears in the writings of Muḥammad Yūsuf Mūsā (d. 1963), who had studied in France under Louis Massignon and who taught ethics at the Faculty of Islamic Theology (*uṣūl al-dīn*) at al-Azhar University. Yūsuf Karam found his writings original and unusual, both in terms of ideas and his methodology of comparative philosophy, and he expected people would find comfort in Mūsā's writings. Muḥammad ʿAbdullāh Drāz (also spelled Muḥammad ʿAbdallāh Darāz, d. 1958), who had studied under Massignon in France as well, developed course material devoted to ethics, which was included in the al-Azhar curriculum and was studied by, for example, the Islamic scholar Yūsuf al-Qaraḍāwī (b. 1926) and his contemporaries (al-Qaraḍāwī 2006; Gräf and Skovgaard-Petersen 2009).

2.3 *The Scholarly Community and the Intellectual Networks*

Tracking the intellectual networks allows for a determining of the extent of interactions between intellectuals of different trends and the factors that made it possible for them to influence and be influenced. Tracing these networks creates a picture of the intellectual environment that contributed to the development of the study of ethics in Egypt, given that there are links between figures representing various intellectual backgrounds: Islamic, liberal, Azharī, Cairo University, Muslim, and Christian.[10] These bonds were intellectual, personal, between teacher and student, or a combination of these.

Examples of the latter form of relationship include that of ʿUthmān Amīn (d. 1978), who was a disciple of Muṣṭafā ʿAbd al-Rāziq and had ties to André Lalande, and Muṣṭafā ʿAbd al-Rāziq, who was a disciple of Muḥammad ʿAbduh. Other examples can be found in the friendship between Yūsuf Karam, Muṣṭafā ʿAbd al-Rāziq, and Muḥammad Yūsuf Mūsā. Yūsuf Karam, whose students included ʿAbd al-Raḥmān Badawī (d. 2002) and Tawfīq al-Ṭawīl (d. 1991), worked as André Lalande's assistant at Cairo University in 1927. ʿUthmān Amīn attended Karam's lectures at Cairo University and later their relationship grew stronger, to the extent that Amīn dedicated one of his books to Karam (Amīn 1953). Yūsuf Karam was working on a book on ethics at the end of the 1940s, but he could not publish it because the manuscript was lost when his house collapsed (Wahba 1986, 62, 521).

10 For instance, Muḥammad Yūsuf Mūsā pointed to the differences between him and Yūsuf Karam, which did not preclude them from entertaining an intellectual and personal friendship (Mūsā 1986, 534).

These intimate bonds and similar ones reflected their proponents' firm belief that ethics was needed as, to put it in Tawfīq al-Ṭawīl's words, *maṣdar li-l-thaqāfa fī Miṣr al-muʿāṣira* ("a source of culture for contemporary Egypt"; al-Ṭawīl 1986, 143). Yūsuf Karam ended his book on the history of modern philosophy in 1949 with the sentence "Our epoch, conflicting views notwithstanding, is eager for a philosophy that supports ethics and religion." (*inna ʿaṣranā al-hāḍir ʿalā taḍārub al-ārāʾ fīhi tawwāq ilā falsafa takfulu al-akhlāq wa-l-dīn*). However, Karam regarded his epoch as having failed to embrace the means that would lead to this kind of philosophy—which include unequivocal faith in reason—and because this was absent, the movement could not succeed (Karam 1949, 440).

2.4 *The Egyptian Context: Discussions in the Leading Journals*

In the Egyptian milieu, it is not possible to separate the rise of ethical thought as a trend from the developments that took place during the *nahḍa* and the reform movements. The intellectual elite, especially those concerned with philosophical studies and whose culture combined traditional knowledge and Western philosophical training, were deeply committed to the idea of comprehensive education, which would include the use of ethical concepts as conveyed in school and university education, as well as through rich discussions in the leading journals of the time, such as *al-Risāla, al-Muqtaṭaf, al-Azhar,* and *al-Hilāl,* among others. Intellectuals were especially interested in the prevalence of moral weaknesses, the need to critique the prevailing culture, and the quest for a "new philosophy" to revive the Egyptian nation. This obsession, which was reiterated from the beginning of the twentieth century, intensified in the 1930s. Glimpses of it can be found in the works of Muḥammad Aḥmad Jād al-Mawlā (d. 1944), who taught Arabic language at Oxford University (1910–13), Yāʿqūb Qām,[11] and Tawfīq al-Ṭawīl (d. 1991), among others.[12] Manṣūr Fahmī even delivered a lecture at the American University in Cairo on "The Impacts of Moral Vulnerability on Our Social Life," which was subsequently published in the journal *al-Hilāl* (Fahmī 1940, 505–13).

One aspect of ethical thinking in the 1930s is reflected in a debate recorded in *al-Risāla* magazine. Aḥmad Ḥasan al-Zayyāt wrote an article titled "Thawra ʿalā l-akhlāq: Hal al-ṣalāḥ ghayr al-najāḥ?" ("Revolutionising ethics: Is the good also the successful?"), in which the author uses an imaginary character to address the problem that while ethics may bring happiness (*al-saʿāda*), it does

---

11 Unfortunately I could not find any biographical information about him.

12 See Tawfīq al-Ṭawīl's introduction to Henry Sidgwick's book *Outlines of the History of Ethics,* (al- Ṭawīl 1949, 36); and Jād al-Mawlā 1932, 1:6. See also Qām n.d., 3, 244; and Ḥusayn 1931.

not provide the way for success (*al-najāḥ*) in life, which requires a material and practical approach. The article provoked an important discussion in which, at a subsequent stage, ʿAbd al-Wahhāb ʿAzzām (d. 1959), Amīn al-Khūlī (d. 1966), and ʿAbd al-ʿAzīz ʿIzzat[13] participated. ʿIzzat argued that this issue could be discussed only on the basis of a philosophical approach to ethics, which might have been, to some extent, missing from previous reactions and responses (al-Zayyāt 1937; ʿAzzām 1937; al-Khūlī 1937; ʿIzzat 1938).

In parallel to these developments, an ethical crisis emerged with the outbreak of World War II, which caused a great deal of destruction and loss of life. The war affected debates about ethics, as one can see from the example of three Egyptian figures. First, there was the debate raised in *al-Risāla* in 1940, where Aḥmad Ḥasan al-Zayyāt wrote a critical article condemning World War II as being antithetical, drawing a comparison between that situation and the war conditions in the pre-Islamic era (al-Zayyāt 1940). Second, Aḥmad Luṭfī al-Sayyid published an article in *al-Hilāl* in 1943 titled "Kayfa yanbaghī an takūn al-akhlāq li-taḥqīq taʿāwun ʿālamī?" (How do we ensure global cooperation regarding ethics?"; al-Sayyid 1943). In this article, the author talks about the idea of *al-salām al-dāʾim,* "a lasting peace," reminiscent of Kant, and the termination of the war, from a critical and philosophical perspective. Third, Muḥammad ʿAbdullāh Drāz wrote a thesis on ethics in the Qurʾān, which he submitted to the Sorbonne University in 1947. Although the thesis does not explicitly refer to a given historical context, it was written in Paris during World War II, apparently under painful circumstances. The three figures, therefore, reflect three different positions vis-à-vis ethics at that time.

3 Main Trends in Modern Ethical Thought in the Next Generations

Openness to European thought drew attention to modern European patterns of thinking, which brought about an evolution in the treatment of ethics and its role from the perspective of the proponents of the *nahḍa*. Initially, ethics was perceived as part of the process of modern civilisation and assumed two forms: The first focussed on the religious and valuation framework adopted by al-Ṭahṭāwī, while the second sought to build an ethical vision in accordance with the classical Islamic perceptions espoused by Muḥammad ʿAbduh.

The scene, however, changed with the next generation of scholars sent to France to study philosophy and ethics[14] and with graduates of the Egyptian

13 Unfortunately I have no biographical information about him.

14 Regarding the names of several of the scholars who were sent to France to study, see Badawī 1992, 153f.

universities, who had deepened their knowledge of philosophy and its doctrines and were influenced by the study of moral philosophy. We notice the emergence of interest in ethics in various trends, which reflected the concerns and backgrounds of these individuals in a manner consistent with the two standards of education in modern Egypt represented in the institutional split between religious education (al-Azhar) and nonreligious education (Cairo University and Dār al-ʿUlūm).

3.1 *Greek Philosophy*

In the context of Greek philosophy, Aḥmad Luṭfī al-Sayyid's translation of Aristotle's *Nicomachean Ethics* constituted "an extraordinary artistic event," as described by Ṭāhā Ḥusayn, who suggested that al-Azhar scholars should consider teaching it (Ḥusayn n.d., 48). What is significant here is that this translation came through the French language, not only because al-Sayyid did not know Greek, but because it was the French renaissance that had drawn his attention to the importance of Aristotle. He understood these advances as having been achieved "because the modern European renaissance had studied Aristotle's philosophy … which was the key to the modern thinking that gave birth to a number of modern philosophical doctrines" (al-Sayyid 1924a). Aiming to provide support for philosophical teachings in the religious schools and institutions, al-Sayyid chose Aristotle for two reasons: The first was that his teachings "do not clash with the national doctrines and do not thwart religious teachings," and the second was "that he [Aristotle] may produce in the Eastern renaissance what he had produced in the Western one" (*rajāʾ an yuntija fī l-nahḍa al-sharqiyya mithla mā antaja fī l-nahḍa al-gharbiyya*; al-Sayyid 1924a).

Aḥmad Luṭfī al-Sayyid had a great impact on a generation of Egyptian intellectuals, to the extent that Ṭāhā Ḥusayn described him as "our first teacher in this age," referring to his being an apologist for Aristotle in the East, whom the Arabs called the first teacher (*al-muʿallim al-awwal*) and whom his disciples described as the "dean of philosophy in the East" (Rajab 1953, 314). One of the central Aristotelian ideas that preoccupied al-Sayyid was that of freedom (*al-ḥurriyya*), as perceived by nineteenth-century liberals, which he considered one of life's necessities. He was attracted to the ideas of the social contract and utilitarianism, which he took from Jeremy Bentham (d. 1832) and John Stuart Mill (d. 1873), advocating for the greatest good for the greatest number of people, and he was equally interested in the ideas of progress and development, seeing translation as a necessary act and part of the civilisational movement (*ḥarakat al-tamaddun*).[15]

---

15 See, in this regard, a conversation with him entitled "Hal nu'allif am nutarjim?" *Muḥādatha maʿa l-ustādh Aḥmad Luṭfī al-Sayyid Bīk*, in *al-Hilāl*, vol. 3, December 1924, 234–36.

While al-Sayyid endeavoured to revive Aristotle, Ismāʿīl Maẓhar (d. 1962) sought to revive the philosophy of Aristippus, a contemporary of Aristotle, whose ideas the latter discussed, without mentioning his name, in his book *The Nicomachean Ethics*. Maẓhar justified this return to Aristippus through his axiomatic belief that the ancient Greeks are the finest people the world has ever known, and the secret behind Aristippus's fame was the rise of individualism and independence in thought and action, away from the influence of the masses. Greek civilisation was that of individuals, while the modern one is that of the masses (Maẓhar 1926, 274–79). The Arabs had been exposed only occasionally to Aristippus; so, Maẓhar decided to write a book about him, in which he included studies about the philosophy of pleasure and pain, considering the doctrine of Aristippus to be nearer to the methods of modern science than Aristotle's. His is a practical doctrine based on established fundamentals in human nature. As opposed to Kant, who advocates supreme ideals, Aristippus reckons with reality and argues that the achievement of instant pleasure is a psychological necessity that we submit to despite ourselves, and recognising this is better than denying it. Thus, we become aware of the reality of being and the self is tamed in order to do good as much as possible.[16]

3.2 *Modern Arab Philosophy*

Apart from Greek philosophy, new and modern philosophical trends emerged in the late 1940s. One of these was the modern Arab trend that considered ethics a branch of sociology in subject matter and in methodology, a view that had been predominant in France since the late nineteenth century and the beginning of the twentieth. It was a view so widespread in education that ʿAbd al-Ḥalīm Maḥmūd (d. 1978), who worked on his doctorate in France in the 1940s under the supervision of Massignon, pointed out that the teaching material in this field was operating within the social sciences framework and that ethics, in this view, "was a human social creation" (Maḥmūd 1985, 172). Clearly, Louis Massignon, when he broached the subject of ethics and ethical trends in his philosophy lectures at Cairo University, made it a branch of the social sciences as well (Massignon n.d., 113–16). Moreover, when Tawfīq al-Ṭawīl translated *Outlines of the History of Ethics* by Henry Sidgwick (d. 1900), in his introduction he pointed to this trend, which he called "idiosyncratic" (*shādhdh*), arguing that it had appeared in France at a time when thought and ethics were obfuscated. He then defined it—Sidgwick and other philosophers

16 *Al-Muqtaṭaf* published some chapters of this work; see Maẓhar 1936. It was republished later; see Maẓhar 2012.

of ethics had neglected to—and, in any case, up until 1949, this trend had not yet been defined in the Arabic language (al-Ṭawīl 1949, 10).

The disciples of this school of thought believed that ethics is a positivistic science, directed towards the study of customs, traditions, and laws as they appear in reality and are experienced by a specific human group, in accordance with the inductive experimental approach. Knowledge of social and moral laws help us improve and promote ethics, and this trend obliterates the traditional perception of ethics by describing it as a standardised science that distinguishes between the theoretical level (that which should be) and the practical one (that which is), which philosophers confuse. Ethics, however, is relative and evolves with society, and this idea is apparent in the context of the transformation of the theory of ethical development into a comprehensive doctrine. It prevailed among the generation of Arab scholars who had studied in France under the pivotal figure in the French sociological school, Lucien Lévy-Bruhl (d. 1939). His students and followers included Manṣūr Fahmī, who came under his influence as his student, as well as ʿAbd al-ʿAzīz ʿIzzat and al-Sayyid Muḥammad Badawī (b. 1916). Maḥmūd Qāsim (d. 1973) translated Lévy-Bruhl's major work, *La Morale et la Science des Mœurs,* in 1953 (it had been published in French in 1903), and had proposed it to the Egyptian Ministry of Education as a revolution in the methodology of research in ethics. Nevertheless he expressed his objection to several of the author's ideas, as is clear from his comments on the translation (Lévy-Bruhl 1953).[17] It seems that Qāsim and Badawī had a different understanding of the sociological trend, which helped alleviate the criticism levelled at it (Badawī 1992, 158).

A new trend, which was different from the sociological one, emerged with ʿAbd al-Raḥmān Badawī (1917–2002), who was the first to introduce the philosophy of existentialism (*al-falsafa al-wujūdiyya*) to the Arab world. His doctoral thesis at Cairo University in 1944 deals with "the existentialist age." He was influenced by the German philosophers Friedrich Nietzsche (d. 1900) and Martin Heidegger (d. 1976). Although Badawī's contribution expanded to include several texts on ethics that he edited and translated, chief among which is his publication of Aristotle in its classical Arabic translation from the Greek, his existentialist orientation is clear in his book *al-Akhlāq al-naẓariyya* ("Theoretical Ethics"; Badawī 1976) and his study titled "Hal yumkin qiyām akhlāq wujūdiyya?" ("Are existentialist ethical values possible?"), which was published in 1953. In this work, he argues that there can be no existentialist ethics, for existence is either the subjective, as experienced by the self (*wujūd li-l-dhāt*),

17 For further details about the ideas of the vanguards of the sociological trend, see ʿAṭiyya 1990, 48–72.

or the objective, as defined by the concrete universe (*wujūd li-l-mawḍūʿ*). Subjective valuation is meaningless because it is an act of self-evaluation, but objective valuation is impossible because the individual is separate and isolated. Thus existentialism and objective valuation cannot be reconciled, and accordingly, one cannot talk about ethics. Badawī rejected the idea of obligation (*al-iltizām*), because it is imposed by others on an individual self, and he rejected the idea of conscience (*al-ḍamīr*), because it is an objective feeling that infiltrates the self. He also rejected both virtue (*al-faḍīla*), because it requires the submission of the self to the dicta of others, and the concept of good (*al-khayr*), because it means that the self is split among other selves (Badawī 1953). Existentialism, however, remained marginal in the Arab world and because it assumed different shapes, one cannot talk about a unique concept of existentialism (Iskandar 1969).

In addition to existentialism, a trend called "modified idealism" (*al-mithāliyya al-muʿaddala*) emerged and became associated with Tawfīq al-Ṭawīl himself. Described as "the pioneer of ethical philosophy in the contemporary Arab world," al-Ṭawīl combined religion and philosophy (ʿAṭiyya 1990, 105). He transcended the critiques levelled at Kant's idealism. Modified idealism means achievement of the self and how it is injected in all the vital forces but without inflicting injustice on the values of society or undermining its standards. Humankind is regarded as an integral and complete whole, harmoniously combining mind and sensation. Al-Ṭawīl also criticised the treatment of pleasure as a standard for conduct. One of his prominent books is *Falsafat al-akhlāq: Nash'atuhā wa-taṭawwuruhā* ("Moral Philosophy: Origins and Developments"; al-Ṭawīl 1967).

Zakī Najīb Maḥmūd's (b. 1905) book *al-Manṭiq al-waḍʿī* represents his first phase in moving toward the "logical positivism" and pleading for it (Maḥmūd 1951a). This positivism was a new movement that was established in 1928 in Vienna by a group of naturalists with philosophical leanings, including Moritz Schlick (d. 1936), Friedrich Waismann (d. 1959), Rudolf Carnap (d. 1970), and others. This movement borrowed from the traditional positivism the material empirical approach, while adding logical explanations. Hence, Maḥmūd differentiated between two types of words: first, words that refer to external facts, which can be verified or determined to be false; and, second, words that are not used to indicate external facts, such as those intended to trigger the emotions of the listener or the construction of a mental state that is internally consistent but has no external meaning (Maḥmūd 1988, 160–62; Maḥmūd 1993, 62). Metaphysics is therefore considered meaningless in that it names what cannot be described as truth or lies. Logical positivism is based on the principle of verification, that is, the meaning of speech is a method of verification—verifying its truth or error by reference to reality, for the meaning of a word and the means of verifying it are the same thing (Maḥmūd 1951a, 16–17). This philosophy was based on belief in experimental science and the veracity of the senses as an indisputable principle. one of the absolute assumptions that underpin modern knowledge and intellectual tendencies. From this point, the function of philosophy became, in the eyes of the logical positivists, the logical analysis of the meaning of terms, determined by verifying them through reference to reality. As for the investigation of the truth of things, that is the function of experimental scientists, because philosophy—according to this brand of positivism—deviates from the description of things in themselves, in that things do not have meanings that refer to sensory meanings in the world of reality (Maḥmūd 1988, 159, 160–181). Maḥmūd calibrated the value of good and beauty based on metaphysics, which, in his opinion, cannot be a science or part of a science (Maḥmūd 1953, 50–52, 110–14). This means that values are relative, because they are subjective. "We are the ones who give things value … basing our estimations on our personal objectives" (Maḥmūd 1951b, 3).

It is noticeable that the above trends—the modernised Greek and the modern European—either lacked completely or marginalised any reference to the Islamic tradition. Although Aḥmad Luṭfī al-Sayyid was in contact with Muḥammad ʿAbduh, the intellectual trajectories of the two men diverged. While ʿAbduh sought a modern civilisation compatible with Islam through the restoration of the *sharīʿa* as an ethical basis for society, al-Sayyid sought a Western model of civilisation through a return to pre-Islamic roots, i.e., Greek philosophy, which is why he embraced philosophical, political, and social ethics. Although ʿAbd al-Raḥmān Badawī and Tawfīq al-Ṭawīl studied under Muṣṭafā ʿAbd al-Rāziq, a disciple of Muḥammad ʿAbduh, they took a completely different direction from that of ʿAbd al-Rāziq, who was a pioneer in the quest for Islamic authenticity (*al-aṣāla al-Islāmiyya*), as articulated in his main thesis, that Islamic legal theory (*uṣūl al-fiqh*) represents authentic Islamic philosophy (*al-falsafa al-Islāmiyya al-aṣīla*).

3.3 *Modern Islamic Ethics*

While the Islamic orientation in ethics espoused by al-Ṭahṭāwī and Muḥammad ʿAbduh represents part of a conciliatory approach that sought to reconcile European civilisation and Islam, it underwent changes with Muḥammad Yūsuf Mūsā and Muḥammad ʿAbdullāh Drāz. Mūsā, who studied in France, taught at al-Azhar, and had links with Yūsuf Karam and Muṣṭafā ʿAbd al-Rāziq, became a trailblazer in the study of ethics in Islam by publishing three books in the 1940s on three issues: chronicling the history of ethics, demonstrating its relation to Greek philosophy, and unravelling the ethical philosophical ideas in Islam, in comparison to Greek and European philosophies. Mūsā embarked on this as a professor in the Faculty of Islamic Theology at al-Azhar University. However, it is clear that Mūsā, by virtue of his training, writings, and relationships, was operating within the Greek concept of ethics, so that no reference to the question of ethics in the Qur'ān and *ḥadīth*, for example, could be found in his work. His focus was chiefly on speculative theology and philosophy (Mūsā 1943; Mūsā 1945; Mūsā 1941.).

Muḥammad ʿAbdullāh Drāz, on the other hand, had the unique privilege of studying ethics in the Qur'ān, driven by modern philosophical queries, especially Kantian philosophy. His book *La Morale du Koran* (the Arabic translation is titled *Dustūr al-akhlāq fi l-Qur'ān*) was originally his doctoral dissertation, published in Paris in 1951, which he submitted to the Sorbonne University in 1947. This was his first attempt at formulating a comprehensive vision of ethics in the Qur'ān, from the perspective of moral philosophy. It is as if Drāz wanted to prove that Islam possesses a comprehensive ethical system, on the one hand, and that there exists a close link between religion and ethics, on the other hand, especially in the French context, where the sociological and positivistic approach prevailed. Drāz chose to return to the Qur'ānic text, free from the legacy of the Islamic tradition and its speculative theological and jurisprudential doctrines, using an inductive approach and a critical viewpoint that transcends the views of the Muʿtazila, the Ashʿariyya, and philosophy in general (Rashwānī 2017, 160).

This inductive trend would take a different direction with Aḥmad Maḥmūd Ṣubḥī, who embarked on the quest for an Islamic ethical pattern, which is distinct from that of Greek philosophy, on the basis that "the pattern mapped out in Aristotle's ethics is nonbinding for all ethical trends," and that ethics must be founded on a metaphysical basis. In his quest, Ṣubḥī resorted to Islamic ethics as adopted by speculative theologians (a reason-based trend "*al-ittijāh al-ʿaqlī*") and Ṣūfis (a direct-experience based trend "*al-ittijāh al-dhawqī*").[18] Moreover, ʿAbd al-Ḥayy Qābīl took the same direction. He studied under Tawfīq al-Ṭawīl and Ibrāhīm Madkūr (d. 1996), and dedicated his book to ʿUthmān Amīn. Qābīl's research focused on the "ethical principles in Islam" as represented in the principles of obligation (*al-wājib*) and happiness (*al-saʿāda*), envisioning a kind of Islamic moral philosophy that is not limited to the referentialities of the Qur'ān and Sunna (Qābīl 1984).

This philosophical orientation declined in influence at the end of the 1980s, with the rise of the behavioural and traditional trends, which searched for pure

18 Ṣubḥī 1983, which was originally an academic dissertation written under the supervision of ʿAlī Sāmī al-Nashshār (d. 1980) at Alexandria University.

Islamic ethics. For instance, Ḥāmid Ṭāhir (b. 1943), who studied in France as well as in Egypt under Maḥmūd Qāsim, wrote a booklet titled *al-Fikr al-akhlāqī fi l-Islām* ("Ethical thought in Islam") for students at the Faculty of Dār al-ʿUlūm. The author's approach is dominated by the perception of ethics in classical behavioural terms, with preliminary theoretical introductions and quotations from the Qurʾān and *ḥadīth*. He annexed to the booklet some classical texts by Ibn al-Muqaffaʿ (d. c.142/759), al-Jāḥiẓ (d. 255/869), al-Muḥāsibī (d. 243/857), Ibn Ḥazm (456/1064), al-Māwardī (d. 450/1058), al-Subkī (d. 756/1355), and Ibn al-Jawzī (d. 597/1200) (Ṭāhir n.d.). Another exponent of this trend, Aḥmad ʿAbd al-Raḥmān (b. 1932), wrote a book titled *al-Faḍāʾil al-khuluqiyya fi l-Islām* ("Ethical Virtues in Islam"), in which he distinguishes between (Greek) philosophical ethics and Qurʾānic ethics. He considered the Greek impact on Qurʾānic studies to be negative, because, in his view, the spirit of the Qurʾān opposes the teachings of Greece. As a religious system (*niẓām dīnī*), Islam has its own system of ethics and virtues, which is different from that of philosophical ethics (ʿAbd al-Raḥmān 1989). Ḥasan al-Sharqāwī[19] criticised "Western ethics" and proposed instead what he termed "pure Islamic ethics apart from any [external] influences," but his proposal lacked a coherent plan or vision (ʿAṭiyya 1990, 199–201). Muḥammad ʿAbdullāh al-Sharqāwī (b. 1952), on the other hand, criticised the dependence of Arab writers on Western ethics as a standard, and he also criticised Tawfīq al-Ṭawīl for his marginalisation of Islamic ethics. To highlight the originality, uniqueness, and sublime nature of Islamic ethics, al-Sharqāwī annexed to his book texts by the distinctive pre-modern Arab authors al-Māwardī, al-Rāghib al-Aṣfahānī (d. early 5th/11th century), and Ibn al-Jawzī, and as well that of Muḥammad ʿAbdullāh Drāz (al-Sharqāwī 1990).

4 Conclusion

This article attempts to show that ethics was an integral part of reformist thought in its various trajectories. Western ideas gave rise to modern discussions in Egypt, and the intellectual response took different positions, ranging from adaptation, critical revision, and rediscovery or reinterpretation of the Islamic tradition. Modern European civilisation and philosophy contributed to the revival of Arabic philosophical and ethical studies to the extent that they became a scientific field and part of the educational curriculum. The division of the educational system in Egypt into religious (*dīnī*) and non-religious (*madanī*) had an impact on the rise of various trends, ranging from

19 Unfortunately I could not find any biographical information about him.

the Western philosophical (Greek and modern) to the Islamic. The Islamic discussions that had been evolving up until the mid-twentieth century were open to the modern philosophical question of ethics, and it was noticeable that philosophy exerted an indelible influence on diverse Egyptian writers, including ʿAbd al-Raḥmān Badawī, Zakariyyāʾ Ibrāhīm (d. 1976), Muḥammad ʿAbdullāh Drāz, and ʿUthmān Amīn, among others. It is true that the reception of Western philosophy was not monolithic and thus had a positive effect on the growth of the philosophical and ethical debate in a critical and open manner. Moreover, the sharpness of the separation between the two institutionalised types of education was mitigated by the spirit of camaraderie that prevailed in France and the relationships among scholars that were established back in Egypt.

Contrary to earlier views that reformist discourse and the modernism associated with it were "largely a product of European influences" (Gibb 1945, 63), this study shows that there is a multiplicity in the perceptions of the reformers and their ideological references. It also identifies several directions in these trends, ranging from conservative virtue ethics, classical Roman or Greek ethics, and modern social, idealistic, and existential ethical theories, to theological and scriptural ethics. For instance, the reform project initiated by Muḥammad ʿAbduh did not remain within ʿAbduh's vision. It has developed into variant and sometimes even conflicting projects because of many factors, such as Egyptian students studying in European universities, the translation movement, and the internal dynamics of Egyptian intellectual discourse.

However, the situation has changed since the 1990s, especially at the Faculty of Dār al-ʿUlūm in Cairo, where the philosophical trend has given way to the more traditional Salafī approach, and some of the advocates of this trend have even claimed that they adhere to the school of ʿAbdullāh Drāz, which raises questions concerning the understanding of Drāz's thesis, which is, to my thinking, profoundly philosophical. Though he seeks to build a textual ethical philosophy, Drāz argues for rationality and is inspired by Kant, toward whose work he openly expressed leanings. It seems, however, that the general religious and political mood since the 1990s has impacted the interpretation of Drāz's thesis and reoriented it toward a Salafī and textual direction that Drāz himself did not intend or pursue. An exploration of these new developments awaits further study.

Bibliography

ʿAbd al-Raḥmān, Aḥmad. 1989. *Al-Faḍāʾil al-khuluqiyya fi l-Islām*. Cairo: Dār al-Wafāʾ.

ʿAbd al-Rāziq, Muṣṭafā. 1922. "Tarjamat al-ustādh al-imām." *al-Manār* 23: 520–30.

ʿAbduh, Muḥammad. 1897. *Risālat al-tawḥīd*. Būlāq: al-Maṭbaʿa al-Kubrā al-Amīriyya.

ʿAbduh, Muḥammad. 1905. *Al-Islām wa-l-Naṣrāniyya maʿa l-ʿilm wa-l-madaniyya*. Cairo: Maṭbaʿat Majallat al-Manār.

Adams, Charles C. 1933. *Islam and Modernism in Egypt: A Study of the Modern Reform Movement Inaugurated by Muḥammad ʿAbduh*. London: Oxford University Press.

Alatas, Syed Farid (ed.). 2009. *Muslim Reform in Southeast Asia: Perspectives from Malaysia, Indonesia, and Singapore*. Singapore: Majlis Ulama Islam Singapura.

Amīn, ʿUthmān. 1953. *Muḥāwalāt falsafiyya*. Cairo: Maktabat al-Anglū Miṣriyya.

ʿAṭiyya, Aḥmad ʿAbd al-Ḥalīm. 1990. *Al-Akhlāq fi l-fikr al-ʿArabī al-muʿāṣir*. Cairo: Dār al-Thaqāfa.

ʿAzzām, ʿAbd al-Wahhāb. 1937. "Thawra ʾalā l-akhlāq." *al-Risāla* 230: 1921–922.

Badawī, ʿAbd al-Raḥmān. 1953. *Hal yumkin qiyām akhlāq wujūdiyya?*. Cairo: Maktabat al-Nahḍa al-Miṣriyya.

Badawī, ʿAbd al-Raḥmān. 1976. *Al-Akhlāq al-naẓariyya*. Kuwait: Wakālat al-Maṭbūʿāt.

Badawī, al-Sayyid Muḥammad. 1992. "Dhikrayātī maʿa l-ustādh al-duktūr Maḥmūd Qāsim." In Ḥāmid Ṭāhir (ed.), *Maḥmūd Qāsim: al-Insān wa-l-faylasūf*. Cairo: Maktabat al-Anglū Miṣriyya, 153–54.

al-Bahy, Moḥammad. 1964. *Al-Azhar: Tārīkhuhu wa-taṭawwuruhu*. Cairo: Wizārat al-Awqāf wa-Shuʾūn al-Azhar.

Commins, David Dean. 1990. *Islamic Reform: Politics and Social Change in Late Ottoman Syria*. Oxford: Oxford University Press.

Comte, de Galarza. 1920. *Lectures in General Philosophy and its History at the Egyptian University*. Cairo: Maṭbaʿat al-Hilāl.

Delanoue, Gilbert. 1982. *Moralistes et politiques Musulmans dans l'Egypte du XIXéme siécle*. Cairo: Institut Français d'Archéologie Orientale du Caire.

Demolins, Edmond. 1899. *À quoi tient la supériorité des Anglo-Saxons*. Trans. Aḥmad Fatḥī Pasha Zaghlūl, *Sirr taqaddum al-Inglīz al-Saksūniyyīn*. Cairo: Maṭbaʿat al-Maʿārif.

Drāz, Muḥammad ʿAbdullāh. 1998. *Dustūr al-akhlāq fi l-Qurʾān al-karīm*. Trans. ʿAbd al-Ṣabūr Shāhīn. Beirut: Muʾassasat al-Risāla.

Gesink, Indira Falk. 2010. *Islamic Reform and Conservativism: Al-Azhar and the Evolution of Modern Sunni Islam*. London and New York: I.B. Tauris.

Ghaly, Mohammed. 2017. "The Journal of Islamic Ethics: A Pressing Demand and a Promising Field." *Journal of Islamic Ethics* 1/1: 1–3.

Gibb, Hamilton A.R. 1945. *Modern Trends in Islam*. Chicago: University of Chicago Press.

Gräf, Bettina, and Jakob Skovgaard-Petersen (eds.). 2009. *Global Mufti: The Phenomenon of Yūsuf al-Qaraḍāwī*. London: C. Hurst & Co.

Guizot, François. 1877. *Al-Tuḥfa al-adabiyya fī tārīkh tamaddun al-mamālik al-Ūrūbbiyya. = Histoire générale de la civilisation en Europe*, 1828. Trans. Ḥanīn Khūrī, Alexandria: Maṭbaʿat al-Ahrām.

al-Ḥaddād, Muḥammad. 2003. *Muḥammad ʿAbduh: Qirāʾa jadīda fī khiṭāb al-iṣlāḥ al-dīnī*. Beirut: Dār al-Ṭalīʿa.

Hourani, Albert. 1970³. *Arabic Thought in the Liberal Age 1798–1939*. London: Oxford University Press = 1968. *Al-Fikr al-ʿArabī fī ʿaṣr al-nahḍa 1798–1939*. Trans. Karīm ʿAzqūl. Beirut: Dār al-Nahār.

Ḥusayn, Ḥusayn Muḥammad. 1931. "Tajdīd al-akhlāq al-miṣriyya." *al-Majalla al-Jadīda* 6: 958–60.

Ḥusayn, Ṭāhā. n.d. *Ḥadīth al-ʾarbaʿāʾ*. Cairo: Dār al-Maʿārif.

Iskandar, Amīr. 1969. "ʿAbd al-Raḥmān Badawī wa-l-wujūdiyya al-ʿArabiyya." *al-Hilāl* 4: 66–75.

ʿIzzat, ʿAbd al-ʿAzīz. 1938. "Al-Fahm al-falsafī li-l-thawra ʿalā l-akhlāq." *al-Risāla* 237: 88–91.

Jād al-Mawlā, Muḥammad Aḥmad. 1932. *Al-Khuluq al-kāmil*. Cairo: Maṭbaʿat Hijāzī.

Jadʿān, Fahmī. 2010. *Usus al-taqaddum ʿinda mufakkirī l-Islām fī l-ʿālam al-ʿArabī al-ḥadīth*. Beirut: al-Shabaka al-ʿArabiyya li-l-Abḥāth wa-l-Nashr.

Karam, Yūsuf. 1949. *Tārīkh al-falsafa al-ḥadītha*. Cairo: Dār al-Maʿārif.

Khalīfa, Ḥājī. 1941. *Kashf al-ẓunūn ʿan asāmī l-kutub wa-l-funūn*. Baghdād: Maktabat al-Muthannā.

al-Khūlī, Amīn. 1937. "Fī wajh al-thawra ʿalā l-akhlāq." *al-Risāla* 232: 2016–2018.

Khūrshīd, Ibrāhīm Zakī. 1984. "Introduction." In Muṣṭafā ʿAbd al-Rāziq and Louis Massignon (eds.), *Taṣawwuf: Dāʾirat al-maʿārif al-Islāmiyya*. Cairo: Dār al-Kitāb al-Lubnānī.

Lalande, André. 1929. *Lectures in Philosophy = Muḥāḍarāt fī l-falsafa li-Andrīh Lālānd*. Trans. Aḥmad Ḥasan al-Zayyāt and Yūsuf Karam, rev. Ṭāhā Ḥusayn. Cairo: al-Maṭbaʿa al-Amīriyya.

Le Bon, Gustave. 1913. *Les lois psychologiques de l'évolution des peuples = Sirr taṭawwur al-umam*. Trans. Aḥmad Fatḥī Pasha Zaghlūl. Cairo: al-Maṭbaʿa al-Raḥmāniyya.

Lévy-Bruhl, Lucien. 1953. *La Morale et la science des mœurs = Al-Akhlāq wa-ʿilm al-ʿādat al-akhlāqiyya*. Trans. Maḥmūd Qāsim, rev. Sayyid Muḥammad Badawī. Cairo: Maṭbūʿāt Muṣṭafā Bābī al-Ḥalabī wa-Awlādih.

Madkūr, Ibrāhīm. n.d. [1983] "Introduction." In Louis Massignon *Cours d'histoirie des termes philosophiques arabes (du 25 novembre 1912 au 24 avril 1913) = Muḥāḍarāt fī tārīkh al-iṣṭilāḥāt al-falsafiyya al-ʿArabiyya*. Ed. al-Khuḍayrī Zaynab. Cairo: Institut français d'archéologie orientale.

Maḥmūd, ʿAbd al-Ḥalīm. 1985. *Al-Ḥamdu lillāh: Hādhihi ḥayātī*. Cairo: Dār al-Maʿārif.

Maḥmūd, Zakī Najīb. 1951a. *Al-Manṭiq al-waḍʿī*. Cairo: al-Maktaba al-Anglū Miṣriyya.

Maḥmūd, Zakī Najīb. 1951b. "Sullam al-qiyam." *Majallat al-thaqāfa* 662: 3–6.

Maḥmūd, Zakī Najīb. 1953. *Khurafat al-mitāfīzīqā*. Cairo: Maktabat al-Nahḍa al-Miṣriyya.

Maḥmūd, Zakī Najīb. 1988. *Qushūr wa-lubāb*. Cairo: Dār al-Shurūq.

Maḥmūd, Zakī Najīb. 1993. *Min zāwiya falsafiyya.* I 4, Cairo: Dār al-Shurūq.

Manṣūr, Fahmī. 1940. "Al-Ḍaʿf al-khulqī wa-atharuhu fī ḥayātinā al-ijtimāʿiyya." *al-Hilāl* 5: 505–13.

Maẓhar, Ismāʿīl. 1926. "Ṭābiʿ al-madaniyya al-ḥadītha: Madaniyyat al-fard wa-madaniyyat al-jamāhīr." *al-Muqtaṭaf* 3: 274–79.

Maẓhar, Ismāʿīl. 1936. "Al-Ladhdha wa-l-sulūk." *al-Muqtaṭaf* 5: 548–53.

Maẓhar, Ismāʿīl. 2012. *Falsafat al-ladhdha wa-l-alam.* Cairo: Kalimāt ʿArabiyya li-l-Tarjama wa-l-Nashr.

Montesquieu, Charles de. 2011. Considérations sur les causes de la grandeur des Romains et de leur décadence. = *Taʾammulāt fī tārīkh al-rūmān: Asbāb al-nuhūḍ wa-l-inḥiṭāṭ.* Trans. ʿAbdullāh al-ʿArwī. Beirut: al-Markaz al-Thaqāfī al-ʿArabī.

Mūsā, Muḥammad Yūsuf. 1943. *Mabāḥith fī falsafat al-akhlāq.* Cairo: Maṭbaʿat al-Azhar.

Mūsā, Muḥammad Yūsuf. 1945. *Falsafat al-akhlāq fi l-Islām wa-ṣilātuhā bi-l-falsafa al-Ighrīqiyya.* Cairo: Maṭbaʿat al-Risāla.

Mūsā, Muḥammad Yūsuf. 1986. "Ilā ṣadīqī al-ustādh Yūsuf Karam." In ʿĀṭif al-Irāqī (ed.), *Yūsuf Karam: Mufakkiran ʿArabiyyan wa-muʾarrikhan li-l-falsafa.* Cairo: al-Majlis al-Aʿlā li-l-Thaqāfa, 532–35.

Mūsā, Muḥammad Yūsuf, 1941. *Fī tārīkh al-akhlāq.* Cairo: Maṭbaʿat Amīn ʿAbd al-Raḥmān.

Naṣṣār, ʿIṣmat. 2009. "Al-Falsafa al-akhlāqiyya bayna ʿUthmān Amīn wa-Zakariyyāʾ Ibrāhīm." *Majallat al-Tasāmuḥ* 28: 247.

Qābīl, ʿAbd al-Ḥayy. 1984. *Al-Madhāhib al-akhlāqiyya fi l-Islām: al-Wājib—al-saʿāda.* Cairo: Dār al-Thaqāfa.

Qām, Yāʿqūb, n.d. *Dirāsāt fi l-akhlāq.* Egypt: no publisher.

al-Qaraḍāwī, Yūsuf. 2006. *Ibn al-qarya wa-l-kuttāb.* Vol. 3. Cairo: Dār al-Shurūq.

Rajab, Manṣūr ʿAlī. 1953. *Taʾammulāt fī falsafat al-akhlāq.* Cairo: Maṭbaʿat Mukhaymar.

Rashwānī, Sāmir. 2017. "Al-Dars al-akhlāqī li-l-Qurʾān." *Journal of Islamic Ethics* 1: 158–94.

Riḍā, Rashīd. 1899a. "Mā lā budda minhu?" *al-Manār* 1: 567–74.

Riḍā, Rashīd. 1899b. "Al-Murshidūn wa-l-murabbūn aw al-mutaṣawwifa wa-l-Ṣūfiyyūn." *al-Manār* 1: 722–35.

Riḍā, Rashīd. 1899c. "Al-Waʿẓ wa-l-wuʿʿāẓ." *al-Manār* 1: 881–85.

Riḍā, Rashīd. 1900. "Āthār ʿilmiyya dīniyya." *al-Manār* 2: 492–94.

Riḍā, Rashīd. 1906. "Tatimmat mulakhkhaṣ sīrat al-ustādh al-imām." *al-Manār* 8: 401–16.

Riḍā, Rashīd. 1907. "Arāʾ al-nās fī mukātabatinā maʿ Lord Cromer." *al-Manār* 10: 312–15.

Riḍā, Rashīd. 1913. "Iḥtifāl li-takrīm Aḥmad Pasha Zaghlūl." *al-Manār* 16: 550–53.

Riḍā, Rashīd. 1914. "Muṣāb Miṣr wa-l-Shām bi-rijāl al-ʿilm wa-ḥamalat al-aqlām." *al-Manār* 17: 472–80.

al-Sayyid, Aḥmad Luṭfī. 1924a. "Introduction." In Aristotle, *The Nicomachean Ethics.* Cairo: Dār al-Kutub al-Miṣriyya.

al-Sayyid, Aḥmad Luṭfī. 1924b. "Hal nu'allif am nutarjim? Muḥādatha ma'a l-ustādh Aḥmad Luṭfī al-Sayyid Bīk, mudīr Dār al-Kutub al-Miṣriyya." *al-Hilāl* 3: 234–36.

al-Sayyid, Aḥmad Luṭfī. 1943. "Kayfa yanbaghī an takūn al-akhlāq li-taḥqīq ta'āwun 'ālamī?" *al-Hilāl* 51/1: 49–57.

Sedgwick, Mark J. 2009. *Muhammad Abduh.* Oxford: Oneworld Publications.

al-Sharqāwī, Muḥammad 'Abdullāh (ed.). 1990. *Al-Fikr al-akhlāqī: Dirāsa muqārana.* Beirut: Dār al-Jīl.

Ṣubḥī, Aḥmad Maḥmūd. 1983. *Al-Falsafa al-akhlāqiyya fī l-fikr al-Islāmī.* Cairo: Dār al-Ma'ārif.

Ṭāhir, Ḥāmid. n.d. *Al-Fikr al-akhlāqī fī l-Islām.* n.p.: no publisher.

al-Ṭahṭāwī, Rifā'a. 1905 [1848]. *Takhlīṣ al-ibrīz ilā talkhīṣ Bārīz.* Cairo: Maktabat al-Mirghānī.

al-Ṭahṭāwī, Rifā'a. 1912. *Manāhij al-albāb al-Miṣriyya fī mabāhij al-ādāb al-'aṣriyya.* Cairo: Maṭba'at al-Raghā'ib.

al-Ṭawīl, Tawfīq. 1949. "Muqaddima." In *al-Mujmal fī tārīkh 'ilm al-akhlāq.* Trans. Tawfīq al-Ṭawīl and 'Abd al-Ḥamīd Ḥamdī = Henry Sidgwick, *Outlines of the History of Ethics*, Alexandria: Dār Nashr al-Thaqāfa, 9–39.

al-Ṭawīl, Tawfīq. 1967. *Falsafat al-akhlāq: Nash'atuhā wa-taṭawwuruhā.* Cairo: Dār al-Nahḍa al-'Arabiyya.

al-Ṭawīl, Tawfīq. 1986. "Dawr al-dīn wa-l-akhlāq fī binā' al-thaqāfa fī Miṣr al-mu'āṣira." In 'Āṭif al-Irāqī (ed.), *Yūsuf Karam: Mufakkiran 'Arabiyyan wa-mu'arrikhan li-l-falsafa.* Cairo: al-Majlis al-A'lā li-l-Thaqāfa, 131–52.

Wahba, Murād. 1986. "Yūsuf Karam: al-Faylasūf al-'aqlī al-mu'tadil." In 'Āṭif al-Irāqī (ed.), *Yūsuf Karam: Mufakkiran 'Arabiyyan wa-mu'arrikhan li-l-falsafa.* Cairo: al-Majlis al-A'lā li-l-Thaqāfa, 55–70.

Wood, Leonard. 2016. *Islamic Legal Revival: Reception of European Law and Transformations in Islamic Legal Thought in Egypt, 1875–1952.* Oxford: Oxford University Press.

al-Zayyāt, Aḥmad Ḥasan. 1937. "Thawra 'alā l-akhlāq: Hal al-ṣalāḥ ghayr al-najāḥ?" *al-Risāla* 229: 181–82.

al-Zayyāt, Aḥmad Ḥasan. 1940. "Al-Akhlāq wa-hādhihi l-ḥarb." *al-Risāla* 388: 1785–86.

CHAPTER 9

Religion as Discourse: Conversion and Commitment to *Jihād* in South Africa

Abdulkader Tayob

1 Introduction*

This essay focusses on the discourse and divergent signification of the life trajectory of Mawlana Moosagie, a South African ISIS supporter. A semiotic analysis suggests meanings of conversion and commitment to *jihād* in South Africa and provides an example of a discourse of *jihād* as it was shaped and reshaped in its enunciation and in exchange, an utterance that was received and rebutted, its meaning recreated and re-fabricated. Traditionalist, modernist, and Islamist ideas and tropes were inflected in the exchange, resulting in creative production of a Muslim political subject for South Africa.

In an article in the widely read South African newspaper *The Daily Voice*, Andrew Robertson, reporting on the 7th Wasatiyyah Conference, held at the Castle of Good Hope in May of 2017, quoted the South African Minister of Police Fikile Mbalula declaring that "Muslims in the Western Cape are the root of global Islamic terrorism" (Robertson 2017). The conference was part of a larger Ramadan Expo before the onset of the month of fasting, and Muslim leaders were invited to reflect on the challenge of radicalism in the country. It was one of a series of annual public conferences and workshops to promote a theology of *wasaṭiyya* (moderation; the middle way) exemplified in the history of the country, particularly during the struggle against apartheid in the 1980s, and in engagement with the democratic government since 1994. The editors of the newspaper withdrew Robertson's report when it was challenged for accuracy by the organisers of the conference. But the report and the event highlighted the diverse signification of *jihād* in South Africa and elsewhere in the twenty-first century among supporters, opponents, and purveyors of news.

* This work is based on the research supported in part by the National Research Foundation of South Africa (Reference number (UID) 85397). The opinions, findings and conclusions or recommendations expressed are that of the author..

In this essay, I focus on the discourse and divergent signification of the life trajectory of one of the South African ISIS supporters, Mawlana Moosagie. I focus on a letter that he sent to his family from Raqqa, which was published on the Website of a satellite radio station, Channel Islam International, on 21 May 2015.[1] The letter remained online briefly before it was removed (Brigaglia 2015). The letter is a plea for *jihād*, written in an autobiographical framework. It opens with a reference to Moosagie's extended family's turn to Islam in the second half of the twentieth century, and concludes with his decision to travel to the new caliphate declared by ISIS. I have been informed that, in later developments, Moosagie escaped the aerial bombardment of ISIS-held areas in 2017, and sought refuge in a camp in Jordan. According to a member of his family, he was waiting for the democratic government of South Africa to facilitate his return to the country.

I propose that a semiotic analysis of the life trajectory of Moosagie will illustrate the meanings of conversion and commitment to *jihād* in South Africa. In semiotics, the central metaphor for religion is not an inner feeling, or belonging, or alienation. It is, rather, a discursive speech act that is made possible by a given set of signifiers and rules. A religious act is akin to speech (*parole*) made possible by a grammar (*langue*), to use the terms coined by the foundational linguist and semiologist Ferdinand de Saussure (1857–1913). Smith and Murphy use the idea of canon to emphasise the linguistic nature of religious acts. Every religious actor is essentially a hermeneut who produces a new meaning through his or her reading of a canon (Smith 1982; Murphy 2003). The new meaning may appear to be a repetition and commitment to the canon, but openly or surreptitiously introduces a novelty. The use of canon should not suggest that interpretation is restricted to the foundational texts of a tradition. In the grammar of a religious act, the canon may also include hermeneutical strategies on how to read texts, and historical, cultural, and political narratives that are woven into these texts. The canon is thus an ensemble of texts, contexts, and strategies that makes interpretation possible. Furthermore, a religious act in its enunciation is addressed to someone. This Bakhtinian addressability of a religious act may be implicit or explicit. Like speech acts, even the solitary or singular religious act assumes and displays a community of listeners who add and create meaning. The true meaning of the act does not belong to the hermeneut. As with a speech act, a multitude of meanings are imputed to the religious act. Meanings may, in fact, be appropriated or stolen from an act that the actor did not intend (Foucault 1977).

---

1 The Moosagie letter has been reprinted as part of this article with an introduction by Andrea Brigaglia, cf. page 196ff.

2 Mawlana Moosagie and His Journey to *Jihād*

Mawlana Moosagie's life trajectory lends itself to semiotic analysis. Such an analysis must include his letter advocating for *jihād*, his predicament after he left ISIS, and the divergent responses among South Africans. For the purposes of this essay, the latter will include the Wasatiyyah Conference of May 2017 cited earlier; the text of a Friday sermon given at the Claremont Main Mosque in Cape Town by Dr. A. Rashied Omar in 2015 (Omar 2015); an interview with a prominent Ṣūfī leader, Fakhruddin Owaisi al-Madani, in Cape Town in 2015 (Dollar 2016); South African-born Notre Dame Professor of Islamic Studies Ebrahim Moosa's opinion piece published in the *Washington Post* (21 August 2015); and a special series of talks and interviews given by religious leaders in and around Johannesburg on a community station called Radio Islam, between 2 June and 8 June 2015. These divergent responses to the letter and life trajectory of Mawlana Moosagie challenge his justification of *jihād* and introduce new meanings to it. Moreover, using signifiers in his letter, they produce novel ideas on modernity, multicultural politics, and interfaith relations. The life trajectory of Moosagie is unique, but a semiotic analysis brings out its shared and discursive character.

This essay is a contribution to ideas first presented by Talal Asad (b. 1932) in his seminal essay of 1986, in which he discussed Islam as a discursive tradition (Asad 1986). Using the idea of semiotics and language, this essay illustrates a change in the discourse of *jihād*. Asad wrote that although he was not talking of modern or Islamist formulations since the nineteenth century, at the same time, he was also not averse to recognising and admitting changes in the discourse of Islam (Asad 1986, 15, 17). Mawlana Moosagie's letter and the responses to it provide an illuminating illustration of this contestation and change in the discourse of *jihād*.

The text of Mawlana Moosagie's letter leaves the impression that the writer believed that the practice of *jihād* as war and active combat against infidels had been neglected by the Muslims of South Africa in general and their religious leaders in particular. *Jihād*, he asserts, was also neglected in the Indian *madrasas* where he and his associates had been trained. He accuses both the Indian Muslim community of South Africa and its religious leadership of promoting a culture of total and unjustified subservience to *buzrugs*. The word *buzrug* (meaning "large" in Persian) refers to revered scholars and saints who attained a high status in the eyes of God and humanity. Moosagie uses the term to refer to what he sees as the subservience of South African Muslims to such individuals and not to God. He contrasts this *buzrug* culture with *jihād*, which, he argues, is represented in exemplary fashion by ISIS. Moreover, he contends, the absence of *jihād* in South Africa has resulted in the subservience of Muslims to the government and to its people. Moosagie declares in his letter that he has decided to join ISIS, even though it may appear to be hell on earth. ISIS, he declares, is preparing Muslims for the end of time predicted by the Prophet Muḥammad. My reading of this letter is meant to familiarise readers with its contents. But it is neither authoritative, nor does it exhaust its signification.

Paul Ricoeur has drawn attention to the narrative structure of identity formation by alerting us to the temporal nature of personal experience recalled as a story (Ricoeur, 1980). Moosagie's letter, with its clear outline of stages, is a good illustration of this narrative identity. The first of these stages is a shift within his extended family to a greater commitment to religious devotion. This is followed by the second stage, a journey to an Indian seminary to pursue religious education. His return to South Africa is marked as the third stage, which he calls an "awakening" to the heretical state of Muslims. Moosagie marks a fourth stage "around 1990, when the Iraq invasion took place." He was then fully convinced of the need for *jihād*, and openly promoted it among South Africans. He is proud of being called a "madman" during this time. The fifth, and what he considers his last stage, is the "Moving to Shaam [Syria]." He describes the Islamic state, and puts it in an eschatological framework. In a semiotic gesture of my own, I am adding a sixth turning point, after this "death" in ISIS. Ultimately he finds himself not in heaven as he predicted in his letter, but in a refugee camp in Jordan. Each of these stages or turning points will be explored in greater detail. In addition to what Moosagie tells us about each, I will also point to his interlocutors, who impute new meanings to his life trajectory.

3 The Six Stages, or Turning Points

Moosagie identifies his first stage as "childhood – 1960s." It is a significant period that marks a major change in his family. He refers to "sparse" religious practices, but notes that family members used to be "regular with *salaah* [ritual prayer] and fasting." His family, he says, was surrounded by "*jahl*" (ignorance), steeped in a business culture and subservient to a dominant "secular system." But the family became more religious, particularly when some members trained in religious education returned from India. This is an important part of the conversion narrative of Moosagie, the first part of a journey that ends in a new vision. The Moosagie letter illuminates the personal significance of an important change that had taken place in a period in the history of South Africa, when apartheid laws were implemented, and which led to a distinct trend toward greater religiosity. The Group Areas Act (1950), in particular, forced

African, Coloured, and Indian communities into separate areas and locations. Among Muslims, it led to increased devotion to Islam in both public and private spheres (Chidester 1992; Tayob 1995).

In his Friday sermon against ISIS, given at The Claremont Main Mosque in 2015, Dr. Omar puts Moosagie's conversion in a different perspective. Drawing on the analysis of the French scholar Olivier Roy (b. 1949), Omar points to "the modern disconnection between faith communities and sociocultural identities [which] produce [...] culturally alienated youth," who are then preyed upon by "demagogues." Moosagie, in Omar's framing, was either a demagogue or one of those "culturally alienated youth" (Omar 2015). Omar was arguing that supporters of ISIS such as Moosagie were promoting a form of cultural alienation by totally rejecting their families and their religious traditions. Moosagie was not turning away from a secular culture as it appears hesitantly in his narrative, but from one steeped in devotion. This claim that ISIS supporters had rejected local Islamic culture was echoed at the 7th Wasatiyyah Conference in Cape Town in May 2017. The resilience of Muslims during colonialism and apartheid was held up as a virtue against radicalisation. Omar and others were suggesting, from a reading of Roy, that local religious and political cultures were a strong defence against radicals.

This is the first example of how Moosagie's self-styled "turning point" was disputed and turned on its head. While he was attempting to draw a personal narrative of awareness and conversion, Omar and others recast it as a rejection of an Islamic culture that was evidently steeped in devotion. Such a reading was possible from hints revealed in Moosagie's conversion narrative. Moosagie admits that his family was fulfilling their required religious duties and devotions. They became more religious than before, but he could not categorically say that the family changed from unbelief to commitment, or total ignorance to awareness. Moosagie seems to suggest that this major change was not sufficient and even false. But his interlocutors—Omar and those who agreed with him, that is—remind him of the religious life that he denigrated.

The next stage of Moosagie's life was his journey to India, which introduced him to Ṣūfism and the hated *buzrug* culture. He concedes that the "sheiks had impeccable character, piety, enviable mannerisms and shining faces." But, he complains, they rendered students unable to pose questions and access the true teaching of Islam. In particular, they said nothing about slavery and *jihād*, omissions that perplexed him and his friends. The revered scholars, according to Moosagie, relegated *jihād* to a distant future "when the Mehdi [Messiah] and Essa [Jesus] ... will appear towards the end of the world." His recollection of this stage in his life, was a strong critique against his teachers and his alma mater.

In his depiction of a younger Moosagie in India, Notre Dame professor Ebrahim Moosa, writing in the *Washington Post,* remembers Moosagie as a student committed to the intellectual culture that he later came to reject. In fact, it was Moosagie who had warned Moosa of modern Islamic politics, which Moosagie considered "heady rhetoric [with] little substance." Moosa's reminder points to the resonance between Moosagie's critique of madrasa education and a minority Muslim youth tradition in South Africa from the 1950s through to the present. In that tradition, mainstream Muslim scholars were castigated for failing to respond to modernity, apartheid, and the democratic state (Tayob 1995; Jeppie 2007). In the 1970s and 1980s, at the height of the struggle against apartheid, the absence of discussion of *jihād* among the *ʿulamāʾ* (religious scholars) was a particularly dominant criticism. Moosagie's letter was drawing on an established modernist rhetoric that had appeared in South Africa and elsewhere (Tayob 1999). A semiotic analysis shows the fluid nature of religious rhetoric, one that adapts itself to new circumstances, and easily applied in unexpected places.

Moosagie's return to South Africa is marked by him as the third stage in his life, which he characterises as an "awakening," during which he was "shocked to discover [his and others'] false beliefs." He rails against the community of Indian Muslims, focussing on the heresy he identifies in three inter-related attitudes: obedience to the state, the dominance of a *buzrug* culture, and affliction by a heretical "virus" called *irjāʾ*. Moosagie seems to be completely oblivious to the presence of Cape Muslims and the growing African communities in South Africa. He is also completely silent on the increasing number of migrant Muslim communities thriving in South Africa since 1994. This blindness has not escaped some respondents. Nevertheless, his representation of South African Indian Muslims was met with critical and creative responses on politics and democracy.

In his criticism of the state of Islam in the country, Moosagie is cynical of Muslim leaders who advocate for obedience to the government "because they [the government] offered us 'freedom of our *deen'* [religion]." He is repeating a common trope among Islamists who believe that Islam demands that the rules of God be followed to the letter. The responses to Moosagie's cynicism offer elements of a political theory that is strikingly different. On Radio Islam, Mawlana Karolia and Mawlana Patel, Muslim religious leaders in Gauteng province, offered a review of Muslim political theory for Muslims living in a secular, democratic country. Karolia gave a learned discourse on key political regimes discussed in the Muslim intellectual tradition, and concluded that there was no reason to reject the secular, democratic state of South Africa. He argued that there was a fundamental equivalence between a secular democratic state and a *dār al-amān* ("abode of peace"), which a leading Ḥanafī jurist, al-Sarakhsī (d. 490/1096), had discussed in the past. He concluded his talk by citing an eschatological verse, "The reward of kindness is nothing but kindness" (Qur'ān 55: 60) (Karolia 2015a). This was an apt quotation and a semiotic application that turned an eschatological meaning into a political ethic, one that emphasises mutual rights and obligations.

In his radio interview with Ummi Abdillah on 8 June 2015, Mawlana Patel supported the same politics but from a different perspective. He points to a history of active engagement of Muslims with the post-apartheid South African state. His prime example is Muslim engagement with the Anti-Terror Bill of 2002; which in his view became less draconian because of this engagement (Patel 2015). Speaking at the Wasatiyyah Conference in 2017, former premier of the Western Cape Ebrahim Rasool also referred to the close involvement of Muslims in the political history of South Africa. He reminded the audience of a long history of struggle by Muslims for a democratic South Africa. Patel was suggesting what Muslims may gain from engagement with a democratic state, while Rasool's frame of reference was Muslim participation in the creation of a democratic state for all. Both views, however, reject Moosagie's argument that Muslims were blindly obeying the government. Moosagie's observation was limited, his interlocutors argued, and gave them a chance to offer an alternative narrative on the politics of Islam in South Africa, one that included a long tradition of political activism or accommodation.

Continuing with his observations on the role of Islam in South Africa, Moosagie placed much of the blame on a dominant *buzrug* culture pervasive in Muslim communities. It was a culture that did not allow an individual believer direct access to and responsibility towards God. He argued that Ṣūfism in particular was responsible for creating a bond of unquestioned loyalty between an initiate (*murīd*) and his or her guide (*murshid*, *pīr*). Moosagie's interlocutors, who included Ṣūfī sympathisers and authoritative religious leaders, treaded carefully on this point. The Radio Islam series accepted the gist of this observation, but used it to emphasise the value of the revered leaders in the history of Islam. Others, such as Omar and Moosa, used the reference to launch their own attack on traditional scholarship in the modern world.

In her introduction to each of the Radio Islam programmes, producer Ummi Abdullah emphasised the value of the *ʿulamāʾ* for Muslims:

> This is part of a Radio Islam series taking apart oft-mentioned contestations of ISIS propagandists. Those who aim ISIS rhetoric at unwitting South African audiences create confusion, mayhem and aim to weaken public faith *in the guidance of our Ulama* [emphasis mine].

The indispensability of religious scholars was repeated and stressed. Moreover, the fifth programme in the series was dedicated to Ṣūfism (Karolia 2015b). Against Moosagie's claim, Karolia argues that the key teachings of Ṣūfism are contained in the Qurʾān and the Sunna. Karolia considers the long history of Islam, including the *sharīʿa*, politics, and other developments. He admits that many new developments may be observed in this history, intimating that there was a common logic in the innovations of Ṣūfism and acceptable innovations in jurisprudence. He stresses, however, that these changes can be traced back to the fundamental teachings of Islam. More significantly, his talk on Radio Islam implies that this connection is guaranteed by the knowledge and sincerity of the true scholars of Islam. Only such *ʿulamāʾ* (religious scholars) could guarantee this continuity between the Prophetic event and the present.

Moosa's response to Moosagie's criticism of the revered scholars (*buzrugs*) is different. He lays the blame for ISIS on Islamic orthodoxy and its custodians (the *ʿulamāʾ*). He calls for "a doctrinal overhaul … [of Muslim theology as] the best long-term antidote to the radicalism and senseless interpretations that masquerade as Islam." Moosa calls Salafism a "formaldehyde," which "prevents decomposition but also creates the illusion that the body is alive" (Moosa 2015). Moosagie, he concludes, "was able to embrace the Islamic state as its lodestar only because Islamic orthodoxy has not offered a humane alternative" (Moosa 2015, 153). Similar sentiments were echoed in the Wasatiyyah Conference in Cape Town in May 2017.

Moosagie's letter points to a key problematic in modern Muslim discourse. While religious scholars stress the central role they play in connecting Muslims to the source of revelation, the also insist that only some scholars—those steeped in knowledge and sincerity—are capable of guaranteeing this connection. This argument concedes that there is a proliferation of scholars who may not enjoy this authority. Moreover, Professor Moosa's criticism of the religious scholars resonates in Moosagie's letter. This rebuttal of Moosagie thus exposes the tenuous link between the origins of Islam and the life of Muslims in the present—potentially sundered by the likes of Moosagie and Moosa. Critics such as Moosa reveal that this self-validation of the religious scholars claiming their paramount value and importance was not accepted by all.

Moosagie's next criticism of the Muslim community is that it has fallen prey to the heretical theology of *irjāʾ*. He calls this heresy a "virus," which has to be combatted and eradicated. The accusation of *irjāʾ* has been used by radical Muslim groups who claim that contemporary Muslims have virtually abandoned the practices of Islam, supposedly satisfied with faith as the guarantee of salvation. In early Islamic history, the theology of *irjāʾ* was a rejected creed that declared that faith was sufficient for salvation (Watt 1962, 22–23). Radical Islamic commentary ignores the turn to greater devotion to prayer, fasting, charity, and adoption of Islamic modes of dress clearly evident among Muslims in South Africa and across the globe. The Conference in May 2017 demonstrated this greater devotion. While a sizable number of members attended the conference against radicalism, hundreds of Muslims paid an entrance fee in order to buy the Islamic goods on offer. Modern radicals focus on states that they claim are not implementing the laws of the *sharīʿa*, and they criticise all Muslims who accept such states—irrespective of the fact that they are devout Muslims in all other respects (al-Qurashi 1997; al-Ṭarṭūsī 2003; al-Maqdisī 2003; Wagemakers 2009). Thus a contemporary radical application of a theological heresy provides justification for declaring as apostates those Muslims who do not follow these radicals.

Moosagie's letter reveals a very South African context. He defines *irjāʾ* as a belief or sentiment "to apologize on behalf of Allah." He then lists five ways in which Muslims in South Africa relate to disbelievers in amiable and friendly ways: "in brief, you are embarrassed by the verses of Allah hence you scramble 'to try and cover up.'" Moosagie urges Muslims to maintain an antagonism with disbelievers, suggesting that in politics and society they should not seek to develop friendly and mutually beneficial relations with disbelievers. He then lists the groups in South Africa and elsewhere whom he sees as following this misguided course of action: "the Sufi sect, the Mouloodi sect and the Tablighi Jamaat sect."

In response to this charge, Mawlana Ally, from Springs, near Johannesburg, asserted on the Radio Islam programme of 3 June 2015 that the key teachings and practices of Ṣūfism and the Tablighi Jamaat can be traced to the earliest venerable scholars and saints of Islam. He clarifies the doctrine of *irjāʾ* for listeners, and stresses the value of good deeds to reach ever higher stations in heaven in the hereafter. But he also concludes the programme with a jibe at the "dry" and "harsh" individuals who reject some of these practices (Ally 2015). Taking a more political approach, Owaisi al-Madani, in an interview with University of Cape Town researcher Cathlene Dollar, addresses the allusion to South African apologetics more directly. Moosagie and his ilk, he declares, reject the "Islam of co-existence" that dominates South Africa, whereby Muslims have learnt to live with people of other faiths (Dollar 2016, 145). In his Friday sermon, Omar accused ISIS supporters of promoting a "toxic theology" that jeopardises the development of a "more peaceful, humane and just world." Mufti Seraj from Port Elizabeth, in an interview with a journalist declared that South African Muslims do not need an Islamic state to be virtuous:

> If you know the Muslim community in South Africa, we've been living here for years, we've been practicing our Islam, we don't make a difference between a Muslim who lives in a modern society and a Muslim who lives in an Islamic society, except on the basis of how much *that particular person is devoted to Islam* [my emphasis].
>
> FINNAN 2015

Mufti Seraj made this statement before Moosagie's letter became public, on the occasion of the South African government preventing a teenage girl from boarding an aircraft, apparently en route to join ISIS. It captures a rejection of Moosagie's particular politics.

The discussion of heresy (*irjāʾ*) in Moosagie's letter shows a creative application to the situation of Muslims living in a minority context. Moosagie's accusation of *irjāʾ* is a meaning snatched from its use in the contemporary Middle East and applied to Muslims living in democratic South Africa. But this innovative reading from Moosagie was in turn rejected by those who emphasised the value and validity of Islam and its practices in a democratic ethos.

Moosagie's fourth stage in his life trajectory turns on his realisation that *jihād* as fighting and dying for the faith is a central teaching of Islam, one that was suppressed by Ṣūfism with its "spiritual Jihad." He also rejects his Indian teachers, whom he characterises as focussing on how to eat sweet melons according to the Sunna of the Prophet Muhammad, but who did not "yearn to be killed in fighting the enemy in accordance with the desire of the *Nabie* [the prophet Muḥammad]…." Moosagie was proud that he was prevented from spreading this message in mosques and radio stations, because, in his view, such was the reception of the prophets in the past.

Moosagie's claim that the *ʿulamāʾ* had abandoned *jihād* was categorically denied by various critics. In opening the series of talks on Radio Islam on 2 June 2015, Mawlana Dockrat, from Pretoria, asserted that the *ʿulamāʾ* in India were and continue to be committed to *jihād*. They waged *jihād* against the British, with Gandhi and his followers in the *Khilāfat* movement of the early twentieth century, and in various political campaigns in the fight against colonial rule. *Jihād* also took the shape of the establishment of a madrasa (the Deobandi) after the Indian War of Independence (Indian Mutiny) of 1857 (Dockrat 2015). The Ṣūfī leader Owaisi al-Madani challenged Moosagie on the rules and processes of *jihād* followed by ISIS. He also declared that ISIS should be rejected as a *khawārij* sect—a reference to a group of dissenters in the early history of Islam who have been rejected by Muslims—both Sunnī and Shīʿa—for taking to *jihād* at the slightest provocation. He was reiterating what many other Muslim scholars have said about ISIS since its establishment (al-Yaʿqūbī 2015; Abdu Baraa and Hasan 2014).

Dockrat's defence of the *ʿulamāʾ* and their *jihād* introduced a nuance that resonates with Islamic modernist thought. In his discussion of the forms of *jihād*, he includes diverse forms of political engagement, all of which were directed at independence from colonial rule. It is a modernist reading of the application of *jihād* in the modern world. Owaisi-Madani, on the other hand, was not as successful in his insisting that the caliphate be founded on proper procedure. Moosagie had pre-empted this argument in his letter by pointing out that the caliphate was not always founded on such procedures, alluding to al-Māwardī (d. 450/1058) and other medieval jurists who accepted the fait accompli of historical caliphs appointed in less than exemplary fashion (Enayat 1982; al-Māwardī 1983). Owaisi-Madani and other respondents to ISIS have not addressed this argument.

Semiotics shows how the interlocution between Moosagie and Dockrat prompted a rethinking of the forms of *jihād*. Dockrat's responses reflect an Islamic modernist argument for *jihād* that justifies all political engagements as *jihād*. A semiotics analysis points to how traditional thinking imperceptibly shifted in comprehension and application of the doctrine. At the same time, on the rules to be followed in *jihād*, semiotics reveals an unresolved issue on the nature of Islamic politics and political authority.

"Moving to Shaam" was the final and inevitable end for Moosagie. He discusses the accusations and "myths" about ISIS in the media, but admits that the *dawla* (the state) fights against all groups and individuals that do not pledge total allegiance to the caliph. He also reports that "right now you will see full Sharia law," where "all crime is strictly controlled." But he devotes considerable space to the *malḥama* (eschatological battle) that would unfold in Syria. The Dajjāl (the evil one) was on his way to usher in the end-time, and ISIS was preparing believers for his arrival. Moosagie focusses on the deceptive promise of the Dajjāl:

> This similar *fitna* [trial] is *Shaam* and *Darul Kufr* [Land of Infidelity]. Externally Shaam does look like hell, full of bombings, killings, unlivable conditions, sicknesses, harsh weather and a host of other difficulties. Yes it does look like Hell.
>
> On the other hand *Darul Kufr* looks like heaven, with all its comforts, foods, wonderful living and luxuries.
>
> Everyone will opt for the *'jannah,'* [heaven], everyone will opt for *Daral Kufr*, but know that this is actually your Hell. A true believer will opt to migrate against all odds to Shaam, he will opt for this Hell, for indeed it is actually *jannah*.

A "vaccine" given to the true believers, ISIS was inoculating them against the deception, helping them develop themselves through the trials of violence and mayhem. Muslims should choose this "hell" of ISIS, which is the true heaven. When the Dajjāl comes, they would have learnt how to choose the truth.

It is perhaps significant that I did not find any direct or indirect references to eschatology among the interlocutors of Moosagie. Journalist Graeme Wood has pointed out that eschatology plays a dominant role in ISIS propaganda but has not been fully appreciated: "Western media frequently miss references to Dabiq in the Islamic State's videos, and focus instead on lurid scenes of beheading." The name of its glossy newsletter *Dābiq* refers to a battlefield mentioned in a Prophetic *ḥadīth* at the end of time (al-Nawawī, Book 54, chapter 9). Wood argues that ISIS is preparing for that battle (Wood 2015). My reading of Moosagie's letter is that he does not only focus on this final battle, but more emphatically on the appearance of heaven and hell, truth and evil, and prosperity and failure. Steeped in a war of images with adversaries, Moosagie's focus on the elusive representations of good and evil is more telling. In his rendering, ISIS is playing the role of a curtain-raiser for this battle between the appearance of heaven and hell. Moreover, the choice that Moosagie offers Muslims in South Africa is closer to home. He is pointing to the luxuries that Indian Muslims enjoy in democratic South Africa, the place they occupy in a rainbow nation of many cultures and traditions. According to Moosagie, they are deluded by such material bounties that must by their very nature be short-lived. Moosagie asks Muslims to rather choose the "hell" of ISIS, which is not what it appears to be. Moreover, Moosagie in 2015 is fully aware, as are his Muslim listeners, that the rainbow heaven of South Africa has begun to unravel.

A life trajectory requires a constantly updated narrative, and this is true of Moosagie's path as well. Life throws up unexpected and unwelcome challenges, and they must be reshaped in the narrative of the self. Moosagie expected to go into battle and emerge in the afterworld. Instead he finds himself sitting in a camp in Jordan, waiting for an official from the South African Department of Foreign Affairs to persuade the Jordanian government to release him into their care and custody. We may have to wait for his return to see if he provides a narrative update. But this scenario may be very unlikely. In 2015, several supporters of ISIS returned to South Africa. Media and security specialists are left guessing about their motivations before and after their return, because their lawyers, defending their clients' rights in democratic South Africa, are advising them not to talk to anyone. Moosagie's apparent trust in the South African government exemplifies the contradictions of those who have nurtured dreams of an Islamic utopia, but lived for another day in a democratic country. Whilst embracing the Islamic state, they were forced to turn to the modern state to give them life.

4 Discussion and Conclusion

I have presented a detailed account and analysis of the life trajectory of Moosagie and its diverse signification. His widely publicised letter provoked numerous South African interlocutors to respond in spoken and written form. Using the letter and responses to it, I have offered an interpretation of the meaning given by the author and by those who responded to him. Moosagie presented a narrative in which he justified his decision to turn away from his educational background, and how and why he chose the theology and politics of ISIS. His interlocutors seized upon the letter and the facts of his life, and argued for a different understanding of *jihād*. Moreover, they offered new meanings to the relationship between Muslims and a modern, democratic state. The exchange underlines the precarious and critical position of religious scholars as the guarantors of authenticity and continuity between the origins of Islam and its history. It also puts into bold relief some of the historical contingencies of Muslim politics in the past and present. Not all issues were resolved and some remain lingering in the aftermath of Moosagie's escape from ISIS. There is no doubt, however, that his life trajectory acts as a reference point for a discourse on *jihād* that is not static but open to constant change.

Talal Asad has been hesitant about modern discourses framed under the concepts of modernism and traditionalism. Such terms are, by their very definition, connected to the history of the social sciences as they emerged in the cultural and political history of the West. Like other post-colonial thinkers, Asad attempted to provincialise the social sciences in general, and anthropology in particular (Chakrabarty 2000; Asad 2003, 269). But he does not rule out the possibility of change: "An anthropology of Islam will therefore seek to understand the historical conditions that enable the production and maintenance of specific discursive traditions, or their transformation—and the efforts of practitioners to achieve coherence" (Asad 1986, 17). With the exception of Bowen's examination of Islamic human rights discourses in France and Indonesia, those who have followed Asad's insight on the discursivity of religions have tended to stay clear of transformation and change in the discourse (Bowen 1993; Mahmood 2001; Pinto 2010; Hirschkind 2001). They have avoided or been unable to address the intersection or convergence between an Islamic discourse that has been inherited from the past and the hegemonic discourses or ideas emanating from the West.

My case study of the semiotics of Moosagie's letter shows that the ideas, tropes, and suppositions of modernity are already present in the debates and discussions of Muslims. Moreover, I have shown that interlocutors draw from a body of literature and debates that have been called modernist, traditionalist, and fundamentalist. Irrespective of the validity and provinciality of these terms, it shows that they are inserted in an enunciation of *jihād*. Using the idea of a religious act as a linguistic act, I have shown how signification takes on a discursive character between actors and interlocutors, among participants ranging from religious scholars to journalists to university professors. The letter and life of Moosagie reveal a semiotic universe centring on *jihād* between the past and the present, between texts and context, and between war and inter-cultural and inter-religious propositions in a modern democratic state. I think such enunciations and their semiotics should be studied more carefully and extensively in order to identify a religious discourse and its clearly evident transformation.

Bibliography

Abdu, Baraa and Abdul Rahman Hasan. 2014. "Debate: Validity on the Khilafah and If They Have the Correct Aqidah or Not." Accessed 20 May 2015. http://dawahukpaltalk.blogspot.com/2014/12/abu-baraa-mp3-audio.html?m=1

Ally, Abbas-Ali Zubair. 2015. "What is Murjia? (Part 2 and 3)." *Radio Islam*. Accessed 8 June 2015. https://ia600509.us.archive.org/26/items/AnsweringISISPropogandistsPart23WhatIsMurjiaAreOurDalyWazaifBidahWed03.06.2015/Answering_ISIS_Propogandists_Part_2__3_What_is_Murjia_are_our_daly_wazaif_bidah-wed-03.06.2015%20.mp3

Asad, Talal. 1986. *The Idea of an Anthropology of Islam*. Washington, D.C.: Center for Contemporary Arab Studies, Georgetown University.

Asad, Talal. 2003. *Formations of the Secular: Christianity, Islam, Modernity*. Stanford: Stanford University Press.

Bowen, John R. 1993. *Muslims Through Discourse: Religion and Ritual in Gayo Society*. Princeton: Princeton University Press.

Bowen, John R. 2001. *Shariʿa, State, and Social Norms in France and Indonesia*. Leiden: ISIM.

Brigaglia, Andrea. 2015. "Open Letter to South African Muslims, Inviting them to Join ISIS, By Mufti Rashied Moosagie." *Annual Review of Islam in Africa* 13: 121–37.

Chakrabarty, Dipesh. 2000. *Provincializing Europe: Postcolonial Thought and Historical Difference*. Princeton: Princeton University Press.

Chidester, David. 1992. *Religions of South Africa*. London: Routledge.

Dockrat, Moulana Ashraf. 2015. "Fake Deobandi Muhajids [sic] and Anti-Jihad South African Ulama (Part 1)." Accessed 8 June 2015. https://ia801501.us.archive.org/10/items/AnsweringISISPropogandistsPart1AreDeobandisSAUlamaAntiJihadTues02.06.2015/Answering_ISIS_Propogandists_%20Part_1_Are_Deobandis_SA_Ulama_anti_Jihad-tues-02.06.2015.mp3

Dollar, Cathlene. 2016. "Probing the Sunni Ulama's Condemnations: An Interview with Fakhruddin Owaisi Al-Madani (Cape Town)." *Annual Review of Islam in Africa* 13: 140–50.

Enayat, Hamid. 1982. *Modern Islamic Political Thought*. Austin: University of Texas Press.

Finnan, Daniel. 2015. "Should South Africa act against ISIS radicalisation, or is Cape Town teenager an isolated incident?" Accessed 21 July 2017. https://muslimsinafrica.wordpress.com/2015/04/08/an-interview-of-professor-hussein-solomon-on-radio-france-international-on-south-african-girl-recruited-by-isis/

Foucault, Michel. 1977. "Nietzsche, Genealogy, History." In Donald F. Bouchard (ed.), *Language, Counter-Memory, Practice: Selected Essays and Interviews*. Ithaca: Cornell University Press, 139–64.

Hirschkind, Charles. 2001. "Civic Virtue and Religious Reason: An Islamic Counterpublic." *Cultural Anthropology* 16/1: 3–34.

Jeppie, Shamil. 2007. *Language, Identity, Modernity: The Arabic Study Circle of Durban*. Pretoria: HSRC Press.

Karolia, Mawlana Muhammad. 2015a. "Explaining the Terms Darul Ieman Darul Kufr Darul-Harb Darul-Ahad Etc.(part 4)." Accessed 8 June 2015. http://www.radioislam.org.za/a/index.php/library/152-opinion-and-analysis/15700-explaining-the-terms-darul-ieman-darul-kufr-darul-harb-darul-ahad-ect.html

Karolia, Mawlana Muhammad. 2015b. "The Concept of Tasawwuf (Part 5)." Accessed 8 June 2015. https://ia600507.us.archive.org/33/items/AnsweringISISPropagandistsPart5TheConceptOfTasawwufExplainedFri05.06.2015/Answering_ISIS_Propagandists_Part%205_The_concept_of_Tasawwuf_explained-fri-05.06.2015.mp3

Mahmood, Saba. 2001. "Rehearsed Spontaneity and the Conventionality of Ritual: Disciplines of Ṣalāt." *American Ethnologist* 28/4: 827–53.

al-Maqdisī, Abū Muḥammad. 2003. "Al-Dīmuqratiyyah Al-Dīn (Democracy is Religion)." Accessed 1 September 2008. http://www.tawhed.ws/files/8.zip

al-Māwardī. 1983. *Al-Aḥkām al-sulṭāniyya*. Cairo: Dār al-Shabāb.

Moosa, Ebrahim. 2015. "My Madrassa Classmate Hated Politics. Then He Joined the Islamic State (Re-Print From the *Washington Post*, 21 August 2015)." *The Annual Review of Islam in Africa* 13: 151–3.

Murphy, Tim. 2003. "Elements of a Semiotic Theory of Religion." *Method & Theory in the Study of Religion* 15/1: 48–67.

al-Nawawī, Yaḥyā b. Sharaf. (n.d). *Ṣaḥīḥ Muslim bi-Sharḥ al-Nawawī*. 18 vols. Beirut: Dār Iḥyā' al-Turāth al- 'Arabī.

Omar, A. Rashied. 2015. "Mitigating the Toxic Political Theology of ISIS: Friday Sermon at Claremont Main Road Mosque Condemning ISIS." *The Annual Review of Islam in Africa* 13: 154–7.

Patel, Mawlana Yusuf. 2015. "The Way Forward for ISIS Sympathizer (Part 6)." Accessed 19 July 2017. https://ia600506.us.archive.org/29/items/101932/101932.mp3

Pinto, Paulo G. 2010. "The Anthropological and the Initiated: Reflections on the Ethnography of Mystical Experience Among the Sufis of Aleppo, Syria." *Social Compass* 57/4: 464–78.

al-Qurashi, Sheikh Muhammad. 1997. "Al-Murji'ah Sect, Its History and Beliefs." *Minbar Tawhed and Jihad* (*Pulpit of Monotheism and Jihad*). Accessed 17 July 2011. http://www.tawhed.net/dl.php?i=1211091c

Ricoeur, Paul. 1980. "Narrative Time." *Critical Inquiry* 7/1: 169–90.

Robertson, Andrew. 2017. "Cape in Muslim Terror Capital." *Voice* 22, May 5.

Smith, Jonathan Z. 1982. *Imagining Religion: From Babylon to Jonestown*. Chicago: University of Chicago Press.

al-Ṭarṭūsī, Abū Baṣīr (ʿAbd al-Munʿim Muṣṭafā Ḥalīma). 2003. "Aʿmāl tukhrij sāḥibaha min al-milla." *Minbar Tawhed and Jihad* (*Pulpit of Monotheism and Jihad*). Accessed 20 July 2006. http://www.tawhed.ws/dl?i=znr63yvm

Tayob, Abdulkader I. 1995. *Islamic Resurgence in South Africa: The Muslim Youth Movement*. Cape Town: UCT Press.

Tayob, Abdulkader I. 1999. "Defining Islam in the Throes of Modernity." *Studies in Contemporary Islam* 2/1: 1–15.

Wagemakers, Joas. 2009. "The Transformation of a Radical Concept: al-Walāʾ wa-l-barāʾ in the Ideology of Abu Muhammad al-Maqdisi." In Roel Meijer (ed.), *Global Salafism: Islam's New Religious Movement*. London: Hurst & Company, 81–106.

Watt, William Montgomery. 1962. *Islamic Philosophy and Theology*. Edinburgh: Edinburgh University Press.

Wood, Graeme. 2015. "What ISIS Really Wants." *The Atlantic*, March 2015. Accessed 31 July 2017. https://www.theatlantic.com/magazine/archive/2015/03/what-isis-really-wants/384980/

al-Yaʿqūbī, Muḥammad Abū l-Hudā. 2015. *Inqādh al-umma: Fatwā mufaṣṣala fī ithbāt anna Dāʿish khawārij wa-anna qitālahum wājib*. Cairo: Dār al-Baṣāʾir.

Appendix

Open Letter to South African Muslims, Inviting them to Join ISIS by Mufti Rashied Moosagie

Introduced, edited and annotated by Andrea Brigaglia, University of Cape Town[2]

---

2 Brigaglia, A. "Open letter to South African Muslims, inviting them to join ISIS, by Mufti Rashied Moosagie." *Annual Review of Islam in Africa* 2015, 13, 121–137.

Introduction

On 21 May, 2015, the Lenasia-based radio station *Channel Islam International* (CII) published on its website the text of an open letter that the radio had received in the form of an email sent by Rashied Moosagie, a well-known Islamic educator based in Port Elizabeth, South Africa. The email was sent from Raqqa (Syria), where the author had recently migrated with his family to join the cause of the religio-political entity known as *al-Dawla al-Islamiyya fi'l-Iraq wa'l-Shams* (DAESH), the Islamic State of Iraq and Syria (ISIS), or simply as "the Caliphate" of Abu Bakr al-Baghdadi. The original text of the letter was available for some time at the link http://www.ciiradio.comtag/rashid-moosagie/, before being deleted by the radio following the polemics that understandably ensued following its publication. The publication of this letter marked the peak of a series of events, all of which occurred in 2015 and confirmed that the ISIS call was starting to make in-roads among the South African Muslim public. The first of these events was an interview with an ISIS fighter of South African nationality. The interview, obtained by *Daily Maverick* via social media, was published in February.[3] The second was the news of the death of a man from Roshnee, a suburb of Vereeniging, who was reportedly fighting for ISIS in Syria. The news was published in April,[4] and it was followed by the revelation that an entire network of people originating from the same suburb had enrolled in the ranks of al-Baghdadi's Caliphate. The third was the attempt by a 15-year old girl from Kenwyn, Cape Town, to join ISIS. Her attempt, which also occurred in April, was thwarted by the South African authorities who had been following her internet exchanges with a recruiter.[5]

It was thanks to the publication of Rashied Moosagie's open letter, however, that the public debate over the presence of ISIS in South Africa reached an unprecedented level. For South African Muslims in particular, this letter was an authentic wake-up call.

This was the first case of a South African individual, with substantial credentials and a background in Islamic studies that had earned him the (informal) title of "Mufti" (Muslim legal expert), who had officially joined an international Jihadist organization.

The powerful effect of Moosagie's case and his open letter was due to the fact that it challenged the popular view that ISIS' propaganda can appeal *only*

3 http://www.dailymaverick.co.za/article/2015-02-22-exclusive-is-this-the-first-south-african-fighting-for-the-isis/#.WCM44mea21s.

4 http://imzansi.co.za/south-african-man-who-joined-isis-killed/.

5 http://www.telegraph.co.uk/news/worldnews/africaandindianocean/southafrica/11519340/South-African-teenage-girl-becomes-first-arrested-for-trying-to-join-Islamic-State.html.

to a disenfranchised, young public devoid of a solid background in Islam—something that is certainly often, but not *always*, the case.

After the publication of Moosagie's open letter, many critical responses to ISIS and its religious ideology (directly or indirectly responding to Moosagie's call) were published by South African Islamic organizations, Muslim public intellectuals and individual religious leaders. Some of these responses resonated in the national media, as well as in mosques and Muslim radios, leading to an interesting engagement which is still, to a large extent, an ongoing one. As part of its effort to document the life of contemporary African Muslim communities in their complexities, ARIA has decided to re-publish the original text of Moosagie's letter, edited to fit ARIA's editorial style, annotated here and there to facilitate the understanding of the many references to Islamic terminology, and followed by a selection of some of the responses to ISIS that have come out of South African Muslim public intellectuals and religious leaders. In the text that follows, all translations in between square brackets, as well as all notes, have been added by the editor.

Moosagie's religious background before his "awakening," followed by his embrace of ISIS' version of Salafi religious ideology, emanates mainly from Deobandi institutions of learning. Rooted in an Indian nineteenth-century reform movement, Deobandism is known for its strict adherence to classical Hanafi jurisprudence, as well as for its endorsement of a sober form of Sufism, "cleansed" from many allegedly spurious ideas and practices. In this sense, Deobandi scholars are usually engaged in a twofold competition; on the one side, with more traditional forms of Sufism (in particular, in the Indian subcontinent as well as in South Africa, the rival Barelvi school), and on the other side, with the Salafi and Wahhabi schools who reject Sufism altogether. Of the former, Deobandis usually criticize practices like festive celebrations for the *Mawlid* (birthday of the Prophet), visiting the shrines of *awliya'* (saints) and belief in the intercession (*tawassul*) of the Prophet and saints. Of the latter, they criticize the non-reliance on the derivative rulings of the scholars of the Hanafi *madhhab* and more generally, their "lack of respect" for the authority of traditional scholars (*ulama'*). In this sense, the Deobandis find themselves in the weird position of being regularly labeled as "Wahhabis" by their Sufi opponents, and as "Sufis" by their Salafi ones. The complex relations between the Deobandi Taliban fighters and the international "Arab legion" of mainly Salafi *muhjahideen* who fought the Afghan war and later gave birth to al-Qaeda, is a reflection not only of the geo-strategic stakes of the conflict and of the multiple interests involved in it, but also of the tension between Deobandism and Salafism as two partly overlapping, but ultimately distinct theological trends.

Deobandi religious schools have often been in the spotlight in the past, due to the theological affinity between Deobandism and the Afghan and Pakistani

Taliban movement. It is important to note, however, that in his letter, Moosagie voices an extremely harsh criticism of his traditional Deobandi training. For Moosagie, Deobandi Islam can be ultimately traced back to the culture and theology of Indian Sufism. Most of the time, in fact, when he uses the term "*buzrug* Islam" or "*hazrat* Islam" as derogatory references to Sufism, the context shows that he is referring in particular to the Deobandi school. Other Sufi trends like the Barelvis and the many Sufi orders that are popular in South Africa, are simply dismissed by Moosagie with the term *Mawloodis* (i.e. those who practice *Mawlid* celebrations) and they are not even considered to be worth any articulate criticism.

On the whole, this document can be considered essentially as a criticism of Deobandi Islam from the point of view of somebody who has recently undertaken a transition—perhaps we can even say a deep "conversion"—to Salafism, who has embraced a particularly extreme version of Salafi political theology, and who has been enchanted by the apocalyptic flavour of ISIS' message.

It is in the presence of this genuine autobiographical element, perhaps, rather than in the theological or political element, that lies the main interest of this document.

Text of the Open Letter by Rashied Moosagie

This is an Important Message to My Family and Colleagues

Since our *hijra* [migration; religiously motivated exile] to *Shaam* [Syria][6] many family members, friends and acquaintances have been thrown into confusion, anger and general disbelief. We were requested to give a detailed explanation leading to this decision. But before the details are presented, a brief history background will be necessary in order to fully understand this issue. Should you find it necessary to respond to this message, please do not counter with insults, rather seek to underline each statement together with your respective answers extracted from the Quran and Sunnah [prophetic practice]. Please also note that any answer offered with a *hazrat* flavor[7] will be ignored.

Childhood—1960's

As children, we grew up in a sparse *deeni* [religious] environment. Although most family members were regular with *salaah* [ritual prayer] and fasting,

6 One of the characteristic aspects of ISIS religious ideology is the call to all Muslims to perform the *Hijra* (migration) to the *Islamic State*. This call is considered obligatory for all adult Muslims. Failure to comply results, for all those who are able to do so, in being automatically considered a *murtadd* (apostate)—unless their decision to remain in an "unbeliever" nation is justified by their commitments to sacrifice their lives in suicide attacks.

7 From the Urdu *Hazrat* (from Arabic *hadrat*, "presence") a title of respect used especially in Sufi circles to express the veneration of religious scholars and Sufi saints.

they were also surrounded by an extremely ignorant society whose day-to-day *ibaadah* [worship] was riddled with *jahl* (ignorance). This society's main concern was business and all that related to it. *Deen* [religion] on the other hand was an inherited subject generally regarded as secondary. We were never prompted to seek *Deeni* [religious] knowledge; in fact it was a rather shunned and disliked topic as it was simply "the lazy person seeking a way out to escape the family shop." Pursuing the secular system was given significant priority, *deen* [religion] was neglected and our day-to-day madrassahs [Islamic schools] were run and taught by ordinary unlearned people. Even basic Quran reading was not taught properly.

Our first encounter with some *deen* [religion] was with the advent of three family *alims* [religious scholars] who had studied in India. They brought to us some *fiqh* [jurisprudence], *tafseer* [Quranic ex-egesis] and above all the *hazrat* system[8] of India. It was fascinating as well as overwhelming. This was the start of our journey to *deeni* [religious] knowledge. Their influence and tuition led us to depart to India to pursue further *Deeni* [religious] studies.

India

Deeni [religious] life in India was also well accepted by us. It was filled with mysticism and Sufism. The sheikhs had impeccable character, piety, enviable mannerism and shining faces. The *madrassahs* taught *tafseer, hadeeth, fiqh* and some philosophical subjects. I could not figure out the actual purpose for philosophy and logic though. "To combat philosophers and their ideologies…" did not make much sense—we really never needed these arts in our entire lives.

During this *madrassah* phase, some very troubling aspects were:

- Lack of *amr bil maroof* [enjoining good] and *nahi anil munkir* [sic; forbidding the evil].[9] *Salah* [ritual prayer] could be performed or left out. No real bother from the authorities. That also applied to fasting, *Juma'* [Friday congregational prayer], etc.

8 The veneration of (usually Sufi) religious leaders.

9 I.e. lack of insistence on enforcing the performance of religious duties on the wider Muslim community. The correct transliteration is *munkar* (disapproved act; wrongdoing), not *munkir* denigrator. The approximate or wrong transliteration of Arabic terms is understandable and very common in people who have not gone through academic training in Arabic. This particular mistake, however, which occurs in several instances in this letter, is quite a surprising one, because it actually changes the meaning of one of the key terms of Islamic theology.

– The stringent adherence to the *mamoolat* (specified zikrs) for the *saalik* (a person on the road to seek Allah).[10] *Mamoolat* were somehow regarded more significant than Sunnah *ibaa-dah*.[11]

However, these matters were not to be taken seriously as the sheikhs knew best. We accepted these *hazrats* [Sufi leaders], submitted wholeheartedly to them and were very involved with their ideologies. In spite of everything,"... were these not those special people that the world revolves upon?...,"[12] "...*abdaals*...,"[13] "...hidden army of Allah...," "...the actual viceroys of Allah on earth...," etc. These concepts were firmly acknowledged and expounded by us for many years to come. Comprehensive *tafseer* of the Quran *Majeed* [Glorious Quran] and Hadith *kitabs* [books] were well expounded. But two aspects always perplexed us; Jihad [holy struggle] and *Raqeeq* (slavery). These subjects were frowned upon. We were made to believe that these two were not actually applicable today any longer.

> Jihad will be only when the *Mehdi* [Messiah] and *Eesa* [Jesus] *Alayh Salaam* [peace be upon him] will appear towards the end of the world. *Raqeeq* [slavery] is disliked in Islam and should be abolished, never to be revived again.

Our entire *madrassah* [religious school] phase was based upon the *buzrug* [*sic;* reverend or saint] element. We were saturated with the *buzrug* system.[14] And ... yes, we loved and adored it. But all along, that nagging of guilt did not leave our inner heart. There was this nagging issue of Jihad. Why do such pious and learned people ignore Jihad? What was happening in Palestine? (Note that in the 70s we only knew of one fighting—in Palestine).

---

10 A reference to the devotional litanies (*dhikr*) that are characteristic of the various Sufi *turuq*.

11 "Sunna *ibada*" is a reference to the supererogatory acts of worship that are not a part of the obligatory aspects of Islam, but which were regularly performed by the Prophet and are, therefore, particularly recommended. Moosagie is criticizing the insistence of many pious devotees of Sufi orders to the zealous recitation of the litanies of their *tariqa,* while neglecting some of the Sunna supererogatory practices.

12 According to widespread Sufi notions, at every age there is a *Qutb* (Pole of a hidden hierarchy of saints) who acts as a sort of spiritual centre of the world.

13 The *qutb* of every age is believed to be assisted by a number of *abdal* (lit. "substitutes"), one of whom is elevated by God at the rank of *qutb* whenever the *qutb* of a particular time dies.

14 *Buzrug*is a Persian and Urdu term, more or less a synonym of *Hazrat.* This is another reference to the veneration of saints that is typical of Sufi Islam.

We were told to ignore their fight as those were simply wretched souls without beards or Indian *kurtas* [long robe] and deserved the punishment and wrath of Allah![15]

Departing for South Africa

Upon departing from India, our next phase required us to return and live in a *kaafir*[unbeliever] country, to practice and preach a *tasowuff* [*sic;* Sufism] and "peaceful" Islam.

Our seniors insisted that we follow and obey the governments of our countries, that we should never fight or oppose them. We should live as obedient servants because they offered us "freedom of our *Deen.*"

We were still trying to figure out what type of freedom of *deen* [religion] ever existed in South Africa. For example, we marry in the name of Allah and the government says that the marriage is illegitimate. This is freedom?

Obviously we had readily obeyed—for the institution of *sheikh-mureed* [master-disciple relation] was the true Islam, or so we thought. We used to express great resentment at those who mocked us: "how dare they mock such a pure system?"

Our lives were spent in teaching this foreign system of Islam and a great chunk of the delivered *bayaans* (lectures) were based upon the lives, actions and *malfoozaat* (sayings) of the *buzrugs* [Sufi saints]. The bulk of the talks included the miraculous feats and tales of the *buzrugs* (which of course were now discovered to be mostly false hearsay, devoid of any authenticity).

And so we continued our lives which also included journeying many times to the "*majlis*" [mosque][16] of our sheikhs…

Awakening

But within the heart, this system was never really acceptable. A system riddled with fantasies, love stories, foreign type *zikrs* [litanies] and *shagls* [devotional recitations], *hazrat* worship [saint worship] and *shirk* [polytheism] type beliefs could definitely not be the truth. One type of *shirk* [polytheism] was to regard your sheikh as *haazir naazir* (constantly present and looking at you) even in *salaah* [ritual prayer]. It was an Islam from the tales of the 1001 Arabian Nights, far from the Islam of the Noble *Sahabah* [the Prophet's companions]

---

15 I.e. we were taught that the Palestinians are suffering Zionist occupation because they are too secular. Indifference to the Palestinian struggle was very common in Indian Muslim circles, due to the secular and leftist orientation of the Palestinian leadership.

16 By putting the term between inverted commas, Moosagie hints that he is not recognizing the mainstream Sunni mosques of South Africa as legitimate, due to their failure to endorse the ISIS.

Radhi Allahu Anhum [may God be satisfied with them]. And to merely question this system was taboo, to be repelled with a torrent of insults.

We were shocked to discover our false beliefs. We realized that the rejection of jihad originated from none other than the notorious *irjah* system[17] which came about centuries ago. And Sufis were among the greatest proponents of the *irjah* system.

What is the [I]rjah or [M]urjiah System?

In a nutshell, the murjiah system can be defined as: "To apologize on behalf of Allah."

Na-oezo-billah [I seek refuge unto God]—imagine wanting to apologize on behalf for the Creator of all things. What greater *shirk* [polytheism] than this, yet Allah says in the Quran "…and never has there been nor will there ever be anyone to take Him to task…"

For example:

- Allah uses the term *Kaafir* [unbeliever] and you apologize and change it to *Ghair Muslim* (Non-Muslim).
- Allah says *Ishiddau* [sic] *alal Kufaar* (harsh on the *kufaar* [unbelievers]) and you apologize and refer it to some soft term. You frown and totally avoid this *Ayat* [verse] of the Quran.
- Allah says to fight and kill the *kufaar* [unbeliever], but you apologize by presenting some weird meaning.

17 This is a reference to the *Murji'a*, an early Islamic theological trend that grew in opposition to the Kharijites. While the latter argued that the believer who commits serious sins becomes automatically an apostate, the Murji'ites believed that his judgment is deferred (*irja'*) to God in the afterlife, and that he still has to be considered a believer, even if only a nominal one. For the Murji'ite, faith and actions are two different affairs, while for Kharijites they are one and the same thing. The Mu'tazilites famously adopted, on this issue, a median position (*manzil bayna al-manzilatayn*), arguing that the Muslim grave sinner cannot be called a believer (*mu'min*) nor an unbeliever (*kafir*), but an impious (*fasiq*). While the Murji'a as an independent school have become extinguished, their position on the issue of the grave sinner was later adopted by most classical Sunni theological trends, including Maturidis and Ash'arites, with the significant addition that while faith and actions are not the same thing, they do influence each other (i.e., the faith of a Muslim is increased by the practice of good actions and decreased by the practice of sins). The term *Murji'a* had virtually disappeared from Muslim theological debates for many centuries. In the last two centuries, however, the Wahhabi school has revived these polemics and has started to use the term Murji'a as a derogatory term for the Ash'aris. Over the last few years, this term has also assumed a special connotation in the Salafi-Jihadi lexicon, where it is applied as a broad label for those (even from among the Salafis) who reject the global Jihad project.

– Allah says that the *Kufaar* [unbelievers] shall burn painfully in Hell and you apologize, referring it to some obscure term such as "won't be near the mercy of Allah." And so you continue to apologize on behalf of Almighty Allah…

In brief, you are embarrassed by the verses of Allah hence you scramble "to try and cover up." *Irjah* also requires that the clear injunction in the Quran (*Al-bara wal Wala* [disassociating from unbelief and showing support for Islam])[18] should be avoided not to offend their "non-Muslim brothers." Yet it clearly means that we are not allowed to befriend *kufaar* [unbelievers] and never aid them against the Muslims.

This *irjah* system was also the worst virus to ever befall the Muslim *ummah* [community] and unfortunately it has now reached its peak level.

The *irjah* system was never rejected because most [S]ufis and learned scholars favored it as a quick way out to side step jihad. Most of the world *ulema* [sic] and sects promote *irjah* fully. It is a disease which only the true *ulema* will be able to combat with the aid of jihad against these sects.[19] People today openly promote *irjah* and they travel far and wide to propagate their *baatil* [null and void] *irjah*. To compound their *baatil*, these *murjiahs* [proponents of *irjah*] believe that their world wide acclaim, large numbers and massive following are directly accredited to its *maqbooliat* (divine acceptance)—May Allah save us. This is a weak argument as Christians, [S]hias [sic] etc. have been around for centuries too and they are much larger in number than these sects.

18 The strict application of the principle of *al-wala' wa'l-bara'* is foundational to the entire edifice of contemporary Salafi thought and practice. Its rigid application, however, is also the reason why contemporary Salafi groups tend to fragment so easily into multiple, mutually exclusionary ones. It is based on the principle of *al-wala' wa'l-bara'*, that the Saudi-based Salafi scholars who supported the Saudi kingdom argued that the Salafi *Sahwa* trend, which was influenced by the Muslim Brothers and called for (*wala'*) a "non-Muslim" system like elections, had committed apostasy. It is based on the same principle, a few years later, that the leaders of al-Qaeda argued that the Saudi kingdom, because of its strategic alliance (*wala'*) with the US, had committed apostasy. When ISIS was created, the followers of al-Baghdadi used the same principle to argue that the al-Qaeda representatives in the Syrian conflict, *Jabhat al-Nusra*, had committed apostasy, because they were collaborating (*wala'*) with the Free Syrian Army who was fighting to establish a "non-Islamic" democratic system, and because they failed to pledge allegiance (*bay'a*) to the Caliphate.

19 In the transition from al-Qaeda to ISIS, the emphasis of Salafi-Jihadi theory has shifted from an attempt to rally the Muslim masses in a war against the West, to a Jihad against all the Muslims who do not join the cause of Jihad. This means that ISIS is at war with virtually all existing Sunni theological and political trends, as clearly stated by Moosagie, echoing standard ISIS literature like the *Dabiq* magazine, in his letter.

But it is apostasy to claim that they could be on the truth due to their large numbers, following, learned priests and scholars.

Common [M]urjiah [S]ects

The current *Khilafa* [Caliphate] is established upon the *Minhaj* [system] of *Nabuwah* (i.e. [sic] as in the time of our *Nabie* [Prophet] *Salallahu Alayhi Wasllam* [*sic;* may God send his blessing and peace unto him]) and it is time now to scrutinize the sects that had penetrated the entire Muslim world.

The three most notable *murjiah* sects today are: Sufi sect, *Mouloodi* sect and the *Tabligh Jamaat* sect.[20]

Unfortunately, the Deoband School today has harnessed all three groups under their own banner.[21] Thus today, as it stands, they are also deviant from the *haq* [sic; truth].

These sects have many features in common; but the [S]ufi sect is the most deviant. Their *teachers* promote a type of passive *shirk*, divine communication and a host of actions justified by terms as: *Ilhaam* (divine inspiration), *Kashf* (divine entry into the unseen)[22] *Ru'ya* (instructions via dreams)[23] and the actions and sayings of the past and present *buzrugs* [saints]. The *Mouloodi* sect is simply a bunch of singing and dancing offshoot of the [S]ufis. They are a totally corrupt and have numerous blasphemous beliefs.[24] The Tablighi movement is a deviant sect promoting passive Islam or rather Mohandis [sic] Ghandi [sic] Islam.

---

20 Such a tripartite categorization is curious and clearly mirrors Moosagie's perception of the internal division of Sunnism as a South African-born, Deobandi-trained and Salafi-converted individual. The Deobandi school promotes a strict adherence to traditional Hanafi practices and a moderate Sufism. The term *Mawloodis* is widely used in Deobandi literature as a derogatory term to label all other Sufi trends, in particular the rival Indo-Pakistani Barelvi school. The *Jama'at al-Tabligh* is not a distinct school of thought, but a Deobandi activist missionary movement, especially popular with the youth.

21 It is clear from Moosagie's tones in the letter that he believes that in principle, the Deobandis are closer than other Muslims to "true" Islam, but that their teaching is so diluted that they cannot be considered as authentic Muslims anymore. This sort of "disappointment" with the Deobandi scholar is one of the major themes of the letter.

22 "Unveiling" of the unseen.

23 *Ru'ya* just means a "dream."

24 As they refrain from celebrating *Mawlid* (the Prophet's birthday), Deobandis often label all non-Deobandi Sufi groups as *Mawludis*. Here, Moosagie uncritically uses a traditional term of Deobandi polemical literature, which does not actually correspond to any specific group.

Tasowuff [Sufism]
Irjah led to the invention of *tasowuff*.[25] The proponents never cease in their futile attempts to verify it from the Quran and Sunnah.

The mere fact that it is named *tasowuff* reveals it as an innovation. Yet the Quran and Sunnah are filled with advice and guidance to perfect any person no matter how bad he may be.

For example, Allah praises the suppressing of anger and the *hadeeth* describes methods of control such as engaging in *salaah* [ritual prayer], to sit or lie down or drink water. These methods will suffice completely. So why should they be replaced with other methods? Why a person should be subjected to foreign tasks unheard of in the Sunnah? In fact some of the methods praised in *tasowuff* are ridiculously absurd, such as hurling faeces upon the *mureed* (follower) for anger testing.[26] These practices were usually mostly derived from the actions and character of "*buzrugs*" and not from the *Sahabah Radhi Allahu Anhum* [the Prophet's companion, may God be satisfied with them]. Actually *tasowuff* is a training ground to indoctrinate its followers upon a *minhaj* [system] of "*akabireen*"[27] (elders) and to finally unmold them to the world as perfect replicas—and the system will have produced "*hazrat* clones" who are able to speak, eat, drink, dress, sleep and even walk like their sheikhs to such an extent that the Sunnah postures of *salaah* are substituted by "*hazrat* brand postures." When they have reached this "lofty" level, they are known to have attained *sier fillah* [sic] (reached into Allah—*Allahu Akbar*).[28] A word of note here: The term "*sier fillah*" is a [S]ufi term which denotes the highest level a

25 There are many contradictory hypotheses about the origins of Sufism that have been advanced by various historians, but the association between the *Murji'a*as a theological school of early Islam and the first Sufis of Iraq is not one of the theories that have currency in historical literature. The Murji'ites were promoted especially by the Umayyad Caliphs in Damascus, while the first Sufis especially grew out of the circles of Kufa and Baghdad who were trying to distance themselves from power. The association of the two terms, however, makes sense emotionally (rather than historically), in the context of Moosagie's critique of Deobandi Sufism as a sort of "disengaged Islam."

26 This is certainly not a known practice in any South African Sufi order, but there might be instances of this sort in certain strands of Indian Sufism, and this is probably what Moosagie has in mind.

27 The Arabic word *kabir* (big; elder) has several plural forms: *kabirin, akabir* and *kibar*. The one used by Moosagie seems to be a weird conflation of the first two.

28 The *sayr fi' Llah* (path in God) is the name given in Sufi literature to the stages of the mystical path *after* the aspirant has completed his *sayr lil-Lah* (path to God) and achieved *fana'* (annihilation). Moosagie seems to conflate the two terms.

human can reach. It literally means that you fade away into the being Allah. What utter *kufr* [unbelief] and *shirk* [polytheism]. In fact some [S] ufi sects even believe that the *kufaar* [unbelievers] can reach this stage—May Allah forbid!

Thereafter they are conferred with a type of holy mantle called "*khilafat*." The result is even more destructive—their fellow colleagues and friends now view this new "*khalifa*" to be a qualified "*buzrug*" with newly assigned status and none among them may dare to oppose this newbie. He can now also expound the mystic four [S]ufi chains, receive *ilhaam* [divine inspiration] and *kashf* [unveiling of the unseen], and he will transcend into a mystique [sic] realm wherein he will be constantly streamed with special "*faidh*" [spiritual emanation] from their sheikhs, even though the sheikh may be deceased. Similar to ancestral worship of the pagans.

A word of note here, *faidh* in [S]ufi terms denotes a constant spiritual light stream emanating from the sheikh, whether he is dead or alive. Thus it is common for them to visit the graves of their sheikhs "to connect further to this line of *faidh*." This is *kufr*[unbelief] and unheard of in the Sunnah!

The Aggression of [T]hese [S]ects

They are willing to spill blood and post henchmen around to physically attack their opponents. Yet the *kufaar* [unbelievers] and *murtadeen* [apostates] mock *Nabie Salallahu Alayhi Wasallam* [the Prophet, may God send his blessings and peace unto him] on a daily basis but they NEVER dream of rising up in defense of *Nabie Salallahu Alayhi Wasallam* [the Prophet, may God send his blessings and peace unto him]. They say "…adopt patience…" And they brand defenders of our beloved *Nabie Salallahu Alayhi Wasallam* [the Prophet, may God send his blessings and peace unto him] as "thugs and hooligans." By Allah I swear that these people have zero love for *Nabie Salallahu Alayhi Wasallam* [the Prophet, may God send his blessings and peace unto him][.]

Personal [E]xperience

Some firsthand experience in this affair should be also mentioned here. None among the followers of this order may dare to oppose this system. If anyone does, his opposing is understood to be directed to the entire [S]ufi clan present, past and future and [–] may Allah forbid—ultimately opposing *Nabie Salallahu Alayhi Wasallam* [the Prophet, may God send his blessings and peace unto him]. Threats and curses are freely cast by these so called "soft" *ulama*, laymen, family members, colleagues and "*mureeds*" [disciples]. They shamelessly expose their rage, but not upon the *kufaar* nor upon the *munafiqeen* [hypocrites] *murtadeen* [apostates] nor upon the enemies of Islam, but upon speakers of truth. Plus it is no ordinary rage but a rage intensified with bitter vengeance flung by saliva squirting lips … yes and so much so for the "*karmakhlaaq*" [sic] (beautiful character) of these [S]ufis!

Torrents of insults and curses are liberally directed to those who challenge them, similar to the actions of the pagans of *Jahiliya* [pre-Islamic times] who tried to scare the Muslims who dared question their idols.

"…And you dare question the words or actions of these *hazrats* [saints]. You *ghinzeer* [pig]! You shall be struck dead!…" (In fact they do narrate stories of people *who* were struck dead merely upon opposing the *hazrats*…. *Subhanallah* [God is transcendent above this]!).

Their concept of someone harming a *wali* [saint] is totally crooked and they misquote the *hadeeth* wherein Allah proclaims: "Whoever harms a *wali* of mine can expect war from me."

They actually have absolutely no clue to the actual meaning of this *Hadeeth*. If they did truly understand its meaning, they would obviously never limit it to "India *buzrugs*" [Indian Sufi saints] and their "*khalifas*" [successors]. In other words a *wali* has attained sainthood through a man-made hereditary system, very similar to the Christian sainthood methodology. Thus this structure effectively denies the description of a true *wali* mentioned in the Quran and Sunnah. When Allah describes a true *mujahid* [holy warrior] as his *wali* [saint], they refuse to acknowledge that and will not hesitate to insult and curse him. Their typical modus is to condemn and curse the mujahedeen daily. Are they not afraid of the "war" which Allah will declare upon them for harming his friends?

World-wide Influence

Unfortunately this *sheikh-mureed* [master-disciple] system is widely acknowledged especially in India and western countries. The more followers the sheikh acquired, the greater his influence and "*maqbooliat*" [acceptance] (accepted by Allah). He receives royal treatment and in most cases they are usually surrounded by the "*laanies*"[29] and other worldly influential doctors, lawyers, and *hazrat* [saint] worshippers—people who are all too willing to sponsor their first class luxurious world tours. The journeys and Disneyland rides are termed "*islah majlis*" [assemblies of moral reform] (whatever that means) and are accompanied by many holiday makers with packages generally packed with

29 An Afrikaans word used in South African English slang meaning "an influential person," or, "a VIP."

expensive tourist's attractions and peppered with daily doses of "*min janibillah malfoozat*" (talks placed into the heart by Allah) [i.e. daily prescribed litanies] litanies dished out on the fly which in turn are so readily swallowed by the most eager head nodding and torso swirling *mureeds* [Sufi disciples]. Plus the generous offerings, sumptuous meals and celebrity quality transport. Their food and drink leftovers are treated as holy and divided as booty among themselves.

But when we ponder the lives of the noble *Sahabah* [Companions] and those after them, the true saints of Allah never do we discover this type of system. They never acquired thousands of *mureeds* [disciples], they never indulged in sumptuous meals and they were never entertained by "*laanies.*"

Buzrug?

A *buzrug* is a Persian term used to denote a *wali*or saint of Allah.

So what is a *wali* in its true sense? Let us search the Quran and Sunnah. The Quran describes them as virtuous, steadfast in *Salah* [ritual prayer], *Zakaah* [alms] AND Jihad [holy struggle]. They were also honest, sincere, noble, faithful, harsh upon the *kufaar* [unbelievers], soft and kind to the Muslims, perpetual in *salaah* [ritual prayer] and never feared the chastising of the chastisers. All the *Sahabah* had these qualities so we could indisputably declare them as *Awliyah* (plural of *wali*) [saints].[30] And their weapons were always strung upon their shoulders or at their sides.

If we search for a true *wali* of Allah we find another description in a *Hadeeth*: "…should he ask for or say anything, not much attention would be paid, should he ask for your daughters, he will be refused…," in brief a person you don't care much about. Allah says that by his honor if this person should even take an oath, Allah will fulfill it accordingly.

Sheikh-Mureed [Master-Disciple]

So now, where did all this really originate from? There are many theories, but the most obvious would be a copycat guru system. The *Sheikh-Mureed* [master-disciple] is based upon the same system implemented by the gurus of India and the pre-Islam fire worshippers of Persia. The *Sheikh-Mureed* system is governed by orders similar to the guru orders and they pass on their "spiritual" blessings down into their successor's hearts with a "chest to chest" connection.

30 The tendency to mythically project an ideal of absolute perfection in *all* the Companions (*sahaba*) of the Prophet is typical of certain strands of Sunni piety. This tendency grows especially after the first three centuries, in an effort to balance Shiite readings of early Islamic history. The "mythicization" of the *sahaba* is a cornerstone of Deobandi pietistic literature. Most early Sunni scholars (e.g., al-Tabari), on the contrary, held a much more historical, balanced and critical view of early Islamic history.

The [S]ufis also claim to have connected chains leading right up to Ali *Radhi-Allahu-Anhu* [may God be pleased with him]. May Allah forbid! Where do they get this information from? Not a single narration or authentic source could verify these chains and "spiritual *khilaafa* [Caliphate]" of the *Sahabah* [companions]. This is another deviant way to divert the true physical *khilaafa* [Caliphate] of the *Sahabah* into the spiritual realm of their "*buzrugs*."[31]

There are also certain dangerous beliefs attached to the sheikh, for example, that they constantly receive *kashf* [unveiling] of every movement of their *mureeds* [disciples]; their actions should never be challenged, even if it be against Sharia. Nor are you allowed to even endorse *nahianilmunkir* [sic] (preventing wrong) amongst them. How could you ever find fault with a "sinless *buzrug*?" Did you ever dream of voicing your dislike for their anti Shariah actions? Do you raise your voice when your sheikh and his *mureeds* are seated in a packed mixed audience watching dolphins and their scantily clad maidens' antics accompanied by corresponding music? You are commanded to believe that their actions should never be questioned as they are perpetually in a "*haal*" (lofty spiritual state) under the throne of Allah. Their followers truly believe that their sheikhs are in contact with Allah and whatever they speak or write is "…a *noor* (divine light) directly from the throne of Almighty Allah." *Na-oezo-billah* [I seek refuge unto God] what *shirk* [polytheism] and blasphemy! Many of the books written by these *buzrugs* contain lies, fabrications and unauthentic *hadeeth*, yet their followers refer to these books as "light directly from the *Arsh* [Throne] of Allah," [m]ay Allah forbid.

Spiritualism

So what does spiritualism actually mean? It is foreign to Islam and cannot be found anywhere in the Quran and Sunnah and the lives of the *Sahabah*.

Most of the books written or orated from the *buzrugs* are filled with spiritualism claimed to be derived from verses of the Quran and *Hadeeth*. However, most of their sources are from the *Mathnawi* by Moulana Rumi.[32] Sufis have branded the *mathnawi* as the "[Q]uran of Persia"—[m]ay Allah forbid. And when they do quote the verses of the Quran and *hadeeth* it is simply presented not to expound the Quran or the Sunnah, but merely as symbols to

31 For Moosagie, Sufism's emphasis on the concept of "spiritual succession" (*khilafa*) and on pledging allegiance (*bay'a*) to a Sufi master, are tools to divert Muslims from the "real" purpose of Islam, i.e. the establishment of a tangible Caliphate (*Khilafa*), which is one of the central themes of ISIS—if not *the* central theme.

32 Made up of 25,000 verses, the *Mathnawi* is the most famous collection of poetry composed by Jalal al-Din Rumi (d. 1273), the most celebrated Sufi poet of Islamic history.

confirm their own spiritual explanations which were claimed to be either received as "*ilhaam*" (revelation) or "*ilqa*" (direct communication from Allah). Millions of rands (and in most cases public funds) are wasted publishing these [S]ufi books and fairy tales which became freely available in all the *masaajids* [mosques] of South Africa with some *masjids* [mosques] boasting entire lined corridors to such an extent that they have replaced the Quran—another cunning method utilized by *shaytaan* [Satan] to remove the Quran from our lives. A similar incident is mentioned in the Quran of a *kaafir* [unbeliever] who attempted to direct the believers away from the Quran with his imported fairy tales from Rome and other ancient cities. Look at his punishment…[33]

Sahr [sic; Magic][34]

In addition to being *murjiahs*, an integral part of this Indian system was their involvement with superstitions, *aamils* [esoteric practictioners] and *sahr* [sic] (black magic). Any "*molvi*" [Quranic teacher] or "*moulana*" [religious scholar] who can "speak" to *jinns* [invisible spiritual beings] or remove *sahr* [magic spells] is known as an "*Aamil*" [spiritual practitioners].[35] They are very similar to the bone throwing. Black *sangomas* [traditional healers and diviners] of South Africa. It has absolutely nothing to do with Islam and in many cases these "*aamils*" practice open *shirk* [polytheism] and *kufr* [unbelief]. Unwary Muslims flock to them but despite constant warnings against these frauds, they are simply too naïve to realize that their association with these *dajjals* [impostors] is plain *kufr* [unbelief] and *shirk* [polytheism]. To compound this *baatil* [invalid belief], many of these "*aamils*" [practitioners] are "*khalifas* [successors] of the great *buzrugs* [saints] of India"—so now these *aamils* are holy people of Allah who can't be wrong, people who are blessed with "special *nusrah* (aid)"—*Subhanallah* [God is transcendent above this!], what blasphemy.

In any case these "*aamils*" always cause more damage than good resulting in numerous family breakups, exactly what *Shaytan* [Satan] desires. It is the *fardh*

33 I have not been able to detect what incident narrated in the Quran is being referred to by Moosagie here.

34 It should be *sihr*, not *sahr*. This is another curious mistake of transliteration in Moosagie's letter.

35 Esoteric practices like the manufacture of protective Quranic talismans (*talasim, ta'awidh,* etc.) used to be (and still are, to a certain extent) a very common activity of Sunni (especially Sufi) religious scholars. A rich literature on these themes has circulated throughout the classical times, both in Arabic and in the main languages of Islam. These practices have declined during the last two centuries as they are under the attack of both "rationalist" trends and Salafi "scripturalist" ones.

[individual obligation] duty of every Muslim to physically eradicate[36] these "*aamils*" from their respective societies.

Journey to the [T]ruth

It was a painful experience to abandon a lifetimes [sic] involvement with a highly treasured system which convinced all of its adherents to be the true *deen* [religion] of Islam. But Allah requires you to forfeit all your idols and only worship him—that is true *imaan* [faith]. The *mushriks* [polytheists] of Mecca knew the truth, but they refused to abandon their dear lifelong idols.

It was not easy to reject the current Deobandi system founded by luminaries who were perhaps not part of the *irjah* camp and who readily supported active Jihad as well as its promotion, but history is scant on such matters.

Although Deoband was allegedly involved in great battles, no historical facts could verify these claims. No *mujahideen* were housed, or produced from this institution. On the contrary, our stay in Deoband did not reflect Jihad at all. The Deobandi institution strictly implements its original Nanotwi[37] constitution without modifications and if any Jihad doctrines ever existed, why did it vanish? In fact the current principal (a grandson of the original founder) at our time was totally against any Jihad or opposing the *mushrik* [polytheist] government. When the Indian *mushrik* government was forcefully castrating the Muslims, he was calling for peace and co-operation with these *mushriks*. Many Deoban- dis will scramble to defend this allegation with claims that some *hazrats* [Sufi saints] were even martyred in a battle. That may be true to a certain extent but Jihad was definitely NOT Deobandi policy, otherwise every Deobandi would naturally be a fully fledged *mujahid*. An institution's products are always reflected in their ideology. If the ideology was Jihad, the graduates would definitely also reflect Jihad—NEVER the opposite. Deobandis will claim that history is full of "the great Jihad of Deoband and their 14,000 Ulama slaughter tale."[38] This is a fabrication with absolute no authentic source[.]

36 This should not be taken as a simple metaphor. In the areas under its control, ISIS has carried out systematic purges of Muslim practitioners (who are often religious scholars) accused of *sihr*(magic).

37 From Muhammad QasimNanotvi (d. 1880), one of the founders of the *Dar al-Ulum* of Deoband, India.

38 Reference to the alleged murder of 14,000 Muslim scholars in India by the British, between 1864 and 1867.

Jihad

Around 1990, when the Iraq invasion took place, we decided to scrutinize the Jihad facet of Islam. How could we ever be subservient to a *kufr* government? Jihad in Islam clearly refers to physical fighting whether offensive or defensive. But [i]n the eyes of the *murjiah* sects, Jihad refers to everything else but the actual physical fighting. Jihad, a tenant [sic] of Islam was being defied, yes defied by famous *ulema* [sic] and learning centers, including Deoband and this was something which could never ever be left unchallenged!

Jihad is Islam and [D]enial is [K]ufr

Note [w]ell: Sufi ideology expressively denies Jihad, not necessarily in word form, but in actions, teachings and intentional elimination of Jihad verses which brought about a new world order of "spiritual Jihad." This ideology clearly opposes the Quran and Sunnah.

Our claim to love and follow *Nabie Sallalu- alayhi-wasallam* [the Prophet, may God send his blessing and peace unto him] is false, for he said "…I would like to fight in the path of Allah, be killed, become resurrected, fight again, be killed, become resurrected, fight again, be killed…" So why don't you also have this love to fight? Why do you present excuses upon excuses? In fact[,] you oppose anyone who even promotes Jihad. Those *"buzrug"* Sunnah love stories of refusal to eat a sweet melon because his love for the Sunnah could not direct him to the actual slicing method? But did he ever yearn to be killed in fighting the enemy in accordance to the desire of *Nabie Sallalu-alayhi-wasallam* [the Prophet, may God send his blessing and peace unto him]? In all my stay in India and association with these sheikhs, I was never encouraged towards Jihad or its preparations. Their so called preparations were masked by flimsy excuses such as "until *islah* [moral reform] of the *nafs* [human soul] has been made…." Once I asked "…and when do I qualify? Or rather is it possible to ever reach the point of accomplishment of the *nafs*? No one could ever reply me until this day."

Actually these are excuses presented by those who refuse to partake in jihad. The Quran mentions one such person who came to *Nabie Sallalu-alayhi-wasallam* [the Prophet, may God send his blessings and peace unto him] at the time of recruiting for the battle of Tabuk.[39] This person claimed that he had a weakness for roman girls.[40] So he would like to be excused from Jihad.

---

39 The battle of Tabuk (northern Arabia) was fought by the Muslims against the polytheist Arabs, in 630.

40 In the hadith, the term *rumi* ("Romans") actually means "Byzantine." According to the event alluded to by Moosagie here, a companion by the name of Jadd b. Qays tried to

So he presented an excuse similar to the [S]ufi excuse "until *islah* of the *nafs* has been made...."

A verse was then revealed wherein Allah reprimanded him severely and described his remaining behind as the actual great *fitna* [in this context, temptation]. Observe how Allah rebukes people who present these false excuses!

My [S]tance

While in S[outh] A[frica], these *irjah* sects were challenged, Jihad was openly promoted and taught; Muslims were incited to rise and fight America and all those who supported them. The *irjah* sects unfortunately control all the *masjids* [mosques] and public platforms whereby they managed to silence the truth for a while though by placing bans on *masjids* and radio platforms.[41] The masses were persuaded not to listen to this "radical madman who will soon be destroyed for opposing their hazrats" ...

Yes we are proud to be labled madmen for those were labels given also to the glorious *Sahabah* [companions] *radhi Allahu anhum* [may God be pleased with them].

Moving to Shaam [Syria]

An in depth study into the Quran, Hadeeth, Sunnah and lives of the *Sahabah* led to only one conclusion—that towards the Hour, *Shaam* [Syria] will have to be the ultimate destiny of a true believer. *Shaam* will be the land of the foretold great battles, the coming of the last *Khilafa* [Caliphate] and the descent of *Eesa* [Jesus] *Alayh Salaam* [peace be upon him], but this document was not intended to present information on that issue but *Inshallah* [God willing] a detailed document relating to *Shaam*, the *Malhama* [end of Time battle] and the events leading up to it will be released soon—with authentic proofs.

Towards the hour *Dajjal* [the Antichrist] will appear and it is the greatest *fitna* [civil strife] ever to surface on earth. The entire assembly of *Ambiya* [prophets] *alayi salaam* [sic; peace be upon him (them?)] warned against this terrible *fitna* [civil strife] to appear, so know that it is going to be a VERY GREAT

---

use his weakness for Byzantine women as an excuse to withdraw from participating into the expedition, claiming that traveling to a place like Tabuk, where Byzantine girls lived, could induce him into temptation. It is in reference to this event that, according to traditional exegetical literature, verse 9:49 of the Quran was revealed to rebuke Jadd b. Qays.

41 It is not clear here to what mosques and radios Moosagie is referring. It can be inferred, however, that for a brief time, he attempted to promote ISIS in the open, but was repressed thanks to the collaboration of the official South African Muslim bodies and the South African security forces.

FITNAH. But Allah is merciful, he will slowly strengthen his true friends with *fitnahs* similar to that of *Dajjal* [Antichrist], to prepare His friends to identify and withstand these approaching *fitnahs* as they continue to appear.

Like vaccines (which are in reality "mini viruses"), doctors induce into their patients to prepare them for the actual virus attack. Today we witness one *fitna* similar to that of *Dajjals fitnahs*—a Heaven and Hell. *Dajjal* will come along and present this "*jannah* and *jahannum*" [Heaven and Hell] and everyone will opt for his "*jannah*." Everyone will be commanding each other to choose his "*jannah*" and NEVER to go towards his hell. It is absolutely absurd to choose the hell of *Dajjal*. Despite all odds, a true believer will opt for *Dajjal's* hell and this action will stir the emotions of everyone—they will become furious, rebuke and even fight with him for making such an "outrageous and despicable" decision. But the believer will insist to jump into *Dajjal's* hell in true obedience to *Nabie* [the prophet] *Salallahu Alayhi Wasllam* [peace be upon him] who had forewarned the *ummah* [community of believers] and instructed them to choose the hell of *Dajjal* as it will in reality be a heaven. And those who opted for his heaven will in realty have chosen Hell.[42]

This similar *fitna* is *Shaam* and *Darul Kufr* [the Abode of Unbelief].[43] Externally *Shaam* does look like Hell, full of bombings, killings, unlivable conditions, sicknesses, harsh weather and a host of other difficulties. Yes it does look like Hell.

On the other hand *Darul Kufr* [the Abode of Unbelief] looks like heaven, with all its comforts, foods, wonderful living and luxuries.

Everyone will opt for the "*jannah*," everyone will opt for *Darul Kufr*, but know that this is actually your Hell. A true believer will opt to migrate against all odds to *Shaam*, he will opt for this Hell, for indeed it is actually *jannah*. By Allah, despite all these difficulties, you experience true serenity as never before found anywhere. To see the name of Allah so high, to witness his law everywhere and to see his soldiers marching against *kufr* [unbelief] brings untold joy to a *Mu'min*'s [believer] heart. Merely to know that we all stand side by side, risking our very lives to be bombed and killed purely for being true believers is truly an amazing and incomprehensible feeling.

---

42 One of the main characteristics of ISIS ideology, distinguishing it from other Salafi-Jihadi groups like al-Qaeda, is its strong emphasis on an apocalyptic reading of contemporary history. For a rich study of ISIS' apocalyptic doctrines, see William McCants, *The ISIS Apocalypse: The History, Strategy, and Doomsday Vision of the Islamic State* (London: Macmillan, 2015).

43 According to ISIS doctrine, the entire world today constitutes *Dar al-Kufr* (land of unbelief), with the exception of al-Baghdadi's Caliphate.

Also you know that you are able to help in some way the oppressed Muslims as Allah commands:

> And why should ye not fight in the cause of Allah and of those who, being weak, oppressed?—Men, women, and children, whose cry is: "Our Lord! Rescue us from this town, whose people are oppressors; and raise for us from the one who will protect; and raise for us from thee one who will help!" [Q 4: 75].

How is it possible for us to continue living in safe and comfortable homes while ignoring the pleas of those Muslims who are being oppressed by the united *kufaar* [unbelievers]? It is better for us to sacrifice our lives and share their grief for indeed it may, Allah willing, be an acceptable excuse in His Gracious Court.

The Khilafah [Caliphate] [*C*]*ondemnation* [*C*]*ampaign and its* [*M*]*yths*

Accusations against the *Khilaafa* [Caliphate][:]

1. America controlled[.]
2. The *Khalifa* [Caliph] is an American, [J]ew, puppet of America[.][44]
3. *Dowla* [the (Islamic) State] kills Muslims and innocent people[.]
4. *Dowla* [the (Islamic) State] *takfeers* [excommunicates] everyone who disagrees with them[.]
5. The *Khilaafa* [Caliphate] is Illegitimate[.]

These are probably the main arguments presented against *Dowla* [the (Islamic) State]. Right now in *Dowla* you see full Sharia Law, absolutely NO *kaafir* court [secular courts] at all. All crime is strictly controlled with Sharia Law. Amongst the laws are:

- Execution for *Irtidaad* [apostasy], *Sahr* [sic; magic] and homosexuality[.]
- Stoning for adultery[.]
- Hands amputation for theft[.]

---

44 The idea that al-Baghdadi and his group are being used by Americans is current, especially among the Iraqi and Syrian public opinions. According to this theory, the goal of American and Israeli strategists, in complicity with the Saudis, would be to create a Salafi island in the Sunni majority areas between the two countries of Iraq and Syria, where ISIS has created its state. The ultimate goal would be to break the "Axis of Resistance" that joins the countries of Iran, Iraq and Syria and that allows weapons and intelligence to be transferred to the Lebanese Hezbollah. For a parody song and video-clip, diffused by the Iraqi TVs in 2014, which portray ISIS under this light, see https://www.youtube.com/watch?v=94YL8eXP30M. Especially promoted by the Iraqi and Syrian governments is the idea that Western powers have used ISIS as an asset to create the "New World Order," which has variously resonated among Muslim publics of various orientation.

- Flogging for *Zina* [adultery][.]
- Prison for *Riba'* [usury] and gambling (if discovered)[.]
- *Salaah* [ritual prayer] is enforced and all businesses to be closed upon *Salaah* times entry[.]
- No music allowed in homes or public areas[.]
- No wine and cigarettes[.]
- Full *hijaab* [female veil] is enforced[.]
- No mixing of sexes in public[.]
- No Cinemas, racecourses, banks, discos or clubs[.]

It is a laughing matter to regard all this as America or American aided[.] Let us assume that if this was the case then know that America must be complimented for accomplishing such a sterling act to fully introduce Shari[a] into *Shaam* [Syria]. For centuries now, even a Muslim country could not achieve this blessing! Many western sources reported that countries upon countries have tried to establish proper law, justice and a crime free environment for decades, but they had failed hopelessly with adverse results compared to the swift achievements of *Dowla* [the (Islamic) State] within 7 months.

Western quote: "…it is amazing to see crime dropping to almost zero within this short time, ISIS is indeed powerful…"[45]

The *Khalifa* [Caliph] [Abu Bakr al-] Baghdadi is a *Qurashi* [from the Arab tribe of Quraysh] Sayed [descendant of the Prophet] [A]rab and a violent enemy of America. It does not mean that since he may have at one stage been a prisoner of this enemy that he now suddenly became one of them.[46] He only speaks the Quran and Sunnah and is a very violent fighter against America so according to this impossible notion, America succeeded in producing a true believer and their greatest enemy!

Dowla does not kill any Muslim. They only fight *kufaar* [unbelievers], [*S*]*hia* [Shiites], [Y]azeedi and *murtad* [apostates]. Currently *Jabhatu Nusrah* [the Nusra Front][47] has joined the coalition and is thus fighting side by side

---

45 We have not been able to trace this quote back to any source. Maybe Moosagie is referring to a westerner who has "migrated" to the ISIS Caliphate.

46 Abu Bakr al-Baghdadi was detained for some time by American forces in Abu Ghraib and Camp Bucca. Reports about the length of his detention are contradictory. According to those who see him as an American asset (see note 42 above), it was during his detention that the American intelligence decided either to co-opt him as a collaborator to infiltrate the al-Qaeda leadership, or to release him and use him indirectly as a tool of their policy.

47 Now known as *Jaysh Fath al-Sham* (Army for the Conquest of Syria), the al-Nusra front was for several years the official representative of the al-Qaeda network in the Syrian conflict, where it has been playing an ambiguous role, at times collaborating with the many Salafi factions (*Ahrar al-Sham, Harakat Nour al-Din al-Zenki,* etc.) which are allied with the Western-backed FSA (Free Syrian Army), and occasionally overlapping with ISIS.

with the *Taghoot* [idolatrous] enemy.[48] *Dowla* regards this as an act of *irtidaad* [apostasy] established from the Quran and Sunnah.

Dowla does not *takfeer* [excommunicate] any Muslim who disagrees with them on any *fiqh* [jurisprudential] law. However, if their *aqeedah* [theology] is against the Quran and Sunnah, then they will most certainly *takfeer* [excommunicate] you. That is absolutely in order according to Sharia.

The *Khilaafa* [Caliphate] is not illegitimate nor was it necessary to "consult" anyone. Throughout history, many Muslim thrones were violently seized and accepted by the Muslim masses without opposition.

Harun Rashied [sic][49] seized the throne yet he was acclaimed to be one of the greatest khalifas [Caliphs] of the Muslim world. Aurengzeb [sic][50] seized the throne from his father, had him imprisoned and executed his two brothers, yet the "hazrats [Sufi scholars] of India" regarded him as the greatest ruler of India. No one accused him as one who acquired an illegitimate throne.

Some [P]oints to [P]onder

I need answers to this question: Do you accept us as Muslims?

There are only two answers to this question, either a NO or either a YES.

If the answer is NO, then present your proof which casts us out of Islam. To this date, no one could forward that type of evidence.

If the answer is YES, which means that you do accept us to be Muslims? [sic] So either we are good Muslims or bad Muslims, but Muslim indeed. Correct?

Then why do you not demonize the current 60 *kufr* countries [unbelieving countries] and the *munafiqeen* [hypocrite] Arab countries that are mercilessly and incessantly pounding us with the most horrendous and devastating bombs. Brothers you have not seen the effects of these bombs, because the [W]est don't [sic] show you. *Dowla* on the other hand does not publicize these atrocities for possible adverse effects upon the weaker *mujahid* [holy fighter] or

---

For Moosagie, the al-Nusra Front is now a full member of the "camp of unbelief" and an enemy to fight.

48 *Taghut* (idolatry) is a term that current Jihadi-Salafi literature uses in particular with reference to nation states ruled by constitutions (secular or Islamic). The "taghoot camp," therefore, is made of all those forces who are fighting for the establishment of a Syrian state ruled by a man-made constitution, including the Islamists (Muslim Brothers) as well as the Salafis who accept the principles of borders and constitutionalism.

49 Harun al-Rashid (d. 809) was the fifth caliph of the Abbasid dynasty.

50 Muhammad Aurangzeb Alamgir (d, 1707) was the sixth ruler of the Mughal dynasty in India.

those who intend *hijrah* [religiously motivated migration]. It is heart rendering to see someone still alive without arms and legs, blinded and deaf. Imagine what a life this person needs to endure. May Allah grant these *mujahedeen* [holy fighters] a very lofty stage. You don't experience true pain like us here. Just a few weeks ago, about 2.5km from us, these *kufaar* [unbeliever] Americans sent in drones to locate a *masjid* [mosque]. The fighter jets followed and tried to bomb this *masjid* [mosque] but missed striking an adjacent block of flats, wiping out three families. Brothers you don't know what real pain is, to see a mother frantically running back to her bombed down apartment, screaming hysterically to her children whose faint screams under masses of rubble dwindle into a silence never to be heard again.

But you don't utter ONE word of disapproval, which leads us to believe that you are quite happy with these cruel attacks and bombing. You simply say: "Yes we condemn them…" But that too is a lie to soothe you. Did you publically condemn them like how you publically condemn *Dowla*? If so, then please oblige and show me ONE article or even a phone chat. But you are willing to condemn us for hours on end. I ask you to mount any *mimbar* [pulpit] for only one day in any *masjid* [mosque] and speak out against America, but you won't dare anger this idol. By condemning the jihad, *Dowla*, the *muhajireen* [those who have migrated to join ISIS] and *mujahedeen* [holy fighters] you clearly demonstrate your lack of fear for Allah and your great fear for this idol. This is absolute *shirk* [polytheism]! I have never heard you deliver one violent lecture condemning America as you so ferociously condemn us. In fact senior *ulema* [Muslim scholars] in Port Elizabeth and S[outh] A[frica] have stooped to gutter level spitting out against us, yet they cannot even whimper against *Taghoot* [idol] America.

My Final Advice

Fighting the coalition has now become very fierce here in *Dowla* and I implore you to please heed this advice very seriously for we do not know whether Allah will allow us ever to meet again.

It is necessary for you to study the Quran and Sunnah and to clear your heart and mind of all doubts regarding the *aqeedah* [theological doctrine] of our *Deen* [religion]. No one should be embarrassed to re-learn *Deen* [religion], no matter the age. Upon entry into *Dowla*, everyone is taught the correct *aqeedah* [theological doctrine] directly from the Quran and Sunnah. Any amount of questions may be asked and they will be answered with clear as daylight proofs. It is also necessary for all Muslims, especially in the western countries to reject all the deviant sects which appeared amongst the Muslims.

Two common groups also need to be rebuked and rejected due to their apostasy.

Kufr [unbelief] Beliefs of:

Mouloodi sect:[51]

- Regard *Nabie* [the Prophet] *Salallahu Alayhi Wasllam* [may God send his blessings and peace upon him] to have unseen Knowledge[.]
- Believe *Nabie* [the Prophet] *Salallahu Alayhi Wasllam* [may God send his blessings and peace upon him] is present everywhere[.]
- They are quite pleased to live under *Taghoot* [idolatry].[52]
- Reject Jihad[.]
- Not allowed to fight the *Taghoot* [idolatrous system] as they give you freedom of *moulood* [celebrating the Prophet's birthday][.]

Tablighi Sect:

- Reject Jihad and make *inkhiraaf* (change) of the Quraan verses pertaining to Jihad.
- Gave Nizamudeen[53] and Raiwind[54] (two manmade structures in India and Pakistan) holy status and attribute *thawaab* (divine reward and blessings) for visitors[.]
- Gave Nizamudeen and Raiwind preference above the holy Haj and Umrah pilgrimage.
- Regard their *Fazaail Amaal* as their Quran and insist that the Quran of Islam cannot be understood or acted upon without this book.[55] Quran of Islam is third on their list.
- They are quite pleased to live under *Taghoot* [idolatry] and firmly believe in their obedience (to *Taghoot*)[.]
- You are not allowed to fight the *Taghoot* as it will curtail their movement.

These sects should abandon their *kufr* [unbelief], *shirk* [polytheism] and blasphemous beliefs immediately, otherwise they will ultimately join the band of the coming *Dajjal* [Antichrist].

May Allah grant us victory upon the *Kufaar* [unbelievers] and *Munafeqeen* [hypocrites] Ameen.

Your brother[,] Rashid Moosagie[.]

---

51 See note 22 above.

52 See note 46 above.

53 A neighbourhood in South Delhi (India), home of the international headquarters of the Tabligh movement.

54 A neighbourhood in Lahore (Pakistan), home to another major headquarters of the Tabligh movement.

55 *Fada-il al-a'mal* (in Urdu, *Faza'il e-amal*), by Muhammad Zakariya Kandhlawi, is a religious text especially cherished in Tabligh circles.

PART 4

Media Perspectives and Material Approaches

CHAPTER 10

From the Pocketbook to Facebook: Maktabat Wahba, Publishing, and Political Ideas in Cairo since the 1940s

Bettina Gräf

1 Introduction*

In the course of the Arab revolutions that took place between 2010 and 2012, many commentators spoke of Twitter and Facebook revolutions, so much so that one might have gotten the impression that the new communication technologies available in the region since the beginning of the 2000s were the main causes of the revolts. Walter Armbrust characterised this approach in 2012 in terms of the technological determinism and presentism of Arab media studies. In his opinion, one should rather concentrate on the interplay of technology and social action from a historical perspective "for the simple reason that change is more often a gradual process" and never directly caused by media technology (Armbrust 2012, 48–49). He argues in favour of including the wider cultural context and suggests the year 1919 as a starting point for researching the cultural history of new media in Egypt, the year when "print culture reached a critical mass" (Armbrust 2012, 34).[1] "Print culture" is a key word here, since the concept of culture in combination with a specific media technology already hints at a complex relationship.

It has been argued further that print culture was an important component in establishing national identities (Anderson 1983). Meanwhile this idea has been challenged: "[I]n a nation like Egypt, where literacy rates were low, nonprint media also played an important role in shaping identities" (Fahmy 2010, 83).

* The research for this article was conducted between 2010 and 2014 within the larger research project *In Search of Europe: Considering the Possible in the Middle East and Africa*, based at what is now the Leibniz-Zentrum Moderner Orient Berlin and funded by the German Ministry for Education and Research (BMBF) (cf. Abdelkarim and Gräf 2013a, 2013b). I would like to thank Schirin Amir-Moazami, Ruth Mas, and Elke Posselt for their valuable support and their comments and suggestions on an earlier version of this article.

1 For the period before 1919 and the developing book market and communities of readers, see Baron 1997, Skovgaard-Petersen 1997, and al-Bagdadi 2010. For the development of nonprint media, the recording industry, and theatre before 1919, see Fahmy 2010.

 | DOI:10.1163/9789004386891_011

Armbrust, who always promoted the value of taking audiovisual media into account, suggested the year 1975 as an endpoint for his cultural history of new media, "when the audiocassette entered the global media scape" (Armbrust 2012, 34). He considered the audiocassette a "small medium" and a "game changer," since it had the capacity to bypass official gatekeepers and could build up "counterpublics" (ibid., 35; see also Sreberny-Mohammadi and Mohammadi 1994). He further suggested that one might see the close of the history of cultural mass mediation in Egypt sometime before the 1990s, namely "before the practical applications of the digital revolution began to become tangible" (ibid., 44). Accordingly "print culture" serves as the starting point for his project and the arrival of "electronic culture" as its end.[2]

Electronic culture is most often associated with "the emergence of the screen as the central point of the communicative and aesthetic experience," and thus with the blurring of boundaries on many levels, including those of the nation and nation-states (Druckery 1996, 13). In what follows I will be taking Walter Armbrust's comments to heart and will merge the two perspectives of print and electronic culture by investigating three generations of publishing in the context of Cairo since the 1940s. The publishing house Maktabat Wahba in Cairo and three generations of the Wahba family will serve as my organising principle.[3] I take the practices of publishing pocketbooks and posting on Facebook as examples of small media practices that thus test the meaning of publishing in connection with ambitions for social change.[4]

2 Maktabat Wahba, First and Second Generation

> It is 29 November 2011. I'm sitting between pocketbooks at Maktabat Wahba in Al-Gomhoreya Street in Abdeen, Cairo, close to the metro station Mohamed Naguib. The books are not buried under dust because Ahmed, one of the employees, runs through the two narrow corridors of the bookshop Maktabat Wahba and hits the books regularly with a frond. The owner of the bookshop Sultan Husayn Wahba calls after his

2 For the term print culture, see Eisenstein 1986; for electronic culture, Druckery 1996, 12–25.

3 During research for my PhD thesis on media fatwās and the Egyptian scholar and activist Yūsuf al-Qaraḍāwī, I became interested in what could be called Islamic publishing. Maktabat Wahba has been one of the main publishers of al-Qaradāwī's books and accordingly I started my investigations there (cf. Gräf 2010, 124).

4 To categorise Facebook as small media might be wrong from today's perspective, yet it can still be a useful concept, as we will see (Burgess 2015).

> son Muhammad: *Mḥmmd, ḥāt al-ḥalāl wa-l-ḥarām, bi-surʿa!* His voice is serious and impatient and Muhammad is not quick enough. *Muhammad, bring me the* [book] *The Lawful and the Prohibited, quickly, hurry up!* The book by Yūsuf al-Qaraḍāwī that the publisher is asking for is at the back of the little bookshop on the left and is given to him immediately.[5]

Later, in the interview, Sultan Husayn Wahba (Sulṭān Ḥusayn Wahba, b. 1954) started telling me the story of how his father, Wahba Hasan Wahba (Wahba Ḥasan Wahba, 1923–2003), had founded the publishing-house-cum-bookshop Maktabat Wahba in the 1940s. It is the first of four interviews I recorded with him and one of many occasions between November 2011 and June 2013 when I discussed with him the politics and culture of publishing in Egypt, Iraq, and the Levant since the 1940s, in general, and the story of his life as a publisher, in particular. The aim of my research has been to understand the relation between the new technology of publishing pocketbooks, new actors in the field of publishing, and the emerging ideologies of communism and Islamism in the 1930s and 1940s.

According to al-Saʿīd Dāwūd's book *al-Nashr al-ʿāʾilī fī Miṣr* ("Family publishing in Egypt"), seven private publishing houses were founded in the 1940s in Cairo: al-Maktaba al-Miṣriyya in 1942, Maṭbaʿ Farūq in 1944, Maktabat al-Qāhira in 1944, Dār al-Fikr al-ʿArabī in 1946, Maktabat Wahba in 1946, Maktabat al-Aṭfāl in 1947, and Maṭbaʿ ʿAbd al-Raḥmān Muḥammad in 1948 (Dāwūd 2008). Maktabat Wahba was the only one dedicated exclusively to Islamic books (*al-kutub al-dīniyya*).[6] The basic idea behind the founding of Maktabat Wahba, according to Sultan Wahba, was to support *daʿwa*, Islamic calling. His father, Wahba Hasan Wahba, is quoted as saying: "*Anā lastu jāmiʿan li-l-māl wa-lākinnanī ṣāḥib al-daʿwa wa-l-risāla*" ("I'm not one who accumulates money but instead I support the call to Islam and spreading the message of Islam").

Wahba Hasan Wahba was born on 23 October 1923 in Ḥayy al-Khalīfa, east of the river Nile in Cairo.[7] His father was a corn dealer (*tājir ghilāl*).[8] Wahba learnt to read and write, studying in a *kuttāb* from 1927 to 1929. His father wanted him to become a corn dealer as well, but Wahba Hasan Wahba refused and instead

5 Account from my work diary, November 2011.

6 For the notion of *kutub dīniyya*, see Gonzales-Quijano 1998, 162. However, Dār al-Kitāb al-ʿArabī was also founded in 1946 as a joint partnership between Saʿīd al-Sahhār and Muḥammad Ḥilmī al-Minyāwī. In the early 1950s, its catalogue included mainly books by Muslim Brothers, especially Muḥammad al-Ghazālī, as well as the Brotherhood's official publications; see Sabaseviciute 2018, 92.

7 Also in the following: Interview with Sultan Husayn Wahba, Cairo, 26 November 2011.

8 According to Safynaz Kazem, he owned a bakery; cf. Kazem 2000.

wanted to do something with books. His uncle on his mother's side worked in the traditional craft of bookbinding (*tajlīd al-kitāb,* or *mihnat al-tajlīd*) and this inspired Wahba. Sultan told me further that his father spent his first five years with Muḥammad Rashīd Riḍā, the publisher of the journal *al-Manār*, at the publishing house Dār al-Manār, where he studied up until the age of eleven, shortly before Riḍā died, in 1935.[9] Then he worked with Muṣṭafā Ḥalabī in his publishing house, Maṭbaʿat Ḥalabī, which was founded in 1919 (Dāwūd 2008, 426) in order to familiarise himself with bookkeeping, bookbinding, and printing. He stayed there until he was sixteen years old.[10] At the beginning of the 1940s, he moved to al-Maktaba al-Ahliyya, a popular bookstore for all kinds of books (*al-nashr al-ʿāmm*). All this took place in Ḥayy al-Khalīfa.

In 1945, at the age of twenty-two, Wahba became a member of the Muslim Brothers and in 1946 he decided to open his own small bookstore near al-Azhar Mosque in Ḥayy a-Ḥusayn, where many Islamic bookstores (*maktabāt dīniyya*) were located. He called it Maktabat Wahba li-l-Ṭibāʿa wa-l-Nashr wa-l-Tawzīʿ ("Wahba Bookstore for Print, Publication, and Distribution"). Wahba went to pray in the Sayyidnā al-Ḥusayn Mosque, next to al-Azhar Mosque, and attended classes with Shaykh Muḥammad Ṣabra. In this circle Wahba Hasan Wahba got to know other students of his generation at al-Azhar, such as Khālid Muḥammad Khālid (1920–96), al-Sayyid Sābiq (1915–2000), and Muḥammad al-Ghazālī (1917–96)—the last two were also members of the Muslim Brothers at that time. In the year 1950, Wahba moved to al-Gomhoreya Street in Abdeen, not far from the Asbakeya Garden and the metro station Ataba, which we know were commercial centres and also the location of newly built department stores (Reynolds 2011, Schulze in this volume). This area is now one of the three centres for Islamic books, along with Ḥayy al-Ḥusayn near al-Azhar Mosque, and al-Faggala in Kamel Sedky Street (Winkler 1997).

If one entered the narrow bookstore Maktabat Wahba in 2011, after passing two glass display cases with the latest and most important publications, one would have found the current publisher, Sultan Husayn Wahba—the second son of Wahba Hasan Wahba—sitting behind a table to the left of the entrance. From his position there he not only sold books but also organised his publishing house, discussing new projects on the telephone or with people seated around him. He also managed his affairs with the printers' offices and did his

9 This is confirmed by Kazem 2000 and by al-ʿAntabalī under: http://www.ikhwanwiki.com, last accessed 1 March 2018. There are different links between Muḥammad Rashīd Riḍā and the Muslim Brothers, one being the fact that Ḥasan al-Bannā was a "diligent reader of *al-Manār*" (Krämer 2010, 16), another that al-Bannā edited *al-Manār* between July 1939 and September 1940 after Riḍā's death (Krämer 2010, 53–54).

10 Muḥammad Ḥilmī al-Minyāwī obviously did the same; see Sabaseviciute 2018, 99 fn 35.

accounts. In his case there is no differentiation between publisher and bookseller, and Sultan Wahba continues the family tradition in the same surroundings as his father, Wahba Hasan Wahba, before him. A photograph of his father reading hangs on the wall behind Sultan Husayn Wahba.

3 From Here We Start

In the first four years of operation, Maktabat Wahba only distributed books. The first book Wahba Hasan Wahba ever published himself was Khālid Muḥammad Khālid's *Min hunā nabdaʾu* ("From here we start"), in 1950 (Dāwūd 2008, 438),[11] which evinced strong support for socialism. The second book he published was the reply by Khālid's close friend Muḥammad al-Ghazālī, *Min hunā naʿlamu* ("From here we learn," or "Our beginning in wisdom") in the same year. Al-Ghazālī defended Islam against socialist ideas and promoted a comprehensive Islamic social order. Both books provoked a public debate about the proper social order, secular ideas, socialism, the equality of women in society, and various forms of democracy.[12] Khālid Muḥammad Khālid's book was at first banned and confiscated and condemned as being an attack on the religious establishment and anti-capitalistic—and Khālid was called a communist by the official censors (*"raʾy fī l-kitāb hujūman ʿalā rijāl al-dīn wa-ʿalā al-raʾsmāliyyīn wa-hādhihi simat al-shuyūʿiyya wa-l-shuyūʿiyyīn"*) (Khālid 1950, ḥ).

As a result, Wahba Hasan Wahba became known in the world of publishing. After Gamal Abdel Nasser came to power, in 1954, Wahba Hasan Wahba, at the age of thirty-one, was sent to prison, as were many of his fellow Muslim Brothers; he stayed there for six years, until 1960.[13]

In the second phase of his career as a publisher, from 1960 to 1965, he started with many new titles and authors, for example Abū l-Ḥasan al-Nadwī, Abū l-Aʿlā al-Mawdūdī, al-Bahī al-Khūlī, and Muṣṭafā al-Sibāʿī. He created a logo and a catalogue—with an introduction to the reader—in 1962. There is no written testimony by Wahba Hasan Wahba himself, except the introduction to the memoirs of Muḥammad al-Bahī, which Wahba had published in

11 This information was confirmed by Khālid Muḥammad Thābit, son of Khālid Muḥammad Khālid and owner of Dār al-Muqaṭṭam, in February 2013. However, the edition from 1950 that I use is published by Dār al-Nīl li-l-Ṭibāʿa. The latter is also cited as the publisher in an article in *al-Ahrām*, no. 23171, 3 April 1950.

12 Cf. Ziadeh 1951, Harris 1964. See also al-Qaraḍāwī 2000, 204–06.

13 In the interview, Sultan Wahba described the torture his father suffered in prison. Similar testimonies of torture in Nasserist prisons were published by the Muslim Brothers in the 1980s and 1990s; cf. Krämer 2010, 80–81 and 126 fn 27.

1983 (posthumously) and this introduction to his first catalogue in 1962.[14] He published books in the following categories: *Dirāsāt Islāmiyya ʿāmma* (general Islamic studies), *Fi l-fiqh al-Islāmī* (Islamic jurisprudence), *Fī falsafāt al-diyānāt* (philosophy of religions), *Fi l-taʾrīkh* (history), and *Adab* (literature). Most of the books he published were in the first category. In the interview, Sultan Husayn Wahba explained to me that books within this category formed a new kind of doctrine (*naẓariyya jadīda*). In contrast to earlier religious books, for example in the categories of jurisprudence (*fiqh*) and heritage (*turāth*), these new books would support the idea of Islamic social movements.

From 1965 to 1970 Wahba Hasan Wahba was again imprisoned. According to his son, the main reason this time was that he had published books by Sayyid Quṭb, the literary figure and intellectual head of the Muslim Brothers, who was hanged in 1966 (Shepard 2003, Sabaseviciute 2018). In the catalogue from 1965 three books of his are listed: *al-Salām al-ʿālamī wa-l-Islām* ("World peace and Islam"), *al-Mustaqbal li-hādhihi al-dīn* ("The future of this religion"), and *Maʿālim fi l-ṭarīq* ("Milestones").[15]

When Muhammad Anwar el-Sadat came to power in Egypt in 1970, Wahba was released from prison. The third chapter in the publishing house's history started in 1972, when it initially operated as a stationery shop, and it continued quite successfully until Wahba's death in 2003. In the 1980s and 1990s, the theme *al-ṣaḥwa al-islāmiyya* (Islamic awakening) became popular and books (mainly pocketbooks) by Islamist thinkers were in great demand and sold well inside Egypt and abroad. Besides members of the Muslim Brothers and similar organisations, independent writers were read and discussed, among them Munīr Shafīq, Aḥmad Kamāl Abū Majd, Fahmī Huwaydī, and Ṭāriq al-Bishrī (Krämer 1999, 36–41), as well as Nādiya Muṣṭafā and younger scholars such as Hiba Raʾūf ʿIzzat (Karam 1998, McLarney 2015, Dennerlein in this volume).

Maktabat Wahba was never regarded as an organ of the Muslim Brothers, since Wahba published different kinds of books, some of which would not

---

14 Muḥammad al-Bahī (1905–1982), a professor of Islamic and Greek philosophy who had studied in Germany with Ernst Cassirer, was the director of the Department of Islamic Culture at al-Azhar University until he became the first president of al-Azhar after its nationalisation in 1961, and at the same time he was appointed Egyptian Minister of Awqāf (religious endowments). Wahba published al-Bahī's more than twenty books and became a close friend. The most important of Muḥammad al-Bahī's books was *al-Fikr al-Islāmī al-ḥadīth wa-ṣilatuhu bi-l-istiʿmār al-gharbī* ("Modern Islamic thinking and its link to Western colonialism"), first published in 1957 with many reprints, among them one in 1973 by Dār al-Fikr, Beirut.

15 Yūsuf al-Qaraḍāwī divides Sayyid Quṭb's books into three phases, the literary, the missionary, and the radical. With the latter phase al-Qaraḍāwī himself does not sympathise; see al-Qaraḍāwī 1998, 128–30.

have fitted in with the Brothers' worldview, such as those of Muḥammad al-Bahī.[16] As mentioned above, the first book Wahba Hasan Wahba published was Khālid Muḥammad Khālid's call for Islamic socialism. Wahba later continued to publish Khālid's books on socialism and democracy (before Khālid himself became closer to Islamism and to Ṣūfī discourse).[17] What the authors Wahba Hasan Wahba published had in common, however, was a new kind of writing by *ʿulamāʾ*, activists, and intellectuals—writing that called for social change and seemed to be sure of achieving it.

Sultan Husayn Wahba, who took over the publishing house from his father in 2003, continued to be financially successful, especially with the books by Yūsuf al-Qaraḍāwī.[18] However, Wahba and his employees took a critical view of the political developments after the rise to power of the Muslim Brothers under the elected president Mohammed Morsi in 2012 and the ensuing military coup that brought Abdel Fattah al-Sisi to power in July 2013. In 2015, the books by Yūsuf al-Qaraḍāwī and Sayyid Quṭb were removed from the shelves of the publishing house Dar El Shorouk (Dār al-Shurūq) at the Cairo International Book Fair by the Egyptian police.[19] Maktabat Wahba, which is much smaller, has however continued to have a presence at the fair, but, according to Sultan, it suffered sizable losses in 2014.[20] Today, in 2017, the publishing-house-cum-bookshop still

16 Serious press activities by the Muslim Brothers started in June 1933 with the weekly *Jarīdat al-Ikhwān al-Muslimīn*. Before the Brothers bought their own printing press in June 1934, the Syrian journalist Muḥibb al-Dīn al-Khaṭīb printed the paper, cf. Krämer 2010, 44. For the important role Muḥibb al-Dīn al-Khaṭīb, the owner of al-Maktaba al-Salafiyya and founder of the literary journal *al-Zahrāʾ* and the weekly *al-Fatḥ*, played for Ḥasan al-Bannā, see Dawn 1988, 80–81, and Krämer 2010, 23. Until 1946, the Brotherhood did not publish any dailies, see Sabaseviciute 2018, 99 fn 37. See al-Qaraḍāwī for the weekly *al-Ikhwān*, the daily *al-Ikhwān al-Muslimūn*, and the journal *al-Shihāb* ("The Flame") in the 1940s, al-Qaraḍāwī 2002, 292–304.

17 Khālid Muḥammad Khālid founded Dār al-Thābit in the 1980s and started to support Ṣūfī discourse: interview with his son Khālid Muḥammad Thābit, Cairo, February 2013. See also Shepard 1995 and Khālid's autobiography *Qiṣṣatī maʿa l-ḥayāt* ("My Story with Life"), published by Dār al-Muqaṭṭam in 2002. Cf. also Aishima and Salvatore 2009.

18 I was personally in a position to witness this during the book fairs in Cairo in 2012 and 2013, when people from Southeast Asia, South Asia, and North, East, and South Africa bought al-Qaraḍāwī's books in great quantities. Al-Qaraḍāwī was present at the fair in 2013 and signed his books (my work diary 27 January 2013).

19 See the information under: https://cairobookstop.wordpress.com/find-a-book-in-cairo/cairo-international-book-fair/. CairoBookStop is a website (in both Arabic and English), produced by Nancy Linthicum and Michele Henjum and installed in 2014, that "seeks to bring together and assist book lovers, book buyers, book makers, and book sellers in Cairo by providing a space on the web that collects and presents basic information and brief descriptions of some of the literary publishers and bookstores in Cairo."

20 Interview with Sultan Husayn Wahba during the book fair in Cairo, January 2014.

operates, although under different conditions, since there has been a rigorous crackdown on the Muslim Brothers since 2013 and they have once again been banned as a terrorist organisation (Grimm and Harders 2017). Those members and sympathisers who did not leave Egypt for Doha, Istanbul, or London withdrew from political debates and engagement. The current demand for books that support the Islamist movement, at least from inside Egypt, is on hold (Mounir 2017).[21]

4 Ownership and Censorship

The general question then is this: What is the relationship between these activist writings, the origins and trajectories of the authors as well as those of the publishers, and the format of the pocketbooks they used? The personal story of Wahba Hasan Wahba is a story of social mobility and social climbing. How is it related, one might ask, to the books that he produced, since he was not an intellectual himself? Could he have published other formats and other ideas as well?[22]

Many new publishing houses were founded under similar circumstances in the 1940s. They differed, on the one hand, from the state-funded printing houses, such as the Būlāq press, which had been installed and used by the government under Muḥammad ʿAlī (r. 1805–48) from the 1820s (Atiyeh 1995, 244–45), and older private publishing houses that had started their enterprises in the last quarter of the nineteenth century (al-Bagdadi 2010, 55). Some of the larger producers of newspapers and journals still exist today, such as *al-Ahrām* (which was founded in 1875), *al-Hilāl* (1892), and *Rūz al-Yūsuf* (1925) (Dupont 2008, Phillipp 2010). Al-Azhar—to cite a third type of publisher, besides the state and private owners—started its own printing house in 1930 (Dubovoy 1998, 12; Reid 2014, 83).

Wahba might have published communist writings, had he not been such a stalwart Muslim Brother, since the success story of leftist publishing began around the same time. These leftist publishers, too, took advantage of cheap publishing, which offered those with limited financial means the ability to suddenly reach larger numbers of people, an audience of young rebels, to use

21 Telephone conversation with Muhammad Sultan in September 2017. Although I have not visited Egypt since 2014, I'm still in contact with the Wahba family. That also includes female family members, even though they do not appear in this essay.

22 These questions counter the somehow simplistic understanding that technology alone would be responsible for social change: see, for example, E. Eisenstein (1986 and 1993) in her books about the relationship between print technology and the enlightenment. For an articulate critique, see Armbrust 2012.

James Jankowski's words, who would search for political guidance, readings, and action (Jankowski 1975). Much has been said about the *effendiyya*, a term that is, according to Lucie Ryzova, "often used to mean some kind of a middle class" and "(over) characterized as the reading public" (Ryzova 2005, 124). However, in her opinion "in the 1930s and 40s, the term effendiya tends to mean a specific, 'rebellious' generation" (Ryzova 2005, 151 fn 4). These very rebels were the possible readers of a different kind of political writing, be it nationalist, Islamist, and/or communist (see also Sabaseviciute 2018, who argues that these writers and their readers had an anti-elite and anti-colonial impetus in common).

The production of pocketbooks benefited from the production of newspapers and journals. New printing machines were used that made large print runs possible. Huge paper rolls were utilised instead of sheets of paper, as with ordinary printing. In addition to this, the paper could be of lower quality. The book covers and bindings were also managed differently than with ordinary books. All in all they were cheaper to produce and light to carry.[23] Founding a small publishing house in the 1940s did not require a big investment and people like Wahba Hasan Wahba, who could not possibly have become publishers at the end of the nineteenth century, were in a position to become publishers and bookstore owners in the 1940s.

Another similar example is Hagg Mohamed Madbouli (Ḥājj Muḥammad Madbūlī, 1938–2008), who started out selling newspapers on the streets of downtown Cairo in the 1940s, founded a kiosk in Talaat Harb Square in 1951, and went into publishing in 1958, eventually founding his bookstore and publishing house, Maktabat Madbouli. The press, which publishes a broad assortment of titles, rose to prominence and has been one of the most successful bookstores in downtown Cairo (Dāwūd 2008, al-Aʿsar 2005).[24]

When investigating the production of pocketbooks, the social and economic conditions, and the various resistive political ideas connected with this new technology, ownership is obviously one important element to consider. Another is censorship, especially censorship by the modern state and its government

23 The historical development of "publishing small books in large numbers … began in Britain in the late eighteenth century, although the 'paperback revolution' did not start till the 1930s," Ebel 2003, 113. The German publishing house Reclam published Shakespeare in paperback format from 1857 and thus pioneered the mass market, cf. Fischer 2004, 282. See also Rössler 1997 and Klussmann and Mix 1998. In the U.S. the company Pocket Books, founded in 1939, had by 1950 become the leading publisher of affordable paperbound titles. See Felsch 2015 for a very interesting account of the protest generation of 1968 and their relation to pocketbooks. I thank Elke Posselt for this reference.

24 The Lebanese film maker Arab Lotfi made a film about him called *El Hagg Madbouli*, cf. Mostafa 2013, 269.

and institutions. As I have mentioned, Wahba Hasan Wahba went to prison under Nasser twice, in 1954 and in 1965. Mohammed Madbouli's kiosk was nearly closed down more than once. He had difficulties with the national security forces under Nasser, although for different reasons than Wahba Hasan Wahba, since Madbouli was not a Muslim Brother. "During the 1950s and 1960s, he was charged with publishing subversive books in twenty-four cases. He never went to jail, though, and was often supported by well-known writers" (al-Aʿsar 2005).

We also know of difficult relationships between publishers who specialised in pocketbooks in other regions governed by different kinds of states:

> The year 1952 was an historical one in the history of American book publishing. A special committee of the U.S. House of Representatives (the Gathings Committee) formed for the express purpose of investigating the influence of paperback books on American society. Never before or since in the history of the book in the United States has a specific format been singled out for this degree of scrutiny; but perhaps never before had one been seen as a serious threat to public morality. The House investigation followed in the wake of diverse and vocal censorship efforts designed to counter the perceived threat of paperback novels, with their suggestive cover art and titillating stories.
>
> SPEER 2001, 153

The reasons for censoring and banning pocketbooks at that time in the United States were moral ones. The cover art and content of these books touched on three main themes: sex, sadism, and murder (Speer 2001, 153). We can conclude that, no matter where, pocketbooks seem to have invited the intervention of the modern censor, namely the state and its inspectors. We can further conclude that the special connection of content, ownership, and censorship forms certain cultures of publishing and therewith recognisable mechanisms of power relations in certain times. It is never the political idea—that is, the content alone—that is at stake. Therefore—and this has been suggested by different authors—one should concentrate on the various practices of publishing connected to the history of political ideas (Armbrust 2006, Gershoni 2006).

5 Wahba, Third Generation

> Again Sultan Wahba sends the 22-year-old Muhammad to bring a book, this time from the storage area on the first floor. Again Muhammad is not

> quick enough and Sultan gets angry with him. Muhammad gets him the book, however not quietly as usual but in a temper. They get in a quarrel and Muhammad says: "I will not be the one who continues your bookshop. If I produce books at all, it will be children's books, which is a huge market and I like it much more." Sultan, however, does not comment on it.[25]

Later that night, while sitting along the banks of the Nile, Muhammad Sultan (b. 1990), son of Sultan Husayn Wahba and grandson of Wahba Hasan Wahba, told me about his life and dreams. He did not have concrete plans but a lot of expectations and ideas about his life. He told me of his secret love, which he didn't want anyone to know about.[26] I asked what he thought about Maktabat Wahba, about the books his father sells, and about politics. He replied that he was not interested in politics. That was in May 2012 and it was a lie, since he had been going constantly to Tahrir Square, chanting along with the other demonstrators for bread (*ʿaish*), dignity (*karāma*), and social justice (*ʿadāla ijtimāʿiyya*), and taking photographs. He documented the demonstrations, songs, and demands of the people in 2011 and 2012. Yes, Muhammad wanted change, but not according to the programme of a particular political party. At any rate, he did not want to have to worry about being beaten up or tortured to death for no reason by the police of his own country at any unforeseen moment.[27] That is what he told me that night. He said, "We will never forget this feeling, Bettina. They will not suppress us so quickly anymore." His photographs are powerful witnesses not only to the days of the revolution in Cairo in January 2011 but also to all the other demonstrations that were held nearly every week until the elections for a new Egyptian parliament in November 2011 and the presidential elections in May and June 2012.[28] Anger was targeted at the military council (*al-majlis al-aʿlā li-l-quwwāt al-musallaḥa*, or *al-majlis al-ʿaskarī* for short), which had continued to govern Egypt despite the Revolution of 25 Yanāʾir. The comments on Facebook that Muhammad and his friends shared during this time were quite outspoken. On the first anniversary of the

25 Account from my work diary in May 2012.

26 At this moment, I was reminded of Tarik Sabry's poetic account "The Bridge and the Queue as Spaces of Encountering," see Sabry 2010, 63–94.

27 Unfortunately, we see an ongoing practice of violence and even torture by the Egyptian state against its own citizens and foreigners too; see Walsh 2017.

28 His photos are a record of the days on Tahrir Square in January and February 2011, which led to the overthrow of Husni Mubarak. They also show the other demonstrations that took place between the parliamentary elections in Egypt in November 2011, in which the party of the Muslim Brothers won 37.5 per cent of the vote, and the presidential elections in May and June 2012, where Mohammed Morsi defeated Ahmed Shafiq.

revolution, they posted calls for demonstrations against the military dictatorship in Egypt at different mosques and churches in Cairo. The aim was still to give power to the people and not to get separated on any cause that was unofficially fuelled, be it religious or otherwise. The poster text in Arabic script read as follows:

> Amākin khurūj al-muẓāharāt yawm 25 Yanā'ir 2012 fi l-Qāhira:
> al-ʿAbbāsiyya: "masjid al-nūr" aw "al-kātidrā'iyya"
> Ramsīs: "masjid al-fatḥ" aw aqrab kanīsa lak (…)
> yasquṭ yasquṭ ḥukm al-ʿaskar
> (Places where one can go for demonstrations on 25 January 2012 in Cairo:
> al-ʿAbbāsiyya: "al-Nour Mosque" or "Saint Mark's Cathedral"
> Ramsīs: "al-Fatḥ Mosque" or the church closest to you (…)
> down, down with the rule of the military)
>
> Facebook, Go Bike, 15.1.2012[29]

One post, dated 25 January 2012, says in Latin script:

> „Deeeh thawraa mesh 7aflaaaaaa:
> :@:@:@:@:@:@:@:@:@:@:@:@:@:@:@:@ (…) za3laaan
> awyyyyyyyyyyyyyyyyyyyyyyyyyyyyyyyyyyyyyyyyyyyyyyyyyyyyyyy."
> (The revolution is not a party:
> :@:@:@:@:@:@:@:@:@:@:@:@:@:@:@:@ (…)
> veryyyyyyyyyyyyyyyyyyyyyyyyyyyyyyyyyyyyyyyyyyyyyyyyyyyyy sad)
>
> Facebook, Go Bike, 25.1.2012

Muhammad had probably not been lying to me. He was not particularly interested in politics, but he did not want to be suppressed either and he wanted to keep his spirits up and fight for the right to live in a non-authoritarian Egypt.

One of the starting points for the movement, which eventually led to the huge demonstration on 25 January 2011, was the Facebook page *We are all Khaled Said/Kullunā Khālid Saʿīd,* initiated by Wael Ghonim in August 2010. The site had another name, *El Shaheed* ("The Martyr"), and it publicised whatever was known about the twenty-eight-year-old computer programmer Khaled Said, who had used the Internet in one of Alexandria's cyber cafes before he was arrested by two Alexandrian police officers, whose business he had published on the Internet. He was beaten to death (Salvatore 2011, 10).

29 Seventeen mosques and churches were named on the poster. If the name of the church close by was not known, it was written "aqrab kanīsa lak" (the church closest to you). All translations of Facebook posts in the following are mine.

Facebook, which was launched in 2004, was used in Egypt by a few "young cosmopolitans" for propagating political ideas (Ftouni 2017). It was often claimed from outside that young people in Middle Eastern countries would use the Internet, and Facebook especially, simply in order to "vent frustrations," nothing more (Salvatore 2011, 10). This claim was wrong, as we know, for example, from the trajectory of the 6 April Youth Movement, which supported worker strikes in El Mahalla El Kubra and started with a Facebook campaign run by Esraa Abdel Fattah in March 2008. With Wael Ghonim's initiative in June 2010, the phenomenon became more popular, and more people than before and also from older generations started to publish their political opinions on Facebook. One of those was the Egyptian political scientist and thinker Heba Raouf Ezzat (Hiba Raʾūf ʿIzzat, b. 1965). In her book titled *al-Khiyāl al-siyāsī li-l-Islāmiyyīn: Mā qabla l-dawla wa-mā baʿdahā* ("The political vision of Islamists: Before and after the state"), she formulates an elaborate critique of the earlier political ideas of Islamists, such as the Muslim Brothers, for capturing the modern nation state for an Islamic project, that is, an Islamic state. Within the book, she describes her first steps on Facebook and Twitter in 2010 as follows:

> The aim of my earlier journalistic writings was to serve as a window for scientific thoughts to a wider public.... But then something entirely new began, with my—at that time passionate—participation on Facebook and Twitter, accounts that my students had installed for me. It allowed me to crystallise precise thoughts and set me free from scientific technical terms. And I allowed the interested reader to participate in my journey, although there was a lot of rejection of my critique and my ambitions to reconsider certain ideals, and a tendency to stick to older political imaginations, and there was also a rise of political polarisation within the field.
>
> EZZAT, 2015, 11; 15; translation mine

Facebook enabled the political theorist to express herself differently for a different audience. Throughout the revolution Ezzat propagated her views, argued with different people, and commented on ongoing events on Facebook and Twitter. However, the last entry on her Twitter account, on 16 August 2013, correlates with the massacre at Rabaa El Adaweya Square in Cairo on 14 August 2013. By that time Ezzat had posted 48,900 tweets and had 747,000 followers on Twitter. Many people were killed that day and many more were silenced. In her last tweet she states the following:

> "Liman saʾalanī: ḥīna takhtār kayfa takhtār isʾal nafsak: mā al-qiyam allatī taʿīsh min ajlihā? wa-bi ayy ikhtiyārāt tuḥibb an talqā rabbak? huwa man yuḥāsib al-nās. wa-huwa akbar. Hashtaq# yawm al-qiyāma." (Those who

> are asking me: if you choose as you choose, ask yourself, what values are you living for? And with what kind of decisions would you like to meet your Lord? He is the one who holds people accountable. He is the Almighty. Hashtag# day of resurrection).
>
> Twitter, DR. HEBA ROUF EZZAT, 16.8.2013; translation mine

Since she closed her Twitter account, her Facebook site has changed as well. She uses it now to announce her work and to teach classes, since she is no longer allowed to teach at Cairo University—in fact, she does not live in Egypt anymore but is still actively teaching and giving lectures in Istanbul, Doha, and London.

The events of August 2013 in Rabaa El Adaweya Square also changed the Facebook publishing habits of Muhammad Sultan and his friends. What that meant in practice I was able to learn in connection with Muhammad's other activities.

6 Go Bike … Go Life

Early in the morning, on a Friday in June 2012, Muhammad took me to the northeast of Cairo, where I was to spend my first morning with the kids and young adults of his mixed-gender biking group *Go Bike … Go Life*. A few months earlier he had founded a club for cycling with three other friends. The four young men, between the ages of twenty and twenty-six, pooled their money and bought seventy bicycles, which during the week are put in storage in Masr al-Jadidah. They like the idea of using bikes instead of cars. Muhammad says it is much healthier and good for the environment. In the past, people used bikes more often, but today you don't see any in the streets of Cairo. Only on Fridays can you ride a bicycle without risking your life; otherwise nobody rides them, with the exception of the boys who sell bread in downtown Cairo.

Actually, it is not only their convictions that lead them to cycle on Fridays; it is also a way to enjoy their lives with each other. As far as I can tell, these activities on Fridays, including sightseeing in their own city, are unique. One of the most important elements for the group, however, is their sharing of photographs and comments on Facebook (and today Instagram) after each ride, like this post by Lamia in Latin script, after cycling to the Citadel of Cairo in July 2012:

> "Ayna3m ana et7ar2t bs f3lan kan ride lazeez gdn w momayaz … bravooooooooo go bike estamerooooooo :)" (yes, I was exhausted but finally it was a very sweet tour and outstanding … bravo go bike, continue :)
>
> Facebook, Lamia, 7.7.2012

Since the start of the group in 2012 I have followed their activities on Facebook in connection to *Go Bike … Go Life*. They use their own language, which is a mix of Arabic in Arabic script, English, and Arabic in Latin script, which is widely used and has been called Arab Easy (Gonzales-Quijano 2014, Aishima 2016). Most of the comments are connected to the biking tours, the pictures that have been uploaded, the energy it takes, and the fun they have. They go on special rides during Ramadan and participate in special events. However, after the massacre at Rabaa El Adaweya on 14 August 2013, which was a Wednesday, no ride took place. One day later, on the *Go Bike* Facebook site, Muhammad and his friends stated in Arabic script:

> "Naẓaran li-ẓurūf al-ḥāliyya al-mawjūda fi l-balad tamma ilghāʾ al-rāyd ghadan" (Because of the actual circumstances in the country the ride tomorrow will be cancelled)
>
> Facebook, Go Bike, 15.8.2013

One of the early comments by their cycling friends reads, in Arabic script: "al-shawāriʿ fāḍiya wa-l-qubūr zaḥma" (The streets are empty and the graves spill over) (Facebook, Abdullah, 14.8.2013).

7 Go Life under Surveillance

After that week, the Go Bikers continued their Friday rides, as they still do today, but I never saw any political comments on their Facebook accounts again, either on the *Go Bike* site or on their personal profiles. Self-censorship plays its part (Herrera 2015). They still use Facebook for publishing and sharing private matters. The pictures they post always show smiling and seemingly happy young people. The group was even invited to the private Egyptian TV channel CBC (Capital Broadcasting Center, on the air since 2011) in November 2014 and took part in one of the episodes of the very popular programme *Khawatir 11*, an Islamic broadcast for young people with Ahmad al-Shuqayri, which was aired during Ramadan 2015 at ARAM TV/mbc, a Saudi channel. The episode dealt with environmental problems and methods of saving electricity. Life seems to go on as usual.[30]

Meanwhile, Facebook claims to have more than one billion users. The uprisings in the Middle East were good for business. While Facebook pages may have helped to organise the start of the revolution in 2011, the media enterprise

30 For *Khawatir*, see Kraidy and Khalil 2009, 110.

has also helped to shut down pages since at least 2013. "For obvious reasons it is impossible for activists to use their real identity to administer political pages on Facebook, but concealing one's identity (even under repressive states) is yet another violation of (FB's) terms and conditions," as Gholam Khiabany states in his article with the polysemous title "Technology of Liberation and/or Otherwise" (Khiabany 2015, 352). Facebook has become the owner and censor of electronic media culture in a single persona. If you don't want to go to jail in Egypt today, you can either censor your own comments on Facebook or leave the country, as Heba Raouf Ezzat and many others did.

Yet Facebook and similar companies are connected to the broader issue of surveillance as well, which is an even more sophisticated practice of controlling people's thoughts and actions than censorship and self-censorship (Burgess 2015). Linda Herrera describes it as follows:

> In Egypt, four years after the uprising, the populist military regime currently under the presidency of 'Abd al-Fatah al-Sisi has returned full throttle to the surveillance state, but this time with eyes wide open to the vast capabilities of digital surveillance.
>
> HERRERA 2015, 355

Muhammad's father, Sultan Wahba, does not necessarily fall under this kind of surveillance, since he has no Facebook page and no Twitter account, and he does not use a smartphone for his phone calls. Maktabat Wahba does not even have a website (and also does not feature on the website CairoBookStop). His life as a publisher and bookseller went on almost as usual during the years 2011 and 2012, interrupted only by electricity cuts, more traffic problems than usual, heated political debates in his bookshop, and very good business before the military coup in 2013. Sultan never went to Tahrir to demonstrate.

Muhammad's generation acts differently than that of his father, Sultan Husayn Wahba, who, of course, himself acts very differently in comparison to his father, Wahba Hasan Wahba. But what is the difference? The differences are certainly the media they use and thus the constraints they face, but, more importantly and connected to the latter, the languages they speak, the worlds they encounter, and the aims they have. They do not at all share the same territory, although all three men have lived their lives in Cairo. Transnational Arab TV and digital applications by American media and communications companies operating in multinational settings have been available to Muhammad since he was under ten (cf. Kraidy and Khalil 2009). He rejects aligning himself with a specific political party or certain political ideals and he certainly will not continue the publishing enterprise of his grandfather and father.

His father grew up in an almost closed Egyptian nationalist culture (in spite of Pan-Arabism and Pan-Islamism; see Abu-Lughod 2005), without much exposure to media content from the U.S., Europe, and Asia, and with strong alliances to the larger project of Islamism. He does not speak any language other than Arabic. His grandfather never travelled outside Egypt, other than making the *ḥajj* to Mecca, despite being a Muslim Brother (which was not supposed to be a nationalist project in the first place), and read only Arabic-language media.

However, what the three Egyptian men—Wahba, Sultan, and Muhammad—all from the same family and representing three generations of publishing (in the broad sense), have in common is their vision for social change, and—it would seem—its failure. Neither print nor electronic media have helped them much with the censoring mechanisms at work in their respective eras. As for pocketbooks and Facebook—each medium has had its own specificities and its own momentum for supporting claims by political and social actors, but only for limited periods of time.

8 Conclusion

Walter Armbrust has suggested investigating the cultural history of new media in Egypt from a historical perspective from 1919 on, as was discussed in the beginning of this article. In order to be able to do this and, at the same time, understand practices in print and in electronic media, I think we need further categories to help us navigate through time. The conceptual pairing of ownership and censorship that binds peers of the same generation together, as has been suggested in this article, is one possibility.

Both print and electronic cultures can be seen as determined by structures of ownership and censorship. This means, first, that more often than not the technology for informing, educating, and entertaining is in the hands of a small elite and not in the hands of the majority of the people. Secondly, the practices of producing, distributing, and reacting to media content (be it news, political ideas, or music) have always been connected to the controlling function of gatekeepers of various kinds (Eickelman 1999). However, as I have tried to show in this article, certain small media technologies—understood as inexpensive and flexible decentralised means of publishing for a specific audience (Armbrust 2012, Sreberny-Mohammadi and Mohammadi 1994)—and the actual processes of mass mediation connected to them, which are used and promoted at specific moments in time, enable people to actively challenge established structures of ownership and censorship, if only momentarily. This, of course, poses new questions (such as the question of how structures of ownership are reproduced and practices of censorship are replicated over time and generations). Time is one factor and space is another.

Let me therefore close with one last remark. The cultural history of new media can be written only from a transregional perspective, that is, a perspective that reflects the borders of the modern states, and their permeability and impermeability. Print culture, on one side, has been associated with the evolution of the modern nation and modern nation-state borders (Anderson 1983), and electronic culture, on the other side, has been connected to global cultural flows (Appadurai 1990, Druckery 1996). Today, in the boom years of electronic culture, nation-state borders have been re-enforced, and, as we have learnt from Edward Snowden, we are almost all under surveillance, be it in the Middle East, in America, or in Europe. It is easy to think that the circumstances Egyptians are living under apply only to Egyptians. We may learn sooner rather than later that this is an illusion.

Bibliography

Abdelkarim, Mohamed, and Bettina Gräf. 2013a. "Re-Introducing Ideology: Neoliberal Islam and Global Capitalism." In Daniela Swarowsky, Samuli Schielke, and Andrea Heister (eds.). *In Search of Europe? In Collaboration. An Experiment*, Heijningen: Jap Sam Books: 44–62.

Abdelkarim, Mohamed, and Bettina Gräf. 2013b. "Taqdīm al-īdiyūlūjiyya min jadīd. al-Islām al-niyūlībrālī wa-l-ra'smāliyya al-ʿālamiyya." In Daniela Swarowsky, Samuli Schielke, and Andrea Heister (eds.). *In Search of Europe? In Collaboration. An Experiment*, Heijningen: Jap Sam Books: 51–65.

Abou El-Magd, Nadia Mahmoud Ibrahim. 1992. *The Political Ideas of Khalid Mohamed Khalid: Islam, Democracy, Socialism and Nationalism*. Master's thesis. American University in Cairo.

Abu-Lughod, Lila. 2005. "Interpreting Culture(s) after Television. On Method." In Lila Abu-Lughod, *Dramas of Nationhood: The Politics of Television in Egypt*. Chicago: University of Chicago Press, 29–53.

Aishima, Hatsuki. 2016. "Are we all Amr Khalid? Islam and the Facebook Generation of Egypt." In Adeline Masquelier and Benjamin F. Soares (eds.), *Muslim Youth and the 9/11 Generation*. Santa Fe: School for Advanced Research Press, 105–22.

Aishima, Hatsuki, and Armando Salvatore. 2009. "Doubt, Faith, and Knowledge: The Reconfiguration of the Intellectual Field in Post-Nasserist Cairo." *Journal of the Royal Anthropological Institute* 15/1 (May): 41–56.

Anderson, Benedict. 1983. *Imagined Communities: Reflections on the Origins and Spread of Nationalism*. New York: Verso Press.

al-ʿAntabalī, Ashraf ʿĪd. n.d. "Wahba Ḥasan Wahba ṣāḥib fikr wa-daʿwa wa-risāla." Available at http://www.ikhwanwiki.com, accessed 1 March 2018.

Appadurai, Arjun. 1990. "Disjuncture and Difference in the Global Cultural Economy." *Theory, Culture and Society* 7: 295–310.

Armbrust, W. 2006. "Audiovisual Media and History of the Arab Middle East." In Israel Gershoni, Amy Singer, and Y. Hakan Erdem (eds.), *Middle East Historiographies: Narrating the Twentieth Century*. Seattle: University of Washington Press, 288–313.

Armbrust, W. 2012. "History in Arab Media Studies: A Speculative Cultural History." In Tarik Sabry (ed.), *Arab Cultural Studies: Mapping the Field*. London: I.B. Tauris, 32–54.

al-Aʿsar, Marwa. 2005. "A Life in Books: Hagg Madbouli Tells of His Rise from Child Newsvendor to Major Publisher." Published in *Cairo Magazine* 29 September 2005. Available at http://permalink.gmane.org/gmane.education.libraries.mela/6042.

Atiyeh, George. 1995. "The Book in the Modern Arab World: The Cases of Lebanon and Egypt." In George Atiyeh (ed.), *The Book in the Islamic World: The Written Word and Communication in the Middle East*. Albany: State University of New York Press, 233–53.

al-Bagdadi, Nadia. 2010. *Vorgestellte Öffentlichkeit: Zur Genese moderner Prosa in Ägypten (1860 bis 1908)*. Wiesbaden: Reichert Verlag.

al-Bahī, Muḥammad. 1957. *Al-Fikr al-Islāmī al-ḥadīth wa-ṣilatuhu bi-l-istiʿmār al-gharbī*. Cairo: Maktabat Wahba.

al-Bahī, Muḥammad. 1983. *Ḥayātī fī riḥāb al-Azhar: Ṭālib wa-ustādh wa-wazīr*. Ed. Wahba Ḥasan Wahba. Cairo: Maktabat Wahba.

Baron, Beth. 1997. *The Women's Awakening in Egypt: Culture, Society, and the Press*. New Haven: Yale University Press.

Burgess, Jean. 2015. "From 'Broadcast Yourself' to 'Follow Your Interests': Making Over Social Media." *International Journal of Cultural Studies* 18/3: 281–85.

Cohen, Anouk. 2016. *Fabriquer le livre au Maroc*. Collection Terres et Gens d'Islam (IISMM). Paris: Karthala: IISMM.

Dawn, Ernest C. 1988. "Pan-Arab Ideology in the Interwar Years." *International Journal of Middle East Studies* 20: 67–91.

Dāwūd, al-Saʿīd. 2008. *al-Nashr al-ʿāʾilī fī Miṣr*. Cairo.

Druckery, Timothy. 1996 "Introduction." In Timothy Druckery (ed.) *Electronic Culture: Technology and Visual Representation*. New York: Aperture Foundation, 12–25.

Dubovoy, Sina. 1998. "Al-Azhar University." In Carol Summerfield and Mary Elizabeth Devine (eds.), *International Dictionary of University Histories*. London and New York: Routledge, 9–13.

Dupont, Anne-Laure. 2008. "The Ottoman Revolution of 1908 as Seen by *al-Hilāl* and *al-Manār*: The Triumph and Diversification of the Reformist Spirit." In Christoph Schumann (ed.), *Liberal Thought in the Eastern Mediterranean: Late 19th Century until the 1960s*. Leiden: Brill, 123–46.

Ebel, Kerstin. 2003. "Can You Paperback a Pocketbook?" *Multilingua: Journal of Cross-Cultural and Interlanguage Communication* 22/2: 113–32.

Eickelman, Dale. 1999. "Communication and Control in the Middle East: Publication and Its Discontents." In Dale Eickelman and Jon W. Anderson (eds.), *New Media in the Muslim World: The Emerging Public Sphere*. Bloomington: Indiana University Press, 33–44.

Eisenstein, Elizabeth. 1986. *Print Culture and Enlightenment Thought.* [Chapel Hill]: Hanes Foundation, Rare Book Collection/University Library, University of North Carolina at Chapel Hill.

Eisenstein, Elizabeth. 1993. *The Printing Press as an Agent of Change.* Cambridge: Cambridge University Press.

Ezzat, Heba Raouf. 2015. *Al-Khiyāl al-siyāsī li-l-Islāmiyyīn: Mā qabla l-dawla wa-mā baʿdahā.* Beirut: Arab Network for Research and Publishing.

Fahmy, Ziad. 2010. "Media Capitalism: Colloquial Mass Culture and Nationalism in Egypt, 1908–1918." *International Journal of Middle East Studies* 42/1: 83–103.

Felsch, Philipp. 2015. *Der lange Sommer der Theorie: Geschichte einer Revolte 1960–1990.* München: C.H. Beck.

Ftouni, Layal. 2017. "Performative Interventions in Public Space: An Interview with Dictaphone Group." In Tarik Sabry and Layal Ftouni, *Arab Subcultures: Transformations in Theory and Practice*. London and New York: I.B. Tauris, 113–25.

Gershoni, Israel. 2006. "The Theory of Crisis and the Crisis in A Theory: Intellectual History in Twentieth-Century Middle Eastern Studies." In Israel Gershoni, Amy Singer, and Y. Hakan Erdem (eds.), *Middle East Historiographies: Narrating the Twentieth Century*. Seattle: University of Washington Press, 131–82.

al-Ghazālī, Muḥammad. 1950. *Min hunā naʿlamu.* Cairo: Dār al-kutub al-ḥadītha fi l-Qāhira.

Ghonim, Wael. 2012. *Revolution 2.0: The Power of the People is Greater than the People in Power: A Memoir.* Boston: Houghton Mifflin Harcourt.

Gonzales-Quijano, Yves. 2014. "Technology Literacies of the New Media: Phrasing the World in the 'Arab Easy' (R)evolution." In Leila Hudson, Adel Iskandar, and Mimi Kirk (eds.), *Media Evolution on the Eve of the Arab Spring*. New York: Palgrave Macmillan, 159–66.

Gonzales-Quijano, Yves. 1998. *Les Gens du livre: Édition et champ intellectuel dans l'Égypte républicaine*. Paris: CNRS Publication.

Gräf, Bettina. 2010. *Medien-Fatwas@Yusuf al-Qaradawi: Die Popularisierung des islamischen Rechts*, ZMO-Studien 27, Berlin: Klaus Schwarz Verlag.

Grimm, Jannis, and Cilja Harders. 2017. "Unpacking the Effects of Repression: The Evolution of Islamist Repertoires of Contention in Egypt after the Fall of President Morsi." *Social Movement Studies* 17/1: 1–18.

Harris, Christina Phelps. 1964. *Nationalism and Revolution in Egypt: The Role of the Muslim Brotherhood.* The Hague: Mouton.

Herrera, Linda. 2015. "Citizenship under Surveillance: Dealing with the Digital Age." *International Journal of Middle East Studies* 47: 354–56.

ʿIzzat, Hiba Ra'ūf. 2015. *Al-Khiyāl al-siyāsī li-l-Islāmiyyīn: Mā qabla l-dawla wa-mā baʿdahā*. Beirut: al-Shabaka al-ʿArabiyya li-l-Abḥāth wa-l-Nashr.

Jankowski, James P. 1975. *Egypt's Young Rebels: "Young Egypt," 1933–52*. Stanford CA: Hoover Institution Press.

Karam, Azza M. 1998. *Women, Islamisms and the State: Contemporary Feminisms in Egypt*. London: Palgrave Macmillan.

Kazem, Safynaz. 2000. "Hagg Wahba: Reference Work." *Al-Ahram Weekly On-line*, No. 513, 21–27 December 2000. Available at http://weekly.ahram.org.eg/Archive/2000/513/profile.htm, accessed 1 March 2018.

Khālid, Khālid Muḥammad. 1950. *Min hunā nabda'u*. Cairo: Dār al-Nīl li-l-Ṭibāʿa.

Khālid, Khālid Muḥammad. 2002. *Qiṣṣatī maʿa l-ḥayāt*. Cairo: Dār al-Muqaṭṭam.

Khiabany, Gholam. 2015. "Technologies of Liberation and/or Otherwise." *International Journal of Middle East Studies* 47: 348–53.

Klussmann, Paul G., and York-Gothart Mix (eds.). 1998. *Literarische Leitmedien: Almanach und Taschenbuch im kulturwissenschaftlichen Kontext*. Wiesbaden: Harrassowitz.

Kraidy, Marwan, and Joe F. Khalil. 2009. "A Short History of Arab Television." In Marwan Kraidy and Joe F. Khalil, *Arab Television Industries*. London: Palgrave Macmillan, 9–32.

Krämer, Gudrun. 1999. *Gottes Staat als Republik: Reflexionen zeitgenössischer Muslime zu Islam, Menschenrechten und Demokratie*. Baden-Baden: Nomos.

Krämer, Gudrun. 2010. *Hasan al-Banna*. Oxford: Oneworld Publications.

Legendre, Bertrand. 2010. "Les Débuts de l'edition de poche en France: Entre l'industrie et le social (1953–1970)." *Mémoires du Livre/Studies in Book Culture* (*MdLSBC*) 2/1.

McLarney, Ellen Anne. 2015. *Soft Force: Women in Egypt's Islamic Awakening*. Princeton: Princeton University Press.

Mostafa, Dalia Said. 2013. "Popular Culture and Nationalism in Egypt: ʿArab Lotfi and Egyptian Popular Music." In Anastasia Valassopoulos (ed.), *Arab Cultural Studies: History, Politics, and the Popular*. London: Routledge, 261–82.

Mounir, Safiya. 2017. "More MB Assets Frozen." *Al-Ahram Weekly* 1358, 24 August–6 September 2017, available at http://weekly.ahram.org.eg/News/22297.aspx, accessed 1 September 2017.

Pannewick, Friederike, Georges Khalil, and Yvonne Albers (eds.). 2015. *Commitment and Beyond: Reflections on/of the Political in Arabic Literature since the 1940s*. Wiesbaden: Reichert.

Philipp, Thomas, 2010. "Progress and liberal thought in *al-Hilāl*, *al-Manār*, and *al-Muqtataf* before World War I." In Christoph Schumann (ed.), *Nationalism and Liberal Thought in the Arab East: Ideology and Practice*. New York and London: Routledge, 132–44.

al-Qaraḍāwī, Yūsuf. 1970. *Al-Waqt fi l-ḥayāt al-Muslim*. Cairo: Maktabat Wahba.

al-Qaraḍāwī, Yūsuf. 1998 [1994]. *Al-Ijtihād al-muʿāṣir bayna l-inḍibāṭ wa-l-infirāṭ*. Beirut: al-Maktab al-Islāmī.

al-Qaraḍāwī, Yūsuf. 2000. *Al-Shaykh al-Ghazālī kamā ʿaraftuhu: Riḥlat niṣf qarn*. Cairo: Dār al-Shurūq.

al-Qaraḍāwī, Yūsuf. 2002. *Ibn al-qarya wa-l-kuttāb: Malāmiḥ sīra wa-masīra*, vol. 1. Cairo: Dār al-Shurūq.

Reid, Donald M. 2014. "Azhar, al-." In Ibrahim Kalın (ed.), *The Oxford Encyclopedia of Philosophy, Science, and Technology in Islam*. Oxford and New York: Oxford University Press, 81–84.

Reynolds, Nancy Y. 2011. "Salesclerks, Sexual Danger, and National Identity in Egypt, 1920s–1950s." *Journal of Women's History* 23/3: 63–88.

Rössler, Patrick. 1997. *Aus der Tasche in die Hand: Rezeption und Konzeption literarischer Massenpresse, Taschenbücher in Deutschland, 1946–1963*. Karlsruhe: Literarische Gesellschaft.

Ryzova, Lucie. 2005. "Egyptianizing Modernity through the 'New Effendiya': Social and Cultural Constructions of the Middle Class in Egypt under the Monarchy." In Arthur Goldschmidt, Amy J. Johnson, and Barak A. Salmoni (eds.), *Re-Envisioning Egypt 1919–1952*. Cairo and New York: The American University in Cairo Press, 124–62.

Sabaseviciute, Giedre. 2018. "Sayyid Qutb and the Crisis of Culture in Late 1940s Egypt." *International Journal of Middle East Studies* 50: 85–101.

Sabry, Tarik. 2010. "The Bridge and the Queue as Spaces of Encountering." In Tarik Sabry, *Cultural Encounters in the Arab World: On Media, the Modern and the Everyday*. London: I.B. Tauris, 63–94.

Salvatore, Armando. 2011. "Before (and after) the 'Arab Spring': From Connectedness to Mobilization in the Public Sphere." *Oriente Moderno, Nuova serie* 91: 5–12.

Shepard, William E. 2003. "Sayyid Qutb's Doctrine of Jāhiliyya." *International Journal of Middle East Studies* 35: 521–45.

Shepard, William E. 1995. "Khālid Muḥammad Khālid." In John L. Esposito (ed.), *Oxford Encyclopedia of the Modern Islamic World*. Oxford and New York: Oxford University Press, 2: 412–13.

Skovgaard-Petersen, Jakob. 1997. "Fatwas in Print." *Culture and History* 16: 73–88.

Speer, Lisa K. 2001. "Paperback Pornography: Mass Market Novels and Censorship in Post-War America." *Journal of American & Comparative Cultures* 24/3–4: 153–60.

Sreberny-Mohammadi, Annabelle, and Ali Mohammadi. 1994. *Small Media, Big Revolution: Communication, Culture, and the Iranian Revolution*. Minneapolis: University of Minnesota Press.

Walsh, Declan. 2017. "Why Was an Italian Graduate Student Tortured and Murdered in Egypt? The Strange Twists in the Case of Giulio Regeni's Disappearance in Cairo." *New York Times*, 15 August 2017.

Winkler, Stefan. 2001. "Distribution of Ideas: Book Production and Publishing in Egypt, Lebanon, and the Middle East." In Kai Hafez (ed.), *Mass Media, Politics, and Society in the Middle East*. Cresskill NJ: Hampton Press, 159–73.

Winkler, Stefan. 1997. *Buchproduktion und Strukturen des Verlagswesens im heutigen Ägypten*. Master's thesis. Bamberg: University of Bamberg.

Ziadeh, Nicola A. 1951. "Recent books on the interpretation of Islam." *Middle East Journal* 5/4: 505–10.

CHAPTER 11

Reading between the Lines: Arabic Script, Islamic Calligraphy, and the Question of Legibility

Alina Kokoschka

1 Introduction

Islamic calligraphy, whether written with a reed, painted with a brush, or laid as a mosaic, is of outstanding importance for Islam and for Muslim religious life and experience. Despite the fact that Arabic script conveys fundamental meaning, instant legibility is not at the centre of Islamic calligraphy. Rather, the calligraphy causes problems to the reader, whether learned or lay: It is hard to read. Sometimes it is barely legible. What is the point of a writing that cannot be read?, literary scholar Akane Kawakami asks, alluding to a quote from Roland Barthes. The latter's answer would most likely be that with illegibility materiality comes to the fore (Kawakami 2011, 388). Materiality is undoubtedly of great importance when thinking about scripts. At least until the dawn of the digital age, writing always happened on something and was done with something.[1] Arabic script has a particularly close connection to materiality and things, given its fundamental role in Islamic art and applied writing of various kinds. This philosophical photo essay argues that, even so, the quasi illegibility of writing in Arabic does not shift attention away from what is written, nor does it focus merely on materiality. It holds that the hindered readability is neither a coincidence nor simply a result of artistic playfulness or pure love of fanciful ornamentation. By graphically coding the obvious way of reading, it opens up different forms of legibility, a legibility beyond words. And this would not be possible without one quintessential graphic element that determines Arabic script's ability to be coded: the line.

Writing in a beautiful manner is commonly regarded as the acknowledged aim of calligraphy. Although Islamic calligraphy is considered to be of

1 See famously Kittler 1985 on this aspect, as well as Nemeth 2017, for material- and technique-informed approaches. I wish to thank Birgit Krawietz for her critical remarks on earlier versions of this article. I am also grateful to the Copenhagen-based David Collection, which has been of great inspiration and generous in allowing me the use of official images from the collection.

 | DOI:10.1163/9789004386891_012

undoubtedly outstanding beauty, the Arabic term *fann al-khaṭṭ* suggests a decisively different perspective: calligraphy as "the art of the line." And indeed, it is lines that shape the very distinct aesthetic qualities of Arabic script and Islamic calligraphy. Lines make material the movement of the hand. Lines connect letters and ornaments. Lines appear on objects, flow around columns and niches, and become large architectural forms. However, it is these same lines that make many calligraphic works barely readable. This essay proposes that in order to grasp this seemingly paradoxical phenomenon of non-readable writing, the "art of the line" has to be seen as calligraphy that reaches beyond words and invites reading between the lines.

The term calligraphy itself has misconceptualised our notion of Islamic calligraphy: when the notion of "beauty" (Greek *kalos*) becomes the focus, inevitably the queries that arise will relate mainly to decoration and adornment. Even though art history and manuscript studies have enriched the debate on Islamic art and writing with valuable insights on their higher aesthetics, interactions with architecture, and historical conditions, the line as the basic element of Islamic calligraphy is commonly not identified as a major actor.[2] For that and other reasons, thinking about Arabic script and Islamic calligraphy with the line at its centre demands a multidisciplinary approach. Furthermore, studies from philosophy, typography, computer science, and anthropology will illuminate the role of this often thin and overlooked yet potentially infinite graphic phenomenon.

2 Art of the Line

Arabic script is a special script not only because of some of its peculiarities. It is the script of a scripture, the language and writing system of the Qurʾān. A calligraphy of Qurʾānic verses can be considered a quasi-manifestation of God's word. According to its fundamental significance for Islam and Muslim religiosity, whether read, written, or merely seen or listened to when enlivened by recitation, Arabic writing "had to achieve a visual beauty, elegance and intricacy that would make writing commensurate with its sacral message" (Kabir 2015, 491f.). Calligraphy as an art developed in its own right, as did Qurʾān recitation. While the term "calligraphy" hints at that aim—to write something

2 There are exceptions: Barbara Brend, in her article "Rasm," *EI2*, who, identifies an "Islamic line" and follows its changing widths, strokes, and appearances through regions and dynasties. Unfortunately no link to calligraphy is made. For Laura U. Marks, the line is an important part of her argument to explain connections between Islamic art and vector graphics; see Marks 2010, 229–40.

beautifully (Greek *kalos*)—the Arabic equivalent to the term "calligraphy" is *fann al-khaṭṭ*, the "art of the line." Neither aim nor outcome are at play in the phrase—only the graphic phenomenon that flows out of the hand and then the pen—without lines there are no letters. Identifying writing with lines shifts the perspective: lines connect, flow, transport, or put an end to certain messages. And so, apart from designating script, *khaṭṭ* might also denote a (pipe) line or track to transport goods or conversations.

These connecting lines affect the Arabic script's capacity to become art and ornament, to join, to digress, and to separate. Arabic is a cursive script, meaning that letters are connected and there is no differentiation between block letters and cursive writing.[3] Furthermore, this script is characterised by its many ligatures that by far exceed the ligatures common to Latin script, such as the "ch" in German or "fi," where the upper end of the letter "f" serves as the dot of the letter "i." In Arabic, ligatures appear between most letters, as twenty-two out of twenty-eight letters require a mandatory connection to the surrounding letters,[4] and some letter combinations result in a particular ligature, such as combinations with *nūn* or *mīm*, which, depending on the font, may be linked even closer than usual so that, for example, the first letter is on top of the second (Illustration 11.1).

Already at this point, legibility might be hindered by intense shrinking through second- or third- degree ligatures (Benatia 2006, 139). A third-degree ligature is well known, as it often appears in the name of the prophet Muḥammad, where the upper ending of the *ḥā'* nearly touches the top of the *dāl* and thus reshapes the name almost into a sphere (Illustration 11.2). *Allāh* and the name *Muḥammad* when designating the Prophet show a special morphology (Benatia 2006, 138), which not only mirrors the significance of those two Islamic words per se but serves almost as a typographic correspondence between the vertical emphasis with the word *Allāh* and the spherical with *Muḥammad*. This special morphology can be considered one reason for the logo-like quality of these most famous Islamic words. It is through the open-endedness of graphic expression that the "Arabic line" allows the Arabic script to take on an "iconic capacity," as Juan E. Campo calls it (Campo 1987, 295). In this case, although less legible in a way, the graphic renderings of *Allāh* and *Muḥammad* are "read"—in the sense of recognised—by Muslims across the

3 As one outcome, there are hardly any abbreviations or acronyms in Arabic. At the same time, as Arabic is a consonantal script, it can be regarded as abbreviated by its very nature; see below.

4 The letters of *alif, dāl/dhāl, rā'/zāy,* and *wāw* are not connected to the letter to the left; cf. Gründler 2001, 139.

ILLUSTRATION 11.1 The letter nūn may take many different shapes depending on the letter that follows. Figure taken from "Text Layout Requirements for the Arabic Script." W3C Editor's Draft 03 August 2017, https://w3c.github.io/alreq/.
Note: The technical issue of text layout requirements for Arabic script is quite complex in nature and, although there are some mistakes, the here cited "Github" documentation is rather comprehensive, especially in view of the fact that literature on this topic is somewhat rare. Github is a major online platform for constant documentation and collaborative review of diverse issues related to programming.

globe, whether literate in Arabic or not. This "legibility" extends even to the realm of the commodities that reach Muslims in non-Arabic speaking cultures and societies, as in the case of an apotropaic talisman bought in Istanbul (Illustration 11.2).

These most prominent "logos" of Islam, along with others, which often function as easily identifiable signs rather than as written words, are what have allowed for Islamic branding of spaces for a very long time, such as is seen in the Hagia Sophia in Istanbul, where, rendered as oversized shields, these logos with their iconic capacity dominate what is at the same time a Christian historical monument. And whether as paintings, wall hangings, or as oversized three-dimensional objects, they have become increasingly fashionable as a means for also branding private spaces as Islamic, as the product range of furnishings and home accessories stores shows (Illustration 11.3).[5]

Ligatures that form a new symbol representing a word or even a more complex figure are rare in Latin script; one such example would be the ampersand, which represents the word *et*, Latin for "and," and appears as a "pretzel" in the worst case.[6] In an Islamic context, whole sentences have become ligatures of their own because of their mandatory and thus frequent use: eulogies praising Allāh or invoking God's blessing upon the Prophet Muḥammad (*taṣliya*) form

5 This is not to say that this is the only use or understanding of representations of Islamic writing. *Baraka* (divine blessing) transferred through writing whether written, read, or just seen is of utmost importance.

6 For an extensive discussion of the history of the ampersand, see the essay by the Bauhaus typographer Jan Tschichold (1981) *Formenwandlungen der Et-Zeichen*, Dresden: Verlag der Kunst.

ILLUSTRATION 11.2 *Nazar* talisman, to ward off the Evil Eye, Turkey 2012. Blue glass, golden glitter, and plastic pearls, with printed motive showing the Kaʿba. From the author's collection.
PHOTOGRAPH BY THE AUTHOR

comparatively rich typographic phenomena and even make an appearance in Islamic texts written in Latin script.[7] Just as headings, initials, or footnotes are considered ideographic in script analysis, since they are methods that make vivid the intellectual structure of a text in a graphic manner (Krämer 2005, 36), the eulogy ligatures are part of the ideography of Islamic texts. They express visually the intellectual structure of an Islamic text, as they clearly mark inserted citations as deriving from authoritative sources—and with that, they convey the author's ideological profile. This formal yet content- and cognition-affecting function has not been elaborated upon sufficiently. Acknowledgment

7 For an example of Arabic eulogies in Latin texts, see https://contemplatequran.wordpress.com/2015/06/05/seerah-series-part-2the-meaning-of-sallallahu-alaihi-wasallam/.

ILLUSTRATION 11.3 Shop window in Istanbul 2012 with oversized "Muḥammad" lettering in an especially twisted ligature.
PHOTOGRAPH BY THE AUTHOR.

comes from unexpected direction: "fdfa" is the unicode standard for *ṣallā 'llāhu ʿalayhi wa-sallam*, "May the prayers and peace of God be upon him."[8]

The already mentioned numerous intra-word ligatures characteristic of Arabic script—connections between the letters that make up a word—are the visual expression of the underlying differences in the functionality of the Arabic writing system. This is closely connected to the act of speaking or reciting Arabic:

> While the approach to spacing in the Roman Script is thus dissecting and analytical, the Arabic script lacks this dissecting function of spatial intervals and thereby produces the opposite effect. Rather than singling out words and letters as separate entities, its spacing mirrors the continous flow of human speech.…Space and script together form an integrated continuum.
>
> SPERL AND MOUSTAFA 2014, *42*

Continua of another sort, as elemental as the "constant flux of the world" (Erzen 2007, 70)—which some would argue is a basic tenet of the Islamic world view—can be graphically expressed with the peculiarities of the line in Arabic script. The lines forming ligatures are not fixed; they "can be stretched or shrunk according to the writing context."[9] What is most commonly referred to as *kashīda* in Arabic graphic design and word processing contexts[10] is specific to the Arabic script and allows for alignment by adjusting the lengths of the words themselves, instead of extending spaces between letters and words as in Latin script justification. By extending the lines of the inscribed space instead of the blank space, words and sentences can be adjusted perfectly to the shape and size of the material carrier. This technique can be illustrated by the many heterogenous applications observable in Islamic art over time.

This ʿAbbāsid silver dirham (Illustration 11.4) dates back to the year 208/823–24.[11] While the circularly arranged writing on the margin shows only

8 Cf. http://www.unicode.org/charts/PDF/UFB50.pdf (accessed 4 October 2017). For a constructive dialogue between Islamic manuscripts and Unicode standards, see Milo 2013. Although invectives just as much as eulogies highlight the author's profile, to my knowledge no standard invective ligatures have been developed in digital text processing.

9 Benatia et al. 2006, 143; see there also for specific rules.

10 *Kashīda* means pulled, lengthened, extended in Persian. Arabic terms are *taṭwīl* (lengthening) or *tamdīd* (extension, lengthening). I will use the term *kashīda*, since it is the more common in contemporary Arabic contexts and clearly denotes the phenomenon of stretched lines in Arabic writing.

11 Ruler and dates are unnamed; the coin dates from the time of the caliph Abū Jaʿfar ʿAbdallāh al-Maʾmūn b. al-Rashīd (198–218/813–33).

ILLUSTRATION 11.4 Silver dirham dated 208/823-24. Photograph by Pernille Klemp for The David Collection, Copenhagen, Inv.No C 32.

the slightest use of prolongation,[12] a literally extended use of the technique can be seen in the inscription that appears in coin's centre. The latter part of the *shahāda* ("Muḥammad is His Prophet"; *Muḥammad rasūl Allāh*) is arranged with a strict baseline and is thus in sharp contrast to the surrounding bended writing. The strong use of *kashīda* leads to a "linearisation," that is a

12 Unclear to me is the role of the upper circular line separating the two levels of writing. This dirham "is an early example of the 'reform type.' This initially involved a rearrangement of the legends, with an additional outer margin bearing words from the Qur'an," here Q 9:33; see description of Inv. no. C 32 of the David Collection, online: https://www.davidmus.dk/en/collections/islamic/dynasties/abbasiderne/coins/c32?back=1&show=design (accessed 11 October 2017).

"formatting of the space to be inscribed."[13] The result is, according to Christian Stetter, an interplay of lines and surface that has no comparison within the realm of the pictorial (Stetter 2005, 121). When looking at early Islamic coins, which contrast with Byzantine coins from the perspective of the line, the revolutionary potential of the graphic comes to the fore and image-centred debates of aniconism are relegated to second place. While in this image, extensions are in use simply for alignment, nevertheless in the case of this ʿAbbāsid dirham there seems to be a rhythm to the stretching. It is always the middle of the word that appears extended and thereby flattened, so that the first word at the top of the centre of the coin, *li-llāh* ("for God"), placed at the start of the latter part of the *shahāda,* is typographically emphasised. Thus, on this coin *Allāh* is set in two different manners. The second mention of God, at the bottom of the roundel, the last word in this latter part of the *shahāda,* shows a rare stretch within the word *Allāh*.[14]

The flexibility of the line developed within the Arabic script becomes significant when it comes to bilingual encounters, allowing for a coherent paralleling of two scripts without producing visually disturbing blanks. This Francophile stationer and gift shop in Beirut's Christian area of Gemmayzeh makes use of *kashīda* in order to graphically present its product range equally in Arabic and Latin letters (Illustration 11.5). This can by no means be regarded as a matter of course, since most bilingual signs in Beirut, one of the centres of Arabic-Latin graphic dialogues in the region, show a dominant Latin part (Abdel Baki 2013). In this case, at least the width and number of lines are the same. Because the graphics here take the Latin typeface's height as the general measurement, the Arabic equivalent appears smaller. It has been "Latinised" (Abdel Baki 2013, 46).

Recent encounters between Latin and Arabic script with a double meaning—between the scripts as writing systems and script as code underlying a computer program—show the aesthetic as well as cognitive dimension of the extendability of the Arabic line. The artist Ramsey Nasser developed a programming language based on the Arabic script. This was done on the one hand in order to draw attention to the up until now rarely criticised or even noticed Latin dominance over any other script in programming code. Latin script's dominance is not limited to the digital realm but here it becomes most evident and limiting. Programmes such as Microsoft Word have had difficulties in displaying Arabic letters with the necessary ligatures, as becomes clear in the photograph of the "Bauhaus" campaign (Illustration 11.6). Most applications

13 Translation by the author.

14 To the best of my knowledge, this is unusual at least in later times. More historical examples would have to be taken into consideration to clarify this conclusively.

ILLUSTRATION 11.5 Beirut 2017.
PHOTOGRAPH BY THE AUTHOR.

just cannot "read" Arabic letters: "A relevant disclaimer: The Arabic spelling won't render in our CMS [Content Management System]," as one online magazine discussing Nasser's programming language *qalb* remarked. On the other hand, Nasser explores and illustrates the mutual vivification that occurs

ILLUSTRATION 11.6 On the fence surrounding the building site for the new Bauhaus Museum, to open in 2018, the slogan "Bauhaus Museum in the city of Dessau" is rendered in various languages. The Arabic version shows the three most common mistakes that word processing programmes cause: All letters are unconnected. Writing is from left to right instead of right to left, while letters are not reversed accordingly.
PHOTOGRAPH BY THE AUTHOR, 2017.

between Arabic calligraphy and code written in Arabic (Illustration 11.7). The "beauty of code" (Chandra 2014) may be confirmed through the connecting lines' capacity to be lengthened in Arabic. The possible alignment of lines of code here contributes to the readability for human readers and concerns aesthetic debates on programming style.[15] What is more, there is a strong parallel between the recursiveness of code and Arabic calligraphy's non-linear and sometimes even circular way of writing, "looping back on itself."[16]

In contrast to this very nonmaterial and somewhat abstract example of digital code are material objects, which too demand recognition as partners for Arabic script and Islamic calligraphy. Lines are not only flexible horizontally—they shrink and stretch in every possible direction. This extraordinary

15 I thank Felix Ostrowski for technical explanations on this subject.
16 Galperina 2014. For the official documentation of the programming process, see ps://github.com/nasser/--- (accessed 5 November 2017).

```
(حدد فيبوناتشي (لامدا (ن)
  (إذا (أصغر؟ ن ٢) ن
    (جمع (فيبوناتشي (طرح ن ١))
         (فيبوناتشي (طرح ن ٢))))))
```

ILLUSTRATION 11.7 Programming Language *qalb* ("heart," a recursive acronym for *lugha barmaja*) with the implementation of the Fibonacci sequence algorithm, which is frequently used in demonstrations of new programming languages. For Nasser's mosaic of recursive code sequence in calligraphic style, see Galperina 2014. Image kindly provided by Ramsey Nasser.

nature of the line—the straight line, the curved line, the twisted line—leads, among other things, to Arabic script's "applicability." Lines of letters and lines of ornament can follow the shape of any object. This is of quite some importance, since the contemporary phenomenon of Arabic writing in an Islamic context extends beyond its "usual" place—or what is considered usual from an outsider's point of view. Elaborate lettering that is known from relief and other forms of calligraphic artistry appears on packaging, in advertisements, and on everyday mass-produced goods in Muslim commodity culture across the globe.[17]

Because of the shapeshifting, the "morph-ability" of connecting lines, whole words and sentences might even become objects in themselves. Just as dissolving Qurʾānic verses in water transfers words written on solid material into a healing solution full of *baraka* (divine blessing), words here might be transformed into something material themselves, something other than what they denote. This allows for fancy designs, so that an online shop called "Kashida" sells bookends formed from the first and last letter of the alphabet, *alef* and *yāʾ*, and bookshelves consisting of the Qurʾānic imperative *iqraʾ* ("read!"), where the stretched lines offer space for books.[18] But this is by no means a new phenomenon. The Ṣūfī dervish's staff shown below illustrates the close connection in Islam between script and material objects, or things, as in this case, the writing/calligraphy itself forms a thing and has even become a thing

17 For a detailed account of contemporary commodities in an Islamic context, see Kokoschka (forthcoming), *Waren Welt Islam*, Berlin: Kadmos.

18 https://kashidadesign.com/alefyaa-bookends-pbl.html, http://kashidadesign.com/iqraa-bookcase.html (both accessed 25 October 2017).

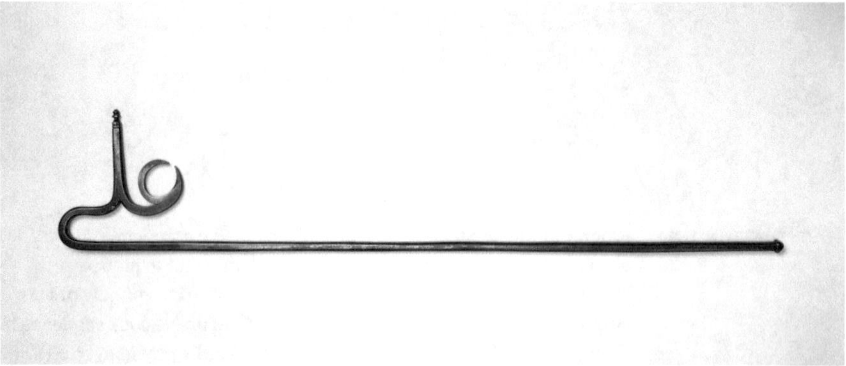

ILLUSTRATION 11.8 Dervish's staff, Iran, 18th-19th century. Photograph by Pernille Klemp for the David Collection, Copenhagen, Inv.No 15/1994.

(Illustration 11.8). The name ʿAlī, referring to Muḥammad's cousin and son-in-law, here becomes a 68.5 centimetre-long staff made of steel, which was used by a dervish during vigil remembrance practice (*dhikr*), in order to "rest his head or arm as he warded off sleep."[19] The *ʿayn*'s round shape might have been comfortable to touch and thereby would help the dervish to maintain focus, while the *lām*'s long neck obviously served as a supporting surface for hands or arms, and then for the head resting on it.

This high degree of flexibility of the connecting line enables further creative bendings—and drawn dialogues between script, things, and images. When it comes to Islamic calligraphy, letters and words seem to begin to lead a life of their own. They leave the baseline, which in some traditional typefaces is already multilevel. As baselines multiply and letters are piled up or intertwined, the observer is asked not only for a "simultaneous linguistic reconstruction" of vocalisation (Gründler 2001, 140), since Arabic script is a consonantal script (*abjad*). The observer of complex calligraphies also has to reconstruct even the "semantic linearity" (Clévenot and Degeorge 2000, 154) and deconstruct images before reading is even possible. Once the single baseline is abolished, bundles spring up from words and verses to generate shapes of falcons and faces, of tulips, flames, and lions.[20] Words can form anthropomorphic, zoomorphic, and phytomorphic images, as well as images of inanimate objects. Here linearity as we know it has come to an end, and readability in the conventional sense has vanished (Illustrations 11.9-11.11).

But instead of the sort of silhouettes known in the Western context—contours cut out along the exact outlines of a recognisable image—these

19 Object description of Inv. no. 15/1994.

20 On zoomorphic and anthropomorphic calligraphies, see Schimmel 1992.

ILLUSTRATION 11.9 In the shop of the Great Mosque of Xi'an, China, this calligraphy was displayed for sale in 2015. It shows a vase full of flowers that is formed out of words. The centre section of the vase reads *raḥmat Allāh* (God's Mercy).
PHOTOGRAPH BY THE AUTHOR.

ILLUSTRATION 11.10 A Turkish restaurant in Berlin uses the basmala in the shape of a tulip as a neon-lit shop sign.
PHOTOGRAPH BY THE AUTHOR 2017.

calligraphies open up a new dimension of pictoriality of script and are given their shape by largely unconnected streams of lines that nevertheless result in a congruent and easily "readable" form, despite the illegibility of the words. These images share the feature that the words they are made of are illegible.

ILLUSTRATION 11.11 In this Bektashi Ṣūfī paper silhouette (1280/1863–64), cut with a sharp knife rather than scissors, ʿAlī is personified as a lion.
Note: Cf. description of Inv. No. 21/1974.
PHOTOGRAPH BY PERNILLE KLEMP FOR THE DAVID COLLECTION, COPENHAGEN, INV.NO 21/1974.

Or, to be more precise, they are quasi-illegible, since once the observer literate in Arabic *knows,* he will be able to decipher at least parts of what is written.

3 Beyond Words, or Reading the Illegible

The case of Islamic script-images or "image-texts," as David Morgan (2005, 64–68) came to call them, illustrates vividly a process seldom recognised: the "letters' disappearance in the process of reading." Aleida Assmann further states that "when the medium retreats, it gains its power over the reader" (Assmann 2012, 235). This "imaginative reading" (Assmann 2012, 243)[21] that allows for images to appear is a transcendence of the written word and becomes possible only through the letters' arbitrariness. And arbitrariness is at the core of many pieces of Islamic calligraphy. The role of the imagination in reading Islamic calligraphy calls for further exploration.

21 Translations mine.

The recurring difficulties in deciphering Islamic calligraphy led early orientalist scholars to the belief that "texts were often meaningless, full of errors, and/or illegible; and that those that had a discernible meaning, such as Qur'ānic verses, were haphazardly chosen, formulaic, and seldom constituted a coherent epigraphic programme" (Gharipour and Schick 2013, 1). Those times are long gone, although some friction remains, in view of a seemingly very different logic and functionality of writing and reading. Only once we acknowledge that words and writing may have a meaning beyond simply the legible word do other reading practices appear meaningful. When we look at the literal meaning of *āyas* (Qur'ānic verses) as signs or epiphanies, they can then be seen as "hints at another sphere" (Beinhauer-Köhler 2011, 38). In order to "read" this sphere—that is, the cosmic order beyond verbal expression—*seeing* has to come first. Seeing before reading requires a deceleration that is enabled through Islamic calligraphy's hindered readability. Islamic calligraphy presents a calculated delay in reading and understanding. According to philosopher Dieter Mersch it is precisely the "alien morphologies" that we encounter in reversed, taken apart, and piled up lines that not only lead to something unseen but to "visibility beyond the visible" (Mersch 2012, 325).

Bärbel Beinhauer-Köhler calls what enables this other way of reading the act of "focussing." According to this concept, grasping cognitively what is written is not central, but, rather, it is catching sight of the calligraphic verses as such and in totality, not dissecting the image (Beinhauer-Köhler 2011, 42). The divine cannot be fully understood—this is beyond human ability. The powerful relation between the written, the seen, and then the read, which leads to a non-graspable realm in between, becomes even more potent when we think about writing in a script that is believed to bear power in and of itself. The language of the Qur'ān and certain verses in particular are believed to carry *baraka,* regardless of whether the believer is able to decipher what is written, whether the reader is literate or illiterate. Coming back to the initial question of "What is the point of a writing that cannot be read?," the answer may now lead in a different direction, away from the written towards the reader: If the writing cannot be read, reading has to be learned anew.

Bibliography

Abdel Baki, Randa. 2013. "Bilingual Design Layout Systems: Cases from Beirut." *Visible Language* 47/1: 39–66.

Assmann, Aleida. 2012. "Lesen als Kippfigur: Buchstaben zwischen Transparenz und Bildlichkeit." In Sybille Krämer, Eva Cancik-Kirschbaum, and Rainer Totzke (eds.),

Schriftbildlichkeit: Wahrnehmbarkeit, Materialität und Operativität von Notationen. Berlin: Akademie Verlag, 235–44.

Beinhauer-Köhler, Bärbel. 2011. *Gelenkte Blicke: Visuelle Kulturen im Islam*. Zurich: Theologischer Verlag.

Benatia, Mohamed Jamal Eddine, Mohamed Elyaakoubi, and Azzeddine Lazrek. 2006. "Arabic Text Justification." *TUGboat* 27/2: 137–46.

Brend, Barbara. "Rasm". In Peri Bearman et al. (eds.), *Encyclopaedia of Islam, Second Edition*. http://dx.doi.org/10.1163/1573-3912_islam_COM_0910. Accessed 3 August 2017.

Campo, Juan E. 1987. "Shrines and Talismans: Domestic Islam in the Pilgrimage Paintings of Egypt." *Journal of the American Academy of Religion* 55/2: 285–305.

Chandra, Vikram. 2014. *Geek Sublime: The Beauty of Code, the Code of Beauty*. Minneapolis: Graywolf Press.

Clévenot, Dominique, and Gérard Degeorge. 2000. *Das Ornament in der Baukunst des Islam*. Munich: Hirmer.

Eldem, Edhem. 2013. "Writing Less, Saying More: Calligraphy and Modernisation in the Last Ottoman Century." In Mohammad Gharipour and Irvin Cemil Schick (eds.), *Calligraphy and Architecture in the Muslim World*. Edinburgh: Edinburgh University Press, 465–83.

Erzen, Jale Nejdet. 2007. "Islamic Aesthetics: An Alternative Way to Knowledge." *The Journal of Aesthetics and Art Criticism* 65/1: 69–75.

Galperina, Marina. May 5 2014. "Artist's Notebook. Ramsey Nasser." http://animalnewyork.com/2014/artists-notebook-ramsey-nasser/. Accessed 3 November 2017.

Gharipour, Mohammad, and Irvin Cemil Schick. 2013. "Introduction." In Mohammad Gharipour and Irvin Cemil Schick (eds.), *Calligraphy and Architecture in the Muslim World*. Edinburgh: Edinburgh University Press, 1–9.

Gründler, Beatrice. 2001. "Arabic Script." In J.D. McAuliffe (ed.), *Encyclopedia of the Qurʾān*. Leiden: Brill, 1: 135–44.

Internationalization Working Group. 2017 "Text Layout Requirements for the Arabic Script. W3C Editor's Draft 03 August 2017." https://w3c.github.io/alreq/. Accessed 7 November 2017.

Kabir, Ananya Jahanara. 2015. "Hieroglyphs and Broken Links: Remediated Script and Partition Effects in Pakistan." *Cultural and Social History* 6/4: 485–506.

Kawakami, Akane. 2011. "Illegible Writing: Michaux, Masson, and Dotremont." *The Modern Language Review* 106/2: 388–406.

Kittler, Friedrich A. 1985. *Aufschreibesysteme 1800–1900*. Munich: Wilhelm Fink.

Krämer, Sybille. 2005. "'Operationsraum Schrift': Über einen Perspektivenwechsel in der Betrachtung der Schrift." In Gernot Grube, Werner Kogge, and Sybille Krämer (eds.), *Schrift: Kulturtechnik zwischen Auge, Hand und Maschine*. Munich: Wilhelm Fink Verlag, 23–57.

Krämer, Sybille, and Rainer Totzke. 2012. "Was bedeutet ‚Schriftbildlichkeit'?" In Sybille Krämer, Eva Cancik-Kirschbaum, and Rainer Totzke (eds.), *Schriftbildlichkeit: Wahrnehmbarkeit, Materialität und Operativität von Notationen*. Berlin: Akademie Verlag, 13–35.

Marks, Laura U. 2010. *Enfoldment and Infinity: An Islamic Genealogy of New Media Art*. Cambridge MA: The MIT Press.

Mersch, Dieter. 2012. "Schrift/Bild - Zeichnung/Graph - Linie/Markierung. Bildepisteme und Strukturen des ikonischen ‚Als'." In Sybille Krämer, Eva Cancik-Kirschbaum, and Rainer Totzke (eds.), *Schriftbildlichkeit: Wahrnehmbarkeit, Materialität und Operativität von Notationen*. Berlin: Akademie Verlag, 305–27.

Milo, Thomas. 2013. "Towards Arabic Historical Script Grammar Through Contrastive Analysis of Qur'ān Manuscripts." In Robert M. Kerr and Thomas Milo (eds.), *Writings and Writing: Investigations in Islamic Text and Script in Honour of Januarius Justus Witkam*. Cambridge: Archetype, 250–92.

Morgan, David, 2005. *The Sacred Gaze: Religious Visual Culture in Theory and Practice*. Berkeley: University of California Press.

Nemeth, Titus. 2017. *Arabic Type-Making in the Machine Age: The Influence of Technology on the Form of Arabic Type, 1908–1993*. Leiden: Brill.

Schimmel, Annemarie. 1992. "Calligraphy and Sufism in Ottoman Turkey." In Raymond Lifchez (ed.), *The Dervish Lodge: Architecture, Art, and Sufism in Ottoman Turkey*. Berkeley: University of California Press, 243–52.

Sperl, Stefan, and Ahmed Moustafa. 2014. *The Cosmic Script: Sacred Geometry and the Science of Arabic Penmanship*. London: Inner Traditions.

Stetter, Christian. 2005. "Bild Diagramm Schrift." In Gernot Grube, Werner Kogge, and Sybille Krämer (eds.), *Schrift: Kulturtechnik zwischen Auge, Hand und Maschine*. Munich: Wilhelm Fink Verlag, 115–35.

CHAPTER 12

Dimensions of "Giving Voice:" Discursive Agency and Intellectual Practice on Swahili Islamic Radio, in Mombasa 2005–2006

Kai Kresse

1 Introduction

This contribution draws from a larger project in which I work through internal debates among coastal Muslims in postcolonial Kenya, tracing and discussing the dynamics of their self-positioning as a religious community that has seen itself marginalised by, as many put it, subsequent "upcountry Christian governments."[1] My study also observes and contextualises internal conflicts within the regional *umma* (community) in everyday life, between "modernist" reformers and Ṣūfī-oriented Muslims, as these conflicts are raised and negotiated in emergent Swahili Muslim publics at different points in time. The first Swahili Islamic newspaper, for instance, was called *Sahifa* and was written and circulated from 1930 by Sheikh al-Amin bin Ali Mazrui (Kresse 2017). His writings exhibit a critical consciousness of the diminishing status of coastal Muslim culture in the British colonial era (which is blamed on the lack of social engagement and religious commitment by coastal Muslims) and an anticipation of increasing external domination by upcountry Africans in the future. A generation later, in the post-independent Kenya of the 1970s, his students were continuing this work by publishing Islamic pamphlets that criticised *bidaa* practices (Ar. *bidʿa*, unlawful innovation) and educational booklets that

1 Acknowledgements: This chapter builds on my larger work on Swahili Muslim publics in postcolonial Kenya, for which fieldwork, by means of consecutive short-term visits to Mombasa and Lamu, was conducted between 2004 and 2014, in annual/bi-annual sequences. The recordings I worked with were partly recorded by me from live broadcasts, but mostly supplied to me by Stambuli A. Nassir himself. It is to him and Abubakar Amin that I owe sincere gratitude for their readiness to talk about the broadcast and related matters. I also thank other friends and interlocutors in Mombasa with whom I was able to discuss this radio show and Stambuli's stance. Earlier versions of this essay were presented at workshops, conferences, and talks at Columbia University, the University of Bayreuth, and the Leibniz-Zentrum Moderner Orient in Berlin during the spring of 2017. The larger project is laid out in Kresse forthcoming; this topic specifically in Chapter 5.

provided historical background and religious guidance. In the particular case discussed here, two generations later, the focus is on a live broadcast discussion programme directed at a more recently constituted radio public based in Mombasa, in the post-Moi era.[2] Hereby, the radio makers build on this modern tradition of public critique and consciousness building introduced by Sheikh al-Amin.

2 Approach and Programmatic Perspective

Let me couch and frame my approach to this study in programmatic terms. My entry-point to the study of intellectual practice is a hermeneutical focus on the forms, uses, and traditions of knowledge in society, and their distribution and contestation (see Lambek 1993). I have drawn from Karin Barber's approach, an anthropology of texts, which explores *oral and written* texts (within one framework) as socially embedded enunciations of meaning-making (Barber 2007). To understand and lay out how my source-texts are reflexive of society, I combine close readings with ethnographic contextualisation, immersing myself in the texts (the language used, vocabulary, rhetoric, patterns, and idioms of speech) as well as their social contexts. Thereby, I sought to cultivate my sensitivity to the multiple layers and dynamics of meaning that shape and affect the community here—which is again re-shaped by its members, in processes of "social formation" and "re-formation" (Meyer 2009).

3 Get Educated with Stambuli!

Stambuli is a charismatic speaker and activist in Mombasa, whom I have known for more than fifteen years. Between 2005 and 2007 he hosted a radio show called *Elimika na Stambuli!*, or "Get educated with Stambuli!" It was a popular show that was aired every Saturday morning from 8am to 9am on *Radio Rahma*, the first Islamic radio station in coastal Kenya in the post-colonial period.[3] People of all backgrounds and ages were invited to call in with their

2 President Daniel arap Moi ruled Kenya between 1978 (when he took over as vice president from the deceased Jomo Kenyatta) until December 2002, when he agreed to leave power peacefully without any contestation, following an assurance of immunity and a so-called "golden handshake" agreement. For a reliable and comprehensive account on the history of post-colonial Kenya, see Hornsby 2012.

3 Previously, between 1947 and 1966, Islamic broadcasts in Swahili (with Qur'ānic and musical recitations also in Arabic) had been popular on the coastal national radio program, "Sauti ya Mvita" (Voice of Mombasa). But that was abolished because of growing popular pressure and

opinions or ask questions live on air, and engage in a wider conversation about current concerns affecting coastal Muslims in Kenya. The discussions were moderated by Stambuli and his co-host, Abubakar. Both men were in their late thirties or early forties: Stambuli, the initiator, was a former musician and social activist, who was already known as an engaged critic who speaks his mind and always had evidence for what he said. Abubakar was a well-educated, like-minded professional moderator and full-time employee of the radio station.[4]

Both Stambuli and Abubakar were discontented with the Muslim elite and its lack of leadership, which they felt had aggravated the marginal status of Muslims in Kenya. They conceived of this radio show as a bottom-up programme for mutual education about social, political, and religious matters, to "give voice" to ordinary people, whose concerns were rarely taken on directly in public. With its innovative concept of live call-in debates, this radio programme created a new Swahili public, and invited listeners to participate actively and "voice" their own concerns. Many engaged, and they did so drawing from common resources of Swahili intellectual practice.

My ethnographic account explores several dimensions of *discursive agency* that come into play, using the term in an exploratory manner that will become clearer as I go along. Hereby, aspects of moral obligation and ethical motivation appear as part of a range of relevant connotations. This links us to the field of "ordinary ethics" as Michael Lambek calls it (Lambek 2010, 2015), in which social actors are enveloped, as speech acts (following Austin 1965), interaction rituals (following Goffman 1967; see also Collins 1998), and ethical commitments intersect (in judgments, promises, or apologies; following Arendt 1998). The ethical, Lambek says, "is immanent to action" in everyday life (Lambek 2015, 45)—and we shall be able to see this here, too.

4 Sociality, Knowledge, and Practice on the Swahili Coast

On the Swahili coast, as elsewhere, knowledge and practice intertwine. Here, a core vocabulary of social interaction reflects sociality and mutual attention,

demands for "Africanisation," and objections to Arabic and Islamic sounds on the airwaves by the demographic majority (Brennan 2015).

4 Stambuli Abdilahi Nassir and Abubakar Amin are their full names. In recent communications, having read a draft of this chapter, both indicated that they wanted their full real names to be used in publication. I already knew Stambuli well before becoming interested in covering this radio broadcast as part of my research, and I got to know Abubakar during my visits to Mombasa in 2005 and 2006. I had a string of conversations with each of them, and I also collected further materials and information from them and other interlocutors in Mombasa.

out of which Swahili publics gradually emerge as discursive spaces in which meaning is negotiated. This applies to everyday encounters that start with the obligatory mutual greetings (*-salimiana*, "to greet each other"), to neighborly *baraza* group meetings as basic places of daily communicative exchange, in conversation, discussion, critique, and jest.[5] A group of basic verbs reflects these relationships of mutually directed sociality in communicative interaction, as an inserted linguistic marker for mutuality (*-an-*)—called a "reciprocative"—qualifies these actions as "doing something with each other":

-ju-an-a	*to know each other*
-wasili-an-a	*to communicate (with each other)*
-kumbush-an-a	*to remind each other*
-elimish-an-a	*to educate each other*
-heshim-i-an-a	*to respect each other*

Indicating mutual familiarity, recognition, and guidance, these expressions mark a discursive space in which *knowledge of* and *obligations to* one another are intertwined. They are at the core of social interaction, and at the same time they represent its basic normative aspects. This sketches out basic idioms, patterns, and values of Swahili intellectual practice, which are commonly invoked in all kinds of discussion, in written and oral form, past and present: in neighbourly *baraza* discussions (Loimeier 2007; Kresse 2007, 72–80; Kresse 2005), in didactic poetry (e.g., Allen 1971), and in religious sermons. Finally, they are also discernible in the radio shows that I followed.

5 Radio Rahma

Radio Rahma, the first Islamic radio station on Kenya's coast, was started in Ramaḍān 2004, by the son of former President Moi's most important political representative on the coast, Shariff Nassir (d. 2005). No religious radio stations had been allowed under President Kenyatta (r. 1963–1978), and radio had been state-owned until the final phase of President Moi's tenure (1978–2002). Under President Kibaki's rule (since early 2003), new private media channels blossomed across the country for the first time. Christian radio stations were

5 Such small social gatherings, commonly among neighbors or otherwise like-minded groups of men, are named after the stone benches (also *baraza*, plural *mabaraza*) that are often built into the outside structures of houses or mosques.

already sprouting up widely when *Radio Rahma* started broadcasting; these Christian radio makers had picked up on the opportunity early on (Branch 2011, 234). All this was set in the ongoing politics of post-9/11, with Kenya helping in the United States-led "war-on terror," a situation that amplified the existent tensions between the Christian upcountry government and the increasingly marginalised Muslim constituency (see Seesemann 2007; Prestholdt 2011).[6]

The show attracted a wide spectrum of listeners and callers, among them many women, some elderly, and even children. The communicative skills of most callers were remarkable, reflecting the importance accorded to proper ways of speaking in society. They seemed at ease and spoke clearly and confidently when raising issues. A young boy called in during the very first broadcast in March 2005 and reminded people in an exemplary way about the need for neighbourhood solidarity (*ujirani*), illustrating this verbal ability most impressively. A sense of openness and common purpose was cultivated by the moderators, as they used this first show as a brainstorming session, asking listeners for important topics and pressing issues that should be addressed and discussed in future broadcasts.

These aspects point to a set of meanings in which discursive agency can be seen as a useful term, understood on the one hand as the *general ability to speak well* (that is, to exercise agency through one's discursive registers and verbal creativity) and thereby push one's goals further; and, on the other hand, as *the provision of discursive space, and with it, the potential to use it* and be heard. Beyond these levels, internal to social action itself, further levels of meaning come into play when we start thinking critically about ethnography, an issue I shall be raising in conclusion.

6 "Educating Yourself through Others"—The Project and Its Makers

In the maiden broadcast in March 2005, Stambuli and Abubakar in effect promised to take on the concerns of a wider audience of ordinary Muslims and to discuss them in thematic sessions where people could participate by calling in or texting messages. The goal was for listeners to educate themselves by participating. Indeed, the chosen title of the programme, *Elimika na Stambuli!*, or in an alternative earlier version, *Jielimishe na Stambuli!* ("Educate yourself with Stambuli!"), emphasises the causative role of participating in the

6 For related earlier and later accounts on Islamic radicalisation and terror in East Africa, see Becker 2006; Mwakimako and Willis 2014; Anderson and McKnight 2014.

processual action of (self-)education. Any relevant matters could be raised for discussion, and callers were held to addressing one another in respectful dialogue. Common Swahili expressions for *educating* and *informing each other* (*elimishana* and *juzana*) were flagged as key words, thus enforcing a sense of mutual engagement. Also callers and moderators alike invoked the common moral obligation of all Muslims, of "commanding right and forbidding wrong to each other" (Cook 2000), in its Swahili idiom, *kuamrishana wema na kukanyana maovu*.

Among the first suggestions for topical discussions were: the problem of drug addiction and the recent spread of forbidden practices seen as polytheism (*shirk*), both brought forward by female callers; and the proper dress-code for men when going for prayers, raised by a man who condemned the wearing of football shirts in mosques as disrespectful. Other topics included how the coastal economy (*uchumi*) was being exploited by upcountry politics; why the coastal Independence movement had failed; how education compared to that in other parts of the Muslim world; complaints about the City Council's negligence, and many more.

The *Elimika* programme became something of an institution in Mombasa, with many tuning in and contributing to live discussions. Off air, *Radio Rahma* started local initiatives on social well-being, and sponsored some public educational, religious, and leisure events (including the public viewing of World Cup football games in the central Makadara grounds, in 2006). On air, the moderators insisted on respectful communication. Insulting language was unacceptable, as was generalising talk about social others (Christians, Hindus, ethnic groups, etc.), as this sounded dismissive. From time to time, the moderators would interrupt callers who violated the rules. In this way, they accorded as much importance to the proper form of discussion as to the actual topics themselves.

7 Listening in: Vicious Circles—Debating Terrorism (*ugaidi*)

While most sessions took a critical stance, the most courageous programme was a discussion of "terrorism" (*ugaidi*), pursued on two consecutive days in July 2005. This programme countered claims, held by some, that acts of terror could be justified as *jihād* (struggle) and thus as acceptable acts of revenge. Stambuli and Abubakar, along with many callers, insisted that there is no way in which killing defenceless victims could be acceptable. A few callers however (both men and women), pledging solidarity with Muslims in places like Iraq and Palestine, justified it as a defensive reaction to the aggressive anti-Muslim policies led by the United States and its "war on terror."[7]

This conflict could not be ignored nor taken lightly, and its discussion presented a dilemma. Stambuli decided to facilitate a frank and painful discussion. He found it important for all those who were affected, as members of the Muslim community, by the claim that violence could be exercised in their name to pay attention, make their own judgment, and speak out. Initiating the discussion here can itself be seen as an exercise by Stambuli of the obligation of "forbidding wrong"; for, as he argued on air, throughout the discussion, such violence was forbidden by Islam.

Later on he told me, during our informal conversations about this broadcast, that his efforts were aimed at making sure that there *could and would* be public debates on fundamentally contentious and divisive matters such as this one in his Muslim community. He believed that those who sympathised with "terror" had not considered the matter properly, nor their own position and their responsibilities to their peers and family members. Making his point on air, Stambuli also described a vivid scenario of global migration,[8] which had led to the fact that now many Kenyan Muslims had relatives living in countries around the world, including the West (where, he said, they were safe and cared for, and given housing and money, before they had contributed a thing):

> Our siblings who are in London these days, how are they? And those who are in Dubai and Saudi Arabia, what about them? Those in Canada or Ireland, how are they? They were chased away, they fled, they were welcomed over there, they were given money before getting a job, they were taken care of until they got jobs and accomodation by social services.[9]

As migrants, Kenyan Muslims had become part of these societies, which, as one caller argued, could be seen as acceptable targets for violent attacks, in retaliation for Muslim suffering (in Iraq, Afghanistan, and Palestine). Asked whether he could justify the deaths of innocent people, or of Muslim peers or relatives who were living abroad, the caller became evasive. He said that this

---

7 For contextual literature on this, see Mamdani 2005 (esp. 45–62; 249–60); for philosophical perspectives on the "war on terror," see Presbey 2007. For East Africa, e.g., Becker 2006; Prestholdt 2011; Mwakimako and Willis 2014; Seesemann 2007.

8 For illuminating essays speaking to the dynamics addressed here, see Graw and Schielke 2013.

9 *Ndugu zetu wako London sasa hivi wako vipi? Walioko Madubai, Saudia wakoje? Canada, Ireland wako vipi? Walifukuzwa, walikimbia, wakapokewa kule, wakapawa pesa kabla hajapata kazi, akawaangaliwa mpaka akapata kazi na nyumba ya social services.*

was lamentable but unavoidable, under the circumstances of the persistent enemy attacks, to which one needed to respond in kind: "an eye for an eye, and a tooth for a tooth," he said, quoting the Qur'ān. Another caller, when pushed on this point, actually conceded that, in order to argue for violence, "we need to put Islam aside" (*Islam tuweke kando*); then, the situation could be addressed in strategic terms.

Stambuli was aware of the vulnerability of his own position in such a loaded discussion. He cautioned the audience that even if some disliked him, they had no right to simply dismiss him as an unbeliever (*mkafiri*) for what he said. He too considered himself a faithful believer, who had the right to speak and to be listened to with respect, just like he listened to others and heard them out:

> [Y]ou, my friend, as a human being *you have the right* to think I am in the wrong–and I don't deny that; as I said yesterday, I respect your opinions. But just like you understand religion in a certain way, *grant me the same right* in the way I understand that religion—even if you hate me for how I understand this religion. It may be that you are in the right, or it may be that I am in the right.[10] [my emphasis, KK]

Why did Stambuli need to subject himself to such situations in which his vulnerability became readily exposed, I asked myself. Why did he decide to endure such difficult confrontational situations live on air? I will take this up for further reflection, also with a view to my own ethnographic practice: why did I need to go through with the coverage of this dificult topic? And what is the benefit of my ethnography here? For now, we can say that Stambuli's programme addressed a particular public, which it helped to create in the first place, and it had a certain impact, also through the style of conversation and argumentation employed, the way in which belief is invoked, and so on. The programme was educational and geared towards self-cultivation, not only in terms of piety in personal life, but also in terms of outright and upfront interaction about issues that matter, in a wider social space in which community members are very different and not all pious (or otherwise committed) in the same way.

At the end of this programme on terrorism, Stambuli invited the senior guest for that show, Prof. Mohamed Hyder, a retired university professor in biology

10 (…) *we mwenzangu mwanadamu unayo haki kuniona mimi na kosa na sipingi kama nilivyoambia jana naheshimu maoni yenu. Lakini unavyo ulivyoelewa dini na mimi nipe ile haki hata kama wanichukia na mimi ninavyoelewa ile dini. Waweza kuwanishinda naweza mimi nakushinda.*

and a long-time activist for social and religious reform, to comment. After having introduced his audience earlier in the show to the American linguist and philosopher Noam Chomsky as a role model political critic, he encapsulated the relevance of Stambuli's programme for ordinary Muslims in his concluding vote of thanks:

> And we, in our ongoing discussions, we can develop ourselves (if God wishes), by discussing more and more amongst ourselves matters such as those covered today. *Radio Rahma gives people a chance to be able to exchange (and possibly change) their thoughts about such matters.* And I would like to congratulate you, I am happy to have been able to be with you here today....[11] [my emphasis, KK]

8 Reflections on Discursive Space

What Prof. Hyder highlights in these closing comments is good for us to think with: the "*Elimika na Stambuli!*" broadcasts are praised, as they provide an open and accessible space for discussion among fellow Muslims, so that, within these dynamics of discursive exchange and mutual education (*-jadiliana*; *-elimishana*) concerns could be raised, addressed, and negotiated. Opinions could be exchanged, (re)shaped, and consolidated (or rejected).[12] Prof. Hyder's comment here emphasises *the fundamental value of being able to engage in discussion as such*. This provides opportunity for mutual engagement, listening to one another's points while also seeking to *convince* one another (through reasoning). Frank talk by all those using this space, those who called in and voiced their concerns, helped to lay out the actual features of internal conflict and divisions, so that they could be better understood and addressed by all.

As Prof. Hyder said, by continuing to exchange arguments with one another, change—or the realisation of the potential for communal self-transformation—became possible, in non-violent ways. Similar observations have been made for a live discussion programme on a new Arab satellite TV channel, which was

11 *Na sisi inshallah katika kujadiliana, na kujadiliana zaidi, kuhusu mambo kama haya, Radio Rahma imewapa watu nafasi ya kuweza kubadilishana fikra kwa mambo kama haya. Na napenda kuwapa pongezi, nafurahi sana kuweza kuwa pamoja na nanyi siku ya leo.*

12 An implicit message here is that the community benefits from such interaction (in that a reasonable consensus may arise), although this is not explicitly said.

also construed to facilitate direct, immediate discussions and to pose to invited guests questions from an audience participating by means of telephone calls (Eickelman 2005, 47–50).[13] The design of Stambuli's radio programme enabled an outspoken exchange within the community, providing all listeners (as potential call-in participants to the live debate) with the opportunity to publicly "give voice" to their fundamental concerns and sentiments, exercising their *discursive agency* in response to what had been said. An egalitarian and critical character was emphasised in this public discursive space, confronting existent hierarchies and assumptions, by "reminding others," and "forbidding wrong" from below, so to speak.[14] These broadcasts cultivated a more leveled and direct debate, as rules and restrictions for personal interaction did not apply here in the same way (regarding gender, seniority, descent, or ethnic background). Women and men, old and young, Arab and Mijikenda under normal circumstances in everyday life would not have opportunity to discuss these topics together.

Stambuli's show ceased to exist in 2007, when the private funder for the programme withdrew his monies, apparently, as Stambuli told me in retrospect, under pressure from Muslim politicians and members of the elite who had come to resent Stambuli's critique. Consequently, the owner of *Radio Rahma*, who had political ambitions himself, did not give Stambuli a chance to continue, despite the popular success his programme had had (and that I had witnessed myself). Today, Stambuli continues to give talks and lectures, some very political, throughout the region and on social media. He remains a popular speaker, and has a strong voice in the Swahili community, including in the diaspora. Part of the power of his agency, I believe, is a direct result of his intellectual practice in performance. Using the right words (and the right kind of knowledge and "sense" of a situation) at the right time is pertinent here. Stambuli did not and would not advocate violence. Yet with his words alone, he sought to mobilise his community, and it is this discursive activity that reveals his ethical commitment within his intellectual practice.

13 For similar dialogical dynamics, see also studies on the use of *fatwa* interaction in new media (e.g., Gräf 2010; Clarke 2009).

14 See Cook (2000, 584), on the everyday, *egalitarian* (and even "democratic") character of command. Note that Cook also calls this an "intellectual tradition," which he seeks to explore within the society in which it flourished, also to see what difference it may have made in the streets (p. xiii).

9 Concluding Thoughts on Stambuli's Discursive Agency and That of Ethnography

Stambuli here was so committed to his obligation to publicly address the issue of "terror" (*ugaidi*),[15] as a kind of promise to himself and to his peers, that in the process he was ready to endure much friction. Similarly, thinking about my own ethnographic practice in relation to this, I also saw it as my self-committed obligation to observe and report on this discussion. On a meta-level, it may be productive to think further about how the doing and writing of ethnography provides us as anthropologists with discursive agency, which we acquire in the process itself (of shared experiences in fieldwork and dialogical reflections on it); ethnography *gives voice to us* as (credible, one would hope) anthropologists, while we (as writers) "create" the ethnography in the first place, giving voice to our interlocutors as the central subjects of our ethnographic narratives, through which we then pass on what we learned by thinking about how they acted.[16]

I would like to emphasise the point that the pursuit of an ethnography of intellectual practice requires us to "listen in" carefully and become sensitive to the motives and ethical dimensions involved in the life-worlds of the actors we attempt to understand. This approach can enable us to exercise our newly acquired "discursive agency" responsibly in our ethnographies (as a promise we give ourselves). Somewhat in parallel to Stambuli, I took it on as my self-ascribed task as ethnographer to write an informed and sensitised account of this local (and yet translocal) internal discussion of "terror"—and to listen and endure in the process—so that a sense of the value of insight into the complex internal dynamics of the negotiation of such a sensitive and contested topic could be passed on, including (perhaps most importantly) a sense of Stambuli's achievement in creating a discursive space for such a discussion to take place in the first place.[17] In this way, I work to build and sustain in turn,

15 This is an abstract noun (i.e., set in the u-class) formed from the noun *gaidi*, meaning "robber" or "plunderer." See, e.g., Johnson 1989.

16 Such reflections link us back to fundamental questions and discussions about the work and responsibilities of the anthropologist as ethnographer (as writer, and as human being living with others), representing one's own experiences and that of others, reported upon, on the basis of a situation of shared time and space; see, e.g., Clifford and Marcus 1986; Fabian 1983, 1996.

17 If "to take seriously points of view and visions of life they do not share" and even strongly disagree with, is a "key task" for anthropologists (Schielke 2014, 13), this challenge was also mastered by Stambuli here.

from my side, a discursive space in academia (addressing a different and wider public), where such exercise of discursive agency (with its struggles and discontents) can then be heard and taken seriously.

Uncomfortable questions and sensitive issues that are of fundamental concern to everyone individually and the community as a whole, such as terror/*ugaidi* here, need to be addressed not only within social communities but also within academia, as a vehicle for mediating knowledge and informing judgments for the wider public. Some colleagues in anthropology and related disciplines have already made some headway in discussing how conceptions of violence and terror, martyrdom, and dedicated religious struggle are controversially discussed in the Muslim world *and* the West (see, e.g., Euben 2002; Asad 2007; Kurzman 2011). It is important to address this further, in order to lay out the existing kinds of diverse opinion, their reasoning patterns, and the contextualisations and justifications brought forward to argue for them. In this way, we obtain a richer and more adequate picture of the discursive dynamics concerning such fundamentally contested and sensitive topics as part of existent life-worlds.

Picking up on my introductory comment on Michael Lambek's conception of an "ordinary ethics" (2010; 2015) and his assumption about the ethical as immanent in everyone's everyday practice, my case study here could be seen to affirm how Stambuli indeed developed and performed his broadcast as part of an *"immanent" ethical practice* in his everyday conduct—yet one that does not by any means seem "ordinary." He had committed himself publicly to directing attention to sensitive and critical matters that needed to be discussed in public, for the betterment of his community, and he managed to deliver on that in an exceptional broadcast.

Insofar as my work contributes to the anthropology of Islam and to understanding the internal diversity of the Muslim world that my interlocutors are part of, I have focused here on the ways in which they address and negotiate internal conflict. I seek to understand their "ways of reasoning, and the reasons for arguing" (see Asad 1986), and thus to explore ethical and other dimensions of intellectual practice on the Swahili coast, with a view to Africa and the Muslim world more widely. Ultimately, my research also seeks to counter the dominance of Eurocentric categories in our analytic language, by drawing from key terms (and idioms and patterns of thinking) from these regions, for the "thinking of society" more generally.

Here, I have highlighted the *discursive* and *intellectual agency* of the radio programme's listeners and makers, also with a view to a wider Western-dominated world (inside and outside of academia), which historically has long been denying, misreading, or ignoring the critical and creative resources of such agency in practice, in large parts of Africa and the Muslim world.

Especially at a time when xenophobia and Islamophobia are again on the rise, research on the exercise of discursive and intellectual agency as part of everyday conviviality within complex political spaces inhabited by the people with whom we do research continues to be important.

Bibliography

Allen, J.W.T. 1971. *Tendi: Six Examples of a Swahili Classical Verse Form.* Nairobi: Heinemann.

Anderson, David M., and Jacob McKnight. 2014. "Kenya at War: al-Shabaab and Its Enemies in Eastern Africa," *African Affairs* 114/454, 1–27.

Arendt, Hannah. 1998[2] [1958]. *The Human Condition.* Chicago: University of Chicago Press.

Asad, Talal. 1986. *The Idea of an Anthropology of Islam.* Washington DC: Center for Contemporary Arab Studies, Georgetown University.

Asad, Talal. 2007. *On Suicide Bombing.* New York: Columbia University Press.

Austin, John. 1965 [1955]. *How to Do Things with Words.* New York: Oxford University Press.

Barber, Karin. 2007. *The Anthropology of Texts, Persons and Publics: Oral and Written Culture in Africa and Beyond.* Cambridge and New York: Cambridge University Press.

Becker, Felicitas. 2006. "Rural Islamism during the 'War on Terror': A Tanzanian Case Study." *African Affairs* 105 (421): 583–603.

Branch, Daniel. 2011. *Kenya: Between Hope and Despair, 1963–2011.* New Haven: Yale University Press.

Brennan, James R. 2015. "A History of *Sauti ya Mvita* ('Voice of Mombasa'): Radio, Public Culture, and Islam in Coastal Kenya, 1947–1966." In Rosalind I.J. Hackett and Benjamin F. Soares (eds.), *New Media and Religious Transformations in Africa*. Bloomington: Indiana University Press, 19–38.

Clarke, Morgan. 2009. *Islam and New Kinship: Reproductive Technology and the Shariah in Lebanon*. New York: Berghahn Books.

Clifford, James, and George Marcus. 1986. *Writing Culture: The Poetics and Politics of Ethnography.* Berkeley: University of California Press.

Collins, Randall. 1998. *The Sociology of Philosophies: A Global Theory of Intellectual Change.* Cambridge MA: Harvard University Press.

Cook, Michael. 2000. *Commanding Right and Forbidding Wrong in Islamic Thought.* Cambridge and New York: Cambridge University Press.

Eickelman, Dale F. 2005. "New Media in the Arab Middle East and the Emergence of Open Societies." In Robert W. Hefner (ed.), *Remaking Muslim Politics: Pluralism, Contestation, Democratization*. Princeton: Princeton University Press, 37–59.

Euben, Roxanne L. 2002. "Killing (for) Politics: *Jihad*, Martyrdom, and Political Action." *Political Theory* 30/1: 4–35.

Fabian, Johannes. 1983. *Time and the Other: How Anthropology Makes Its Object.* New York: Columbia University Press.

Fabian, Johannes. 1996. *Remembering the Present: Painting and Popular History in Zaire.* Berkeley: University of California Press.

Goffman, Erving. 1967. *Interaction Ritual: Essays in Face-to-Face Behavior.* New York: Doubleday.

Gräf, Bettina. 2010. *Medien-Fatwas@Yusuf al-Qaradawi: Die Popularisierung des islamischen Rechts.* Berlin: Klaus Schwarz Verlag.

Graw, Knut, and Samuli Schielke. 2013. *The Global Horizon: Expectations of Migration in Africa and the Middle East.* Leuven: Leuven University Press.

Hirschkind, Charles. 2006. *The Ethical Soundscape: Cassette Sermons and Islamic Counterpublics.* New York: Columbia University Press.

Hornsby, Charles. 2012. *Kenya: A History Since Independence.* New York: I.B. Tauris.

Johnson, Frederick. 1989 [1939]. *A Standard Swahili-English Dictionary.* London and New York: Oxford University Press.

Kresse, Kai (ed.). 2017. *Guidance (Uwongozi) by Sheikh al-Amin Mazrui: Selections from the First Swahili Islamic Newspaper. A Swahili-English Edition.* Trans. Hassan Mwakimako and Kai Kresse, foreword by Alamin Mazrui and Hammad M.K. Mazrui. Leiden: Brill.

Kresse, Kai. 2005. "At the *Baraza*: Socializing and Intellectual Practice at the Swahili Coast." In Toyin Falola (ed.), *Christianity and Social Change in Africa: Essays in Honor of J.D.Y. Peel.* Durham NC: Carolina Academic Press, 613–31.

Kresse, Kai. 2007. *Philosophising in Mombasa: Knowledge, Islam, and Intellectual Practice on the Swahili Coast.* Edinburgh: Edinburgh University Press for the International African Institute.

Kresse, Kai. Forthcoming. *Swahili Muslim Publics and Postcolonial Experience.* Bloomington: Indiana University Press.

Kurzman, Charles. 2011. *The Missing Martyrs: Why There Are So Few Muslim Terrorists.* Oxford and New York: Oxford University Press.

Lambek, Michael 1993. *Knowledge and Practice in Mayotte: Local Discourses of Islam, Sorcery, and Spirit Possession.* Toronto: University of Toronto Press.

Lambek, Michael. 2010. "Introduction" and "Towards an Ethics of the Act." In Michael Lambek (ed.), *Ordinary Ethics: Anthropology, Language, and Action.* New York: Fordham University Press, 1–36; 39–63.

Lambek, Michael. 2015. "Living As If It Mattered." In Michael Lambek, Veena Das, Didier Fassin, and Webb Keane, *Four Lectures on Ethics: Anthropological Perspectives.* Chicago: Hau Books.

Loimeier, Roman. 2007. "Sit Local, Think Global: The Baraza in Zanzibar." *Journal for Islamic Studies* 27: 16–38.

Mamdani, Mahmood. 2005. *Good Muslim, Bad Muslim: America, the Cold War, and the Roots of Terror*. New York: Three Leaves Press.

Meyer, Birgit, ed. 2009. "Introduction: From Imagined Communities to Aesthetic Formations: Religious Mediations, Sensational Forms, and Styles of Binding." In Birgit Meyer (ed.), *Aesthetic Formations: Media, Religion, and the Senses*. New York: Palgrave Macmillan, 1–28.

Mwakimako, Hassan, and Justin Willis. 2014. "Islam, Politics, and Violence on the Kenya Coast." *Observatoire des Enjeux Politiques et Sécuritaires dans la Corne de l'Afrique*, Note 4.

Presbey, Gail M. (ed.). 2007. *Philosophical Perspectives on the "War on Terrorism."* New York: Rodopi.

Prestholdt, Jeremy. 2011. "Kenya, the United States, and Counterterrorism." *Africa Today* 57/4: 2–27.

Schielke, Samuli. 2014. "There Will Be Blood: Expecting Violence in Egypt, 2011–2013." *ZMO Working Papers* no. 11 (2014), 1–16.

Seesemann, Rüdiger. 2007. "Kenyan Muslims, the Aftermath of 9/11, and the 'War on Terror.'" In Benjamin F. Soares and Rene Otayek (eds.), *Islam and Muslim Politics in Africa*. London: Palgrave Macmillan, 157–76.

CHAPTER 13

Shāh Walī Allāh of Delhi, His Successors, and the Qur'ān

Muhammad Qasim Zaman

1 Introduction

This paper is concerned with the writings on the Qur'ān by Shāh Walī Allāh (d. 1176/1762) of Delhi and his immediate successors and the impact those writings came to have on Qur'ānic studies in South Asia. Walī Allāh is widely seen as a major Ṣūfī figure and one of the most significant scholars of the Qur'ān, *ḥadīth*, and law in South Asia.[1] Although hardly the first to render the Qur'ān into Persian on the Indian subcontinent, Walī Allāh's Persian translation had considerable influence on generations of translators and exegetes. He is often credited with helping to bring the study of *ḥadīth* closer to the centre of concerns of the South Asian *'ulamā'*. The pronounced interest that many South Asian *'ulamā'* have evinced in *ḥadīth* and in writing commentaries on major canonical works owes much to Walī Allāh's initiative in that field. Adherents of almost all major doctrinal orientations that emerged in Sunnī Islam in the colonial era revere his memory; this is a significant measure of his influence, given the rivalries that have long continued to beset relations among the different orientations.

Given Walī Allāh's stature and the respect with which his sons and successors have often been viewed by many Sunnīs in South Asia, it would seem to be unremarkable that his writings should have come to enjoy great influence in scholarly and other circles. Yet a closer look at some of his work quickly reveals the considerable, if often muted, ambiguity that has also accompanied his legacy. Walī Allāh was a harsh critic of his contemporary Ṣūfīs and jurists, whom he accused of making the practice of Islam excessively cumbersome and of putting forth unwarranted claims to authority (Walī Allāh 1967–70, 1: 271–82). Such criticism has appealed to modern critics of the *'ulamā'* and Ṣūfīs more than it has to either of the latter, and many among Walī Allāh's contemporaries

1 For a useful anthology of scholarly work on Walī Allāh, see Chaghatai 2005. An assessment of the scholarship on him until the late 1980s is provided by Hermansen in Chaghatai 2005 (Hermansen's article was first published in 1988).

 | DOI:10.1163/9789004386891_014

could not have warmed to it. Walī Allāh was also unusual in his age for his emphasis on *ijtihād*, that is, the articulation of new legal rulings in light of the foundational texts. This underlies some of his appeal to latter-day Salafīs and to Muslim modernists such as the poet and philosopher Muḥammad Iqbāl (d. 1938), but, at a time when many among the *ʿulamāʾ* viewed *ijtihād* with considerable misgiving, Walī Allāh's view on this subject too could not have endeared him to them. In his magnum opus, the *Ḥujjat Allāh al-bāligha*, Walī Allāh sought to demonstrate how Islamic legal and other norms and even the core Islamic rituals promoted recognisable human interests (*maṣāliḥ*; singular, *maṣlaḥa*), a notion that resonates with those who seek to present Islam as a "rational" religion, one in tune with human nature. But once again, this view creates some anxiety among traditionalist *ʿulamāʾ* insomuch as they see it as fueling the modernist propensity to not just explain particular norms in light of their underlying rationale but to explain them away as needed. Walī Allāh was a great admirer of the *Muwaṭṭaʾ* of Mālik b. Anas (d. 179/795), the foundational text of the Mālikī school of Sunnī law. He wrote two commentaries on it, but that preference never caught on in what has remained a predominantly Ḥanafī South Asia. Some of Walī Allāh's writings also reveal an unusual interest in what in modern parlance would be called socio-economic justice. Indeed, some social critics have made a point of invoking Walī Allāh in their own appeals to social justice; others, however—among them many *ʿulamāʾ*—have remained uncomfortable with such constructions, often by way of arguing that Walī Allāh's views have been distorted by interested parties (Zaman 2012, 221–60). Finally, it is worth noting that one of Walī Allāh's grandsons, Shāh Ismāʿīl (d. 1831), had become part of an early nineteenth-century puritanical movement that the British would long characterise as "Wahhābī." Many of the ideas espoused by the leaders of that movement were at a considerable distance from the Ṣūfī-inflected piety of Walī Allāh and his other successors. Yet the fact that members of that movement, too, looked to Walī Allāh for some of their inspiration has made for added discomfort in traditionalist and Ṣūfī circles.

The reverence for Walī Allāh, then, is scarcely unqualified. Yet his Persian rendering of the Qurʾān has arguably exercised a major influence on generations of subsequent translations into Urdu. Two of his sons, Shāh ʿAbd al-Qādir (d. 1814) and Shāh Rafīʿ al-Dīn (d. 1818) produced translations of the Qurʾān into Urdu; and the best known of his sons, Shāh ʿAbd al-ʿAzīz (d. 1824), wrote a commentary in Persian on portions of the Qurʾān. Almost a century later, in the early twentieth century, Maḥmūd Ḥasan (d. 1920), a much respected scholar associated with the Deoband madrasa as well as with what proved to be an abortive anti-colonial movement, produced an Urdu translation of the Qurʾān that was billed as a more accessible rendering of Shāh ʿAbd al-Qādir's early Urdu translation. That translation has continued to be widely influential in South Asia and beyond. The question of how Walī Allāh and his sons were able to put their stamp on subsequent translations of the Qur'ān merits some explanation, and it is the purpose of this paper to provide it.[2]

2 The Qur'ān and the Common Believer

In the introduction to his translation of the Qur'ān, completed in 1151/1738, Walī Allāh made it clear that the work was intended for a popular, lowbrow audience, among them the children of soldiers and craftsmen, as well as ordinary believers not having the ability or the leisure for the pursuit of advanced learning. People who sat together to listen to medieval classics such as the *Mathnawī* of Rūmī, the *Gulistān* of Saʿdī, and the *Manṭiq al-ṭayr* of ʿAṭṭār would only benefit more, he said, from listening to the word of God. And even scholars could gain something from the translation (Walī Allāh 2001, 15–17). This was no mere rhetoric. Rather, it was clearly part of Walī Allāh's goal from relatively early in his career to facilitate people's practice of their faith, to anchor it in the foundational texts, and to cut down to size juristic and Ṣūfī claims to authority as intermediaries between God and ordinary believers.

In a later work setting out the principles of Qur'ānic exegesis, Walī Allāh sought to reorient the commentators' concerns away from the stories they liked to tell about the "occasions" on which particular Qur'ānic passages were supposedly revealed (*asbāb al-nuzūl*) and towards an explication of the Qur'ān's universals (*kulliyyāt*; Walī Allāh n.d., *al-Fawz*, 11, and Walī Allāh 1914, 20).[3] For, in his view, not only did a focus on such stories divert attention from seeking guidance from the Qur'ān's teachings, it also threatened to tie those teachings to a particular time, a particular people, and thereby to undercut their timelessness (Walī Allāh n.d., *al-Fawz*, 11; Walī Allāh 1914, 20). Yet Walī Allāh is also famous in Muslim modernist circles for the idea that God had tailored His laws, even the mandatory rituals, to the customs and habits of the people He had addressed through His revelation (cf. Walī Allāh 1877, 1: 117; Hermansen 1996, 341–42). From this it could be inferred that other people were to be

2 As might be expected, Walī Allāh's work on the Qur'ān and that of his sons has received some scholarly attention. As regards Walī Allāh, notable discussions include Sindhī 1998, 45–97 (first published in 1944); Jalbani 1967, 5–28; Rizvi 2004 (first published in 1980), 229–41; and Baljon 1986, 136–51. On Shāh ʿAbd al-ʿAzīz, see Rizvi 1982, 103–38. And on Shāh ʿAbd al-Qādir, see Qāsimī 1977 and Khalid 2016.

3 The work is undated. Rizvi 2004, 222, lists it among Walī Allāh's writings produced between 1739–40 and 1747.

guided by the example of the revelation's first addressees without, however, being bound by the norms in question (cf. Iqbal 1934, 163). This is not an unreasonable inference, especially in light of Walī Allāh's overarching concern to show how scriptural teachings took account of their addressees' particular circumstances. Walī Allāh did not explicitly say, however, that Qur'ānic laws could continue to evolve according to changing circumstances. What he did say was that one could understand how people's interests were served by revelation by looking at how the Qur'ān had taken account of *Arab* customs in articulating its teachings (Walī Allāh n.d., *al-Fawz*, 13; Walī Allāh 1914, 25). In any case, his concern with finding ways of continuing to guard people's interests as they went about their lives and practised their faith was palpable throughout his writings. Among other things, this meant being able to interpret the Qur'ān in a variety of different ways in order to find a meaning that would fit people's needs. Indeed, as he put it in quoting Abū l-Dardā', a companion of the Prophet Muḥammad, one could hardly claim to be a scholar of the law without that ability (Walī Allāh n.d., *al-Fawz*, 19; Walī Allāh 1914, 38).

In what appears to have been a concerted effort, the project of bringing the teachings of the Qur'ān to ordinary people continued with Walī Allāh's sons. Shāh Rafīʿ al-Dīn produced a more or less literal translation of the Qur'ān.[4] That enterprise sought to minimise the translator's intrusiveness, in the process helping not only to preserve the foundational text's authenticity but also to affirm the translation's closeness to the original. It also made it difficult to use, however, except for the more indefatigable readers. For his part, Shāh ʿAbd al-Qādir produced an idiomatic Urdu translation, much like Walī Allāh's Persian version. At a time in the early nineteenth century, when Urdu was coming into its own as the spoken language of people in north India and when important poets had begun using it as their principal literary language, ʿAbd al-Qādir's translation—*Mūḍiḥ al-Qur'ān*—came to establish itself as a landmark work. Completed in 1205/1790, one of its first print editions, if not the very first of them, dates to 1829 (on the completion date, see ʿAbd al-Qādir 1829, preface [not paginated]). Significantly, ʿAbd al-Qādir had made a conscious effort not to render the Qur'ān into literary Urdu, then often called "Rekhta." Instead, he translated it into "commonly used Hindi[-Urdu]" (*Hindi-i mutaʿārif* [ʿAbd al-Qādir 1829, preface]). Where other translators would have employed Arabic or Persian words to denote key Qur'ānic terms, ʿAbd al-Qādir went out of his way to find indigenous terms for them. For instance, Walī Allāh had rendered the Qur'ānic word *al-ṣamad,* an attribute used to describe God

4 See *Qur'ān-i majīd chahār tarjama* (1882), which contains Rafīʿ al-Dīn's translation as the third of the four printed together.

("Eternal," "Self-sufficient"; Q 112:2) as *bī-niyāz* and Rafīʿ al-Dīn as *bī-iḥtiyāj*, using respectively a Persian and an Arabic term for it. ʿAbd al-Qādir, however, chose a Sanskrit term for it: *niradhar* ("without support"). And he translated the term *al-furqān* in Q 2:53 ("Remember when We gave Moses the scripture and the means to distinguish [right and wrong] (*al-furqān*), so that you might be guided") with the Hindi term *chakwatī* ("decision," "settlement").[5] Walī Allāh had translated *al-furqān* as *ḥujjat* (Arabic *ḥujja*: "proof") and Rafīʿ al-Dīn as *muʿjiza* (an Arabic term often understood as "miracle").[6] ʿAbd al-Qādir's translation was not merely an exercise in virtuosity—to show that he could produce a rendering of the Qurʾān that avoided Arabic and Persian loan words and could therefore be reckoned a "genuine" Hindi-Urdu translation. It is best seen, rather, as an effort to make the Qurʾān intelligible to people in their putative idiom, without the expectation that they would know the religious connotations of particular Arabic and Persian terms.

Shāh ʿAbd al-ʿAzīz's commentary, too, had employed "simple Persian language in accordance with the common usage of this land" (ʿAbd al-ʿAzīz 1886, 3). Like his father, he was also in the habit of giving public lessons (*waʿ ẓ*) on the Qurʾān. He would do that every Tuesday and Friday, and "thousands" of people would attend the sessions (ʿAbd al-Raḥmān 1875, 28–29). The learned ones in the audience would bring particular classical exegetical works with them and be called upon by ʿAbd al-ʿAzīz to say how a Rāzī (d. 606/1210), an Ibn al-ʿArabī (d. 638/1240), or a Bayḍāwī (d. 710/1310)—all commentators of great authority—had explicated a particular passage, to be followed by ʿAbd al-ʿAzīz's own explanations. The sermons in question are said to have been accessible to the ordinary believers, too (ʿAbd al-Raḥmān 1875, 29). To underscore the continuity of such sessions with his father's, ʿAbd al-ʿAzīz had begun his lessons where Walī Allāh had left off, at Q 5:8 ("… adhere to justice, for that is closer to awareness of God"). And Shāh Muḥammad Isḥāq (d. 1846), a maternal grandson of ʿAbd al-ʿAzīz and a distinguished scholar in his own right, would later commence his lessons precisely where ʿAbd al-ʿAzīz had left off, at Q 49:13 ("… In God's eyes, the most honoured of you are the ones most mindful of Him" [ʿAbd al-Raḥmān 1875, 30]). Engagement with the Qurʾān for the benefit of ordinary believers was something of a family enterprise for Walī Allāh, his sons, and some of their descendants. As if to underscore this, some printed editions

5 On the meaning and early usage of these terms, see Ṣiddīqī et al., 1977–2010, 19: 856 (*niradhar*); ibid., 7: 522 (*chakwatī*). Translations from the Qurʾān in this chapter follow Abdel Haleem 2004, with occasional modification.

6 For a useful list of the Hindi-Urdu terms used in the translation, see Khālid 2016, 104–10, 154–213.

of the Qur'ān carried three translations simultaneously: Walī Allāh's and Rafī' al-Dīn's interlineally, and 'Abd al-Qādir's in the margins, together with the explanatory notes that both Walī Allāh and 'Abd al-Qādir had provided to their respective translations (*Qur'ān-i majīd* 1872).

3 The Rhetoric of Authority

Although a good deal of the work on the Qur'ān by Walī Allāh and his successors was intended for a broad, non-scholarly audience, it was backed by claims to religious authority that seem intended to satisfy even the most demanding of Ṣūfī and scholarly rivals. Such claims are not uncommon in the writings of some of Walī Allāh's predecessors.[7] They may reasonably be assumed nonetheless to have helped garner scholarly attention even to works not primarily intended for a scholarly audience. Walī Allāh was not diffident in his assertions. In his brief treatise on the principles of exegesis, he employed a distinctly Ṣūfī idiom to note several times that an understanding of matters relating to the Qur'ān had been "unveiled" (*fatḥ*) to him or "poured down from the sea of divine effulgence" upon him (Walī Allāh n.d., *al-Fawz*, 32, 35).[8] In matters of exegesis, he said, he had approximated the rank enjoyed by a master jurist in his school of law (*mujtahid fi l-madhhab*). Indeed, "I am a direct student of the Qur'ān, insomuch as I am an Uwaysī of the Prophet's unveiling spirit" [Walī Allāh n.d., *al-Fawz*, 35; Walī Allāh 1914, 71]).[9] Speaking at the end of the book about some special mystical qualities (*khawāṣṣ*) of the Qur'ān, Walī Allāh noted that "a new door [to such forms of knowledge] has been opened to ... [me]. God the exalted once put His beautiful names (*asmā'-yi ḥusnā*), the great verses (*āyāt-i 'uẓmā*), and the blessed supplications beside me and said that all this was His gift for my use. However, every verse and [divine] name and supplication is tied to conditions that cannot be encompassed in any guiding

7 Shaykh Aḥmad Sirhindī (d. 1034/1624), is one notable example of such claims. See Friedmann 2000, 23–31.

8 On the sense of *fatḥ* (literally: opening) as mystical unveiling in the work of Ibn al-'Arabī, a significant influence on Walī Allāh, see Chittick 1989, xii–xiv, 168–70, 222. Cf. ibid., 378 on "the Prophet [as] the possessor of perfect unveiling."

9 Walī Allāh's reference here is to Uways al-Qarnī, a contemporary of the Prophet Muḥammad, who had become a "Companion" of the Prophet without having ever met him. While Ṣūfīs are typically tied to one another through formal initiation at the hands of a Ṣūfī master into a particular order, the Uwaysīs comprise an order of their own that does not depend on formal Ṣūfī genealogies. Although he referred to himself as an Uwaysī in this instance, Walī Allāh had been initiated into the major Ṣūfī orders of the time. For a similar claim by Shaykh Aḥmad Sirhindī, see Friedmann 2000, 28.

principle [for it]. Its guiding principle is rather that one wait for an indication from the world of the unseen.… [Till then,] the verse or divine name in question should be recited as stipulated by the experts of recitation" (Walī Allāh, *Fawz* n.d., 40–41; Walī Allāh 1914, 83; Walī Allāh 1985, 80).[10] This formulation seeks to preserve the exegetical tradition but it reserves for a Walī Allāh the authority to reorient it. That, of course, is precisely what he had attempted to do in this treatise on the principles of exegesis and in many other works.

That Walī Allāh has come to be seen as a crucial link in the onward transmission of religious learning from earlier times is also an important basis of his authority. Despite a thriving book culture, the authenticity and authority of *ḥadīth* texts has continued well into modern times to depend on a chain of identifiable human links going back all the way to Muḥammad (Graham 1993). In early modern South Asia, Walī Allāh was among the most prestigious of these links (Najībābādī 1986, 1: 35–36). That authority would be inherited by his sons and successors, to whom significant other claims are attributed as well. An anecdote about Shāh ʿAbd al-Qādir, which occurs in a hagiographical work concerned largely with his brother, Shāh ʿAbd al-ʿAzīz, is worth noting here. One Shams al-Dīn, an associate of ʿAbd al-Qādir, once had a dream in which he saw the latter address a wall facing him with a startling command: "'If I am a true prophet (*nabī-yi ṣādiq*), then testify to my prophethood (*nubuwwat*).' Suddenly, there was an agitation in the wall and a voice called out of it: 'You are a true prophet.'" On being told about this dream, ʿAbd al-Qādir is said to have taken it as a sign that his translation of the Qurʾān had, indeed, found favour with God (ʿAbd al-Raḥmān 1875, 18–19). When such stories had originated is not clear, but their scandal-free circulation in the late nineteenth century, at a time when Mirzā Ghulām Aḥmad (d. 1908), the founder of the Aḥmadī community, was busy articulating his own prophetical claims in the Punjab, is extraordinary. To the hagiographer who reported it a century and a half ago, there is nothing remarkable about it other than an affirmation of his protagonist's eminence. Shāh ʿAbd al-ʿAzīz is quoted by the same hagiographer as saying that "two streams flowed on [his] … shoulders from the Preserved Tablet" when he discoursed on the Qurʾān on the appointed days. He experienced no such effulgence (*fayḍān*) at other times and could not even answer people's questions about what he had said on those occasions (ʿAbd al-Raḥmān 1875, 29–30).[11]

10 I draw on the Urdu and English translations of this passage, but my translation of the Persian diverges in some respects from them. Also see Baljon 1986, 149–50.

11 The Preserved Tablet (Q 85.22) is commonly understood to refer to the primordial record of all scriptures as well as of privileged knowledge, including people's destinies. On its invocation in Ṣūfī circles, see Schimmel 1975, 101–2, 194, 224, 414.

4 Print and Patronage

In nineteenth-century India, the technology of print helped bolster and broadcast claims to religious authority in unprecedented ways. There is some uncertainty about when ʿAbd al-Qādir's translation of the Qurʾān was printed for the very first time, but the edition produced in 1829 is widely recognised as among the earliest. The influence of that translation as well as of other writings by Walī Allāh and his sons and successors owes much to the technology of print.

The publication of the 1829 edition was at the initiative of one Sayyid ʿAbdallāh, a disciple of Sayyid Aḥmad of Rae Bareli (d. 1831). Sayyid Aḥmad had spent some time under the tutelage of Shāh ʿAbd al-Qādir and he went on to organise a movement to purify Muslim beliefs and practices in light of what he saw as authentic Islamic teachings. He was joined in the effort by Shāh Muḥammad Ismāʿīl (d. 1831), Walī Allāh's grandson. ʿAbd al- Ḥayy (d. 1828), who was married to a daughter of Shāh ʿAbd al-ʿAzīz, also became part of the movement. These men, together with a number of Sayyid Aḥmad's disciples, traveled to Mecca for pilgrimage in 1822–24. Also accompanying them was Sayyid ʿAbdallāh, who would go on to publish ʿAbd al-Qādir's translation at the insistance of ʿAbd al- Ḥayy and of Shāh Muḥammad Isḥāq, a grandson of ʿAbd al-ʿAzīz (Sayyid ʿAbdallāh, "Khātima," in ʿAbd al-Qādir 1829).[12] Some years after his return from the pilgrimage, Sayyid Aḥmad of Rae Bareli made what turned out to be a failed effort to establish a polity on India's northwest frontier. He, Shāh Muḥammad Ismāʿīl, and a number of their followers died there fighting the Sikhs in 1831.[13]

Over the course of the nineteenth century, ʿAbd al-Qādir's translation would be printed numerous times, sometimes independently but often, as noted, with those of Walī Allāh and Rafīʿ al-Dīn and in combination with some other, older works.[14] It was this translation that Christian missionaries in India chose to publish in Roman transliteration, first in 1844 and again in 1876, illustrating the authority it had come to enjoy in the years since its first appearance in print. As the Reverend T.P. Hughes noted in his preface to the 1876 edition:

12 Sayyid ʿAbdallāh's "Epilogue" (*khātima*) is appended to ʿAbd al-Qādir's translation. It is not paginated.

13 On the life and career of Sayyid Aḥmad, see Gaborieau 2010; Gaborieau 2013. On Sayyid ʿAbdallāh, see Gaborieau 2010, 155–56.

14 For one notable example, see *Qurʾān-i majīd chahār tarjama* 1882. Besides the Persian rendering by Walī Allāh and those in Urdu by Rafīʿ al-Dīn and ʿAbd al-Qādir, this work also contains a translation ascribed to the great Persian poet and moralist Saʿdī, as well as a work said to be by him on the "occasions of revelation." On this work, see Blumhardt 1909, 217.

> Although there is no *authorized* translation of the Qurān in any language, that by Abdul Qādir is held in high estimation by learned Muslims.... A quotation from this translation will, therefore, be accepted by Muhammadan doctors as being a correct rendering of the original Arabic and it is hoped that its publication will be of some service to the Christian Evangelist, as it will enable him to quote the Quran in idiomatic Urdu from a translation of admitted authority....
>
> *THE QURĀN* 1876, iii

In another telling indication of ʿAbd al-Qādir's stature, a commentary was circulating in his name in late nineteenth-century India. Although its publisher took great pains to highlight its importance, it is considered by most scholars to have been misattributed to ʿAbd al-Qādir.[15]

The translation, as opposed to the spurious commentary, that ʿAbd al-Qādir produced was a more widely published work than Walī Allāh's was destined to be. The latter, however, was the more eminent scholar and some of ʿAbd al-Qādir's authority no doubt owed itself to his illustrious father's. In turn, the success of ʿAbd al-Qādir's translation may have contributed to the appeal of his father's writings. Those writings, too, had found some enterprising publishers in mid-to-late nineteenth-century India. A notable instance is represented by Muḥammad Aḥsan Ṣiddīqī (d. 1895) and his stepson ʿAbd al-Aḥad (d. 1920).

Ṣiddīqī, a versatile scholar and entrepreneur, taught Persian at colleges in Benaras and Bareilly before and after the Mutiny of 1857, which marked the last major challenge to the formal onset of colonial rule in India. While a number of prominent religious scholars, including those who would go on to found the famous madrasa at Deoband in 1866, are known to have participated in the events of the Mutiny, Ṣiddīqī was opposed to it. In fact, he preached against it, which caused much public anger in Bareilly and forced him to temporarily leave the town (Qādirī 1966, 50–51).[16] It was in the same town that he subsequently established a printing press, the Maṭbaʿ-i Ṣiddīqī, and it was there that he published Walī Allāh's magnum opus, the *Ḥujjat Allāh al-bāligha*, in 1869. Ṣiddīqī's edition was subsequently published from Egypt

15 (Pseudo)-ʿAbd al-Qādir n. d. [1890]. See the poem on p. 180 underscoring its importance and its usefulness for the scholar and the ordinary believer alike, including women and children. Also see the poem on the back cover. On the misattribution, see Qāsimī 1977, part 2, appended to the volume with independent pagination, 73–75.

16 The most detailed account of Ṣiddīqī's life is Qādirī 1966. Qādirī refers to Ṣiddīqī as Muḥammad Aḥsan Nānotawī, with reference to his hometown; but he had usually referred to himself as Muḥammad Aḥsan Ṣiddīqī, which is how I, too, will refer to him. As will be evident from the following, I am deeply indebted to Qādirī's learned work.

as well, complete with occasional Persian glosses to explain difficult Arabic terms.[17] Ṣiddīqī also edited and published in 1869 Walī Allāh's *Izālat al-khafāʾ ʿan khilāfat al-khulafāʾ*, a major work on the virtues of the caliphs Abū Bakr and ʿUmar, the first two successors of the prophet Muḥammad, in which Walī Allāh vigorously defended them against Shīʿī critiques of their legitimacy.[18] Neither book had been printed in India before that time. Both the *Ḥujjat Allāh al-bāligha* and the *Izālat al-khafāʾ* were published under the patronage of the chief minister of the Indian princely state of Bhopal.[19] That these works were published just over a decade after the Mutiny, at a time when the Muslims of India were under a dark cloud for their role in its events, is worth noting here. With his loyalist credentials established during the Mutiny, Ṣiddīqī may have had the political cover to pursue his publishing activities and, in the process, to promote Walī Allāh's writings. There was nothing subversive about those writings, so far as the British were concerned. Yet, for loyalist devotees of Walī Allāh's legacy, there may be some irony in the fact that his son ʿAbd al-Qādir's translation had found one of its earliest publishers in what the colonial authorities had come to see with great misgivings as "Wahhābī" circles. And Bhopal's own first spouse—the noted scholar Ṣiddīq Ḥasan Khān (d. 1890), consort of the Begum of Bhopal—would be deprived in the mid-1880s of his royal titles by the British, on suspicion of his connection to Wahhābī networks.

Ṣiddīqī was also a translator. Among Walī Allāh's works, he translated an Arabic treatise on *ijtihād* into Urdu (Qādirī 1966, 143). He also produced an Urdu translation of al-Ghazālī's (d. 505/1111) most famous work, *Iḥyāʾ ʿulūm al-dīn*; fittingly perhaps, in view of his devotion to the Walī Allāh family, the Qurʾānic passages from that book were given in Urdu in the translation of Shāh ʿAbd al-Qādir (Ṣiddīqī 1913, 1: 3 [preface]). Unusual among traditionally-educated scholars of his age, Ṣiddīqī knew English and he is said to have also translated Godfrey Higgins' early nineteenth-century book on the prophet Muḥammad (Higgins 1829; Qādirī 1966, 141–42).[20]

17 For the Indian edition, see Walī Allāh 1869 and for the Egyptian edition, Walī Allāh 1877. For the publication date of the latter edition, see 2: 201; and Kāndhlawī 2001, 76–77.

18 On the publication date of Ṣiddīqī's edition, see the publisher's note to Walī Allāh n.d., *Izāla*, Urdu translation (Karachi: Muḥammad Saʿīd, n.d.), 1: 3.

19 See Walī Allāh 1976, 2: 284. On the chief minister, Muḥammad Jamāl al-Dīn (d. 1881), see Preckel 2000, 70.

20 The Urdu translation gives the translator's name as ʿAbd al-Wadūd, although Qādirī 1966, 141, identifies it as in fact the work of Ṣiddīqī. The latter is said to have been embroiled in some controversies at the time and thought it politic not to take credit for the translation. The translation, according to Qādirī, was done at the instance of Sayyid Aḥmad Khān (d. 1898), the pioneering modernist of the late nineteenth century. I have not been able to see the Urdu translation: *Ḥimāyat-i Islām* (Bareilly: no publisher, 1873).

Following in the footsteps of his stepfather, ʿAbd al-Aḥad too was a scholar in his own right as well as a publisher. He was the proprietor of the Maṭbaʿ-i Mujtabāʾī, and it was at his insistance that Ṣiddīqī had edited some of the writings of Walī Allāh as well as the *fatwā* collection of Shāh ʿAbd al-ʿAzīz (Qādirī 1966, 148–49).[21] Among ʿAbd al-Aḥad's own writings was a history of Arabic literature (ʿAbd al-Aḥad 1909) and a two-volume compilation, in Urdu translation, of the discourses of the leading Ṣūfī masters of the Chishtī order (ʿAbd al-Aḥad 1901). ʿAbd al-Aḥad's loyalism went much further than his stepfather's. At the outset of World War I, he had actively supported the war effort, helped with the colonial regime's recruitment efforts, contributed to the war fund, and even given a loan to the government as part of that effort (Qādirī 1966, 165). The honours he received in turn from the government seem to have become a liability for him by the time the war ended. A movement in defence of the Ottoman caliphate, which had fought Britain and the Entente Powers and faced collapse and dismemberment upon its defeat in the war, galvanised British India as nothing else had. Loyalists like ʿAbd al-Aḥad, who had become rich because of business success but presumably also on account of the government's patronage, could not have had many sympathisers among the masses of people drawn to the Khilāfat movement. In a poignant illustration of just how strongly anti-colonial the popular mood had become, ʿAbd al-Aḥad's funeral procession, in 1920, itself was disrupted by some people (Qādirī 1966, 165–68).

Maḥmūd Ḥasan, the noted Deoband scholar, had also died that same year, 1920. His politics were at the opposite end of the spectrum from ʿAbd al-Aḥad's: until shortly before his death, Maḥmūd Ḥasan had been interned on the island of Malta on account of having been associated with a pan-Islamic anti-colonial effort that had taken him to the Ḥijāz in 1915. He had returned to India to a hero's welcome in 1920. During his internment, Maḥmūd Ḥasan had completed an Urdu translation of the Qurʾān. Published posthumously, it is arguably among the most influential of the Qurʾān's Urdu renderings today. Even before he had left India on his ill-fated anti-colonial enterprise, there was the expectation in some publishing circles that his translation would bring dividends to the Deoband madrasa.[22] By the time he returned to India, his religious and political stature was such that the madrasa's publishing house had decided to put out just the introduction to the translation, with the translation itself to be published later (Ḥasan n.d., *Muqaddima*).

---

21 Ṣiddīqī also translated Walī Allāh's *al-Inṣāf fī bayān sabab al-ikhtilāf*, a work on juristic disagreements in early Islam. The book was published by the Maṭbaʿ-i Mujtabāʾī in 1889. See Qādirī 1966, 142–43.

22 The National Archives, UK: FO 686/149: Silk Letters Case (Statement by Matlub-ur-Raḥmān, 25 September, 1916), 221–22.

The translation, as Maḥmūd Ḥasan made clear in the introduction, was based on that of Shāh 'Abd al-Qādir. Indeed, as he saw it, the principal justification for attempting a new translation at all was that many of the words 'Abd al-Qādir had used in his work were no longer easily understood by ordinary people and some of 'Abd al-Qādir's renderings had been rather too concise for their meaning to be entirely clear (Ḥasan n.d., 6).[23] The Deoband scholar's self-appointed task, then, was to update 'Abd al-Qādir's language and expression, but he had been guided even in that effort by 'Abd al-Qādir's translation as a whole and, to a lesser extent, by Walī Allāh's (Ḥasan n.d., 6). This is not pro forma modesty, expressed merely to justify a new translation, for Maḥmūd Ḥasan's rendering does hew very closely to 'Abd al-Qādir's. Maḥmūd Ḥasan's decision to follow 'Abd al-Qādir in this manner testifies to the classic status that the latter's work had achieved by then. Yet it was hardly inevitable, of course, that Maḥmūd Ḥasan should have done this. For instance, an Urdu translation of the Qur'ān by Ashraf 'Alī Thānawī (d. 1943), a highly influential jurist and Ṣūfī contemporary of Maḥmūd Ḥasan from within the circles associated with the Deoband madrasa and the Sunnī doctrinal orientation spawned by it, speaks deferentially of 'Abd al-Qādir's work but shows no comparable dependence on it (cf. Thānawī 1978, 1: 3 n. 1). Maḥmūd Ḥasan's translation was not merely an expression of marked deference to 'Abd al-Qādir, however. It served equally to *replace* it. Once the style and language of 'Abd al-Qādir had been suitably updated for a contemporary audience, and new glosses had been added by both Maḥmūd Ḥasan and another Deobandī stalwart, Shabbīr Aḥmad 'Uthmānī (d. 1949), 'Abd al-Qādir's *Mūḍiḥ al-Qur'ān* would retain only antiquarian appeal. Anyone interested simply in understanding the Qur'ān—rather than in consulting, say, an early Urdu specimen of it—would find Maḥmūd Ḥasan's work to be the best guide.

Yet even as the earlier work was effectively replaced by Maḥmūd Ḥasan's, the very conspicuous acknowledgment of the latter's dependence on the former served also to affirm the bond between Walī Allāh and his sons, on the one hand, and the Deobandīs, on the other. Despite considerable ambivalence towards Walī Allāh in some Deobandī circles, as has been observed, he remains the most important figure in the intellectual genealogy of the Deobandī orientation. Then there are those who have embraced him without reservation. The most notable among them was 'Ubayd Allāh Sindhī (d. 1944), a Sikh convert to Islam who was Maḥmūd Ḥasan's student at Deoband and subsequently the

23 My references to the introduction are to the text as it forms part of the Qur'ān translation. That text diverges only superficially from the separately published *Muqaddima* (Ḥasan n.d. [ca. 1920]).

ringleader of the abortive anti-colonial movement that had taken Maḥmūd Ḥasan out of India. Later in his career, Sindhī would write books in explication of Walī Allāh's thought as well as more than one commentary on the Qurʾān.[24] The Deobandī establishment has never warmed to Sindhī, although its members have often tried, with varying degrees of success, to disentangle Walī Allāh, and even Maḥmūd Ḥasan, from him. In any case, the fact that the bond between Walī Allāh and the Deobandīs that Maḥmūd Ḥasan had worked to strengthen rested on the Qurʾān meant that other Deobandis could continue to benefit from it without having to accept the full package of Walī Allāh's oeuvre.

As noted, Maḥmūd Ḥasan's translation has come to acquire the status of a modern classic among South Asian translations of the Qurʾān. In the mid-1940s, it was translated into Persian by a team of Afghan *ʿulamāʾ* under the patronage of the Afghan king, Ẓāhir Shāh (r. 1933–73). That work has been reprinted several times, often under the title of the *Kābul tafsīr*. The subtitle of the 1996 edition—"From the Sunnī Viewpoint" (*az dīdgāh-i ahl-i sunnat*)—suggests some of the authority it is meant to carry as representing *the* Sunnī perspective.[25] It was Maḥmūd Ḥasan's Urdu translation, too, that the Saudis chose to publish in a new edition in 1993 as part of their programme to disseminate the Qurʾān in reliable local translations throughout the world (*al-Qurʾān al-karīm* 1993).

5 Conclusion

Three points are worth noting in concluding this brief study. First, my attention in this chapter to the impact of print and patronage, of claims to authority, and efforts of devotees to promote particular authors and their work should not be construed as suggesting that the success and influence of these authors and their works are necessarily reducible to those factors. Walī Allāh's Persian translation of the Qurʾān and ʿAbd al-Qādir's *Mūḍiḥ al-Qurʾān* are important achievements in their own right. Walī Allāh's *Ḥujjat Allāh al-bāligha* is a major contribution to *ḥadīth* and legal studies and it can be justly counted among

24 On the abortive movement, see Zaman 2012, 11–14; on Sindhī's work on the Qurʾān, ibid., 223–30.

25 The original edition, which I have not seen, was titled: *Qurʾān-i majīd ba-tarjama o tafsīr, ba-amr-i pādshāh-i sharīʿat parwar al-mutawakkil ʿala l-lāh aʿlā-ḥaẓrat Muḥammad Ẓāhir Shāh, pādashāh-i Afghanistān, taḥt-i naẓar-i hayʾatī az ʿulamāʾ-yi īn kishwar, az tarjama o tafsīr-i ḥaẓrat shaykh al-Hind Maḥmūd Ḥasan Deobandī* …, 6 vols., Kabul: Maṭbaʿ-i ʿumumī-yi Kābul, 1944. Later editions, published in 1966 and 1996, have continued to be published in six volumes. For the most recent edition, see *Tafsīr-i Kābulī* 1996.

the most important works ever written on how sacred law ought to be understood in terms of the human interests it putatively serves. Similar claims could be made of some of his other writings as well. Put another way, the attention Walī Allāh has received in modern Muslim circles is well justified by the depth and subtlety of his work. Nonetheless, as any publisher or publicist knows, the intrinsic quality of a work does not necessarily suffice to bring attention to it, let alone to make it a classic. It takes a great deal of work *besides* intellectual labour to do so. Thus it was not inevitable, in light only of their intellectual merit, that Walī Allāh's Persian translation of the Qur'ān, or ʿAbd al-Qādir's *Mūḍiḥ al-Qur'ān,* or Maḥmūd Ḥasan's Urdu rendition should have become as influential as they did. Other competing works had their own merits, and it is by examining some of the ways in which particular writings were promoted—by the authors themselves and by their successors—that we gain some understanding of their relative success and influence.

Second, some of the examples provided in this paper are suggestive of how, intentionally or not, claims to authority can be piled up on one another to powerful cumulative effect. That no less than three full translations of the Qur'ān, as well as a substantial, if partial, commentary should have been produced between Walī Allāh and three of his sons adds up to a quite remarkable body of work. Many even among those who had not read any of those writings are likely to have found this amount of focussed work impressive, even intimidating. Equally impressive were the mystical claims that accompanied this and related work—of an understanding of the Qur'ān cast into one's heart from on high, distinctive forms of knowledge gifted by God to the exegete, and so forth. Mystical claims were bolstered by those of impeccable scholarship: already before the Mutiny of 1857, as observed, Christian missionaries had thought it politic to utilise ʿAbd al-Qādir's rendering in their polemics on Islam on the grounds that no one could then accuse them of having mistranslated the Qur'ān.

Finally, although it might be tempting to trace a direct line from Walī Allāh and his sons to certain scripturalist circles of the late nineteenth and the twentieth centuries, Walī Allāh's world stands in fact at a considerable distance from the latter. For instance, the Salafīs, who have often seen him as a progenitor and have published many of his writings, have tended to ignore his mysticism.[26] His mystical discourses have ruffled other feathers, too. In his *Fuyūḍ al-ḥaramayn*, Walī Allāh had observed that many Ṣūfī saints were

26 Several of Walī Allāh's books were published by the Maṭbaʿa al-Salafiyya of Cairo, among them *ʿIqd al-jīd fī aḥkām al-ijtihād wa-l-taqlīd* (1965) and *al-Inṣāf fī bayān sabab al-ikhtilāf* (1965). The Maktaba al-Salafiyya of Lahore, too, has published some of his writings, among them *al-Fawz al-kabīr fī uṣūl al-tafsīr* (1951) and *Qurrat al-ʿaynayn fī tafḍīl al-shaykhayn* (1976).

recipients of inspiration (*ilhām*) from on high, to the effect that God had excused them from the *sharīʿa* obligations that were otherwise binding. His father, too, Walī Allāh said, had received such inspiration. Yet he had continued in the performance of his *sharīʿa* obligations, although without questioning the validity of the inspiration in question. Walī Allāh's point was that, for the elect, the *sharīʿa*'s commands tended to become second nature, so that they discharged them even without being required to do so (Walī Allāh n.d., *Fuyūḍ*, 23–24; cf. Jalbani 1967, 69). It is telling that Amīn Aḥsan Iṣlāḥī (d. 1997), a noted exegete who was once associated with the Jamāʿat-i Islāmī of Sayyid Abū l-Aʿlā Mawdūdī (d. 1979), found this to be an abhorrent idea, and he went to some length in reprimanding Walī Allāh for it in unusually strong terms (Iṣlāḥī 1977, 65–71.).

Another example is also instructive. In speaking of the Qurʾān's aesthetic qualities, Walī Allāh invoked Indian ragas—which he had heard country folk perform—and noted that what people had in common was their ability to find pleasure in melody, although the principles governing it and their particular tastes necessarily varied from place to place (Walī Allāh n.d., *Fawz*, 30; Walī Allāh 1914, 60–61). Given their longstanding misgivings about music, such comments would probably not sit well with puritanical reformers, least of all in discussions of Qurʾānic aesthetics. For his part, Shāh ʿAbd al-ʿAzīz had "complete mastery in the science of music" (ʿAbd al-Raḥmān 1875, 24); he had also written a treatise on the subject. Once again, a mid-twentieth-century scholar candidly admitted that his "reverence [for ʿAbd al-ʿAzīz] had yet to allow an acceptance of the work's attribution" to him (Barakātī 1976, 58). The point is not, of course, that Walī Allāh and his sons were unconcerned with boundaries between Islam and other faiths or—despite what he said about *sharīʿa* obligations in relation to saintly figures—that they were indifferent to *sharīʿa* norms. It is rather that their understanding of Islam was closer in at least some important ways to that of the cultural elite of their own age than it was to that of the scripturalists of a later era (cf. Alam 2004, 171–72). And yet, in their sustained attention to the Qurʾān and to the study of *ḥadīth*, Walī Allāh and his immediate successors were not typical of their age either. Their legacy in those areas would allow later reformers to claim them more successfully for their particular causes than might have been possible otherwise.

Bibliography

ʿAbd al-Aḥad. 1901. *Panj ganj: Malfūẓāt-i khawājagān-i Chisht-i ahl-i bihisht*. 2 vols. Delhi: Maṭbaʿ-i Mujtabāʾī.

ʿAbd al-Aḥad. 1909. *ʿArabī adab kī taʾrīkh*. Delhi: Maṭbaʿ-i Mujtabāʾī.

ʿAbd al-ʿAzīz, Shāh. 1886. *Tafsīr-i ʿAzīzī*. Bombay: Maṭbaʿ-i Fatḥ al-Karīm.

Abdel Haleem, M.A.S. 2004. *The Qurʾān: A New Translation*. Oxford: Oxford University Press.

ʿAbd al-Qādir, Shāh. 1829. *Mūḍiḥ al-Qurʾān*. Calcutta: Maṭbaʿ-i Aḥmadī. British Library, London, MS 14507.d.16. Accessed through the Princeton University Library, http://library.princeton.edu, 2 July 2017.

(Pseudo-)ʿAbd al-Qādir, Shāh. n.d. [1890]. *Tafsīr-i Mawlānā Shāh ʿAbd al-Qādir al-maʿrūf ba-Mūḍiḥ al-Qurʾān*. Delhi: Maṭbaʿ-i Aḥmadī. British Library, London, MS 14507.c.18. Accessed through the Princeton University Library, http://library.princeton.edu, 19 July 2017.

ʿAbd al-Raḥmān, Muḥammad. 1875. *Maqālāt-i ṭarīqat maʿrūf ba-faẓāʾil-i ʿAzīziyya*. Hyderabad: Maṭbaʿ-i Matīn Kartān. (http://digitool.library.mcgill.ca/webclient/DeliveryManager?&pid=108856 [accessed 16 July 2017]).

Alam, Muzaffar. 2004. *The Languages of Political Islam: India 1200–1800*. Chicago: University of Chicago Press.

Baljon, J.M.S. 1986. *Religion and Thought of Shāh Walī Allāh Dihlawī, 1703–1762*. Leiden: E.J. Brill.

Barakātī, Maḥmūd Aḥmad. 1976. *Shāh Walī Allāh awr unkā khānadān*. Lahore: Majlis-i ishāʿat-i Islām.

Blumhardt, J.F. 1909. *A Supplementary Catalogue of Hindustani Books in the Library of the British Museum Acquired during the Years 1889–1908*. London: The British Museum.

Chaghatai, M. Ikram (ed.). 2005. *Shah Waliullah (1703–1762): His Religious and Political Thought*. Lahore: Sang-e-Meel Publications.

Chittick, William C. 1989. *The Ṣūfī Path of Knowledge: Ibn al-ʿArabi's Metaphysics of Imagination*. Albany: State University of New York Press.

Friedmann, Yohanan. 2000. *Shaykh Aḥmad Sirhindi: An Outline of his Thought and a Study of his Image in the Eyes of Posterity*. Delhi: Oxford University Press.

Gaborieau, Marc. 2010. *Le Mahdi incompris: Sayyid Aḥmad Barelwi (1786–1831) et le millénarisme en Inde*. Paris: CNRS Éditions.

Gaborieau, Marc. 2013. "Barelwī, Sayyid Aḥmad." *Encyclopedia of Islam, THREE*.

Graham, William A. 1993. "Traditionalism in Islam: An Essay in Interpretation." *Journal of Interdisciplinary History* 23: 495–522.

Ḥasan, Maḥmūd (trans.). n.d. *Ḥamāʾil sharīf mutarjam*. Bijnor: Madīna Press.

Ḥasan, Maḥmūd. n.d. *Muqaddima-i tarjama-i Qurʾān-i majīd*. Deoband: Maṭbaʿ-i Qāsimī (ca. 1920).

Hermansen, Marcia. 1996. Trans. *The Conclusive Argument from God: Shāh Walī Allāh's Ḥujjat Allāh al-bāligha*. Leiden: Brill.

Hermansen, Marcia. 2005. "The Current State of Shāh Walī Allāh Studies." In M. Ikram Chaghatai (ed.), *Shah Waliullah (1703–1762): His Religious and Political Thought*. Lahore: Sang-e-Meel Publications, 683–93.

Higgins, Godfrey. 1829. *An Apology for the Life and Character of the Celebrated Prophet of Arabia, Called Mohamed, or the Illustrious*. London: Rowland Hunter.

Iqbal, Mohammad. 1934. *The Reconstruction of Religious Thought in Islam*. London: Oxford University Press.

Iṣlaḥī, Amīn Aḥsan. 1977. *Tazkiya-i nafs*. Faisalabad: Malik Sons.

Jalbani, G.N. 1967. *Teachings of Shāh Walīyullāh of Delhi*. Lahore: Sh. Muḥammad Ashraf.

Kāndhlawī, Nūr al-Ḥasan Rāshid. "Ḥujjat Allāh al-bāligha: Makhṭūṭāt, ṭibāʿat, takhrīij, ḥawāshī, tarājim." *Fikr o naẓar* 39: 2 (2001): 57–90.

Khālid, Muḥammad Salīm. 2016. *Shāh ʿAbd al-Qādir ke Urdu tarjama-i Qurʾān ka taḥqīqī o lisānī mutālaʿa*. Karachi: Idāra-i yādgār-i Ghālib.

Najībābādī, Muḥammad Ṣiddīq. 1986. *Anwār al-Maḥmūd ʿalā sunan Abī Dāwūd*. 2 vols. Karachi: Idārat al-Qurʾān wa-l-ʿulūm al-Islāmiyya.

Preckel, Claudia. 2000. "The Roots of Anglo-Muslim Cooperation and Islamic Reformism in Bhopal." In Jamal Malik (ed.), *Perspectives of Mutual Encounters in South Asian History 1760–1860*. Leiden: Brill, 65–78.

Qādirī, Muḥammad Ayyūb. 1966. *Mawlānā Muḥammad Aḥsan Nānotawī*. Karachi: Rohilkhand Literary Society.

Qāsimī, Akhlaq Ḥusayn. 1977. *Maḥāsin-i Mūḍiḥ al-Qurʾān*. Delhi: Idāra-i Raḥmat-i ʿālam.

al-Qurʾān al-karīm wa-tarjamat maʿānīhi wa-tafsīruhu ila l-lughat al-Urdiyya. 1993. Medina: Majmaʿ khādim al-ḥaramayn al-sharīfayn al-malik Fahd li-ṭibāʿat al-muṣḥaf al-sharīf.

Qurʾān-i majīd chahār tarjama maʿa shaʾn-i nuzūl-i Saʿdī. 1882. Delhi: Maṭbaʿ-i Mujtabāʾī. British Library, London, MS 14507.d.20. Accessed through the Princeton University Library, http://library.princeton.edu, 30 August 2017.

Qurʾān-i majīd-i mutarjam bil-tarājim al-thalāth. 1872. Delhi: Maṭbaʿ-i Mujtabāʾī.

The Qurān translated into the Urdu by Shaikh Abdul Qādir Ibn i Shāh Walī Ullah of Delhi, A.D. 1790. 1876. Lodiana: The Mission Press.

Rizvi, Saiyid Athar Abbas. 1982. *Shāh ʿAbd al-ʿAzīz: Puritanism, Sectarian Polemics, and Jihad*. Canberra: Maʿrifat Publishing House.

Rizvi, Saiyid Athar Abbas. 2004 [1980]. *Shāh Walī-Allāh and his Times*. Lahore: Suhail Academy.

Schimmel, Annemarie. 1975. *Mystical Dimensions of Islam*. Chapel Hill: University of North Carolina Press.

Ṣiddīqī, Abū l-Layth et al. 1977–2010. *Urdu lughat taʾrīkhī uṣūl par*. 22 vols. Karachi: Taraqqī-i Urdu Board.

Ṣiddīqī, Muḥammad Aḥsan. 1913[5]. *Madhāq al-ʿārifīn*. Urdu translation of Ghazālī, *Iḥyāʾ ʿulūm al-dīn*. 4 vols. Lucknow: Naval Kishore Press.

Sindhī, ʿUbayd Allāh. 1998 [1944]. *Shāh Walī Allāh awr unkā falsafa*. Compiled and edited by Muḥammad Sarwar. Lahore: Sindh Sāgar Academy.

Tafsīr-i Kābulī az dīdgah-i ahl-i sunnat. 1966. n.p.: Nashr-i iḥsān.

Thānawī, Ashraf ʿAlī. 1978. *Bayān al-Qurʾān*. 12 vols. Lahore: Maktabat al-Ḥasan.

Walī Allāh, Shāh. n.d. *Al-Fawz al-kabīr maʿa Fatḥ al-Khabīr fī uṣūl al-tafsīr*. Lahore: Maṭbaʿ-i ʿilmī.

Walī Allāh, Shāh. 1914. *Al-Fawz al-kabīr fī uṣūl al-tafsīr*. Translated into Urdu by Rashīd Aḥmad Anṣārī. Aligarh: Maṭbaʿ-i Aḥmadī.

Walī Allāh, Shāh. 1985. *Al-Fawz al-kabīr fī uṣūl al-tafsīr*. Translated by G.N. Jalbani. Islamabad: National Hijra Council.

Walī Allāh, Shāh. n.d. *Fuyūḍ al-Ḥaramayn*. Arabic text and Urdu translation. Delhi: Maṭbaʿ-i Aḥmadī.

Walī Allāh, Shāh. *Ḥujjat Allāh al-bāligha*. 1869. Ed. Muḥammad Aḥsan Ṣiddīqī. Bareilly: Maṭbaʿ-i Ṣiddīqī (http://archive.org/details/McGillLibrary-rbscislḤujjat BP160W31869-16842, accessed 21 July 2017).

Walī Allāh, Shāh. *Ḥujjat Allāh al-bāligha*. 1877. Ed. Muḥammad Aḥsan Ṣiddīqī. 2 vols. Cairo: al-Maṭbaʿa al-Miṣriyya.

Walī Allāh, Shāh. 1976. *Izālat al-khafāʾ ʿan khilāfat al-khulafāʾ*. Ed. Muḥammad Aḥsan Ṣiddīqī. 2 vols. Lahore: Suhayl Academy.

Walī Allāh, Shāh. 2001. *Al-Qurʾān al-karīm ba-tarjama ba-zabān-i fārsī*. Islamabad: Daʿwa Academy.

Walī Allāh, Shāh. 1967–70. *Al-Tafhīmāt al-Ilāhiyya*. Ed. Ghulām Muṣṭafā al-Qāsimī. 2 vols. Hyderabad: Shāh Walī Allāh Academy.

Zaman, Muḥammad Qasim. 2012. *Modern Islamic Thought in a Radical Age: Religious Authority and Internal Criticism*. Cambridge: Cambridge University Press.

PART 5

The Politics of Body and Gender

CHAPTER 14

#ItsMensTurn: Of Hashtags and Shīʿī Discourses in Iran

Katajun Amirpur

1 Introduction

In December 2009, a Facebook post put out this call to men: *Be a man, send us your photo as a woman.* Many men did, and what had not been intended by its instigators to be a display of solidarity with Iranian women was nevertheless interpreted as such and made global headlines. What became the media campaign *Men in Hijabs* was originally intended instead to display support for a particular man, Majīd Tavakkolī, who, on National Student Day, 8 December 2009, had given a speech decrying the crackdown on election fraud protests that summer and against oppression in general. He fled when police tried to arrest him, and the next day, FARS, a state news agency, published a photo of him in women's clothing.[1]

Showing Tavakkolī in female garb was a transparent reference to an incident involving Abolhasan Bani Sadr (b. 1933), the first president of the Islamic Republic. In fact, pictures of both men were published side by side by the news agency. It is alleged that a disgraced Bani Sadr fled Iran in 1981 disguised in a hijab, although doubt has been cast on this account. Bani Sadr, now living in Paris, has never commented on the matter, but the fact that he was not captured during his escape suggests that the photograph is likely to be a fake. The trope referred to here of a dissident fleeing disguised as a woman is a familiar one, and its use in this more recent incident was intended to send a message: there are no real men in the opposition. They are weaklings, women, in fact. The social media initiative *Men in Hijabs* turned this message on its head.

2 Rethinking Gender

Not only did *Men in Hijabs* deconstruct an important marker of the Islamic Republic, it provided an opportunity to rethink gender. It was aimed at an Iranian

1 http://www.farsnews.net/newstext.php?nn=8809171609, 8.12.2009. Accessed 24 November 2017.

 | DOI:10.1163/9789004386891_015

public both within and outside Iran. The community of exiles and expatriates is becoming ever more strongly joined with the community of Iranians at home, in a discourse community that constitutes itself as a "counter-public" (*Gegenöffentlichkeit*), in the sense defined by the German sociologist and philosopher Jürgen Habermas (b. 1929). Its forum is the Internet, which has broad penetration throughout Iran, a country with 46 million users. This online agora is still shaped mainly by exiles, but in dialogue with Iranians within the country.

It is because of this Internet community's function that the question of democracy is more strongly linked to that of women's rights in Iranian discourse today. Until a few years ago, that had simply not been the case. In the years following the Iranian revolution of 1978–79, the legal question of inequality was seen primarily as a women's problem, something that did not concern men and had no connection to the opposition's reform efforts. Women's issues were addressed exclusively by women (Mir-Hosseini 2002).

This phenomenon is remarkable not least because the opposite was true in pre-revolutionary Iranian discourse. Reformist thinkers of the 1960s and 1970s saw women's rights and the role of women in society as a matter that concerned them very much. The religious reform debate on the topic was opened by Ayatollah Morteżā Moṭahharī, in a widely read 33-part series of articles published between 1966 and 1967 in the popular journal *Zan-e Rūz* ("Today's Woman"). In it, Moṭahharī tried to frame a religious response to changing social circumstances and above all to the demands of young women from more traditional families that they be allowed to share in the rights and opportunities that more Westernised middle-class women enjoyed.

Moṭahharī took a middling position, arguing that Islam, if properly understood, was not opposed to women enjoying education, working outside the home, and actively determining their own lives. He cites the Prophet as an example who, when ʿAlī requested the hand of his daughter Fāṭima in marriage, responded that he would need to ask her (Moṭahharī 1994, 90). Moṭahharī also accommodates modernist positions with his statement that monogamous marriage represents the norm while polygamy is an exception. Nonetheless, he insists that polygamy may at times be necessary and that men and women in Islam do not enjoy equal rights (*tasāvī*), but only similar ones (*tashābeh*) (Moṭahharī 1994, 144).

The voice of Iranian sociologist ʿAlī Sharīʿatī (1933–77) was even more important in the discourse on women's role. Unlike Moṭahharī, he did not allow himself to be caught up in legal reasoning, but went to the heart of constructing a new prototype of Shīʿī womanhood in his famous lecture *Fāṭima is*

Fāṭima. It was presented in 1971 at the Ḥosayniyyeh Ershād, a scholarly centre that had been founded as a counterweight to the traditional institutions of Qom, which were seen as too remote from real-world concerns.

To Sharīʿatī, the Prophet's daughter represents the ideal woman. He draws her as a perfect mother and companion to her husband, but also as actively standing up for her rights, for example, when she faced down the first caliph, Abū Bakr, when he tried to expropriate her inherited estate at Fadak. Thus, Fāṭima is distinguished from what he calls "Western Twiggies," a type of woman Sharīʿatī disparages as ineffectually dependent on men. This does not mean he is setting up Fāṭima in contrast to European women as such. She has her Western counterpart in a scientist who, as he puts it, sacrifices a decade of her life to study the language of ants in the desert, which he considers a commendable pursuit. The European woman as Iranians know her through their glossy magazines, he insists, is a fiction found nowhere in Europe. What Iranians had presented to them as the European woman was instead an Iranian media product, a homemade montage (*sākht-e īrān, mūntāzh-e mellī*). Thus, Sharīʿatī at once criticises both the aspects of Western emancipation reaching Iran and traditional religiosity that reduces women to mere ceremonial mourners (Sharīʿatī 1990, 70–71).

In broad strokes we can say, though, that the Islamic Revolution's laws passed after 1979 enshrined the views of Ayatollah Ruhollah Khomeini (d. 1989) rather than those of Moṭahharī. Khomeini had laid down his position as early as 1961 in his *Tawżīḥ al-masāʾel*, a collection of *fatwā*s that he published in his role as a Source of Emulation (*marjaʿ*), to provide guidance to the faithful on what is permitted and what is forbidden. Khomeini allowed both polygamy and temporary marriage, viewed divorce as the privilege of men, and stated that women may not marry without the consent of their fathers or travel abroad without the permission of their husbands (Khomeini 1990, 334–35; 350).

3 The Female Voice, Male Support, and Calls for Justice

Although Khomeini's vision of ideal womanhood ended up becoming law, the vision laid out by Sharīʿatī was far more influential in the socialisation of many religious women. They were unwilling to settle for the role the government sanctioned for them as homemakers. One exemplar of these views is Shahla Sherkat (b. 1956), editor of the journal *Zanān* ("Women") since the early 1990s. *Zanān* initiated political campaigns, for example, calling for women to be allowed to stand for president. At the heart of its calls to action lay the demand to break the male monopoly on interpretation. It was not that the Qurʾān was patriarchal, the journal argued, but the problem lay in the reading of its interpreters, men whose perspective was shaped by their specific interests and prejudices. There was no such thing, the journal insisted, as an unprejudiced reading. The vocabulary used makes it unmistakably clear that the work of the German philosopher Hans-Georg Gadamer (1900–2002) plays an important role in this discourse. His stance on hermeneutics and the requisite terms had become widely known in Iran following the publication of a book on the subject by Iranian philosopher Moḥammad Shabestarī (b. 1936; Shabestarī 1996). Gadamer's thinking had also been adapted by the women of *Zanān* as the basis of their approach to Qurʾānic interpretation: One can understand a text and its meaning only by recognising the question the text answers, Gadamer had stated—and Shahla Sherkat agreed.

That the context must be included in the interpretation and that, above all, the female voice needs to be heard was the creed of the women's movement that had formed around *Zanān*. Accordingly, it seemed an abdication of principle when, in 2005, the campaign *One Million Signatures for Women's Rights* sought out the legal opinion of a male authority. The goal of the campaign was to collect a million signatures in order to pressure parliament into changing the law (Amirpur 2013, 97–125). The supporting *fatwā* of a senior male authority figure was intended to add weight to the campaign's demands. The principle of *taqlīd* (imitation, or emulation), which calls on the faithful to choose a religious authority to follow, could be a useful tool here. It may be taking things too far to argue this, but the principle of adherence to authority in Shīʿa Islam may hold great potential for positive change that Sunnī Islam, in the absence of such clearly defined authorities, lacks. In our example, this means that using the support of established male authorities in the fight for women's rights is a valid strategy. The support their opinion provides may legitimise a demand and shield it from being criticised as un-Islamic. Gaining the support of a senior Source of Emulation (*marjaʿ*), who by definition would have a significant following, can be decisive. The history of Shīʿa Islam is rich in such examples, from the tobacco protests of 1891 to the call by Ayatollah Sīstānī (b. 1930) for citizens to vote in the 2004 general elections in Iraq.

Iranian women's rights activists found a religious authority to support their views in Ayatollah Yūsuf Ṣāneʿī (b. 1937). His position in favour of changing discriminatory laws is rooted in the principle of justice, which is particularly important in the Shīʿī tradition, where it is counted among the core principles of religion (*uṣūl al-dīn*). Thus, Ṣāneʿī is thoroughly anchored in Shīʿī tradition when he argues:

> It is a great error for us to say that something is not compatible with justice, but very well, if religion calls for it we will accept it, whether it is just or not. We must instead weigh our laws against justice. Where they are unjust, we must consider an approach that is founded on justice.[2]

One example: Under current law, the compensation payable for the death of a woman, referred to as blood money (*diya*), is only half that for a man. Ṣāneʿī argues that although this may have been just in the past because men were the family breadwinners, it is no longer acceptable today, when women often contribute equally to the family income. As a result, the compensation money must be adjusted.

> We must ponder Islam with reason (*bāyad eslām-rā bā ʿaql besanjīm*). It is not acceptable for us to allow our Islam to dictate terms to reason.[3]

Accordingly the criterion by which to judge what is just and what is unjust is reason, not the text of the Qurʾān. This, too, is in keeping with Shīʿī tradition, where reason is thought to be capable of independently leading to insights that the Qurʾān also offers. To Shīʿī theologians, reason is a source of understanding that stands independent of the sacred texts, which is why their tradition places much greater emphasis on individual reasoning than does mainstream Sunnī Islam.

4 Solidarity across Gender Lines

To return to the *Men in Hijabs* campaign, it demonstrated that women's rights activists today are more willing to involve men in their efforts than was previously the case. A similar change of attitude can also be observed among men in the reformist movement where, as we saw above, for decades no connection was made between the struggle for women's rights and political reform. This absence becomes especially glaring when we study the works of reformist authors from the 1990s. Most of them had nothing at all to say on gender issues. ʿAbdolkarim Soroush (b. 1945), the most important protagonist of the reform movement, barely addresses the question, and where he does, it is from a very traditional perspective (Mir-Hosseini 2002). *Kiyan*, the leading reformist

2 http://saanei.xyz/?view=01,00,05,00,0 Interview: 5.7.1380 (27.9.2001). Accessed 22 November 2016.

3 Ibid.

paper, for which Soroush was the main author, did not publish even a single gender-themed article. Asked about this, Soroush explained that there were more important questions to address and that women's issues could be written about in women's magazines (Mir-Hosseini 1999, 243). Gender did not feature as a real category in the thinking of these reformists.

Instead, a hierarchy was posited in which democracy was cast as a first-order right of the highest priority, as opposed to women's rights, which were seen largely as second-order concerns. This ultimately led to the view that primary efforts should be directed toward the struggle for democracy and that women's rights activism represented a distraction or deviation from that course. ʿAbbās ʿAbdī (b. 1956), a leading reformist, used this very image to explain the situation and concluded that although it was legitimate for specific groups to fight for their rights, in the process they needed to be careful not to disturb the greater and more important overall struggle for democracy (Paidar 2001, 28).

Of course, women protested against this view: They could not accept a scale of priorities that placed their equal rights below an abstract notion of democracy (Moṭīʿ 2000). Yet regardless of their criticism, the male-dominated reformist discourse long retained the habit of consigning gender issues to the realm of Shīʿī jurisprudence, or *fiqh*. The reformers, though, did not see *fiqh* as a field in which the reinterpretation of Islam would be undertaken. Intellectuals such as Soroush did not concern themselves with *fiqh* in the narrow sense, and those who did, like Mohsen Kadivar (b. 1959), limited that concern to matters of government. This has changed now.

The shift in awareness also encompasses the group of so-called non-religious intellectuals, to adopt a questionable designation that has been current at least since the revolution. The regime then had divided intellectuals into two classes, the religious and the non-religious. The latter were persecuted or dismissed from universities, as the ruling ideology counted them as "not-our-own" (*ghayr-e khodī*). The former, on the other hand, were counted among "our own" (*khodī*) and assumed to be at least capable of basic loyalty to the regime, since they had *taʿahhod*, an affiliation with Islam. Some degree of dissent on their part was tolerated on that basis. The reformist ideas proposed by both groups are ultimately not as dissimilar as this strict divide would suggest, though. Many who are counted among the non-religious are not as irreligious as the designation would seem to suggest, and it was not uncommon for intellectuals to move from the status of *khodī* to *ghayr-e khodī* as they became more reformist.

Another trait that religious and non-religious intellectuals long shared was their blindness to issues of gender. Non-religious intellectuals, too, have only recently begun to self-critically examine their past conduct. Hamid Dabashi

(b. 1951), Professor of Iranian Studies at Columbia University, in New York City, and one of the most important Iranian public intellectuals worldwide, welcomed the opportunity to finally show solidarity with the headscarf protest. He also pointed out that Iranian men were late in doing so. The proper time to show such solidarity would have been thirty years ago, when women had been forced to wear headscarves in the first place (Bower 2009).

A similar self-criticism is expressed in Farsi literature by Shahriar Mandanipour (b. 1957). He writes, in his novel *Censoring an Iranian Love Story*:

> Sara goes to the dressing room. This is the perfect opportunity for Dara to savor the bitter taste of Sara's tooth-shattering retort. Well, like many enlightened Iranian men, he is subconciously ashamed of his own incompetence and inaction, when after the revolution, mothers, sisters, and wives, through coercion and by having pushpins stabbed into their foreheads, were forced to wear headscarves and chadors, and year after year, their human rights were taken away from them. And at this very moment, the stinging slap of a political inspiration lands on his ear. Dara discovers that during all the years that he and his generation fought for utopia in Iran, they were wrong, and they should have instead fought for this small and basic right.
>
> MANDANIPOUR 2009, 187

That sort of insight might have been the underlying reason for the hashtag *ItsMensTurn,* which provided the title for this essay. This is its history: Nīlūfar Ardalān is known in Iran above all under the name of Lady Goal; she heads the women's national soccer team. Yet when this team qualified for the Asian Championships in Malaysia for the very first time, in 2015, Lady Goal was conspicuous not through her performance on the pitch, but through her absence. It turned out that her husband had refused her permission to travel abroad. This was his right under Iranian law: a married woman may not leave the country without her husband's consent. The public outcry that followed resulted in the campaign *#ItsMensTurn*. Husbands affirmed their commitment online, posting: "It's men's turn: I restore the right to travel to my wife." Another hashtag read: "Human rights have no gender." Thousands of such statements were posted on Facebook.[4] The Iranian vice president responsible for women's issues received thousands of e-mailed complaints against Lady goal being forced to stay at home.

4 http://mystealthyfreedom.net/en/campaigns/. Accessed 24 November 2017.

In November of 2015, an Iranian court accorded Lady Goal the right to travel without her husband's permission to lead the Iranian team in the World Cup Competition in Guatemala. It is not known for certain whether this verdict was guided by the Islamic principle of *maṣlaḥa* ("the common good"), which places the benefit to the Islamic community above strict adherence to the law, but it is certainly possible (Reissner 1988). The fact that Iran won the World Futsal Championships under the leadership of Lady Goal has since been used as an argument for women's freedom to travel, and thus for women's rights in general.

5 Conclusion

It remains difficult to predict what will come of civil society activism of this kind. Observing discourses on women's rights is bound to remain interesting, though. Awareness that women's rights are not a second-order matter but part of the greater issue of human rights has increased noticeably. This is an achievement that reflects progress in Islamic feminism, which has managed to connect to extant reformist discourses by integrating arguments from Shīʿī theology and jurisprudence. It is also the result of social media functioning as a political forum, in which we have seen not only the Iranian and the expatriate counter-public unite with one another, but also men and women joining together in support of women's rights.

Bibliography

Sources

Khomeini, Ruhollah. 1990. *Tawżīḥ al-masāʾel.* Tehran: Imam Khomeini Foundation.

Mandanipour, Shahriar. 2009. *Censoring an Iranian Love Story: A Novel.* Trans. Sara Khalili. New York: Alfred A. Knopf.

Mir-Hosseini, Ziba. 1999. *Islam and Gender: The Religious Debate in Contemporary Iran.* Princeton: Princeton University Press.

Mir-Hosseini, Ziba. 2002. "Religious Modernists and the 'Woman Question:' Challenges and Complicities." In Eric Hooglund (ed.), *Twenty Years of Islamic Revolution: Political and Social Transition in Iran since 1979.* Syracuse, NY: Syracuse University Press, 74–95.

Moṭahharī, Mortażā. 1994. *Nezām-e ḥoqūq-e zan dar eslām.* Tehran: Tahr-e nou.

Moṭīʿ, Nāhīd. 2000. "Zanān moʿaṭṭal dar ṣaff-e demūkrāsī." *Zanān* 62: 37–38.

Paidar, Parvin. 2001. *Gender of Democracy: The Encounter between Feminism and Reformism in Contemporary Iran.* Geneva: United Nations Research Institute for Social Development.

Shabestarī, Moḥammad. 1996. *Hermenūtīk, ketāb va sonnat.* Tehran: Tarh-e nou.

Sharīʿatī, ʿAlī. 1990. *Zan.* Tehran: Mazarandan.

Studies

Amirpur, Katajun. 2013. "'Wir sind die Hälfte der Bevölkerung Irans'—Die Frauen in der Grünen Bewegung." In Susanne Schröter (ed.), *Geschlechtergerechtigkeit durch Demokratisierungen?* Bielefeld: transcript Verlag, 97–125 (106–110).

Bower, Ewe. "New Protest Statement Builds in Iran—Men in Head Scarves." Accessed 2 November 2017, CNN: http://edition.cnn.com/2009/WORLD/meast/12/14/iran.headscarf.protest/index.html.

Reissner, Johannes. 1988. "Der Imam und die Verfassung. Zur politischen und staatsrechtlichen Bedeutung der Direktive Imam Khomeinis vom 7. Januar 1988." *Orient* 29/2: 213–36.

CHAPTER 15

Contested Genderscapes: Islamic Languages of Women's Rights in the Arab Region

Bettina Dennerlein

1 Introduction

This contribution enquires into the intellectual dynamics of current debates on gender in the Arab World, based on a close reading of a programmatically Islamic critique of transnational women's rights and their implementation in the Middle East and North Africa (the MENA region). The point of departure is a text by Hiba Ra'ūf 'Izzat (Heba Raouf Ezzat, b. 1965), an Egyptian political scientist and Islamic thinker, written to serve as a background paper for the 2005 *Arab Human Development Report* (AHDR), which was subtitled "Towards the Rise of Women in the Arab World."[1] While explicitly grounding her critique of transnational women's rights activism in the tradition of modern Islamic thought, 'Izzat asserts herself into differently aligned debates and addresses diverse national and international publics. She provides an example for further exploring the ideological and conceptual intricacies of transnational genderscapes. Her background paper can be considered an instructive case in point that illustrates the emergence of what Margot Badran has called the "middle ground" or "middle space" of current gender debates in the MENA region, where, in spite of the ideological dominance of the secular-religious binary, both categories are basically enmeshed (Badran 2001).

Abundant research exists on the "politics of" as well as the "politics for" women's rights (to borrow a distinction introduced by Upendra Baxi in critical human rights studies) in the MENA region, with research strongly focussed on Egypt.[2]

1 AHDR 2005, annex 1, 246. A reference to the text can be found on the Arabic website of the AHDR among the resources on the topic of gender (*al-nauʿ al-ijtimāʿī*) (http://www.arab-hdr.org/arabic/resources/publications.aspx?tid=979; accessed 27 July 2017). However, the background papers currently can no longer be downloaded from this page. The version referred to here was downloaded on 7 April 2014. 'Izzat is also mentioned as a contributor to the AHDR of 2005 (AHDR 2005, IX) and repeatedly cited in the text of the report (AHDR 2005, 203, 208, 211).

2 Cf. for example Abu-Lughod 2010; Al-Ali 2000; Hatem 2005; Jad 2007; Stachursky 2013; Tadros 2016.

 | DOI:10.1163/9789004386891_016

Numerous researchers have investigated the multifaceted and at times vexing interplay of local yet transnationally connected women's rights groups, authoritarian regimes, and international developmental agendas. Likewise, Islamic opposition to human rights in general and women's human rights in particular has attracted ample attention, especially during the 1990s.[3] In contrast, trends within Islamic discourse that have sought to accommodate human rights in order to gain new credibility have gained much less consideration. This holds all the more true for the explicitly self-critical Islamic approaches to women's empowerment as illustrated by the writings of Hiba Raʾūf ʿIzzat. ʿIzzat, a professor of political science at Cairo University, was trained in Egypt and Great Britain. She is a prolific writer in both Arabic and English and since the 1990s has continuously contributed to national, regional, and international debates on Islam, gender, and globalisation, combining research and activism.[4] Considered to be close to the ideological brand of the Egyptian Muslim Brotherhood, ʿIzzat bases her thought on the writings of influential contemporary scholars, most notably Muḥammad al-Ghazzālī (1917–96) and the well known and highly mediated Yūsuf al-Qaraḍāwī (b. 1926; Stowasser 2001; ʿIzzāt 1999). She has figured prominently among the regular authors on the Internet platform IslamOnline (https://islamonline.net/author/h-ezzat).[5] Her master's thesis, titled *al-Marʾa wa-l-ʿamal al-siyāsī* ("Woman and political action"), was published by the Washington D.C.-based International Institute of Islamic Thought (IIIT) in 1995, and in it and in later works, ʿIzzat has suggested renewing *ijtihād* (interpretation of the sources of Islamic law) in order to overcome the limitations of contemporary Islamic and secular approaches to issues of women's rights (ʿIzzāt 1995 and 1999).

2 Women's Rights, Islam, and the Family

On the national level, modern Islamic personal status law as codified by the Egyptian state institutionally and programmatically fuses religion, gender, and the family.[6] As a result of the political construction of both the secular and the religious "as discrete conceptual categories" enmeshed with the highly

3 To mention just two titles, see Mayer 2013, and Ali 2000.

4 On ʿIzzāt, see McLarney 2010 and 2015, 219–53; Esposito 2010, 119–21. See also Bahi 2011, Daly 2010, Hatem 2002, Hatem 2006, Mehrez 2007.

5 This website was founded in 1997 in Qaṭar, supported by, among others, Yūsuf al-Qaraḍāwī. ʿIzzat was involved in the establishment of its Cairo office. On the establishment and background of the website, see Gräf 2008.

6 For a comparative perspective on this phenomenon see Cady and Fessenden 2013, 3–24.

gendered separation of public and private spheres, the issues of "woman" and "family" became increasingly sacralised (Badran 2013, 106). "'The woman' and 'the family' were the last domain left to the religious, over which they were in principle free to rule" (Badran 2013, 107). At the same time, the issues of "woman" and "family" were turned into sites of ideological competition. "Confining *sharīʿa* to domestic matters politicized the family both as a sphere of intimate, affective relations and as a repository of group identity of which religious affiliation was a defining legal and moral characteristic.... Languages of privacy that entered the legal discourse around personal status matters concurrently with the limiting of the *sharīʿa*'s jurisdiction served to create 'the family' both as a private space and one which was central to political order" (Bier 2011, 104). Against this background, it was difficult for secular women's rights groups to directly challenge Islamic personal status law because of its association with religion. In contrast to this, Islamists systematically politicised the family, turning it into a model for a liberated and Islamic social and political order.[7]

Concurrently, the growing valourisation and institutionalisation of women's rights as human rights on the international and the national levels allowed for new forms of politicisation. Since the 1990s, feminist activists have successfully pushed for women's rights to become an integral part of international discourse and the politics of human rights and human development. Major international conferences, along with the Declaration on the Elimination of Violence against Women of 1993, the optional protocol to the major women's rights declaration of 1979, the Convention on the Elimination of all Forms of Discrimination Against Women (CEDAW), which entered into force in 2000, and the UN millennium goals formulated in 2000 all indicate the increasing weight women's rights issues have gained internationally. The protection of women's rights has also been put on the agenda of international politics and foreign policies of Western countries, especially with respect to the Muslim world (for example, in justifying military interventions in Afghanistan and Iraq).[8] As far as Egypt is concerned, important accomplishments on the national level were the ratification of CEDAW in 1981 as well as the establishment of the National Council for Women in 2000, created by presidential decree and, until the revolutionary events of 2011, headed by Egypt's then first lady, Suzanne Mubarak (Stachursky 2013, 98–101, 107f.).

---

7 For the secular women's rights movement up through the 1990s, see Al-Ali 2009, 154f., 165f. For Islamic positions on family law in the same period, see Hatem 2002.

8 On human rights and the foreign policy of the U.S. in general, see Mertus 2004. On discourses on gender, sexuality, and the war against terror in the U.S., see Puar 2005 and Oliver 2007. For the Muslim and Arab world, see Al-Ali and Pratt 2009, and Kandiyoti 2011.

For women's rights activists and for non-governmental organisations (NGOs) in Egypt, as elsewhere in the Arab region, promoting women's human rights has thus become a powerful means for acquiring international recognition and for mobilising funds. Yet, there are also several problems connected to this process that have led to women's rights groups at times being subject to sharp criticism.[9] First, the role of authoritarian regimes is seen to be an ambiguous one in this context. While transnational human rights and women's rights discourses open up a political space for opposition and change, the implementation of human rights depends on the state. Official human rights policies tend to strengthen the authority of the state and enhance the state's role in the field of women's and human rights. Another point of critique is the link between human rights discourse and neoliberal notions of reform in the political, social, and economic fields. Human rights-based development agendas are seen as promoting a politics of privatisation and structural adjustment, irrespective of the social problems it creates—not least with respect to gender inequality. Finally, the normative notions of individual autonomy, choice, and secularism that come as part and parcel of transnational human rights norms are seen as marginalising or displacing other possible approaches to issues of social justice.

At the same time, Islamic resistance to transnational women's rights has intensified since the 1994 Cairo Conference on Population and Development and the 1995 United Nations Conference on Women held in Beijing, with its Platform for Action putting women's rights groups under additional pressure. Not only in Egypt has opposition to the term "gender" tightened since then. Gender was and continues to be perceived by different religious and other conservative forces worldwide as a major threat to norms of sexual difference and clearly defined heteronormative gender roles. Opposition to the term "gender" is most often staged as a defence of the family or of "family values," which are increasingly framed in terms of human rights (cf. Dennerlein 2017).

A telling illustration of this kind of opposition to transnational women's rights expressed in Islamic terms is a booklet by Yūsuf al-Qaraḍāwī titled *al-Usra kamā yurīduhā al-Islām* ("The family as wished-for by Islam"), published in 2005 (al-Qaraḍāwī 2005). The booklet is based on two papers delivered by al-Qaraḍāwī at the 2004 Doha International Conference on the Family, which was

9 Cf. Moghadam 2005 and Moghadam 2009, among others. For an ethnographic study of transnational activism against violence against women, see Merry 2006. On transnational women's rights activism with respect to the Arab world, see Abu-Lughod 2009 and 2010, among others. For a more general discussion of the link between the state and women's rights in the Middle East, see Hatem 2005. For Egypt, see Al-Ali 2000; Stachursky 2013. On the Arab world, see Abu-Lughod 2009, Adely 2009, and Hasso 2009.

organised on the occasion of the tenth anniversary of the United Nations International Year of the Family (al-Qaraḍāwī 2005, 6).[10] The Doha conference served as a forum for different conservative forces targeting the defence, or rather the promotion, of the family. It is concomitant with a broader strategy involving United States-based organisations such as the World Family Policy Center and the Family Research Council, which refer to article 16, paragraph 3, of the Universal Declaration of Human Rights, which guarantees protection of the family as the "natural and fundamental group unit of society," in order to call for the respect of family values as a human right (Bob 2012, esp. 53–6).[11] In his booklet, al-Qaraḍāwī claims respect for marriage and the family as sacred institutions—an idea completely absent from traditional Islamic law. According to al-Qaraḍāwī, this assumption is shared by all "religions of the book." At the same time, he claims the right to protect Islam's particularities (*khaṣāʾiṣ*) with respect to other religions (al-Qaraḍāwī 2005, 5–7). Among these particularities, Qaraḍāwī mentions repudiation and polygyny, thereby marginalising a longstanding tradition of Muslim self-critique of exactly these two institutions that has persisted since the turn of the nineteenth into the twentieth century.

Another example of Islamic opposition to transnational women's rights is a declaration issued in 2013 by the International Union of Islamic Scholars (IUIS; al-Ittiḥād al-ʿĀlamī li-ʿUlamāʾ al-Muslimīn)—headed by al-Qaraḍāwī—on the topic of CEDAW and UN declarations against violence against women. The 2013 declaration of the IUIS opens with a demand for recognition of the principle of gender complementarity in Islamic family law as opposed to gender equality in the name of religious diversity (*al-tanawwuʿ al-dīnī*).[12] It fundamentally rejects the assumption that gender differences considered legitimate according to Islam should be denounced by international law as being conducive to violence against women. As a consequence of this argument, the concept of marital rape as a criminal offence, for instance, is explicitly rejected in the document.

In UN discourses on the Arab world such as the *Arab Human Development Report*—which was officially declared to constitute an advocacy tool prepared and owned by Arabs (http://www.arab-hdr.org/about/intro.aspx)—women's rights, Islam, and the family are major issues of concern. The AHDR in general

10 For the declaration of the conference on the official website of the Doha Institute, see https://www.difi.org.qa/doha-declaration/.

11 See article 16, paragraph 3, Universal Declaration of Human Rights: "The family is the natural and fundamental group unit of society and is entitled to protection by society and the State."

12 For the complete text of this declaration see http://iumsonline.org/ar/aboutar/nt-lnhd/s72/.

has been criticised for its tendency to culturalise socio-economic and political problems of the region in terms of an assumed "Middle Eastern Exceptionalism" (Bayat 2005, 1225). Regarding the 2005 AHDR, entitled "Towards the Rise of Women in the Arab World," Lila Abu-Lughod more particularly criticises the negative image drawn of the family, based on the assumption of a specific "pathology of Arab gender culture" (Abu-Lughod 2009, 85).[13] Abu-Lughod reproaches the authors of the AHDR 2005 for one-sidedly portraying the family as patriarchal, tribal, and fundamentally opposed to the "rise of women." According to Abu-Lughod, the AHDR posits women's "differentiation from family" as a key to their empowerment and she critiques that underlying ahistorical and normative depiction of the family for being based on liberal feminist theories (Abu-Lughod 2009, 89f.). She concludes that the AHDR fails to properly understand the "more relational basis of women's selfhood and decision making" in Middle Eastern societies, as well as different forms of negotiations or bargains that take place in asymmetrical family settings (Abu-Lughod 2009, 90 f.).

A closer look at the reports, however, reveals a more complex picture. Both the AHDR of 2005 and, perhaps even more so, the AHDR of 2009 on "Challenges to Human Security" tend to set up an opposition between the traditional family, portraying it as a refuge for all sorts of violence against women and patriarchal oppression, and the modern normative family, which is seen to need and deserve protection by the state. According to the report, the normative family is based on family planning and rights, which in turn are based on societal reform. The AHDR of 2005 explicitly praises women's roles in the realm of the normative family: "Thus, enabling women to build their capabilities is the crucial foundation that prepares them to play a positive, creative role as women in raising children, strengthening family bonds of affection and cohesion, and empowering all family members to participate effectively in the project for Arab renaissance" (AHDR 2005, 220). Women's familial roles are even seen to be an asset for societal development: "[D]iscrimination against women violates the principles of equality of rights and respect for human dignity, is an obstacle to the participation of women, on equal terms with men, in the political, social, economic and cultural life of their countries, hampers the growth of the prosperity of society and the family and makes more difficult the full development of the potentialities of women in the service of their countries and of humanity" (AHDR 2005, 275). This model of the modern, normative family also informs the 2016 AHDR devoted to the topic "Youth and the Prospects for Human Development in a Changing Reality." For instance, the AHDR

13 For other critical appraisals of the 2005 AHDR, see Adely 2009 and Hasso 2009.

of 2016 deplores the fact that youth cannot form their own conjugal families early enough because of economic problems—a situation that is said to lead to frustration (AHDR 2016, 5; 33). In contrast to the normative family, the male-oriented "traditional" family is again portrayed as the soil that nurtures the "seeds of discrimination embedded in cultural beliefs and traditions" and is held responsible for young women's exclusion (AHDR 2016, 32).

3 Hiba Ra'ūf 'Izzat on Women's Political Empowerment and Islamic (Self-)Critique

'Izzat's background paper for the 2005 AHDR, which figures importantly in the final report in the chapter "Political Structures" (AHDR 2005, 202–12), is devoted to the topic *"Ḥawla mawāqif al-quwwa al-siyāsiyya khāṣṣatan al-ḥarakāt al-Islāmiyya wa-l-ḥarakāt al-dīniyya min tamkīn al-nisā' fi l-buldān al-'Arabiyya"* ("About the positions of political forces, especially of Islamic/Islamist movements and religious movements, on the topic of women's empowerment in the Arab countries"). The fact that 'Izzat did not contribute a background paper on the family might seem surprising at first glance, given the prominence of the topic in her writings. However in the author's view, women's political empowerment and the family are intrinsically linked.

This is congruent with the intellectual heritage of modern Islamic thought that reaches back to the turn of the nineteenth into the twentieth century and in which 'Izzat explicitly grounds her ideas. Women and the family were central political and intellectual-philosophical themes of Arab reformist thought in addition to or, rather, cutting across other core themes of political justice, science, religion, and the progress of civilisation (Kassab 2010, 20–21). The topic of women and the family has been equally prominent in discussions among reformist Islamic scholars and intellectuals. Research on early debates on the status and rights of women has convincingly shown how gender emerged as a major factor in modernist projects on the metaphorical as well as the institutional and structural levels. A brief look at journals of the early cultural-political reform movement of the *nahḍa* (the Arab "awakening" of the second half of the nineteenth century), such as *al-Muqtaṭaf* and *al-Hilāl,* shows recurring discussions of the issue of women, not least in the sections devoted to letters to the editors, which served as important forums of public debate.[14]

14 See, for example, the debates raised by a contribution by Amīn al-Khūrī under the title "Hal li-l-nisā' an yaṭlubna kulla ḥuqūq al-rajul," published in *al-Hilāl,* 15 February 1894, 366–9. See also El Sadda 2006.

Women as well as men from different regional and religious backgrounds participated in these debates, commenting on and contradicting one another.

In early reformist writings from the late nineteenth and early twentieth centuries as famously illustrated by Qāsim Amīn's (1863–1908) influential book *Taḥrīr al-marʾa* ("The liberation of woman"; 1899), gender relations inside the family were seen to mirror the greater political order. At the same time, they were thought to constitute the refuge of the nation's most authentic characteristics. Marriage and the family were portrayed as the realm of conjugal love and intimacy. Women's rights could thus refer to different things at the same time—to more basic natural and/or human rights, to civil rights (especially with a view to the exercise of economic activity), to the right of access to education and/or certain professions, and, last but not least, to rights in the field of Islamic personal status law or the realm of the family. In *Taḥrīr al-marʾa,* Amīn, explains that the Islamic *sharīʿa* conferred on women equality (*musāwāh*) and full human rights (*ḥuqūq al-insān*) before any other legal system in the history of mankind did so. With respect to women's education he declares that the enhancement of personal capacities constitutes a "natural right" (*ḥaqq ṭabīʿī*) of every human being—that is, including women.[15] This position does not prevent Amīn from asserting that women are naturally predisposed to modesty and domesticity as well as more inclined towards monogamy, although the latter is presumed to be the desirable orientation of both men and women. Amīn explicitly states that the currently observable differences in the intellectual capacities of women and men are a result of the low status or position imposed on women, not grounded in any anatomical difference (Amīn 1899, 47–8.).

Other intellectuals from the same period insisted on women's rights being essentially different from men's rights as a result of natural differences between the sexes, if not openly claiming women's natural inferiority to men. Interestingly, while such supposedly natural differences were referred to by secular as well as Islamic intellectuals, it seems that it was especially the first group who insisted explicitly on women's inferiority. A telling example of this attitude is an article by Shiblī Shumayyil (1850–1917) under the title "al-Marʾa wa-l-rajul wa-hal yatasāwayān?" ("Woman and man: Are they equal?"), published in two consecutive issues of the journal *al-Muqtaṭaf* in March and April 1887, in which the author bases his argument on modern science that, according to him, has proved the inferior status of females in evolutionarily advanced species (as opposed to the more equal status of males and females in lower species).

15 For different notions of "rights" (natural rights, rights endowed by the Islamic *sharīʿa*, or political rights) referred to by the author, see, for example, Amīn 1899, 11–12, 22, 109–13.

This article elicited several critical comments, to which the author reacted with a reply published later the same year in the same journal (Shumayyil 1887a, b, c).

With the further development of modernist reformist trends in Islam in line with the thinking of Muḥammad ʿAbduh (c. 1849–1905), Rashīd Riḍā (1865–1935), and the Muslim Brotherhood and similar movements, the issue of women's rights continued to be discussed, being differently linked to the foundationalist concepts of nature and/or revelation. In an article titled "al-Marʾa al-muslima" ("The Muslim woman"), published in 1940 in two consecutive issues of the famous Islamic journal *al-Manār*, established by Rashīd Riḍā, Ḥasan al-Bannā (1906–49), the founder of the Egyptian Muslim Brotherhood, presents his point of view on the issue of women's rights, explaining that the Islamic *sharīʿa* indeed prescribes different rights for men and women, based on the obvious "natural" differences between the sexes (al-Bannā 1987, 7). In this article, al-Bannā firmly defends practices such as veiling and gender segregation, which had been openly criticised earlier by reformist scholars, notably Muḥammad ʿAbduh and Qāsim Amīn. This determined stance against women's rights taken by al-Bannā has to be explained in light of the general intellectual and political competition during the interwar period, with the more liberal Muslim intellectuals and women's rights activists arguing for women's rights likewise citing Islamic references in support of their views.[16] A major shift in Islamic positions on women has again been observed in the 1990s—most notably in the writings of scholars such as Muḥammad al-Ghazzālī and Yūsuf al-Qaraḍāwī (Stowasser 2001). It is especially their accommodative attitude towards women's political participation from which Hiba Raʾūf ʿIzzat substantially draws.

In her study of female voices of the religious awakening in Egypt since the 1970s, Ellen Anne McLarney depicts Hiba Raʾūf ʿIzzat as representing a generation of Islamic writers who see themselves as supporters of a liberal Islam, as opposed to the state's illiberal secularism (McLarney 2015, 192). ʿIzzat is an internationally well-connected, very visible public intellectual and frequent presenter at conferences. In her book *al-Marʾa wa-l-ʿamal al-siyāsī*, published in 1996, as well as in a programmatic article published in the Cairo-based scholarly journal *Alif* in 1999, ʿIzzat positions herself in the line of Islamic reformist thought, more particularly that of Muḥammad al-Ghazzālī and Yūsuf al-Qaraḍāwī, while suggesting a renewal of *ijtihād* that bridges the gap between Islamic scholarship and social sciences and in which women should actively

16 On the use of Islamic references in liberal thought of the same period, see Gershoni 1999; McLarney 2015; Hatem 1989; Cooke 1986; Khater and Nelson 1988; Baron 2005, 189–213; Baron 2001.

participate. This renewal of *ijtihād* is presented by ʿIzzat as a collective national task and political project (ʿIzzat 1999, 114–5).

On several occasions ʿIzzat has voiced her fundamental opposition to what she considers to be Western secularist feminist or gay and lesbian assaults on the family (Ezzat 2002). In her writings, she defends a hierarchical structure of the family with the man as head, while asserting that leadership has to be exercised in a consultative (*shūrī*) manner (McLarney 2010, 139). ʿIzzat bases her argument on the definition of the family as a political institution, which, as such, is subject to general criteria of political justice. She strongly criticises the private-public binary of family versus the political—a position shared, according to ʿIzzat, by secularists as well as Islamists (ʿIzzat 1999, 113–4). Opposing this binary, ʿIzzat defines the family as the basic unit of the Islamic polity. This allows her in turn to interpret *qiwāma* (male superiority) in terms of political leadership (*riyāsa*). Political leadership for its part is tied to the moral notion of *ṣalāḥ* (exemplary uprightness; McLarney 2010, 138–40). At the same time, *qiwāma* is connected to the notions of *wilāya* (sovereignty) and citizenship, making it a realm of rights and (political) participation (ʿIzzat 2005, 16). A key term introduced by ʿIzzat in claiming a political role for women as women in their everyday familial life is the "politics of presence"—as opposed to (formal) "politics of representation."[17]

McLarney has argued that by claiming a political role for women inside the family, ʿIzzat questions the de-politicisation of the family as well as the privatisation of religion (McLarney 2015, 219–53). The politicisation of the family simultaneously allows ʿIzzat to intervene in Islamic as well as feminist debates. She actually pleads for a renewal of Islam(ism)'s political imaginary, which she argues needs to draw also on Western (secular) political thought and Western experiences. While herself strictly opposing secularism—especially in her more polemical contributions on the Internet platform IslamOnline, notably on the topics of human rights and feminism (ʿIzzat 2013; 2014)—in her scholarly work ʿIzzat urges surmounting the polarisation between Islamism and secularism which, according to her, works at the expense of women (ʿIzzat 1999). In this context she refers to the model of the Nationalist-Islamic Conferences held in the 1990s which, in her view, have remained so far unsuccessful.[18]

ʿIzzat starts her background paper for the 2005 AHDR with a general appraisal of how different political forces have adjusted their positions since the mid-1990s in reaction to the International Conference on Population and Development held in Cairo in 1994 and to subsequent women's rights

17 On this notion as developed by ʿIzzat, see also Esposito 2010, 119–21.

18 On the different initiatives of this kind, see Browers 2006.

conferences. She rightly observes that Islamic forces especially have mainly focused on women's political rights, thereby trying to limit the socio-cultural implications of women's human rights in other realms (ʿIzzat 2005, 1–2). Before discussing select positions of different political forces in different countries, ʿIzzat explicates the basis for her critical analysis with three points: First, she starts from the assumption that women's issues (*qaḍāyā al-marʾa*) cannot be separated from more general controversies (*jadaliyyāt*) and debates in the region. Second, she maintains that, in women's issues, internal and external disputes and conflicting agendas are inevitably interconnected. Third, very much in congruence with the critique from Middle East women's studies specialists, ʿIzzat asserts that standardised indicators and quantifying approaches to the question of women's empowerment are not capable of rendering the complexities of women's lives and the different forms of their active participation in the Arab region.

As far as Islamic or Islamist positions are concerned, ʿIzzat makes a clear separation between what she calls the *salafī* trends (*tayyārāt salafiyya*) and the school of the Muslim Brothers (*madrasat al-ikhwān al-muslimīn*) (ʿIzzat 2005, 7). According to her analysis, followers of the *salafī* trend place the principle of *qiwāma,* or male superiority, over questions of *wilāya,* or political sovereignty. They thereby reduce women as wives and mothers exclusively to their roles in the sphere of the family—in opposition to the sphere of politics (ʿIzzat 2005, 7). In spite of certain differences among themselves, movements of the *salafī* trend are seen as sharing a strong focus on morals as the main cause for political crises—thereby neglecting the absence of democracy as a major factor (ʿIzzat 2005, 10). At the same time, ʿIzzat observes that women in these movements nevertheless have started to question certain ideological positions on the basis of Islamic law itself.

In contrast, movements of the *ikhwān* trend are characterised by ʿIzzat as a middle way position (*mawqif wasaṭī*). To justify this characterisation, she refers to a document issued by the Egyptian Muslim Brotherhood just before the Cairo Conference of 1994 titled "al-Marʾa al-muslima fi l-mujtamaʿ al-muslim" ("The Muslim woman in Muslim society"). However, ʿIzzat asserts that in movements of the *ikhwān* trend, women are still not prominently involved, even if the principle of their political participation is widely recognised (ʿIzzat 2005, 11). The major problem here, according to ʿIzzat, is again the private vs. public binary. The solution she suggests is a more holistic and, at the same time, more genuinely Islamic definition of politics and political participation (ʿIzzat 2005, 13). ʿIzzat strongly criticises Islamists' focus on issues of morals and sexuality, calling instead for a vital "innovative dialectical Ijtihad" (Engl. original; ʿIzzat 2005, 15). A key sentence for understanding ʿIzzat's point of view is rendered verbatim in English translation in the AHDR 2005. After having clarified that women's empowerment indeed needs to be considered not a result of but a pre-condition for building the Islamic society, ʿIzzat states: "In this way, women's participation in the shaping of the model would become part of the empowerment [Ar. *tamkīn*] of the model, not simply their own empowerment, and 'the woman's voice' would take part in creating, developing and renewing the model as one of the pillars of its 'Islamicity' [Ar. *Islāmiyya*]" (AHDR 2005, 211; ʿIzzat 2005, 23). With this kind of argument, which deliberately draws on the *ikhwān* strain of Islamic thought, ʿIzzat actually ultimately contradicts the *ikhwān* tendency to naturalise and sacralise marriage and the family in order to seal them off from politics. Up until now, this substantial difference in how the family is viewed does not seem to have been further developed by the author in order to more systematically distinguish her views from established Islamic discourses on the family. It may rather be seen to have prepared the author's turning away from the topic of the family as such to address seemingly more general political issues such as those she addressed in her book *Naḥwa ʿumrān jadīd* ("Towards a new civilization"), published in 2015—an equally daring enterprise of post-secular, or, as the author labels it, post-nation-state Islamic (self-)critique.

Bibliography

Abu-Lughod, Lila. (ed.). 1998. *Remaking Women: Feminism and Modernity in the Middle East*. Princeton: Princeton University Press.

Abu-Lughod, Lila. 2009. "Dialectics of Women's Empowerment: The International Circuitry of the *Arab Human Development Report 2005*." *International Journal of Middle East Studies* 41: 83–103.

Abu-Lughod, Lila. 2010. "The Active Social Life of 'Muslim Women's Rights': A Plea for Ethnography, not Polemic, with Cases from Egypt and Palestine." *Journal of Middle East Women's Studies* 6/1: 1–45.

Adely, Fida J. 2009. "Educating Women for Development: The Arab Human Development Report 2005 and the Problem with Women's Choices." *International Journal of Middle East Studies* 41: 105–22.

Ahmed, Leila. 1992. *Women and Gender in Islam: Historical Roots of a Modern Debate*. New Haven: Yale University Press.

Al-Ali, Nadje. 2000. *Secularism, Gender and the State in the Middle East: The Egyptian Women's Movement*. Cambridge: Cambridge University Press.

Al-Ali, Nadje, and Nicola Pratt. 2009. *What Kind of Liberation? Women and the Occupation of Iraq*. Berkeley: University of California Press.

Ali, Shaheen Sardar. 2000. *Gender and Human Rights in Islam and International Law: Equal before Allah, Unequal before Man?* The Hague: Kluwer.

Amīn, Qāsim. 1899. *Taḥrīr al-mar'a*. Cairo: Maktabat al-Taraqqī.

Arab Human Development Report (2005): "Towards the Rise of Women" (http://www.arab-hdr.org/Reports/2005/2005.aspx).

Asad, Talal. 2003. *Formations of the Secular: Christianity, Islam, Modernity*. Stanford: Stanford University Press.

Badran, Margot. 1995. *Feminists, Islam, and Nation: Gender and the Making of Modern Egypt*. Princeton: Princeton University Press.

Badran, Margot. 2001. "Locating Feminisms: The Collapse of Secular and Religious Discourses in the Mashriq." In *Agenda* 50: 42–57.

Badran, Margot. 2013. "Gendering the Secular and the Religious in Modern Egypt: Woman, Family, and Nation." In Linell Elizabeth Cady and Tracy Fessenden (eds.), *Religion, the Secular, and the Politics of Sexual Difference*. New York: Columbia University Press, 103–20.

Bahi, Riham. 2011. *Islamic and Secular Feminisms: Two Discourses Mobilized for Gender Justice*. EUI Working Papers 25. Florence: European University Institute.

al-Bannā, Ḥasan. 1987. *Al-Mar'a al-muslima*. Ed. Muḥammad Nāṣir al-Dīn al-Albānī. Beirut: Dār al-Jīl. First published in *Majallat al-Manār* 35 (May 1940) 550–3 and (September 1940) 765–73.

Baron, Beth. 2001. "An Islamic Activist in Interwar Egypt." In Kathleen D. McCarthy (ed.), *Women, Philanthropy, and Civil Society*. Bloomington: Indiana University Press, 225–44.

Baron, Beth. 2005. *Egypt as a Woman: Nationalism, Gender, and Politics*. Berkeley: University of California Press.

Baxi, Upendra. 2004. *The Future of Human Rights*. Oxford: Oxford University Press.

Bayat, Asef. 2005. "Transforming the Arab World: The *Arab Human Development Report* and the Politics of Change." *Development and Change* 36/6: 1225–37.

Bier, Laura. 2011. *Revolutionary Womanhood: Feminisms, Modernity and the State in Nasser's Egypt*. Stanford: Stanford University Press.

Bob, Clifford. 2012. *The Global Right Wing and the Clash of World Politics*. New York: Cambridge University Press.

Browers, Michaelle. 2006. "The Centrality and Marginalization of Women in the Political Discourse of Arab Nationalists and Islamists." *Journal of Middle East Women's Studies* 2/2: 8–34.

Cady, Linell Elizabeth, and Tracy Fessenden (eds.). 2013. *Religion, the Secular, and the Politics of Sexual Difference*. New York: Columbia University Press.

Cooke, Miriam. 1986. "Telling Their Lives: A Hundred Years of Arab Women's Writings." *World Literature Today* 60/2: 212–6.

Cuno, Kenneth M. 2015. *Modernizing Marriage: Family, Ideology, and Law in Nineteenth- and Early Twentieth-Century Egypt*. Syracuse: Syracuse University Press.

Daly, Suny. 2010. "Young Women as Activists in Contemporary Egypt: Anxiety, Leadership, and the Next Generation." *Journal of Middle East Women's Studies* 6/2: 59–85.

Dennerlein, Bettina. 2017. "Kulturalisierung transnational: Der Streit um Ehe, Familie und Sexualität 'im Islam'." *Freiburger Zeitschrift für Geschlechterstudien* 23/2: 37–51.

El Sadda, Hoda. 2006. "Gendered Citizenship: Discourses on Domesticity in the Second Half of the Nineteenth Century." *Hawwa* 4/1: 1–28.

Esposito, John L. 2010. *The Future of Islam*, Oxford: Oxford University Press.

Euben, Roxanne L., and Muhammad Qasim Zaman. 2009. "Yusuf al-Qaradawi." In Roxanne L. Euben and Muhammad Qasim Zaman (eds.), *Princeton Readings in Islamist Thought: Texts and Contexts from al-Banna to Bin Laden*. Princeton: Princeton University Press, 225–9.

Gershoni, Israel. 1999. "Egyptian Liberalism in the Age of 'Crisis of Orientation': Al-Risāla's Reaction to Fascism and Nazism, 1933–1939." *International Journal of Middle East Studies* 31/4: 551–76.

Gräf, Bettina. 2008. "IslamOnline.net: Independent, interactive, popular." *Arab Media and Society*: http://www.arabmediasociety.com/?article=576, January 2008.

Gräf, Bettina. 2010. *Medien-Fatwas@Yusuf al-Qaradawi: Die Popularisierung des islamischen Rechts*. ZMO-Studien 27. Berlin: Klaus Schwarz Verlag.

Gräf, Bettina, and Jakob Skovgaard-Peterson (eds.). 2009. *Global Mufti: The Phenomenon of Yūsuf al-Qaraḍāwī*. London: Hurst & Co.

Grami, Amel. 2014. "Islamic Feminism: A New Feminist Movement or a Strategy by Women for Acquiring Rights?" In Jean Said Makdisi, Noha Bayoumi, and Rafif Rida Sidawi, (eds.), *Arab Feminisms: Gender and Equality in the Middle East*. London: I.B. Tauris, 317–32.

Grewal, Inderpal. 2005. *Transnational America: Feminisms, Diasporas, Neoliberalisms*. Durham NC and London: Duke University Press.

Hasso, Frances S. 2009. "Empowering Governmentalities Rather Than Women: The Arab Human Development Report 2005 and Western Development Logics." *International Journal of Middle East Studies* 41: 63–82.

Hasso, Francis. 2011. *Consuming Desires: Family Crisis and the State in the Middle East*. Stanford: Stanford University Press.

Hatem, Mervat. 1989. "Through Each Other's Eyes: Egyptian, Levantine-Egyptian, and European Women's Images of Themselves and of Each Other (1862–1920)." *Women's Studies International Forum* 12/2: 183–98.

Hatem, Mervat. 2002. "Gender and Islamism in the 1990s." *Middle East Report* 22 (spring): 44–47.

Hatem, Mervat. 2005. "In the Shadow of the State. Changing Definitions of Arab Women's 'Developmental' Citizenship Rights." *Journal of Middle East Women's Studies* 1/3: 20–45.

Hatem, Mervat. 2006. “In the Eye of the Storm: Islamic Societies and Muslim Women in Globalization Discourses.” *Comparative Studies of South Asia, Africa and the Middle East* 26/1: 22–35.

ʿIzzat, Hiba Raʾūf. 1995. *Al-Marʾa wa-l-ʿamal al-siyāsī.* Herndon VA: International Institute of Islamic Thought.

ʿIzzat, Hiba Raʾūf. 1999. “Al-Marʾa wa-l-ijtihād: Naḥwa khiṭāb Islāmī jadīd.” *Alif: Journal of Comparative Poetics* 19: 96–120.

ʿIzzat, Hiba Raʾūf [Ezzat, Heba Raouf]. 2002. “Rethinking Secularism … Rethinking Feminism.” *Islamonline* (https://archive.islamonline.net/?p=17501). Accessed 19 June 2018.

ʿIzzat, Hiba Raʾūf. 2005. *Ḥawla mawāqif al-quwwa al-siyāsiyya, khāṣṣatan al-ḥarakāt al-Islāmiyya, wa-l-ḥarakāt al-dīniyya, min tamkīn al-nisāʾ fī l-buldān al-ʿArabiyya.* Background Paper to the 2005 AHDR. (http://www.arab-hdr.org/arabic/resources/publications.aspx?tid=979; downloaded 7 April 2014; text no longer available on this site).

ʿIzzat, Hiba Raʾūf [Ezzat, Heba Raouf]. 2011. “The Umma: From Global Civil Society to Global Public Sphere.” In Denisa Kostovicova and Marlies Glasius (eds.), *Bottom-Up Politics: An Agency-Centred Approach to Globalization*: New York: Palgrave, 40–49.

ʿIzzat, Hiba Raʾūf. 2013. “al-Niswiyya … Biḍāʿa fāsida.” *IslamOnline.* https://islamonline.net/3796. Accessed 19 June 2018.

ʿIzzat, Hiba Raʾūf. 2014. “Ishkāliyyāt mafhūm ḥuqūq al-insān.” *IslamOnline.* https://islamonline.net/6490. Accessed 19 June 2018.

ʿIzzat, Hiba Raʾūf. 2015. *Naḥwa ʿumrān ğadīd.* Beirut: al-Shabaka al-ʿArabiyya li-l-abḥāth wa-l-nashr.

Jad, Islah. 2007. “NGOs: Between Buzzwords and Social Movements.” *Development in Practice*, 17/4–5: 622–29.

Joseph, Suad (ed.). 2000. *Gender and Citizenship in the Middle East.* Syracuse: Syracuse University Press.

Kandiyoti, Deniz (ed.). 1991. *Women, Islam and the State.* Basingstoke: Macmillan.

Kandiyoti, Deniz. 2011. *Islam und Geschlechterpolitik: Überlegungen zu Afghanistan.* Berlin: EUME Lectures.

Kassab, Elizabeth S. 2010. *Contemporary Arab Thought: Cultural Critique in Comparative Perspective.* New York: Columbia University Press.

Khater, Akram, and Cynthia Nelson. 1988. “Al-Harakah al-nisaʾīyah: The Women's Movement and Political Participation in Modern Egypt.” *Women's Studies International Forum* 11/5: 465–83.

Khouloussy, Hannan. 2010. *For Better, For Worse: The Marriage Crisis that Made Modern Egypt.* Stanford: Stanford University Press.

Krämer, Gudrun. 2006. “Drawing Boundaries: Yūsuf al-Qaraḍāwī on Apostasy.” In Gudrun Krämer and Sabine Schmidtke (eds.), *Speaking for Islam: Religious Authorities in Muslim Societies.* Leiden: Brill, 181–217.

Krämer, Gudrun. 2009. "'New Fiqh' Applied: Yūsuf al-Qaraḍāwī on Non-Muslims in Islamic Society." *Jerusalem Studies in Arabic and Islam* 36: 389–405.

Kreil, Aymon. 2011. "La St Valentin au pays d'al-Azhar: Éléments d'ethnographie de l'amour et du sentiment amoureux au Caire." In M. Gross, S. Mathieu, S. Nizard (eds.), *Sacrés familles: Changements religieux, changements familiaux*. Toulouse: Erès.

Latte Abdallah, Stéphanie. 2010. "Féminisme islamique, vingt ans après." *Critique internationale* 46/1: 9–23.

Mahmood, Saba. 2001. "Feminist Theory, Embodiment, and the Docile Agent: Some Reflections on the Egyptian Islamic Revival." *Cultural Anthropology* 16/2: 202–36.

Mahmood, Saba. 2005. *Politics of Piety: The Islamic Revival and the Feminist Subject*. Princeton: Princeton University Press.

Mayer, Elizabeth. 2013. *Islam and Human Rights: Tradition and Politics*. Boulder: Westview Press.

McLarney, Ellen Anne. 2010. "The Private is Political: Women and Family in Intellectual Islam." *Feminist Theory* 11/2: 129–48.

McLarney, Ellen Anne. 2015. *Soft Force: Women in Egypt's Islamic Awakening*. Princeton: Princeton University Press.

Mehrez, Samia. 2007. "Translating Gender." *Journal of Middle East Women's Studies* 3/1: 106–27.

Merry, Sally Engle. 2003. "Rights Talk and the Experience of Law: Implementing Women's Human Rights to Protection from Violence." *Human Rights Quarterly* 25: 343–81.

Merry, Sally Engle. 2006. *Human Rights and Gender Violence: Translating International Law into Local Justice*. Chicago: University of Chicago Press.

Mertus, Julie A. 2004. *Bait and Switch: Human Rights and U.S. Foreign Policy*. New York: Routledge.

Moghadam, Valentine. 2005. *Globalizing Women: Gender, Globalization, and Transnational Feminist Networks*. Baltimore: Johns Hopkins University Press.

Moghadam, Valentine. 2009. *Globalization and Social Movements: Islamism, Feminism, and the Global Justice Movement*. Lanham: Rowman and Littlefield.

Oliver, Kelly. 2007. *Women as Weapons of War*. New York: Columbia University Press.

Puar, Jasbir. 2005. *Terrorist Assemblages: Homonationalism in Queer Times*. Durham NC: Duke University Press.

al-Qaraḍāwī, Yūsuf. 2005. *Al-Usra kamā yurīduhā al-Islām*. Cairo: Maktabat Wahba.

Rhouni, Raja. 2010. *Secular and Islamic Feminist Critiques in the Work of Fatima Mernissi*. Leiden: Brill.

Salime, Zakia. 2011. *Between Feminism and Islam: Human Rights and Sharia Law in Morocco*. Minneapolis: University of Minnesota Press.

Shumayyil, Shiblī. 1887a, b. "Al-Mar'a wa-l-rajul wa-hal yatasāwayān?" *al-Muqtaṭaf* March 1887: 355–60 (Part 1) and *al-Muqtaṭaf* April 1887: 401–5 (Part 2).

Shumayyil, Shiblī. 1887c. "Al-Mar'a wa-l-rajul wa-hal yatasāwayān: al-Radd." *al-Muqtaṭaf* October 1887: 50–9.

Soage, Anna Belén. 2008. "Shaykh Yusuf al-Qaradawi: Portrait of a Leading Islamic Cleric." *Middle East Review of International Affairs* 12/1: 51–68.

Stachursky, Benjamin. 2013. *The Promise and Perils of Transnationalization: NGO Activism and the Socialization of Women's Human Rights in Egypt and Iran.* New York: Routledge.

Stowasser, Barbara. 1994. *Women in the Qur'an, Traditions, and Interpretation.* Oxford: Oxford University Press.

Stowasser, Barbara. 2001. "Old Shaykhs, Young Women, and the Internet: The Rewriting of Women's Political Rights in Islam." *The Muslim World* 91: 99–120.

Stowasser, Barbara. 2009. "Yūsuf al-Qaraḍāwī on Women." In Bettina Gräf and Jakob Skovgaard-Petersen (eds.), *Global Mufti: The Phenomenon of Yūsuf al-Qaraḍāwī*, 181–212.

Tadros, Mariz. 2016. *Resistance, Revolt, and Gender Justice in Egypt.* Syracuse: Syracuse University Press.

Welchmann, Lynn. 2007. *Women and Muslim Family Laws in Arab States.* Amsterdam: Amsterdam University Press.

CHAPTER 16

On Coming to Grips with Turkish Oil Wrestling: Conceptualising Muscular Islam and Islamic Martial Arts

Birgit Krawietz

1 Introduction

This programmatic essay reflects on how to frame modern Turkish oil wrestling from a wider Islamic studies perspective.[1] In contrast to the homogenising and for many decades utterly nation-bound narrative of republican Turkey imposed on the sport, this article points to a broader scope of influences. Following the late Shahab Ahmed (2016) conceptually, this proposal uses Islam in the sense of a perplexing yet inclusive cultural multiplicity. In order to grasp the complex and elusive topic, this contribution uses extremely broad strokes:

(i) To start with, it suggests that the—deficient and hitherto underdeveloped—conceptions of "Muscular Islam" (Section 1) and "Islamic martial arts" (Section 2) might become analytically more productive in the future. It roughly relates both, in historical perspective, to institutionalised slavery and military chivalry (*furūsiyya*) (section 3) in (not only, but notably) the Mamlūk and Ottoman Empires, with a side glance also to the Persian realm and pre-Islamic times.

(ii) It identifies heritage wrestling as the most popular and the main extant remnant of the Islamic *furūsiyya* tradition, with the Turkish city of

1 The research on oil wrestling in Edirne was initially part of a project at the Zentrum Moderner Orient (ZMO) in Berlin, see https://www.zmo.de/forschung/projekte_2008_2013/bromber_contest_sports_e.html, accessed 14 September 2017. Here, I draw on my hitherto unpublished conference presentations: "Hegemoniale Männlichkeit und Martial Arts in der Islamischen Welt," given at the workshop *Körper und Moral: Ordnungsvorstellungen in mehrheitlich muslimischen Ländern*, an event shared by the Asien-Afrika-Institut of the University of Hamburg and the Akademie der Wissenschaften in Hamburg on 22–23 July 2011; I am indebted to its organisers, Monika Arnez and Katja Niethammer. The second is my paper "Muscular Islam with Shamanistic Features: The Many Layers of Turkish Oil Wrestling," given at the conference *The Aesthetics of Crossing: Experiencing the Beyond in Abrahamic Traditions*, which took place on 19–21 March 2015; I thank the organisers of this conference in Uetrecht, Simon O'Meara and Christian Lange. I am further grateful to Katrin Bromber, Bettina Gräf, and Alina Kokoschka for taking a critical look at earlier versions of this essay.

 | DOI:10.1163/9789004386891_017

Edirne as a modern national centre of this type of martial art and Muscular Islam. On closer inspection, the physical practice of oil wrestling and its established festival structure abounds, with an enormous variety of cultural registers (Section 4). This vast reservoir for identity construction cannot be reduced to merely a Turkish national, narrowly defined Islamic or nostalgic (Neo-)Ottoman activity.

(iii) Side glances to recent developments in Turkey can help to relativise and fine-tune the suggested conceptions. The idea of physically assembling heritage sports, together with their imagined trans-Asian background, resonates with the "Turkish history thesis." This is played out not only in Edirne but has started to take place also in the global city of Istanbul, although within a much different and wider framework, as shall be indicated (Section 5).

2 "Muscular Christianity" and "Muscular Judaism" as Challenges to Oil Wrestling

The heritage sport of oil wrestling (*yağlı güreş*) is a particular form of freestyle wrestling performed on unmown grass, with the protagonists and their trousers completely drenched in olive oil, turning victory over the opponent into an extremely slippery and demanding task. It is quite popular, especially in the western half of Turkey, was chosen as *the* national style of traditional wrestling in Turkey, and is officially labelled as "the sport of the ancestors" (*ata sporu*). In 2010, it was accorded by UNESCO the status of "Intangible Cultural Heritage"; it is practised within a series of outdoor festivals, the most important of which is staged annually on the outskirts of Edirne, a city in northwestern Turkey, close to the borders of Greece and Bulgaria. Instead of calling the Kırkpınar oil wrestling festival of Edirne an "invented tradition," an expression that insinuates feigning, it might be more helpful to subsume it under the rubric of "neo-traditional or 'modified' wrestling practices [that] have reached some degree of sportification [but] they do not seem to be among the 'sufficiently' disciplined ones precisely because they were never fully disconnected from their festive context" (Bromber et al. 2014, 1). Hence, it is not advisable to assume for such types of athletic enterprise sharp dichotomies between "traditional" and "modern" sports with the consequence of "understanding the latter as the sole expression of the 'modern'." Therefore, "these 'modified' forms exist simultaneously and relate to 'traditional' as well as Olympic-style wrestling" (Bromber et al. 2014, 1–14; for the aspect of sportification, Krawietz 2010). Some wrestlers practise both types of wrestling, as does Recep Kara, the Turkish oil wrestling champion of 2004, 2007, 2008, and 2016.

Despite the sport's rich cultural background, it is quite astonishing that neither Islamic, Middle Eastern, Ottoman, nor Turkish studies have had much to say about wrestling practices and narratives, with the clear-cut exception of Iranian studies, the perspective of which will be sketched out below. Male bodies have not been the central focus of Islamic studies and related disciplines in any case, so that it comes as no surprise that these disciplines also do not pay much attention to wrestling.[2] A nevertheless decisive publication was written nearly forty years ago by the Turkologist and historian Hans-Peter Laqueur (1979). Anthropologists have also made important contributions to the role of wrestling in Turkey. Carl Hershiser (1998) emphasises: "Within the context of Turkish folk culture, traditional wrestling is more than just a sport. It is both a performance and an elaborate physical ritual that celebrates the traditional construction of an ideal Turkish masculinity."[3] The Bulgarian anthropologist and wrestling expert Petăr Petrov is also relevant here, as he has done research on the afterlife of traditional wrestling and its (re)production of a social order in some of the former Ottoman strongholds under conditions of nationalism and socialism (Petrov 2007). In one chapter of her *Faces of the State*, Yael Navaro-Yashin deals with national Greco-Roman wrestling, although many of her observations are also applicable here:

> What cricket is for India, soccer and wrestling turned out to be for Turkey. In the development of the culture of sport in the twentieth century, soccer and wrestling distinguished themselves as the most popular and most promising in the incitement of national fervour. They were construed as Turkey's national games."
>
> NAVARO-YASHIN 2002, 124

Although she is not concerned with modified wrestling and its heritage-style variants, her insights should nevertheless be tested for the case of oil wrestling.

2 There are, of course, several examples to the contrary, but it is not necessary to assemble here pertinent literature. As compared to other topics, the percentage of works on this subject is still rather low. The spread of modern sports seems to garner more attention, not least due to the influence of gender studies and spatial studies that take an interest in sportscapes.

3 The anthropologist Carl Hershiser, who has a Turkish Muslim mother and familiarity with wrestling, describes his status among the oil wrestlers with whom he travelled to athletic events as that of a "native outsider" (Hershiser 1998, 38).

There is a flood of popular Turkish literature and rich visual archives on oil wrestling that are only partly digitised for "the long twentieth century."[4] Taken together with academic studies such as Turkish dissertations, this constitutes a vast body to be explored. Although the state of Turkey repressed for many decades public expressions of Islam, the influence of religion has nevertheless become manifest in various branches of popular culture. For instance, Brockett analyses provincial newspapers from the middle of the twentieth century and argues in favour of "the dynamic relationship between the elite vision and popular experience" (Brockett 2011, xii). His study demonstrates creative forces of self-expression on the regional level beyond top-down and even counter to centralistic state expectancies, notably a cherishing of the Ottoman past and a "Turkish-Islamic synthesis" *avant la lettre* (Brockett 2011, 23, 175, 196, 223, and passim). The rise of heritage-related popular culture in various provinces of Turkey, including cultural manifestations of religion, has yet to be explored on a wider scale. Pertinent developments should be analysed with regard to Republican oil wrestling, combining texts, visuals, interviews, and field research (not to mention other cultural sport practices). From an Islamic studies perspective, it is desirable to transcend the narrow perspective of the nation-state, all the more so since the actual presentation of Turkish oil wrestling has opened up considerably to further influences, especially in the last one and a half decades.

A concept that could help in analysing this type of freestyle wrestling is "Muscular Islam." Furthermore, it may be eye-opening to look at various (Muslim) movements, institutions, organisations, and particular festivals or other events that are aimed at fighting purported cultural decay. These activities combine the staging of athletic elements with narratives that suggest a rekindling of Islamic ideals and a revival of the religious-cultural heritage in action, its group spirit, and technologies of the self. The problem is, however, that the notion "Muscular Islam" has, to the best of my knowledge, not yet been systematically outlined and explored in the aforementioned disciplines or in sports studies. While "Muscular Christianity" and "Muscular Judaism" are familiar scholarly concepts, an analysis of this concept as it relates to Islam is not yet available (Putney 2001; Ladd and Mathisen 1999). This raises the question of its historical causes and the particular social reasons for its emergence. Muscular Christianity, for comparison, came into being in specific contexts in the middle of the nineteenth century, when philosophical and moral ideas about the physical enactment of masculinity, self-discipline, and team-spirit became

4 For digitised oil wrestling publications presented by the Edirne municipality, see http://www.edirnekirkpinar.com/en/arsiv/1-books, accessed 6 October 2017.

popular in England and beyond, notably in the United States and Australia. Protestant Christians advocated initiatives to combat the moral and physical decay of, first of all, young men, and aspired to the creation of a New Man through various associations. This idea of spiritual and physical male reinvigoration in modern times shaped institutions such as boarding schools, YMCAs in many countries around the globe, the Red Cross, the Boy Scout movement, etc., was advocated in sports magazines, and is mainly associated with athletic disciplines, such as basketball, football, gymnastics, and rugby. Although it was most virulent for the British Victorians and spread quickly in that period to various realms of influence, it lingers on in certain milieus until today.

Like Muscular Christianity, which was a response to the negative effects of the industrial revolution and the understanding of society as an organism or even a machine that invites enhancement via social engineering, Muscular Judaism was also a reaction to a discourse of decay and decadence. The term Muscular Judaism dates back to the turn of the nineteenth century, was coined by Max Nordau, and is related to "the so-called Jewish question in European modernity" (Presner 2007, xxiv). Fueled by Zionism and the impact of exclusion from emerging national sports clubs, along with the stigmatisation and mass migration of Jews from Eastern Europe beginning in the 1880s, it addressed physical strength, dauntlessness, and complete determination; it related not only to the founding of specific sports clubs in this new spirit, but already in 1921 led to the establishment of the Maccabi World Union, which came to stage the international Maccabiah Games, beginning in 1932.

Despite the strong evidence of these two concepts—Muscular Christianity and Muscular Judaism—with a variety of well-documented phenomena, an Internet search in 2017 produces hardly any titles on Muscular Islam.[5] Up until now there have been no monographs on the topic and just a few chapter titles or scientific articles that refer to the term: in her contribution of 2011, Samaya Farooq explores the specific subjectivities of Muslim males in "an all-male Islamic independent school situated in England" who have a Pakistani background, which makes them suspicious in the Islamophobic climate after 9/11, and who employ football as a means to craft themselves as moral people (Farooq 2011). She explicitly states that:

> [T]he concept of "muscular Islam" was first used by Nauright (1997) in his exploration of masculinity and "Coloured" rugby in Cape Town, South

5 I got to read the unpublished paper of Krais 2017 only after the submission of my article. He primarily "aims at filling a gap in the transnational history of the missionary encounter and Muslim-Christian relations in the colonial Arab world."

> Africa. Exposing how "Coloured" men utilised rugby to bolster their subordinate position during apartheid, his work alludes to the important roles of sport and religion in restructuring the contours of demoralised masculinities.
>
> FAROOQ 2011, 147f.

The article by Nauright (1997) that Farooq mentions refers to research carried out in South Africa, a country in the Global South, once a part of the British Empire, but obviously the Muscular Islam dimension has hitherto not been explored for Muslim majority countries, neither before 9/11 nor after, nor has it been discussed in wider Islamic studies in relation to any other trigger events or developments.

A challenging and highly reflexive contribution has been made by Wilson Chacko Jacob, who focusses on a "class of Egyptian men (the *effendiyya*)" for the period between 1870 and 1940, whom he describes vaguely as "a cultural bourgeoisie" (Jacob 2011, 4). This group is characterised by a shared concern for civilisational enhancement via a double reconfiguration of caring for body and soul through indulging in activities that had been advocated by the emerging Boy Scouts movement since the 1920s, groups of local toughs, the Young Men's Muslim Association (YMMA), the Muslim Brotherhood, paramilitary youth organisations in general, the Egyptian Olympic movement, established in 1914, and physical culture magazines. Although he intermittently refers to the appropriation of Islam, such as with the presentation of the prophet Muḥammad as "the original über-Scout" (Jacob 2011, 109), he does not suggest "Muscular Islam" as a concept and does not mention this term. To these usual suspects identified as agents of physical and psychic transformation as a response to colonial regimes or to the demands of Western influences and the founding of modern nation-states in general, sports clubs need to be added. For such broader developments in the Middle East, bits and pieces have already been scientifically covered, especially for Lebanon.[6] Nevertheless, all-encompassing comparisons of such groups for different nations are hitherto not available; also, for example, a monograph that would give an overview on the Olympic movement in the Middle East is still missing. However, what has been rather hidden from view concerning endeavours in this direction are modified versions of traditional sports.

We have to turn to the region of Iran and further eastward, especially to Indonesia, in order to encounter more frequent research on tradition-bound

6 See, for instance, publications of Jennifer M. Dueck, Sune Haugbolle, Michael Johnson, and Keith David Watenpaugh.

phenomena of "Muscular Islam," although the term itself is rarely used. The most famous example is Zurkhane athleticism, which comprises a number of activities with specific instruments, but which used to include wrestling as well (Chehabi 2002; Ridgeon 2010; Rochard 2002). The sport came into being presumably in response to the Mongol invaders in the thirteenth century and was practised in certain indoor sites, usually in urban settings, for training mostly with mock-martial weaponry; the wrestling style that has meanwhile been separated from its historical canon is widely known in Iran and South Asia as Kushti or Pahlevani wrestling (Krawietz 2013, 148–49, 151). A short BBC article of 2004, in a popular science fashion, uses the title "Muscular Shias Return to Roots" and informs us that the institution of houses of strength (*zūrkhāna*) hosts "ritual martial arts training" and that "[m]artial arts rituals go to the heart of Shia tradition" (Irving 2004). However, Muscular Shīʿism as such has not been sufficiently researched, although there are many publications about Zurkhane athletism and also about ʿĀshūrāʾ practices. Concerning the latter, the rituals of mourning and self-flagellation in the Islamic month of Muḥarram seem to be at the centre of academic interest, but less so their subversive message of strength through the display of muscular bodies, performances with a martial appeal, and invigorated religious-political dedication. Furthermore, Muscular Shīʿism should not be understood in a reductionist manner or be studied only as a confessionally confined phenomenon, but it would be useful to also analyse it in relation to developments spreading among majoritarian Sunnīs. Both major Islamic groups and many subdivisions refer to Muḥammad and his cousin and son-in-law ʿAlī and draw on comparable though distinct patterns of reference and performativity from the sources.

We do not know how exactly forms of traditional wrestling (among other practices) spread throughout the post-formative Persianite realm. Shahab Ahmed drew attention to what he calls the often neglected "Balkans-to-Bengal complex." For the "rough period 1350–1850" Ahmed perceives, with respect to "the societies living in the vast region extending from the Balkans through Anatolia, Iran and Central Asia down and across Afghanistan and North India to the Bay of Bengal," something that may come close to "a relatively distinct and integrated world (sometimes termed a 'civilization,' or a 'cultural zone' within Islamic civilization)" (Ahmed 2016, 73). Ahmed calls this realm he uses as "the primary socio-historical case" in his book "at once a major and a dominant historical paradigm of Islam—but [one that] is largely unrecognized as such" (Ahmed 2016, 83). According to him, "the Balkans-to-Bengal complex is certainly the dominant paradigm of Islam in the long historical period that directly preceded the violent irruption of European modernity into societies of Muslims" (Ahmed 2016, 82). Ahmed is not merely concerned with extensive literary canons, but he significantly draws on Sufi practices in particular to boost his argument of an extremely variegated yet inclusive Islam. However, similar explorations into athleticism are not (yet) available and modern anthropology with its methdological tool of fieldwork in any case sets in only much later in the nineteenth century.

For many years, the study of traditional wrestling under the conditions of (colonial) modernity in the case of the Indian subcontinent was associated with the name of the anthropologist Joseph Alter, a dominant figure in the field, who does not, however, focus on Islamic influences (Alter 1992).[7] Only recently, Muslim Pakistani equivalent practices have become more visible in academia, especially through Jürgen Frembgen and Paul Rollier. However, they argue *against* the influence of Islam, claiming that "there are also many cultural fields in Muslim societies that are not directly informed by religious belief or ritual. There is, for instance, the dimension of traditional sports and pastimes, games and play, entertainment and amusement" (Frembgen and Rollier 2014, xiii, 3–45). At the same time they acknowledge: "Many of these cultural practices, some of which still survive, were informed by Persian influences," and they mention, notably, references to ʿAlī as "Father of the *pahlwan*s," i.e., of the traditional wrestlers (Frembgen and Rollier 2014, xv, 22–23). Such statements can serve as an illustration of an all too narrow understanding of what Islam comprises, the widespread attitude that Shahab Ahmed deplores and which he attempts to deconstruct in his ambitious project.[8]

For Turkey, the concept of Muscular Islam looks at first glance even less convincing in view of the Kemalist state institutions and politics that used to shy away from Islamic references. However, certain ministries, such as the Turkish Ministry of Youth and Sports and the Ministry of Tourism, engage with and foster that dimension, notably with respect to oil wrestling as national cultural politics (Krawietz and Riedler forthcoming). The open, though limited, inclusion of and emphasis on certain Islamic elements has grown in the last one and a half decades, a circumstance that has not been followed up upon sufficiently through research. Hence, this essay argues that not only the—somewhat Islamically tinted—adoption of what were originally Western sports that have since become global athletic disciplines should be considered in the future in a

7 Alter has, for instance, also written about yoga and Muscular Christianity with a "Hindu" twist (Alter 2006).

8 Ahmed's overall message is underlined by this quote: "We are confronted with a range of apparently contradictory and mutually non-commensurate statements and actions—whether that apparent contradiction is between doctrine and doctrine, doctrine and practice, or practice and practice—all of which claim, to their own satisfaction, to be representative of and integral to a putative object, 'Islam'" (Ahmed 2016, 109).

Muscular Islam perspective, but also—and perhaps even more so—modified sports with an indigenous tradition that have been turned into "heritage" of sorts. *Both* large strains participate in the (post-)modern enunciation and production of a strong Muslim body, a better self, and a better community.

In his unpublished dissertation of 2015, historian Murat Yıldız examines, for the period from the late nineteenth century to the early twentieth, the evolving new-style physical culture, but he does not include in his study wrestling in Istanbul and its discussion in the late-Ottoman local sports press, despite the commercial success of Turkish wrestlers in Europe, who were known as the "Terrible Turks" (Krawietz 2012a).[9] He emphasises tropes and practices shared by different communities, a result that allows him to state that "these discussions serve as a unique vantage point from which we can trace inter-communal connections in the empire and challenge the notion that Turks, Armenians, Greeks, and Jews from similar educational and socio-economic backgrounds inhabited entirely separate spatial and cultural spheres" (Yıldız 2015, 201). As a consequence, he is barely interested in distinguishing the notions of Muscular Judaism or Muscular Christianity, despite the fact that he variously refers to their standard carriers and methods when he looks at "schools, voluntary athletic associations, the Ministry of Public Education, the press, and newly constructed urban spaces" (Yıldız 2015, 255). However, Yıldız does not mention Muscular Islam. Studies of this type are very important for the emerging discourses about the necessity of physical strength and fitness.[10] Therefore, we should not only pay attention to "the global spread of modern sports" (Yıldız 2015, 16–17, n36), but, as an important part of that, also to modified, often heritagised versions of sports.

Furthermore, we need publications that also take a comparative approach, looking at physical practices (modern and re-fashioned local ones) and techniques aimed at fighting moral corruption and setting one's energies on personal betterment with reference to Islam in (emerging) national theatres of self-presentation. The states in which these practices can be observed range from those attaining independence quite early, such as Saudi Arabia in 1932, or very late, such as the small countries in the Arab Gulf at the beginning of the 1970s, Bahrain, Qatar, and the United Arab Emirates. All of them heavily employ—to varying degrees Islamically framed, but in any case, technologically

9 However, Yıldız mentioned this phenomenon and highlighted its importance at the ZMO-conference *"New Man" in Africa, Asia and the Middle East: Practices, Networks and Mobilization, c. 1910–1960*, in September 2017.

10 See for the early Turkish Republic, Akın 2004. In this essay, it is not possible to ponder the potential overlap between wrestling bodies, physical culture, and later, body building; see Krawietz 2012a, 209–12.

enhanced and otherwise modified—sports of the desert (camel races, falconry, and horse races) in their cultural politics. That is to say, Muscular Islam as an umbrella term and a research perspective for certain developments can comprise especially, but not exclusively, periods before and after state formation, be relevant until today, and be shaped by state and non-state actors. Since Muscular Judaism is strongly related to the rise of Zionism, it would make sense to look for expressions of Muscular Islam also in relation to breaking points in the Islamic world, such as the abolishment of the caliphate in 1924, the founding of the State of Israel in Palestine in 1948, the crushing defeat of Egyptian and other Arab forces in the Six Day War of 1967 against Israel, the Iranian Revolution of 1978–79, September 11 of 2001, and the Arab Spring, all of which already make for quite a long list.

3 Exploring Islamic Martial Arts

Another concept for framing modified traditional sports—apart from Muscular Islam—could be Islamic or Muslim martial arts. However, as the term is widely understood, martial arts are seldom associated with the Islamic world but usually with Southeast Asia and most of all with countries such as China, Japan, and Korea, or religions such as Buddhism, Taoism, and Shintoism. There are some diligent case studies for Southeast Asian contexts, such as Hallenberg's analysis of an Islamic appropriation of standardised Chinese martial arts (*wushu*) in Northern China by the Hui, China's largest Muslim minority (Hallenberg 2002). Another part of the world that has been tackled from the viewpoint of its rich martial arts tradition is Indonesia and Southeast Asia in general, although those who do research on this region often do not pursue an Islamic studies dimension in any depth.[11] There is an even greater lack of historically and Islamically informed martial arts studies for a large number of Arab countries. The surge of traditional Southeast Asian martial practices on a global level is a result of the rise of new visual media in the twentieth century. In *Modernity at Large,* Arjun Appadurai states:

> The transnational movement of martial arts, particularly through Asia, as mediated by the Hollywood and Hong Kong film industries (Zarilli 1995)

---

11 See the *Journal of Asian Martial Arts* for perspective on the dominance of other research aspects. An important exception is Farrer (2009), who writes about Malay culture and the employment of the Islamic Ḥaqqānī-Naqshbandī Ṣūfī order of martial arts. Rashid (1990, 64) explains the still "relative seclusion"—at least at that time—of Malay martial arts (*ilmu pencak silat*).

> is a rich illustration of the ways in which long-standing martial arts traditions, reformulated to meet phantasies of contemporary (sometimes lumpen) youth populations, create new cultures of masculinity and violence, which are in turn the fuel for increased violence in national and international politics.[12]
>
> APPADURAI 2005, 40F.

For the country of Iran, Chehabi alerts us to the fact that, in the "1970s one new element came to enrich Iran's sports scene, and that was East Asian martial arts. Here the impetus came from a nephew of the Shah, Prince Shahryar Shafiq, an accomplished athlete who introduced martial arts to the armed forces, but the great popularity of Chinese kung fu films also played a role" (Chehabi 2002, 281). A striking popular expression of such developments with an Islamic twist is related to the Mujahideen, or Afghan guerilla fighters, who ousted Soviet troops from their country after a century of occupation. The Russians started to withdraw from Afghanistan in 1988, the year the blockbuster film *Rambo III* appeared on screen. It featured the super-hero, Sylvester Stallone, alias John Rambo, a Vietnam veteran who undertakes to rescue his former instructor, held captive by the Russians in the Afghan borderland. Rambo is presented as being familiar with Asian martial arts: he had retreated to Thailand after the disaster of the Vietnam war and was involved in stick fighting to make a living. However, the *ad-hoc* helpers he recruits for this mission impossible to rescue his dear friend (with victims of this rescue numbering in the three-digits) appear as archaic Muslim forces: a troop of Afghan riders trained in Buzkashi, a sort of polo centred on the corpse of a dead goat (Azoy 1982; Levine 2000). Actually, there is some historical realism in this setting, insofar as the scenes in the film of the martial arts folk-game Buzkashi may be perceived as a faint reminder that polo, as an ancient "sport of kings," was invented on the Iranian plateaus and spread in many directions (Chehabi and Guttmann 2002, 385). As this example suggests, not only Old Iranian and Shīʿī influences[13] may need to be better integrated into the analysis of martial arts in the extremely wide and complex Islamicate world, but also into media studies—the latter always with the necessary caveat that martial arts should not be understood as something stemming exclusively from East Asia, appearing only since around the 1970s via Kung-Fu films and the like. One of the most important reference works for martial arts worldwide duly includes entries on "Ottoman Oiled Wrestling,"

12 Such inspirations may not necessarily produce only violence, but also expressions of hedonistic self-fashioning in fitness clubs or body-building studios.

13 This relates to contributions about *javānmardi* (the Persian equivalent of *futuwwa*) movements and the early phenomenon of juvenile martial arts vagabonds (*ʿayyārūn*).

"Ottoman Martial Arts," and "Iranian Martial Arts" (Green and Svinth 2010, 85–87), however, it misses out on much of the literature mentioned here (of course, only publications prior to 2010 could have been included) as well as on the role of Islam with respect to "Belief Systems" and "Performing Arts" as dealt with in the work's second volume. Obviously, larger research gaps have to be addressed, one of which is that studies on Muscular Islam should be better woven into the wealth of scholarship on the Ottoman army.

4 Remarks on Chivalry in the Mamlūk and Ottoman Empires

The Ottoman spoils of war from the sixteenth to eighteenth centuries (German *Türkenbeute*) assembled as trophy collections or bought for the historic armories of Europe (Budapest, Dresden, Karlsruhe, Krakow, Moscow, Munich, and Vienna) as well as the largest and most complete Turkish national reservoir of Ottoman weaponry culture, which is displayed in the Istanbul Military Museum (Askerî Müze) not far from Taksim Square, abound with sumptuous martial artefacts and trappings. They range from weaponry of all sorts to horse armour and precious textiles. However, what such types of expositions and archives of knowledge usually do *not* reveal are the regular physical training and leisure activities of Ottoman soldiers (and civilians) that did not leave behind traces in such impressive arts and crafts. One of the rather blind areas that such a focus on precious artefacts creates is the wrestling tradition—notably, that of the Janisseries (*yeni çeri*), as the empire's infantry troops (abolished in 1826)—not to speak of ordinary civilians who also wrestled on various occasions. Although Ottoman miniature paintings attest to high-level wrestling events for festivities at court, neither the above-mentioned permanent museum collections nor academic scholarship have contributed much to elucidate this performative athletic dimension and the social role of wrestling as combat preparation as well as a joyous celebration activity.[14]

Such gaps get even wider for earlier historical settings. The sub-discipline of Mamlūk studies, which is dedicated to the dynasty of the same name (r. 648–922/1250–1517), is thriving and, David Ayalon (1914–98) notably and many others in his wake have written extensively about the historical process of introducing firearms and the system of military slaves (sg. *mamlūk*). Such slaves were imported from outside the Arab and Muslim realm and educated in martial arts and Islam, but the analysis of their training patterns, and

14 The thick volume by Faroqhi and Öztürkmen 2014 mentions various sports activities, including wrestling, only in passing, but does not offer a closer analysis of any of them.

especially those for wrestling, still poses problems as to the concrete quotidian and festive athletic practices.[15] It would make sense to sift through the manifold scholarly publications and to better link findings from Mamlūk studies (and the many other earlier and later dynasties since the time of the ʿAbbāsids, r. 132–923/750–1517, that also relied on the Islamic institution of imported one-generation military slaves and held athletic festivities) to modern Muscular Islam phenomena, including wrestling.

The most promising genres in this regard are chivalry, equestrianism, and knightly martial exercise (*furūsiyya*) in preparation for warfare, which also includes archery, the use of lances, swords, maces, war engines, the strategic art of war planning, and, according to some authors, even hunting and polo. The wealth of *furūsiyya* manuscripts, which date back to times even long before the Crusaders appeared in the Middle East, is largely untapped. Shihab al-Sarraf has diligently sifted through this vast Arabic corpus, which presents material from different perspectives, such as the normative, the philological, and the veterinary. Al-Sarraf distinguishes between "higher chivalry" (*furūsiyya ʿulwiyya*), directed from horseback, and "lower chivalry" (*furūsiyya sufliyya*), performed on foot, such as wrestling (*muṣāraʿa*) (al-Sarraf 2004, 144).[16] Although Ḥadīth literature abounds in descriptions of the physique and the physical practices of the prophet Muḥammad (and certain of his Companions) and elaborates on his wars and raids, a systematic Islamic appropriation of his martial physical culture occurs only later in *furūsiyya* literature, the normative branch of which attaches great importance to the legitimising force of the Prophetic role model.[17] Such documents have become a main source from which Muscular Islam renderings of the Prophet and certain of his Companions as strong bodies empowered by a superior religion gather inspiration to mould modern ideals from pious Arab ancestors (*salaf ṣāliḥ*) (al-Sarraf 2004, 144). Hence, some athletic disciplines appear as divinely blessed, such as riding, archery, and wrestling. A certain extraordinarily strong wrestler named Rukāna is said to have converted to Islam only when the Prophet himself defeated him athletically. However, it is not mighty Rukāna who dominantly re-emerges as a figure of reference in twentieth-century oil wrestling, as shall be demonstrated in the next section.

---

15 A welcome contribution is Guo (2013), who emphasises that "it is evident that in the medieval Islamic world men were engaged in various physical exercises, competitive or recreational fencing, boat racing, swimming, and weightlifting (also relevant were animal fighting, falconry, and hunting)" (Guo 2013, 6).

16 For a hyper-modern version of proud chivalry, see Bromber and Krawietz 2013, 205–206.

17 For a glimpse into Islamised versions of this genre, see Conermann 2009.

5 The Lurking Cultural Multiplicity of Oil Wrestling

Oil wrestling is also important insofar as it shows that a narrow understanding of the concept of Muscular Islam as merely a somewhat Islamically tinted appropriation of modern "Western" sports—along the lines of Muscular Christianity and Muscular Judaism—would blind us to appreciating modified heritage-style sports as important elements in the realm of the modern. From the 1920s until today, the Turkish border town of Edirne can lay claim to being, in terms of oil wrestling, *the* national centre of Muscular Islam. That is not to say that it has constantly striven towards the 2010 UNESCO heritage success that was to come or that Islamic elements have really dominated the scene. What is of interest here is the cultural multi-layeredness of the annual Kırkpınar festival, which represents the most important event of all modified traditional wrestling competitions throughout Turkey. Taking oil wrestling merely as the tip of the iceberg, a vast cultural reservoir for Muscular Islam becomes visible.

The Friday sermon in the famous Selimiye mosque in the city centre of Edirne on the day the tournament starts infuses wrestlers and other visitors with familiar national and religious tropes, clustered around expressions such as *Allah için ölmek güzeldir, bareket, bayrak, istiklal, kuvvet, millet, rahmet, şehit oldukları, ülkelerimiz, vatan* ("It is excellent to die for God, *baraka*, flag, independence, power, nation, mercy, martyrs, our country, fatherland"), etc. With this spirited prelude to the oil wrestling games in the nearby Sarayiçi quarter, the framework of the Turkish nation-state looms large, and many parts of the connected ceremonies veer towards hyper-nationalism (Krawietz 2014b). However, Turkish popular literature on oil wrestling and its festival components also emphasise the Central Asian Turkic background of modern Turks as a decisive part of that national narrative. This is in line with the "Turkish history thesis" (*Türk tarih tezi*) as the founding doctrine of the heavily shrunken Ottoman sucessor state of modern Turkey. Şükrü Hanioğlu puts it in a nutshell: "According to the Turkish history thesis, the cradle of human civilization was Central Asia, the Turkish homeland. From here the Turks had migrated to all Old World continents, establishing major states," although the Kemalists' handling of that narrative for the most part failed to reach the broader masses to create effective emotional bonds (Hanioğlu 2011, 164–65). Ersanlı claims that the architects of the early Turkish Republic "were unable to confront peacefully the multiplicity of Turkicness, the plurality in the merging styles of Islam and Turkishness, the originality of Europeanness and Asianness" so much so that they "tried to squeeze all this richness into a very confined identity based on a[n] a-historical interpretation of Ur-Turks of Aryan race, the best of which were believed to have moved to Anatolia," coming from various regions of Central Asia (Ersanlı 2001, 8). But the main deficiency of this doctrine was that it "bypassed the Ottoman past" (Hanioğlu 2011, 165).

Hans-Peter Laqueur, who visited the competitions in the second half of the 1970s, describes oil wrestling, in his dissertation of 1979, as a "sports discipline within the Ottoman-Turkish order of culture and society" (Laqueur 1979, i) and argues that these games were "stamped by a clearly nationalistic and chauvinistic tendency and served first and foremost propagandistic goals" (Laqueur 1979, 98). In a similar manner, Navaro-Yashin states, concerning freestyle wrestling in the following decade:

> In the 1980s, wrestling, with a history that preceded the building of the republic, was symbolically associated with a tradition of Turkish power: *Turkic-to-Ottoman-to-Turkish statecraft* personified in the image of the wrestler as Leviathan. The government and presidency of Özal, with its Ottomanist revivalism combined with a version of laissez-faire Westernism, provided special support to the sport of wrestling.
>
> NAVARO-YASHIN 2002, 124

This also applies to my observations about oil wrestling throughout recent years. However, despite its strongly determined nationalistic imprint, reminders of prior and other cultural registers have not completely been eradicated, suppressed, or transformed in a no longer identifiable manner, and they are more complex than the "Turkic-to-Ottoman-to-Turkish statecraft" formula suggests. The question is to what broader cultural entities the ceremonial actions performed in the course of this type of wrestling and its paraphernalia actually belong. The point I want to make here is that the Kırkpınar wrestling festival is a striking example of how the massive national paradigm overlaps with manifold cultural influences from an extremely broad geographical and historical range.

Yet, although the UNESCO oil wrestling nomination statement lists a number of these elements as typical, no discernable efforts are made to differentiate systematically between the various cultural influences and to take pride in their multiplicity. Being granted Intangible Cultural Heritage status already recognises and cherishes a cultural artefact's peculiarity, but this does not automatically mean that the applicants who have proposed this status themselves have an interest in revealing its potentially hybrid character. The narrow focus of the Kırkpınar application—despite its national appropriation—has to do with the fact that traditional wrestling was not presented to the international organisation as a shared physical practice of a larger realm, but as tied to a very particular place, at the very border of the Republic of Turkey and to a specific annual festival time.[18] The borderland position and battered wartime history of Edirne resonates with the national message of gathering strength against external enemies.

It is worthwhile noting that in 2010, three different (neo-)traditional or modified sport forms independently applied for and were granted Intangible Cultural Heritage status by UNESCO: Kırkpınar oil wrestling (UNESCO 2010, Kırkpınar); the Naadam Festival in Mongolia, which comprises wrestling, archery, and riding (UNESCO 2010, Nadaam; Krist 2014); and for Iran, Zurkhana ("House of Strength") rituals and athletic practices (UNESCO 2010, Pahlevani).

The latter also traditionally included wrestling. Such showcase events get heavily mediatised and foster not only national pride but also impressions of similar, if not intersecting, shared practices across national frameworks. Against the widespread tendency of essentialism, the philosopher Ludwig Wittgenstein (d. 1951) made the famous conceptual proposal of family resemblance (*Familienähnlichkeit*) in order to pay more attention to the similarities, though they may be vague, rather than to sharp differences between similar entities. His focus on similarities that observes sense, instead of the insistence on hierarchical genealogies (Kimmich 2017, 89), has been widely adopted in cultural studies.

Throughout recent years, international visitors not only from across Asia, but from other parts of the world as well, have regularly come to attend the main annual tournament in Edirne and to appreciate it also in the sense of such family resemblance. Nevertheless, the three victorious countries of 2010 did not opt to pick up on their prospective "family resemblance" and to submit a shared application with traditional wrestling as its common denominator or take even more countries on board.[19]

Despite the national fine-tuning but local framing of the Edirne event, the multiplicity of cultural registers in Turkish oil wrestling remains striking. To start with, the practice of applying olive oil to male wrestling bodies was taken over from the Byzantines when Turkic migration waves originally from Central Asia populated not only Anatolia but expanded also into Southeastern Europe. Some regions of what became much later the modern state of Bulgaria were

18 On the historical phenomenon of festivals, including oil wrestling, being related to a market fair (*panayır*), see Laqueur 1979, 14–18.

19 There are other successful Intangible Cultural Heritage applications to UNESCO that are backed by a certain number of countries, the largest one being the falconry project, submitted by 18 countries together and officially inscribed in 2016.

known during Ottoman times as a hotbed for producing oil wrestling masters. Further Western influences of decisive impact go back to the later nineteenth century, when a number of Turkish wrestlers went to Europe and even to the United States, creating the vaudeville hype about "Terrible Turks" and the like (Krawietz 2012a, 210). Their return to Ottoman, then national Turkey, and the general trend towards sportification strongly modified the rules and cultural framing of oil wrestling (Krawietz 2012b, 2151). The revival of the Olympic idea, with the first organised event taking place in Athens in 1896, and globalisation in general led to the international spread of certain previously regional forms of wrestling, such as Greco-Roman wrestling and Judo, so that distinct forms, such as Japanese Sumo, Swiss wrestling, and Turkish *yağlı güreş* were united under the umbrella term "wrestling" (Laqueur 1979, 50). However, the Turkish word for wrestling itself (*güreş*) had already entered many languages, a circumstance that may also indicate the dynamic, cross-cultural capacity of this deeply engrained activity (Erdem 2010, 9).

In general, the Turkish Republic wanted to exclude religion from public space and limit it to a matter of merely private concern. Yet, in the second half of the twentieth century, certain concessions had to be made, and since the beginning of the new millennium, the Justice and Development Party (*Adalet ve Kalkınma Partisi*) had in any case started its ascendancy, although not on the local level of the city of Edirne. Nevertheless, this trend has led nationwide to a more explicit presence of religion in the form of Sunnī Islam, but religious influences could be felt already in many domains much earlier. However, the trend by which "traditional games are invariably stripped of their religious associations as they evolve into modern sports" (Guttmann 2004, 11) cannot be confirmed for oil wrestling. The complete dissolution of religious references within the realm of sports and specifically for oil wrestling did not happen when it was included in the Turkish Wrestling Federation that has promoted and organised oil wrestling events from 1999 onwards, together with the also popular non-oil version, Karakucak. There are other versions of wrestling in Turkey, such as Aba and Şalvar (Dervişoğlu 2014, 49–53) that are likewise promoted by the state, as will be shown towards the end of this article.

The religion of Islam is variously intertwined with Kırkpınar rituals, beginning with the collective visit[20] to the Wrestlers' Cemetery in the city centre, a practice that is led by the Muftī of Edirne, and it is the habit of many wrestlers

20 Collective in the sense that in attendance are the main representatives of the political and cultural administration, plus several residents of the town, journalists, and tourists, but not the majority of the wrestlers. Space is in any case limited in and around the tiny cemetery.

to attend the official Friday prayer and sermon in the central Selimiye mosque. In the quarter of Sarayiçi, Islamic elements are most perceivable through the professional ceremonial moderators (sg. *cazgır*), whose mainly formulaic announcements are nowadays broadcast via loudspeaker. Turkish booklets published in the last decades list the most widely used stanzas (*salavat, dua*), which show a certain number of Islamic references.[21] Laqueur points out that the *cazgır*s as a wrestling institution go back to pre-Islamic times, but that after the advent of Islam, they copiously employed Islamic religious formulae (Laqueur 1979, 6). This is only to a certain degree in accordance with my own experience listening to the Kırkpınar soundscape about three decades later. The ceremonial announcers, who have some liberty to improvise and rearrange the familiar building blocks in their stylised speeches, seem to have only limited religious knowledge and religion does not become dominant in their cultural framing of the event. Often used is the—evidently malapropised—confession of faith, *Allah Allah İllâlah* (instead of *lâ ilâha illâ Allâh*), followed by an invocation of the Prophet Muḥammad and, significantly, his cousin and son-in-law ʿAlī (*Ya Muhammad, ya Ali*). The latter is also acknowledged in Shīʿite Islam as the first rightful caliph, while, according to the Sunnīs, he is merely the fourth one and was not divinely sent to establish a certain sequence of impeccable leaders. This Shīʿte twist may have to do with the fact that the heterodox Shīʿite Dervish order of the Bektaşis played a considerable role in "the Balkans."

The strong shamanistic character of the opening ritual (*peşrev*) evolves from the Central Asian origins of Turkic wrestling (Krawietz 2014a, 452ff). However, such an interpretation is often preemptively cast aside by assurances that this ritual should instead be understood as some sort of pre-modern "warming up." Hence, some wrestlers do not even knowingly complete the ritual sequence that mimics the flapping wings of an eagle about to fly, but occasionally insert the waving of a hand to greet fans in the arena or even combine the retracting of the raised arm with further rubbing of oil into the skin or with an arm rotation that resembles standard arm circle training. Although the practice of *peşrev* is of shamanistic origin, the term itself is Persian, which used to be the cultural lingua franca for a vast realm of the Middle East and beyond. In any case, there are a number of additional Persian words that appear across a wide region, thus bearing testimony to a huge Persianate realm in which such athletic practices played a considerable role. *Cazgır*s often shout the Persian

21 Wrestling performances were often related to lifecycle rituals such as circumcisions or marriages.

expression "wrestler" (*pehlivan*; instead of Turkish *güreşçi*)[22] to summon in rhyme athletes to the field of action (*meydan*), another Persian term of wrestling importance.

Many recurrent stanzas appeal to the "Master of the Wrestlers, His Excellence and Friend of God Hamza" (*Pehlivanların piri Hz. Hamza'yı veli*) (Erdem 2010, 49).[23] In his Turkish sport history, Doğan Yıldız explains that every occupation or trade used to have its own forefather (*pir*)—yet another word of Persian origin—and that the uncle (*amca*) of the Prophet and so-called "Lion of God" (*Allahın Arslanı*), who died in 625 CE as a martyr in the Battle of Uḥud, was known as the "Patron of Wrestlers" (*pehlivanların piri*) (Yıldız 1975, 202; Kowalski 1940, 171). Ḥamza b. ʿAbd al-Muṭṭalib is known as a fearless fighter, notably in the Battle of Badr, in 2/624. However, it is not his historically established seventh-century role in what is nowadays Saudi Arabia, but much later legendary embellishments that have prompted his popularity (Heath 1990, 432–35; Leder 2009, 170). His mythical lifecycle narrative (*Sīrat Amīr Ḥamza*) gained widespread acclaim, although the "rich material often contradicts itself" and some time "between the tenth and fifteenth century at the latest the legend must have reached the Indian subcontinent." From there, it spread widely, so that apart from "Urdu, it is known to exist in Arabic, Persian, Turkish, Sindhi, Malay, Javanese, Georgian, Balinese, Sudanese, Pashto, Bengali, and Hindi versions" (Lakhnavi and Bilgrami 2008, 910–12; Seyller 2002, 12–13). According to Stefan Leder, the Ḥamza narrative is the geographically most widespread "example of a type of narratives that are initially identifiable in Iran already in the early Middle Ages (9th century) and then multiplied since the 13th century in the Arabic realm and that were henceforth highly successful until the 20th century" (Leder 2009, 171f.).

Interestingly, it is not the wrestler Rukāna, whom the Prophet is said to have converted through his athleticism and who is known from Ḥadīth and *furūsiyya* literature (Ibn Qayyim al-Jawziyya 2005, 76–80), but the popular "Balkans-to-Bengal" hero Ḥamza who takes centre stage—also in Edirne:

> Unlike many Muslims of today, the Muslims of the Balkans-to-Bengal complex did not feel the need to articulate or legitimate their Muslimness/their Islam by mimesis of a pristine time of the earliest generations of the community (the *salaf*). Rather, they felt able to be Muslim in explorative, creative, and contrary trajectories ... taking as a point of

---

22 The Turkish language absorbed the Persian term *pehlivan* (Erdem 2010, 10).

23 Actually, the story is more complicated in many presentations, but cannot be detailed here; see Erdem 2010, 61–69.

> departure the array and synthesis of the major developments of the preceding centuries.
>
> AHMED 2016, 81

Hence, there seems to be a vast cultural backdrop to support the designation of Ḥamza as the epitome of a fearless fighter. This rich cultural tapestry appears as a vivid Islamic narrative and martial arts example of Shahab Ahmed's "Balkans-to-Bengal complex" that also had an impact on Arabic-speaking Muslims under Ottoman rule and, as in this case, the mythical Ḥamza made it to nowadays Turkish-speaking communities and resurfaces in oil wrestling.

Thus, besides the genre of *furūsiyya*, a second promising postclassical source for insights into popular martial arts stories with an Islamic twist is the host of heroic legends with their oral presentations and vivid enactments that are full of combat situations and in particular wrestling scenes. Besides the *Ḥamzanāmeh*, extended epic tales of the hero's exploits, there are further heroes who are, to differing degrees, related to historical core figures. They are embedded in groups of martial stories that are enriched by manifold magical stories about heroic traversers of time and space.[24]

Also from the perspective of materiality, there are many similarities, such as the shape and decorative style of the *kıspet*, the leather wrestling trousers, which are a clear reminder of (Shīʿite) Persian Zurkhane wrestling, although the Zurkhane trousers have a much more ornamental design. For manifold reasons, it makes sense to perceive a striking family resemblance among several traditional modes and rituals of wrestling, its paraphernalia, soundscape, and moral or ethical attitudes. This diverse landscape would need another, more in-depth and comparative type of investigation that cannot be carried out here. Suffice it to say that oil wrestling is full of reminders of cultures the Turks passed through on their long journey from Central Asia to Anatolia and Southeastern Europe, plus all sorts of cultural crosspollinations that occurred when the Ottoman Empire (and its athletic practices) extended across three continents.

Despite its regular display of hyper-nationalism on the ground, the annual oil wrestling tournament of Kırkpınar has attracted a larger and much more mixed audience than a merely national or a restricted regional forum. Many journalists show up, mainly from Asian and European countries, some of

---

24 All these heroes, such as Sayf b. Dhī Yazan, ʿAntar b. Shaddād, Dhāt al-Himma, and al-Malik al-Ẓāhir Baybars, should be studied more closely so as to ascertain their precise wrestling and martial arts credentials.

them working on behalf of TV stations. An even larger number of more-or-less professional photographers attend the festival. This mixed crowd must sense a family resemblance or reminders of a "Balkans-to-Bengal complex" and convey it to broader audiences. Paradoxically, it must have been the mediatised visibility created, first of all, by increased national pride and its promotion, that resulted in many more and very different people starting to pay attention to oil wrestling. However, contrary to the considerable homogenising efforts of its official Turkish-national on-site presentation, the new audiences from abroad as well as from Turkey itself have sensed the nevertheless still palpable diversity of cultural, ethnic, and religious components of oil wrestling.

6 The Ethnosport Cultural Festival in Istanbul

In the winter of 2016, those who got onto or descended from the tube at Taksim Square, the well-known central destination and transportation hub of modern Istanbul, were all of a sudden confronted with astonishing vistas. Standing or walking on the flat moving floor on both sides of the middle lower level, commuters were transported into a fancy time tunnel with pictures of exotic, yet vaguely familiar figures. The permanently attached sequence of photographs had received unexpected interim company: below the historic photos a row of temporary easels had been placed, each of them carrying a different tablet. When I stumbled onto that scene in December 2016, there were on one side a series of coloured photographs taken at a huge sports and cultural event called "Etnospor Kültür Festivali I,"[25] and on the other, plates that introduced in Turkish the athletic disciplines involved in that festival by name, followed by descriptions of a few sentences. Moving back and forth between the two rows, I noted that the display comprised: the Cirit game on horses (*Atlı Cirit Oyunu*) (Diem 1982, 86–100), Kuşak wrestling (*Kuşak Güreşi*), the Mangala game (*Mangala*), goat polo (*Kökbörü*; above-mentioned as Buzkashi), the Aşık game (*Aşık Oyunu*), Mas wrestling (*Mas Güreşi*), Şalvar wrestling (*Şalvar Güreşi*), oil wrestling (*Yağlı Güreş*), traditional archery on foot (*Geleneksel Yaya Okçuluğu*), Aba wrestling (*Aba Güreşi*), and archery on horses (*Atlı Okçuluğu*). The explanatory text blocks mentioned various people and large tribes throughout wider

25 I do not want to dwell here on the term "Etnospor." Suffice it to say that in 1996 the "Turkish Traditional Sport Branches Federation" (*Türkiye Geleneksel Spor Dalları Federasyonu*) was set up on the national level, https://gsdf.gov.tr/tr/, accessed 23 October 2017. See its activities report (*Faaliyet raporu*) of 1997/1998.

regions in Asia, while the time ranges given started with the year 5000 BCE. This geographic and chronographic radius resonates with the Turkish history thesis and its historical theatres of Turkic—in the widest sense—action in Central Asia and Anatolia.

Obviously, the biggest contingent included vaguely ethnically identified wrestling activities or, in the language of this essay, modified wrestling styles—making up five of the eleven disciplines or games. The protagonists from across Asia were shown in combat, wearing typical costumes, partly equipped with historical weaponry, underlining the diversity of martial combat styles. The competitively organised activities evolved on a large field, where dozens of mostly white, but also some black, Mongolian-style tents and rows of booths for traditional arts and crafts (*geleneksel el sanatları atölyeleri*) were set up (such as carpet weaving, embroidery, and wood engraving). Notably, the horse races and equestrian games, as well as the various archery contests, necessitated a considerable scope of action. High-rise buildings in the background reminded one of the actual time and place: the first Festival was staged on 26–28 August in 2016 at the western outskirts of Istanbul in Küçükçekmece, more precisely at the Place of Bezirganbahçe.[26] The photographs showed two logos: one of the Municipality of Greater Istanbul (*İstanbul Büyükşehir Belediyesi*), which had organised this youth convention (*Gençlik Meclisi*), the other one a sort of an neo-archaic "E"-shaped logo for "World Ethnosport Confederation."[27]

The colourful pictures presented dressed-up athletes, sports functionaries from different countries, politicians, administrators, and many children and teenagers of both sexes (girls and women with and without headscarves) as the main beneficiaries. Young people were shown in conversation and sportive interaction with the protagonists. Traditional dance groups such as the Whirling Dervishes and a large Mehter-band rounded out the scene. The Chairman of the World Ethnosport Confederation, Necmeddin Bilal Erdoğan, is a son of the current President of Turkey and is also a proficient archer. In an English-language booklet entitled *The Age of Sport Awareness*, he deplores in his introduction the fact that "[s]adly, the numerous sports inherited by our ancestors now take a backseat in the world of sports. This is a starting point

26 Istanbul's historical venue for riding and archery contests was the Hippodrome (*At Meydanı*), near the Blue Mosque, which serves meanwhile as a hot spot for tourism.

27 See the coulored *Dünya Etnospor Konfederasyonu* booklet of 96 pages; it also lists eleven disciplines, but mentions instead of (the traditional intelligence and strategic game) Mangala, two sorts of archery, *Dünya Etnospor Konfederasyonu*, 5. I collected these and other materials from a promotional tent set up next to the oil wrestling arena in Edirne during the annual games of 2017. For a comparison, see "Global Zurkhane Sports," in Krawietz 2013, 156–57.

of our movement to revive these sports" (1). Obviously, Turkey plans to take a leading role in "Developing Ethnosport as a World Sport,"[28] and decided to host in 2018 the 3rd World Ethnosport Cultural Festival (*Etnospor Kültür Festivali*), again in Istanbul, on behalf of the World Ethnosport Confederation. The far-ranging scope of these games, the various new members from all over the world, and increasing number of athletic disciplines included point way beyond the mental landscape of the Turkish history thesis. Judging from the early founding members of this organisation, which was set up in 2011 (one year after the triple modified-wrestling UNESCO success, which included Turkish oil wrestling), it appears that Central Asian athletes may have initially been the main target group of this movement. However, meanwhile the larger narrative is about a general counter-model to the Olympics, which dominated the twentieth century, "where sportive success was the sole aim of sports" (*The Age of Sport Awareness*, 1). And it is about Turkey as an emerging global player, as well as about enhancing the dynamics of Istanbul as a world city, and the revival of trans-Asian and new global axes of cooperation.

After submitting this contribution, I had the opportunity to actually attend the five-day festival (9–13 May 2018), close to the Bosphorus and with the skyline of Istanbul's quarter of Fatih in the background. About 880 athletes competed in 13 categories; it was also announced that oil wrestling was prominently represented by 300 athletes, of whom 45 belonged to the highest category of head wrestlers (*başpehlivanlar*). Included were even countries like Japan, with mounted archery (*Yabusame*) and Qatar with falconry (*şahin gösterisi*). There were ample hands-on opportunities to familiarise oneself also in pratical terms with old-style Ottoman weaponry before the introduction of firearms. Nevertheless, the main organising principle was the hosting of athletic disciplines across various ethnicities and with roots in different religious faiths.

7 Conclusion

This essay captures my endeavours to come to grips with Turkish oil wrestling in Edirne and its resurfacing in the Etnospor Kültür Festavali, which has been held since 2016 in Istanbul by the World Ethnosport Confederation (Dünya Etnospor Konfederasyonu).[29] It looks for concepts to adequately frame this athletic and cultural practice and to relate it to wider concerns of Islamic studies

28 *The Age of Sport Awareness*, 24. The 2017 transfer of the 2016 site of the games from Küçükçekmece to Yenikapı demonstrates the high priority given this event.

29 For pictures and further details, see http://etnosporfestivali.com, accessed 15 May 2018.

in historical perspective and in today's world of rapidly developing nation-states. Understanding Islamic tradition upfront as a variegated process helps in perceiving its immensely rich ways of growing. Two quick side glances on recent Turkish settings alone indicate the multiplicity of shaping future (cultural) developments. The concept of "Muscular Islam" was suggested for this and further studies, not simply because muscular bodies and sportive references to Islam are involved, but because of complex wider narratives and practice patterns in the sense of fighting loss and defeat, of moral re-strengthening, self-empowerment, and group solidarity built through self-confidence in one's own cultural heritage, including spiritual Islamic elements. Historical role models, whether appropriated from *furūsiyya* literature or from the widespread popular culture of fantastic heroic stories, may be more influential for Muscular Islam phenomena than, say, the European culture of knights is for Muscular Christianity. The subject requires considerable research aimed at exploring the potential Muscular Islam dimension of the waning Ottoman Empire and of other political entities in the larger Islamic world and also beyond Muslim-majority countries. There is no lack of deep experiences of loss, weakness, and decay from which Muscular Islam might have emerged and continues to take shape. Hitherto, modified wrestling forms have been rather hidden from the study of multiple modernities and (the barely existing) research perspectives of Muscular Islam and of Islamic martial arts, but they possess the longest historical continuity, while creatively incorporating meaningful developments of cultural transformation. The hypernationalisation of oil wrestling developed as a response to the dramatic founding of the Turkish republic, but has lately been somewhat softened through processes of sportification and heritagisation. Furthermore, the so-called Ethnosports Cultural Festival has been fostered as a cultural response to the new trans-Asian axes and as a showcase for Turkey's projected new place in the world.

Bibliography

Ahmed, Shahab. 2016. *What Is Islam?: The Importance of Being Islamic*. Princeton and Oxford: Princeton University Press.

Akın, Yiğit. 2004. *Gürbüz ve Yavuz Evlatlar: Erken Cumhuriyet'te Beden Terbiyesi ve Spor*. Istanbul: İletişim Yayınları.

Alter, Joseph S. 1992. *The Wrestler's Body: Identity and Ideology in North India*. Berkeley: University of California Press.

Alter, Joseph S. 2006. "*Fin de Siècle*: Muscular Christianity with a 'Hindu' Twist." *The International Journal of the History of Sport* 23/5: 759–76 (Special Issue: *Muscular Christianity in Colonial and Post-Colonial Worlds*).

Appadurai, Arjun. 2005[7] [1996]. *Modernity at Large: Cultural Dimensions of Globalization*. Minneapolis and London: University of Minnesota Press.

Azoy, G. Whitney. 1982. *Buzkashi: Game and Power in Afghanistan*. Philadelphia: The University of Pennsylvania Press.

Brockett, Gavin D. 2011. *How Happy to Call Oneself a Turk: Provincial Newspapers and the Negotiation of a Muslim National Identity*. Austin: University of Texas Press.

Bromber, Katrin and Birgit Krawietz. 2013. "The United Arab Emirates, Qatar, and Bahrain as a Modern Sport Hub." In Katrin Bromber, Birgit Krawietz, and Joseph Maguire (eds.), *Sport Across Asia: Politics, Cultures, and Identities*. New York: Routledge, 189–211.

Bromber, Katrin, Birgit Krawietz, and Petăr Petrov. 2014. "Wrestling in Multifarious Modernity." *The International Journal of the History of Sport* 31/4: 1–14 (Special Issue: *Wrestling with Multiple Modernities*).

Chehabi, H.E., and Allen Guttmann. 2002. "From Iran to All of Asia: The Origin and Diffusion of Polo." *International Journal of the History of Sport*, 19/2–3: 384–400.

Chehabi, H.E. 2002. "The Juggernaut of Globalization: Sport and Modernization in Iran." *International Journal of the History of Sport* 19/2–3: 275–94.

Conermann, Stephan. 2009. "Muḥammad zu Pferde im Kampf: Ein Beispiel für das Genre der *Furūsiyya an-nabawiyya* während der Mamlukenzeit (1250–1517)." In Bert Fragner et al. (eds.), *Pferde in Asien: Geschichte, Handel und Kultur*. Vienna: Verlag der Österreichischen Akademie der Wissenschaften, 51–59.

Dervişoğlu, Mehmet. 2014. *Halk Bilimi Açısından Kırkpınar Güreşleri*. Istanbul: Edirne Valikliği Kültür Yayınları.

Diem, Carl. 1982[2] [Berlin 1942]. *Asiatische Reiterspiele: Ein Beitrag zur Kulturgeschichte der Völker*. Hildesheim, Zurich, and New York: Olms.

Dueck, Jennifer M. 2007. "A Muslim Jamboree: Scouting and Youth Culture in Lebanon under the French Mandate." *French Historical Studies* 30/3: 485–516.

Dünya Etnospor Konfederasyonu [booklet of 96 pages, n.d., n.p.].

Erdem, Halis. 2010[2] [2009]. *Doğuşundan Günümüze Kırkpınar Güreşleri*. Edirne: Ceren Yayıncılık.

Ersanlı, Büşra. 2001. "'Turkish History Thesis' and its Aftermath: A Story of Modus Operandi." *Asien Afrika Lateinamerika* 29: 7–29.

Farooq, Samaya. 2011. "'Tough Talk', Muscular Islam and Football: Young British Pakistani Muslim Masculinities." In Daniel Burdsey (ed.), *Race, Ethnicity and Football: Persisting Debates and Emergent Issues*. Oxford: Routledge, 145–59.

Faroqhi, Suraiya, and Arzu Öztürkmen (eds.). 2014. *Celebration, Entertainment and Theatre in the Ottoman World*. London, New York, and Calcutta: Seagull Books.

Farrer, D.S. 2009. *Shadows of the Prophet: Martial Arts and Sufi Mysticism*. New York: Springer.

Frembgen, Jürgen Wasim, and Paul Rollier. 2014. *Wrestlers, Pigeon Fanciers, and Kite Flyers: Traditional Sports and Pastimes in Lahore*. Karachi: Oxford University Press.

Green, Thomas A., and Joseph R. Svinth (eds.). 2010. *Martial Arts of the World: An Encyclopedia of History and Innovation*. Santa Barbara: ABC-Clio, vol. 1.

Guo, Li. 2013. *Sports as Performance: The Qabaq-game and Celebratory Rites in Mamluk Cairo*. Berlin: EB-Verlag.

Guttmann, Allen. 2004. *Sports: The First Five Millenia*. Amherst and Boston: University of Massachusetts Press.

Hallenberg, Helena. 2002. "Muslim Martial Arts in China: *Tangping* (Washing Cans) and Self-Defence." *Journal of Muslim Minority Affairs* 22/1: 149–75.

Hanioğlu, M. Şükrü. 2011. *Atatürk: An Intellectual Biography*. Princeton and Oxford: Princeton University Press.

Haugbolle, Sune. 2012. "The (Little) Militia Man: Memory and Militarized Masculinity in Lebanon." *Journal of Middle East Women's Studies* 8: 115–39.

Heath, Peter. 1990. "Arabische Volksliteratur im Mittelalter." In Wolfhart Heinrichs (ed.), *Orientalisches Mittelalter*. Wiesbaden: Aula-Verlag, 423–39.

Hershiser, Carl Mehmet. 1998. *Blood Honor and Money: Turkish Oiled Wrestling and the Commodification of Traditional Culture*. PhD dissertation, University of Texas at Austin.

Ibn Qayyim al-Jawziyya, Shams al-Dīn Muḥammad. 2005. *Al-Furūsiyya*. Beirut: Dār Ibn Ḥazm, (section *muṣāraʿat al-rasūl li-Rukāna wa-rihānuhu ʿalā dhālik*).

Irving, Mark. 2004. "Muscular Shias return to roots." In *BBC News*. http://news.bbc.co.uk/1/hi/world/middle_east/3647621.stm, accessed 7 September 2017.

Jacob, Wilson Chacko. 2011. *Working out Egypt: Effendi Masculinity and Subject Formation in Colonial Modernity, 1870–1940*. Durham and London: Duke University Press.

Johnson, Michael. 1977. "Political Bosses and Their Gangs: Zuʿama and qabadayat in the Sunni Muslim Quarters of Beirut." In Ernest Gellner and John Waterbury (eds.), *Patrons and Clients in Mediterranean Societies*. London: Duckworth, 207–24.

Kimmich, Dorothee. 2017. *Ins Ungefähre: Ähnlichkeit und Moderne*. Konstanz: Konstanz University Press.

Kowalski, Tadeusz. 1940. "Ringkämpfe bei den Balkantürken." *Pubblicazioni dell'Istituto Universitario Orientale di Napoli* n.s. 1: 163–75.

Krais, Jakob. 2017. "Christian Clubs, Muscular Muslims and New Nationalism: Competing Youth Movements in Late Colonial Algeria." ZMO conference *'New Man' in Africa, Asia and the Middle East: Practices, Networks and Mobilization, c. 1910–1960*, September 2017, unpublished paper.

Krawietz, Birgit. 2012a. "Big Bodies That Matter: Making a Difference in Turkish Oil Wrestling." In Hinrich Biesterfeldt and Verena Klemm (eds.), *Differenz und Dynamik im Islam: Festschrift für Heinz Halm zum 70. Geburtstag*. Würzburg: Ergon, 201–17.

Krawietz, Birgit. 2012b. "The Sportification and Heritigisation of Traditional Turkish Oil Wrestling." *International Journal of the History of Sport* 29/15: 2145–61 (Special Issue: *Sport in the Middle East – Power, Politics, Ideology and Religion*).

Krawietz, Birgit. 2013. "Martial Arts Iranian Style: Zurkhane Heavy Athletics and Wrestling Contested." In Katrin Bromber, Birgit Krawietz, and Joseph Maguire (eds.), *Sport Across Asia: Politics, Cultures, and Identities*. New York and London: Routledge, 144–66.

Krawietz, Birgit. 2014a. "Prelude to Victory in Neo-traditional Turkish Oil Wrestling: Sense Perceptions, Aesthetics and Performance." *International Journal of the History of Sport* 31/4: 445–58 (Special Issue: *Wrestling in a Multifarious Modernity*).

Krawietz, Birgit. 2014b. "Sport and Nationalism in the Republic of Turkey." *International Journal of the History of Sport* 31/3: 336–46.

Krawietz, Birgit, and Florian Riedler. *Forthcoming*. "Outlook on Ottoman Heritage as Edirne's Future." In Birgit Krawietz and Florian Riedler (eds.), *The Heritage of Edirne in Ottoman and Turkish Times: Continuities, Disruptions, and Reconnections*. Berlin et al.: De Gruyter.

Krist, Stefan. 2014. "Wrestling Magic: National Wrestling in Buryatia, Mongolia and Tuva in the Past and Today." *The International Journal of the History of Sport* 31/4: 423–44.

Ladd, Tony, and James A. Mathisen. 1999. *Muscular Christianity: Evangelical Protestants and the Development of American Sport*. Grand Rapids MI: Baker Books.

Lakhnavi, Ghalib, and Abdullah Bilgrami. 2008. *The Adventures of Amir Hamza: Lord of the Auspicious Planetary Conjunction*. Trans., introduction, and notes, Musharraf Ali Farooqi. New York: The Modern Library.

Laqueur, Hans-Peter. 1979. *Zur kulturgeschichtlichen Stellung des türkischen Ringkampfes: Einst und jetzt*. Frankfurt am Main, Bern, and Cirencester: Peter Lang.

Leder, Stefan. 2009. "Religion, Gesellschaft, Identität – Ideologie und Subversion in der Mythenbildung des arabischen >Volksepos<." In Anja Bettenworth and Christine Schmitz (eds.), *Mensch, Heros, Gott: Weltentwürfe und Lebensmodelle im Mythos der Vormoderne*. Stuttgart: Steiner, 167–80.

Levine, Emma. 2000. *A Game of Polo with a Headless Goat*. London: André Deutsch.

Nauright, John. 1997. "Masculinity, Muscular Islam and Popular Culture: 'Colored' Rugby's Symbolism in Working-class Cape Town c. 1930–70." *The International Journal of the History of Sport* 14/1: 184–90.

Navaro-Yashin, Yael. 2002. *Faces of the State: Secularism and Public Life in Turkey*. Princeton and Oxford: Princeton University Press.

Petrov, Petăr. 2007. "'Sultan werden': Über die politische Ausnutzung traditioneller Ringkämpfe in Bulgarien" In Arié Malz, Stefan Rohdewald, and Stefan Wiederkehr (eds.), *Sport zwischen Ost und West: Beiträge zur Sportgeschichte Osteuropas im 19. und 20. Jahrhundert*. Osnabrück: Fibre Verlag, 221–36.

Presner, Todd Samuel. 2007. *Muscular Judaism: The Jewish Body and the Politics of Regeneration*. New York: Routledge.

Putney, Clifford. 2001. *Muscular Christianity: Manhood and Sports in Protestant America, 1880–1920*. Cambridge MA: Harvard University Press.

Rashid, Razha. 1990. "Martial Arts and the Malay Superman." In Wazir-Jahan Karim (ed.), *Emotions of Culture: A Malay Perspective*. Singapore, Oxford, and New York: Oxford University Press, 64–95.

Ridgeon, Lloyd. 2010. *Morals and Mysticism in Persian Sufism: A History of Sufi-futuwwat in Iran*. London and New York: Routledge.

Rochard, Philippe. 2002. "The Identities of the Iranian *Zurkhānah*." *Iranian Studies* 35/4: 313–40.

al-Sarraf, Shihab. 2004. "Mamluk *Furūsīyah* Literature and Its Antecedents." *Mamlūk Studies Review* 8/1: 141–200.

Seyller, John. 2002. *The Adventures of Hamza: Painting and Storytelling in Mughal India*. London and New York: Smithsonian Institution.

Tietze, Nikola. 2001. *Islamische Identitäten: Formen muslimischer Religiosität junger Männer in Deutschland und Frankreich*. Trans. from the French by Ilse Utz. Hamburg: Hamburger Edition.

Türkiye Geleneksel Spor Dalları Federasyonu, https://gsdf.gov.tr/tr/, accessed 23 October 2017.

Türkiye Geleneksel Spor Dalları Federasyonu: *1997/1998 Faaliyet raporu* [booklet of 136 pages, n.d., n.p.].

UNESCO. 2010a. "Kırkpınar Oil Wrestling Festival." In *UNESCO, Intangible Cultural Heritage*. https://ich.unesco.org/en/RL/kirkpnar-oil-wrestling-festival-00386, accessed 3 October 2017.

UNESCO. 2010b. "Naadam, Mongolian Traditional Festival." In *UNESCO, Intangible Cultural Heritage*. https://ich.unesco.org/en/RL/naadam-mongolian-traditional-festival-00395, accessed 3 October 2017.

UNESCO. 2010c. "Pahlevani and Zoorkhanei Rituals." In *UNESCO, Intangible Cultural Heritage*. https://ich.unesco.org/en/RL/pahlevani-and-zoorkhanei-rituals-00378, accessed 3 October 2017.

Watenpaugh, Keith David. 2006. *Being Modern in the Middle East: Revolution, Nationalism, Colonialism, and the Arab Middle Class*. Princeton: Princeton University Press.

World Ethnosport Confederation: *The Age of Sport Awareness* [booklet of 36 pages, n.d., n.p.].

Yıldız, Doğan. [ca. 1975]. *Türk Spor Tarihi*. Istanbul: Yayıncılık.

Yıldız, Murat Cihan. 2015. *Strengthening Male Bodies and Building Robust Communities: Physical Culture in the Late Ottoman Empire*. PhD dissertation, University of California, Los Angeles, 16–255; n36.

Yıldız, Murat Cihan. 2017. "Physical Culture and the New (Ottoman) Man in Early-Twentieth-Century Istanbul." ZMO conference *'New Man' in Africa, Asia and the Middle East: Practices, Networks and Mobilization, c. 1910–1960*, September 2017, unpublished paper.

PART 6

Dominant Minorities and Dominant Majorities

CHAPTER 17

Domination, Resilience, and Power: Religious Minorities in the Imperial and Post-Imperial Middle East

Hamit Bozarslan

1 Introduction

In Iraq, Syria, and Yemen, after decades of nationalist, left-wing, and Islamist contests, which presented themselves as more or less universalistic—or at least integrative—movements, these societies have become theatres of wide-scale confessional wars with irreversible disruptive effects that will continue for years to come. Sectarian tensions also play a structuring role in the very shaping of power relations, modes of segmentation and stigmatisation, and expressions of allegiance and dissidence in Turkey and Iran, two important Middle Eastern countries that share with these other countries an imperial past (Massicard 2012, Dudoignon 2017).

As I have suggested elsewhere (Bozarslan 2015), this sectarian burden has certainly not been fatal. Not only has the "sectarian map" of these countries changed many times throughout the last centuries, the sectarian conflicts played a barely significant political role in Iraqi, Syrian, and Yemeni societies during the "revolutionary heydays" of the 1950s and 1960s. Still, the centrality that they have established over the last two decades or so poses serious challenges to the social sciences and invites scholars to reconsider some of their assumptions of the 1990s and 2000s. Ethnic and religious groups, both majorities and minorities, may well constitute "imagined communities" or be products of modernity (Gellner 1983, Anderson 1991). Yet, they have an historical thickness (Valensi 1986), and the conflicts they experience produce "real victims" (Hayden 1996). Analysis of these groups thus requires not only erudition, sociological and anthropological investigation, and empirical data gathering through constantly renewed fieldwork, but also specific attention must be paid to the transformative effects of conflicts and coercive or regulated modes of domination and/or violent contest. Only such a multi-disciplinary approach can enable us to understand historical continuities and new configurations in which radical ruptures take place—either in one single

 | DOI:10.1163/9789004386891_018

country or in a region as vast as the Middle East—and the power relations, group discourses, narratives, and subjectivities that are intrinsically linked to them.

2 Imperial Legacy

The available documentation on religious minorities in the Middle East (Longva and Roald 2011) confirms the existence of a "tacit contract" (Mardin 1977) that excluded neither violence nor negotiation between the rulers and their subordinated "subject-groups" under the past imperial order. A "tacit contract" can be defined as official or unofficial recognition of subordinated social, professional, tribal, and religious groups by a central power, which grants them some rights, among them the right to be represented through the intermediary of their dignitaries. In turn, these groups owe a constrained allegiance to the state and accept the status (as well as different forms of visibility and specific regimes of taxation) it imposes upon them.

Internal autonomy accorded to non-Muslims, to non-dominant Muslim confessions, and to some sectarian "apostate" groups that were deemed to have left Islam constituted one of most significant features of the "tacit contract" both in Iran and in the Ottoman Empire. These groups, in turn, accepted and internalised imperial rule, which transformed them into de jure or de facto dominated and subordinated communities. Explicit renunciation of the possibility of holding power and attaining equality with the dominant community was the very condition of survival for the Christian and Jewish groups, whose religious dignitaries were able to negotiate different privileges with the state both for themselves and for their communities (Iognat-Prat and Veinstein 2003). The *dhimma* regime, which some Islamic scholars present as a specific form of religious plurality in the Dār al-Islām, was not synonymous with religious equality. Whatever the concrete modes of accommodation might have been between the non-Muslim religious establishments and the central state, various measures—such as regulations regarding the organisation of space; the obligation to manifest one's religious affiliation, namely through dress codes; and the official preservation of discriminatory measures, such as the interdiction on constructing new places of worship or the bearing of arms—were meant to reproduce both the imperial system and the superiority of the dominant Muslim confession in time and in space.

Some exceptions notwithstanding (Scholem 2008), the scholarly research I am aware of does not portray the subjectivities of dominated religious groups and their hierarchies before the reforms of nineteenth century. There is no doubt, however, that these groups were keen to preserve their autonomy vis-à-vis the central state, but within their historical trajectories and specific traditions, as well as the autonomy of their hierarchies, vis-à-vis each other. The juxtaposition of ethnic/linguistic and confessional boundaries, as was the case for Armenian, Greek, and Aramaic communities in Mesopotamia, and Orthodox communities in the Balkans, has certainly increased their self-consciousness in forming subordinated territorial or supra-territorial entities within a broader imperial framework.

Moreover, both in the Ottoman Empire and in Iran, imperial rule had to deal also with other religious communities that did not belong to the *ahl al-kitāb,* "people of the book," and thus could not enjoy official recognition: Zoroastrians, who preceded Islam; confessions that had openly left Islam, such as as the Yazīdīs, Druzes, and Baha'is; and "heretics," who interpreted Islam in a strong ʿAlid tradition, such as the Nuṣayrī/ʿAlawī, the Alevi/Kızılbaş, and the Ahl-i Ḥaqq communities. Without being officially recognised as "legitimate" religious groups, these communities were also integrated into the imperial "tacit contract" and, except for some periods of repression, as those of the sixteenth century against the Kızılbaş dissidence in the Ottoman Empire (Çakmak and Gürtaş 2015) and the nineteenth-century campaigns of "Islamisation" of the Yazīdī communities (Gökçen 2012), they could enjoy a de facto autonomy.

Imperial engineering functioned as a permanent producer of inter-communitarian boundaries, further reinforced through the sacralisation of three specific fields: the *matrimonial domain*, the warrant of the internal reproduction of the community, which was in principle exclusively intra-confessional; *places of worship,* which gave a metaphysical meaning to each religious community; and *cemeteries,* which attested to a group's intergenerational continuity in a given territory much more than real or fictive genealogies. Transgression of inter-communitarian frontiers in these three domains, as it was observed in the twentieth century, particularly but not exclusively, during the Armenian genocide, could not but undermine the tacit contract with the state, or the "civility" warranting the peaceful coexistence among different communities. Calendars and rituals (such as Eastern celebrations for Christian groups, or public presentation of the Peacock Angel for the Yazīdīs), autonomous production and transmission of theological knowledge, and religious hierarchies and chains of relationships between masters and disciples constituted other intra-communitarian landmarks and were widely "immunised" if not sacralised.

An empire is a system based on the categorisation of populations and their direct or indirect representation effected by the recognition of dignitaries of religious, tribal, professional, and in some cases ethnic groups as the *most favoured lords*. The Muslim empires did not constitute exceptions to this rule.

There is no doubt that in the Ottoman Empire as well as in Iran, power was ultimately exerted by Muslims (even though, in some cases, rulers of these two entities themselves violated this supreme principle codified by Muslim legists). With the major exception of the Roman Empire, an empire is not "a fabric of citizens"; its durability depends on the immunity of the centre, which is attained through its (theoretical) externality vis-à-vis its subjects. Whatever their religious affiliation might be, the subjects are not integrated into the political system. As Şerif Mardin suggests for the Ottoman case, the "centre" of the Empire does not define a territorial space but rather the "central power," wherever it might be effectively present; the highly complex "periphery," on the other hand, includes the entire society, regardless of linguistic or religious affiliations (Mardin 1973).

3 Civility of the Empires, Citizenship of the States

This supra-social nature of the central power explains why the concepts of majority and minority could not be applied to empires. These categories became a reality only with the diffusion of nationalism, a doctrine and a set of praxis that presupposes or establishes an explicit link between the state and the "nation," and its transformation into the "identity" of the "nation-state." From a Kantian perspective (Kant 1784), the term "minority" would describe a group deprived of the right to think and act of its own will without being dictated to by an external authority, and not possessing the same rights as the religious or linguistic majority that constitutes the "nation." In this sense, the term "minority" constitutes indeed "a sociological euphemism" (Nibert 1996) for oppressed or more-or-less marginalised groups. Defining a group as a *minority* is in fact closely linked to power relations. If Christians in the late Ottoman Empire or post-imperial Iraq, Syria, or Egypt constitute "minorities," the reason is not only that they are numerically far less important than Muslim subjects of these countries, but because they are de facto or de jure excluded from the *nation*, which is defined as Muslim. Likewise, the nation and state formation process in the Balkans has led to the minoritisation of the Muslim groups from the Balkan nations, not because of their obvious numerical weakness (except in Bosnia and Albania), but because most of the Balkan states formed in the nineteenth and twentieth centuries were defined, implicitly or explicitly, as Christian.

Commenting on Nikos Kazantzakis's well-known novel *Liberty or Death* (1950), the French political scientist Jean Leca underlined the importance of a paradox observed in the Ottoman Empire in the nineteenth and twentieth centuries: the process of the invention of citizenship, which theoretically offers more equality than ever before to the members of a given *nation* (no matters how artificial or imaginary it is), in fact produces much more inter-sectarian (or inter-communitarian) inequality and violence than existed during the highly stratified pre-modern periods (Leca 1991). In spite of mechanisms of domination, subordination, and stratification dividing imperial subjects into dominant and dominated categories, the pre-modern periods were marked by a codified civility among different religious communities. Ivo Andrič's masterwork, *The Bridge on the Drina* (1945), shows that the dominant Muslim and dominated Christian communities not only had to be respectful towards each others' "sacralised domains," they also had to to stand in solidarity against Istanbul/Constantinople's interventions in their common remote territory. In his *Âge de Sable* (French translation Mireille Robin 2000), Dževad Karahasan, a contemporary Bosnian author, also insists on the importance of this inter-communitarian civility and adds that in pre-war Sarajevo, each inhabitant of the city had to be an "amateur ethnographer" in order to live in a perfect harmony with the others. Likewise, André Raymond observes that different religious communities in Cairo were keen (or at least obliged) to cooperate which one another in order to preserve the autonomy of their city (Raymond 1986). Even before the collapse of the Syrian and Iraqi Arab-Sunnī community in the year 2010, some forms of peaceful coexistence, which one should certainly not confound with cosmopolitanism, could be observed in Mosul and Aleppo. Many decades after the decline of the Ottoman Empire, in fact, some cities, such as Sarajevo (before the 1992–95 war), Aleppo, Istanbul (until the anti-Christian pogroms of 1955), Jerusalem, Mosul, and Kirkuk remained as "imperial cities," not because they were chosen as privileged cities by the Ottoman rulers, but because they kept alive means of inter-communitarian coexistence, which challenged the nation-state's claims to homogeneity. In all these cases many interactions did exist between different religious communities, separated by marriage, places of worship, and cemeteries, but united around and in shared urban spaces.

Citizenship, in turn, was not only about introducing a theoretical equality between citizens, but also about defining the boundaries of "one single family," unified on the basis of shared linguistic and/or religious denominators, or even of a total homogeneity. Limiting equality solely to the members of a supposedly existing *nation* could thus but go hand-in-hand with the exclusion or the de facto minoritisation of those who did not fulfil the criteria of homogeneity. In a worldview determined by social Darwinism (Doğan 2012, Elsharky 2016), the "otherness from within" could thus easily be assimilated to the "enmity from within," leading to the state's repression and violent dissidences.

The association of citizenship with a religious or linguistic entity not only explains the intensity of symbolic violence against minorities, as it is reflected in nationalist historiography, curriculum, or the arts; it also allows us to understand why, in some cases, even genuine attempts to suppress segregation and discrimination against non-Muslim communities were doomed to fail.

The evolution of the late Ottoman Empire is from this point of view quite significant. To some extent, the late Ottoman reforms (Tanzimat), namely those introduced by the 1839 (*Hatt-ı Serif*) and 1856 (*Hatt-ı Humayun*) imperial edicts, were aimed at suppression of the inequalities between Muslims and non-Muslims that had been codified for many centuries within the framework of the *millet* system. The 1863 Armenian constitution (*Nizamname-i Millet-i Ermeniyan*) and the 1865 General Regulations of the Rabbinate (*Hahamhane Nizamnamesi*) created wide avenues for these communities and could be seen as important democratic reforms for the entire Ottoman Empire. For the first time confessional groups were organised through their elected "assemblies" (sing. Ar. *majlis*, Turk. *meclis*). But at the same time, these edicts and *nizamnames* imposed new codifications on the status of non-Muslims and allowed the Sublime Porte to intervene much more openly in their internal organisation and in the appointment procedures of their hierarchies. The Ottoman constitution and law of elections of 1876 to 1877 also had two radically contradictory outcomes: on the one hand they aimed at a genuine representation of Ottoman "citizens" and particularly of Christian communities. But on the other hand, the constitution officially defined the state as Muslim, determining thus its official identity in religious terms. Attributing an official religious identity to the state was much more than recognising that the Ottoman Empire was indeed a Muslim state; it was a means of affirmation, or even reinforcement of the Islamicity of the state *in spite* of other, rather egalitarian, changes introduced by the constitution (Bozarslan 2004). The constitution, thus, could only accelerate the process of politicisation of the non-Muslim communities, mainly those of Asia Minor and the Balkans, who were tempted to affirm their own identity in religious *and* political terms.

Similarly, partly in order to answer positively to European demands, the election code created separate electoral lists for non-Muslims, allowing their representation in the short-lived Ottoman parliament; by so doing, however, it was also condemning them to a rigid status. They could thus *exclusively* be non-Muslims and enjoy the right of representation *es qualité*—that is, in an official capacity—but not as political actors. The election code constituted the starting point of a new process, which "locked up ... people in identity categories, instilling supposedly primordial differences in the political culture, submitting political negotiation to supposed immutable rules and paralyzing governmental decision in the name of power sharing" (Picard 2012, 11). In the Ottoman Empire and then, after its dissolution, in Turkey, as well as, in much less repressive conditions, in the post-World War I Arab states, formal juridical equality between citizens went hand in hand with much more codified and stratified relations between states and religious minorities.

One should also mention new forms of discrimination against religious (and later on, linguistic) minorities, which had no juridical ground, but were justified in the combined name of nationalism and science. Research conducted by Taner Akçam (2008), Fuat Dündar (2010), and Erik-Jan Zürcher (2010) shows that statistics and a variety of scientific methods, including fieldwork and highly sophisticated ethnographic investigations, were used in order to demonstrate an overwhelming "demographic superiority" of Muslims (and in some cases of Turks) in Anatolia and Ottoman Thrace before, during, and after the 1915 Armenian genocide. The Committee of Union and Progress (CUP), which created a single-party regime in 1913, used social Darwinism in order to portray Armenians and Greeks as "vital threats" to a nation that had yet to be built, and also mobilised available scientific tools to monitor their existence and project changes in the demographic texture of the Anatolian population.

This link between the state and the formation of a "majority" also explains how it was that "the Christians of Syria and Lebanon, Armenians of Asia Minor and Assyrians of Kurdistan or even in the border areas in Persia experienced massacres or systematic deportations" not under "the *dhimma* regime" (Heyberger 2003: 17), but only after its abolition. As Hans-Lukas Kieser (2000) shows, the collective protection assured by Western powers to these communities appeared to be simply inefficient, or even counterproductive, as was seen during the wide-scale massacres of Armenians in 1894 to 1896 and during the genocide of 1915, whose victims also included many Assyrians and Chaldeans.

4 Grounding the Nation in a Confession

As the Azeri (Iran), Baluch (Iran and Pakistan), Arab (Iran and Turkey), and region-wide Kurdish cases show, one of the consequences of the state-formation (or re-formation) process in the twentieth century has been the transformation of many linguistic groups into minorities. As living proofs of an imperial past, these status-less groups, among them the well-studied Kurds, still constitute strong challenges to the very claim of building homogeneous nations or reaching "national unities" that would ignore linguistic differences.

Still, the religious minorities distinguish themselves from the linguistic ones in the sense that they show, by their very existence, other paradoxes of Middle

Eastern (and Balkan) nationalisms, which found their source of inspiration in nineteenth-century European experiences. In the Middle East as elsewhere, "nations" were supposed to be meta-historical entities existing by the "law of the nature" or according to the "rules" of social Darwinist selection, condemning them to a war of "survival" against one another. To some extent, the claim was that such a nation had to be self-sufficient, that is, without any link with other identities such as the religious ones. In spite of this claim to exclusivity, however, nationalism in the Ottoman space, for instance, could achieve viability and legitimise itself only through its references to the religious/sectarian sphere. In order to come into existence, the "nation" needed a deeper history than its own, which could be found only in religion and in its remote monasteries and *zāwiyas*.

This paradox has obviously marked nationalisms of Christian populations in the late Ottoman Empire; but Muslim nationalisms in no way constituted exceptions to this rule. Both Arab and Turkish nationalisms included, explicitly or implicitly, religion as part of their official identity-equation. One of the most radical Arab nationalists, Michel Aflaq (1910–89), who was a Christian, accepted Islam as one of the cultural-historical boundaries of the Arab nation (and converted at the end of his life to Islam) (Aflaq 1977). Even the "revolutionary Arab regimes" of the 1950s and 1960s maintained the Islamic identity of the state and nation. In Turkey, following the legacy of one of the most influential ideologists of the CUP, Ziya Gökalp (1876–1924), the nationalists defined the Turkish nation *simultaneously* as Turkish, *Muslim,* and secular (Gökalp 1976). Secularisation (and in the 1930s, Kemalist laicism) were not understood as contradicting Islam, commonly accepted as a component of the national identity and as a boundary separating Anatolian Muslims from non-Muslims; secularism was simply considered a set of measures regulating the place of religion in a nation that was a priori defined as Muslim. There is no need to insist here on the consequences of such a religiously determined definition of the nation: suffice it to say that the proportion of non-Muslims, who represented more than 20% of the population in 1914 within the territorial framework of current Turkey, declined to some 2% after the Armenian genocide of 1915 and the Muslim-Orthodox population exchange with Greece in 1924. This figure has further decreased to 0.5% in the 1970s to 1980s (Courbage and Fargues 2005). The remaining Christian and Jewish communities have been victims of many waves of repressions throughout the twentieth century, and the Lausanne Treaty of 1923, which officially regulates their status and accords them some degree of autonomy, has never been fully applied.

In the Arab world, the definition of the nation as Muslim went hand in hand with the systemic exclusion and segregation of non-Muslims, but, with the exception of the more-or-less forced departure of the Jewish communities in the aftermath of the creation of Israel in 1948 (Trigano 2009), these policies did not lead to waves of repression and massacres similar to those seen in the late Ottoman period in Asia Minor or in republican Turkey. In some cases, the rulers of Arab countries have even tried to "assimilate" Christianity into the "national" culture. In the wake of a long tradition going back to the Sassanid period analysed by Michael Strausberg (2011), the marriage of the "ruler" (such as Yasser Arafat or King Hussein of Jordan) to a Christian woman, whether a convert to Islam or not, has been presented as a sign of integration of the Christian community into the nation. In Egypt and Jordan, "homeland" has been presented as a part of the "holy land," an expression that explicitly refers to a nineteenth- and twentieth-century Christian imaginary. Notwithstanding the sporadic repression directed against them, in other cases religious minorities have been "folklorised" and presented as a part of "authentic" culture (*turāth*), as in Iraq, Syria, and Egypt. In these three countries, the "presidential courts" have always included some Christian members, who could mediate between power and the Christian communities broadly speaking. In Iran of today, Christians (but also the country's small Zoroastrian and Jewish communities), who are obviously not capable of claiming any kind of equality with Muslims, nevertheless, as totally subordinated and therefore politically ignored communities, may feel they can escape from the repression targeting so many members of the dominant Shīʿī majority. These religious minorities have in fact no interest in turning their backs on their communities, which "bloc them up" (Longva and Roald 2011) in their rigid status, but which in turn, also give them some protection, while Muslim opponents of the regime have no choice but to break free from the ties of their own oppressive community, which prevents them from becoming full citizens.

5 Subjectivities of Religious Minorities

One of the characteristics of any system of domination is that it denies the dominated group the right to define itself through its own subjectivities, to have a voice of its own. The dominant group defines the dominated through its own words: it "reifies" the dominated, including by the use of gender-based categorisations, defining, for instance, non-Muslim women as "licit" to Muslims in the context of war, as was the case with Armenian women during the Armenian genocide of 1915 and with Yazīdī women during the rule of the so-called Islamic State in Iraq in 2014 and after (Ter Minassian 1999, Médecins Sans Frontières 2017). But "reification" also means that the dominating imposes upon the dominated its own requirements and expectations. The most important of these expectations is that this dominated group's discourses and narratives should not contradict the image that the dominant group wants to convey of itself. "Harmony" with the state and with the majority is possible only at the cost of satisfying this condition.

This denial of subjectivity explains why the dominant groups' discourses present Islam as an intrinsically "tolerant" religion and strongly invite religious minorities to confirm this "evidence" through their own public discourse and narratives. One faces thus a fundamental gap between experience, in-depth subjectivities, and public discourses of these communities. In Turkey, for instance, the discourses of religious dignitaries of the Christian and Jewish communities, which insist on the perfect harmony between them and Muslims, are not only in complete contradiction to available data on their history and current situation, but also to the narratives of their "dissident" members. Similarly, the Christians and Jews in Iran, where they have a "value of life" inferior to that of Muslims, are obliged to show an "impressive resilience" as a "survival technique" and confirm in their public statements the utmost "care" with which the Muslim state treats them (Longva and Roald 2011, 1–23).

Presenting oneself as a "happy" religious community in a "tolerant" country living in "perfect harmony" with the majority is obviously a constraint imposed by an objective process of minoritisation, subordination, discrimination, and in some cases, also physical repression, that leaves no other choice than capitulation to the dominant religious groups. But while conforming to this obligation, religious minorities also try to maintain some means of resistance. The groups' survival depends largely on their capacity to develop "hidden transcripts" (Scott 1990) that can take, in some cases, truly esoteric forms, as may be observed in the Alevi community in Turkey. Public visibility, internationally recognised status of victimhood, public display of the minority group's cultural and artistic creations based on its own narratives—these are also important resources that all oppressed groups use in order to resist but also to create community-based power.

In turn, however, production of such a counter-space requires the existence of "doorkeepers" of the esoteric knowledge, producers of discourses, frames, and narratives, and those who are able to "translate" them into "foreign," that is, extra-group languages. Here, as in the cases of other subaltern groups, resistance would be simply impossible to imagine without internal power and power relations and their legitimisation by the group's members; the submission to internal authorities or to religious hierarchies appears however to be the very condition of some degree of resistance against the domination imposed by the dominant group, its state, or its agencies.

6 Historical "Apostate" Groups, Muslim Minority Confessions, and Esoterism

As is well known, since the caliphate of Abū Bakr (11–13/632–34), Muslim states and legists have formally prohibited abandoning Islam in favour of another religion (*ridda*). Whether national legislations authorise it or not, Muslims who convert to another religion are effectively threatened with their lives, as the assassination of a German Protestant pastor and two Turkish converts in Malatya on 18 April 2007 illustrates. Albeit a marginal phenomenon, conversion from Islam to Christianity constitutes, however, an increasing tendency in many Middle Eastern societies. The convert populations in Turkey and also in North African countries, who live their faith in almost underground conditions, may well form in the future new numerically small and politically close to invisible minorities. This issue seems to constitute one of the most sensitive taboos of these societies, which research has yet to deal with (Guirguis 2008).

Legally founded or not, the prohibition on "leaving Islam" in order to adopt another faith is seldom defended solely on a theological basis. Two arguments are constantly evoked to justify this ban: that of "protection of public security order" (Chaumont and Urvoy 2007) and that of the impossibility of abandoning Islam, not as a faith, but as an organic community. As Ghassan Salamé suggested years ago, abandoning the community is associated with *khurūj*, that is, betrayal of the sort that ultimately led to the assassination of the caliph ʿAlī (Salamé 1994, 23).

The issue of apostasy is a more complex one, as far as some historical communities that left Islam are concerned. The Baha'is, the Yazīdīs (Fuccaro 1999), and the Druze community in Lebanon and Syria (and in very peculiar conditions in Israel; see Rivoal 2000) have had naturally different historical trajectories. Except in the specific case of the Baha'is, victims of a systematic repression under the Islamic Republic of Iran, however, they are often socially and publicly accepted or even implicitly assimilated to Islam and this, in spite of the fact that they are still seen as theological threats to Sunnī and Shīʿa Islam.

In their beginnings, these new religions often had some millenarian expectations; but thanks to their institutionalisation, they went simultaneously through a double process of axiological de-radicalisation and theological radicalisation, leading ultimately to their rupture with Islam. As for the other religions, the de-radicalisation manifested itself through investment in the earthly world and an eschatological *aggiornamento*. The radicalisation in turn, took place namely in the fields of cosmogony and anthropology: these communities have often accepted the principle of *tanāsukh* (metempsychosis, a belief that is strictly forbidden by Islamic legists) and, in order to avoid the re-incarnation of their members in inferior human bodies or even in animal bodies (*masūkhiyya*), prohibited out-group marriages. The principle of *tanāsukh* and a highly sophisticated esoteric doctrine appeared to be efficient mechanisms of group cohesiveness and internal social control, allowing them to dispose of their own internal authorities and separating them from others. There is no doubt that the principles of *tanāsukh* and esotericism have blocked these communities into rigid frameworks, but also have offered them some means of resistance and survival.

Esotericism has also been an arm of resilience for minority Muslim groups that, in the context of repression by the dominant Muslim group, sought to avoid any kind of public visibility. One observes, indeed, a movement of the pendulum between periods of invisibility, imposed by repression, and those in which the minority tries to re-conquer visibility through its mobilisations, if not violence (Mardin 1977; Nakash 2006; Louer 2012). This swing of the pendulum between dissimulation and quest and conquest of visibility attests that *taqiyya* (hiding one's religious beliefs) and esoteric knowledge (and esoteric knowledge production) are not only important theological issues, but also highly political ones. To be sure, in almost every historical context, esotericism as knowledge, but also as a lifestyle and as an obligation to tell the truth only inside a clandestine "we-group" is a constraint and not a choice (Koyré 1988). In the Muslim world as elsewhere, esotericism is a revelator of asymmetric relations between the dominant and dominated Muslim communities, but also an arm of resistance.

Neither the dominant confession, nor the state that adopted it as its official or *par default* religion, need to overemphasise their Sunnī identity (or in the Iranian case, Shīʿī). They are simply "Muslim" and their dominant position allows them to define Islam as de facto Sunnī or Shīʿī, without according to the other confession full equality. From that point of view, neither their Islamicity, nor their hegemonic power to say what the "true" Islam or "true" religion is, can be questioned. This attribute of domination leaves no choice to the minority group other than to hide itself or, when possible, to overemphasise its Alevi, Nuṣayrī/ʿAlawite, Shīʿī or Sunnī affiliation, the only available identity option left to them. The condition for these groups to renounce to this exclusive but constrained identity is that the state itself renounce its confessional nature. From this perspective, the identity politics of the Muslim minority confessions, which at first glance seem to be highly moderate, constitute in fact a form of radicalism no less because they *radically* question the very identity of the state and of the dominant group.

The periods in which dominated groups overemphasise their specificity and try to conquer the space of visibility are also those of crisis for states' hegemonic syntaxes (Billig 1995). What some scholars have called the "Alevi revival" in Turkey is significant from this point of view (White and Jongerdeen 2003). The Alevis, who have been victims of many pogroms in the past, are still hesitant to publicly confess their religious affiliation. In spite of this fact, the Alevi movement, which does not have a structuring reference actor but a plurality of associations, won momentum during the past two decades, partly as a consequence of the weakening of the state's official ideology based on Turkicity, Islam, and "contemporeanism" (i.e., "secularism"; Massicard 2012). From the very beginning of the Turkish Republic, founded in 1923, these terms excluded Kurdish, Alevi, or conservative/Islamic groups. The crisis of this official identity in the 1990s could not but push these excluded groups to express themselves through violence (in the Kurdish case), more openly outspoken identity politics (the Alevi case), or desire for the conquest of power (Islamism). As Laure Guirguis (2012) shows, Egypt has experienced a similar process. Coptic activism and religious radicalism were inevitable consequences of sporadic but very costly Islamist violence targeting the Coptic community; but they were also an outcome of and an answer to the crisis of the Egyptian state, which could not or did not want to impose on the state an official, non-sectarian identity. In all these cases, the crisis of the state and its official ideology allowed for the emergence of new political and cultural actors, who were able to codify, at least to some extent, historical narratives of various groups and propose to them new options and horizons.

How have states responded to these crises in recent times? Except in Lebanon, where confessionalism is not only recognised but has also constituted the very basis of the unwritten "national pact" since 1943, the states can, according to their local contexts, try to conceal their own confessional identities and/or strengthen the overall Islamicisation of their societies. In the Syrian case, for instance, the dominant religious group, the ʿAlawīs, whose high-ranking dignitaries in fact control the state, uses esoterism and *taqiyya* in order to hide members' own identity and appear as genuinely "Muslim." The Sunnī domination in Iraq under Saddam Hussein presented similar features, with those in power attempting to hide the state's more and more exclusively Sunnī nature; today, in contrast to aggressively Shīʿa militia forces, some Shīʿī actors in Iraq also try blend in as simply Muslim Iraqis.

7 Power-Building Strategies of the Religious Minorities

As many cases in the Middle East attest, for religious minorities the space for manoeuvring and the acquisition of some degree of immunity often requires formal acceptance of the dominant discourse and loyalty to the state. Thus, loyalty to the dominant group, discussed by Elizabeth Picard (2012) following the well-known model of Albert Hirschman (1970), becomes a constrained one and ceases to be a choice. In order to become a genuine alternative decided by the group itself, *loyalty* has to be accepted, by the state, the majority group, and the minority itself, as a fully legitimate political position or behaviour, as much as *exile* and *voice*, two other strategies mentioned by Hirschman. It is only when the state and the majority consider exile and voice not as betrayals, but as legitimate forms of expression and contest, that the minority can cease to consider the loyalty of its members to the state or to the society, broadly speaking, as a form of betrayal to the group. That means, ultimately, the end of the system of domination in which one group constitutes the majority and the others are constrained to become de facto or de jure minorities. Reaching such an aim, however, requires the invention of another conception of politics, in which the oppositions are formulated not according to primordial—or rather, primordialised—categories, but according to political divisions, programmes, and projections.

As I mentioned earlier, religious minorities' reproduction of their subaltern status through silence and formal loyalty to the state and to the majority group, as we observe it as a general rule in the Middle East, does not mean that these religious minorities have no capacity for resistance. I have already insisted on the importance of "hidden transcripts" introduced by Scott (1990), as specific narratives, myths, counter-heroes, and counter-calendars, and becoming invisible through *taqiyya* and esotericism, as strategies of resilience and resistance. Establishment of intra-communitarian associations such as charity organisations, formation of an economic elite or middle class, establishment of new print or distant electronic media, performance of everyday rituals (baptisms, marriage, burials, etc.), which constitute the main prerogatives of religious authorities, constitute both important resources of survival, resilience, and resistance, and instruments of power. In some cases, when conditions allow, direct collective actions or political commitments can also be used as power-creating resources. Autonomous Alevi activism in Turkey but also political participation, namely (but not exclusively) through the Republican People's Party, and collective actions and public demonstrations by the Copts in Egypt and their engagement in different political movements (the Wasaṭ Party, the Kifāya movement) before the 2011 revolution are examples of this form of access to power resources (Norton 2005). In spite of the lack of in-depth and comparative studies, but on the basis of many empirical observations, one can also assume that education becomes a strategy for survival, resistance, and in some cases also of power-conquest for religious minorities. Throughout the nineteenth century, Christian and Jewish communities in harmony with education by the past; thanks to the missionary schools and the Alliance israélite universelle, they constituted the very first agents implementing modern Western education in the Middle East. Their schools were in fact the cradle of an intelligentsia and of many new ideas, including left-wing ideologies. In the twentieth century, education seems to have become both a decisive pawn and a battlefield for Muslim and/or "heterodox" communities. The ʿAlawīs in Syria, for instance, already by the 1920s and 1930s, were sending their children to the then widely overlooked military schools. Nothing suggests that this choice obeyed a "reflexive" strategy; however it ultimately allowed them to come to power through the 1966 and 1970 coups d'etat. The Shīʿa case in Lebanon, studied, among others, by Catherine Le Thomas (2011), is also significant from this point of view. Obviously, following the tradition of the late Musa Sadr (1928–78?), many Shīʿī associations, Amal, and particularly Hezbollah were and still are keen to build a wide network of education, which today serves the purposes of forming an elite; but it also allows enrollment and control of the Shīʿī population and its voluntary or coercive mobilisation when required. Thanks to generous grants given by Shīʿī endowments, schooling also permits the creation of client groups, such as children of the martyrs. In that sense, education appears to be a real power resource vis-à-vis other confessional groups, but also within a given community. Esoteric knowledge and memory constructions are also important power resources, allowing minorities to establish an internal chain of transmission of what is not known, not thought, and not diffused by the state or by the dominant religious group. Minority group members have in fact to learn, through the official system of education, what the dominant group produces and its hegemonic syntaxes, but also, through their own channels, what it excludes, and in some cases, forbids. Thus, production and transmission of knowledge create an overall differentiation vis-à-vis the dominant group and constitute a resource of symbolic superiority.

Departure into exile or diaspora formation can also be considered as a power resource. Exile is, no doubt, before everything else, a constraint, attesting to the group's unease with its situation. No doubt either that the process of diaspora formation provokes unprecedented problems for an exiled group, such as the control of the youth and the preservation of an endogamic matrimonial system. These issues are particularly sensitive ones for small communities like the Yazīdīs, who believe in the principle of *tanāsukh* and forbid exogamic marriages. But diaspora formation can also mean new opportunities for a religious minority, such the Assyrians and Chaldeans from Turkey or for the Yazīdīs. Not only can they thus proceed to a new communitarian restructuring around their religious authorities, but they can also produce new historical narratives and formulate political, cultural, and social claims, while trying to tightly control group members and present their values and worldviews as truly universal ones.

8 The Issue of Universalism

At the turn of the twentieth century, Zoroastrians, during the Iranian revolution of 1906, assumed important political roles, while Armenian revolutionaries as trans-border actors were diffusing revolutionary ideas across the Ottoman, Iranian, and Russian Empires (Motika and Ursinus, 2000). In her book dedicated to the study of the role of the non-Muslim militants in the in the Middle East, Taline Ter Minassian (1997) uses the concept of "Colporteurs of the Komintern," in other words, the bearers and diffusors of leftwing ideas in the region. Even after the genocide, many surviving Armenian intellectuals and their descendants participated in left wing movements (Marchand and Perrier 2013). In many cases, in fact, non-Muslim or non-dominated religious groups played an important role in country-wide or region-wide horizontal mobilisations. As Gudrun Krämer has shown, many Jewish public figures participated actively in the intellectual and political life of Egypt as *Egyptians*, defending the idea of social justice and identifying themselves with the struggle for independence (Krämer 1989, 5–7). Palestinian Christians, as well as Iraqi Christian, Jewish, and Shīʿī intellectuals, such Muḥammad Mahdī al-Jawāhirī (1899–1997), have played nationwide roles in political mobilisation for decades (Zubaida 2003). Shīʿīs in Iraq also participated in great numbers in the country's left-wing movements before the 1968 Baʿth coup and, as is well known, many Alevis were affiliated with radical left-wing organisations in Turkey of the 1970s.

Beyond the understandable will to show loyalty to the nation through participation in a horizontal political struggle, one could analyse these forms of action undertaken by minorities as an expression of a quest for universalism. As Jean Leca (1991) suggests, universalism legitimises the demands of particular groups seen as victims of a global repressive system. In this sense, the universalist dissidence of minorities, through which they interpret their sacrifices as the price they pay for the "emancipation of humankind" as a whole, is also synonymous with prestige and symbolic power. The weakening of horizontal social mobilisations in the Middle East as well as the impact of Islamism, which excludes almost all the religious minorities (with the exception of Sunnīs in Iran and Shīʿīs in some parts of the Arab world), have, more than ever, condemned minorities to their "bounded categories."

Bibliography

Aflaq (Aflak), Michel. 1977. *Choix des textes de la pensée du fondateur du parti Baʿth. Unité-Liberté-Socialisme*. Madrid: Impr. Litografia Eder.

Akçam, Taner. 2008. *Ermeni Meselesi Hallolunmuştur: Osmanlı Belgelerine Göre Savaş Yıllarında Ermenilere Yönelik Politikalar*. Istanbul, İletişim Yayınları.

Anderson, Benedict. 1991. *Imagined Communities: Reflections on the Origin and Spread of Nationalism*. London: Verso.

Billig, Michael. 1995. *Banal Nationalism*. London: Sage.

Bozarslan, Hamit. 2004. "Islam, laïcité et la question d'autorité dans l'Empire ottoman et en Turquie kémaliste." *Archives des sciences sociales des religions* 125: 99–113.

Bozarslan, Hamit. 2015. *Révolution et état de violence. Moyen-Orient 2011–2015*. Paris: CNRS.

Çakmak, Yalçın, and Imran Gürtaş (eds.). 2015. *Kızılbaşlık, Alevilik, Bektaşilik, Tarih-Kimlik-Inanç-Ritüel*. Istanbul: Iletişim.

Chaumont, Eric, and Marie-Thérèse Urvoy. 2007. "Apostasie." In Mohammad Ali Amir-Moezzi (ed.), *Dictionnaire du Coran*. Paris: Robert Laffont, 63–66.

Courbage, Youssef, and Philippe Fargues. 2005. *Chrétiens et juifs dans l'Islam arabe et turc*. Paris: Payot.

Doğan, Atila. 2012. *Osmanlı Aydınları ve Sosyal Darwinizm*. Istanbul: Küre Yayınları.

Dudoignon, Stéphane. 2017. *The Baluch, Sunnism and the State in Iran: From Tribal to Global*. London: Hurst.

Dündar, Fuat. 2010. *Crime of Numbers: The Role of Statistics in the Armenian Question (1878–1918)*. New Brunswick NJ and London: Transaction Publishers.

Elshakry, Marwa. 2016. *Reading Darwin in Arabic, 1860–1950*. Chicago: University of Chicago Press.

Fuccaro, Nelida. 1999. *The Other Kurds: Yazidis in Colonial Iraq*. London and New York: I.B. Tauris.

Gellner, Ernst. 1983. *Nations and Nationalism*. Ithaca NY: Cornell University Press.

Gökalp, Ziya. 1976. *Türkleşmek, Islâmlaşmak, Muasırlaşmak*. Ankara: Kültür Bakanlığı.

Gökçen, Amed. 2012. *Osmanli ve Ingiliz Arşiv Belgelerinde Yezidiler*. Istanbul: Bilgi Üniversitesi.

Guirguis, Laure (ed.). 2008. *Conversions religieuses et mutations politiques: Tares et avatars du communautarisme égyptien*. Paris: n.p.

Guirguis, Laure. 2012. *Les Coptes d'Egypte: Violences communautaires et transformations politiques, 2005–2012*. Paris: Karthala.

Hayden, Robert M. 1996. "Imagined Communities and Real Victims: Self-Determination and Ethnic Cleansing in Yugoslavia." *American Ethnologist* 23/4: 783–801.

Heyberger, Bernard (ed.). 2013. *Chrétiens du monde arabe: Un archipel en terre d'Islam*. Paris: Autrement.

Hirschman, Albert O. 1970. *Exit, Voice, and Loyalty: Responses to Decline in Firms, Organizations, and States*. Cambridge MA: Harvard University Press.

Iognat-Prat, Dominique, and Gilles Veinstein. 2003. *Histoire des hommes de Dieu dans l'Islam et le Christianisme*. Paris: Flammarion.

Kant, Immanuel. 1784 (2004). "Beantwortung der Frage: Was ist Aufklärung?" *UTOPIE kreativ* 159: 5–10. Available at https://www.rosalux.de/fileadmin/rls_uploads/pdfs/159_kant.pdf.

Kieser, Hans-Lukas. 2000. *Der verpasste Friede: Mission, Ethnie und Staat in den Ostprovinzen der Türkei 1839–1938*. Zurich: Chronos.

Koyré, Alexandre. 1988. *Réflexions sur le mensonge*. Paris: Alia.

Krämer, Gudrun. 1989. *The Jews in Modern Egypt, 1914–1952*. London: I.B. Tauris.

Le Tomas, Catherine. 2011. "Education and Minority Empowerment in the Contemporary Middle East." In Anh Nga Longva and Anne Sofie Roald (eds.), *Religious Minorities in the Middle East: Domination, Self-Empowerment, Accommodation*. Leiden: Brill, 267–88.

Leca, Jean. 1991. "Nationalisme et Universalisme." *Pouvoirs* 57: 33–42.

Longva, Anh Nga, and Anne Sofie Roald (eds.). 2011. *Religious Minorities in the Middle East: Domination, Self-Empowerment, Accommodation*. Leiden: Brill.

Louer, Laurence. 2012. *Shiism and Politics in the Middle East*. Trans. from French by John King. London: Hurst.

Marchand, Laure, and Guillaume Perrier. 2013. *La Turquie et le fantôme arménien: Sur les traces du génocide*. Arles: Solin, Actes-Sud.

Mardin, Şerif. 1973. "Center-Periphery Relations: A Key to Turkish Politics ?" *Daedalus* 102/1: 169–90.

Mardin, Şerif. 1977. "Youth and Violence in Turkey." *European Journal of Sociology* 19/2: 229–54.

Massicard, Elise. 2012. *The Alevis in Turkey and Europe: Identity and Managing Territorial Diversity*. New York: Routledge.

Médécins Sans Frontières. 2017. "Le cauchemar des Yézidies." Available at https://www.medecinsdumonde.org/fr/actualites/irak/2017/03/08/le-cauchemar-des-yezidies.

Motika, Raoul, and Michael Ursinus (eds.). 2000. *Caucasia between the Ottoman Empire and Iran, 1555–1914*. Wiesbaden: Reichert.

Nakash, Yitzhak. 2006. *Reaching for Power: The Shiʿa in the Modern Arab World*. Princeton: Princeton University Press.

Nibert, David. 1996. "Minority Group as a Sociological Euphemism: A Note on the Concept of 'Privileged/Oppressed Groups.'" *Race, Gender & Class* 3/3: 129–36.

Norton, Augustus Richard. 2005. "Thwarted Politics: The Case of Egypt's Hizb al-Wasat." In Robert Hefner (ed.), Remaking Muslim Politics: Pluralism, Contestation, Democratization. Princeton: Princeton University Press, 133–60.

Picard, Elizabeth. 2012. "Conclusion: Nation-Building and Minority Rights in the Middle East." In Anh Nga Longva and Anne Sofie Roald (eds.), *Religious Minorities in the Middle East: Domination, Self-Empowerment, Accommodation*. Leiden: Brill, 230–55. Also available at https://hal.archives-ouvertes.fr/halshs-00715384/document.

Raymond, André. 1994. "Le Caire traditionnel: Une ville administrée par ses communautés?" *Maghreb-Machrek* 143: 9–16.

Rivoal, Isabelle. 2000. *Les Maîtres du secret: Identité communautaire et ses manifestations au Proche-Orient. Le cas des Druzes en Israël.* Paris: EHESS.

Salamé, Ghassan (ed.). 1994. *Démocraties sans démocrates: Politiques d'ouverture dans le monde arabe et islamique*. Paris: Fayard.

Scholem, Gershom. 2008. *Sabataï Tsevi: Le Messie mystique 1626–1676*. Lagrasse: Verdier.

Scott, James C. 1990. *Domination and the Arts of Resistance: Hidden Transcripts*. New Haven: Yale University Press.

Strausberg, Michael. 2011. "From Power to Powerlessness: Zoroastrism in Iranian History." In Anh Nga Longva and Anne Sofie Roald (eds.), *Religious Minorities in the Middle East: Domination, Self-Empowerment, Accommodation*. Leiden: Brill, 171–93.

Ter Minassian, Taline. 1997. *Colporteurs du Komintern: L'Union soviétique et les minorités au Moyen-Orient*. Paris: Sciences-Po.

Ter Minassian, Anahide. 1999. "Un exemple: Mouch 1915." Available at http://www.imprescriptible.fr/cdca/mouch.

Trigano, Shmuel (ed.). 2009. *La Fin du judaïsme en terre d'Islam*. Paris: Denoël.

Valensi, Lucette. 1986. "La tour de Babel: Groupes et relations ethniques au Moyen-Orient et en Afrique du Nord." *Annales Économies, Sociétés, Civilisations* 41/4: 817–38.

White, Paul Joseph, and Joost Jongerden (eds.). 2003. *Turkey's Alevi Enigma: A Comprehensive Overview*. Leiden: Brill.

Zubaida, Sami. 2003. "Grandeur et décadence de la société civile irakienne." In Hosham Dawod and Hamit Bozarslan (eds.), *La Société irakienne: Communautés, pouvoirs et violences*. Paris: Karthala, 47–61.

Zürcher, Erik-Jan. 2010. "The Late Ottoman Empire as Laboratory of Demographic Engineering." Accessed July 2010. http://www.sissco.it/fileadmin/user_upload/Pubblicazioni/Mestiere_di_storico/1-2009/zurcher.pdf.

CHAPTER 18

Carving Out a Space for Equal Political Citizenship? Muslim Politics of Remembrance in Uganda

Dorothea E. Schulz

1 Introduction

In the spring of 2012, while doing research on the history of Muslim education in Mbale, Eastern Uganda, I inadvertently came across a documentary that piqued my interest. Produced by the Media Studies Department of the Islamic University in Uganda in Mbale, the documentary "The Forgotten Muslims" covered a protest rally held by Muslims, which, because it publicly staged Muslim claimants as the main protagonists, marked an extraordinary moment in the history of the Ugandan nation-state. For more than three months in 2011, about two hundred Muslims—men, women, and children—camped out in Sheema, a rural district in southwestern Uganda, to call for public recognition of a massacre carried out against members of the local Muslim minority in 1979, in the aftermath of President Idi Amin's fall from power. The spokesmen of the protest interviewed in the documentary spelled out the three goals of the protest: First, to pressure the government to openly acknowledge that the massacre had taken place and "left unhealed wounds in the memory of the local Muslim population"; second, to garner public support for their claim that "justice should finally be done" and Muslims receive material compensation for the land and property lost in the aftermath of the massacre; and third, to create public awareness that the massacre was "only one of many injustices inflicted on Muslims in Uganda's history" and that, to overcome "Muslims' ongoing discrimination," Muslims should be granted greater representation in national politics.

The documentary was not broadcast on national or local media, nor could the organisers of the Sheema protest register success. President Yoweri Museveni's government never responded to their call for dialogue and compensation. Eventually, the protesters were obliged to pack up their tents and return to wherever their families had relocated after the 1979 massacre.

In view of the violent history of Uganda, a history of consecutive, protracted periods of bloodshed and regional civil wars, which, cast in the language of ethnic and religious altercation, lasted until recently (2004), the Muslim

 | DOI:10.1163/9789004386891_019

protest camp, its media coverage, and apparent political failure are noteworthy in several respects. The protesters publicised their grievances by linking an idiom of hurt, loss, and victimisation to a language of political rights and citizenship on one side, and to a call for material recompense, on the other. In a political climate shaped by the National Resistance Movement (NRM) government's attempts to quell various oppositional forces through a combination of coercion, co-optation, and infiltration of non-governmental structures of political mobilisation, the organisation of the protest required considerable courage. Also, coverage of the protest in a documentary produced at a prestigious university that targets the country's Muslim minority reflects transformations in the national educational system, which, since colonial times, has contributed to the systematic marginalisation and stigmatisation of Muslims (Kiyimba 1986, 1989, 1990; Schulz 2013a,b). The media coverage of the protest camp testifies to the emergence of a self-confident Muslim middle class that draws on a language of citizenship and justice to call for greater political representation. Moreover, by publicly addressing an instance of Uganda's tradition of politically and socially motivated bloodshed, the documentary breaks with the NRM policy of silencing, in the name of national reconciliation, past atrocities related to the NRM government's rise to power (Twaddle 1988).

This article focuses on questions of remembrance and commemoration as a means of addressing possibilities of peaceful coexistence and equal treatment in contemporary Ugandan society, in which various Christian denominations dominate—in terms of numbers and political strength—in a society of considerable religious plurality, which includes Muslims and practitioners of various other religions traditions.[1] The article asks how, under current political conditions, members of the Muslim population in southwestern Uganda deal with their historical experiences of violence, bereavement, and a state-orchestrated silencing of these historical experiences; and what social, political, and physical spaces they carve out in this process. With these questions, I join the debate on religious pluralism and coexistence in religiously diverse settings, a debate to which Gudrun Krämer made a significant contribution. As Krämer put it succinctly in her 1995 chapter "Islam and Pluralism," regardless of the different theoretical positions adopted by Islamic scholars, the actual practice of religious and political pluralism in societies shaped by Islamic legal,

1 Muslims make up approximately 12 per cent of the population, while adherents of other faiths, among them Jews, Hindus, Bahais, and practitioners of indigenous religious traditions religions, are estimated at about 4 per cent (source: US 2015 Uganda International Religious Freedom Report, https://www.state.gov/documents/organization/256295.pdf, accessed 30 August 2017).

political, and moral traditions depends on what those in power consider and impose as being consistent with the public order and with dominant conceptions of morality, religion, and custom.

Gudrun Krämer's interest in social praxis and in relations of power and authority is congruent with the perspective adopted in this article. Yet whereas hers was an effort to lend a critical eye to debates on "Islam's" capacity to make room for liberal values and for those critical of officially endorsed readings of Islam, I explore possibilities *for Muslims* to enjoy equal political rights and civic liberties in a country dominated by Christians, and to speak about injustices endured *as* a religious minority.

In taking the fact that Muslims were permitted to publicly address and commemorate past atrocities as an indicator of their political and civic rights as a religious minority, the article contributes to a burgeoning scholarship on memory, commemoration, and violence. Much of the scholarship highlights the political dimension of remembrance, focusing on the role of the commemoration of violence in nation-building and in identity politics by groups that seek to gain political leverage and claim specific social and/or cultural identities (Last 2000; Greenberg 2005; Khalili 2005). Yet, whereas this scholarship demonstrates the interplay between violence, memory, and the making of political community, it evinces a curious disregard for religion. Only rarely have scholars asked how religious affiliation and difference play into the (always selective) remembrance of past events and inform power relations between religious groups (see Scheffler 2002; Stier and Landres 2006). Yet these questions need to be addressed in order to understand how various markers of difference, whether framed as "religious," "ethnic," or "cultural," factor into possibilities for peaceful coexistence after incidents of violence and substantial material loss. In short, we need to bridge the divide between debates on religious pluralism and scholarship on memory politics.

As an anthropological contribution to this endeavour, this article investigates the political space that Muslim protesters could claim and the kinds of claims they were allowed to articulate as indicators of the political rights of Muslims in Uganda and of their location within the national body politic.[2]

2 My understanding of "space" is threefold. First, I study "space" as a sphere of socially and politically relevant action, in which Muslims intervene with a political agenda and in this process invoke and remake an imaginary collectivity of believers. Second, I also understand "space" as an at once physical and social entity that gains particular significance because of historical events or present practices associated with it. Third, I consider the public platform generated by the documentary "The Forgotten Muslims" as a "media space" that creates opportunities for Muslims to publicly address some of their grievances, yet that simultaneously forecloses the mention of other concerns.

It explores the implications, for individuals and entire families, of the officially "allotted" (or denied) space for remembrance. For this, the article pays close attention to the specific nature of the "silence" that the NRM government imposed on Muslims from Sheema District, and also to the forms of silence or articulation in which these Muslims engage in turn. Of particular relevance, here, is Karin Willemse's (2005, 10) insightful distinction between two forms of silence. The first omits what the speaker assumes (or, I would add, knows) to be common knowledge shared by speaker and interlocutor. The second silence refers to something remaining unmentioned because its articulation would expose the speaker to social sanction or, in the Ugandan case, to political repression.

An investigation into the practices of remembrance and mourning and related silences by Muslims also contributes to a critical appraisal of the heuristic value and transcultural applicability of the concepts of "trauma." This critique is aimed at literature on post-war and post-disaster settings that address the coping strategies of victims of war, forceful migration, and "natural" disasters through the concepts of "traumatic memory" and "post-traumatic stress disorder."

Critics who work at the intersections of transcultural psychiatry, memory studies, and the anthropology of violence increasingly question the possibility of designating a fixed set of psychological and medical symptoms with the term "trauma" (Antze and Lambek 1996; Young 1995; von Peter 2008, 2009; Luig 2010). They also express doubt about the effectiveness of corresponding therapeutic interventions (such as dialogical counselling) that draw on the assumption that the discursive, imaginary revisiting of past traumatic events generates a cathartic release and provides victims with a sense of closure about the past.[3] The critics stress the cultural biases and specific conceptions of psycho-social well-being and "mental health" that inform "talking cure" approaches (Neuner et al. 2001; WHO 2005), and maintain that the curative effectiveness of forms of remembrance and mourning depends on culturally specific conceptions of decency, honour, and agency, and on the historical and political setting within which this form of remembering takes place. Whether "talking" is considered an adequate and effective healing strategy also depends on the existence of alternative, culturally validated, and historically entrenched modes of restoring socio-moral order and personal well-being.

Rather than taking for granted that people's silences about past experiences indicate their "traumatic" nature, the following discussion examines

3 Similarly fallacious assumptions about the curative effects of public talk and discursive remembrance underlie truth commissions (see Solomon 2001; Byrne 2004; Bronéus 2008).

how Muslims conceive of these experiences, how and why they chose to commemorate—or silence—them, and in what possibly alternative spaces and forms of remembrance and mourning Muslims engage to deal with past experiences of violence and victimhood.

To give a sense of the restrictive nature of the space within which Muslims in Uganda might engage in commemoration and mourning, the following sketch outlines how religious and other forms of difference have been treated in Uganda's fraught post-colonial history.

2 A Nation-State Riven by Antagonism and Strife

The Ugandan national body has been historically divided by multiple lines of conflict. These lines of conflict shifted and sometimes evolved in concentric circles, yet they nevertheless congregated around a main north-south divide, which, in several regions of today's Uganda, often date back to nineteenth-century political struggles. These struggles were exacerbated by a British colonial *divide-et-impera* strategy and were expressed in terms of ethnic confrontation and, on the part of the southern populations, privileged by missionary-school education and colonial administration, as a civilisational gap between them and the peoples from the northern regions. Social antagonisms and differences in status and accomplishment were often expressed through references to the different political organisations that put northern segmentary societies in opposition to the kingdoms of southern Uganda. Some of these antagonisms had portentous consequences for post-independence politics, when they translated into protracted periods of ethnic strife and civil war in several regions of the country. Among these conflicts is the civil war, which, since the establishment of the current NRM regime under President Yoweri Museveni in 1986, has set Acholiland (Northern Uganda) in opposition to the central state in Kampala. The origins of these tensions can be traced at least to the regime of Idi Amin (1970–79). A fragile and precarious situation of peace in Acholiland has held since 2004. Over the last fifteen years, another important regional divide, which, after Idi Amin's fall from power, opposed the populations of the West Nile Region (the home region of Dictator Amin) in the country's northwest to the central state, has been attenuated through the incorporation of leading representatives of the region into the NRM government under President Museveni (see Bogner and Neubert 2012).

In the political and social spaces the conflicting parties created through their actions, physical violence was presented as a legitimate and necessary means to achieve a just social order. Similar to many other conflicts in Uganda's political history, in which the torture, mutilation, and execution of civilians, military, and "rebels" or "freedom fighters" were the order of the day, each side claimed for itself a rightful exercise of violence and justified its actions as a means of self-defence or in the name of national security (e.g. Finnstrom 2003). Additional social and political frictions within the country's north and south were, and still are, locally expressed and reified through the idiom of ethnic and religious difference and confrontation.[4] At the national level, in contrast, these lines of conflict and competition have been glossed over by an official discourse of national reconciliation and integration imposed since the early years of the NRM government.

Muslims' historical experiences of marginality, forceful expulsion, and existential threat in southwestern Uganda (and also in other regions, such as West Nile and Northern Uganda) should be understood against the backdrop of these long-standing, ethnicised rifts in local political fields, and of a state-orchestrated memory politics that depends on the selective silencing of past events. Even if Muslims constitute approximately 10 to 25 per cent of the population in these regions, the government of President Museveni has treated their experiences of violence as if they were of lesser importance than atrocities committed in the name of ethnic difference.

In view of this governmental policy of selective silencing and omitting certain elements of local history that do not fit the official narrative, one might wonder about the position Muslims from Sheema District have been able to assume in local political arenas, and how the officially imposed selective silence about local history affects the possibilities for Muslims (and their motivation) to carve out spaces for collective and personal remembrance and mourning, to assign responsibility, and to call for compensation. It also raises the question as to how these activities and spaces of remembrance initiated by the families of Muslim victims in the rural southwest relate to the struggle for public recognition undertaken by Muslim intellectuals and activists in the national arena.

To address these questions, the following subchapter outlines the historical event to which the protest camp in Sheema District referred, and discusses the contemporary political conditions that determine how and to what extent relatives of victims can now talk about the massacre.

4 These rifts pit against each other inhabitants of the West Nile Region, Acholiland, and the Karamoja region in Uganda's north; they also nourish resentment and competition among people from eastern, western, and central Uganda.

3 The 1979 Massacre against Muslims in Sheema District

In 1979, in the midst of the turmoil surrounding the forceful removal of the Amin regime by a liberation army in which Yoweri Museveni held an influential position, different regions of the country experienced outbursts of anti-Muslim sentiment. Depending on local power balances between Muslims and Christians, the outbursts ranged from the illegal appropriation of land and property, to forceful expulsion, and to violent, sometimes murderous attacks. In the early months of that year, several groups of armed fighters that made up the liberation army, which had invaded the country from across the Tanzanian border, operated next to each other in Uganda's southwest. In a situation of general insecurity, exacerbated by indecisive leadership structures within the military, many Muslims were forcefully expelled from their home villages and in this process lost all their property. The situation improved moderately during Yusuf Lule's two-month presidency, but not for Muslim members of the local population. The harassment and destruction of crops and property that Muslims had endured in numerous villages since early April 1979 took a deadly turn in June in an area near the regional capital, Mbarara. At this time, Yoweri Museveni had become the defence minister of President Yusuf Lule's government. On 26 June, about sixty Muslims—men, women, and children from several villages in the Bushenyi area (Sheema District, near the regional capital Mbarara)—were rounded up by angry mobs of villagers, led to the river Rwenzi, located in close proximity, and hacked to death with machetes or simply thrown into the river. In other areas of the southwest (and in other regions), Muslims were threatened and forced to leave the land they had sometimes been cultivating for generations.

Nobody was ever prosecuted for these acts and for the next twelve years, the Muslim massacre was not treated as a subject of public debate or as a matter for which relatives of those who had perished could claim compensation. The situation changed in 1991, when a group of Muslim intellectuals and activists from Kampala systematically interviewed survivors. Abasi Kiyimba, a professor at Makerere University in the capital, Kampala, compiled their oral testimony in the form of a report that, eleven years after its original publication (1990), was put online, in July 2012. In the introduction to the report, Kiyimba portrays the 1979 massacre as a "holocaust." He also links the massacre to a politics of recognition, by, for instance, insisting on the need for its public remembrance as a precondition for "peace and stability" (Kiyimba 2012, 2).

The decision by Kiyimba and fellow members of the Makerere University Muslim Students' Association (MUMSA) to make the collected testimonies publicly accessible marked an important step in Muslim politics of mourning.

It made past injustices against Muslims a topic of public debate and recognition. While atrocities committed against Muslims from the West Nile region in the north of the country could be more easily justified by reference to the material advantages and political privileges Muslims from the region had enjoyed under Amin, addressing the victimisation of Muslims in the southwest was a much more sensitive issue; after all, this region is President Museveni's home base but it also constitutes the breeding ground for the most powerful opposition to his government.

The sensitive nature of the massacre makes its public mention a difficult, even dangerous affair. Even questions of Muslims' position in national and regional politics cannot be easily addressed.[5] The secretiveness surrounding the events gives room for multiple versions of what actually happened: the events that prompted the killings; who is responsible[6]; whether certain individuals masterminded the killing of Muslims; to what extent those in military control of the region lent support to the killings or simply let it happen; and to what extent villagers initiated the attacks by themselves and hence should be held responsible. Of particular salience and sensitivity were questions about the nature and extent of involvement by members of the current government.

What emerges from the report by Kiyimba and his colleagues, from an account written by American journalist Andrew Rice (2009), and from the different, sometimes inconsistent or even contradictory accounts I gathered is that responsibility for the killings and for their silencing in official discourse should be assigned at the local and national levels. Most accounts had four points in common. They depicted the killings against the backdrop of longstanding competition over political influence at the village level and traced this competition back to the first presidency of Milton Obote (1962–71). The second common point of most accounts was that they represented the killings as revenge killings, that is, they argued that the massacre was instigated by people resentful of influential Muslims who, under the regime of Idi Amin, had capitalised on their connections to the district commissioner (DC) in the regional capital of Mbarara to increase their property (for example, access to fertile land that before had been cultivated by other families). Other accounts made a similar point; they identified the killing of a wealthy, influential (and widely unpopular) Christian in the village of Kiziba (where quite a number of

5 These constraints impeded my conversations not only with relatives of former victims of the massacre, but also with official representatives of the Muslim national organisation in Mbarara.

6 For obvious reasons, during group interviews with relatives of victims and other villagers, all responsibility for the atrocities was assigned to individuals outside the village, such as persons who at that time were highly placed in the military hierarchy.

the victims had been living) as the triggering moment that led to the slaughter of the more than sixty Muslims. Third, the perpetrators of the massacre were neighbours and other villagers, in some cases members of families with whom the victimised families had "exchanged wives," that is, maintained matrimonial alliances. Fourth, perpetrators and those relatives of victims who were able to relocate to their home village still live together today and meet each other regularly; Muslims eye their neighbours with a mixture of unresolved hurt and of resignation to the need to forgive and move on, without being able to forget (Rice 2009, 213–19). Out of this shared history, an atmosphere of silent suspicion continues to prevail among villagers, an atmosphere that palpably overshadowed my research in 2012 and 2013, too.

Similar to its response in other regions in which Muslims experienced harassment, expulsion, and deathly confrontation, the NRM government has been reluctant to address these past atrocities and injustices. This policy has affected Muslims, as much as it has affected other religious and ethnic groups who, at some point, had adopted an oppositional position to the NRM government or to one of the preceding regimes. Any attempt to publicly address these past events and the grievances that victimised groups could raise against members of the current government and state administration have been sacrificed in the interest of national stability and "reconciliation."[7]

The fact that Muslims in southwestern Uganda, particularly relatives of victims of the massacre, abstain from publicly talking about their historical experiences of violence can be seen as a way of engaging this NRM-orchestrated memory politics. For obvious reasons, Muslims are particularly reluctant to address details of the massacre that touch on the alleged involvement of leading members of the NRM government. Certainly, the protest staged by Muslims in Sheema District in 2011 shows that the times are over in which the massacre cannot be publicly addressed. Still, the public declarations of protest spokesmen suggest that for Muslims it is easier to frame their public interventions as a struggle for material recompense and for recognition, rather than as an attempt to define and inhabit a public space designed as a site of mourning and collective remembrance. This is an instance of a silence that results from the decision of relatives of the Muslim victims not to speak about commonly shared knowledge; in the national public arena, in contrast, the silence muffles

7 Official memory politics regarding the West Nile region is a prominent example of this politics of silencing and purposeful forgetting (Bogner & Neubert 2012), which, in the name of national security and a strong NRM government, privilege the strategic integration of a few well-placed Muslim politicians into the current government over the recognition of the experiences of violence and persecution endured by the majority of the Muslim population of this region.

broader awareness of what happened to the Muslim minority in the aftermath of President Amin's ouster.

It is now time to compare the response by Muslims in Sheema District to governmental memory politics, notably the Sheema District protestors' refusal to engage in a public politics of mourning, to that of Muslim activists and intellectuals at the national level; and to ask how differences between these responses reveal the different opportunities for political action open to Muslims at the local as opposed to the national level.

The following subchapter sketches out how the political space claimed by Muslims in contemporary national politics emerged out of the changing conditions for political action generated since the regime of President Idi Amin.

4 Muslims' Changing Position in Postcolonial Politics

Whereas the first presidency of Milton Obote by and large perpetuated the historically marginal position of many Muslims, President Amin's regime had deeply ambiguous implications for Muslims. Many non-Muslims came to associate Islam with the atrocities committed by Amin and his cronies, and also with political opportunism and nepotism.[8] Muslims, too, who were not closely associated with Amin's regime, had many reasons not to feel secure and to question Amin's claims about promoting Islam (Rowe 1988, 274ff.; see Kiyimba 1990, 102ff.).[9] Nevertheless, Idi Amin's regime became a stepping-stone in Muslims' self-organisation and in the politicisation of their religious identity, not only because it granted unprecedented privilege to (selected) supporters of Amin's regime but because it improved Muslims' access to higher education. At the same time, governmental policy under President Amin fostered new divisions within the Muslim community (Chande 2000, 354–55; Schulz 2013a,b), which, starting in the late 1980s, resulted in confrontations between more radically minded Salafi activists and an older generation of Muslim leaders (Kiyimba 1990; Kayunga 1993). These confrontations were forcefully repressed by the NRM government. Partly as a result of the peace process initiated in the West Nile region, several high-ranking Muslim politicians (some of whom had

8 Kiyimba (1990, 102) offers a nuanced assessment of the allegation that Muslims in politically influential positions were beneficiaries of political nepotism. He lists individual Muslims whose appointment to high-ranking posts could not be explained by merit; but he also argues that because of their competence, several Muslims managed to stay in office after Amin's departure.

9 Their fears became true after the collapse of Idi Amin's regime, when, in a broad move toward revenge, Muslims were massacred in different regions of the country.

close ties to Idi Amin's regime) are currently members of the NRM government. Nevertheless, according to some Muslim public intellectuals, the interests of Muslims as a religious minority are not sufficiently represented in national and local governmental structures. Their sense of occupying a precarious political position has been confirmed in the time since Uganda declared its participation in the "global war on terror" (2001) and the 2009 Kampala bombings at the hands of al-Shabaab militias, events that reinforced the tendency of the government to liken Muslim political activism to a radical, politically subversive Islam. Strife within the national Muslim association, Uganda Muslim Supreme Council (UMSC), also weakens the organisation's political clout.[10] Muslims in Uganda thus find themselves in a dilemma that, according to Constantin (1995), characterises the situation of Muslim minorities throughout East Africa. To gain a voice in the political process, Muslim minorities need to organise themselves in structures recognised by the state. But mobilisation through these structures of representation also reproduces internal rifts and lessens chances that these activists can represent the interests of a unified Muslim community.

Still, the protest rally organised by Muslims in Sheema District and the fact that they joined hands with Muslim public intellectuals who struggle for a recognition of Muslim interests in the national political arena are signs of an incipient Muslim self-confidence. Key proponents of the emergent Muslim assertiveness are members of a small education-based Muslim middle class, of which Abasi Kiyimba, the main author of the 1990 report on the massacre, is a prominent example. Well aware that past victimisation does not form part of their collective memory, they struggle to overcome the government-imposed silencing of past events and the structural amnesia that follows from it. At the national level, their activities take the form of public speeches, publications, and the organisation of rallies; they have also materialised in Muslim structures of self-organisation.[11]

The efforts of Muslim intellectuals and activists go far beyond attempts to publicise formerly silenced details of a violent past. In their public interventions at the national level, they join the ranks of other Muslim activists and politicians who call for the recognition of Uganda's Muslims as a religious minority that has been marginalised in social and political life. They frequently frame their call for full inclusion in the political community as a matter of

10 At present, a conflict opposes the supporters of the Mufti of Uganda, Sheikh Shaban Mubajje, to a faction of the UMSC that contests his legitimacy, charging him for selling UMSC property for his own personal gain.

11 Some of these structures, such as the Uganda Muslim Education Association (UMEA) and the Makerere University Muslim Students' Association (MUMSA), date back to the 1930s and 1960s respectively. They have gained new momentum over the last fifteen years.

religious diversity; and they plead for an ordering of collective life in ways that make room for their particular, religiously sanctioned needs, such as the regulation of economic activity (framed as a matter of Islamic banking) and of everyday life. Their public interventions at the national level thus differ in tone and purpose from the call for compensation voiced by Muslims during the protest camp in Sheema District, southwestern Uganda. It also differs with respect to the motivations that inform their effort to overcome the deafening silence imposed by the NRM government.

Still, there also exist overlaps between the claims that Muslim intellectuals voice in the national political arena in Kampala and the rhetoric employed by the same or other activists at the local level. This is evident in the ways in which spokesmen of the Sheema protest frame their concerns and aims. In the passage from the documentary "The Forgotten Muslims" I quoted in the introduction, key terms of an international discourse on civil and political rights are mobilised. Take, for instance, the proposition that "justice" should be finally accorded to Muslims through a public recognition of past offences and injustices. This echoes the argument by Kiyimba (in the introduction to his 1990 report) that "remembering" is a precondition for "peace and stability," and his portrayal of the 1979 massacre as a "holocaust."

In employing these discursive strategies in national and local arenas, Muslim intellectuals such as Kiyimba seek to lend support to the initiative of local Muslims. At the same time, their political aims and the arguments they provide differ from what local families of victims privilege in their struggle to rebuild their existence and move on with their lives.

5 Muslim Practices of Remembrance and Mourning

The Sheema protest camp was meant to be a platform for Muslims to claim material compensation for wasted lives and property and the restitution of lost land. But their efforts were to no avail. The government never responded to their call; nor did it address their grievances in any other form. While the reasons for the refusal on the side of the government to acknowledge what had happened in 1979 are certainly complex,[12] they point to the limited political leverage of the victims' families, all of them farmers without connections to the

12 Possible reasons are the probable lenient stance by leading members of the government toward perpetrators at the times of the massacre and in its aftermath; the (realistic) assumption that any restitution of land would open a Pandora's box; and the (equally well-founded) assumption that monetary compensation would trigger a flood of court cases and publicly endorsed grievances.

centre of political power in Kampala. The failure of the public protest not only highlighted the difficulties ordinary Muslim farmers face when seeking public redress. It also confirmed the suspicion of those Muslims who, as they told me, had been hesitant to participate in the protest camp. Although their fear of reprisals on the part of the government had not materialised, they stressed that to "stay away from the public" and to "keep silent about what we can neither forget or remedy" would have been "the wisest thing to do."

Given the reluctance of numerous Muslims in Sheema District to publicly voice their grievances about their relatives' violent death during the 1979 massacre, it is worth considering how they, as well as other Muslims in the area, relate to the 1979 massacre today. What deserves further scrutiny here are whether there are practices and social spaces in which these Muslims commemorate or bemoan their family's history of victimisation and what significance they attribute to these practices.

Earlier in this chapter, I mentioned that the atrocities conducted against Muslims in the region are an issue that sits like a stone in the stomach of local collective memory and renders assertions of the existence of a village "community" obsolete. Relatives of victims can still identify the perpetrators and their children, yet all parties feel that, for the security and stability of their own lives, they should move on and keep silent about past events (Rice 2009). Muslims are also reluctant to publicly express their feelings of grief and pain or even to remind others of the past, for fear of being intruded upon by government spies and of being charged with treason and the instigation of opposition to the current regime.

The atmosphere of suspicion and distrust in which I conducted my interviews with family members of the deceased in the spring and summer of 2012 rendered difficult any attempt to move beyond the wall of silence Muslims had built around themselves.

What my interlocutors did address, however, were questions regarding the commemoration of the massacre. Relatives of victims described in detail, with a mixture of relish, reservation, and solemnity, how on the occasion of the anniversary of the massacre, Muslims from different villages of the area would come together in the courtyard of one family and engaged in joint prayers for the deceased. My interview partners tended to describe this collective prayer as a religious observance and as a family event. As Abdu, whose uncle and aunt perished in the massacre, put it to me in August 2012:

> I often think of my uncle and aunt, of what happened to them, and there is little to stem my sadness. But this is not something I want to mention,

> even to my own family. No, there is little we can do together as Muslims to bring back memories of those who died. We have to move on with our lives, even if the thought of what happened to our relatives and of what we lost pains us. No need to talk about it publicly, this is a family affair and one that only concerns us as Muslims.
>
> We meet once a year, on the anniversary of the bloodshed, in the courtyard of one of us. There, we engage in a collective prayer, to pray for our beloved ones, that God may have mercy on their souls. This is a moment of collective sadness about what happened to us. It helps that so many people come and attend the event. Then, we entrust those who died and our own fate and that of our children to God the Almighty.... Other than that, we have to move on.

Abdu describes the prayer as a temporal space for individual and collective mourning, and also as an act aimed at confirming the family's ancestral ties and future existence. He frames the ritual as an act of commemoration performed in a social and physical space located at the interstices of public village life and the domestic sphere, and outside the religious sphere proper and outside a public realm of debate. The particular nature of the ritual, that is, its function as a prayer, hints at the forceful death of relatives without explicitly mentioning what it entails. The ritual thus subsumes both forms of silence that I defined in the introduction. The same applies to other acts that are equally framed as elements of religious rituals and that similarly serve the combined purposes of mourning, commemoration, and future-oriented restoration.

The personal and religious nature of these acts of commemoration prevent them from serving as a platform for Muslims to render public their grievances and claims to compensation. The ritual acts create a personal space of mourning from which non-Muslims are automatically excluded. By defining the prayer ritual as one of family commemoration and personal mourning, and by performing it in the space of the courtyard, Muslims from the Bushenyi area carve out a physical and social sphere outside and beyond struggles over public recognition, political influence, and compensation. By the same token, it is this reframing as a "religious" practice that makes these ritual practices not only genuine, culturally specific forms of mourning and remembrance, but also ones that are protected from state interference. It is these ritual practices, I would argue, that deserve further scholarly attention if we want to understand culturally accepted and effective forms of restoring psycho-emotional well-being and what people envisage as a desirable socio-moral order.

6 Conclusion

In her reflections on post-September 11 political culture in the United States, Judith Butler stresses the future-oriented effects of collective mourning (2004). Butler's insistence on the productive effects of mourning are highly insightful, even if the positive effects she highlights are predicated on the particular political conditions under which collective mourning could be conducted in post-September 11 U.S. society. In contemporary Uganda, such conditions conducive to collective mourning and public commemoration are nonexistent for Muslims. Given the long-standing and deep divisions that fracture the Ugandan national community, the 1979 Muslim massacre could not yield similar community-generating effects. Instead, the massacre, and Muslims' efforts to remember it, reflected and refracted existing social and political divisions. The failed attempts of victimised Muslim families to raise public awareness of the 1979 massacre through a protest camp and its media coverage illustrate the inhibiting power of the memory politics imposed by President Museveni's government. Official memory politics revolve on the selective remembering of past atrocities and hence on the implicit cordoning off of those instances of violence that served the establishment and legitimation of the current government. The overarching and deeply ambivalent political culture of partial erasure and selective remembrance engineered by the NRM ruling party prompts relatives of former victims to at once remember and keep silent about past experiences of violence but also about their own involvement in violent acts vis-à-vis non-Muslims, so as to enable a life in close proximity to former perpetrators and victims.

As we have seen, Muslim activists and intellectuals who intervene in the national political arena point to the silencing of discussion of the massacres conducted against Muslims in 1979 as proof of the continued marginalisation of Muslims as a religious minority. Thus, what these activists highlight in their critique of governmental memory politics is that the government fails to grant a crucial condition for peaceful religious coexistence and pluralism. They claim to speak for the entire Muslim community and refer to past atrocities committed against Muslims in their call for recognition as a religious minority; they also frame their struggle as a matter of civil and political rights.

This view and political agenda differs from that of Muslims from Sheema District, who fight for public recognition of the violence and injustices they and their relatives endured. The protestors refer to the same historical events and experiences, but mainly with the aim of claiming material compensation. Also, whereas Muslim activists at the national level refer to religious difference to call for equal citizenship, at the local level, religious affiliation and difference allows for the cordoning off of a realm of commemoration—from state interference and from Christian neighbours. In fact, at the village level, religious ritual constitutes the only sphere in which Muslims can conduct with impunity their practices of mourning and remembrance.

This insight not only points to significant divisions among Muslims, along the lines of educational and economic inequality, contrary to the view frequently referenced by Muslim activists of Ugandan Muslims as a "community of fate." It also returns the discussion to the possibilities of coming to terms with past experiences of victimhood and violence, and about the role played in these practices by culturally specific forms of remembrance and mourning.

The diversity of practices of remembrance and mourning by Muslims presented in this chapter disrupts what has been commonly viewed as an unproblematic connection between "traumatic" experience, talking, and healing, and instead widens scholarly understanding of how these different interventions relate to one another and unfold their respective potential to restore psycho-emotional well-being.

As we have seen, Muslims are not only reluctant to frame their experiences as a matter of traumatic history but also consider such an endeavour to be pointless. To them, dealing with memories of victimhood and pain through religious ritual has a strongly future-oriented orientation, one directed at the restoration and continuity of family, faith, and religiously coined tradition. The terminology of traumatic experience and treatment, and the related connotations of hurt and destruction, would miss the essentially productive, restorative thrust of these locally sanctioned forms of spiritual and emotional healing.

Bibliography

Antze, Paul, and Michael Lambek (eds.). 1996. *Tense Past: Cultural Essays in Trauma and Memory*. New York and London: Routledge.

Bogner, Artur, and Dieter Neubert. 2012. "Die Komplexität der Akteursfigurationen bei 'Konflikttransformation' und 'Postkonfliktprozessen.'" In Dierk Spreen and Trutz von Trotha (eds.), *Krieg und Zivilgesellschaft*. Berlin: Duncker, 374–406.

Brounéus, Karen. 2008. "Truth telling as 'talking cure'? Insecurity and Retraumatization in the Rwandan Gacaca Courts." *Security Dialogue* 39/1: 58–76.

Butler, Judith. 2004. *Precarious Life: The Powers of Mourning and Violence*. London and New York: Verso.

Byrne, Catherine. 2004. "Benefit or Burden? Victims' Reflections on TRC Participation: Peace and Conflict." *Journal of Peace Psychology* 10/3: 237–56.

Chande, Abdin. 2000. "Radicalism and Reform in East Africa." In Nehemia Levtzion and Randall Powels (eds.), *The History of Islam in Africa.* Athens OH: Ohio University Press, 349–69.

Constantin, François. 1995. "The Attempts to Create Muslim National Organizations in Tanzania, Uganda and Kenya." In Holger Bernt Hansen and Michael Twaddle (eds.), *Religion and Politics in East Africa: The Period Since Independence.* London: James Currey, 19–31.

Finnstrom, Sven. 2003. *Living with Bad Surroundings: War and Existential Uncertainty in Acholiland, Northern Uganda.* Uppsala: Uppsala University Library.

Greenberg, Jonathan. 2005. "Generations of Memory: Remembering Partition in India/ Pakistan and Israel/Palestine." *Comparative Studies of South Asia, Africa and the Middle East* 25/1: 89–110.

Kayunga, Sallie Simba. 1993. *Islamic Fundamentalism in Uganda: A Case Study of the Tabligh Youth Movement.* Kampala, Uganda: Centre for Basic Research.

Khalili, Laleh. 2005. "Places of Memory and Mourning: Palestinian Commemoration in the Refugee Camps of Lebanon." *Comparative Studies of South Asia, Africa and the Middle East* 25/1: 30–45.

Krämer, Gudrun. 1995. "Islam and Pluralism." In Rex Brynen, Baghat Korany, and Paul Noble (eds.), *Political Liberalization and Democratization in the Arab World*, vol. 1, *Theoretical Perspectives.* Boulder CO: Lynne Rienner, 113–28.

Kiyimba, Abasi. 1986. "The Problem of Muslim Education in Uganda: Some Reflections." *Institute of Muslim Minority Affairs Journal* 7/1: 247–58.

Kiyimba, Abasi. 1989. "Christian-Muslim Relations in Uganda." *Current Dialogue* 16: 28–31.

Kiyimba, Abasi. 1990. "The Muslim Community in Uganda through One Hundred and Forty Years." *Journal of African Religion and Philosophy* 1/2: 85–105.

Kiyimba, Abasi. 2012. "A Detailed Account of the 1979 Massacre of Muslims in Western Uganda." Published online 31 July 2012 <http://campusjournal.ug/index.php/special-report/investigation>, accessed 15 October 2013.

Last, Murray. 2000. "Reconciliation and Memory in Postwar Nigeria." In Veena Das et al. (eds.), *Violence and Subjectivity.* Berkeley: University of California Press, 315–32.

Luig, Ute. 2010. "Über das Erinnern von Gewalt und die Verarbeitung des Schmerzes am Beispiel von ausgewählten Flüchtlingsgruppen und den Ex-Kämpferinnen der äthiopischen TPLF." *Curare* 33/1–2: 60–71.

Neuner, Frank, Margarete Schauer, and Thomas Elbert. 2001. "Testimony-Therapie als Psychotherapie für Überlebende staatlicher Gewalt." *Zeitschrift für politische Psychologie* 9/1: 585–600.

Rice, Andrew. 2009. *The Teeth May Smile but the Heart Does Not Forget: Murder and Memory in Uganda*. New York: Metropolitan Books.

Rowe, John. 1988. "Islam Under Idi Amin: A Case of Déjà Vu?" In Holger Bernt Hansen and Michael Twaddle (eds.), *Uganda Now: Between Decay and Development*. London: James Currey, 267–79.

Scheffler, Thomas (ed.). 2002. *Religion Between Violence and Reconciliation*. Beirut: Ergon.

Schulz, Dorothea. 2013a. "What Makes a Good Minority Muslim? Educational Policy and the Paradoxes of Muslim Schooling in Uganda." *Contemporary Islam* 7/1: 53–70.

Schulz, Dorothea. 2013b. "(En)gendering Muslim Self-Assertiveness. Muslim Schooling and Female Elite Formation in Uganda." *Journal of Religion in Africa* 43/4: 396–425.

Solomon, Andrew. 2001. *The Noonday Demon: An Atlas of Depression*. New York: Scribner.

Stier, Oren Baruch, and J. Shawn Landres (eds.). 2006. *Religion, Violence, Memory, and Place*. Bloomington: Indiana University Press.

Twaddle, Michael. 1988. "Museveni's Uganda: Notes toward a Provisional Analysis." In Hansen Bernt and Michael Twaddle (eds.) *Uganda Now: Between Decay and Development*. London: James Currey, 313–35.

von Peter, Sebastian. 2008. "The Experience of 'Mental Trauma' and Its Transcultural Application." *Transcultural Psychiatry* 45/4: 639–51.

von Peter, Sebastian. 2009. "The Concept of 'Mental Trauma' and Its Transcultural Application." *Anthropology & Medicine* 16/1: 13–25.

WHO. 2005. *Manual for Community Level Workers to Provide Psychosocial Care to Communities Affected by the Tsunami Disaster*. Electronic document: <http://www.searo.who.int/entity/emergencies/documents/List_of_Guidelines_for_Health_Emergency_community_level-workers.pdf?ua=1>, accessed 21 September 2017.

Willemse, Karin. 2005. "Mapping Selves: Biographic Narratives of Working Women Negotiating the Sudanese Islamist Moral Discourse in Darfur, West Sudan." Paper presented to the conference *Conversion, Modernity and the Individual in Africa and Asia*, Leibniz-Zentrum Moderner Orient, Berlin.

Young, Allan. 1995. *Harmony of Illusions: Inventing Post-Traumatic Stress Disorder*. Princeton: Princeton University Press.

PART 7

Arab Revolutions and Their Impact on Research about the Middle East

CHAPTER 19

Understanding Transformation, Elite Change, and New Social Mobilisation in the Arab World: An Actor-Centred and Policy-Oriented Research Project

Muriel Asseburg

1 Introduction

The protests and upheavals that swept through the Arab world in 2010 and 2011 constituted a historic turning point in the relations between Arab societies and the autocratic systems that had shaped much of the region's political culture throughout the past decades. For the first time, political mobilisation of large parts of the population in several Arab countries successfully challenged regimes that were, it seemed, well entrenched through stable elite coalitions and loyal security apparatuses. The upheavals precipitated dynamics of change and conflict, ranging from gradual or piecemeal reform to authoritarian retrenchment, deepened internal conflict, and all-out civil war.

In four countries—Egypt, Libya, Tunisia, and Yemen—the formal prime decision makers of the authoritarian regimes that had been in power for decades were forced out of office by combinations of popular movements, military defections, coups, and—with the exception of Tunisia—external involvement, ranging from verbal encouragement (Egypt), to robust mediation and the threat of sanctions (Yemen), to military intervention (Libya). As a result, these four countries have since been in the throes of drawn-out transformation processes.

However, whether the change of leadership that took place in these four countries actually constituted regime change and encompassed a comprehensive reconfiguration of the political elite was an open question. Who exactly were the new players, would they be capable of exerting sustainable influence, and how would they relate to what remained of the previous elite that was still represented in the structures of power? Would mass political mobilisation contribute to the emergence of a more inclusive national identity, or would it prepare the ground for populism and radicalisation, compounding existing conflicts? Would changes in the balance of power also translate into significant

 | DOI:10.1163/9789004386891_020

changes to the political order? Finally, in what way could external actors such as Germany and the European Union provide constructive support to transformation processes in the region?

2 The Project and Its Advisory Council

To tackle these questions, Stiftung Wissenschaft und Politik (SWP), the German Institute for International and Security Affairs in Berlin, in 2012 conceived an actor-centred and policy-oriented research project titled "Elite Change and New Social Mobilization in the Arab World." Over the four years of its duration, nearly thirty researchers, some two-thirds of them from Arab countries or of Arab origin, cooperated in the endeavour (for varying periods and with differing levels of intensity). They investigated the attitudes, priorities, and actions of different actors, such as the military, the representatives of the ancien régime, business elites, labour movements, youth, civil society, various strands of Islamist movements and parties, and so forth. Beyond working on their individual case studies, project fellows collaborated in devising a conceptual framework that would allow researchers to grasp the complex dynamics operating among the relevant actors and their impact on the path of transformation.[1]

One of the project's main outputs was a Special Issue of the journal *Mediterranean Politics*, published as Issue 1 of 2016, with contributions examining the transformations in Egypt, Libya, Tunisia, and Yemen between early 2011

1 The project was generously funded by the German Federal Foreign Office and the Robert Bosch Stiftung, and benefited from cooperation with the Alexander von Humboldt Foundation and the Friedrich-Ebert-Foundation, as well as the doctoral programmes of the Heinrich Böll Foundation and the Hanns-Seidel-Foundation. The project's Advisory Council was headed by Gudrun Krämer and assembled representatives of academia, donors, partner organisations, and the German Bundestag. Its other academic members were: Cilja Harders, Marianne Kneuer, Claus Offe, Rachid Ouaissa, and Ulrike Freitag. Gudrun's familiarity with policy-oriented research, her trans-disciplinary experience, and topical interventions in the public debate, combined with her academic excellence, were crucial in bringing to bear the wide-ranging knowledge and experience of the council. In doing so, she was able to draw on her insights from previous positions, such as being a senior research fellow at Stiftung Wissenschaft und Politik (1982–1994), a member of the Advisory Council to the Bundeszentrale für politische Bildung (the Federal Agency for Civic Education, 2005–2013), and a member of the Advisory Council to the Ministry of Economic Cooperation (1996–2009), to name but a few of the positions in which she bridged academia and politics. For an overview of the project fellows and publications please refer to the project website at https://www.swp-berlin.org/en/projects/completed-projects-compl/arab-elites-and-social-mobilization-compl/introduction/.

and late 2014.[2] The overall objective of the study was to identify crucial actors and understand the dynamics behind the cycles of contestation that shaped these processes and led to a significant variety of preliminary outcomes, ranging from state failure, civil war, and de facto partition (Yemen and Libya), to authoritarian restoration (Egypt), to precarious consensus on a more participatory and liberal order (Tunisia).

3 Why an Actor-Centred Approach to Understanding Transformation?

The inquiries assembled in the Special Issue start from the premise that the developments that unfolded in Egypt, Libya, Tunisia, and Yemen after 2011 cannot be characterised as linear, or centrally crafted and steered transitions from authoritarian orders towards preconceived outcomes. Rather, the studies approach these developments as "dynamic, ambivalent, and open-ended processes of transformation" (Bouziane et al. 2013, 2), driven by actors who negotiate, struggle, and at times violently fight over rules of governance and representation, as well as norms and values, all of which serve as means or political resources potentially influencing the trajectory of the transformation.[3] Therefore, the authors of these studies do not strive to identify causal links between structural factors and preliminary outcomes. Rather, legacies and structural conditions are seen as one of the sets of political resources or as part of "a good or a bad 'hand' to play in the political struggle over new institutions" (Ahmed and Capoccia 2014, 9). Institutional arrangements, such as new constitutions, are conceived as the expression of specific balances of power as evolved during the transformation process.[4] To understand how these new institutions are created, Ahmed and Capoccia (2014, 9) propose "focus[ing] on the strategic interaction of key actors in fighting over institutional innovations."

The actor-centred approach adopted in the Special Issue is based on the central assumption that an analytical focus on the strategies, choices, and

2 The following is an abbreviated and slightly adapted version of the introductory article by Asseburg and Wimmen 2016, reprinted by permission of the publisher, Taylor & Francis Ltd, http://www.tandfonline.com.

3 The term *political resource* is used here in the broad sense proposed by Dahl (1961, 226) as "anything that can be used to sway the specific choices or strategies of another individual."

4 Francis Fukuyama noted that paying "too much attention to the formal rules obscures the fact that things are so fluid in these early democracies that everything really depends on the ability of the underlying social groups to mobilize and to get their way" (Diamond et al. 2014, 97).

performances of those actors who wield significant influence over the political process, as well as the evolving relations between them, can help identify the key dynamics at work in the four cases discussed here. In addition, consideration is given to the criticism advanced in many studies on political transformation: the "over-emphasis on the role of the state, ruling elites and traditional political and civil society actors to the detriment of societal forms of unstructured mobilization and non-traditional, leaderless and horizontal social and political actors" (Pace and Cavatorta 2012). Hence, half of the case studies focus on what we refer to as "mobilised publics." The analysis also focuses on the dynamics between the two sets of actors, asking first how the politically relevant elite were constrained by sustained social mobilisation and to what extent they engaged with bottom-up participation, ignoring and suppressing it or utilising and exploiting it, and second, investigating whether the extended scope of popular mobilisation generated increased opportunities for participation and whether this contributed to the legitimacy and stability of the emerging political order or caused instability and conflict.

4 The Politically Relevant Elite

Such an approach first requires identifying the people and groups who play relevant parts in the struggle, thus affecting the transformation process. A look at nominal positions of power—such as the presidency, leadership of the armed and security forces, and leadership of political parties—offers some information helpful in identifying the actors involved but does not ascertain their relative weight. It also tends to omit actors with significant influence who do not hold nominal positions (for example, business elites), especially as informal institutions and arrangements remain of crucial importance in the political orders analysed here. Therefore, a combination of positional, decisional, reputational, and network approaches used in elite studies are used to identify a wider array of relevant actors.[5]

In their analysis of the changing power structures of Arab regimes in the early 2000s, Perthes and his colleagues (2004, 5) proposed the term *politically relevant elite* (PRE), defined as "those individuals, groups, and networks … in a given country who wield political influence and power in that they make strategic decisions or participate in decision making on a national level, contribute to defining political norms and values (including the definition of 'national interests'), and directly influence political discourse on strategic issues."

5 For an overview of the terminology and approaches of elite studies, see Knoke 1993.

This implies that even in the unmistakably authoritarian orders preceding the uprisings, political power was not restricted to a narrowly circumscribed core elite. Around a president or king, the model describes a significantly larger secondary elite—middle ranks of the ruling party, the officer corps, representatives of large businesses and state institutions—that wields influence on the centre and trades loyalty for shares of resources and local or sectoral franchises of power. A tertiary elite—clerics, representatives of interest groups, prominent journalists, and so on—may at times or in regard to certain issues of national relevance have the power to set and influence agendas. Distribution of power may vary between actors in different phases and manifestations of the regime, and the influence and bargaining power of individual actors are likely to wax and wane in response to changes in the economic order, challenges in the areas of security and foreign policy, the type of opposition the regime encounters, and so on. As Migdal points out, it often remains ambiguous as to what extent the core elite of an authoritarian regime is indeed in control, or rather, rests its power on mediation between actors who constitute semi-autonomous centres of power and may be subdued only at significant cost (Migdal 2001, 36).

The contributions in the Special Issue start from this understanding of the PRE. It is assumed that in the four countries under consideration, the ouster of the formal prime decision maker provided actors located in the second layer of the PRE with far greater autonomy and control over resources of power than they previously wielded. The opening up of the political sphere also allowed players formerly excluded from the three elite circles or admitted only in a very restricted fashion, as well as some entirely new actors, to enter the political arena. The transformation processes were perceived by these actors as opportunities to establish a new balance of power and lay down rules of the game to ensure their dominant (or improved) position.

5 Mobilised Publics

A significant cohort of the protesters who took to the streets in 2011 did not restrict their ambition to the overthrow of a detested dictator or regime, but kept pushing for significant changes in the ways their societies were ruled. Consequently, the PRE encountered recurrent cycles of contentious action that challenged its monopoly over the formal transformation processes and concrete policy decisions. As the 2011 uprisings consecrated the inherent legitimacy of such manifestations of the popular will, the PRE initially faced difficulties in dismissing or repressing such challenges.

While the heuristic model of the PRE acknowledges the potential of leaders of mass movements or prominent representatives of civil society organisations (CSOs) to become part of the PRE, it does not foresee or conceptualise sustained influence from broader parts of society through contentious action. This is an omission it shares with the (likewise elite-centred) models for transition from authoritarian rule forged in response to the largely peaceful transfers of power from authoritarian to democratic rulers in Southern Europe and Latin America since the mid-1970s. While these approaches recognise the importance of a popular upsurge in initiating a transition, their authors expected and even required such forms of mobilisation to be "always ephemeral" (O'Donnell and Schmitter 1986, 55–56), as they were considered a liability with the potential to generate radicalisation and jeopardise the transfer of power to institutionalised political parties and the establishment of a liberal democratic order (Przeworski 1986; Huntington 1991).

As many observers have noted (for example Cavatorta 2012; Beinin 2014; Bayat 2014), the 2011 uprisings were initiated neither by Islamists nor by liberal CSOs. A significant contingent of these "activated citizens" (Cavatorta 2012, 78) continued to challenge the PRE outside and beyond formal channels of representation, clearly not thinking that their immediate influence on and intervention in the political process should be ephemeral. As a consequence, the original PRE model is complemented here by the category of mobilised publics, which is significantly broader than "civil society" but at the same time more specific. Mobilised publics should be understood to include any collective of citizens that becomes active and mobilises others to do so, with the explicit objective of exerting immediate influence on the political process. Describing these actors as "publics" denotes their defining characteristic: namely, a mode of operation predominantly geared towards obtaining broad support, and hence leverage, for their claims and agendas through representation in the public sphere. Thus the category covers an array of collectives that includes, among others, fully institutionalised associations and impromptu and partly or entirely non-formal social movements, as well as interest groups and political parties.

Including political parties in this category is an indication that the PRE and mobilised publics often overlap. Groups and individuals who are part of mobilised publics frequently seek out allies within the PRE to leverage their influence, and some (such as leaders of mass movements) might accumulate enough resources to become part of the PRE themselves. PRE actors in turn attempt to use—or even create—mobilised publics to generate evidence of popular legitimacy for themselves and their agendas (or to counter and undermine that of rivals) and as a resource in inter-PRE struggles for influence.

One of the challenges of investigating mobilised publics therefore lies in assessing the degree to which they retain autonomous agency and where agency gives way to co-optation and top-down conformity.

The Special Issue's chapters concerned with mobilised publics combine ethnographic approaches with some of the tools developed in the study of social movements, such as political opportunity structures, resource mobilisation, framing strategies, and network analysis (for overviews of the various approaches, see McAdam et al. 1996; Opp 2009).

6 Research Results—Substantial Elite Change and New Elite Bargains

By late 2014, in all four countries substantial change had occurred in the composition of actors involved in political decision making and agenda setting as well as in relations between them. The extent of these changes covers the wholesale removal of core PRE (as in Libya), to the entry of new major players and dramatic advances by formerly marginalised or outlawed groups in the political process (as in Tunisia and Egypt). In Yemen, the power-sharing deal between different segments of the old PRE and the traditional opposition initially provided a degree of continuity, but in the fall of 2014 Anṣār Allāh (the Houthi movement, al-Ḥūthiyyūn) imposed itself by force of arms, ousting parts of the old PRE and seeking agreements with others, including the former president.

Parties and actors propagating variations of political Islam initially achieved significant popular support in competitive elections in Tunisia, Egypt, and Libya, and hence solid representation in transition governments and constituent assemblies. The power-sharing arrangement in Yemen likewise gave the Muslim Brotherhood-affiliated Iṣlāḥ party a say in government. These Islamist groups therefore appeared well positioned to exert significant leverage over the transformation processes that were to follow. By late 2014, however, in none of the four countries had they been able to realise an Islamic order or substantial progress towards it.[6]

At the same time, a significant number of actors who had been involved with the old regimes as beneficiaries or in official capacities managed to retain or reclaim significant footholds within the PRE. The most obvious example is Egypt, where the leadership stemming from the 2013 coup reinstated a number

6 For a discussion of what would constitute an Islamic order and the evolution of Islamists' thinking in this regard see Krämer 1994, 1995, 1999, 2005, 2013, among others.

of prominent actors from the Mubarak era in pursuit of a new authoritarian elite bargain under the vanguard of the military. In Tunisia, Nidāʾ Tūnis succeeded in providing a platform resurrecting the central tenets of the rule of Zayn al-ʿĀbidīn b. ʿAlī (president of Tunisia 1987–2011), while simultaneously distancing itself from the abuses of the regime and, in contrast to Egypt, allowing for the continued inclusion of forces of political Islam. Even in Libya, realignments of political alliances have increasingly worked towards the return of some prominent figures of the Qadhdhāfī regime in parts of the country. Although the Gulf Cooperation Council (GCC) road map for Yemen explicitly sidelined then-President ʿAlī ʿAbdullāh Ṣāliḥ, it preserved a role for his political camp and allowed his family continued influence and power, in particular in the military.

With the partial exception of Yemen, the persistence of influential elite segments did not occur as the result of a preconceived strategy engineered by remnants and partisans of the old regime to roll back the 2011 uprisings. Rather, the intense polarisation that ensued when the new arrivals to the PRE attempted to convert their assumed leverage into control engendered the creation of heterogeneous political alliances against them. For these initially defensive coalitions, the support of the core constituencies of the former regimes was an extremely valuable political resource. Whether for reasons of vested interest, social prejudice, or ideological antagonism, these circles remained mostly hostile towards the new arrivals to the PRE. Political actors who could plausibly be identified with positive aspects of the old order without being too obviously tainted by its abuses were attractive for these constituencies. In addition, their position within the emerging political landscape received added boosts, as populations became increasingly tired of drawn-out and chaotic processes that failed to bring them tangible benefits.

With regard to the evolving balances of power, political resources clearly mattered more than the procedural frameworks of the transformations. Thus, in the four cases analysed here, institutional designs were largely the outcome of power politics rather than formative of these outcomes, as the literature concerned with constitutional and institutional "engineering" assumed they would be (Diamond 1999; Von Beyme 2001; Reynolds 2011) and as expected by external actors promoting democratisation.

Alleged influence by external actors on domestic power dynamics loomed large in domestic discourses and contributed to heightened suspicions about hidden agendas and resources. Yet the struggle for power was driven first and foremost by domestic actors, who requested and accepted foreign support in pursuit of their own interests and agendas. Above all, external actors ultimately failed to steer the process according to their objectives. Even in Yemen, where they intervened most consistently and where dependency on external aid and a credible threat of international sanctions provided significant leverage to them, they were not able to determine outcomes.

The cases discussed here also do not support the notion that the "tyranny of starting conditions" (Diamond et al. 2014) ties the outcome of "noncooperative transformation processes" (McFaul 2002) to the distribution of political resources in a linear, path-dependent relationship. Resources matter, but they are not fixed assets, and the effectiveness of their use depends on how and by whom they are deployed and at what point within the broader dynamics of contention.

Despite the attention paid to ideological conflict, in particular concerning the role of political Islam in Tunisia and Egypt,[7] ideological positions have turned out to be an equally insufficient predictor of the behaviour of actors, formation of alliances, and course of transformations. In Egypt after the July 2013 coup, many self-styled liberals had no qualms about cooperating with the Salafist Nūr party and endorsing arbitrary arrests and extra-legal killings. In early 2014 in Tunisia, the Islamist Ennahḍah party (Ḥarakat al-Nahḍa) endorsed a constitution that won wide praise for its liberal content. Heterogeneous, albeit sometimes temporary, alliances between actors who had little in common or were former adversaries (for example, the military and the Muslim Brotherhood in Egypt, and Ennahḍah and Nidāʾ Tūnis in Tunisia) offered an opportunity to pool complementary resources, thus making the combined power of the alliance more than the sum of its component parts.

In Egypt and Tunisia, strong coalitions formed around the priority of restoring state authority and fending off challenges to the existing social order, including the networks of privilege that had thrived in the shadow of the anciens régimes. It remains doubtful, however, whether the elite bargains[8] struck in Tunisia and Egypt will usher in stable and legitimate orders. Technocratic rule, in Egypt augmented with a heavy dose of authoritarianism, may generate a modicum of legitimacy, and hence support among populations weary of turmoil and dysfunctional governance. Yet a reproduction of the alliances between privileged business actors and the military (the latter with a much more prominent role than before 2011) in Egypt, and the restoration of networks of privilege connecting the political, business, and administrative sectors in

7 For an overview of the Arab debate, see Kanie 2014.

8 Elite bargain is understood here as "the particular way in which the elite agrees among itself and organizes support around … a common understanding about the 'rules of the game,' especially concerning property rights, law enforcement and access to resources" (Hesselbein 2011, 1).

Tunisia are unlikely to yield legitimacy, and hence stability, in the medium to long term. Bound by the rationale of shared interest, such coalitions will be inherently incapable of uprooting clientelist networks.

At the same time, in both Egypt and Tunisia, there was a clear tendency (albeit to very different degrees) to restrict the scope for non-formalised participation and contentious action. Securitisation of public spaces, restrictions on associations, the lack of reform of state institutions (in particular the security sector), and the persistence of patronage networks all suggested that the PRE would continue to perceive demands for participation and transparency as threats to the social and political order.

In Libya and Yemen, the confrontational strategies of the PRE drove both countries to state failure, civil war, direct military intervention, and de facto partition. Armed conflict rather than institutional processes ultimately emerged to determine realities. In Libya, old and new elites tried to control cities, regions, and critical infrastructure, and thus grab a share of the country's wealth, rather than coalescing around political agendas or engaging in building a new political order. In Yemen, the GCC-initiated transformation process was severely undermined by the (longstanding) lack of state control, an upsurge in violence by groups affiliated with al-Qāʿida, and a reinvigorated drive by militant movements, such as Anṣār Allāh, to realise their demands through the barrel of a gun, after being side-lined in the transformation process.

7 The Limits of Politics from Below

Mobilised publics persistently rallied to influence the transformations and challenge the exclusive control of elite actors over these processes, but the results were limited and ambiguous in all four countries. The few independent activists and civil society representatives directly involved in the formal transformation processes (as members of transitional governments or constituent assemblies) had very limited influence on deliberations. Only in Yemen were they able to push through progressive reform proposals in the National Dialogue Conference. Yet the international actors who had championed and strongly supported a broad-based dialogue later declined to pressure a government deemed a strategic ally in the so-called War on Terror to implement the assembly's reform agenda. In Tunisia and to a lesser degree in Egypt, protest and lobbying campaigns influenced public debate, and through it the deliberations in the formal transition bodies to a certain extent. Yet such influence remained restricted to specific policy fields (for example, the legal status of women) to the exclusion of others (such as social and economic issues) and did not mount serious challenges to the PRE's control over the political agenda.

Paradoxically, in three out of the four cases, it was precisely at the apex of polarisation, with the PRE paralysed by deep division and transformation processes on the verge of breakdown, that mobilised publics gained renewed relevance. In the summer of 2013, the Egyptian Tamarod (Tamarrud, "rebellion") movement was instrumental in generating the wave of public protest that tilted the balance of power against President Muḥammad Mursī.[9] Against the backdrop of the July coup in Egypt, in Tunisia, the Tunisian General Labour Union (Union générale tunisienne du travail), backed by large demonstrations, took the lead in getting the warring political camps to compromise. In Libya, a popular movement against militia rule emerged as the political process ground to a halt, while the inability of the central government to control large parts of the country allowed mobilised publics to organise locally and push the demands of marginalised groups and areas, a trend also observed in Yemen. Yet, as they stepped into the void, a significant part of these mobilised publics assumed a partisan character and disintegrated or fractured as a result. Those who chose alignment with the PRE quickly lost their autonomy, in particular where and when rising levels of violence furthered discourses that demanded unquestioning loyalty to those supposedly leading the fight against an existential threat. Their capacity and even will to challenge the political leadership all but disappeared.

Conversely, political movements—among them the Muslim Brotherhood in Egypt, Nidāʾ Tūnis (during the fall 2013 protests), and even the militant Anṣār Allāh in Yemen (in 2014)—integrated into their repertoire of political contestation popular mobilisations that mimicked the outward appearance of the 2011 uprisings. Thus, rather than being forged into a political force for change, the momentum of the 2011 uprisings was instead appropriated by old and new PRE actors who increasingly mastered new forms and tools of mobilisation and in this way voided forms of political expression with participatory and emancipatory potential.

There remained residual groups of activists who continued to develop their skills and sustain the social memory of resistance. It is conceivable that in the

9 Tamarod serves as a case in point for the ambiguous character that mobilised publics can assume and their vulnerability to penetration and appropriation by the PRE. Many reports have documented the role of the military and the Egyptian business elite in launching, funding, and facilitating Tamarod. This, however, does not detract from the autonomous agency of the heterogeneous initiatives and citizens who joined the movement, including many with "revolutionary" credentials dating back to 2011 and before.

long run they will become part of an evolutionary build-up towards effective repertoires of activism and leaderships that constitute a more serious challenge for the PRE in the next cycles of contention. The more imminent result of disappointed expectations, fruitless engagement, and deteriorating living conditions, however, might well be that significant parts of society translate the lost hope of 2011 into rejection of any involvement in the public arena or into support for populist, chauvinist, or radical tendencies.

Bibliography

Ahmed, Amel, and Giovanni Capoccia. 2014. "The Study of Democratization and the Arab Spring." *Middle East Law and Governance* 6/1: 1–31.

Asseburg, Muriel, and Heiko Wimmen. 2016. "Dynamics of Transformation, Elite Change and New Social Mobilization in the Arab World." *Mediterranean Politics* 21/1: 1–22, available online: http://www.tandfonline.com/doi/full/10.1080/13629395.2015.1081448.

Bayat, Asef. 2014. "Foreword: Arab Revolts in Post-Islamist Times." In Are Knudsen and Basem Ezbidi (eds.), *Popular Protest in the New Middle East: Islamism and Post Islamist Politics*. London: I.B. Tauris, xv–xxiv.

Beinin, Joel. 2014. "Civil Society, NGOs, and Egypt's 2011 Popular Uprising." *South Atlantic Quarterly*. 113/2: 396–406.

von Beyme, Klaus. 2001. "Institutional Engineering and Transition to Democracy." In Jan Zielonka (ed.), *Democratic Consolidation in Eastern Europe*, vol. 1: *Institutional Engineering*. Oxford: Oxford University Press, 3–24.

Bouziane, Malika, Cilja Harders, and Anja Hoffmann. 2013. "Analyzing Politics Beyond the Center in an Age of Transformation." In Malika Bouziane, Cilja Harders, and Anja Hoffmann (eds.), *Local Politics and Contemporary Transformations in the Arab World: Governance Beyond the Center*. New York: Palgrave Macmillan, 1–21.

Cavatorta, Francesco. 2012. "Arab Spring: The Awakening of Civil Society. A General Overview." *IEMed. Mediterranean Yearbook Med.2012*, Barcelona: European Institute of the Mediterranean, 75–81.

Dahl, Robert A. 1961. *Who Governs? Democracy and Power in an American City*. New Haven: Yale University Press.

Diamond, Larry. 1999. *Developing Democracy: Toward Consolidation*. Baltimore: Johns Hopkins University Press.

Diamond, Larry, Francis Fukuyama, Donald L. Horowitz, and Marc F. Plattner. 2014. "Reconsidering the Transition Paradigm." *Journal of Democracy* 25/1: 86–100.

Hesselbein, Gabi. 2011. *Patterns of Resource Mobilisation and the Underlying Elite Bargain: Drivers of State Stability or State Fragility*. London: London School of Economics, Crisis States Research Centre, Working Paper 88, July.

Huntington, Samuel P. 1991. "How Countries Democratize." *Political Science Quarterly* 106/4: 579–616.

Kanie, Mariwan. 2014. *Transition Debates in a Transforming Middle East*. The Hague: Hivos, Knowledge Programme Civil Society in West Asia, Special Bulletin 4, February.

Knoke, David. 1993. "Networks of Elite Structure and Decision Making." *Sociological Methods and Research* 22/1: 23–45.

Krämer, Gudrun. 1994. "The Integration of Integrists. A Comparative Study of Egypt, Jordan and Tunisia." In Ghassan Salamé (ed.), *Democracy without Democrats? The Renewal of Politics in the Muslim World*, London: I.B. Tauris, 200–26.

Krämer, Gudrun. 1995. "Islam and Pluralism." In Rex Brynen, Bahgat Korany, and Paul Noble (eds.), *Political Liberalization and Democratization in the Arab World*, vol. 1, *Theoretical Perspectives*, Boulder and London: Lynne Rienner, 113–28.

Krämer, Gudrun. 1999. *Gottes Staat als Republik: Reflexionen zeitgenössischer Muslime zu Islam, Menschenrechten und Demokratie*. Baden-Baden: Nomos.

Krämer, Gudrun. 2005. "Gute Regierungsführung. Neue Stimmen aus der islamischen Welt." *Verfassung und Recht in Übersee* 38/3: 258–75.

Krämer, Gudrun. 2013. "Modern but Not Secular. Religion, Identity and the *ordre public* in the Arab Middle East." *International Sociology* 28/6: 629–44.

McAdam, Doug, John D. McCarthy, and Mayer N. Zald (eds.). 1996. *Comparative Perspectives on Social Movements: Political Opportunities, Mobilizing Structures, and Cultural Framings*. Cambridge: Cambridge University Press.

McFaul, Michael. 2002. "The Fourth Wave of Democracy and Dictatorship: Noncooperative Transitions in the Postcommunist World." *World Politics* 54/2: 212–44.

Migdal, Joel S. 2001. *State in Society: Studying How States and Societies Transform and Constitute One Another*. Cambridge: Cambridge University Press.

O'Donnell, Guillermo, and Phillippe C. Schmitter. 1986. *Transitions from Authoritarian Rule*, vol. 4: *Tentative Conclusions about Uncertain Democracies*. Baltimore: Johns Hopkins University Press.

Opp, Karl-Dieter. 2009. *Theories of Political Protest and Social Movements: A Multidisciplinary Introduction, Critique, and Synthesis*. London and New York: Routledge.

Pace, Michelle, and Francesco Cavatorta. 2012. "The Arab Uprisings in Theoretical Perspective: An Introduction." *Mediterranean Politics* 17/2: 125–38.

Perthes, Volker, ed. 2004. *Arab Elites: Negotiating the Politics of Change*. Boulder: Lynne Rienner Publishers.

Przeworski, Adam. 1986. "Some Problems in the Study of the Transition to Democracy." In Guillermo O'Donnell, Phillippe C. Schmitter, and Laurence Whitehead (eds.),

Transitions from Authoritarian Rule, vol. 3: *Comparative Perspectives*. Baltimore: Johns Hopkins University Press, 47–63.

Reynolds, Andrew. 2011. *Designing Democracy in a Dangerous World*. Oxford: Oxford University Press.

CHAPTER 20

Understanding Politics in Egypt "From Below"

Cilja Harders

1 Introduction

In the winter of 2018, the Egyptian Revolution, it seems, is dead. A civilian government under military control with re-elected president and former general ʿAbd al-Fattāḥ al-Sīsī rules with severe infringements on citizens' rights while waging a brutal "war on terror" against Islamists. Many prominent human rights activists, among them Gamal Eid, Hossam Bahgat, Mozn Hassan, Azza Soliman, Negad al-Borai, and Ahmed Ragheb are banned from travelling and faced with severe legal charges (Magid 2016). Many other, less well known activists and citizens are in prisons, where torture and arbitrary police violence have again become a normality (HRW 2017). The only non-governmental organisation (NGO) that caters to the needs of victims of torture, the Nadim Centre, was shut down.[1] The new NGO law, which was passed by parliament in 2016, is highly restrictive and puts civil society under the scrutiny and at the mercy of the security apparatus (HRW 2017). In addition, with austerity measures in place, the country is going through a deepening economic crisis. Not the least of concerns, given the unstable regional environment, European and American governments have prioritised their own security interests over human rights concerns and do "business as usual" with the Egyptian government, depriving civil society of much needed international support.

This narrative describes many of the harsh realities of post-revolutionary Egypt and highlights the continuities of authoritarian and military rule by a small and powerful elite that controls state institutions. But such a focus is problematic in two ways. First, it taps into older narratives of seemingly stable "oriental despotism" and feeds into a discourse on "Arab exceptionalism 2.0." Seven years after the revolutionary moments[2] of 2011, both the regimes and the

1 http://www.alnadeem.org/en.

2 In political science, a revolution is a sudden, comprehensive, and usually violent change of the political order. As the labelling of the events under discussion is highly contested among scholars and the Egyptian public, I use McAdam, Tarrow, and Tilly's (1996, 165) proposition to differentiate between "revolutionary situations" and "revolutionary outcomes," where the latter can also signify a fundamental reorganisation of the political system. Clearly, the mass

 | DOI:10.1163/ 9789004386891_021

discipline seem to be back to business as usual. The productive mood of self-criticism that touched the fields of political science and area studies, which were stunned after most observers failed to anticipate uprisings on such a scale, has evaporated. And thus, secondly, the analytical shifts, which began while scientists were struggling with the unfolding events, also tend to be ignored again. A regime-and elite-centred perspective that focusses on structures rather than on agency could not explain the uprisings (Harders 2013, Grimm 2015, Cavatorta 2015), and it is not useful for understanding the mid-and long-term effects of the revolutionary situations either, I argue.

Rather than wondering if "the revolution failed" I suggest looking at the long-term, less visible, but quite transformative impacts the mass mobilisations have had since 2011, which are often more tangible on the local scale. I thus look at the productivity of the events with a focus on political participation, using the approach of a "state analysis from below," which I will illustrate in Section 1. A "state analysis from below" can help us to capture processes of authoritarian rule "from above" and how these power structures are challenged and re-negotiated "from below." In addition, this perspective sheds light on the local dynamics of mobilisation in informal networks, which are crucial in three ways. First, these networks are used for coalition building and help protect against violent repression (Grimm and Harders 2017). Second, they structure the less visible engagements of ordinary citizens with the "every-day state" (Ismail 2006). Third, these networks of families, neighbours, friends, and colleagues are spaces in which change—for example, in gender relations or political subjectivities—was and is negotiated and practised (Singerman 1995, Bayat 1997).

While applying this perspective, I hold that the revolutionary moment of 2011 was indeed transformational and that it even created new types of political participation, such as the *lijān shaʿbiyya*, the popular committees, which will be discussed in more detail in Section 2 of this essay. In such a reading, the most important results of the revolutionary uprisings are the dynamic processes of politicisation and pluralisation, which went on well beyond the bloody summer of 2013. The fact that people protested en masse and brought down Husni Mubarak (president from 1981 to 2011) is already an important achievement and a fundamental rupture of a deeply rooted system of authoritarian rule embedded in a social contract of informality, as I will explain in Section 2. While unprecedented numbers of people were actively reclaiming the right to have rights (Arendt 1949), they were also reclaiming the political as a space

protests of 2010/2011 in the Arab world were a major rupture and thus constitute a revolutionary moment. The outcomes are, at least in the short run, mostly authoritarian restoration.

of meaningful participation and citizens' rights. The political experiences and practices of the years after the uprisings had indeed a lasting impact on many people even though this can no longer be translated into autonomous or even oppositional action on a larger scale. The more long-term effects of such experiences cannot be easily captured when looking at the regime level, as many political scientists would do. Thus, in a current research project in the framework of the collaborative research centre "Affective Societies 1172," Bilgin Ayata, Derya Özkaya, Dina Wahba, and I propose to use the lens of emotion and affect research to trace the impact of the transformative event of 2011, but also its limits. Building on the example of Egypt's popular committees, we traced the ambivalences and possibilities of these new political spaces. Dina Wahba and I argue that political practices in and of the committees can feed into more inclusive and less patriarchal and authoritarian political subjectivities (Harders and Wahba 2017)—but very often, they also remain within the limits of the established class and gender order of the authoritarian social contract.

2 Conceptualising the "State from Below"

What is "state analysis from below"? It is an analytical framework that draws on critical, feminist, constructionist, and ethnographic works as sources of inspiration.[3] It is embedded in the qualitative paradigm, is empirically grounded,[4] and uses critical feminist methodologies (Haraway 1988). It begins with French political scientist and sociologist Jean-Francois Bayart's observation that "contemporary cultures of the state are created by all social actors, including those from 'below,' even if their contribution does not necessarily contradict that of the powerful" (Bayart 1991, 65). The approach aims to expand upon our understanding of state-society relations in the broadest sense, while looking at microdynamics on the local scale, thus inscribing itself thoroughly

3 The following paragraphs are taken from Harders 2013 and have been partly revised.

4 My conceptual reflections build on data and material gathered through more than fifteen months of qualitative research in different popular neighbourhoods in Cairene districts (al-Waili (al-Wāyalī), al-Sayyida Zaynab, Bassatin (al-Basātīn), and Dār al-Salām) between 1994 and 1997. Since then, I have regularly visited some of the neighbourhoods, and since 2011 on a yearly basis. In September 2011, November 2012, and October 2016, I did systematic fieldwork in Bassatin, Dar al-Salām, and Bulaq Abu Eila (Būlāq Abū l-ʿAlā). The latter fieldwork was done with Dina Wahba in the framework of our research project on emotion, affect, and political participation. Fieldnotes, informal conversations, online documents, and media reports complement the interview data. All quotes are anonymous so as to not compromise the security of my interlocutors.

in theory-oriented critical area studies (Amar 2013, Derichs 2015, Korany and El-Mahdi 2012). Thus "state analysis from below" examines local issues, since it is at that level that power relations become tangible on this scale and abstract concepts such as "the state," "governance," and "politics" take concrete form. In the following, I will flesh out some of these concepts in more detail.

In our 2013 volume, Anja Hoffmann, Malika Bouziane, and I start from the basic assumption that so-called peripheral spaces and seemingly marginal actors have been vital in triggering major change on the regime level (Bouziane, Harders, and Hoffmann, 2013). The uprisings of 2011, as well as the ensuing and ongoing transformations in the region, are rooted in earlier practices of small scale, localised, and formal or informal forms of politics, which often occur beyond the political and geographical centres. Thus, years before the 2011 mass mobilisations, local (and surely national) authoritarian governance was not only reproduced on the local level but also contested locally. A perspective "from below" entails both a spatial and a material stratification dimension as it focusses on poor, excluded and/or marginalised communities. Space is socially constructed and needs to be understood in relational terms. "The 'local' is conceptualized in spatial terms and understood as a territorialized small-scale *place* that is demarcated from and interlinked to other *scales*" (Hoffmann, Bouziane, and Harders 2013, 5). The "local" is a political space, which is both a testing and a contested ground for changing state-society relations and thus deserves closest scrutiny. It is relevant in three respects. First, it is a place where the networks of mobilisation and participation materialise. Second, these informal structures are both a building ground for new mobilisation and political change and a repository for authoritarian practices and attitudes at the same time. Third, local networks can have compensatory functions when state institutions and actors are dysfunctional or disappear. Thus, there is a link between these micro-level dynamics and the macro-level developments in Egypt and beyond.

On the macro-level, "state analysis from below" focusses on the dynamic and contradictory relations between "the state" and "society" rather than on the formal institutions and organisations, national arenas, and political elites. The approach stresses the agency of actors, their resources, interests, and belief systems, within the given material and non-material structures. This implies a heuristic notion of the state (Trouillot 2001). Instead of assuming that the state and its agents deliver public services and contribute to the welfare, security, and inclusion of citizens, it starts from the local practices of an "everyday state" (Ismail 2006, Amar 2013) with limited hegemony, in which networks, as "institutions of the people" (Singerman 1995) play a major role. The state, then is a "translocal institution that is made visible in localized practices" between citizen and the bureaucracy (Gupta 1995, 376). It is a space of contestation and power struggles structured by a social contract. These struggles are embedded in specific historical, symbolic-discursive, social, institutional, cultural, and economic contexts. They constitute "politics," which is understood here in a broad sense.

Descriptively, "politics" can be conceptualised as participation, which I define as involvement in the social, political, and economic processes of formal and informal resource-allocation in a society (Harders 2002, 55). Political participation includes informal, individual, hidden, illegal, and "nonpolitical" actions and networks, as well as organised public collective actions inside and outside of institutionalised frameworks. State analysis from below uses an intersectional lens. This means that it pays special attention to how class, race, ethnicity, and gender structure access to and use of specific resource flows and participation patterns (Crenshaw 1989).

Even though I stress the relevancy of agency, including its often contingent outcomes, state-society relations are structured power-relations. The metaphor of the social contract is one way to capture this structure. This means that state-society relations are regulated according to certain general rules or "logics of action" (Jünemann et al. 2013), which in the Egyptian case entails an implicit "deal'" of political acquiescence for access to welfare (Büttner and Büttner 1993). In Egypt since the days of Gamal Abdel Nasser (president from 1956 until his death in 1970), this deal meant swapping independent political voice for access to welfare. The social contract was authoritarian in nature and it changed as the welfare state became weaker and services diminished. Over time and in the face of ongoing economic and political challenges, regimes in the region relied on five major adaptation and modernisation strategies: informalisation, Islamisation, repression, limited economic liberalisation, and limited political liberalisation. Informalisation became a distinctive feature of state-society relations over the last fifteen years—hence my characterisation of the social contract as a "social contract of informality" (Harders 2002).

This informalisation first became tangible when Cairo and other cities began to grow substantially and informally, and the so-called informal settlements (*ʿashwaʾiyyāt*) began to spread (Denis 2012). Especially in poor-to-lower-middle-class neighbourhoods, informal family and neighbourhood networks were constantly used to organise savings and housing. People built on these relations of trust and reciprocity for the collective or individual appropriation of public resources (Singerman 1995, Harders 2002, Ismail 2006). I take networks of neighbours, families, villages, and workplaces to be informal institutions, which include non-hierarchical and hierarchical relations such as patron-client relationships.[5]

5 I cannot engage with the literature on informality here in any detail. Whereas Bourdieu (1987) basically understands social networks as the incorporation of social capital, Singerman takes

For example, people dug wastewater canals in order to keep their neighbourhood clean. They appropriated electricity by tapping into power stations, and they squatted on land or built homes without official permission. Asef Bayat describes these practices as massive, visible, and informal "non-movements," engaged in a "quiet encroachment of the ordinary" (Bayat 1997, 57). The aim of these everyday practices is the improvement of living conditions, not the direct delegitimising of state authority. It is through these individual actions that "ordinary people change the Middle East," Bayat argued, years before the uprisings (Bayat 2007).

Many other dimensions of life became informal, too. Students in schools and even university students were drawn into a system of officially illegal private tutoring in order to finish their educations (Hartmann 2008). Patients in public hospitals had to pay for food, medication, and doctors' attention while being officially treated. The formal transportation system of the city did not extend to the growing settlements, and people established informal services, among them the infamous cheap motorised rickshaw taxis called tuk-tuks. This in turn was linked with police corruption and racketeering (Harders 2002). For the rich, informal spaces of action often allow for individual enrichment and corruption. Even though these modes of action were not completely new to the Egyptian state-society relations, their degree and scope decisively increased during the last twenty years. In this "social contract of informality," the state offers space for informal types of agency and participation rather than citizenship rights and a functioning welfare system, while still expecting loyalty and political demobilisation.

But the formal and the informal, the local and the national are closely linked. Informal appropriation of resources is based on the state's tacit toleration of these practices. In the social contract of informality, rights and claims of citizens are replaced by hard-to-regulate possibilities of informal action within informal organisations and institutions. Still, citizens maintain expectations of at least minimal delivery of services. As the Egyptian state cannot cater to

---

them to be informal institutions of the *sha'b* (people) because networks structure agency and represent a widespread logic of action (Singerman 1995, 244ff.). Helmke and Levitsky state that informal institutions are "socially shared rules … that are created, communicated, and enforced through channels outside of officially sanctioned channels" (Helmke and Levitsky 2004, 727). They stand in clear contrast to formal institutions, which rely on official channels for rule-enforcement. Bouziane shows that informal institutions can be available even in written form. She suggests distinguishing formal and informal institutions according to scope and addressee: "While informal institutions are spatially and politically limited in their scope, formal institutions claim validity within certain state territories in the Weberian sense" (Bouziane 2013, 142).

these expectations in the long run, the social contract of informality also generates a crisis of legitimacy, as citizens are increasingly aware of the lopsidedness of the contract. This crisis of legitimacy, in addition to rising activism (Mossallam 2012), a deepening economic crisis (Bogaert 2013), and massive state violence, was crucial in bringing about the uprising of 25 January 2011. Since then, Egyptian citizens have been struggling intensively to re-negotiate the social contract and its dominant logics of action, that is, limited political and economic liberalisation, Islamisation, informalisation, and repression. They have challenged all restrictions on political participation, they criticise repression and dominant economic policies, they engage in new ways with political Islam, and they have greatly expanded informal political and economic spaces. The wealth of social and political activism and mobilisation in the last years provides empirical proof to this claim (Ibrahim and Singerman 2014, Shenker 2016, Abd Rabou 2016, Abdalla 2016, Korany and El-Mahdi 2012). Meanwhile, repression and state violence continued and intensified after the summer of 2013 (Abdelrahman 2015).

3 Local Activism and *lijān shaʿbiyya*[6]

The popular efforts to re-appropriate the state from the local and national elites in power after 2011 involved a huge array of formal and informal community-oriented activities in which citizens took urgent issues into their own hands. Innumerable youth initiatives, local development groups, independent radio stations, urban development groups, popular committees (*lijān shaʿbiyya*), and artistic activities spread throughout the country. Although all *lijān shaʿbiyya* carry the same name, they represent a broad variety of people, ideas, and actions.[7] They all share a sense of local empowerment and—at least between 2011 and 2013—all possessed a huge sense of enthusiasm. They all focus on local issues, using different strategies in reaching out to their areas' inhabitants and to the authorities.

Self-organised local political committees and groups providing security materialised on 28 January 2011, when residents of Cairo and other Egyptian cities activated their neighbourhood networks (Bremer 2011a,b, Hassan 2015,

6 The following paragraphs are taken from Harders and Wahba 2017 and have been slightly revised.

7 In this sense, some of these activities can also tap into earlier practices, notably the existence of national defense committees carrying that same name, which were set up in war times in Egypt (Mossallam 2012)

El-Meehy 2012). The aim was to safeguard life and property under circumstances of extreme uncertainty and repression. This was mostly an urban phenomenon, crossing class boundaries: neighbourhood committees were set up in rich and poor areas alike (Saleh 2016). They were predominantly male. Citizens took over police functions in securing lives and property in the face of real and imagined insecurity. Umm Hassan, a resident of an informal settlement, recounted:

> When we heard about the events in Taḥrīr and about the burning of police stations, the men of our street went out in order to protect us. But nothing really happened. The people who were really scared were our Christian neighbours. They felt threatened. But nothing happened. And after the eighteen days, we all went back home and the committee stopped.

Popular committees took over security functions on the local level during critical periods of mass mobilisation in January and February 2011. This experience led to closer social relationships even in neighbourhoods that were not traditionally close knit. As a result, some of these new networks served as resources for activism after the eighteen days of revolution. But as Saleh rightly points out, as much as the committees influenced the balance of power to the detriment of the police during those eighteen days, they did not challenge the politics of the army, and except for some revolutionary committees occupying Taḥrīr Square, they mostly maintained traditional class, property, and gender relations (Saleh 2016, 57–63).

After the overthrow of President Mubarak, the paths of the popular committees immediately diverged: some disbanded, some formalised or merged with newly established parties, some continued in a revolutionary spirit, and others became rather developmental in outlook (Mossallam 2011). A youth activist recounted: "As a popular committee we had three main goals: to foster community participation, to establish popular monitoring of local government, and to try to create alternative media." An activist from a different neighbourhood said that they "wanted to bring the revolution" to their quarter. "Now, finally, we can implement plans to make the neighbourhood cleaner and better," a female head of a development NGO said. "We had these plans for years, but the authorities did not listen to us."

Especially vulnerable interviewees presented proud stories of self-empowerment and successful conflict with the local administration over water and electricity shortages during the first year of the post-Mubarak transformation. "We went to the building of our district's administration. We confronted them with our demands," said a woman from a poor neighbourhood in Cairo who talked about this new and empowering experience after the uprisings. "We were loud! And can you imagine that these people really talked to us? They never did that before. But after the revolution, they were afraid." More than one initiative in Giza mobilised inhabitants to collect their garbage and throw it on the steps of the governor's office. By mobilising publicly, the local inhabitants gained a voice and were able to exert pressure on the authorities to either finally implement projects they had approved years ago, or to react to the grievances of the inhabitants. They found local solutions to local problems, such as streets in need of paving and missing access to the city's cooking gas lines, and even acted in place of the dissolved local councils, as in the case of Maspiro.

Some committees developed close affiliations with formal political organisations such as political parties; others were careful to avoid making such alliances. Activists were also frustrated with the often service-oriented attitude of the population and the ways in which political forces exploited it. As one activist of a local initiative in Cairo, who wishes to remain anonymous, pointed out in 2012 when discussing the difference between his committee's work and the charity work of the Muslim Brotherhood on the ground: "They are giving the people fish, we want to teach them how to fish."

Political divisions intensified during the 2012 electoral campaigns for parliament and the presidency. Activists joined various parties, and parties competed for locally embedded actors in order to enhance their electoral success on the ground, just as in Mubarak's time (Harders 2002). Many popular committees and youth initiatives later became involved in the Tamarrud ("rebellion") campaigns and nonviolent efforts to oust then-president Muḥammad Mursī. In the bloody summer of 2013, some of them turned into direct support groups for ʿAbd al-Fattāḥ al-Sīsī, then-minister of defense and president since June 2014. Many people have since retreated from politics in the face of repression and polarisation, which destroyed earlier personal or political bonds. Others turned to development activities after more transformative political action was once again criminalised. Jennifer Bremer, Hatem Hassan, and Asya El-Meehy in their studies hint at the ambivalent qualities of the committees. El-Meehy argues that they were neither entirely democratic nor fully inclusive (El-Meehy 2012). Our data also indicate that the internal dynamics of popular committees have contained many contradictions, most prominently between older and younger people, between men and women, and between rich and poor. Many activists have sought to challenge class hierarchies, the disrespect of women, and the devaluation of the young. But we find that translating their criticism into new practices was a daunting undertaking. This is partly the case because the groups were deeply rooted in existing social and political structures. Their members built them on the networks they already had access to, such as those provided by family, friends, neighbours, and work. By tapping into existing networks, the committees were able to quickly take on some of the responsibilities of the state as its agencies broke down. However, this also meant that they inherited some of the problems of the informal social contract that had evolved in the context of authoritarianism. But the committees are also spaces for people new to the process testing new ways of doing politics.

The sheer number of groups that came to life after the eighteen days of uprising in 2011 made for a substantial change in the local political landscape. This experience of empowerment cannot be erased, and in many ways it was highly productive: it changed the perceptions and the actions of social and political actors. After years of acquiescence, people spoke out and used the committees to struggle both for a better life and to have a voice. These processes then, can feed into new political subjectivities, which are more inclusive and less patriarchal and authoritarian—as many of our interview partners and some academics have suggested, including Hania Sholkamy (2012), Asef Bayat (2015), Sari Hanafi (2012), Mohamed Bamyeh (2013), and Samuli Schielke (2015). Dina Wahba and I conclude our study of the popular committees with the view that "neighborhood committees can be empowering spaces, especially for young men and some women. This new type of political participation feeds into emerging new political subjectivities, which are more inclusive and less authoritarian. Thus, even as the regime stayed more or less the same by many measures, the people changed. They are transformed by the revolutionary experiences and by the new political practices they have engaged in. This is one of the most important results of the events the Egyptian people lived through since 2011. But the committees are also highly ambiguous, contentious, and power-loaded spaces. Here, actors constantly renegotiate notions of gender, age, class-relations, political orientation, and creed. They challenge and at times accommodate the logics that stabilize the authoritarian social contract." (Harders and Wahba 2017, 19).

4 Conclusion

Looking at the Egyptian revolution "from below" illuminates the microdynamics of political mobilisation and de-mobilisation. It focusses on popular efforts to re-appropriate the state from the local and national elites in power after 2011, which involved a huge array of community-oriented activities in which citizens took urgent issues into their own hands. This experience of empowerment cannot be erased, and in many ways it was highly productive: it changed the perceptions and the actions of social and political actors, with long lasting effects on state-society relations. Drawing on original fieldwork in several neighborhoods of Cairo and Giza, this essay argues that the committees embody a new form of political participation in Egypt, which has endured despite the country's sharp return to authoritarianism since the summer of 2013. As such, the committees—as imperfectly democratic and as varied as they are—are a dividend of the revolution that will continue to be relevant in Egypt's political future. These findings dovetail with reflections of our interlocutors and academic analysts. However, the state seems to have become even more elusive than before. Levels of repression and localised violence have been high under all regimes since the uprisings. But ever since President al-Sīsī came to power, the regime has systematically cracked down on autonomous political spaces and actors, forcing people off the streets and back into informal and more invisible ways of participation. Thus, today, the structure of the social contract of informality and major strategies for wielding power have not changed substantially as a "state analysis from below" can show. Nevertheless, the seeds of a different world are encapsulated in the participatory experiences of the last years, waiting for new opportunities to arise, while many activist struggle on.

Bibliography

Abdalla, Nadine. 2016. "The Quest for Accountability and Socio-political Change in Egypt: Repertoires of Actions and Challenges for Youth Activism at the Local Level." In Sylvia, Colombo (ed.), *Youth Activism in the South and East Mediterranean Countries since the Arab Uprisings: Challenges and Policy Options*. EuroMeSCo Joint Policy Study 2: 27–44.

Abdelrahman, Maha. 2015. "Report Thy Neighbor: Policing Sisi's Egypt." *openDemocracy* 23 February.

Abd, Rabou, Ahmed 2016. "Not a revolution yet." *The Tahrir Institute for Middle East Policy*, 25 April 2016, available at https://timep.org/commentary/not-a-revolution-yet/

Amar, Paul. 2013. *Dispatches from the Arab Spring: Understanding the New Middle East*. Minneapolis: University of Minnesota Press.

Arendt, Hannah. 1949. "Es gibt nur ein einziges Menschenrecht." *Die Wandlung* 4/3: 754–70.

Bamyeh, Mohammed. 2013. "Anarchist Method, Liberal Intention, Authoritarian Lesson: The Arab Spring Between Three Enlightenments." *Constellations*. 20/2: 188–202.

Bayart, Jean-François. 1991. "Finishing with the Idea of the Third World: The Concept of the Political Trajectory." In James Manor (ed.), *Rethinking Third World Politics*. London: Longman, 51–71.

Bayat, Asef. 1997. "Un-Civil Society: The Politics of the 'Informal People.'" *Third World Quarterly* 18/1: 53–72.

Bayat, Asef. 2007. *Life as Politics: How Ordinary People Change the Middle East*. Stanford: Stanford University Press.

Bayat, Asef. 2015. "Revolution and Despair." *Mada Masr*, 25 January 2015, available at https://www.madamasr.com/en/2015/01/25/opinion/u/revolution-and-despair/, accessed 9 September 2018.

Bogaert, Koenraad. 2013. "Contextualizing the Arab Revolts: The Politics behind Three Decades of Neoliberalism in the Arab World." *Middle East Critique* 22/3: 213–34.

Bourdieu, Pierre. 1987. "What Makes a Social Class? On the Theoretical and Practical Existence of Groups." *Berkeley Journal of Sociology*, 32: 1–17.

Bouziane, Malika. 2013. "Negotiating (Informal) Institutional Change: Understanding Local Politics in Jordan." In Malika Bouziane, Cilja Harders, and Anja Hoffmann (eds.), *Local Politics and Contemporary Transformations in the Arab World: Governance Beyond the Center*. Basingstoke: Palgrave Macmillan, 137–57.

Bremer, Jennifer Ann. 2011a. "Leadership and Collective Action in Egypt's Popular Committees: Emergence of Authentic Civic Activism in the Absence of the State." *International Journal of Not-for-Profit Law* 13/4.

Bremer, Jennifer Ann. 2011b. "Leadership and Collective Action in Egypt's Tahrir Revolution: Emergence of Civic Activism in Response to Repression." Paper presented at the International Association of Schools and Institutes of Administration Annual Conference in Rome, Italy.

Büttner, Friedemann, and Veronika Büttner. 1993³. „Ägypten." In Dieter Nohlen and Franz Nuscheler (eds.), *Handbuch der Dritten Welt*. Bonn: Dietz, 154–89.

Cavatorta, Francesco. 2015. "No Democratic Change … and Yet No Authoritarian Continuity: The Inter-paradigm Debate and North Africa After the Uprisings." *British Journal of Middle Eastern Studies* 42/1: 135–45.

Crenshaw, Kimberle. 1989. "Demarginalizing the Intersection of Race and Sex: A Black Feminist Critique of Antidiscrimination Doctrine, Feminist Theory and Antiracist Politics." *University of Chicago Legal Forum*, Article 8, 139–68.

Denis, Eric. 2012. "The Commodification of the Ashwa'iyyat: Urban Land, Housing Market Unification, and De Soto's Interventions in Egypt." In Myriam Ababsa, Baudouin Dupret, and Eric Dennis (eds.), *Popular Housing and Urban Land Tenure in the Middle East: Case Studies from Egypt, Syria, Jordan, Lebanon, and Turkey*. Cairo: The American University in Cairo Press, 227–58.

Derichs, Claudia. 2015. "Shifting Epistemologies in Area Studies: From Space to Scale." *Middle East: Topics & Arguments* 4/1: 29–36.

El-Meehy, Asya. 2012. "Egypt's Popular Committees: From Moments of Madness to NGO Dilemma." *Middle East Report* 42/4: 29–33.

Grimm, Jannis. 2015. "Eine Schwalbe macht noch keinen Frühling: Die arabischen Umbrüche in der politikwissenschaftlichen Literatur." *Zeitschrift für Vergleichende Politikwissenschaft* 9/1–2: 97–118.

Grimm, Jannis, and Cilja Harders. 2018. "Unpacking the Effects of Repression: The Evolution of Islamist Repertoires of Contention in Egypt after the Fall of President Morsi." *Social Movement Studies* 17/1: 1–18. Available at http://dx.doi.org/10.1080/14742837.2017.1344547.

Gupta, Akhil. 1995. "Blurred Boundaries: The Discourse of Corruption, the Culture of Politics, and the Imagined State." *American Ethnologist* 22/2: 375–402.

Hanafi, Sari. 2012. "The Arab Revolutions: The Emergence of a New Political Subjectivity." *Contemporary Arab Affairs* 5/2: 198–213.

Haraway, Dona. 1988. "Situated Knowledges: The Science Question in Feminism and the Privilege of Partial Perspective." *Feminist Studies* 14/3: 575–99.

Harders, Cilja. 2002. *Staatsanalyse von unten: Urbane Armut und politische Partizipation in Ägypten. Mikro-und mesopolitische Analysen unterschiedlicher Kairoer Stadtteile.* Hamburg: Deutsches Orient-Institut.

Harders, Cilja. 2013. "Bringing the Local Back In: Local Politics between Informalization and Mobilization in an Age of Transformation in Egypt." In Malika Bouziane, Cilja Harders, and Anja Hoffmann (eds.), *Local Politics and Contemporary Transformations in the Arab World: Governance Beyond the Center*. Basingstoke: Palgrave Macmillan, 113–36.

Harders, Cilja. 2015. "'State Analysis from Below' and Political Dynamics in Egypt after 2011." *International Journal of Middle East Studies* 47/1: 148–51.

Harders, Cilja, and Dina Wahba. 2017. "New Neighborhood Power: Informal Popular Committees and Changing Local Governance in Egypt." In Thanassis Cambanis and Michael Wahid Hanna (eds.), *Arab Politics Beyond the Uprisings: Experiments in an Era of Resurgent Authoritarianism.* New York: The Century Foundation Press, pp. 400–419. Available at https://tcf.org/content/report/new-neighborhood-power/

Hartmann, Sarah. 2008. "'At School We Don't Pay Attention Anyway'–The Informal Market of Education in Egypt and Its Implications." *Sociologus* 58/1: 27–48.

Hassan, Hatem M. 2015. "Extraordinary Politics of Ordinary People: Explaining the Microdynamics of Popular Committees in Revolutionary Cairo." *International Sociology* 30/4: 383–400.

Helmke, Gretchen, and Steven Levitsky. 2004. "Informal Institutions and Comparative Politics: A Research Agenda." *Perspectives on Politics* 2/4: 725–40.

Hoffmann, Anja, Malika Bouziane, and Cilja Harders. 2013. "Analyzing Politics beyond the Center in an Age of Transformation." In Malika Bouziane, Cilja Harders, and Anja Hoffmann (eds.), *Local Politics and Contemporary Transformations in the Arab World. Governance Beyond the Center*. Basingstoke: Palgrave Macmillan, 3–21.

Horst, Jakob, Annette Jünemann, and Delf Rothe. 2014. *Euro-Mediterranean Relations after the Arab Spring: Persistence in Times of Change*. London: Routledge.

Human Rights Watch (HRW). 2017. "Egypt." In *World Report 2017*, 233–41.

Ibraheem, Karim, and Diane Singerman. 2014. "Urban Egypt: On the Road from Revolution to the State? Governance, the Built Environment, and Social Justice." *Egypte-Monde Arabe* 11: 101–20. Available at http://ema.revues.org/3255.

Ismail, Salwa. 2006. *Political Life in Cairo's New Quarters: Encountering the Everyday State*. Minneapolis: University of Minnesota Press.

Korany, Bahgat, and Rabab El-Mahdi. 2012. *Arab Spring in Egypt: Revolution and Beyond.* New York and Cairo: The American University in Cairo Press.

Krämer, Gudrun. 2013. "Modern but not Secular: Religion, Identity and the *ordre public* in the Arab Middle East." *International Sociology* 28/6: 629–44.

Magid, Pesha. 2016. "Understanding 554 Travel Bans Since 2011." *MadaMasr* 28 June.

McAdam, Doug, Sidney Tarrow, and Charles Tilly. 1996. "To Map Contentious Politics." *Mobilization: An International Quarterly* 1/1: 17–34.

Mossallam, Alia. 2011. "Popular committees continue the revolution." *Al-Masry Al-Youm* (*English Edition*) 18 June. Available at http://www.egyptindependent.com/popular-committees-continue-revolution/

Mossallam, Alia. 2012. *Hikāyāt sha'b–Stories of Peoplehood: Nasserism, Popular Politics and Songs in Egypt, 1956–1973*. PhD dissertation. The London School of Economics and Political Science (LSE).

Saleh, Ahmed. 2016. *The Popular Committees: The Local, the Ordinary and the Violent in the Egyptian Revolution.* Master's thesis, Budapest: Central European University.

Schielke, Samuli. 2015. *Egypt in the Future Tense: Hope, Frustration, and Ambivalence before and after 2011*. Bloomington: Indiana University Press.

Shenker, Jack. 2016. *The Egyptians: A Radical Story.* London: Allen Lane.

Sholkamy, Hania. 2012. "Women Are Also Part of This Revolution." In Bahgat Korany and Rabab El-Mahdi (eds.), *Arab Spring in Egypt: Revolution and Beyond.* New York and Cairo: The American University in Cairo Press, 153–74.

Singerman, Diane. 1995. *Avenues of Participation: Family, Politics, and Networks in Urban Quarters of Cairo.* Princeton: Princeton University Press.

Trouillot, Michel-Rolph. 2001. "The Anthropology of the State in the Age of Globalization: Close Encounters of the Deceptive Kind." *Current Anthropology* 42/1: 125–38.

PART 8

Muslims Inside Out

CHAPTER 21

Recognition and its Traps in Liberal Secular Conditions: The Case of Muslims in Europe

Schirin Amir-Moazami

1 Introduction[1]

In recent decades, the increasing visibility of Muslims in European public spheres has not only generated a number of controversies but also given rise to a series of political measures designed to regulate religious plurality. In the face of far-reaching and readily mobilised international terror networks, security technologies have been expanded, and these increasingly impinge on Muslim spheres and thus, of necessity, shape religious practice. On the other hand, the permanent (that is, no longer temporary) presence of Muslims in Europe has also set in motion political procedures aimed at social inclusion. To date, however, few scholars have taken critical note of the fact that the logics of recognition and securitisation are closely interlinked (Peter 2008, Birt 2006, Schiffauer 2008, Tezcan 2012). Moreover, security and recognition policies are often seen as divergent political strategies for dealing with marginalised minorities who are viewed as suspect. Security discourses fall within the realm of Islamophobia because they lump together various sectors of the population and place them under blanket suspicion. Recognition, meanwhile, is regarded as a welcome (counter)measure. Most recently, this has been shown in striking fashion by the widely expressed public avowal that Islam is part of Germany. Although a series of voices have doggedly insisted that it does *not* belong, the affirmative belief remains oddly intact, so that the ensuing questions are rendered redundant: Under what conditions does Islam belong? Which Islam are we talking about here, and who determines the point at which the belonging starts? Because recognition seems at first to be the opposite of exclusion or indeed aversion, the cunning that is sometimes embedded in efforts at inclusion, as reflected in the currently flourishing integration paradigm, is often exempted from criticism.

In the following essay, I would like to complicate this common opposition, by focussing more on the relationships between recognition and the regulation of religious plurality in the liberal secular conditions that pertain in European

1 Translated from German by Simon Cowper.

 | DOI:10.1163/9789004386891_022

nation-state contexts. Above all, because recognition is touted in many places or tacitly accepted as an overdue measure of multicultural politics, it is worth taking a closer look at the contradictions and exclusionary mechanisms it contains.

Looking at recognition as one amongst a number of other political aporias, I proceed in two steps. In the first step I would like to consider recognition policies for Muslims in Europe in the context of a political theoretical reflection on the contradictions inherent to the recognition of minorities in nation-state contexts.[2] My analytical lens builds upon Patchen Markell's (2003) critique of recognition by substantiating some of his arguments using the example of the "Muslim question" in Europe. Markell's objections to Hegelian-inspired recognition policies contain two key elements that I would like to touch on by way of introduction: first, recognition requires a clearly defined subject to be recognised, one that often gains contours through the act of recognition.[3] Secondly, this subject of recognition requires an authority that articulates and administers recognition. Since Hegel, this recognising authority has taken material form in the more-or-less centralised nation-state, which, at the same time, experiences an increase in sovereignty through the act of recognition. Since this body determines the regulatory framework of recognition in close accord with national customs and legal conventions, the recognition of (religious) minorities can be seen as an aporia inasmuch as it is constantly manoeuvring between marking and dissolution, assimilation and segregation, exceptionalisation and normalisation.

If I "apply" Markell's critique in these two areas with respect to Muslim struggles for recognition in Europe, it is not so much because I am following his core concern—which is to read Hegel against the grain and to derive a theory of acknowledgement from his recognition theory. Rather, I will give a more specific twist to his discussion by focussing on the question of the recognition of *religious* minorities in Europe's liberal secular nation-states. The current attempts at and requests for recognition by Muslims in Europe more or less oblige us to look more specifically at questions concerning the arrangements

2 Here I presuppose the empirical finding that Western European countries with high rates of immigration have agreed in different ways to the basic approach of recognising religious cultural minorities (on this, see Peter 2008; Tezcan 2012; Brunn 2012).

3 Although this is not central to my argument, it should be noted that Markell formulates this criticism more radically. At the same time, he transfers the subject of recognition into a genealogy, according to which the modern subject is imagined as self-determined and autonomous. As critics of liberalism from Isaiah Berlin to Wendy Brown have shown, this conception of the autonomous, self-determining subject is as much based on presuppositions as it is normative. It requires the capacity, the will, and the preconditions for independent action and thinking, and it deliberately conceals power relationships.

of state, church, and nation, and thus to also think of political secularism as a structuring mechanism for regulating religious plurality and as a source of either recognition or non-recognition for Muslims. To this extent, the focus on political aporia allows us to more clearly illuminate the structural mechanisms of inclusion and exclusion that recognition policies also entail. In this way the research on Islam and Muslims in Europe, which is still perplexingly ahistorical and often void of broader theoretical questions, can be transferred to a substantial discussion of political theory.

A final word by way of preface: it is not my intention to extol non-recognition or outright exclusion as an alternative. I also set little store by assumptions of an authenticity of minority identities that precedes recognition and becomes tainted by it. Rather, I see the critical practice of reflection and dissection as a necessary prior step to be taken before it makes sense to ponder policy models in pluralist societies.

2 The Recognising State and the Muslim Subject to be Recognised

If we first look at the contemporary contexts in which the recognition of Muslims is negotiated, we can conclude that the Muslim question in Europe has generated a veritable proliferation of discourse. Muslims are in the cross hairs, their religious practice the subject of fierce political controversy; they are researched, surveyed, under surveillance, scrutinised, regulated, stigmatised, or: recognised. A series of critical analyses has drawn attention in different ways to the related process of how a Muslim subject is produced (Mas 2006; Birt 2006; Peter 2008; Spielhaus 2011; Brubaker 2013; Tezcan 2012; Amir-Moazami 2014). In one way or another these works have pointed to the fact that through the invocation and self-invocation as particular religious subjects, the "Muslimisation of Muslims" has been promoted by a range of different actors with very different expectations. The question of the concrete political rationalities that become manifest in the process of invoking Muslims as Muslims, and hence also the question of the ways in which the incitement to and shortage of discourse on Islam and Muslims also entails gestures and policies of recognition is strangely disregarded. Not only this, but the question of what deep-seated patterns the interpellation of Muslims as problematic subjects draws on is scarcely mentioned (exceptions are Mas 2006 and Peter 2008). These approaches leave out another question, one that is pressing in terms of political theory and crops up within a national and supranational setting: How can a minority that has been minoritised demand legal, political, or cultural participation beyond identity politics without perpetuating problematic ascriptions? In the following, my intention is not so much to answer this question but rather to examine in more detail the aporias inherent to it.

Markell's critique of politics of recognition is particularly helpful here. He takes as his starting point political theoretical discussions that have, since the 1990s, increasingly turned away from policies focussed on redistributing material goods, favouring instead policies that recognise cultural identity.[4] In general terms, Markell (2003, 3) makes the criticism that these theories, mostly based on Hegel, proceeded from the more or less idealistic standpoint that inequalities and exclusionary mechanisms were to be overcome with the help of a fairer policy for distributing the commodity, constituted by the "recognition" of cultural identities. According to him, the idea of mutual recognition thus emerges, on the one hand, from false assumptions, in particular because it masks power structures. On the other—and this is more important for my argument—Markell shows that policies of recognition are based on a sovereign but at the same time unmarked *We*, which controls recognition and decides what is and is not worthy of it. In Markell's view, this would be a way of reproducing the hegemonic framework: instead of being put under scrutiny, the politics of recognition would misconstrue deep-seated structures of inequality and relationships of power. In fact, in the worst-case scenario, they would even advance them:

> Thus, even those exchanges of recognition that express a spirit of inclusion—such as Jewish emancipation or contemporary multiculturalism—deal, at best, with the symptoms and effects of subordination, while simultaneously working to reproduce the problematic aspiration to sovereign agency in which those effects are rooted. At times, this may mean that existing relations of injustice will be preserved or even reinforced, albeit cloaked in a superficial layer of reform.
>
> MARKELL 2003, 31

Thus a policy of recognising minorities tends to presuppose and thus codify the identity of the person to be recognised as a fait accompli. Even if identity is conceived as dynamic, hybrid, or fragmented, and the struggle for recognition is seen as a permanent and open-ended condition (as we find, for example, in Honneth 2010), codifications are inevitable. The creation of the sovereign "Muslim" subject identified by the above-mentioned authors is thus bound

4 The reasons for this are evident: marginalised groups, especially in the United States, have increasingly challenged standards of justice and demanded political and, to some extent, legal recognition of their particularity.

into the recognition process and can hardly be circumvented by an appeal to the complexity, dynamics, or volatility of identity.

Over and above these more general considerations, I am primarily interested in the question of how paradoxically, in the context of the nation-state, state recognition policies perpetuate the marking of minorities, while reproducing the majority as unmarked. Admittedly, a politics of recognition should compensate for the blind spots in liberal rights of freedom by bringing to the fore the needs of vulnerable minorities. Ultimately, however, it reproduces the dichotomy of the majority population and minority groups that is engendered in nation-states (Markell 2003, 6). Of particular value in this context are Markell's reservations about the sovereignty assigned to the (nation) state in the course of seeking recognition—regardless of whether the state manifests as a neutral, and at the same time absent, mediating institution or as an active subject. Here, Markell refers primarily to the close interconnectedness of state and civil society and thus opposes the idea anchored in many recognition theories that the state is a more or less autonomous and above all neutral instance that can mediate the commodity of recognition and distribute it from afar (Markell 2003, 26–7).

Understood in this way, the recognition instance of the state can then be read in Foucauldian terms as conceiving of the state as an *effect* of diverse and somewhat diverging power techniques, instead of an abstract or a priori given object. It is through the act of recognition itself that state sovereignty is created or that the state recovers sovereignty. More importantly, a growth in state sovereignty is therefore not only a product of disciplinary or sanctioning measures but is also at work in provident precautionary practices such as recognition.

According to Markell, this happens principally because the state becomes the identity-forming body for the groups or people struggling for recognition, from which they hope for independence and agency (Markell 2003, 125ff.). He terms this "displacement through identification":

> That mode of address, after all, furthers the state's project of rendering the social world "legible" and governable: to appeal to the state *for* the recognition of one's own identity—to present oneself as knowable—is already to offer the state the reciprocal recognition of its sovereignty that it demands.
>
> MARKELL 2003, 31

Markell thus suggests an aspect that I would like to elaborate further: The subject who is to be recognised must be legible within a specific political system.

In this connection, Markell's chapter—framed in the context of the history of ideas—on Jewish emancipation in the nineteenth century is particularly instructive. Here, he concretises his critique of the Hegelian ideal of the state as an independent institution, detached from social conflicts, that dispenses, promotes, and administers recognition.

In this historical case, Markell sheds light on how civil rights entailed new forms of subordination, domestication, and reshaping in relation to Jews, namely re-enacting the self-image of the sovereign Prussian state and helping to relocate Jewish identification with this very state (Markell 2003, 126 and 131ff.). In this regard, he opposes not only a paean to the long sought-after emancipation, as expressed by Hegel and subsequent interpreters of his work, such as Robert Williams, but also the premature condemnation of the state as the mere reproducer of social inequality, as envisioned by Marx and others:

> Far from merely declaring Jewishness to be irrelevant to political membership, emancipation was at once a removal of restrictions on Jewish life and an active effort to reshape Jewish, and German, identity. Indeed, the policy was shot through with tensions that arose from the fact that it was designed in substantial part to secure an impossible sovereignty for the state; and many of the most troubling consequences of the policy for Jews arose less from the fact that it succeeded in making the state neutral (for it did not) than from the fact that it made Jews bear, disproportionately, the weight of its own failure to achieve its quixotic goals.
>
> MARKELL 2003, 131

It would thus be easy to glorify Jewish emancipation as a successful policy of recognition or, conversely, to denounce its failure. Both views are misguided because they misconstrue the ambivalence of the process of emancipation via the emerging nation-state. The guarantee of civil rights was also coupled with the conditions of becoming compliant citizens, even as "Jewishness" was persistently emphasised (cf. Bauman 1991, 107). This paradox in a strange way gains currency in light of the present-day excessive focus on Muslims' adaptability or inadaptability to liberal secular orders in Europe.

The recognising, unmarked general thus does not simply interpellate the particular seeking recognition in an asymmetrical fashion. It is also dependent on the construction and repetition of a moral norm, whose contours first appear in the process of recognition or, more generally, the marking of the particular. In the present case, this is configured in the consistently articulated appeal to Muslims that they must first of all affirmatively subscribe to the fundamental norms and values of Europe (or of particular nation-states), before they can be regarded in any sense as legitimate candidates in the struggle for recognition.

3 The Liberal Secular Matrix as a Qualification Space for Recognition

In particular because the politics of recognition are linked to conditions that have an impact on lifestyle, sensibilities, and religious practice, which they also help to shape, they are ultimately tied to the paradigm of integration. Its aporia consists in marking a community in its particularity and otherness and at the same time making it invisible. However, my concern here is not to simply translate the historical case of the Jewish question into the present or to claim, for example, that nothing has changed since then. The conditions for recognising minorities in nation-state contexts have changed not only through institutionalised individual rights and freedoms but also through the dilution of national borders in the course of Europeanisation and globalisation.

Islam's institutionalisation in Germany and elsewhere in Europe nonetheless shows that certain structures and mechanisms continue to be pertinent, despite the changes in circumstances. The political aporias of recognition therefore remain in new configurations. For in this case too, the state-regulated recognition of Muslims in Europe has an influence on the shaping of identities and affects organisational structures and religious practice.

If, with Markell, we assume that the *We* remains abstract, universal, and unmarked, while the individual seeking recognition is particular and marked, one task should be to reveal the supposedly universal, abstract, and unmarked in its particularity and in its embodied forms. In the case of Muslims, it is the claim to universality in the liberal secular setting, which comes into its own in the marking of the *religious* other ("Muslim"). In what follows, I will characterise this setting as a liberal secular matrix and thus more specifically thematise the connection between recognition and conditionality.

The promise of the secular state to grant all religions the right of representation in equal measure, or even to banish them all from the public space, thus implies an array of fundamental contradictions that the notion of political aporia neatly encapsulates: to be sure, the religious community enjoys an increase in rights in the process of recognition. At the same time, however, it entrusts itself to the state administration, in this way exposing itself to the process of (self-)formation brought into the equation by Markell.

The application made by a wide variety of Islamic groups for state recognition as a religious community or even as a statutory body under public law in Germany, for example, requires the extremely heterogeneous and dynamic

Islamic movements to organise themselves hierarchically in quasi-ecclesiastical structures and to merge into the representative point of contact required by the state. On the other hand, through this verticalisation of an intrinsically heterogeneous tradition, the state increases its authority because recognition as a religious community entails state control and a homogenisation of organisational structures such that they can be managed.

More specifically, this can also be seen in the measures used to establish Islamic religious education in state schools, in the state-sponsored education and training of *imāms*, or more recently in the establishment of institutes of Islamic theology at universities in Germany and in other parts of Europe. Anne Schönfeld (2014), for example, has found that current state efforts to institutionalise the training and further education of *imāms* in Germany are not just aimed at satisfying the religious needs of Muslims. Rather, she argues, these measures are primarily an instrument of regulation and control of the social milieu from which *imāms* are potentially recruited. Above all, Schönfeld demonstrates how these state education and training programmes are geared to the social imaginary of a tamed and democratic Christianity and are thus a component part of an instrument of government that is meant to help propel Islam in a modernising direction. Similarly, when university chairs of Islamic theology are instituted, it becomes patently obvious that a recognition logic is tied in with a civilising project, expressed in this case in the desired secularisation of Islam promised by the process of its academicisation. The former president of Germany Joachim Gauck put this in a nutshell in a speech on the occasion of his visit to the Centre for Islamic Theology at Münster University, which was founded in 2012:

> In our cities there are more than two thousand mosques and houses of prayer that have for the most part only appeared in the last fifty years. And now Islam is also becoming one of the academic disciplines at our universities. Behind this is a reciprocal act of recognition: our society is changing, because it includes an increasing number of Muslims—just as Islam for its part is developing in contact with our society. This entails demands being imposed on both sides—that is all part of it. Admittedly, some people who are resistant to change try to make mileage out of it. But the majority knows that we can only live in fruitful coexistence if we treat each other with respect and come together in a spirit of openness. The foundation for this is *our* basic rights and freedoms, *our* history and language [emphasis added].[5]

5 28 November 2013, http://www.bundespraesident.de/SharedDocs/Downloads/DE/Reden/2013/11/131128-Themenbesuch-Islam.pdf;jsessionid=A57CBA276E6AB695D00E0742D6EFBE5D.1_cid371?__blob=publicationFile.

Here, the conditionality of recognition consists in the fact that reform-oriented, secularising movements in particular become prominent vehicles of the recognition process, or that recognition is expected to be accompanied by adaptive capacities. Furthermore, the appeal to speak in the name of a unified and pliant voice provokes splits within the Muslim community, because every individual voice vies for the favour of the state and each devalues the other as an illegitimate or inauthentic representative of Islam. Currently this is clearly shown by the example of Germany's Alevi community, which, interestingly, mutated from a *cultural* into a *religious* community only as the politics of recognition launched by the state intensified. Precisely because the struggle by groups marked as minorities for the patronage of political authorities does not take place in a religious and political vacuum but is loaded with preconditions, the Alevi community shows itself to be a candidate for recognition that is particularly worthy of support as an Islamic *religious* community. On the one hand, this is because it explicitly eschews any form of dogmatism. In this way it earns itself the seal of approval as being a moderate, open, and liberal religious community, making it worthy of recognition—a community in which religious practice has, first and foremost, a spiritual dimension and thus demonstrates an internalisation of its faith compatible with Protestant thinking. On the other hand, representatives Alevi communities have increasingly gone along with the call to speak as Muslims and to develop into an interlocutor of the state. Yet, precisely because they declare central sources of Islamic discursive traditions to be of secondary or indeed negligible importance, while at the same time asserting Islam's stipulated entitlement to representation in Germany, they tend to give affront to the overwhelming majority of organised or pious Muslims in the country.

The commonly heard statement that Islam does not recognise any authoritative entity that brings together all the different tendencies under one roof and can be represented by a single voice is thus only a part of the whole truth, even if it carries some substance. We should also keep in mind the predefined arrangement of state, church, and nation. There is thus a framework into which non-Christian and, more particularly, non-ecclesiastical organised religious communities must assimilate without any fuss, regardless of what structures of authority they have. Here too, it is important to show once again the historicity of this process.

In a recent genealogy, Anya Topolski (2017) follows the mechanisms of inclusion and exclusion that currently manifest across Western Europe in the establishment of representative Islamic councils, tracing them back to, among other things, the political/theological structure of *shtadlanut* (intercession, mediation). In the case of the Jewish minorities in Europe, Topolski makes clear how Jewish communities tried to use this institution to gain favour with the ruling elites in order to achieve the integration they desired. Since this mediation process required an intercessor in each case, Jews were split—especially in the course of the emergence of the nation-state in the nineteenth and twentieth centuries—into "good" (submissive and compliant) and "bad" (closed-minded and bound to religious traditions) ones. This reinforced hegemonic structures and internal frictions:

> This fact, when put into the historical context of the theological-political practice of *shtadlanut*, understood in terms of a structural mechanism of power, sheds light on similar mechanisms used to communicate and control other minority religious communities. Many of its features, such as its disempowering and depoliticizing effects, are part and parcel of most majority–minority political struggles.
>
> TOPOLSKI 2017, 11

So when I speak of a liberal secular matrix, I also intend it to mean an element of the secular that lies outside formal legal codes. Moreover, its effectiveness consists not in a religious norm that is laid down once and for all but rather in the fact that the secular nation-state is entitled to decide where to draw the borders between religion and politics and which kind of religiosity is (il)legitimate in public life (Agrama 2010).

Despite different arrangements of state, church, and nation, political secularism thus remains ambiguous as a state instrument of separation or cooperation between state and religion. For it is reliant on demarcations between the political and the religious; and these demarcations are neither innocent nor static but full of preconditions, dynamic, and invariably constrained by dynamics of power. Secularism is thus not a neutral overlay but rather one world view among others, not least because the secular state also moulds its citizens and presides over the legitimate borders between the religious and the secular.

It is precisely for this reason that we should also give more serious consideration to the relationship of religion to secularity, which has a strong connection with affects, sensibilities, and embodiments. This tension can, for example, be seen in the cyclically recurring debates on Islamic practices of the individual in public arenas in Europe, which have long since taken on legal proportions. Thus, it is mostly non-conformist religious practices, such as veiling, the physical performance of prayers, or more recently male circumcision, that not only break through inscribed and largely habitualised social conventions but also reveal the inherent power structures of secular spaces. This is what makes it so difficult for subordinate groups to make themselves heard publicly, whose marked and suspect difference remains in urgent need of explanation.

It is in these religious practices, which both confuse and bring to the fore inscribed sensibilities, but at the same time are not outside what is legally permitted, that the terrain of all-inclusive individual rights is often abandoned and generally available freedoms are filled with moral substance. In particular, with religious practices that affect moral sensibilities, the conditions and limits of recognition are very clearly marked and it is also apparent who is recognising whom, at what point in time, and at what price. These moral enhancements of the secular are thus not in the first instance of a formal legal character and are thus hard to verify as an exclusionary mechanism in recognition politics. Yet they resonate with the set of conditions for recognition—albeit often unarticulated.

In this respect, the general questions about the boundaries between religion and politics, between state and civil society, and between public and private also structure the questions that a recognising body poses to the religious minority seeking recognition: Does it fulfil the predetermined criteria of the state–church relationship? Does it bear loyalty to the state or to the liberal constitution? Is it actually capable of democracy? Does it share the principles of freedom and equality? To this extent, the commodity that is recognition for Muslims can be had in Europe only if they are able to legitimise their religious practice in the language audible to liberal ideals (freedom of choice, gender equality, religious freedom, etc.)—that is, if Islam becomes a "religion" in the modern sense (Asad 1993).

Specifying the criteria of recognition inevitably eventuates in the scenario posited by Markell, a one-sided view of the (in)compatibility of the other, whose identity is contoured in this very process. Meanwhile, the criteria of the majority remain universal, unmarked, and non-negotiable, while the minority can survive the struggle for recognition only if it subordinates its marking to the universal—that is, if its demands for recognition are legible within an existing liberal secular framework. And yet at the same time it remains marked.

Instead of cosmetically redistributing recognition and thus treating only the symptoms of disregard, this kind of understanding of the secular as a matrix that regulates and shapes religion might thus help to generate awareness that a secular structure is more contingent than is frequently assumed. This brings me to my conclusion.

4 Conclusion

Given the current climate in Europe, where crude forms of racism and overt aversion to Muslims prevail, a critique of the politics of recognition is somewhat counterintuitive at first glance. If anything, however, recognition seems attractive as a political strategy for solving multicultural dilemmas. While words of welcome are undoubtedly necessary in terms of symbolic politics, scholarly analyses should, however, go beyond the events of everyday politics and avoid models based on hasty reactions that provide only transitory solutions.

But what alternatives are we left with if we see recognition as problematic because it does not identify structural inequalities and exclusionary mechanisms inscribed in the nation-state but merely displaces them? Or should a right to indifference follow from the problematic right to difference? It is in the nature of aporias that they cannot be skirted around but may be only recognised and named, and this because they are structural and not temporary or rudimentary.

It is thus difficult for me to see an alternative, a way out of the dilemma of a state-controlled politics of inclusion and exclusion. However, critical practice seems to me to be a key step if we are to have any understanding of the aporias that lurk out of sight in strategies of recognition. Even before we contemplate more sensible political models, an important step would need to involve an in-depth exploration of the structures of inequality and exclusion that are revealed, under closer scrutiny, in the liberal secular setting, an essential preliminary before we can even attempt to remedy these structures.

A further, more specific step is to shift the line of enquiry and to look at the extent to which the Muslim question is indicative of other questions that are obscured by it: What contingencies and breaches can be determined in the norms and values negotiated at the European level? What function does the interpellation of Muslims have in necessitating repeated comment on the same issue, and how do the questions structure the conditions in which speaking is possible? What forms of political and epistemic violence are connected with this appeal and the mechanisms of inclusion and exclusion inherent to them? To what extent does the reiteration of the same framework of interrogations also serves to hide these forms of power?

The question of secular accretions, for example, obliges us to expand our focus and to desist from a one-sided interrogation of Muslims, sounding out their attitude to their religion in a secular constitutional state. Rather, we should understand secular embodiments as learned and inscribed dispositions, as practices and affects that often remain unmarked on account of their incorporated character.

Besides the general problems that the recognition theorem contains within it—described with recourse to Markell—it would thus be important to call attention to the infiltration into power of embodied secular conventions and institutions like the secular state, which is often seen as a neutral guardian of religious plurality. A critical view of different ways of regulating religious plurality can thus reveal at the same time inscribed and embodied forms of the secular—above all paradoxically, by emphasising the connections between the exceptionalisation and normalisation of the Other.

To bring Markell into the discussion one last time, he makes a distinction here between acknowledgement and recognition. While recognition is inevitably directed at and to the Other, thus playing a part in its particularity, and while the recognising body remains neutralised and naturalised, the politics of acknowledgement is primarily addressed to one's own self:

> What draws us to or bars us from a just relation to others is, in many instances at least, not the state of our knowledge of them, but the state of our understanding of ourselves–in the first feature of my use of "acknowledgment": although the presence or absence of acknowledgment may have important implications for others, the direct object of acknowledgment is not the other as in the case of recognition; it is, instead, something about the *self*.
>
> MARKELL 2003, 35

Identity politics is not circumvented by the classification into Self and Other, as Markell points out in the next step (ibid.); but it does at least alter the line of enquiry. Markell's understanding of acknowledgement implies a "coming to terms with, rather than vainly attempting to overcome, the risk of conflict, hostility, misunderstanding, opacity, and alienation that characterizes life among others" (Markell 2003, 38). In this respect, we should not succumb to the illusion that the act of acknowledgement—or understanding, as Gadamer (1990 [1960]) would have it—resolves normative conflicts in pluralistic societies or precludes misunderstandings. Rather, consideration should be given both to the finite nature of one's own horizon of understanding and to the unpredictability of the outcome.

Bibliography

Agrama, Hussein Ali. 2010. "Secularism, Sovereignty, Indeterminacy: Is Egypt a Secular or a Religious State?" *Comparative Studies in Society and History*, 52/3: 495–523.

Amir-Moazami, Schirin. 2014. "Wer spricht wie für wen–und warum? Zur Anerkennung, Authentizität und Repräsentation von Muslimen unter liberal-säkularen Bedingungen." In Bertelsmann Stiftung (ed.), *Vielfältiges Deutschland: Bausteine für eine zukunftsfähige Gesellschaft*. Gütersloh: Verlag Bertelsmann Stiftung, 357–77.

Asad, Talal. 1993. *Genealogies of Religion: Discipline and Reasons of Power in Christianity and Islam*. Baltimore MD: Johns Hopkins University.

Bauman, Zygmunt. 1991. *Modernity and Ambivalence*. Cambridge: Polity Press.

Birt, Yayha. 2006. "Good Imam, Bad Imam: Civic Religion and National Integration in Britain post-9/11." *Muslim World* 96/4: 687–705.

Brubaker, Rogers. 2013. "Categories of Analysis and Categories of Practice: A Note on the Study of Muslims in European Countries of Immigration." *Ethnic and Racial Studies* 36/1: 1–8.

Brunn, Christine. 2012. *Religion im Fokus der Integrationspolitik: Ein Vergleich zwischen Deutschland, Frankreich und dem Vereinigten Königreich*. Wiesbaden: Springer VS.

Gadamer, Hans-Georg. 1990 [1960]. *Wahrheit und Methode: Grundzüge einer philosophischen Hermeneutik*. Frankfurt am Main: Suhrkamp.

Honneth, Axel. 2010. *Kampf um Anerkennung: Zur moralischen Grammatik sozialer Konflikte*. Frankfurt am Main: Suhrkamp.

Markell, Patchen. 2003. *Bound by Recognition*. Princeton NJ: Princeton University Press.

Mas, Ruth. 2006. "Compelling the Muslim Subject: Memory as Post-Colonial Violence and the Public Performativity of 'Secular and Cultural Islam'." *Muslim World* 96/4: 585–616.

Peter, Frank. 2008. "Political Rationalities, Counter-Terrorism and Policies on Islam in the United Kingdom and France." In Julia Eckert (ed.), *The Social Life of Anti-Terrorism Laws: The War on Terror and the Classifications of the "Dangerous Other."* Bielefeld: Transcript, 79–108.

Schiffauer, Werner. 2008. "Zur Konstruktion von Sicherheitspartnerschaften." In Michael Bommes and Marianne Krüger-Potratz (eds.), *Migrationsreport 2008: Fakten–Analysen–Perspektiven*. Frankfurt am Main: Campus, 205–37.

Schönfeld, Anne. 2014. "Regulierung durch Wissensproduktion, Staatliche Versuche einer Institutionalisierung von Imamen in Deutschland." In Oliver Hidalgo, Holger Zapf, Ahmet Cavuldak, and Philipp W. Hildmann (eds.), *Demokratie und Islam: Theoretische und empirische Studien*. Wiesbaden: Springer VS, 399–424.

Spielhaus, Riem. 2011. *Wer ist hier Muslim? Die Entwicklung eines islamischen Bewusstseins in Deutschland zwischen Selbstidentifikation und Fremdzuschreibung*. Würzburg: Ergon.

Tezcan, Levent. 2012. *Das muslimische Subjekt: Verfangen im Dialog der Deutschen Islam Konferenz*. Paderborn: Konstanz University Press.

Topolski, Anya. 2017. "Good Jew, Bad Jew … Good Muslim, Bad Muslim: 'Managing' Europe's Other." Ethnic and Racial Studies, open-access-publication: http://www.tandfonline.com/doi/full/10.1080/01419870.2018.1391402

CHAPTER 22

The Refugee and the Dog

Ruth Mas

This essay begins with a profound recognition of the reality of deracination and radical displacement that characterised my time in Berlin as a visiting researcher at the Berlin Graduate School for the Study of Muslim Cultures and Societies (BGSMCS).[1] I was there from 2015 to 2017 and the city was awash with refugees pouring out of countries levelled by the brute force of economic misery and political bloodshed. Images of refugees embarking on an overland journey into Europe or spilling out of boats in the high seas of the Mediterranean inundated screens across the world. Germany was reeling from the decision of its Chancellor, Angela Merkel, to let in Syrian refugees by the hundreds of thousands, its liberal left clearly incredulous at such a revelation of political morality. Refugees were suddenly everywhere, exhausted, dusty, and disoriented, filling the Hautbahnhof, and U-Bahn stations, entire families with sleeping bags in tow. Thousands of German citizens rushed to the train stations with cardboard signs raised to welcome them. They brought food and clothing, and took them into their own homes. They stepped in to support the refugees when the state, too underprepared and too overwhelmed with processing close to 800,000 asylum applications, simply could not or did not.[2]

"Camps" to accommodate these newcomers were nevertheless quite quickly set up anywhere and everywhere. They were complete with guards, reminiscent of another era, who were posted at the door with lists that monitored comings and going for the "protection of the refugees," and who were somehow immune to the sensitivity that such camps and such lists should elicit in such a country. Tales of refugees getting "lost" in Germany were already spreading and it was more important to control their displacement than to worry about how doing so would evoke history. Newspapers proudly displayed the meticulously engineered plans of spacial confinement. Bright red T-Mobile signs advertising "refugee plans" dotted the streets. In the midst of this, groups

1 My thanks go to Schirin Amir-Moazami and to Bettina Gräf for their tenacity and singular focus in supporting my presence at the BGSMCS. I am sincerely grateful to them both.

2 Mention should also be made of the fact that in Berlin, for example, refugees were nonetheless receiving an advance allowance for six months of clothing and six weeks of spending money.

 | DOI:10.1163/9789004386891_023

ILLUSTRATION 22.1 Arrival. Illustration by Anton Jones, 2018.
Anton Jones is an illustrator living in Berlin. His drawings for "The Refugee and the Dog" are part of an ongoing series depicting the plight of refugees in Europe.

of graduate students from the BGSMCS ventured into the camps, helped refugees with German bureaucracy, and translated documents.

During the first year of my stay I lived on Torfstrasse, an ordinarily quiet street with African grocers and specialty shops that led off the U-Bahnhof Amrumer Straße, in the working class and immigrant neighbourhood of Wedding. The street had been transformed overnight into a busy pathway that every weekday morning channelled a stream of people out of the metro—some on crutches, some in wheelchairs, many elderly, entire families, countless solitary men—over a bridge arching a narrow canal to the Ausländerbehörde, Berlin's Foreigners' Office, to register, and to apply for residency.[3] As I wove my way through the crowds every morning, all I could sense was how differently fate had spat us out on that street after having had its way with us. I had landed in

3 For a first-hand account of an anthropologist's experience of this office, see Feldman-Savelsberg 2016, 171ff. Feldman-Savelsberg also points out that the last scene in the novel *Snare,* written by the Cameroonian writer Priscillia Mahnjoh, describes how the main character is emotionally incapable of walking over this bridge (Mahnjoh 2013).

the welcoming home of a family of friends, where throughout an entire year I heard about Germany's own variegated history of refugees, one that had also marked these Berliners very deeply. Solidarity, a way of being and a sensibility that refused to go down with the ashes of East Berlin, strongly energised them as they recounted efforts to resist the mounting xenophobic opposition to Syrian refugees seen across the country.[4] Their voices may have been inflected by the euphoria that had overcome Berlin, but they were also tinged with the knowledge of how the welcome of refugees into the country could go wrong.

Some of these accounts were humorous, like the story of how the members of one city's local opera troupe came out to sing at the top of their lungs, in the hopes of drowning out the protests of the right-wing group that had situated themselves in front of the opera house. Others were outright stupefying. When Olaf, one of these friends, asked me, "Ruth, have you seen the article about the refugee and the dog?" he was shaking his head in disbelief. The article had appeared in the 11 November 2016 issue of *Der Tagesspiegel*, one of Berlin's daily newspapers. It seems that a shopkeeper had posted on his store window a sign bearing the image of a dog and stating, "*Asylanten müssen draußen bleiben*" ("Asylum seekers must remain outside").[5] The sign "Dogs must remain outside" is commonly used to prohibit dogs from public places that need to comply with hygiene regulations. Unfortunately, the shopkeeper had crossed out the word "dog" but *not* the image of the dog. In doing so, he had contravened Germany's laws against *Volksverhetzung*—section 130, paragraph 1 of Germany's Penal Code, to be precise—and as a result found himself in front of a judge, accused of incitement against a particular group, and attempting to defend his right to freedom of expression.

4 I experienced this solidarity first-hand. My stay in Berlin would not have been possible without the incredible generosity of Ingrid Hehmeyer, who welcomed me into her home and shared her friends and family. I will never forget the warmth, care, and friendship that she, her sister Kirsten Hehmeyer, and Olaf Freese extended to me during my stay. The daily and lengthy exchanges I had with Bettina Gräf, many of which were about the continued importance of East Germany in the moral, intellectual, and political landscape of unified Germany, was a very important example to me of how this solidarity could be intellectually expressed, and experienced in an academic institution. In this regard, I would also very much like to thank Christoph Rother for his very intelligent and professional research help throughout my stay.

5 I use the term "refugee" instead of "asylum seeker" throughout this essay with the same hope for the recognition of the refugee that is articulated by Amnesty International, when it distinguishes between the two terms: "Not every asylum seeker will ultimately be recognised as a refugee, but every refugee is initally an asylum seeker" (Amnesty International, 2018). The German language has several equivalencies for "asylum seeker." *Asylsuchende* or *Asylbewerber* are the official terms adopted by the press. *Asylanten,* the term the shopkeeper used, is more of an insult, a denunciation, or a condemnation.

The law, which was introduced in the early 1900s, condemns incitement against an individual or attacks against the dignity of a human that are found to be "vicious," "disrespectful," or "defamatory." It was updated in 1959 in the wake of the collapse of the Nazi regime to address hate speech, and it prohibits disturbing public peace by calling for violence against a certain group, a section of the population, or an individual, or attacking them based on their ethnicity, race, or national origin. The prosecution argued that replacing the word "dogs" with "asylum seekers" was a hateful degrading of a specific group seeking sanctuary in Germany, and asked for €6,600 in fines. The judge held a slightly different point of view and eventually fined the shopkeeper €1,800.[6] For the judge, this was a case of "stupidity" (*Dummheit*). One could perhaps not agree more, but probably not for the same reasons as the judge, who insisted that the breaking point in terms of the law was the dog. "You could have written 'Asylum seekers have no business here' on your door, without the dog," the judge instructed him. It appears that the shopkeeper would have been well within his rights to do so. But the picture of the dog was a different story for the court.

The shopkeeper didn't fare as well in the court of public opinion, where, on social media, he was cursed out as a racist and a lunatic. It seems that notwithstanding the foul and dangerous vandalism the shopkeeper experienced—faeces were smeared on his shop window, and the bolts on his car tires were loosened—the uproar reflected a clear civic view of what constitutes racism. The shopkeeper, who apparently had no issue, hygienic or otherwise, with dogs, and who had been sketched with his "grey Schnauzer" in court, was astounded at the storm he had caused with his signage. He really had not wanted to attract attention, nor had he wanted to be hounded by either the media or crowds of dog owners.[7] But, the judge insisted before delivering his verdict, putting up the sign had disturbed public peace.

6 The 54-year-old will have to pay the €1,800 to two kindergartens. If he defaults, he will then be required to pay a penalty of €4,950.

7 Anthropological studies have been conducted on the "special relationship" that Germans cultivate with their dogs. This relationship may very well explain why the dog owner was afraid of the reaction of other dog owners. It also may be tempting to read some sort of irony into the "debasement" of refugees to dogs, given the almost "human" care some of these dogs receive. One need only point to the recent account of the petition that was signed by more than 250,000 Germans to save a dog that had mauled its owners to death (Connolly 2018). Another perspective on the nature of this relationship occurred to me in a conversation with Sara Abbas, a doctoral student at the BGSMCS, when she asked if I had noticed how uncannily well-behaved dogs are in Berlin. Upon reflection, I considered the reasons for their discipline with respect to Cole Moreton's tongue-in-cheek article, "Why All Dog Owners are Fascists" (Moreton 2014). In this case, I am exploiting the journalist's punning introduction of the material presence of the dog (grauem Schnauzer) into the court room.

There is much to parse in this event, or at least in its account in the newspaper, especially the way in which the division of public and private becomes determinative of racism or racist speech. For example, the sign was found to be racist only because of its potential to disturb public peace. But nothing stands out as much as the jaw-dropping legal silence over the racist exclusion and barring of a certain group from a shop, except perhaps the contention of stupidity.[8] That this exclusion was from a place of business instead of a private home, for example, does not make it any more racist, but it does make the irresponsibility of the law more jarring. How deftly stupidity and racism each determine the other! Apparently, if only the shopkeeper had been less "stupid," he could have had freer rein over his racism.

There are many things one might have expected the judge to say in the face of such blatant prejudice and discrimination, but admonishing the accused for not being "smart" enough to game the legal system into allowing his racism is likely not one of them. For the sake of our own stupefaction, we will need to consider how "stupidity" stands in silence's stead on the issue of racism. To do so we must turn to the dog, who figures all over the story. What we can gather is this: First, it is permissible to put a picture of a dog on a sign, but not on this sign. Then, a dog can enter a shop, but it probably shouldn't. There is a dog in court, but it probably shouldn't be there either. The dog is considered unhygienic by many, and being compared to one is supposed to be degrading. But at the same time, the dog is the shopkeeper's companion, and some dog owners, it seems, might be upset that the dog has been lowered to the ranks of a refugee. The poor dog, who has no choice but to be this "man's best friend," ambivalently marks the limits of a humanity rendered civilised only in measure with the compassion that moves it.[9] The dog signals the judge's attempts to legislate stupidity and points to the limits of the law that recognises racism only if it is manifested as speech. If we agree with Jacques Derrida, who, in *The Animal That Therefore I Am,* with reference to his own pet, a cat, speaks of the animal as more than just an object of the human gaze, and as more than simply a figure or an allegory, then we must ask what we are to make of the refugee in this court proceeding. After all, as Derrida argues, the animal can respond

8 Peter Hirschmann, who is now living in the United States, remembers how the signs "Juden und Hunde Verboten" were posted in his hometown of Nuremberg before his family fled the Nazi regime in 1939. Nuremberg was the site where the Nuremberg Laws that deprived Jews of citizenship were created in 1935 (Rosenberg 2017).

9 Perhaps unsurprisingly, the dog's long history of domestication can be traced as far back as 14,000 years ago, to a burial site in Bonn-Oberkassel, Germany, where humans and dogs were buried side by side (Hirst 2017).

even if it cannot speak, but, in this example, the refugee is not necessarily afforded the same possibility (Derrida 2008).[10]

That the dog does not speak or respond, even though it is physically and figuratively present in this court case, gives way to the fact that the legal proceedings all but erase refugee subjects, who were not in attendance in court, let alone invited to respond or speak for themselves. Despite the shopkeeper's insistence on his freedom of expression, he also remains mute, so that his speech is communicated through the law and by way of his barrister, who maintains that his client is not racist because he married a Russian woman and has friends who are foreigners. This parsing of "foreigner" from "asylum seeker" frames the rationale given for the exclusion of refugees from the store: the shopkeeper had had "negative experiences" with refugees in traffic, and he had found two of them smoking a joint in his previous shop, even though it contained flammable material. At this point, and since we are forced to substitute our imaginations for the lack of clarity on the shopkeeper's unspecified "negative experiences" with refugees, it is most difficult to avoid clichés about German infatuation with rules and regulations, the sort that might make a German fret over the behaviour of non-German pedestrians and drivers on their much beloved roads. Moreover, Germany has not exactly been at the vanguard of banning smoking in enclosed public places, and refugees are certainly not the only ones to smoke in places where they shouldn't, or to smoke ambivalently criminalised substances they "shouldn't." But I digress. The point is that refugees are evoked, and inflected into the law, by virtue of the fear of their impending feral criminal status, and the anticipation that their agency will apocalyptically end in flames. The reasoning that frames their degradation to the status of an animal, the dog, unmasks the hypocrisy of the law in which the animality of the refugee may be feared and articulated but not figured.

In *The Beast and the Sovereign*, Derrida describes how in the history of European thought the portrayal of political sovereignty as monstrous animality has allowed for a depiction of humans and animals alike as submitted to the will of the Sovereign. He points out, though, that this comparison hinges on conferring the quality of bestiality on the animal, a quality that is actually proper

10 Donna Haraway (2007) has convincingly argued that the idea of a *mutual* response, where the human meets the gaze of and recognises the animal's non-linguistic and embodied communication, is necessary to an understanding of humans and animals as relational and reciprocal companion species that then expands and renders more complex epistemological, political, and ethical panoramas of our world. I suspect I have not been capable of fully satisfying Haraway's admonishing to not use the dog simply to think with. In my defence, however, I will be letting the dog take the lead in this investigation and will eventually consider how its behaviour sets the standard for moral human behaviour.

only to the human (Derrida 2009, 26, 101). In this way, both the animal-as-beast and the Sovereign are located outside the law, where they are joined together by their status as outlaws and as rogue outsiders to the law, who instil fear in others (Derrida 2009, 32ff.). Derrida adds that between the beast and God there also lies the intermediate state of politicity, "the being-political of the living being called man [*sic*]," which yields another political double beyond the conjoined opposition of Sovereign and beast, which is that of the human, whose "sovereignty consists in raising himself [*sic*] above the animal or appropriating it," and the political being of state sovereignty as monstrous bestiality (Derrida 2009, 25–26). The dog's subsequent rise in status in the ranking established by human sovereignty and empire—we can think here of Napoleon's captivation with dogs—may explain the attempts throughout history to fold the dog into the monstrous bestiality of the state and its processes of sovereignty.

In the account of the shopkeeper and the dog, the ambivalently domesticated animal signals the human taming of the monstrosity of sovereignty and its law. The dog is figuratively and physically conscripted to collude with the secularised imperial politics of the German (and European) judicial assembly.[11] The law attempts to domesticate the unsecularised terror-producing refugee, who, like the dog, stands ambivalently in relationship to it: refugee and dog are at once subjugated and situated both within the confines of the law and outside of it, and as such are not fully political beings. Unlike the dog, whose taming is made evident by its accompaniment of the shopkeeper into the court of law, refugees are physically absent from the court proceedings, their exclusion an echo of their racist exclusion from the shop. Their existence with respect to the law is marked in terms of fear, which is coupled with their denigration to the status of animals, such that their exclusion is deemed racist only at the moment they are figured as animalistic, which in turn paradoxically exposes the bestial monstrosity of the law. This monstrosity is underscored by the attempt at sovereignty by the shopkeeper, who, already elevated above a dog, now wants to raise himself above the refugee. And here, the dog—the dog who may be banned from some shops but who is nevertheless present in the court—points to the continued monstrosity of the law by signalling how the

11 It is certainly not the first time a dog appears in court. A case of a dog's appearing in a London court to testify in his own defence was reported in the New York Times in 1911. Indeed, the expression "Every dog has its day" (in court) has of late acquired new resonance. In the United States, for example, service dogs (or "court dogs") are now sitting in witness stands to comfort traumatised witnesses while they testify against their attackers. And, throughout the last decade or so, dogs have been called to the witness stand in numerous countries to help in identifying perpetrators.

refugee can be barred from the shop as a refugee but not as a dog. However, this exposure is unbearable to the law, and so the shopkeeper gets fined.

The exclusion of dogs might have raised the imperial hackles of Napoleon, whose love of the subjugated beasts led Aldous Huxley to ironically proclaim, "To his dog, every man is Napoleon, hence the constant popularity of dogs" (Moreton 2014). Huxley's remark intimates that perhaps only dogs could love Napoleon back. Thus, and in keeping with the imperious aspirations of human nature, to a Napoleon, every human is a mute and dumb dog, which, when not cast out, i.e., when taken in and *housebroken* or domesticated (from the Latin *domesticare,* meaning "to bring in to dwell in a house") into what is by now, the politically secularising house, home, and family of empire, it is necessarily stupefied into silence. We can conclude that what is at stake in this account of the racism against refugees is not stupidity but the glossing over of their racist exclusion by the realm of the law that deflects it as a lack of human intelligence that allows for the abasement of human to animal. Upsetting the naturalised position of the animal as lower with respect to the higher human is especially egregious to the law because this hierarchy leverages the law's sovereignty. "Stupidity" is thus jerry-built into the epistemological limits of the law, in which the dog functions as the marker of what is known, what should be known, and what cannot, or should not, be known.

Derrida's inquiry into the role of animality in determining the political status of humans unsurprisingly leads him to Aristotle's famous dictum at the beginning of the *Politics* that humans are by nature political animals. For Aristotle, inclusion in the *polis,* or the city, is a qualifying factor in an individual's status as human, and the capacity for speech is what distinguishes the human from other animals. Aristotle states, "From these things therefore it is clear that the city-state is a natural growth, and that humans are by nature political animals, and a person that is by nature and not merely by fortune citiless is either low in the scale of humanity or above it (like the "clanless, lawless, hearthless" individual reviled by Homer, for those by nature unsocial are also "lovers of war") inasmuch as they are solitary, like an isolated piece at draughts. And why a human is a political animal in a greater measure than any bee or any gregarious animal is clear … humans alone of the animals possess speech" (Aristotle 1944).[12] Aristotle's statement leads us to consider how the "exclusion" of refugees from the city, or the shopkeeper's store, is what defines and gives measure to their status as human. In other words, the humanity of humans is legitimised once they belong to a city. Since refugees are searching for acceptance and entrance into a city, their status as humans is ambiguous at best. This ambiguity is heightened and confirmed upon their entry into the shop.

12 I have modified the English translation.

When the shopkeeper denies them access into his store, he is also denying refugees their status as humans, which is an act of racism that exists prior to the perceived equivalency he draws between them and a dog.

By the time of Aristotle, the dog had already made its philosophical appearance at the very heart of the state of politicity in Plato's *Republic*. Here the dog can be found at the edge of the Greek polis, where its presence is tied both to knowledge and to ignorance, a close cousin of stupidity. Socrates is talking to Glaucon, one of his principle interlocutors, and asks him about the qualities necessary for individuals who guard a city. Glaucon agrees that they have to be quick, strong, and courageous. Because such qualities might lead to their behaving like savages, Socrates insists that a good guardian should also be kind and gentle as well as high-spirited. These characteristics stand in opposition to each other and are therefore a difficult mixture to find, but Socrates believes their combination is best exemplified by the "noble hound," or dogs who "are gentle as can be to those they are familiar with and know, but the opposite to those they do not know" (Plato 2004, 55). The guardian of a city must also be philosophical, which is to say have "intellectual curiosity" or be "wanting knowledge for its own sake" (Plato 2004, 55). This is a quality Socrates believes is also found in the dog, "[i]n that when a dog sees someone it does not know, it gets angry even before anything bad happens to it. But when it knows someone, it welcomes him, even if it has never received anything good from him." Socrates continues, "[I]t judges anything it sees to be either a friend or an enemy on no other basis than that it knows the one and does not know the other. And how could it be anything besides a lover of learning if it defines what is its own and what is alien to it in terms of knowledge and ignorance?" (Plato 2004, 56).

Socrates's dog is a philosophical dog, an epistemological dog, a dog able to reflect on the limits of knowledge and how those limits determine entrance into the polis. A guard's ability to patrol the barriers to the polis with knowledge lies precisely in its capacity to know that it doesn't necessarily know. The questions that this poses for us are about the type of knowledge that will determine the inclusion of individuals into the city, and the ignorance of what exactly will bar them: that is, on what grounds will the confines, border, boundary, or limits of the polis be set? The refugee approaching the gateway of the city tests the limits of that knowledge. Thankfully, the guardian of the polis, an animal that can teach a person a thing or two about human behaviour, is curious, and a lover of learning. At first glance, this may seem like a guarantee that, ultimately, the refugee will not be denied entry, since all s/he has to do is to wait until the dog—an inquisitive and analytic dog who wants to know—comes to (re)cognise her or him. Socrates's dog, however, like any other philosopher, is not engaged in neutral inquiry, and it does bark its ignorance *before* anything bad happens to it. Neither the grounds on which its knowledge is founded, nor the process of reasoning through which it achieves such knowledge, nor that knowledge's trajectory, that is, the ongoing conditions that encase that knowledge and upon which that knowledge is deemed acceptable, are objective.

This means that once "recognised," the refugee seeking entry through the city gates can only be accepted into the polis based on the grounds of that polis's knowledge. This also probably means that refugees will be able to remain in the polis only so long as they continue to fulfil the changing conditions that deem that knowledge—the city's (re)cognition of them—acceptable. The refugee is thus subject to the natural extension of the process Socrates refers to when he speaks about the guard's defining what is its "own." The refugee, of course, can befriend the dog, or, like any other foreigner to the city, can also assess that knowledge beforehand and present herself as already adapted to its foundations. There is a possibility too that the dog might recognise the partiality of the grounds on which the limits of the polis are founded and change them. The dog that guards the polis would then have no need to bark, and would allow the refugee, who would eventually be followed by others, to enter the city—their presence would even begin to structure a new foundation for the polis.

Some will warn that thinking in this way would involve bringing the dog and refugee into close proximity in a manner that risks the equivalency that was rejected by the German court. But isn't the question really that for many others the problem with drawing an equivalence between a dog and a refugee is actually that this could also make of the refugee a philosopher? There is, after all, no reason why the refugee could not become the philosophical guard dog of the city. Why this possibility is construed as frightening to the polis has to do with the madness of the revolutionary potential for speech of some philosophers, because, as the Greeks knew, not all philosophical dogs tell you the same thing. The Cynics, those radical philosophers who were considered especially mad, were likened to dogs. We see this, for example, in Aristotle, who in his *Rhetoric*, referred to the great Cynic philosopher Diogenes as "The Dog"; his sobriquet has been ascribed to the fact that the Greek word "cynic" (*kynikos*) originally meant to have the qualities of a dog (*kyôn/kynos*) (Aristotle 2004, 126). In her discussion of the Cynics, Claire Huot explains: "Like dogs, the Cynics lived a liminal existence, either outdoors, or in the marketplace. They had no property. They were the first western pariahs" (Huot 2017, 44).[13] Huot also notes that

13 See also Huot's discussion of how the "sole originating centre of dogs" may be China, where, she states, they were "active partners of the human" (45). One can only imagine what Napoleon's expeditions would have looked like had he known about the status of dogs in China.

the Tamil origin of the term "pariah" signifies "to say or to tell something" and "applies to both humans and dogs as outcasts or lower caste" (Huot 2017, 44). The assumed insanity of the city's pariah can be read into the perceived unsecular and thus violent deviancy and liminality of refugees, which lies in the undomesticated energy of animality that potentially fuels their speech. Is not the approximation of dog to refugee deemed unacceptable precisely because it would enable the refugee's speech, a speech that would be radical for its deemed unsecularity and thus terrifying in its madness?

Key to the approximation between a dog and a refugee that is being formulated in this essay is an understanding that what humans share with dogs is their animality and not the quality of violent bestiality that is, as Derrida argues, mistakenly imputed to animals and concomitantly attributed to the refugee's foreign (ir)rationality and madness. Huot is aware of the distinction between bestiality and animality when she discusses Foucault's treatment of the Cynics. To begin with, she emphasises the importance that they "accorded to the body as a vital ground for philosophy, and also the view of the human as an integral part of nature" (Huot 2017, 44). Huot connects the embodiment of the Cynics to Foucault's discussion of *animalité* in *History of Madness,* from which she extrapolates that "The natural fury of the insane is a testimony of the immediate (non-mediated) violence of '*animalité*.'… The insane are violent and have outbursts of fury …" (Huot 2017, 48).[14] Glossing Foucault's thinking, Huot brings the Cynics and dogs into a metaphoric alignment that highlights the spoken and performative power of this type of mad agency. She states, "Dogs, like the Cynics, are the force of *scandale* which, at root, is noise" (Huot 2017, 52). The problem with the English translation of *animalité* as "animality" is that it mistakenly dichotomises animal and human, and in doing so, weakens the significance that Foucault ascribes to the potential for the fierceness of will, namely, the will to power in humans that exists in us in the form of our animal agency (Huot 2017, 48–50).

The energy of the Cynics and the quality of their speech set an excellent standard for the liberty of *parrhesia*—the freedom of fearless speech—because of their potential for challenging the political limits imposed upon entry to the polis and life within it. Following from this, the folding of Socrates's philosophical dog into the Cynic, the wild, mad, undomesticated dog of rationality that is being argued for here, is thus meant to incite a consideration of the conditions by which a refugee, who, as the city's newly appointed irrational pariah, certainly has something to say, is therefore silenced in the realm of the law.

14 Indeed, Foucault speaks of the manner in which humans become the object of the gaze of animals who mirror the insanity of humans (Foucault 2006, 19).

After all, the dog-like behaviours honed by the Cynics were meant as "transgressions of social and political orders" (Huot 2017, 42). Because it is a danger to the normative boundaries of the polis, the undomesticated "*animalité*" of refugees—namely their will to power that, once harnessed, determines their behaviour and speech—is construed as violently animalistic, and hence, mad. But what this construal actually uncovers is the monstrous bestiality of the sovereign state's rationality that legitimises its own violence.

Insanity is the precursor to confinement, which is the natural precursor to the domestication of the sovereignty of dogs and mad Cynics, which the Cynics naturally contested. Huot describes their resistance in the following way: "Cynics and their entourage of dogs ... in a sovereign fashion, ignore rules—[they are] in other words, the deviants" (Huot 2017, 47). But their lawless freedom, which is the independence that they exercised over themselves inside the polis, also resulted in their confinement. Huot writes, "For their deviance and defiance, they are reined in, treated as dogs, or segregated like chained beasts" (Huot 2017, 47). There is much at stake in this issue of confinement, as Foucault has demonstrated in relation to the "unreason" of the insane, and it hinges on how we understand his discussion of "absolute freedom," which Leonard Lawlor summarises in the following way: "Absolute freedom in Foucault is heteronomy. But more precisely, it is less than heteronomy. Like heteronomy, it is a relation to alterity, but this other is not the laws of nature and it is not the laws of another human.... Absolute freedom in Foucault is this: a movement between forces that come from elsewhere—from the 'outside.'... Its ability to escape from all forms of determinism and all others is what makes freedom absolute" (Lawlor 2017, 60). We know from the rest of Foucault's work, and indeed also from his treatment of the Cynics, that the chances for this escape are less than slim and that the conditions for its achievement are structured into the political restrictions of such power. What the discussion of absolute freedom by Foucault nevertheless highlights is the importance of the "forces that come from elsewhere," or from the "outside," in determining the politics of its confinement, that is, the political restriction to which this undomesticated mad thought is subjected.

In the *History of Madness,* "unreason" is the condition of insanity, the confinement of which opposes the indefinite labour of absolute freedom, and this last is linked by Foucault to the notion of *animalité*. Foucault traces the evolution of confinement as a reaction to the absolute freedom of unreason from the fourteenth-century example of the ship of fools, where the insane travel the "freest and most open of all routes," to the confinement of the insane in the asylum in the nineteenth-century (Lawlor 2017, 59–60; Foucault 2006, 3–43). Such a history clarifies how the ability to enact the freedom of expression embodied by *parrhesia* presupposes freedom of thought. But freedom of thought is also derived from a set of conditions, which are the conditions that it will seek to oppose. Lawlor specifies, "For Foucault, the act that undergoes the formations and modifications is freedom, freedom of thought.... [It] is a thinking that negates the modes into which it has been formed" (Lawlor 2017, 62). If we consider Lawlor's definition of absolute freedom in Foucault's thought as a movement between forces that comes from elsewhere, we can conclude that freedom of thought derives from and engages a thinking that comes from the "outside," or at the very minimum, which seeks its "outside."

One of the ways to understand the resistance to this access to the exteriority of thought and the political imperative to cure its impulse is through an examination of the processes of desacralisation. Lawlor explains, "What Foucault calls desacralisation is what we commonly call the secularisation of Western culture. But unlike the word "secularisation," the word "desacralisation" (referring more directly to the decline of Christianity) contains the association to transcendence" (Lawlor 2017, 64). Foucault contends that the way we perceive madness (i.e., the perception of unreason as the condition of insanity), shapes our impulse to confine it, and is inextricably linked to the process of desacralisation in Western society. This means that desacralisation is thus a turning away from "going beyond," if not going beyond Christianity itself, which in its institutionalised form will continue to remain at the service of secularisation. Of course, secularisation, a state-endorsed project that in many ways is propped up by institutions of Christianity, also paradoxically presupposes the idea of transcendence at the same time as it is opposed to it; this is because there would be no need for secularisation if there were no sacred to begin with. In other words, insofar as the turning away from a thought from outside stems from the process of desacralisation that would identify thought from outside as unreason—the insanity inherent in the indefinite labour of the absolute freedom of thought—and seek to confine it, then secularism, the political mechanism by which desacralisation is achieved and maintained, will also be an agent in that process of turning away. Secularism thus maintains the logic by which unreason and madness are identified and defined, and in turn, these are both shaped by and built into the rationalisation for confinement that secularisation will provide and guarantee the polis. Accordingly, secularism founds the knowledge to the city guarded by Socrates's philosophical dog.

The yet-to-be-tamed, yet-to-be-domesticated, or still-to-be-detranscendentalised sacredness of the unsecularised Muslim refugee will be thus subjected to the process by which the movement of desacralisation has identified unreason and insanity. Lawlor sketches Foucault's historicising of this process:

"At first, as the lepers were before, the [mad are] understood through a 'sacred distance.' Although excluded from society and the church, the mad, like the lepers, still made God manifest. But soon, as verticality starts to disappear, the reference the mad made is displaced to this world" (Lawlor 2017, 64–65). For Foucault, verticality speaks to the "going beyond" capacity of transcendence and of the sacred.[15] Lawlor summarises the historical argument behind Foucault's study of freedom thus: "At first, with the Renaissance, the ravings of the mad refer to the 'elsewhere' of divine or supernatural forces that will bring about the end of the world. Desacralisation moves those forces to 'here'" (Lawlor 2017, 78). Foucault describes this apocalyptic end: "Rather, the rise of madness, its insidious, creeping presence showed that the final catastrophe was always near: the madness of [the human] brought it nigh and made it a foregone conclusion" (Foucault 2006, 15). This passage brings into focus the ways that Muslims, refugees or not, but especially refugees now, and specifically male Muslims, are stereotyped as enraged and violent madmen bent on bringing unsecularised chaos into the world (Mas 2017; 2011). And yet, what we find in that vertical descent from the "up there" of the sacred to the worldly "here" is that what the lawless refugee would have to say and that which is being silenced is more than simply "madness," and that whatever side of the axis it is anchored to, the refugee's speech is produced from a very earthly if not outright ungodly experience of this world.

The potential for danger currently attributed to the sacred realm of Islam in the speech of refugees lies in the fact that the refugees who have recently been arriving in Berlin are more often than not Muslims. The dangerous sacrality that is correlated with them is perceived as being diametrically opposed to the political project of Germany's secularising realm, and it also has the potential to displace the logic of sacrality institutionalised as Christianity that underpins the country's secularisation and legitimises and authorises secularisation's necessary separation from Christianity. Lawlor describes how the stakes of mad speech were transformed in the advance of desacralisation: "The mad seemed no longer to manifest God, but to possess a secret knowledge of the truth of this world. Just as the mad themselves raged and were furious, the knowledge they possess is about the rage and fury of the world, of its disorder; they seem to know about the 'great unreason of the world'" (Lawlor 2017, 65). Exposing the great unreason of the world may be the scandalous project of non-Western knowledge that has been deemed non-secular. But, there is more

15 As Lawlor points out, despite Foucault's initial use of the term "transcendence" (which is associated with verticality) to designate a "going beyond," he later rejects the term (Lawlor 2017, n.19).

that is at stake, of course, in what the refugee speaks, and it has to do with the perversion of justice in this world, the very injustice they are subjected to. This injustice is the responsibility of the polis and the savage logic of neo-capitalism that drives its relation to and competition with other poleis.

The rage, fury, and disorder of the world, a disorder that dissimulates its own unreason by confining the mad, is also produced by the lack of the fulfilment of the promise of the Enlightenment, and not because the latter has been thwarted by the likes of Muslims, whose reference points, worldly and sacred, are being shattered and displaced. Instead, as Foucault clarifies, the failure of the Enlightenment is attributable to the domination of reason over freedom. He states, "Could we not conclude that the promise of the *Aufklärung* to attain freedom through the exercise of reason has in fact reversed itself into a domination of reason itself, a reason that more and more usurps the place of freedom? This is a fundamental problem with which all of us are struggling."[16] It needs to be stated explicitly that the miscarriage of the Enlightenment is not due to the alleged domination of the sacred over reason that is generally attributed to the discourses and practices of the "sacredly motivated" adherents to the Islamic tradition. Foucault is not lamenting our inability to be free of the manifestation of an idealised secularity. Instead, he is emphasising how the notion of reason that is inherent to our secular ideals has produced a logic that subjugates those very ideals—and us in the process.

The dog reappears in Foucault's *Discipline and Punish: The Birth of the Prison*, at a public execution. The book begins with gruesome reports of the 1757 torture in Paris of Robert-François Damiens, who was tried and condemned as a regicide, and whose body was mutilated, burnt, quartered by several horses, and finally thrown into a pit, where it was consumed by fire. One of these reports commented, "There were those who made something of the fact that a dog had lain the day before on the grass where the fire had been, had been chased away several times, and had always returned. But it is not difficult to understand that an animal found this place warmer than elsewhere" (Foucault 1995, 4–5). Damien's body had been submitted to the last vestiges of Christian power, and like the body of monarchical power that he had unsuccessfully attacked but that was soon to be abolished by the French Revolution, it was disassembled. Foucault writes, "In the darkest region of the political field the condemned man represents the symmetrical, inverted figure of the king" (Foucault 1995, 29). This dismantling of the body by the Catholic Church and its monarchy would eventually find its political double in the secular body politic.

---

16 Foucault is here quoted in Lawlor, who has modified the English translation (Lawlor 2107, 59).

The dog's return to the site of the ashes is a reminder that this power and its Christian structuring will never really disappear.

Throughout the rest of *Discipline and Punish*, Foucault details the subsequent secular reassembling of the body, which he describes as a "political anatomy" wherein "The human body [enters] a machinery of power that explores it, breaks it down and rearranges it" (Foucault 1995, 138). The body is disciplined into a docile body through a process that involves reordering the body's movements into measurable movements, a secular modern repetition of the "correct" use of the body contained within and according to established linear sequencings of time. The body is thus temporally rearranged into the "strict spatial partitioning" of modernity's secularised norms. Foucault dedicates a large part of his book to demonstrating how the new organisation of modern bodies in spaces of confinement is accompanied by their surveillance and "permanent registration" (Foucault 1995, 196). The present influx of bodies onto European soil has generated more places of confinement, the camps in which refugees are held and registered, in the hopes of turning them into modernity's docile and secularly rationalised subjects. The mad subject, as Lawlor draws out, is thus "liberated within the new space of confinement, [and] comes to behave more like a tamed animal." He adds that "through this 'semi-freedom,' the mad seem to be cured. Through the 'internal restructuring' of space, confinement takes on the value of a cure" (Lawlor 2017, 68). The creation of the "refugee camps" as an internal restructuring of the space of the city is a natural process of the unreason of the secularising state that seeks to tame refugees so that they become domesticated animals and cure them from the madness of their thought, i.e., their thought from elsewhere.

1 Das Narrenschiff

A clearer sense of the knowledge that the mad possess about the world's chaos and savagery, that is, its unreason or its insanity, emerges in the famous literary example discussed by Foucault, Sebastian Brant's widely translated and best-selling book, *The Ship of Fools* (*Daß Narrenschyff ad Narragoniam*, 1494). The satire, which depicts a ship full of fools that sails off to Fool's Paradise, was written two years after Columbus set sail for the "new world," and parodies those who ambitiously set off to discover foreign lands but who have no knowledge of themselves. The very type of voyage that Brant scorned, was, of course, more than simply a fool's errand of an adventure—it was an integral part of sustaining the Christian Holy Roman Empire he cherished so deeply. Edwin H. Zeydel, the most recent English language translator and editor, states that the

Ship of Fools was considered "a compendium of maxims for righteous Christian living … [and] was widely recognised as Germany's most brilliant book for good Christians since the invention of printing and as a sort of layman's [*sic*] Bible" (Zeydel 1944, 32). The book was also a call for the renewal of the Church and the Roman Empire, as well as a supplication for action to be taken against the advancing Turkish Ottoman Empire (Zeydel 1944, 4). Given the success of his "Christian compendium," it is obvious that Brant found a German audience as distraught as he was at the Church's state of affairs and as desirous of assailing the Turks and their empire.

Brant's liberally expressed opposition to the Ottoman Empire finds a place for Muslims ("Turks" and "Saracens") in the *Ship of Fools* along with the other pagans, atheists, heretics, and witches who don't adhere to the notion of the Christian godhead (Brant, 1944, 314). But the insanity that Brant afflicts on the Muslim "fool" is beyond that of the foolishness, or lack of judgment and common sense that he ascribes to the other passengers. The madness of the Muslim is a *savage* assault on Christianity, which Brant frames by way of his

ILLUSTRATION 22.2 Crossing. Illustration by Anton Jones, 2018.

portrayal of Mohammed as a "shameful" and "cruel heretic," who "tears and wounds" the "Christian's faith," and "abuses" it with "base intent" (Brant 1944, 316). The conventionality of the Christian European image of a rapacious wolf to connote an enemy, and which hangs over Brant's depiction of Mohammed's cruelty, is made more explicit with the Turk, whom he figures as a terrifying wolf—a wild dog—bent on Christian blood.[17] It circles in on Europe, makes its "inroads" through Europe's "open wide" gates to penetrate Christian Europe's "stall," and feasts on the sheep it steals from the Holy Church's flock (Brant 1944, 317–18). In line with the medieval Christian European imaginary of the time, Christianity and its geography are folded into each other as the object of the Turks' wolfish viciousness (Brant 1944, 316–18).

Brant does not explicitly rely on the image of the werewolf, which finds its source in Christianised German paganism and folklore, and which burgeoned in the fifteenth century, where it was commonly associated with witchcraft trials. The Turk is thus a figure that merges violence and insanity; located within the ship of fools, he is simultaneously understood as an internal threat to Christian European sovereignty. In this doubled aspect as wolf-man, he assumes the "outlaw" status of the werewolf, a figure that, as Derrida explains, was a man afflicted with the mental illness of lycanthropy, and is equated to that of "an atheist," that is, to someone "without faith or law," who "does not recognise the sovereignty of God, neither religious law nor the church, especially the Christian church…" (Derrida 2009, 98–100). Hence, the Muslim as werewolf is a miscreant because he is without the Christian faith or its law, and is in a state of terrorism and ready to wage war—he is the Antichrist (Derrida 2009, 100). Located in the in-between state of politicity, the werewolf signals the mediating function of the human between the sovereign and the beast, which exposes *how,* in which ways and under what circumstances, the condition of cruelty is ascribed to a human: what makes the cruelty *human* is that it derives from the human's insanity. The idea of a Muslim werewolf thus

17 As Derrida discusses in *The Beast and the Sovereign*, the wolf emerged as a figure of political tyranny with the ancient philosophers, and has represented the figure of the Sovereign and the rationality of sovereignty. Accordingly, the "voracious and violent and cruel savagery" of the wolf has been attributed to the male figure of the tyrant (Derrida 2009, 81, 98). For example, the title of "Wolf" was ascribed to the "Father of a Nation," or heads of state, such as Mustapha Kemal (i.e., Atatürk, or "Father of the Turks"), who was characterised as the "gray wolf" (Derrida 2009, 17). For a discussion of the feminine and masculine in the lexicography of the beast, see Derrida 2009, 1–31. On the genealogy of the "she-wolf" see Derrida 2009, 63–65. The "wolf" presented by Brant is figured as male. The female "fools" on his ship include prostitutes, wenches, and witches. As such, the language in this text will reflect this masculinisation; for example, the depiction of the Muslim as a wolf and werewolf is a masculine one and will be referred to as such.

heightens this attribution of insanity, because it is the irrationality—the war-mongering terrorising irrationality—of a human whose thought is from outside and from elsewhere. Derrida's pithy declaration—"In other words, to be a Christian or a philosopher is to cease being a beast and a wolf"—clarifies how the notions of "Christian" and "rationality" came together in the longstanding history of accusations levelled against Muslims and their Islamic (ir)rationality (Derrida 2009, 99; Mas 2017, 2011).

Brant's appeal to close Europe's gates, especially against Muslims, has been normalised in rhetoric at the centre of today's politics aiming to bar the entry of foreigners into Europe. The stakes of barricading a (post)-Christian Europe have to do with who gets to define sovereignty and enact the law, as well as the shape that law's tyranny will take, and the ways in which this has already been decided. In other words, if, as Derrida so succinctly puts it, "The law (*nomos*) is always determined from the place of some wolf," then better that the wolf be a Christian one than not (Derrida 2009, 96).[18] Let us briefly consider Derrida's critical response to Carl Schmitt's *The Concept of the Political,* where he likens European sovereignty to a wolf:

> What is fearsome is not only treating [humans] as beasts, but the hypocrisy of an imperialism that gives itself the alibi of universal humanitarianism (therefore beyond the sovereignty of a nation-state) in order *in fact* to protect or extend the powers of a particular nation-state.... At bottom, when a hypocritical imperialism combats its enemies in the name of human rights and treats its enemies like beasts, like non-[humans], or like outlaws, like werewolves, it is waging not a war but what would today be called a state terrorism that does not speak its name. It is itself behaving like a werewolf.
>
> DERRIDA 2009, 74

The humanitarian discourse around Germany's decision to accept refugees is increasingly articulating the necessary sealing off of Europe and the expansion

18 That determination will have much to do with the relationship of the human to Christian law, and will be compounded with the *Muslim* werewolf. If the werewolf exposes those conditions at the level of human cruelty, the figure of Mohammed as the Wolf unmasks how cruelty has already been established and compounded at the level of Sovereignty; this is not only because Mohammed is situated outside the law and understood as competing for and threatening European sovereignty and law, but also because he is aspiring to God's Sovereignty (God's Law) as *the Prophet,* the non-Christian Prophet. Read in this way, the Muslim werewolf is the spawn of this over-determined and conjoined opposition between a beast and a Sovereign.

of Germany's power overseas (Keilberth et al. 2017). The worst of this rhetoric, which is long practised in depicting Muslims as the bloodthirsty foe of Christian Europe, has increased in the face of the plight of the refugees seeking asylum in Germany.

The image of the ship of fools is currently being reimprinted on our imaginations by the spectacle of refugees clinging onto their boats and drowning off the shores of Europe. The illustration is a grotesque reflection in history's mirror, which distorts the unreason of the world by placing it squarely on the shoulders of Muslims. To understand what this distortion conceals, let us turn to Foucault once again for his description of the meaning, symbolism, and social force of the ship of fools. He writes,

> Navigation brought humans face to face with the uncertainty of destiny, where they are left to themselves and every departure might always be the last. The mad on their crazy boats set sail for the other world and it is from the other world that they come when they disembark. This enforced navigation is both rigorous division and absolute Passage, serving to underline in real and imaginary terms the *liminal* situation of the mad in medieval society. It was a highly symbolic role, made clear by the mental geography involved, where the mad were *confined at the gates of the cities*. Their exclusion was their confinement, and if they had *no prison* than the *threshold* itself they were still detained at this place of passage. In a highly symbolic position, the mad individual is placed on the inside of the outside, or vice versa.
>
> FOUCAULT 2006, 11[19]

Instead of navigating the rivers of the Rhineland or the canals of Flanders, refugee boats are launching from ports all over the Mediterranean. At one end, they cross from Turkey to Greece through the Aegean Sea, then from Libya into Italy; on the other, from Morocco to Spain across the Mediterranean's gateway, the Strait of Gibraltar. To say the area is in a state of chaos is a rhetorical compromise in the face of the unspeakable turmoil that enforces the navigation of refugees, and that meets them once they disembark.

The detainment and confinement of refugees at the gates of Europe and its cities is the transposing of the reason that shapes Europe's politics with its correlative madness. Refugees expose the madness of the world that is projected outside of European borders. "Madness," Foucault tells us, "becomes a form related to reason, or more precisely madness and reason enter into a perpetually reversible relationship which implies that all madness has its own reason by

19 I have modified the English translation.

which it is judged and mastered, and all reason has its madness in which it finds its own derisory truth. Each is a measure of the other, and in this movement of reciprocal reference, each rejects the other but is logically dependent upon it" (Foucault 2006, 28–29). "Which means," as he writes further on, "that if madness can only exist in reference to some form of reason, the whole truth of reason is to allow a form of unreason to appear and to oppose it, only to disappear in turn in a madness that engulfs all" (Foucault 2006, 31). The truth of Europe's reason, a reason that was shored up and structured as Enlightenment reason and that shapes Europe's forms of governance, allows the form of unreason to appear so that it can assert its own dominance. In doing so, it reinforces the need for European political rationality as well as Europe's role and standing in the world. The ship of fools located at the beginning of the unreason of the world now returns in the form of refugee boats filled with Muslims threatening to engulf Europe. Its sails are propelled by the capitalist madness driving the Westernising movement of the world, a historical gust from its Christian colonising past.

Angela Merkel's 2016 decision to allow refugees into Germany has quickly been subverted. Refugees are now caught between the madness that forced their departure and the madness that welcomes their arrival. The ports found at each end have been turned into smugglers' coves or slave-trade camps. Refugees are locked up, tortured, raped, and penned in by the dozens in the faeces-infested cells of Libyan camp-prisons (Keilberth et al. 2017). The German Foreign Ministry has compared these prisons to Nazi concentration camps; the European Union describes them as modern-day slave camps where "inmates, mostly Africans, are sometimes 'sold back and forth'" (Keilberth et al. 2017). The Nigerians, Libyans, Ethiopians, Sudanese, Chadians, and Nigeriens who don't die there and who don't drown on their journey across the Mediterranean will eventually meet up with the Syrians escaping from years of civil war.[20] Many Syrians will have been stranded on the Greek "prison islands," where the conditions are horrifyingly dangerous, violent, and unsanitary, or have been stuffed into the overflowing hotel ships that are anchored in their

20 Many refugees travel without passports. In his *Flüchtlingsgespräche* ("Refugee Dialogues") Bertolt Brecht wrote, "The passport is the noblest part of a human being, and it does not come about as easily as a human being. A human can go anywhere, in the most reckless manner and without a deliberate reason, but never a passport. If the passport is good, it is recognised, but a human, no matter how good, may not be recognised" (Brecht 2000, 7). Brecht's statement is a reminder that the recognition of refugees as human and as deserving of asylum is largely dependent on their access to and experience of the bureaucratic process involved in possessing a passport. The title of Bruno Moll's documentary about Brecht's life in Switzerland, *Der Mensch ohne Pass ist ein Hund* ("The Human Being without a Passport is a Dog"), speaks to the tenuous status of the humanity of an individual without a passport.

harbours (Christides and Kuntz 2017). Those who make it out will be joined on their journey by Afghans, Iraqis, Pakistanis, and Egyptians.

Detention awaits on the mainland of an increasingly sealed-off Europe for those refugees who manage to make it across. Its once open borders and roads through the Balkan route leading to Hungary and then to Austria through to Germany are crisscrossed with fences that barricade against the marching masses. The registration facilities once located throughout have now been revamped as prisons. Austria is shutting down the Brenner Pass through the Alps. Forests, fields, and mountains are being patrolled. Police in riot gear have confronted the hordes in train stations. Turkey has entered into a treaty with Europe devised by Germany's Angela Merkel to shut down the Aegean route by closing Turkey's borders to Syria and to Greece; Italy is following suit with the central Mediterranean route (Keilberth et al. 2017). Germany's attempt to hold back the flood of refugees now involves pushing African nations to process asylum requests and implementing "an EU border protection mission on the southern Libyan border" (Keilberth et al. 2017). The description of these efforts by Germany's weekly news magazine *Der Spiegel* rehearses and produces Brant's imperial fantasy of expanding the Empire's geographical and territorial limits to its former Christian glory: "Now Merkel is trying to create a similar project in Africa, by essentially shifting Europe's external borders to North Africa" (Keilberth et al. 2017). The European Union will funnel millions of Euros to this new colonising mission and will supply the armies and police forces of some African countries with the equipment that they need to carry it out (Keilberth et al. 2017). As *Der Spiegel* reports, "Italian warships ensure that the Libyan coast-guard forces refugee boats to return to land. Most private aid organisations have been forced to abandon their efforts to rescue refugees" (Keilberth et al. 2017). The imperial border insecurity of Germany and Europe is now a paramilitarised fantasy of yore that dreams of a sealed off Europe, from where the mad will set sail once again and leave.

2 *Die Hunde auf jemanden hetzen…*

On 1 January 2018, Germany passed a new law called the "Act to Improve Enforcement of the Law in Social Networks," demanding Twitter and Facebook remove any hate speech from the accounts of its members. At almost the same time, Cologne's police force sent out a tweet in Arabic, German, English, and French wishing everybody a Happy New Year. It was then that Beatrix von Storch, the deputy far-right leader of the AFD (Alternative for Germany) party, responded on Twitter: "What the hell is going on in this country? Why is an official police site from the North Rhine-Westphalia tweeting in Arabic? Do you think this will subdue the barbaric, Muslim, group-raping gangs of men?" When her message was blocked, Alice Weidel, an AFD MP and one of its parliamentary leaders, tweeted, "Our authorities submit to imported, marauding, groping, beating, knife-stabbing migrant mobs" (Olterman and Collins 2018). Her message was also blocked, which those on the right predictably objected to, based on their right to the freedom of speech and freedom from censorship.

Several hundred criminal complaints have been filed against both members of the AFD, and Storch and Weidel could face criminal charges for incitement to hatred, that is, for contravening Germany's laws against *Volksverhetzung* (Ahmad et al. 2018).[21] The term *Volksverhetzung* means "the incitement of the people" and is used to refer to the incitement to hatred caused by racist speech.

ILLUSTRATION 22.3 Detention. Illustration by Anton Jones, 2018.

21 This is not the first time the AFD, known for its militant stance against the presence of refugees in Germany (the platform on which it became Germany's third largest party in the federal election of September 2017), has angered large segments of the German population. A year earlier, von Storch, "whose grandfather served as the finance minister under Hitler," answered "yes" to a Facebook survey question on whether "firearms should be used against women and children trying to cross the German border" (Olterman and Collins 2018).

Its root, the substantive *Hetze,* can loosely be translated as "incitement, agitation, baiting," or even "hounding." The verbal construction of *hetzen* includes within it the notions of "incitement" and "hatred," which are tied together etymologically by the figure of the dog through the root of "hetzen," which was derived from the language of hunters driving (agitating, inciting) their dogs to hunt. "Incitement" quickly became coupled with the notion of hate, that is, to hate (*hassen*) as that which moves to pursuit, drives away, and persecutes. Racist speech is thus an unleashing of the dogs on somebody, *die Hunde auf jemanden hetzen,* which is to hate them, or to drive or incite others to hate them.

Angela Merkel may be Germany's top-dog, and even Europe's, but the moment she came close to momentarily embodying the philosophical dog of Socrates, when she made the decision to let in refugees, she was circled in on by the pack of AFD wolves howling and snarling their racism at her heels. Muslims, of course, have not been the only ones on the receiving end of the viciousness of racist rhetoric, which has also been directed against black people, and the anti-Semitism directed against Jews has never ceased. Neo-Nazi propaganda, swastikas, SS symbols, and accounts bearing the name and title of Hitler have been removed from Twitter. Yet, the criticism by Alexander Gauland, also of the AFD, that the law reminds him of the "Stasi methods" used by the GDR is a diversion that seeks to depict a battle for Germany's national identity, where opposing parties pit internal histories against each other (*Die Zeit* 2018). What this distraction is obfuscating is the moment in which free speech becomes the vociferation of sovereignty, which is the occasion for its devouring of its internal and external others.[22]

Is not the insistence on stupidity with which we began this essay, not just a ploy to cover up the unreason—the ferocity and cruelty—of the law and of the state?[23] This question needs to be asked especially in view of the self-appointed role of Europe, with Germany at its helm, as the executor of the Enlightenment's promises. Those of us situated in, and thus benefitting from, its representative institutions of "higher learning" are thus accountable for its normative reach. Our response should require the same infinite labour of the

---

22 See Derrida 2009, 23ff., for his discussion of how the notion of vociferation arises in the lexicon of devourment.

23 See Avital Ronell's study of the instability of stupidity as a concept and its consequent untranslatability. See especially her discussion of the political implications of *Dummheit* and the Christian-derived redemptive qualities that are associated with it (Ronell 2002, 41ff.). See too Derrida's discussion of Ronell's work, where he poses the question of whether "stupidity" is *bêtise,* which is derived from *bête,* the French word for animal; *bêtise,* he argues, is a characteristic that is proper to the human (Derrida 2009, 155).

freedom of thought of the dog-like Cynics' *parrhesia,* which necessarily precedes and is a condition for the freedom of speech so lauded in racist quarters.

We can begin by heeding the warning of Brant, who, despite his xenophobia, was rightfully concerned with the "parade of learning" he was witnessing in his day (Zeydel 1944, 44). The first character in his *Ship of Fools* is a scholar who, "In dunce's dance [takes] the lead," and appears surrounded by masses of unread books (Brant 1944, 62). He declares:

> I, too, have many books indeed
> But don't peruse them very much.
> Why should I plague myself with such?
> My head in booklore I'll not bury.
> Who studies hard grows visionary;
> A Dominie I well could be and pay someone to learn for me.
>
> BRANT 1944, 62–63[24]

Commenting on this chapter, Foucault writes, "But if knowledge is important for madness, it is not because madness might hold some vital secrets: on the contrary, it is the punishment for useless, unregulated knowledge. If it is the truth about knowledge, then all it reveals is that knowledge is derisory, and that rather than addressing the great book of experience, learning has become lost in the dust books and in sterile discussions, knowledge made mad by an excess of false science" (Foucault 2006, 22). Liberating such thought with a thinking from elsewhere will break through the political and epistemological barriers of the modern polis. We really will have no choice, lest we become, like one of the dogs of Napoleon, the lap-dog of power.

Bibliography

Ahmad, Hussein, Melanie Amann, Sven Röbel, and Marcel Rosenbach. 2018. "Germany's New Hate Speech Law: Populists Fight for Their Right to Racism." In *Der Spiegel* 4 January. Accessed 10 April 2018. http://www.spiegel.de/international/germany/german-populists-take-on-twitter-and-the-judiciary-a-1186233.html.

Amnesty International. 2017 "What's the Difference Between a Refugee and an Asylum Seeker?" Accessed 10 April. https://www.amnesty.org.au/refugee-and-an-asylum-seeker-difference/.

24 As a scholar, one cannot help but attend to Brant's admonition against higher learning: *Some fools seek knowledge high and higher, To M.A. Ph.D. aspire, Though people deem them very bright, These fools can't understand aright* (345).

Aristotle. 1944. *Aristotle in 23 Volumes*, vol. 21. Translated by H. Rackham. Cambridge MA: Harvard University Press. Accessed 10 April 2018 at the Perseus Digital Library: http://www.perseus.tufts.edu/hopper/text?doc=Perseus:text:1999.01.0058:book=1

Aristotle. 2004. *Rhetoric*. Trans. W. Rhys Roberts. Mineola NY: Dover Publications.

Brant, Sebastian. 1944. *Ship of Fools*. Trans. Edwin H. Zeydel. New York: Columbia University Press.

Brecht, Bertolt. 2000 [1961]. *Flüchtlingsgespräche*. Expanded edition. Frankfurt: Suhrkamp Verlag.

Christides, Giorgos, and Katrin Kuntz. 2017. "Europe at its Ugliest: The Refugee Scandal on the Island of Lesbos." In *Der Spiegel* 24 November. Accessed 10 April 2018. http://www.spiegel.de/international/europe/conditions-on-lesbos-worsen-for-refugees-and-residents-a-1180209.html.

Connolly, Kate. 2018. "German Dog that Killed Owners May Not Be Put Down After Outcry." In *The Guardian* 9 April. Accessed 10 April 2018. https://www.theguardian.com/world/2018/apr/09/germany-chico-dog-that-killed-owners-petition-hanover.

Derrida, Jacques. 2008. *The Animal That Therefore I Am*. Trans. David Wills. New York: Fordham University Press.

Derrida, Jacques. 2009. *The Beast and the Sovereign*. Ed. Michel Lisse, Marie-Louise Mallet, and Ginette Michaud. Trans. Geoffrey Bennington. vol. 1. Chicago: University of Chicago Press.

Der Spiegel Staff. 2016. "Two Weeks in September: The Makings of Merkel's Decision to Accept Refugees." In *Der Spiegel* 24 August. Accessed 10 April 2018. http://www.spiegel.de/international/germany/a-look-back-at-the-refugee-crisis-one-year-later-a-1107986.html.

Der Tagesspiegel Staff. 2016. "'Asylanten müssen draußen bleiben': Mann geht mit Schild zu weit." In *Der Tagesspiegel* 17 November. Accessed 10 April 2018. https://www.tagesspiegel.de/politik/angeklagt-wegen-volksverhetzung-asylanten-muessen-draussen-bleiben-mann-geht-mit-schild-zu-weit/14858498.html.

Die Zeit Staff. 2018. "Hunderte Anzeigen gegen AfD-Fraktionsvize von Storch." In *ZEIT ONLINE* 2 January. Accessed 10 April 2018. http://www.zeit.de/politik/2018-01/volksverhetzung-beatrix-von-storch-strafanzeigen-silvester.

Feldman-Savelsberg, Pamela. 2016. *Mothers on the Move: Reproducing Belonging between Africa and Europe*. Chicago: University of Chicago Press.

Foucault, Michel. 1995[2]. *Discipline and Punish: The Birth of the Prison*. Trans. Alan Sheridan. New York: Vintage Books.

Foucault, Michel. 2006. *History of Madness*. Trans. Jonathan Murphy and Jean Khalfa. New York: Routledge.

Haraway, Donna J. 2007. *When Species Meet*. Minneapolis: University of Minnesota Press.

Hirst, Krist K. 2017. "Dog History: How and Why Dogs were Domesticated. Recent Scientific Findings about our First Domesticate Partner." In *ThoughtCo* 12 December. Accessed 10 April 2018. https://www.thoughtco.com/how-and-why-dogs-were-domesticated-170656.

Huot, Claire. 2017. "Chinese Dogs and French Scapegoats: An Essay in Zoonomastics." In Matthew Chrulew and Dinesh Joseph Wadiwel (eds.), *Foucault and Animals*. Leiden: Brill, 37–58.

Keilberth, Mirco, Peter Müller, and Maxmilian Popp. 2017. "Stemming the Flow: Why Europe's Migrant Strategy is an Illusion." In *Der Spiegel* 6 September. Accessed 10 April 2018. http://www.spiegel.de/international/europe/europe-seeks-to-shut-down-the-mediterranean-migration-route-a-1166228.html.

Lawlor, Leonard. 2017. "Violence and Animality: An Investigation of Absolute Freedom in Foucault's *History of Madness*." In Matthew Chrulew and Dinesh Joseph Wadiwel (eds.), *Foucault and Animals*. Leiden: Brill, 59–86.

Manjoh, Priscillia M. 2013. *Snare*. Kansas City MO: Miraclaire Publishing.

Mas, Ruth. 2011. "On the Apocalyptic Tones of Islam in Secular Time." In Markus Dressler and Arvind-Pal S. Mandair (eds.), *Secularism and Religion-Making*. Oxford: Oxford University Press, 87–103.

Mas, Ruth. 2017. "Crisis and the Secular Rhetoric of Islamic Paradise." In Sebastian Günther and Todd Lawson (eds.), *Roads to Paradise: Eschatology and Concepts of the Hereafter in Islam*. Leiden: Brill, 2: 1290–1321.

Moreton, Cole. 2014. "Why All Dog Owners Are Fascists." In *The Telegraph* 18 June. Accessed 10 April 2018. https://www.telegraph.co.uk/men/thinking-man/10906046/Why-all-dog-owners-are-fascists.html.

Oltermann, Philip, and Padráig Collins. 2018. "Two Members of Germany's Far-Right Party Investigated by State Prosecutor." In *The Guardian* 2 January. Accessed 10 April 2018. https://www.theguardian.com/world/2018/jan/02/german-far-right-mp-investigated-anti-muslim-social-media-posts.

Plato. 2004. *Republic*. Translated by C.D.C. Reeve. Cambridge: Hackett Publishing Company.

Ronell, Avital. 2002. *Stupidity*. Chicago: University of Illinois Press.

Rosenberg, Eli. 2017. "Nazis Seized His Home During World War II: A Letter Recently Arrived, Expressing Remorse." In *The Washington Post* 25 October. Accessed 10 April 2018. https://www.washingtonpost.com/news/retropolis/wp/2017/10/25/nazis-seized-his-home-during-world-war-ii-a-letter-recently-arrived-expressing-remorse/?noredirect=on&utm_term=.c7e98dfoe08a.

Schmitt, Carl. 2007. *The Concept of the Political*. Expanded edition. Trans. George Schwab. Chicago: University of Chicago Press.

Zeydel, Edwin H. 1944. "Introduction: The Life And Works of Brant." In *The Ship of Fools*. Trans. Edwin H. Zeydel. New York: Columbia University Press, 1–54.

Index

À quoi tient la supériorité des Anglo-Saxons (Demolins) 161
ʿAbbāsids 69, 70, 339
ʿAbd al-Aḥad 290
ʿAbd al-ʿAzīz, Shāh 281, 284, 286, 294
ʿAbd al-ʿAzīz ibn Saʿūd 69
ʿAbd al-Ḥalīm Pāshā, Muḥammad (Prince) 29
ʿAbd al-Qādir, Shāh 281, 283–284, 285, 291
  authority of 287–288, 292, 293
ʿAbd al-Rāziq, ʿAlī 74–75
ʿAbd al-Rāziq, Muṣṭafā 164, 166, 173
ʿAbdallāh, Sayyid 287
ʿAbdī, ʿAbbās 306
ʿAbduh, Muḥammad 37, 61, 159, 160, 173, 176
  ethical thinking of 162–163
  Riḍā's association with 62, 73
Abdülhamid II (Ottoman Sultan/Caliph) 58, 61, 63–64
  criticism on 66
  Riḍā's support for 76
Abdillah, Ummi 187
Abessinia, war with Egypt (1869) 36
Abū Bakr (1st Caliph) 303
Abū l-Dardāʾ 283
Abū l-Suʿūd, ʿAbdallāh 31, 37
Abu-Lughod, Lila 315
Abubakar (Amin) 267, 269, 270
Abushouk, Ahmed Ibrahim xvii, xxxvii
academic institutions, ethnographies of xxvi–xxvii
academic journals, on Oriental/Islamic studies 16n28
Acholiland (Northern Uganda) 380
acknowledgement, politics of 439
actor-centred research approaches 399–400
AFD (Alternative für Deutschland) party 462–463, 464
Affective Societies 413
al-Afghānī, Jamāl ad-Dīn 36–37, 60, 62, 64
Afghanistan 24, 271, 312, 333
Afghanistan, Mujahideen in 337
Aflaq, Michel 364
Africa, Muslim minorities in xx
Âge de Sable (Karashan) 361
The Age of Sport Awareness (Necmeddin Bilal Erdoğan) 348–349
agency, discursive 267, 269
  on Kenyan Muslim radio 273–274
  research on 277
Ägypten
  Armee 35–36
  Ausbildungsreformen 39–40
  Eliten 27, 28, 44–45
  Geschichte 27
  Moderne, in der 27, 29, 44, 45, 46
  und *mondialisation*/globalisation 27
  Öffentlichkeit in der 38
  im Osmanischen Reich 32, 35–36, 40, 45–46
  politische Freiheit in 37–38
  Sprachen in 28–29
  Traditionsliteratur in 28n2
  Universitäten 31
  Wirtschaft 33, 43, 45–46
  Zivilisation 29
  see also Egypt
ägyptisch-abessinischer Krieg (1869) 36
Ägyptisches Museum (Kairo) 31
AHDR (Arab Human Development Reports), on women's rights and modern families 314–316, 319–320
ahl al-ḥall wa-l-ʿaqd 71, 72–73
ahl al-kitāb (people of the book) 359
Aḥmad, Mirzā Ghulām 286
Aḥmad ibn Hanbal 71
Aḥmad of Rae Bareli, Sayyid 287
Aḥmadiyya movement 286
al-Aḥmaq al-basīṭ (*Der einfältige Narr oder einfach der Simplicius*, Theaterstück, Mālṭī) 29
Ahmed, Shahab xix, 327, 333–334, 345–346
akhlāq 157, 158, 161, 163, 164, 167, 168, 171, 172, 174, 175
ʿAlawīs, in Syria 371
Aleppo 361
Alevis
  in Germany 435
  in Turkey 369
ʿAlī (Prophet's cousin and son-in-law), graphic expressions of 257–258

ʿAlī Bāshā, Meḥmed Emīn (Grand Vizier) 40
Allāh, graphic expressions of 248–249, 254
Ally, Mawlana 189
Alter, Joseph 334
American Anthropological Association xviii
Amīn, Aḥmad 165
Amin, Idi 380, 383, 385
Amīn, Qāsim 317
Amīn, Uthmān 166
ʿAnaza tribal confederation 99–104
Andrič, Ivo 361
ʿAnhūrī, Salīm 36
animality 451, 452
animals
  and bestiality 451
  distinction from humans 448
  human relationships with 446
  outlaw status of 446–447
  refugees reduced to status of 447
anthropologists, discursive agency of 275
anthropology
  of Germans and their dogs 444n7
  of Islam 193, 276
  of traditional wrestling 329, 334
  see also ethnography
anti-colonialism
  in India 290
  of Riḍā 55, 57
anti-Muslim violence, in Uganda 376, 382–385
anti-Muslim/anti-Islam polemics, in Islamic studies, in Russia 9
apartheid 184
apostasy, in Islam 204n17, 367
Appadurai, Arjun 336–337
ʿāqila 86n3
Arab Easy 237
Arab nationalism
  and religion 364
  Riḍā's attitude towards 55, 56, 68
Arab revolts (2010–2012) xx, 397–398
  elites in and after 400, 401–402, 403–404, 406, 407
  mobilised publics in 402, 406–408
  regime changes/political transformations resulting from 397–398, 403–408, 411–412, 414, 421
  research on 398–400, 401, 413
  social media in 223, 233–236
  see also Egypt, revolts in (2011/2012)
Arab World
  Christianity in 365
  colonisation of 58, 104n27
  elites in 400–401
    and Arab revolts 401–402, 403–404, 406, 407
  gender relations in 310
  religious minorities in 364–365
  social contract in 415
Arabia, origins of Islam in 8–9
Arabic Chrestomathy (Girgas) 14
Arabic language
  classical, formality of 148–149
  modern literature in, Russian study of 13, 20–22
  study of, in Russia 6, 14, 17–18
  translations from
    into Russian 9
    into Ukrainian 19
    into Urdu 289
  translations into 160–161, 169–170
  vernacular 148–149
Arabic script xviii, 247, 248, 252
  and Latin script encounters 254–255
  legibility of 248–249
  ligatures in 248, 249–252
  lines in 252, 254, 256–257
  and materiality 246
  prolongation in 252–256
Arabic-Russian Dictionary for the Arabic Chrestomathy and the Qur'an (Girgas) 14
Arabs, and Turks, re-unification of 68
Arḍ al-nifāq, (al-Sebaï) 147
Ardalān, Nīlūfar (Lady Goal) 307–308
Aristippus 170
Aristotle 448, 450
  study in Egypt of 169–170
Arkoun, Mohammed 154
Armbrust, Walter 223, 224, 239
Armenian genocide (1915) 363
Armenians
  left-wing politics of 372
  in Ottoman Empire, photography of 113–127
armies, Egyptian 34–36

'art of the line' (*fann al-khaṭṭ*, calligraphy) 248
al-ʿArūsī, Muṣṭafā 39–40
Asad, Talal 183, 193
ʿAshūrāʾ practices 333
Asseburg, Muriel xx, xxxvii
assertiveness, of Muslims in Uganda 386
Assmann, Aleida 261
asylum seekers 443n5
  see also refugees
Atatürk, Mustafa Kemal 69, 74, 458n17
  Riḍā's criticism of 69–70
Attaya, Mikhail 19
audiocassettes, impact of introduction of 223–224
Ausbildungsreformen, in Ägypten 39–40
Ausländerbehörde, in Berlin 442–443
authoritarianism
  challenged from below 412
  in Egypt 405, 411, 415, 421
authority
  recognition by 428
  religious
    claims of 285–286, 293
    in Shīʿa Islam 304
autonomy 87
  individual 428n2
  internal, of minorities 358–359
  in Ottoman Empire
    of Egypt 36, 40, 46
    of village communities 91, 95–97, 98
  of secondary elites 401
Ayalon, David 338
aʿyān 90–91
Ayni, Mehmed Ali 137
al-Azhar university (Cairo) 160
  printing house of 230
  scholars of 39–40, 75

Badawī, ʿAbd al-Raḥmān 171–172
Badawī, al-Sayyid Muḥammad 171
Badran, Margot 310
Baer, Gabriel 87, 88
al-Baghdadi, Abu Bakr 217
al-Bahī, Muḥammad 228n14
Baker, Samuel White 32, 36
Balkans, state formation in, and minorities 360
Balkans-to-Bengal complex (Ahmed) 333–334, 345–346
Bani Sadr, Abolhasan 301
al-Bannā, Ḥasan 76–77, 226n9, 318
baraka (divine blessing) 249n5, 262
baraza 268
Bareilly (India) 288
Barthes, Roland 246
Bartol'd, Vasilii 16, 19, 24
Batunskii, Mark 16
bayʿa (oath of allegiance) 71
Bayart, Jean-François 413
Bayat, Asef xx, 416
The Beast and the Sovereign (Derrida) 446–447
Becker, Carl Heinrich xii
Bedouins, representatives of, in Ottoman Empire 102–103
Beersheba 104n27
Beirut, Arabic - Latin script encounters in 254–255
Berlin, refugees in 441, 442–443
Berlin Congress (1878) 60
Bernstein, Leonard xxxii
bestiality, animality and 451
BGSMCS (Berlin Graduate School Muslim Cultures and Societies, Freie Universität Berlin) xv–xvi, xxxiii–xxxiv, xxxv
Bīk, Amīn Wāṣif 165
Bin ʿAlī, Zaīn al-ʿĀbidīn 404
Birdwood, George 58
Blunt, Wilfrid Scawen 58–59, 60
Boguslvaskii, Dmitrii 7n7
Boldyrev, Aleksei 17–18
books
  Islamic, publishing of 225, 228, 287–292
  paperbacks 225, 231, 232
bookstores, Islamic, in Cairo 226
Bourdieu, Pierre xxvii, 415n5
Bowen, John R. 193
Bozarslan, Hamit xix, xxxvii
Brant, Sebastian 456–459, 465
Brecht, Bertolt 461n20
The Bridge on the Drina (Andrič) 361
Brugsch, Heinrich Ferdinand Karl 31, 43
Būlāq press (Egypt) 230
Büssow, Johann xvii, xxxvii, 91
Butler, Judith 390

Buzkashi (game, Afghanistan) 337
Buznipar, Ş Tufan 59
buzrug culture, Moosagie's criticism of 183, 187, 201, 209–210

Cairo 27–28
  book publishing and selling in 224–231
  culture in 32, 38, 42–43
  Europeans in 32, 41–42
  Ezbekīya quarter in 28–30, 33
  informal settlements in 415–416
  modernity in 46
  political freedom in 37–38
  urban development in 30, 32–33, 39
Cairo University 165
CairoBookStop (website) 229n19
caliphate 56
  Moosagie on 191, 216–218
  al-Rāziq on 75
  revival attempts 77
  Riḍā on 57, 70–74, 76
  see also Ottoman caliphate
caliphs 58
  Riḍā on 65–66, 71–74
calligraphy xviii, 247–248
  Islamic 246–247
    graphic design 247–256
    and/on material objects 256–258, 259–260
    readability of 246–247, 258–262
canon notion 182
Catherine the Great (Tsarina of Russia) 4
Caucasus, Arabic texts related to 9
Çemberlitaş University (Istanbul) 134
Censoring an Iranian Love Story (Mandanipour) 307
censorship
  in Egypt xviii, 227, 229, 231–232
    social media 237, 238
  and print/electronic culture 239
  in Russia 18
  in United States 232
Central Asia, origins of Turks/Turkish nation in 340
Cevdet, Ahmed 102, 103
Chaadaev, Pyotr 18
Charmoy, François-Bernard 10
China, status of dogs in 450n13
chivalry, military tradition of (*furūsiyya*) 327–328, 339
cholera epidemics, in Egypt 33
Chomsky, Noam 273
chrestomathies, Russian 14, 17
Christianity
  in Arab world 365
  conversion to, by Muslims 367
  muscular 330–331
  in Ottoman Empire 100
  and rationality 459
  in Russia, missionary activities by 6–7
  turning away from 453
cities, imperial, inter-communitarian coexistence in 361
citizenship
  minoritisation caused by 361–362
  in Ottoman Empire 32, 360–361
civil society, in Egypt, restrictions on 411
civil wars, in Uganda 380
civilisations
  Egyptian 29
  history of xii
  and Islam 160
  modern 162
civilising project, of Islam in Europe 434
civility, intercommunitarian 361
classical Arabic, formality of 148–149
clothing
  female, Iranian men wearing 301
  as means of communication 126
  see also dress styles
codes, digital, in Arabic 256–257
coins, Arabic inscriptions on 252–254
Colet, Louise 44n38
collective identities, Muslim, and religion 150
collective mobilisation, in Muslim societies 155–156
collective mourning 389, 390
colonialism
  in Arab World 58, 104n27
  in Egypt 46
commemoration *see* remembrance/commemoration
communication
  clothing as a means of 126
  face-to-face 92–93
communities

expatriate, in Iran 302
religious 435
village, in Ottoman Empire 94–99
Companions of the Prophet (*sahaba*), perfection of 209n29
comportement moral 147–156
computer programming, in Arabic 254–257
The Concept of the Political (Schmitt) 459
confessional identities *see* religious identities
confessional wars, in Middle East 357
confinement
of insane 452, 460
of refugees 456, 460, 461–462
conflicts
after Arab revolts, in Libya and Yemen 406
in Muslim communities
in Germany 435
in Kenya 265, 276
in Uganda 385, 386, 391
in post-colonial Uganda 380–381
sectarian, in Middle East 357–358
see also wars
Considérations sur les causes de la grandeur des Romains et de leur décadence (Montesquieu) 161
Constantin, François 386
conversion
of Muslims, to Christianity 367
narrative of Moosagie 184–185, 202–205
to Salafism 199
Cook, Michael 274n14
corporations 87
Ottoman 88–90
corporatism 87
in Middle East 86–87
Ottoman 83, 85, 87–94, 104–105
tribal groups 99–104
village communities 94–99
counter-public (*Gegenöffentlichkeit*) 302
courts of law, dog appearances in 447n11
cultural alienation, of youth 185
cultural studies 342
cultures xvi, xxx–xxxi
in Cairo 32, 38, 42–43
electronic 224, 239, 240
Ottoman, in Egypt 28
physical 335
print 223–224, 239, 240
curricula, of Islamic studies in Russia 11–12
cursive scripts 248
cycling, in Cairo 236–237
Cynics 450, 451, 452
Czada, Roland 87

Dabashi, Hamid 306–307
The Daily Voice (newspaper, South Africa) 181
Damiens, Robert-François 455
Dār al-Kitāb al-ʿArabī (publishing house, Cairo) 225n6
Darülfünun (university) 135–136, 137, 138–139
dead persons, photographs of 115, 118
Demange, Jean-François 10
democracy
early 399n4
in Iran, and women's rights 302, 306
Muslim acceptance of 186–187
Demolins, Edmond 161–162
Dennerlein, Bettina xix, xxxvii
Deobandism 198–199
Moosagie's criticism of 205, 212
Walī Allāh's place in 291–292
deportations, and nation-state formation 363
Der Matossian family 123, 124
Derrida, Jacques 445, 446–447, 458, 459
dervish staffs 257–258
desacralisation 453
dhimma regime 358
dialogues
interfaith xxix
respectful, in Swahili 270
diasporas, formation of 371–372
dictionaries, Arabic-Russian 14
digital codes, Arabic 256–257
Diogenes 450
Discipline and Punish: The Birth of the Prison (Foucault) 455–456
discursive agency 267, 269
through ethnography 275
on Kenyan Muslim radio 273–274
research on 277
discursive analysis 182–183
discursive spaces 268, 269, 273–274
discursive traditions xv, 183, 193

dissidents fleeing Iran disguised as a woman trope 301
Dockrat, Mawlana Ashraf 190, 191
dogs
being compared with
Cynics 450, 452
degradation of 445
refugees 443–445, 450, 451
court appearances of 447n11
domestication of 445n9
human relationships with 444n7, 445, 447–448
philosophical 449–450
Doha International Conference on the Family (UN, 2004) 313–314
Drāz, Muḥammad ʿAbdullāh 166, 168, 174, 176
dress styles, Armenian-Ottoman 120–126
Duff-Gordon, Lucy 38

École d'Égyptologie (Cairo) 31
economy, Egyptian 33, 43, 45–46
Edirne (Turkey), oil wrestling festival in 328–329, 340, 342–343, 349–350
education
in Egypt 160–161, 164–165, 175–176
in France 162, 164–165
Muslim religious 149
in India 183, 185–186, 200–201
and recognition policies 434
Muslim thought on/conceptions of 163–164
al-nahḍa's focus on 161
as power building strategy of religious minorities 370–371
reform of
in Egypt 39–40
in Ottoman Empire 132–136, 137–140
effendiyya (middle class, Egypt) 231, 332
egalitarian character, of radio discussion programmes 274
Egypt
army of 35–36
authoritarian rule in 405, 411, 415, 421
British rule/occupation of 60
censorship in xviii, 227, 229, 231–232
social media 237, 238
economy in 33, 43, 45–46
education in
higher 160–161, 164–165, 175–176
reforms of 39–40
electronic culture in 224
elites of 407n9
European influences on 27, 28, 44–45
ethics/ethical thinking in 157, 161, 162–176
history of 27, 29
informal networks in 415–420, 421
Islamic personal status law in 311–312
language use in 28–29
literature 28n2
modernity in 27, 29, 44, 45, 46
nationalism in 59–60
Ottoman rule of 32, 35–36, 40, 45–46
political freedom in 37–38, 411
politics in 411, 419
print culture in 223–224
public sphere in 38
reform movement in 167
religious minorities in 269, 372
revolts (2011/2012) in 233, 417
mobilised publics in 407, 412–413
popular committees in and after 412, 413, 417–419
and regime change 397–398, 403–404, 405, 406, 411–412, 421
social media use in xviii, 223, 233–238
taxation in 91
universities in 31, 165
women's rights in xix, 312–313
Egypt-Abessinia war (1869) 36
Egyptian Museum (Cairo) 31
electronic culture
and censorship 239
in Egypt 224
and globalisation 240
Elimika na Stambuli! ('Get educated with Stambuli!', radio programme) 266–267, 269–270
and discursive agency 273–274
terrorism, discussions of 270–276
elite bargains 405n8
'Elite Change and New Social Mobilization in the Arab World' (research project, SWP, Germany) 398–400

elites
in Arab World 400–401
and Arab revolts (2010–2012) 401–402, 403–404, 406, 407
Egyptian 407n9
focus on Europe/France of 27, 28, 44–45
language use of 29
formation of, through education 371
Iranian 306
modern, gentling of manners of 151
Muslim religious, and popular Islam 149
Ottoman 90
see also intellectuals
emancipation, of Jews 432
Empire libéral 30, 37
empires 360
Egyptian ambitions for 35, 36, 40
empowerment, after Arab revolts 420–421
Emrullah Efendi 138
Enayat, Hamid 56–57
Encyclopaedia of Islam, THREE (*EI3*) xv
Encyclopedia of Brockhaus and Efron 19
engineering schools, in Ottoman Empire 132–133
Enlightenment, failure of 455
Ennahḍah party (Tunisia) 405
enseignement religieux, Musulman 149
Erdmann, Franz (Fedor) 5
Erdoğan, Necmeddin Bilal 348–349
eschatology, in ISIS propaganda 192, 215
esotericism, in Islam off-shoot religions 368
ethics 267, 276
in Egypt/Egyptian thought on 157, 161, 162–176
Islamic xvii–xviii, 161
in classical era 157–158
modern 158–159, 173–175
European influences on 159–160, 161–162
ethnic groups 357
ethnography
of academic institutions xxvi–xxvii
discursive agency through 275
of Kenyan Muslim radio discussions on terrorism 275–276
see also anthropology
Etnospor Kültür Festivali I and III (Istanbul) 347–349, 350
eulogies, Arabic 250–252
Eurocentrism, in Islamic studies xiii
Europe
closing of 459, 462
Egyptian ties with 34–36
influences of
on Egyptian elites 27, 28, 44–45
on Islamic ethics 159–160, 161–162, 175
on Ottoman dress styles and furnishings 121–123
on Ottoman higher education 133, 136
Islam/Muslims in 434
acceptance of xx–xxi
recognition of xx, 427–428, 429, 432–435, 436–437
visibility of 427
Islamic studies in 22
Jews in, recognition/emancipation of 432, 435–436
public sphere in 36
renaissance in 169
see also West
Europeans
in Cairo/Egypt 32, 41–42, 43
Middle Eastern studies by 83, 84–85
in and on Ottoman Empire 81, 126–127
women, Iranian images of 303
exclusion
of minorities 360
of refugees 447, 448–449
exile 370, 371–372
existentialism, Arab world 171–172
expatriate communities, Iranian 302
extended families, photographs of 115
Ezbekīya Square/neighbourhood (Azbakiyya, Cairo) 28–30, 33, 43, 46
Ezzat, Heba Raouf *see* ʿIzzat, Hiba Raʿūf

face-to-face communication 92–93, 95
Facebook 224n4
Egyptian revolts postings on 233–235, 236
Go Bike site on 236–237
Iranian *Men in Hijabs* campaign on 301, 305
shutdown of Egyptian political pages by 237–238
Fadʿān (Fedʿān) tribal group (Syria) 101–102

Fāḍil, Muṣṭafā 33, 37
Fāḍila, Jamīla 34
Fahmī, Manṣūr 165, 167, 171
families
in early modern societies 92
Islam on protection of 314, 319
and women 316–321
Islamic law on 311–312
modern normative, Arab Human Development Reports on 315–316
photography of
as historical source 112–113
Ottoman 113–127
family, politicisation of, by Islamism 312
famines, in Egypt 33
Farooq, Samaya 331–332
Faroqhi, Suraiya 338n14
Fāṭemeh is Fāṭemeh, (lecture, Sharīʿatī) 302–303
Fāṭima (daughter of the Prophet) 303
fears
of Muslims 458–459
of refugees 446, 454
feminism, Islamic 308
festivals, oil wrestling at 328
fezzes, in Ottoman dress 121
fief-holders, Ottoman 96, 98
Filali-Ansary, Abdou xvii, xxxvii
fiqh, Iranian reform movement's views on 306
Fleischer, Heinrich Leberecht xvi, 15
Flüchtlingsgespräche (Refugee Dialogues, Brecht) 461n20
'The Forgotten Muslims' (documentary, Uganda) 376, 377, 378n2, 387
Fossati, Gaspare 134
Foucault, Michel 451, 452–456, 460–461, 465
Frähn, Christian-Martin 5
France
education in 162, 164–165
influences of
on Egyptian elites 27
on Egyptian ethical thinking 160–161, 164–165, 170–171
on Islamic ethics 159–160, 161–162
on Ottoman education 133–134
Tunisia ruled 60
Franz, Julius 29
Französische Sprache, in Ägypten 29
freedom
absolute 452, 453
political, in Egypt 37–38, 411
reason dominating over 455
of speech 464–465
of thought 453
Freie Universität Berlin, Islamic Studies at xiv–xvi, xxxii, xxxiii–xxxiv
Freitag, Ulrike xxxii
French language
in Egypt 29
translations of texts in, into Arabic 160–161
Frolov, Dmitrii 7n7
Fromentin, Eugène 42
Fukuyama, Francis 399n4
funerals, photographs of 115n10
furūsiyya tradition (military chivalry) 327–328, 339
The Future of Islam (Blunt) 59n4
Fuyūḍ al-ḥaramayn (Walī Allāh) 293–294

Gadamer, Hans-Georg 304, 439
Galarza, Comte de 165
Gauck, Joachim 434
Gauland, Alexander 464
Gautier, Théophile 41–42
Gegenöffentlichkeit 302
gender, Islamic opposition to use of term 313
gender relations
in Arab World/MENA region 310–311
in Iran xix, 301–305, 307–308
General Labour Union (Union générale tunisienne du travail) 407
gentling of manners 151, 155
Germany
incitement prohibition in 443–444
Islam/Muslims in xiii, 427, 435
religious education in 434
Islamic studies in xii–xvi, 22, 23
Ottoman philosophy education influenced by 135
refugees in 441–442, 461
Gérôme, Jean-Léon 43
al-Ghazālī, Abū Ḥāmid 289
al-Ghazālī, Muḥammad 227, 311, 318
Ghonim, Wael 234, 235
Ghubayn (Shaykh) 102n25

Girgas, Vladimir 12–14, 15
Github (online platform) 249
Gladstone, William E. 59
Global Mufti (Gräf and Skovgaard-Peterson eds.) xxxiii
globalisation 27, 240
Go Bike … Go Life (biking group, Cairo) 236–237
goat hair, textiles made from 123
Gökalp, Ziya 137, 364
Gökmen, Mehmed Fatin 137
Goldziher, Ignaz 15
Gottwald, Joseph (Iosif) 6
government administration, Ottoman 99, 102–104
graphic expressions
  of *Allāh* and Muḥammad 248–249, 251, 254
  of intellectual structure of texts 250
  of *shahāda* 253, 254
Great Britain
  Egypt ruled by 60
  India ruled by 288, 289
  Ottoman caliphate opposed by 58–59
Greek philosophy, Egyptian ethical thought influenced by 169–170, 174, 175
Grunebaum, Gustav von xviii
guilds, in Ottoman Empire 81, 82, 87
Guirguis, Laure 369
Guizot, François 162
Gülizar case 123

Haarmann, Ulrich xxxii
Habermas, Jürgen 302
Haddad, Mahmoud 56, 57
Ḥadīqat al-akhbār ('The garden of news', newspaper, Lebanon) 13
ḥadīth, study of, in South Asia 280
Hagia Sophia (Istanbul) 249
hagiographies, of religious scholars 286
Hakkı, İzmirli Ismail 137
Ḥalabī, Muṣṭafā 226
Ḥalīm (Prince, Egypt) 33–34
al-Ḥāmūlī, ʿAbduh 38
Hamzah, Dyala 57
Ḥamzanameh 345–346
Ḥanafī school of law 40
Hanioğlu, Şükrü 340
Haraway, Donna 446n10
Harders, Cilja xx, xxxviii, 413, 414
Hartmann, Elke xvii, xxxviii
Ḥasan, Maḥmūd 281, 290–291, 292
Ḥasana tribal group (Syria) 101
hate, prohibition on incitement to 443–444, 463–464
hate speech, on social media, removal of 462–463
al-Ḥayy, ʿAbd 287
Ḥazrama (village) 96
Hebrew University (Jerusalem), Islamic studies at xxxiii
Hegel, Georg Wilhelm Friedrich 428, 432
Henri v (Comte de Chambord) 44
heritage sports 328, 335, 342
  in Turkey 328, 347–349
heroes 346
Herrera, Linda 238
Hetze 464
hidden transcripts, of religious minority groups 370
Higgins, Godfrey 289
higher education
  in Egypt 160–161, 164–165, 175–176
  Ottoman 133–136, 137, 138–140
Ḥijāz 69, 73
Hijra notion (migration) 199n5
al-Hilāl (journal) 168
Hirschmann, Peter 445n8
Histoire générale de la civilisation en Europe (Guizot) 162
'The Historical Novel in Contemporary Arabic Literature' (article, Krachkovskii) 21
historiography
  of Middle East 85
  Ottoman 83–84
history
  of civilisations xii
  of Egypt 27
  of Muslim world, breaking points in 336
  of philosophy xvii
  religion in 16
  sources of, family portraits 112–113
  of Uganda, post-colonial 380–381
History of Madness (Foucault) 452
History Museum of Armenia (Yerevan) 119
Hodgson, Marshall 151–152, 154, 155
Ḥosayniyyeh Ershād (Qom) 303
households, Ottoman, size of 118–119

Houshamadyan collection (photography) 113–127
'How do we ensure global cooperation regarding ethics?' (article, al-Sayyid) 168
Hügel, Carl Alexander von 41
Hughes, T.P. 287–288
Ḥujjat Allāh al-bāligha (Walī Allāh) 281, 288–289, 292–293
human bodies, disciplining of (Foucault) 456
human rights
 Islam on 311
 neoliberalism associated with 313
 protection of family values as part of 314
 violations, in Egypt 411
 see also women's rights
humanities 3
humans
 and animals/animality 448, 451
 status of refugees as 448–449
Hunger, in Ägypten 33
Huot, Claire 450–451, 452
Ḥusayn, Ṭāhā 165, 169
Huxley, Aldous 448
Hyder, Mohamed 272–273

Ibn ʿAbd al-Muṭṭalib, Ḥamza 345–346
Ibn Khaldūn, ʿAbd al-Raḥmān 153–154
Ibn Miskawayh 164
iconisation/iconic mode of representation 93, 103
idealism, modified 172
identities
 Muslim collective, and religion 150
 national
  and print culture 223
  Turkish 340–341, 364
 recognition of 430
 religious
  of Muslim minority groups in Middle East 368–369
  of states 362, 369
identity politics 368–369, 439
Iḥyāʾ ʿulūm al-dīn (al-Ghazālī) 289
IIAS (International Institute for Asian Studies) xxvii
ijtihād (renewed interpretation of the sources of Islamic law)
 ʿIzzat's views on 311, 318–319
 Walī Allāh's views on 281
Il'minskii, Nikolai 7
imagination
 modes of 84
 role of, in reading Islamic calligraphy 261
imāms, training of, in Germany 434
imperial ambitions, of Egypt 35, 36, 40
imperial rule
 of Egypt 60
  Ottoman 35–36, 40, 45–46
 of minorities 358–360, 361
 of Tunisia 60
Imperial School of Naval Engineering (Muhendishane-i Bahr-i Hümayun) 132–133
imperialism
 British/French 60
 Derrida on hypocrisy of 459
incitement to hate prohibition 443–444, 463–464
India
 anti-colonialism in 290
 book publishing in 287–292
 Mutiny in (1857) 288, 289
 ʿulamāʾ in 190
Indian community in South Africa 183, 186
Indigénat égyptien (*al-raʿāwīya al-jinsīya al-maḥallīya*) 31
indirect rule, Ottoman 100
individualism 152, 170
individuals, autonomy of 428n2
inequalities in power distribution, and recognition policies 430–431
informal institutions 416n5
informal networks
 in Egypt 415–420, 421
 mobilisation in 412, 418
informalisation
 in Arab World 415
 in Egypt 416–417
injustice, experienced by refugees 455
insanity 451, 452–454
 confinement of 452, 460
 Foucault on 460–461
 Western associations of Muslims with 458–459
Institute for Islamic Studies (Freie Universität Berlin) xxxii

'Integrating Media and Transcultural Communication Research within Islamic and Area Studies' (conference, Berlin) xxxiv
intellectual structure of texts, graphic expressions of 250
intellectuals
  Arab, formal classical Arab spoken by 148–149
  Egyptian 166–167
  Iranian 306–307
  Muslim, in Uganda 386–387
interfaith dialogues xxix
Internet, penetration in Iran of 302
An Introduction to Islamic Law (Schacht) 87
Iran
  elites/intellectuals in 306–307
  gender relations/women's rights in xix, 301–305, 307–308
  martial arts in 337
  Men in Hijabs social media campaign in 301, 305, 307
  reform movement in 302, 305–306
  religious minorities in 359–360, 365, 366
  traditional wrestling in 333
Iraq, confessional identity of 369
irrationality, of Muslims 458–459
ISIM (International Institute for the Study of Islam in the Modern World) xxvii–xxviii, xxxi
ISIS (Islamic State of Iraq and Syria)
  jihād notion of 204n18
  Moosagie's support for 181–182, 183, 185, 191–192, 193, 194–199, 214–220
Iṣlāḥī, Amīn Aḥsan 294
Islam 327, 334
  anthropology of 193, 276
  apostasy prohibition in 204n17, 367
  in Arab nationalism 364
  Arabian origins of 8–9
  in Europe, civilising project of 434
  in Germany xiii, 427, 435
  on human rights 311
  in Kenya xviii–xix
  'logos' of 249
  and modernity 152–153, 154–155, 159, 193–194
  muscular 327, 330, 331–336, 339, 340, 350
  off-shoot religions of 367–369
  and political authority 191, 202
  popular versus intellectual 149
  on protection of family values 314, 319
    and women 316–321
  rationality of 281, 305
  and religious pluralism/tolerance 366, 377–378
  religious practices in public sphere of 436–437
  in Russian Empire 4
  and secularisation 364
  in South Africa 182, 184–185, 186–192
    and support for ISIS 181–182, 183–185, 190–192, 193, 194–220
  in Turkey 330, 343
  on unbelievers/heresy 188–190, 203–204
  and violence 271–272
  and women's rights 302, 313–314, 316–321
    see also reform movement
Islam and the Foundations of Government (al-Rāziq) 75
'Islam and Pluralism' (essay, Krämer) 377–378
Islamic books, publishing of 225, 228, 287–292
Islamic calligraphy 246–247
  graphic design 247–256
  and/on material objects 256–258, 259–260
  readability of 246–247, 258–262
Islamic ethics xvii–xviii, 161
  in classical era 157–158
  modern 158–159, 173–175
    European influences on 159–160, 161–162
Islamic feminism 308
Islamic law
  legal personality concept in 86
  women and family in 311–312
Islamic martial arts 327, 333, 336–338, 350
Islamic philosophy 159, 163, 173
Islamic state, political philosophy of 56
Islamic studies xi–xii, xvi–xvii, xxi, xxviii–xxx
  in Europe 22
  in Germany xii–xvi, 22, 23

Islamic studies (*cont.*)
  Krämer's reshaping of xxvi–xxviii, xxx–xxxv
  in Russia 3–4, 22–24
    at Kazan University 4–9, 10–11
    at Moscow 17–20
    at St. Petersburg University 6, 10–17, 23
  in Ukraine 21
Islamic texts, ligatures in 249–252
Islamism 372
  after Arab revolts 403, 404
  Hiba Ra'ūf 'Izzat's criticism of 235, 320
  politicisation of family by 312
IslamOnline website/platform 311, 319
Islamophobia 427
Ismāʿīl Pasha (Khedive of Egypt) 31–32, 33–36, 37, 38, 40, 46, 160
Ismāʿīl, Shāh 281
Ismāʿīlīya (Cairo neighbourhood) 30, 46
Istanbul
  Hagia Sophia in 249
  heritage sports in 328, 347–349, 350
  Military Museum in 338
  Ottoman photography in 111
  universities in 134–135
Istanbul University 135
Istituzioni di diritto musulmano (Santillana) 86
ItsMensTurn hashtag (Iran) 307
IUIS (International Union of Islamic Scholars), opposition to women's rights activism by 314
Ivanov, Mikhail 9n14
Izālat al-khafāʾ ʿan khilāfat al-khulafāʾ (Walī Allāh) 289
ʿIzzat, ʿAbd al-ʿAzīz 168
ʿIzzat, Hiba Raʾūf xix, 235–236, 310
  on women's rights and family values 311, 316, 318–321
İzzet, Mehmed 139

Jacob, Wilson Chacko 332
Jacoby, Günther 135
jamāʿa/cemaʿat concept 89–90
Jamʿīyat al-Maʿārif (Gesellschaft der Schönen Künste, Kairo) 37
Jankowski, James 231
jeweller's guild (Ottoman) 81, 82
Jews
  in Egypt 372
  in Europe, recognition/emancipation of 432, 435–436
jihād notion 183
  of ISIS 204n18
  of Moosagie 183, 185–186, 190–191, 201, 204–205, 213–214
  semiotic analysis of 191, 194
  in South Africa xvii, 181, 191, 193
Johansen, Baber xvi, 86–87
Jones, Anton 442, 457, 463
Journal Officiel (Gautier) 41
journalism, of Riḍā 57
Judaism, muscular 331, 336
'Juden und Hunde Verboten' signs in Nuremberg 445n8
justice
  in Shīʿa Islam 304–305
  social, Walī Allāh's views on 281
  see also injustice

Kaboulian, Boghos 116
Kadivar, Mohsen 306
Kairo 27–28
  Europäer in 32, 41–42
  Ezbekīya-Viertel in 28–30, 33
  Kultur in 32, 38, 42–43
  Moderne in 46
  Orientreisender in 32, 41–42
  politische Freiheit in 37–38
  Stadtentwicklung in 30, 32–33, 39
  see also Cairo
al-Kanākir (Syria) 94–95
Kananov, Georgii 18
Kant, Immanuel 165, 360
Kara, Recep 329
Karahasan, Dževad 361
Karam, Yūsuf 166, 167
Karolia, Mawlana Muhammad 186–187, 188
Kasabashian, Arshalous and Yervant 117
kashīda (lengthened), use in Arabic graphic design of 252–256
Kawakami, Akane 246
al-Kawākibī, ʿAbd al-Raḥmān 66
Kawtharānī, Wajīh 57, 69
Kazan University, Islamic studies at 4–9, 10–11
Kazantzakis, Nikos 360
Kazem-Bek, Aleksandr 5–6, 23

Kemal, Mustafa *see* Atatürk
Kemalists 70, 73, 74
Kenya, Islam/Muslims in xviii–xix
  marginality of 265–266, 267
  radio stations/programs of 266–267, 268–276
Kerr, Malcom 56, 148, 149, 150
Khālid, Khālid Muḥammad 227, 229
Khalidov, Anas 21n35
Kharijites 203n16
Khar'kov University 5n4
al-Khaṭīb, Muḥibb al-Dīn 229n16
al-Khatib, Mutaz xvii, xxxviii
Khawatir 11 (television programme) 237
Khiabany, Gholam 238
al-Khiyāl al-siyāsī li-l-Islāmiyyīn: Mā qabla l-dawla wa-mā baʿdahā (The political vision of Islamists: Before and after the state, Hiba Raʾūf ʿIzzat) 235
Khomeini, Ayatollah Ruhollah, on womanhood 303
Kiev University, Islamic studies at 21
Kırkpınar festival (Edirne) 340, 341, 346–347
  Islamic elements of 343–344
  opening ritual of 344
  UNESCO Intangible Cultural Heritage status of 341–342
Kiyimba, Abasi 382, 383, 385n8, 386, 387
knowledge
  Foucault on 465
  production and transmission of 371
  traditions of 266
Knysh, Alexander xvi–xvii, xxxviii
Kokoschka, Alina xviii, xxxviii, 327n1
Kolonialismus, in Ägypten 46
Krachkovskii, Ignatii 8n9, 13, 17, 21–22
Krämer, Gudrun xi, 372
  on autonomy 87
  on corporations 89
  Islamic/Middle Eastern studies reshaping by xii–xiii, xv–xvi, xxvi–xxviii, xxx–xxxv, 84–85
  on notables as intermediaries 90–91
  on Ottoman reforms 136–137
  on religious pluralism 377
  research projects/approaches of xiv, xv, xxi, 83, 398n1
Krawietz, Birgit xix, xxxviii
Kresse, Kai xviii–xix, xxxviii
Kriege, Ägypten-Abessiniien (1869) 36
Krymskii, Agafangel 19–21
Küçek Hanum 44n38
kufaar (unbelievers), Islam on 203–204
Kultur, in Kairo 32, 38, 42–43
Kurkjian family 122
Kushti wrestling 333

Laqueur, Hans-Peter 329, 341, 344
Lady Goal (Nīlūfar Ardalān) 307–308
Lalande, André 165, 166
Lambek, Michael 267, 276
land ownership, in Ottoman Empire 98
languages
  and politics xviii
  use of, in Egypt 28–29
Latin script
  dominance of 254
  encounters with Arabic script 254–255
  ligatures in 249
law
  courts of, dog appearances in 447n11
  Egyptian, personal status 311–312
  monstrosity of 447
  Ottoman, penal 97
  and stupidity 448
  tyranny of 459
  see also Islamic law
Lawlor, Leonard 452, 453–454, 456
Lazarev Institute of Oriental Languages (Moscow) 18–20
Le Bon, Gustave 162
Le Thomas, Catherine 371
Lebanon
  confessional identity of 369
  Shīʿa Islam in 371
Leca, Jean 360–361, 372
Leder, Stefan 345
left-wing politics
  book publishing by, in Egypt 230–231
  involvement of religious minorities in 372
legal personality concept 86
legends 345, 346
legibility
  of Arabic script 248–249
  of Islamic calligraphy 246–247, 258–262

legitimacy crises, in Egypt 417
Lepenies, Wolf 3
letters, arbitrariness of, in Islamic calligraphy 261
Levitsky, Steven 416n5
Lévy-Bruhl, Lucien 171
liberal secular matrix 436
Libya, revolts in (2012–2012)
 mobilised publics in 407
 and regime change 397–398, 403, 404, 406
ligatures
 in Arabic script 248, 249–252
 in Latin script 249
lijān sha'biyya (popular committees, Egypt) 412, 413, 417–420
Linant Pasha, Louis Maurice 39
linearity, abandonment in Islamic calligraphy of 258
lines
 in Arabic script 252, 254, 256–257
 in Islamic calligraphy 247, 248, 254
 see also 'art of the line'
Linthicum, Nancy 229n19
literature
 Egyptian 28n2
 modern Arabic, Russian study of 13, 20–22
 Russian, Oriental influences on 17
local space 414
logical positivism 172–173
logistical power, of states 84
'logos' of Islam 249
loyalty, of minorities to dominant groups 369–370
Lule, Yusuf 382

Maccabiah Games 331
al-Madani, Fakhruddin Owaisi 183, 189, 190, 191
Madbūlī, Ḥājj Muḥammad 231, 232
madness *see* insanity
madrasas
 in India, Moosagie's criticism of 183, 185–186, 200–201
 in Ottoman Empire 132, 137
Madrasat al-Alsun (School of Languages, Egypt) 160
al-Mahdī, Muḥammad al-'Abbāsī 39, 40
Mahdist revolution (Sudan) 60
Maḥmūd, 'Abd al-Ḥalīm 170
Maḥmūd, Zakī Najīb 172–173
Mahmud II (Ottoman Sultan) 133
Mahnjoh, Priscillia 442n3
majorities
 dichotomy with minorities, reproduction of 431
 formation of 363
 Muslim, portrayal of tolerant Islam by 366
Makerere University (Kampala) 382
al-Maktaba al-Ahliyya (publishing house/bookstore, Cairo) 226
Maktabat Madbouli (publishing house/bookstore, Cairo) 231
Maktabat Wahba (publishing house/bookstore, Cairo) 224–230, 233
Malche, Albert 135
male solidarity, for Iranian women's rights activism xix, 301, 304–305, 307
Mālik b. Anas 281
Mālikī school of law 281
Malov, Efim 8
Mālṭī, Ḥabīb Ablā 29
Mamlūk studies 338–339
Manāhij al-albāb (Rāfiʿ al-Ṭahṭāwī) 28
al-Manār (journal) xvii, 62–63, 161, 226n9
 on Ottoman caliphate 63–64, 68
 on Ottoman Consultative Society 67
 on pan-Islamism 64
Manasse, Séraphin 34
Mandanipour, Shahriar 307
Mann, Michael 84
al-Mar'a al-muslima (The Muslim woman, article, al-Bannā) 318
al-Mar'a al-muslima fi l-mujtamaʿ al-muslim (The Muslim woman in Muslim society, Muslim Brotherhood) 320
al-Mar'a wa-l-'amal al-siyāsī (Woman and political action, Hiba Ra'ūf 'Izzat) 311, 318
al-Mar'a wa-l-rajul wa-hal yatasāwayān? (Woman and man: Are they equal?, article, Shumayyil) 317–318
Mardin, Şerif 360
Marilhat, Prosper 41
Markell, Patchen 428, 430, 431–432, 433, 437, 439
Marks, Laura U. 247n2

al-Marrākushī, Muḥammad Ṣāliḥ 73–74
martial arts, Islamic 327, 333, 336–338, 350
Mashanov, Mikhail 8–9
massacres
of Armenians, in Ottoman Empire 127
of Muslims in Uganda 376, 382–385
commemoration of 388–389, 390
and nation-state formation 363
on Rabaa El Adaweya Square (Cairo) 235, 237
Massignon, Louis 165, 166, 170
Maṭbaʿat Ḥalabī (publishing house, Cairo) 226
material objects, Islamic calligraphy on/and 256–258, 259–260
materiality, and Arabic script 246
Mathnawi (Rumi) 210
al-Māwardī, Abū l-Ḥasan ʿAlī b. Muḥammad b. Ḥabīb 65–66, 71, 73
Mawloodis 199
Maẓhar, Ismāʿīl 170
Mazhar Paşa, Mustafa 102n25
Mazrui, Sheikh al-Amin bin Ali 265
Mbembe, Achille xxi
McGill University, Islamic studies at xviii–xxix
McLarney, Ellen Anne 318, 319
The Meaning and End of Religion (Smith) xxix
meanings, of Qur'ān, and people's needs 283
Mecca, as seat of Ottoman Caliphate 58
media coverage, of Muslim protests in Uganda 377
media representations, study of xviii
media space 378n2
media studies, and Islamic studies xxxiv
Mediterranean Politics (journal), special issue on Arab revolts 398–399
Mednikov, Nikolai 15
Meier, Astrid xvii, xxxviii, 94, 97
*mekteb*s, Ottoman 134, 136
memory
photography as a means of 112, 115, 118
see also remembrance/commemoration
Men in Hijabs campaign (Iran) xix, 301, 305, 307
MENA region (Middle East and North Africa), gender relations debates in 310–311
Merkel, Angela xiii, 441, 461, 462, 464
metaphysics 173
Middle East
confessional wars in 357
conversion of Muslims to Christianity in 367
corporatism in 86–87
European studies of 83, 84–85
historiography of 85
minorities in xix
internal autonomy of 358–359
religious 358, 363–372
politics in 105
sectarian conflicts in 357–358
state and society in 85
see also MENA region
migration, of Kenyan Muslims 271
milieux urbains, et milieux tribals 153–154
military chivalry tradition (*furūsiyya*) 327–328, 339
military slaves 338–339
Min hunā nabda'u (From here we start, Khālid) 227
Min hunā naʿlamu (From here we learn, al-Ghazālī) 227
Minié Bey, Claude-Etienne 35
minorities 360
denial of subjectivities of 365–366
in Middle East xix, 357, 363–372
imperial rule over 358–360, 361
Muslim, in Uganda xx, 378
in Ottoman Empire 359–361, 362
political representation of 362–363
and social Darwinism 363
recognition of 428, 431–432
in Turkey 364, 366, 369
see also religious minorities
minoritisation, and citizenship/nation-state formation 360, 361–362, 363
missionary activities, of Russian Orthodox Church, among Muslims 6–7
Mitchell, Timothy 84, 99
mobilisation
collective 155–156
in informal networks 412, 418
mobilised publics 400, 402–403
in Arab revolts 402, 406–408
Modern Islamic Political Thought (Enayat) 56

modernisation
  different modes of 154
  in Ottoman Empire 132–133, 136–137
    of education 133–136, 137–140
modernity 151–152
  Egyptian 27, 29, 44, 45, 46
  and Islam 152–153, 154–155, 159, 193–194
  religion in xxix–xxx
Modernity at Large (Appadurai) 336–337
modified idealism 172
moeurs, adoucissement des 151
Mohammed *see* Muḥammad
Moi, Daniel arap 266n2
Mombasa, Muslim radio in 266
mondialisation, of Egypt 27
Montesquieu, Charles-Louis de 161
Moosa, Ebrahim 183, 185–186, 188
Moosagie, Mawlana Rashied 181, 182–183
  childhood of 199–200
  conversion narrative of 184–185, 202–205
  criticism by
    of *buzrug* culture 183, 187, 201, 209–210
    of Islam in South Africa 186–187, 188–190, 192
    of Ṣūfism 187, 199, 205–212
  ISIS supporter 188, 191–192, 193, 194–199, 214–220
  jihād notion of 183, 185–186, 190–191, 201, 204–205, 213–214
  narrative identity of 184–185
  religious education in India 183, 185–186, 200–202
moral conduct, religion and 147–156
moral philosophy xvii
La Morale du Koran (Drāz) 174
La Morale et la science des moeurs (Lévy-Bruhl) 171
Moreton, Cole 444n7
Moscow, Islamic studies at 17–20
Mosul 361
Moṭahharī, Ayatollah Morteżā 302, 303
Mott, Thaddeus Phelps 35
mourning, collective 389, 390
Moustafa, Ahmed 252
Mubārak, ʿAlī 31, 39, 40
Mubarak, Husni 412
Muḥammad (Prophet) 8, 339
  graphic expressions of 248–249, 251
  Western perceptions of 457–458, 459n18
Muḥammad, Sulṭān Bīk 165
Muḥammad III al-Ṣiddīq (Bey of Tunisia) 60
Muḥammad Aḥmad b. ʿAbdallāh (mahdī) 60
Muḥammad ʿAlī Pāshā (Khedive of Egypt) 38, 40, 159, 160
Muḥammad Isḥāq, Shāh 284, 287
Muḥammad Ismāʿīl, Shāh 287
Muḥammad Tawfīq (Khedive of Egypt) 59–60
Muhanna (Shaykh of the Ḥasana) 101
Mujahideen, in Afghanistan 337
münevver (enlightened scholars) 134
Muqaddima (Ibn Khaldūn) 153
Murji'as 203–205
Murkos, Georgii 19
Murphy, Tim (2003) 182
Mursī, Muḥammad 407, 419
Musa Bey 123
Mūsā, Muḥammad Yūsuf 166, 173–174
muscular Christianity 330–331
muscular Islam 327, 330, 331–336, 339, 340, 350
muscular Judaism 331, 336
Museveni, Yoweri 380, 382
music, Islamic views of 294
Muslim Brothers (Egypt) 226n9, 228–229
  crackdown of xx, 230
  founding of 76
  ʿIzzat's support for 320–321
  publishing by 229n16
Muslim world
  breaking points in 336
  modernity in 152–153
  sciences in, European influences on 159
Muslims
  appeals for closure of Europe to 459
  conversion to Christianity by 367
  in Europe
    acceptance of xx–xxi
    recognition of 427–428, 429, 432–435, 436–437
    visibility of 427
  in Germany xiii, 435
  in Kenya
    marginality of 265–266, 267

radio programmes/stations of 266–267, 268–276
religious education of 149
in India 183, 185–186, 200–201
and recognition policies 434
in Russian Empire 4, 6–7
stereotyping of 454
in Uganda xx, 376, 385
political representation of 385–386
political rights of 378
politics of recognition by 382–383, 386–387, 390–391
protests by 376–377, 384, 387–388
remembrance/commemoration practices of 379–380, 384–385, 388–389, 390, 391
governmental repression of 381, 384, 390
Sheema district massacre of (1979) 376, 382–385
Western werewolf images of 458–459
Mu'tazilī school of law 160, 203n16
Mutiny (1857, India) 288, 289
mutual response, idea of 446n7
mutuality, Swahili markers of 268
Muwaṭṭa' (Mālik ibn Anas) 281
al-Muwayliḥī, Ibrāhīm 37
Muzio, Emanuele 42
mysticism, of Walī Allāh 293–294

Naadam Festival (Mongolia) 342
al-Nābulusī, 'Abd al-Ghanī 96
Nadim Centre (Egypt) 411
al-nahḍa (Arab renaissance) 13, 158
education focus of 161
in Egypt 165, 167
on women's rights 316–317
Naḥwa 'umrān jadīd (Towards a new civilisation, Hiba Ra'ūf 'Izzat) 321
Naim, Babanzade Ahmed 137, 138
Najarian, Rebecca 116
Najd region 100, 102
Nanotvi, Muhammad Qasim 212n36
Napoleon 448
Daß Narrenschyff ad Narragoniam (Brant) 456–459, 465
Foucault on 460
Nasser, Gamal Abdel 415
Nasser, Ramsey 254–257
national identities
and print culture 223
Turkish 340–341, 364
nationalism
Arab, Riḍā's attitude towards 55, 56
in Egypt 59–60
in Muslim world 155
and minorities 360, 363–364
in Ottoman Empire 364
nations
formation of, minoritisation and 360, 361–362, 363
psychology of 162
Navaro-Yashin, Yael 329, 341
Navrotskii, Mikhail 17
Negev 104n27
neoliberalism, human rights associated with 313
Nerval, Gérard de 41
networks 415–416n5
informal
in Egypt 415–420, 421
mobilisation in 412, 418
intellectual 166
neutrality of states, perceptions of 431, 432
Nicholas I (Tsar) 10n18
Nicomachean Ethics (Aristotle), translation into Arabic 169–170
Nidā' Tūnis 404
al-niẓām al-jadīd (new order, Egypt) 27
Nöldeke, Theodor 8
norms, and reality, in Muslim societies/Islam 148, 149
North Africa *see* MENA region (Middle East and North Africa)
NRM government (National Resistance Movement, Uganda)
Muslim politicians in 385–386
silence/national reconciliation policies imposed by 377, 379, 381, 383, 384
Nūbār Pāshā, Bōgōṣ 44
Nūr party (Egypt) 405
Nuremberg 445n8
Nuzhat al-Afkār (journal, Egypt) 37

obedience to secular authorities, requirement of 191, 202
Obote, Milton 383, 385
Öffentlichkeit
ägyptische 38
europäische 36

oil wrestling in Turkey xix, 327, 328–330, 340–341, 349–350
cultural elements of 341–343, 344–347
Islamic elements of 334–335, 343–344
nationalistic elements of 341
Omar, A. Rashied 183, 185, 189
'On Difference and Understanding: The Use and Abuse of the Study of Islam' (essay, Krämer) xviii
One Million Signatures for Women's Rights campaign (Iran) 304
opera theatre, in Cairo 42–43
Orient
orientalisation of, in Egypt 43–44
Western nostalgia for 41, 43
Orientalism
Islamic calligraphy seen as meaningless in 262
negative connotations of 3
Orientalism (Said) 3
Orientreisender nach Kairo 32
Orthodox Christianity, missionary activities among Muslims by 6–7
osmanische Kultur, in Ägypten 28
Osmanisches Reich
Ägypten als Teil vom 35–36, 40, 45–46
Staatsbürgerschaft im 32
Ostroumov, Nikolai 8
others, just relations to 439
Ottoman caliphate 55, 56, 58, 61, 76
abolition of 74–75
British opposition to 58–59
al-Kawākibī on 66–67
religion and state in 64–65, 69
Riḍā on 63–64, 66, 68, 69–71, 72, 76
Ottoman Consultative Society (Jamʿiyyat al-Shūrā al-ʿUthmāniyya) 67–68
Ottoman culture, in Egypt 28
Ottoman Empire xvii
citizenship in 32, 360–361
corporatism in 83, 85, 87–94, 104–105
tribal groups 99–104
village communities 94–99
Egypt ruled by 32, 35–36, 40, 45–46
guilds in 81, 82, 87
historiography of 83–84
household size in 118–119
minorities in 359–361, 362
political representation of 362–363
and social Darwinism 363
modernisation in 132–133, 136–137
of education 133–136, 137–140
nationalism in 364
photography in 111–112
family portraits 113–127
reforms in *see* modernisation; *tanẓīmāt*-reforms
religion and state in 58
see also Ottoman Caliphate
religious groups in 100, 105
state-society relations in xvii, 83, 90–94
Syria ruled by 99, 102–104
taxation in 96–97, 98
textile production in 123–124
Özervarlı, M. Sait xvii, xxxix

Pakistan, traditional wrestling in 334
pan-Islamism
Ottoman 61, 64
of Riḍā 56, 61, 64
paperbacks *see* pocketbooks
pariahs 450–451
Paris
Egyptian elites' focus on 27
as model for Cairo's urban development 30
world exhibition in (1867), Egyptian contribution 30, 31
parrhesia 451, 453, 465
Pasha, Ahmed Vefik 138–139
passports 461n20
pastoralism, in Syria 100–101
Patel, Mawlana Yusuf 186, 187
patronage 91n11
peaceful coexistence 361
penal law, Ottoman 97
perpetrators, of Sheema district massacre 383–384
Persian language
influences in Turkey of 344–345
Qur'ān translations into xviii, 280, 282–283
personal status law, Egypt in 311–312
Peter the Great (Tsar of Russia) 4
petitioning 91
Petrov, Pavel 18
Petrov, Petăr 329

philosophy 173
education
in Egypt 160
in France 164–165
in Ottoman Empire 135, 137, 138–140
Greek, influences on Egyptian ethical thought of 169–170, 174, 175
history of xvii
Islamic 159, 163, 173
political, of Islamic state 56
photography
European, of Ottoman Empire 127
family portraits, as historical source 112–113
Ottoman 111–112
family portraits 113–127
physical culture 335
Plato 449
pluralism, religious
and Islam 366, 377–378
regulation of 439
in Uganda 377
pocketbooks
and censorship 232
publishing of 225, 231
political freedom, in Egypt 37–38, 411
political Islam *see* Islamism
political philosophy, of Islamic state 56
political power, of elites 400–401
political representation of minorities
Muslims in Europe 435
Muslims in Uganda 385–386
in Ottoman Empire 362–363
political resources 399n3
in/after Arab revolts 404, 405
political rights, of Muslims in Uganda 378
political transformations
from Arab revolts 399, 401, 404–408, 411–413, 414, 417–419
research on 400, 402
politicisation
of family 312, 319
of women's rights 312
politics 415
in Egypt 411, 419
of identity 368–369, 439
Islamic 191
and languages xviii
left-wing 230–231, 372
Middle Eastern 105
Ottoman, community-based 97–98
participation in 415
after Egyptian revolts 412–413, 417–420, 421
of women 319, 320
primacy of 85
of recognition, of Muslims in Uganda 382–383, 386–387, 390–391
of remembrance/commemoration 378
of Muslims in Uganda 379–380, 384–385, 388–389, 390
of Ugandan government 384, 390
Ugandan 377
Politics (Aristotle) 448
polygamy/polygyny, Islam on 302, 314
popular committees, after revolts in Egypt 412, 413, 417–420, 421
portrait photography, Ottoman 111–112
positivism
logical 172–173
of Russian Islamic studies 16
post-mortem photographs, Ottoman 115, 118
Postnikov, Piotr 7n7
poverty, in Ottoman Empire 127
power
exclusion of minorities from 360
inequalities in, and recognition policies 430–431
political, of elites 400–401
relations, at local level 414
resources of 371
strategies for building of, by minorities 369–372
pratique religieuse, et comportement moral 147–156
prayer, as collective mourning 389
PRE (politically relevant elite) 400–401
in/after Arab revolts (2010–2012) 401–402, 403–404, 406, 407
and mobilised publics 402, 407
Preserved Tablet 286n11
print culture
and censorship 239
in Egypt 223–224
and nation state formation 240
private-public binary 320
progress, European thought on 162

prolongation, in Arabic writing 252–256
propaganda of ISIS 197
eschatology in 192, 215
prophets/prophecies, al-Afghānī on 37
protests
of Muslims in Uganda 376–377, 384, 387–388
see also Arab revolts (2010–2012)
psychology, of nations 162
public sphere
Egyptian 38
European 36
Islamic religious practices in 150–151, 436–437
and private sphere 320
publishing industry
in Cairo/Egypt 224–231
in India 287–292
in United States 232
puritanical movements, Islamic 281, 287

al-Qābīl, ʿAbd al-Ḥayy 174
Qādirī, Muḥammad Ayyūb 288n16
al-Qaraḍāwī, Yūsuf 224n3, 225, 228n15, 229, 311, 318
opposition to women's rights activism by 313–314
Qāsim, Maḥmūd 171
Qurʾān
commentaries on 284
ethics in 174, 175
interpretations of
by Iranian women 304
by Walī Allāh 282–283
translations of xviii, 284–285, 293
in Persian xviii, 280, 282–283
in Russian 7–8
in Urdu 281–282, 283–284, 287–288, 290–291, 292
verses, *baraka* of 262
Quṭb, Sayyid 228

Rabaa El Adaweya Square (Cairo), massacre on (2013) 235, 237
racism
in exclusion of refugees 448, 449
verdicts, and stupidity accusations 445
radicalism, of minorities, and crises of states 369
Radio Islam (South Africa) 183, 186–188, 189, 190
Radio Rahma (Islamic radio, Kenya) xviii–xix, 266–267, 268–270
and discursive agency 273–274
terrorism discussions on 270–273
Rafīʿ al-Dīn, Shāh 281, 283, 284, 285
Rambo III (film) 337
Rasool, Ebrahim 187
rationality
and Christianity 459
Foucault on 461
freedom dominated by 455
of Islam 281, 305
see also irrationality
readability
of Arabic script 248–249
of Islamic calligraphy 246–247, 258–262
reading, and seeing 262
recognition
criticism of theory of 430–431, 437–439
of Jews in Europe 435–436
of minorities 428, 431–432
of Muslims in Europe xx, 427–428, 429, 432–435, 436–437
conditionality of 434–435, 436–437
and security issues 427
of Muslims in Uganda 382–383, 386–387, 390–391
of refugees 461n20
The Refinement of Morals (*Tahdhīb al-akhlāq*, Ibn Miskawayh) 164
reform movement 157, 176
in Egypt 167
in Iran 302, 305–306
on women and family 316–317, 318
see also al-nahḍa
refugee boats, as 'ships of fools' 461
'The Refugee and the Dog' (article, *Der Tagesspiegel*) 442, 443
refugees
acceptance of 450
animality of 452
compared to dogs 443–445
confinement of 456, 460, 461–462
Europe closing its borders to 462
exclusion of 447, 448–449

fears of 446, 454
in Germany 441–443, 461
pariah status of 451
speech of 454–455
regime change, after Arab revolts (2010–2012) 397–398, 403–408, 411–412, 421
reification, of minorities 365–366
religion
and commemoration of violence 378
discursivity of 193
history of mankind shaped by 16
in modernity xxix–xxx
and moral conduct 147–156
and nationalism, in Ottoman Empire 364
return to/external marks of 147, 150
and state
Ataturk on 69
al-Kawākibī on 67
in Ottoman Empire/caliphate 58, 64–65, 69
and recognition policies 436
Riḍā on 65–66, 69–70
religious acts 182
religious communities 435
religious education/learning, Muslim 149
in India 183, 185–186, 200–201
and recognition policies 434
transmission of 286
religious groups 357
in Ottoman Empire 100, 105
religious identities
of Muslim minority groups in Middle East 368–369
of states 362, 369
religious minorities
in Egypt 369, 372
in Europe, recognition of 428–429
in Middle East 358, 363–366, 369–370
internal autonomy of 358–359
Muslim 367–369
power building strategies of 369–372
in Turkey 364, 366, 369
religious pluralism
and Islam 366, 377–378
regulation of 439
in Uganda 377
religious practices
Islamic, in public sphere 150–151, 436–437
and moral conduct 147–156
and spirituality 150
remembrance/commemoration
curative effects of 379
by Muslims in Uganda 379–380, 384–385, 388–389, 390, 391
governmental repression of 381, 384, 390
photographs as 112, 115, 118
political dimension of 378
rituals of xx, 389
renaissance 169
Arab, *see al-nahḍa*
Republic (Plato) 449
repudiation, Islam on 314
resistance of religious minorities 370
to images of tolerance by dominant groups 366
Muslim minorities 368–369
revelations, Walī Allāh's claims of 285–286
revolts
in Egypt (2011/2012) 233
social media use in 233–238
see also Arab revolts (2010–2012)
'Revolutionising ethics: Is the good also the successful?' (article, al-Zayyāt) 167–168
revolutions 411–412n2
Mahdist (Sudan) 60
'Urābī (Egypt) 59, 60
Rhetoric (Aristotle) 450
Ricoeur, Paul 184
Riḍā, Muḥammad Rashīd xvii, 55, 57–58, 61–62, 226
and Arab nationalism 55, 56, 68
ethical thinking by 163–164
journalism of 57, 62–63
pan-Islamism of 56, 61, 64
reformist project of 55–57, 63–66, 67–70
on caliphate 57, 70–73, 76
implementation of 74
al-Kawākibī's criticism of 66–67
loss of appeal of 75
support for 76–77
al-Risāla (journal) 167–168

rituals
of opening of Kırkpınar festival 344
of remembrance/commemoration
xx, 389
Rorty, Richard xviii
Roy, Olivier 185
Rozen, Viktor 9n16, 15–17
Rukāna 339, 345
Rumi, Jalal al-Din 210
Russia/Russian Empire
Islamic studies in 3–4, 22–24
at Kazan University 4–9, 10–11
at Moscow 17–20
at St. Petersburg University 6, 10–17, 23
Muslims in 4, 6–7
Russian language, translations into
of Arabic texts 9
of Qur'ān 7–8
Ryzova, Lucie 231

Sablukov, Gordii 7–8
Sacy, Silvestre de 10, 17, 22
Sadr, Musa 371
sahr, *see* magic
Said, Edward 3, 22
Said, Khaled 234
saints, Sufi veneration of 208
Sakne (Egyptian singer) 38
Salafism 176
conversion to 199
criticism on 188, 320
and Deobandism 198
dissociation from unbelievers in 204n17
Walī Allāh's influence on 293
Salamé, Ghassan 367
Ṣāliḥ, 'Alī 'Abdullāh 404
Ṣāne'ī, Ayatollah Yūsuf 304–305
Sängerinnen, ägyptischen 38
Santillana, David 86
Ṣanū', Ya'qūb 37–38
Sarajevo 361
Saussure, Ferdinand de 182
al-Sayyid, Aḥmad Luṭfī 164, 165, 168,
169–170, 173
Schacht, Joseph 86
Schimmelpenninck van der Oye, David 23
Schmitt, Carl 459
Schneider, Nadja-Christina xxxiv
scholars, religious 188, 193
of al-Azhar 39–40, 75
hagiographies of 286
Ottoman 134
South Asian 190, 280, 281
'School of Propagation and Guidance'
project (Riḍā) 68
Schulz, Dorothea xix, xx, xxxix
Schulze, Reinhard xvi–xvii, xxxix
sciences
in Muslim world, European influences
on 159
teaching of, in Ottoman Empire 138
scripts
Arabic 247, 248, 252
legibility of 248–249
ligatures in 248, 249–252
lines in 252, 254, 256–257
and materiality 246
prolongation in 252–256
encounters between Arabic and
Latin 254–255
Latin
dominance of 254
ligatures in 249
al-Sebaï, Youssef 147
secondary elites 401
sectarian conflicts, in Middle East 357–358
A Secular Age (Taylor) 150
secular authorities
and recognition policies 436–437, 438
requirement of obedience to 191, 202
secularisation 150, 453
and Islam 364
'Izzat's opposition to 319
in Muslim societies, absence of 150–151
security
functions performed by popular
committees 418
and recognition of Muslims in
Europe 427
Seehofer, Horst xiii
seeing, and reading 262
Seeing Like a State (Scott) 89
segmentation 85
self-censorship, on Egyptian social
media 237
self-government 90
self-organisation, of Muslims in Uganda 386
self-portrayals

of Ottoman Empire 126
in photography 112
of religious minorities, in Iran and Turkey 366
self-transformation, as part of civilisation 162
Selim III (Ottoman Sultan) 133
Selimiye mosque (Edirne) 340
semiotics 182
of *jihād* notion 191, 194
Senkovskii, Osip 10, 17
Seraj, Mufti 189–190
shahāda, graphic expressions of 253, 254
Shahinian, Hagop 118
sharīʿa, obligations of, Walī Allāh on 294
Sharīʿatī, ʿAlī 302–303
Sharīf Ḥusayn 68–69
al-Sharqāwī, Ḥasan 175
al-Sharqāwī, Muḥammad ʿAbdallāh 175
shaykhs
in European colonial rule 104n27
Ottoman 102, 103, 104
Sheema (Uganda)
massacre against Muslims in (1979) 376, 382–385
commemoration of 388–389, 390
Muslim protests at 376, 384, 387–388
Shīʿa Islam
authority in 304
justice principle in 304–305
in Lebanon 371
martial arts in 333
Shihābī 101–102
The Ship of Fools (Brant) 456–459, 465
Foucault on 460
refugee boats as 461
shtadlanut (intercession, mediation) 435–436
Shumayyil, Shiblī 317–318
Ṣiddīqī, Muḥammad Aḥsan 288–290
sihr, *see* magic
silence 379
on Sheema district massacre of Muslims 383, 388, 390
Ugandan government policies of 377, 379, 381, 383, 384
similarities, focus on 342
Sindhī, ʿUbayd Allāh 291–292
singers, Egyptian 38
sinners, Islamic thought on 203n16
Sirat Amir Ḥamza (Ibn ʿAbd al-Muṭṭalib) 345
al-Sīsī, ʿAbd al-Fattāḥ 411, 419, 421
slaves, military 338–339
Snare (Mahnjoh) 442n3
social change
in Egypt xviii
and technology 230n22
social contract
in Arab World 415
of informality 416–417
social Darwinism, in Ottoman Empire 363
social interaction, Swahili 268
social justice, Walī Allāh's views on 281
social media
in Egyptian revolts xviii, 223, 233–238
in Iran, *Men in Hijabs* campaign on 301, 305, 307
removal of hate speech on 462–463
surveillance of 238
in women's rights activism 308
social organisation 85
Social Science Research Council (SSRC, United States) xxx
social stratification 88
societies xvi
knowledge traditions in 266
Muslim
collective mobilisation in 155–156
norms and reality in 148, 149
religion in 150–151
and states 83, 415
in early modernity 92
in Egypt 416
microdynamics of 413–414
in Middle East 85
in Ottoman Empire xvii, 83, 90–94
sociology, ethics as part of 170–171
Socrates 449–450
solidarity
intellectual expression of 443n4
of men with Iranian women's rights activism 304–305, 307
Soroush, ʿAbdolkarim 305–306
South Africa
apartheid in 184
Indian community in 183, 186
Islam in 182, 184–185, 186–192

South Africa (*cont.*)
and support for ISIS 181–182, 183–185, 190–192, 193, 194–220
jihād notion in xvii, 181, 191, 193
South Asia, religious scholars in 190, 280, 281
Southeast Asia, martial arts in 336
sovereignty
monstrous/wolf images of 446–447, 459
of states, in assigning recognition 431–432
spaces 378n2, 414
discursive 268, 269, 273–274
Islamic branding of 249
local 414
media 378n2
of mourning 389
Speaking for Islam (Krämer and Schmidtke eds.) xxxiii
speech
freedom of 464–465
hate, removal on social media of 462–463
of the mad 454
of refugees 454–455
speech acts, religion as 182
Der Spiegel (journal) 462
spirituality
and religious practices 150
Sprachenerlass (Ägypten, 1870) 28
St. Petersburg University, Islamic studies at 6, 10–17, 23
Staatsbürgerschaft, des Osmanischen Reiches 32
Stadtentwicklung, in Kairo 30, 32–33, 39
Stambuli (Abdilahi Nasser) 266–267, 269, 270–272, 274–275, 276
'state analysis from below' 412, 413–415
State Museum of Ethnography (Sardarabad, Armenia) 119
state-society relations 83, 415
in early modernity 92
in Egypt 416
microdynamics of 413–414
in Middle East 85
in Ottoman Empire xvii, 83, 90–94
states 83–84
control of, and recognition policies 434
crises of, and minority radicalism 369
democratic, Muslim acceptance of 186–187
formation of, and minoritisation 360, 361–362, 363
Islamic, political philosophy of 56
and religion
Ataturk on 69
al-Kawākibī on 67
in Ottoman Empire/caliphate 58, 64–65, 69
Riḍā on 65–66, 69–70
religious identities of 362
secularity of, and recognition policies 436–437, 438
sovereignty of, in assigning recognition 431–432
stereotypes, of Muslim males 454
Stokhof, Wim xxvii
Storch, Beatrix von 462–463
stupidity 464n23
accusation in racism verdict of 445
and law 448
subaltern status, of religious minority groups 370
Ṣubḥī, Aḥmad Maḥmūd 174
Sudan, Mahdist revolution in 60
Suez Canal, opening of 27, 34, 38, 40–41, 43
Ṣūfī orders 285n9
Ṣūfism
Koralia on 188
study of, in Russia 20
Surname-i Vehbi 81, 82
surveillance
needs for 456
omni-presence of 240
of social media 238
survival, tribal versus urban modes of 153–154
Swahili Islamic radio (Mombasa) *see* Radio Rahma
Swahili language
mutuality markers in 268
respectful dialogue in 270
Syria
'Alawīs in 371
confessional identity of 369
Ottoman rule of 99, 102–104

tribal groups in 100–103
village communities in 94–99

Tablighi movement, Moosagie's criticism of 205, 220
tacit contracts, between minorities and states 358, 359
Der Tagesspiegel (newspaper) 443
Taḥrīr al-mar'a (The liberation of woman, Qāsim Amīn) 317
al-Ṭahṭāwī, Rifāʿa Rāfiʿ 28, 159–160, 161
talismans 250
Tamarod/Tamarrud movement (Egypt) 407, 419
tanāsukh beliefs (metempsychosis) 367–368
al-Ṭanṭāwī, Muḥammad ʿAyād 19n33
tanẓīmāt-reforms (Ottoman Empire) 36, 133, 362
taqlīd (imitation/emulation) principle 304
Tavakkolī, Majīd xix, 301
al-Ṭawīl, Tawfīq 167, 170–171, 172, 175
Tawżīḥ al-masā'el (Khomeini) 303
tax farmers, Ottoman 96, 98
taxation 91
in Egypt 91
Ottoman system of 96–97, 98
Taylor, Charles 147, 150
Tayob, Abdulkader xvii, xxxix
technicalisation 151, 152
technology, and social change 230n22
Ter Minassian, Taline 372
terrorism discussions on Kenyan Muslim radio 270–273
ethnography of 275–276
tertiary elites 401
testimonies, of survivors of Sheema district massacre 382
textile production, Ottoman 123–124
Thānawī, Ashraf ʿAlī 291
theatre, Egyptian 29
therapies for dealing with trauma, effectiveness of 379, 391
tolerance, of Islam, Muslim majority image of 366
Tolstoy, Leo 19
tourism, in Cairo 41–42
'Towards the Rise of Women in the Arab World' (essay, Hiba Ra'ūf ʿIzzat) 310
traditions
discursive xv, 183, 193
of knowledge 266
of military chivalry 327–328, 339
neo/modified 328
Traditionsliteratur, Ägyptische 28n2
Transactions of the Oriental Division of the Imperial Russian Archeological Society (journal, Russia) 16
transcendence 454n15
public references to, in Muslim world 150–151
transformations
political
from Arab revolts 399, 401, 404–408, 411–413, 414, 417–419
research on 400, 402
of self 162
translations
of Arabic texts
in Russian 9
in Ukrainian 19
in Urdu 289
of French texts, into Arabic 160–161
of Greek texts, into Arabic 169–170
of Qur'ān xviii, 284–285, 293
in Persian xviii, 280, 282–283
in Russian 7–8
in Urdu 281–282, 283–284, 287–288, 290–291, 292
transmission
of knowledge 371
of religious learning 286
transmutation Occidentale 151
dans cultures Musulmans 152–153
trauma, strategies for coping with 379, 391
travellers, European
in Cairo 32, 41–42
in Ottoman Empire 126–127
tribal groups
corporatism of 99–104
modes of survival in 153–154
'Trouble in Tahiti' (musical, Bernstein) xxxii
truth commissions 379n3
Tunisia
French rule of 60
revolts in (2012–2012)
mobilised publics in 407

Tunisia (*cont.*)
and regime change 397–398, 403, 404, 405, 406
Turkey
founding of state of 73, 74
heritage sports in 328, 347–349
higher education in 135
Islam in 330, 343
muscular 334–335
national identity of 340–341, 364
oil wrestling in xix, 327, 328–330, 340–341, 349–350
cultural elements of 341–343, 344–347
Islamic elements of 334–335, 343–344
nationalistic elements of 341
religious minorities in 364, 366, 369
traditional wrestling in 338
Turks
and Arabs, re-unification of 68
Central Asia origins of 340
Riḍā on 70
Western images of violence and insanity of 458
Twitter, use of, in Egypt 235–236

UCLA (University of California, Los Angeles), Islamic studies at xxxii–xxxiii
Uganda
Muslims in xx, 376, 385
political representation of 385–386
political rights of 378
politics of recognition by 382–383, 386–387, 390–391
protests by 376–377, 384, 387–388
remembrance/commemoration practices of 379–380, 384–385, 388–389, 390, 391
governmental repression of 381, 390
Sheema district massacre of (1979) 376, 382–385
national silence and reconciliation policies imposed by government in 377, 379, 381, 383, 384
post-colonial history of 380–381
religious pluralism in 377
Ukrainian language, translations of Arabic texts into 19
ʿulamāʾ
in South Africa 187–188
in South Asia 190, 280, 281
ʿUmar b. al-Khaṭṭāb (Caliph) 69–70
umma
leadership of 58
unity of 55
Ottoman concerns with 61
Riḍā on 56, 64, 68, 76
unbelievers, Islam on 203–204
UNESCO, Intangible Cultural Heritage status granted to Kırkpınar oil wrestling 341–342
United States
book publishing in 232
Egyptian ties with 35
Unity and Variety in Muslim Civilization (von Grunebaum) xviii
universalism, quest of religious minority groups for 372
universities
Egyptian 31, 165
Ottoman 134–136, 137, 138–140
Russian, Islamic studies at 4–9, 10–17, 23
ʿUrābī revolution (Egypt, 1881) 59, 60
urban areas, modes of survival in 154
urban development, in Cairo 30, 32–33, 39
Urdu, translations of Qurʾān in 281–282, 283–284, 290–291, 292
publication of 287–288
al-ʿUrwa al-Wuthqā (journal) 61–62
al-Usra kamā yurīduhā al-Islām (The family as wished-for by Islam, al-Qaraḍāwī) 313–314
ʿUthmān, Muḥammad 38

Vehbi (Abdülcelil Levnî) 81, 82
Verdi, Guiseppe 42
vernacular languages
Arabic 148–149
Qurʾān translations into 283–284
victimhood, of religious minority groups 372
Vienna World's Fair (1873) 126
village communities, Ottoman 95–96, 98–99
as corporate group 96, 99

politics of 97–98
violence
commemoration of 378
as communication form 93
of insanity 451
and Islam 271–272
in Uganda 380–381
against Muslims 376, 382–385
voice strategy of minorities 370
Volksverhetzung 443–444, 463–464

Wādī n-Nīl (journal) 37
Wahba, Sulṭān Ḥusayn 224–225, 226–227, 229, 232, 232–233, 238–239
Wahba, Wahba Ḥasan 225–226, 227–228, 230, 239
Wahba family 224, 230n21
Wahhābī networks, in India, British suspicions of 289
Walī Allāh, Shāh xviii, 280
authority of 280–282, 285–286, 288, 292–293
and Deobandism 291–292
mysticism of 293–294
Qur'ān translation and interpretation by 282–285
waqf institutions, Ottoman 96, 97
wars
confessional, in Middle East 357
Egypt-Abessinia (1869) 36
Uganda civil wars 380
World War II 168
wasaṭiyya (moderation, the middle way) 181
water distribution systems, Ottoman 94–95
Weber, Max 84, 85
wedding photography, Ottoman 115, 116–117
Weidel, Alice 463
Weltausstellung Paris (1867), ägyptische Anteil 30, 31
West
images of Muslims in 458–459
influences on Turkish oil wrestling of 342–343
nostalgia for Orient in 41, 43
see also Europe
Wirtschaft, ägyptische 33, 43, 45–46
Wittgenstein, Ludwig 342
wolf/werewolf images, of Muslims 458–459
women
dress styles of, in Ottoman Empire 121–122
European, Iranian images of 303
Islamic law on 311–312
women's movements, in Iran 304
women's rights 308, 320
activism
in Egypt xix, 313
international/transnational 310, 312, 313
Iranian male solidarity with xix, 301, 304–305, 307–308
Islamic opposition to 313–314
in Egypt xix, 312–313
in Iran xix, 302–304, 306, 307–308
and Islam 302, 313–314, 316–321
word processing, Arabic 256
World Ethnosport Confederation 348–349
world exhibition in Paris (1867), Egyptian contribution 30, 31
World's Fair (Vienna, 1873) 126
world history xii
World War II, impact in Egypt of 168
wrestling
Islamic views of 339
regional forms of 343
traditional 342
in Iran 333
in Pakistan 334
in Turkey 338
see also oil wrestling
Wuld 'Alī tribal group (Syria) 101
Wulff, Christian xiii

Xi'an (China), Great Mosque in 259

Yazīdīs 371
Yemen, revolts in (2010–2012), and regime change 397–398, 403, 404, 406
Young Turks, government of 68
youth, cultural alienation of 185

Zaghlūl, Aḥmad Fatḥī Pasha 161
Zaman, Muhammad Qasim xviii, xxxix
Zan-e Rūz (Today's Woman, journal, Iran) 302
Zanān, (Women, journal, Iran) 303–304

Zhuze, Panteleimon (Bandali Saliba Jawzi) 9
Zivilisation, ägyptische 29
Zivilisationsdiskurs, in Ägypten 27–28
ZMO (Zentrum Moderner Orient; today Leibniz-Zentrum Moderner Orient) xxxii
Zurkhane athleticism 333, 342, 346

Printed in the United States
By Bookmasters